The Politics of Liberty in England and Revolutionary America

With in-depth analysis of political philosophy and careful attention to historical context, this study locates the philosophical origins of the Anglo-American political and constitutional tradition in the philosophical, theological, and political controversies in seventeenth-century England. By examining the quarrel between the proponents of the doctrine of natural liberty and the champions of divine right theory, this study identifies the source of modern liberal, republican, and conservative ideas about natural rights and government in the seminal works of the Exclusion Whigs Locke, Sidney, and Tyrrell and their philosophical forebears Hobbes, Grotius, Spinoza, and Pufendorf. This study illuminates how these first Whigs and their diverse eighteenth-century intellectual heirs such as Bolingbroke, Montesquieu, Hume, Blackstone, Otis, Jefferson, Burke, and Paine contributed to the formation of Anglo-American political and constitutional theory in the crucial period from the Glorious Revolution to the American Revolution and the creation of a distinctly American understanding of rights and government in the first state constitutions.

Lee Ward is Assistant Professor of Political Science at Campion College, University of Regina. He was a Postdoctoral Fellow in the Program on Constitutional Government at Harvard University. He has published articles on early modern and ancient political thought and has received several academic honors including the Bradley Teaching Fellowship (Kenyon College), the Fordham University Dissertation Fellowship, the Ontario Graduate Scholarship, and Brown and McNiece Scholarships (University of Toronto).

The Politics of Liberty in England and Revolutionary America

LEE WARD

Campion College
University of Regina

CAMBRIDGE
UNIVERSITY PRESS

PUBLISHED BY THE PRESS SYNDICATE OF THE UNIVERSITY OF CAMBRIDGE
The Pitt Building, Trumpington Street, Cambridge, United Kingdom

CAMBRIDGE UNIVERSITY PRESS
The Edinburgh Building, Cambridge CB2 2RU, UK
40 West 20th Street, New York, NY 10011-4211, USA
477 Williamstown Road, Port Melbourne, VIC 3207, Australia
Ruiz de Alarcón 13, 28014 Madrid, Spain
Dock House, The Waterfront, Cape Town 8001, South Africa

http://www.cambridge.org

First published 2004

Printed in the United States of America

Typeface Sabon 10/12 pt.   *System* LaTeX 2$_\varepsilon$ [TB]

A catalog record for this book is available from the British Library.

Library of Congress Cataloging in Publication Data

Ward, Lee, 1970–
The politics of liberty in England and revolutionary America / Lee Ward
    p.   cm.
Includes bibliographical references (p.) and index.
ISBN 0-521-82745-0
1. Political science – Great Britain – Philosophy – History – 17th century.
2. Political science – Great Britain – Philosophy – History – 18th century.
3. Political science – United States – Philosophy – History – 17th century.
4. Political science – United States – Philosophy – History – 18th century.
5. United States – History – Revolution, 1775–1783 – Causes.   6. Liberty.
I. Title.
JA84.G7W37   2004
320′.01–dc22   2003068725

ISBN 0 521 82745 0 hardback

For Ann, *kaloskagathos*

Contents

Acknowledgments   *page* ix

Introduction: Reexamining the Roots of Anglo-American
Political Thought   1

PART ONE: THE DIVINE RIGHT CHALLENGE TO NATURAL LIBERTY

1 The Attack on the Catholic Natural Law   23
2 Calvinism and Parliamentary Resistance Theory   48
3 The Problem of Grotius and Hobbes   71

PART TWO: THE WHIG POLITICS OF LIBERTY IN ENGLAND

4 James Tyrrell: The Voice of Moderate Whiggism   105
5 The Pufendorfian Moment: Moderate Whig
   Sovereignty Theory   133
6 Algernon Sidney and the Old Republicanisms   152
7 A New Republican England   172
8 Natural Rights in Locke's Two Treatises   209
9 Lockean Liberal Constitutionalism   247
10 The Glorious Revolution and the Catonic Response   271
11 Eighteenth-Century British Constitutionalism   305

PART THREE: THE WHIG LEGACY IN AMERICA

12 British Constitutionalism and the Challenge of Empire   327
13 Thomas Jefferson and the Radical Theory of Empire   351
14 Tom Paine and Popular Sovereignty   375

15 Revolutionary Constitutionalism: Laboratories of
   Radical Whiggism   396
   Conclusion   426

Bibliography   433
Index   451

Acknowledgments

This project grew out of my dissertation at Fordham University. My teachers Mary Nichols and Michael Zuckert have generously offered me their support, friendship, probity, and wisdom throughout my studies and career. Without them this book simply would not have been possible, and I am deeply grateful for their mentorship. I would also especially like to thank Paul Rahe, whose careful and imaginative reading of my manuscript made the revision process a challenging and invaluable experience and made this a deeper and richer study by his great contribution. Michael Davis, H. T. Dickinson, David Nichols, Paul Seaton, and Vickie Sullivan also helped me either by reading versions or parts of the manuscript or by otherwise offering their expertise. All remaining errors and shortcomings are, of course, entirely my own.

For the many stimulating conversations about political philosophy at the Tinker and Hatch Lake, I thank my friends and colleagues at Fordham, especially David Alvis, Susan Benfield, Patrick Bernardo, Natalie Fuehrer, Paul Howard, Harold Kildow, Carly Kinsella, Paul Kirkland, Erin Larocca, Sara McDonald, Paul Seaton, Bryan Smith, Flagg Taylor, and Scott Wolland. While working on this book, I was fortunate to be a part of the Department of Political Science at Kenyon College. I cannot imagine a better place to teach, write, and think about political philosophy than Gambier, Ohio. I thank my wonderful students at Kenyon for making every class a real joy and the superb librarians at the Kenyon College Library for their expert help. My colleagues in Political Science, especially Pam Jensen, Fred Baumann, Tim Spiekerman, Kirk Emmert, Devin Stauffer, Dana Jalbert-Stauffer, and Ron Lee, I cannot thank enough for their friendship and support.

I would also like to thank my editor at Cambridge University Press, Lewis Bateman, for his unstinting support for this project and his editorial assistant, Sarah Gentile, for her expert advice and guidance. Fordham University and the Bradley Foundation provided generous financial support while I was working on this project, for which I am very grateful. I would also like to

thank the editors of *Interpretation* for their permission to use parts of an
earlier article on Sidney in Chapters 6 and 7.

To my mother, Catherine, my father, Charles, and my brother, Sean Ward,
I offer my love and gratitude for their unwavering support over the years
and hope my efforts prove worthy of them.

To Ann Ward, my wife, friend, and colleague, I owe everything.

Introduction

Reexamining the Roots of Anglo-American Political Thought

This project is as an effort to address some of the problems contemporary political theorists and intellectual historians have encountered in writing about the Anglo-American political tradition. At least since the demise of Marxist and progressive methods of interpretation, with their emphasis on subrational interests and economic and material forces as the major, if not only, motivational springs for political and constitutional thought and practice, scholars of the Anglo-American tradition have largely agreed on one fundamental interpretive and conceptual premise: ideas matter.[1] The broad, almost universal, consensus among scholars of the field is that early modern Anglo-American thought is defined by a set of principles and deeply held commitments to certain notions of government and law, rights and citizenship. It is now generally assumed that Anglo-American political thinkers and actors in the seventeenth and eighteenth centuries operated within a distinctive framework, or perhaps distinct frameworks, with established categories of thought, ideological assumptions, and philosophical premises.

The bad news, or at least the other side of this overarching "superconsensus," is the deep contentiousness that has characterized the study of seventeenth- and eighteenth-century Anglo-American thought in the past four decades. Ideas matter, but as we have come to realize, scholarly interpretations of these ideas may matter even more. The deepest fault line in contemporary scholarship on Anglo-American thought lies in the divide between the liberal and republican, or Lockean and civic humanist, schools of interpretation. This by now familiar, perhaps all too familiar, dispute pits different interpretive lenses often in search of comprehensive paradigms for understanding our political and constitutional tradition. A typical feature

---

[1] For the classic example of the progressive school of interpretation in America, see Charles Beard, *An Economic Interpretation of the Constitution* (New York: Macmillan, 1935, orig. pub 1913): esp. chs. 5–7.

of the liberal-versus-republican debate is the dispute over the dominance, the relative importance, or even the existence of one or the other system of thought in Anglo-American early modernity.

The roots of the current debate go back at least as far as the middle of the last century. At that time, numerous distinguished scholars like Louis Hartz, Carl Becker, Clinton Rossiter, and Richard Hofstadter established a "liberal" consensus regarding the dominant mode of thought in the Anglo-American political and constitutional tradition.[2] These scholars agreed that the pre-vailing mode of political discourse and constitutional theory in America was profoundly shaped by the overwhelming influence of Lockean-liberal ideas at the time of the Founding. This assertion of a dominant Lockean-liberal paradigm in American political thought mirrored the work of po-litical theorists studying the early modern period such as Leo Strauss and C. B. MacPherson, who proclaimed that early modernity marked the tri-umph of Lockean-liberal notions of rights and government over the classical and Christian assumptions and principles of the premodern era.[3] The distinc-tive features of this liberal consensus in the fields of both Anglo-American and early modern studies were an assertion of the centrality of individual natural rights, an instrumentalist or conventionalist understanding of gov-ernment as a product of human artifice designed and directed to the securing of rights, and a statement of the importance of private property rights and the unleashing of essentially selfish and materialist passions channeled through the political and economic institutions of a competitive, individualistic, and capitalist society. In sum, early liberal modernity peaked in Locke, and Locke was America's philosopher.

The liberal consensus began to unravel in the late 1950s and 1960s when a body of scholarship emerged questioning the alleged univocity of Lockean liberalism ("Locke et praetera nihil") in the Anglo-American tradition. Robert Shalhope coined the phrase "republican synthesis" to describe this

---

[2] For the seminal statements of the liberal consensus, see Louis Hartz, *The Liberal Tradition in America* (New York: Harcourt, Brace, 1955): pp. 3–86; Carl Becker, *The Declaration of Independence: A Study in the History of Political Ideas* (New York: Knopf, 1942, orig pub. 1922); Richard Hofstadter, *The American Political Tradition* (New York: Vintage, 1957): pp. v–xi, 3–17 and Clinton Rossiter, *Seedtime of the Republic* (New York: Harcourt, Brace, 1953). While Rossiter did identify Locke as "primus inter pares" among the formative thinkers in America, it is important to note that he also did much to identify the influence of Opposition Whigs and "continental libertarians" on Anglo-American thought (cf. pp. 358–9).

[3] Leo Strauss, *Natural Right and History* (Chicago: University of Chicago Press, 1953): esp. ch. 5 (though, note Strauss' identification of classical and premodern elements of the British Constitution in "German Nihilism," *Interpretation*, 26, 3 [Spring 1999]: pp. 353–78, esp. pp. 372–3) and C. B. MacPherson, *The Political Theory of Possessive Individualism: Hobbes to Locke* (Oxford: Oxford University Press, 1962). For a recent study that follows the Strauss–MacPherson path, see Pierre Manent, *An Intellectual History of Liberalism*, Rebacca Balinski, trans. (Princeton: Princeton University Press, 1994): esp. ch. 4.

diverse, but interrelated, body of work.[4] Caroline Robbins's classic *Eighteenth Century Commonwealthman* began the process of dethroning Locke by identifying him as only one of many figures in a diffuse stream of republican thought in Britain from the civil war and interregnum periods to the late-eighteenth-century radicals like Burgh, Priestley, and Price.[5] In Robbins' analysis, long-neglected thinkers like Harrington and Sidney, as well as Trenchard and Gordon, took on new importance as influential voices in the English radical and libertarian traditions. Robbins' work was an impetus to other scholars and initiated a largely salutary correction to the monolithic Lockean-liberal consensus. J. G. A. Pocock, spurred in part by Hannah Arendt's rediscovery of classical republican politics, took Robbins' analysis to another level. In a vast collection of articles culminating in the monumental *The Machiavellian Moment*, Pocock identified a civic humanist republican tradition of thought originating in the city-states of Renaissance Italy. He argued that this civic humanist mode of thought, with its emphasis on mixed government, civic virtue, property as instrumental to citizenship, and the importance of participatory politics, was transmitted to the Anglo-American world via Machiavelli and his English followers, most notably Harrington. It was from this civic humanist tradition, Pocock argued, that Anglo-American thought inherited and developed a profoundly anti-Lockean and anti-individualist notion of liberty. This idea of liberty hearkened back to the classical Aristotelian ideal of citizenship as the fulfillment of the human personality through common political discourse and action. At some points, Pocock even suggests that civic humanism was more than a competing paradigm with Lockean liberalism – that it was actually the dominant political philosophy in eighteenth-century America.[6] The impact of Robbins and Pocock's work on the study of American political thought was enormous.

Bernard Bailyn, for example, while not an advocate of the classical republican or civic humanist interpretation, plays down the significance of Locke in the formation of the eighteenth-century Whig mind by identifying Robbins' English Commonwealthmen as the chief inspiration behind the pre-Revolutionary American idea of liberty. It was in the subtradition of "Opposition" or radical "Country" party Whigs epitomized by Trenchard

---

4 Robert Shalhope, "Towards a Republican Synthesis," *William and Mary Quarterly*, 20 (January 1972): pp. 49–80.
5 Caroline Robbins, *The Eighteenth Century Commonwealthmen* (New York: Atheneum, 1968). 1959).
6 J. G. A. Pocock, *The Machiavellian Moment: Florentine Political Thought and the Atlantic Republican Tradition* (Princeton: Princeton University Press, 1975): pp. 545–7 and J. G. A. Pocock, "Virtue and Commerce in the Eighteenth Century," *Journal of Interdisciplinary History*, 3 (1972): p. 122. Cf. Quentin Skinner, "Machiavelli," *Great Political Thinkers* (Oxford: Oxford University Press, 1992): pp. 3–100 and Skinner, *Liberty Before Liberalism* (Cambridge: Cambridge University Press, 1998).

and Gordon's *Cato's Letters,* rather than primarily in Locke, that Bailyn discovered the most important and comprehensive statements on liberty and
power, and virtue and corruption, in Revolutionary America.[7] For Bailyn,
the English radical opposition Whigs provided the conceptual frame of reference for American Whigs regarding the most important questions about
government and liberty. Gordon Wood went further than Bailyn, and even
Pocock, in developing the classical republican influence on Anglo-American
thought. Like Pocock, and in contrast to Bailyn, Wood found the great alternative to Lockean-liberal interpretations of eighteenth-century American
thought to be a tradition of republicanism rooted in classical antiquity. In
Wood's formulation of the republican hypothesis, American Whigs were essentially classical republicans dedicated to an idea of community as a natural
organic whole in which sacrifice of individual self-interest for the sake of the
common good lay at the core of their notion of virtue. The deep tension
between republican virtue and liberal individualism, which Pocock identified in the Whig distrust of commerce, becomes, in Wood's reinterpretation,
open warfare, as Wood's classical republican Whigs are now seen as staunch
anticapitalists and anti-individualists.[8] For both Wood and Pocock, political
liberty – the public share in government – is the central classical assumption
underlying eighteenth-century Whig thought.

   Thus, the crux of the liberal–republican debate centered on two pivotal issues. While the proponents of the republican interpretation were by no means
monolithic in their positions (indeed, the term "republican synthesis" may
itself be misleading), they did share a common tendency to de-emphasize, or
at least seriously question, the once thought formative influence of Lockean-
liberal thought on the Anglo-American tradition. For Bailyn, Wood, and
Pocock, other voices such as Machiavelli, Harrington, and the Opposition
Whigs gained a prominence hitherto unseen in the field. The other major
question at issue between the liberal and republican schools was the status
of premodern, especially classical, thought in the eighteenth-century Anglo-
American world. On one point at least the proponents of the liberal and
republican theses were in agreement: Locke was thoroughly modern, and

---

[7] Bernard Bailyn, *The Ideological Origins of the American Revolution* (Cambridge, MA: Harvard
University Press, 1967): esp. p. 34. Bailyn's findings emerged almost contemporaneously with
John Dunn's influential article claiming that Locke's *Two Treatises* were not nearly as important
or even as widely read as was previously thought. See John Dunn, "The Politics of Locke in
England and America," in *John Locke: Problems and Perspectives,* John Yolton, ed. (Cambridge:
Cambridge University Press, 1969): pp. 56, 80.

[8] Gordon Wood, *The Creation of the American Republic, 1776–87* (Chapel Hill: University of
North Carolina Press, 1969): pp. 29, 53, 58, 60, 417. For his part, Wood sees the end of this
classical politics in America and the ideological victory of liberalism occurring at the time of
the enactment of the U.S. Constitution. For an argument that sees the classical republican
influence extending well into the nineteenth century via the Jeffersonians, see Lance Banning,
The Jeffersonian Persuasion (Ithaca: Cornell University Press, 1978).

so is liberalism. Pocock and Wood, for example, argued that it was not from Locke's modern natural rights theory that the Whigs in England and America learned the fundamentals of government, but rather from the classical Romans and Greeks. It was from this classical source transmitted through the Italian civic humanists that the Whigs developed their most formative ideas about constitutionalism, virtue, property, and citizenship.

In the past two decades, following a steady republican onslaught, Locke and liberalism have made something of a comeback. In the wake of the bygone era of "Locke et praetera nihil" and the "omnia praeter Lockem" spirit of the republican school, another generation of scholars arose to challenge the newly minted republican orthodoxy– it was Locke redivivus.[9] These scholars such as Joyce Appleby, Steven Dworetz, Isaac Kramnick, Thomas Pangle and John Patrick Diggins contested the republican interpretation on several counts. Thomas Pangle and Steven Dworetz argued that the republican interpretation overstated the importance of nonliberal thought in the eighteenth-century Anglo-American tradition while systematically muting and neglecting unmistakably Lockean modes of thought and discourse.[10] Both Dworetz and Pangle attacked the civic humanist or non-Lockean credentials of Trenchard and Gordon's *Cato's Letters*, a central text in the Whig canon of Robbins, Bailyn, Wood, and Pocock. If, as the neoliberal school argued, *Cato's Letters* and other English Whig writings are fundamentally Lockean, then it was not civic humanism that was transmitted to the colonies via Cato and the others, but rather Locke, albeit in somewhat modified form.[11] Joyce Appleby argued that it was the Lockean account of the origins of government to which American Whigs turned during the imperial crisis with Britain in the 1760s and 1770s. Whatever traces of classical republicanism there may have been in eighteenth-century America, she claims, disappeared with the demise of the Federalists and the rise of the thoroughly Lockean liberal philosophy of individualism and capitalism she associates with the Jeffersonians.[12] Isaac Kramnick looks to late-eighteenth-century British radicals like Priestley, Price, Paine, and Burgh to illustrate the formative impact of Locke on the political thought of the period. By uncovering the Lockean roots of late-eighteenth-century British radicalism, Kramnick observed an

---

[9] For "Locke et praetera nihil," see Pocock, "Virtue and Commerce," p. 107. "Omnia praeter Lockem" is the catchy phrase, I believe, coined by Steven Dworetz in *The Unvarnished Doctrine: Locke, Liberalism, and the American Revolution* (Durham, NC: Duke University Press, 1990): p. 23.

[10] Dworetz, *Unvarnished Doctrine*, and Thomas Pangle, *The Spirit of Modern Republicanism* (Chicago: University of Chicago Press, 1988).

[11] Dworetz, *Unvarnished Doctrine*, pp. 10, 89 and Pangle, *Spirit*, pp. 30–3 (though note John P. Diggins, *The Lost Soul of American Politics* [New York: Basic Books, 1984]: pp. 19–20 for a republican reading of *Cato's Letters*).

[12] Joyce Appleby, *Capitalism and a New Social Order: The Republican Vision of the 1790's* (New York: New York University Press, 1984): pp. 8–9, 14, 21–3.

underlying continuity of liberal thought from at least the 1760s on.[13] John
Patrick Diggins, in his study *The Lost Soul of American Politics*, regretfully but
firmly confirms the centrality of Locke's teaching of economic individualism
for the shaping of American political discourse. While Diggins bewailed the
demise of the alternative nonliberal stream of American political thought,
which he identifies with Calvinist Protestantism rather than classical republicanism, he nonetheless confirmed the great importance of Lockean liberalism
in forming the American mind.[14]

In many respects, the neo-liberal Locke *redivivus* school is no more united
than the republican synthesis it sought to correct or replace. It was not always the same Locke who appeared to reclaim his place on the stage. One
essentially Hobbesian Locke would not have much truck with another theistic Locke. Likewise, the bourgeois capitalist Locke was not identical to the
radical dissenting Protestant Locke. Where the new Lockean-liberal school
did stand together, however, was in their criticism of the republican revi-
sionists' tendency to mute or silence what the neoliberals took to be Locke's
enormous influence on the Anglo-American tradition. They often attacked
what they took to be weak (or nonexistent) evidence of classical influences
on eighteenth-century Anglo-American thought.[15] And they questioned the
coherence of forming a republican paradigm out of materials – that is, books
and authors – deeply penetrated by the pervasive spirit of Lockean liberalism.

Thus, the state of the debate in the wake of the republican revision and
the liberal restoration is one of stalemate. Despite the fundamental differences between the two schools of interpretation, there is, however, almost
universal agreement on at least one central question. One legacy of the
republican revision of the old liberal consensus and the recent liberal response is the general concurrence regarding the importance of understanding
the roots and character of English Whig political philosophy. In a sense, the
liberal–republican debate has become an interpretive battle over the heart
and soul of Whiggism. This is not to suggest that there are no other important
elements in eighteenth-century Anglo-American thought such as Protestant
theology or British constitutional custom and practice, but rather to observe
the obvious and yet controversial influence of Whig thought in the period.
The overwhelming evidence supplied by the republican and liberal revision-
ists suggests that English and American Whigs in the eighteenth century read,
studied, quoted, plagiarized, and digested the works of both Locke and the
radical Opposition Whigs. Is Whiggism essentially liberal or republican? Is
Locke a Whig? Is there any reasonable basis to identify a Whig "canon"
that excludes or marginalizes Locke? Does it make sense to speak of two
competing, even contradictory, strains of thought emerging from the same

[13] Isaac Kramnick, *Republicanism and Bourgeois Radicalism* (Ithaca: Cornell University Press,
1990): esp. pp. 35–40, 172–85.
[14] Diggins, *Lost Soul*, pp. 5, 14, 17, 30.
[15] See especially Pangle, *Spirit*, pp. 28–9.

root in late-seventeenth-century England? These are the questions that confront us, along with a growing suspicion that the stark liberal–republican
dichotomy in the current debate in Anglo-American thought rests largely on
distinctions and assumptions foreign to the subject matter itself.

I believe Lance Banning's 1992 restatement of the liberal–republican debate can help guide us through the conceptual minefields facing the contemporary student of Anglo-American early modern thought. Banning, himself
a veteran of the liberal-versus-republican interpretive wars, observed that
the most important legacy of republican and liberal revisionist scholars has
been to show the deep complexity in seventeenth- and eighteenth-century
Anglo-American thought. Unfortunately, he argued, they have often not paid
enough attention to the subtleties of each other's positions. While criticizing Pocock for perhaps going too far in the direction of minimizing Locke's
influence, Banning also noted that the republican revision properly understood should be seen not as a replacement for, but as a vital supplement to,
scholarship demonstrating the Lockean-liberal dimension in the tradition.[16]
Republican scholarship, in this view, brought to light important, but previously neglected, writers, ideas, and modes of thought. Banning observed that
by illuminating the part, we often cast a shadow on the whole. By identifying
diverse strains of thought and constructing paradigms based on this process
of speciation, scholars have broken into disputing parts principles and ideas
that often coexisted in a distinctive combination in the eighteenth-century
Anglo-American Whig mind. Banning suggests that one approach to understanding the distinctive combination of liberal and republican elements in the
Whig intellectual and political tradition is "to start with further exploration
of its origins in seventeenth century England."[17]

In a number of important respects, this study reflects Banning's suggestions and concerns.[18] First, we will examine the origins of the Whig politics
of liberty in late-seventeenth-century England. Through detailed analysis of
the major Whig Exclusion era tracts by James Tyrrell, Algernon Sidney, and
John Locke, we will observe the emergence of distinctively liberal and republican modes of thought and discourse. Why start with the Exclusionists?
On the one hand, it seems to be the most natural place to begin. It was
during the Exclusion crisis that the uniquely modern term "Whig" made
its first appearance in the political lexicon of the tradition.[19] On a more

---

[16] Lance Banning, "The Republican Interpretation: Retrospect and Prospect," in *The Republican Synthesis Revisited: Essays in Honor of George Athan Bilias*, Milton M. Klein, Richard D. Brown, and John Hench, eds. (Worcester: American Antiquarian Society, 1992), pp. 156, 171–2.

[17] Ibid., p. 176.

[18] Of course, this is not to suggest that Lance Banning envisioned with his suggestion my specific approach in this study.

[19] The classic study of the political and social dynamics of the Exclusion crisis is J. R. Jones, *The First Whigs: The Politics of the Exclusion Crisis, 1678–1683* (London: Oxford University Press, 1961). A recent and generally insightful study of this period is found in Mark Kishlansky, *A*

fundamental level, the major Exclusion era writings of Tyrrell, Sidney, and Locke mark the first time three distinctive voices in the English libertarian mold were raised against a common enemy. It is often forgotten amid the contemporary clamor over competing paradigms that the "conservative" or "moderate" Whiggism of Tyrrell, the "republicanism" of Sidney, and the "liberalism" of Locke all entered the world at the same time, battling in common cause against Robert Filmer's defense of divine right monarchy, which was republished by the Tories during the turbulent days of the Exclusion crisis.[20] Perhaps by understanding what it was that united the Exclusion Whigs – their opposition to seventeenth-century divine right absolutism – we may be in a better position to understand and account for the various strains of Whiggism that characterized the following century.

At this point, I should explain the principles of selectivity in my approach to the study of Exclusion period Whig thought and writings. In contrast to the historiographical methodology of Caroline Robbins and Bernard Bailyn, for example, who have elaborated the writings of innumerable figures in the Anglo-American tradition, this study focuses in its central part on the formative impact of three major tracts from among the vast collection of Exclusion Whig writings. However, this methodological approach is not idiosyncratic. The basis for the selection of Tyrrell, Sidney, and Locke rests on three criteria. First, *Patriarcha, Non Monarcha*, the *Discourses Concerning Government*, and the *Two Treatises of Government* evince, as I hope to demonstrate, a level of philosophical sophistication and depth that make them not just *pieces d'occasion*, but rather serious works of political theory in their own right. While an understanding of the historical context in which Tyrrell, Sidney, and Locke operated in the late 1670s and early 1680s provides invaluable insights regarding their motivations, assumptions, and rhetorical strategies, the works selected for special attention possess a degree of intellectual rigor and ideological clarity that surpassed that of the vast majority of the over 200 hastily crafted pamphlets and equally expeditious responses by the

---

Monarchy Transformed (London: Oxford University Press, 1996). While Locke's *Two Treatises* and Sidney's *Discourses* were not published until after the Exclusion crisis (in 1690 and 1698, respectively), whereas Tyrrell's *Patriarcha, Non Monarcha* was published during the crisis in 1681, it is now generally agreed, thanks to the pathbreaking research of Peter Laslett and Richard Ashcraft, that all three of these works were composed wholly or in large part during the period 1679–82. See Peter Laslett, introduction to Locke's *Two Treatises of Government* (Cambridge: Cambridge University Press, 1988): pp. 52–64 and Richard Ashcraft, *Revolutionary Politics and Locke's Two Treatises of Government* (Princeton: Princeton University Press, 1986).

[20] Banning, "Republican Interpretation," p. 155. For Tyrrell as a "conservative" Whig, see Robbins, *Commonwealthmen*, pp. 73–4; and for a sample of Sidney's characterization as a "republican," see Zera Fink, *The Classical Republicans* (Chicago: Northwestern University Press, 1962) and Pocock, *Machiavellian Moment*, p. 422. While the literature identifying Locke as a "liberal" is truly enormous, and will be the subject of Chapters 8 and 9 of this study, one interesting presentation of a nonliberal Locke to note is James Tully, *A Discourse on Property: Locke and His Adversaries* (Cambridge: Cambridge University Press, 1980).

protagonists in this period.[21] Tyrrell, Sidney, and Locke distill and articulate logical premises and philosophical principles typically implicit or inchoate in the works of their Whig associates. Second, I argue that the three Whig thinkers on whom I focus in Part Two are uniquely representative of the underlying philosophical and ideological strains among the Whigs. While Tyrrell's moderate constitutionalism reflected the political vision of most English Whigs at the time and long afterward, Sidney and Locke developed arguments for natural rights and popular sovereignty that took Whiggism in different and competing directions. These alternative directions, moreover, emerged as species of thought deriving their particular character from the logical thrust of the basic Whig position in the Exclusion Crisis. Tyrrell, Sidney, and Locke exemplify differing and discrete arguments that are still identifiably Whiggish.

Third, the selectivity of my approach is validated by the judgment of the historical development of the Anglo-American tradition in the seventeenth and eighteenth centuries. Historically, Tyrrell, Sidney, and Locke were among the most influential Whig writers working (as opposed to publishing) in the earliest stages of the formation of the Whig ideology. The initial impact of Tyrrell's work during the Exclusion era, and the notoriety of Locke and Sidney's work in the years following the Glorious Revolution, ensured their prominence in the pantheon of early Whig champions of limited government. Whereas Tyrrell's moderate Whig argument represented the core of English Whiggism in the eighteenth century, among radical Whigs in England and America Locke and Sidney became the widely accepted authorities on the fundamental principles of popular resistance, political obligation, and constitutional government. Thus, the selection of these major Whig thinkers and their works as a kind of fulcrum for this study is justified by their degree of theoretical sophistication, their representative quality of important strains of Whig thought, and their historical legacy and impact.

The second element of Banning's restatement of the current debate that informs this study is his suggestion to resist the temptation to create "Kuhnian" paradigms or mutually exclusive interpretive syntheses. This study takes to heart Aristotle's caution to the student of political things not to expect the same degree of precision in moral and political studies as in the mathematical and natural sciences.[22] Imagine this study as an archeological project of exploration into the very foundations of early modern Anglo-American

---

[21] For good general surveys of the Exclusion pamphlet literature, see O. W. Furly, "The Whig Exclusionists: Pamphlet Literature in the Exclusion Crisis, 1679–81," *Cambridge Historical Journal*, vol. 13, issue 1 (1957): pp. 19–36 and Charles D. Tarlton, "The Exclusion Controversy, Pamphleteering, and Locke's Two Treatises," *The Historical Journal*, vol. 24, no. 1 (March 1981): pp. 49–68.

[22] Aristotle, *The Nicomachean Ethics*, H. H. Rackham, trans. (Cambridge: Harvard University Press, 1934): 1094b12–28. Cf. Thomas Engeman, "Liberalism, Republicanism, and Ideology," *Review of Politics*, 55 (Spring 1993): p. 331.

political thought. Locke, Sidney, and Tyrrell each had access to the same theoretical and intellectual resources in the philosophical milieu of late-seventeenth-century England in their critique of divine right, yet they created substantially different edifices in response to the divine right challenge to the principle of natural liberty. Rather than following a synthesizing or paradig-matizing impulse, this study adopts a syncretic approach. The three major Exclusion Whig champions produced distinct but frequently intersecting and overlapping arguments. As such, we will illuminate the deep complexity and diverse streams of reasoning inherent in the Whig tradition. Only by dig-ging down to the very roots of Whig thought will we find the materials necessary to reconcile the different strands of this early modern philosophy into the complex heterogeneous whole it originally was. We are faced with the prospect that seventeenth- and eighteenth-century English and American Whigs could and did draw on much richer theoretical and philosophical resources than our prevailing paradigms will admit.

In my attempt to gain a fuller understanding of the Anglo-American po-litical tradition by reexamining the classic Whig texts of the late seventeenth century, this study builds on a number of previous efforts. Paul Rahe's land-mark *Republics Ancient and Modern* traced the origins and development of re-publicanism from Greek antiquity until the early American Republic.[23] In his breathtaking coverage and careful treatment of over 2,000 years of ancient and modern political and constitutional thought, Rahe demonstrated the profound conceptual and philosophical differences between classical thought and the early modern successors of the republican ideal. Rahe challenged prevailing assumptions about the republican project and exposed the deep antagonism of modern theorists such as Machiavelli, Hobbes, Locke, and Madison toward the classical republican principles of moral education and distributive justice.[24] Rahe's work illuminated the formative impact early modern political theory had on the republican dimension of the Anglo-American political and constitutional tradition.

Jerome Huyler's *Locke in America* also went a considerable distance to point beyond the confining paradigms characterizing the contemporary liberal–republican debate. He argued persuasively that Lockean liberalism and classical republicanism were not antithetical modes of thought for eighteenth-century American Whigs. In the Opposition Whig classic *Cato's Letters*, Huyler discovered a carefully crafted synthesis of Lockean individu-alism and natural rights, on the one hand, and the "Old Whig" constitutional republicanism of Algernon Sidney, on the other. This synthesis of liberal and republican elements was ready made for digestion into the bloodstream of

---

[23] Paul Rahe, *Republics Ancient and Modern: Classical Republicanism and the American Revolution* (Chapel Hill: University of North Carolina Press, 1992).
[24] See ibid., esp. Book II, "New Modes and Orders in Early Modern Thought."

pre-Revolutionary America.[25] A third important study, and one to which this project is deeply indebted, is Michael Zuckert's *Natural Rights and the New Republicanism*. Zuckert drew on a vast knowledge of the seventeenth-century natural rights and natural law tradition to illuminate distinct but related and connected strands of Whig thought. Zuckert examined *Cato's Letters* and made the same connection between the Lockean-liberal philosophy of natural rights and the Whig republican political science that Huyler identified. However, Zuckert identified both a distinctly Lockean form of Whiggism and a separate brand of Whig thought he associated with the philosophical authority of Hugo Grotius.[26] Zuckert argued that it was Grotius who was the inspiration and guiding light for most English Whigs, while Locke's influence penetrated only on the margins of eighteenth-century English political discourse, though ultimately finding a home in the American colonies. Rahe's, Huyler's, and Zuckert's findings compel the contemporary student of the Anglo-American tradition to look anew and with fresh eyes at the rich and complex veins of argumentation and theoretical principles underlying the Whig politics of liberty.

The Whig Politics of Liberty

This study is at once broader and more focused than most previous efforts to understand the origins of Anglo-American thought. This study is more focused than many of its predecessors in the sense that I pay primary attention to examining the philosophical foundations of Anglo-American early modernity. This is not intended to deny or diminish the importance of historical, economic, or theological influences in the formation of Whig political thought, but rather to focus on one very important influence that has not been properly understood or fully appreciated hitherto. Thus in Part One of this study I examine the relation of Whig thought to the ideas of its predecessors in the great natural liberty tradition of the seventeenth century. The central element in the Whig critique of divine right in the Exclusion tracts was the response to Filmer's rejection of the doctrine of natural liberty. In his bold and uncompromising assertion of the English divine right position, Filmer, the "most prominent royalist theorist" in England, systematically countered every major form of this natural liberty school extant in mid-seventeenth-century Europe.[27] The natural liberty tradition was by no means uniform in every, or even most respects, but all the adherents to the principle of natural liberty agreed on the premise that human beings are naturally free and equal,

---

[25] Jerome Huyler, *Locke in America* (Lawrence: University Press of Kansas, 1995): pp. 224–46.

[26] Michael Zuckert, *Natural Rights and the New Republicanism* (Princeton: Princeton University Press, 1994): esp. chs. 4, 5, and 7–9.

[27] Mark Goldie, "The Reception of Hobbes," in *Cambridge History of Political Thought*, J. H. Burns and Mark Goldie, eds. (Cambridge: Cambridge University Press, 1991): p. 595.

and that the particular form of government for a given people is the product of consent. Filmer assaulted this tradition with guns blazing, leveling scathing criticisms of the Catholic natural law, Calvinist politics and theology, English civil war era parliamentary contractarianism, and Hobbesian and Grotian natural jurisprudence. Thus, in critiquing Filmerian divine right, the Whigs explicitly defended the principle of natural liberty associated with these schools of thought. The political thought of Filmer's Whig critics, then, emphatically did not emerge from an intellectual and philosophical vacuum.

Each of the major Exclusion Whigs attacked divine right; however, they each did so in defense of a particular understanding of the doctrine of natural liberty. By carefully examining the arguments of Tyrrell, Sidney, and Locke, I have found that the most fundamental source for Whig thought was the philosophic principles of early modern natural jurisprudence. There is, I admit, a paradox at the origin of the Whig politics of liberty. The natural liberty tradition that preceded the Whigs may be broken into two general camps. The first was the anti-absolutist strain typically associated with the later scholastic, Calvinist, and parliamentary radical thought of the English Civil War period. These arguments tended to rest on either a classical natural teleology, the Christian understanding of the divine ordination of political power, or a combination of these elements. For these philosophical and theological partisans of natural liberty, absolute monarchy was antithetical to God's and/or nature's plans for human flourishing.

The Whigs Tyrrell, Sidney, and Locke, however, generally eschewed this respectable anti-absolutist tradition and the classical and Christian assumptions underlying it. They turned rather to the second camp of the seventeenth-century natural liberty tradition: modern natural jurisprudence.[28] Herein lies the paradox. The two most influential natural law and natural rights theorists of the period prior to the Whigs were Hugo Grotius and Thomas Hobbes. Yet these thinkers produced theories of right more or less consistent with absolutist models of political legitimacy. Grotius and Hobbes presented arguments that offered no necessary or even easy connection between natural rights and the principle of limited government so dear to the Whigs. Thus, the first Whigs present a complicated relation to their forbears in the natural liberty tradition eschewing a bona fide anti-absolutist tradition in favor of a modern natural jurisprudence with at least a dubious connection to limited constitutionalism. This study will try to demonstrate how and why

---

[28] My argument runs counter to that of scholars such as Tierney and Oakley, who maintain that the language, and to some extent the logic, of modern natural rights derive from the medieval period (see, for example, Brian Tierney, *The Idea of Natural Rights: Studies on Natural Rights, Natural Law, and Church Law, 1150–1625* [Grand Rapids, MI: William B. Eerdmans, 1997]: pp. 5, 8, 54–69 and Francis Oakley, *The Politics of Eternity: Studies in the History of Medieval and Early-Modern Political Thought* [Leiden: Brill, 1999]: pp. 217–48 dealing with Locke). In contrast I argue that seventeenth-century modern natural rights theory represents more than simply a modification of earlier concepts of right and law; rather, it marks a decisive break from the theological and classical foundations of the medieval concept of natural justice.

the Whigs came to square the natural rights circle and develop principles of natural jurisprudence consistent with limited government.

In other respects, this study is considerably broader than similar efforts. For example, it is surprising, given the enormous scholarly attention paid to Locke over the years, that there is still a relative paucity of thematic treatments of Locke's *Two Treatises* in their proper context, in bas relief as it were, in comparison and contrast with the contemporaneous offerings of other influential Whigs such as Tyrrell and Sidney.[29] On a more fundamental level, however, the present study demands that we expand even further the analytical horizons traditionally employed in investigating the theoretical foundations of the Anglo-American tradition. A principal aim of this study is to demonstrate the seminal influence of seventeenth-century natural jurisprudence on the formation of the early modern Anglo-American mind. I propose that Whig philosophy represented the political instantiation in the English-speaking world of intellectual forces that are fully intelligible only in the context of the massive civilizational changes in the West introduced by the European Enlightenment. The key development in the formation of the Whig politics of liberty, and eighteenth-century Anglo-American thought generally, was the infusion of the concepts, premises, and categories of seventeenth-century continental natural jurisprudence into the fundamental debate over English constitutional theory and practice in the Exclusion and Glorious Revolution periods. This was the critical point when the Whig political philosophy that shaped the eighteenth-century Anglo-American mind was first conceived.

The transformative impact of modern natural law and natural rights philosophy on the essential structure of political and moral reasoning in the Anglo-American world not only radically altered the constitutional landscape of late-seventeenth-century England. The theoretical and ideological aftereffects of the political revolution in 1680s England extended far in time and space, providing the philosophical touchstone for the way British and American Whigs articulated their deepest moral and political commitments up to and beyond the American Revolution. In order to fully appreciate the palpable connection between the ideas produced during what Jonathan Scott calls "England's Troubles" in the 1600s and the renewed series of imperial "troubles" that culminated in American independence, we must unearth the complex and multifarious character of Whig political philosophy in the context of the great natural liberty tradition of seventeenth-century Europe.[30]

---

[29] Notable exceptions are Ashcraft, *Revolutionary Politics*; Julia Rudolph's welcome recent study of Tyrrell, *Revolution by Degrees: James Tyrrell and Whig Political Thought in the Late Seventeenth Century* (New York: Palgrave, 2002); and Martyn P. Thompson, *Ideas of Contract in English Political Thought in the Age of John Locke* (New York: Garland, 1987): esp. chs. 6–10.

[30] Jonathan Scott, *England's Troubles: Seventeenth Century English Political Instability in European Context* (Cambridge: Cambridge University Press, 2000).

Thus, in Part Two of this study I examine the genesis of the three strains of Whig thought that came to define the various dimensions of Anglo-American modernity: Tyrrell's conservative restorationism, Sidney's modern republicanism, and Locke's liberalism. Each of these distinct strains of thought originated in the same source, namely, the modification of key principles of early modern natural jurisprudence and the introduction of these modified notions of natural rights and natural law into British constitutional and political discourse. The results of this process of modification differ, however, in each case.

Tyrrell's moderate Whig restorationism relies on the philosophical authority of the celebrated German jurist Samuel Pufendorf. Tyrrell inaugurated the distinctive subtradition of Whig thought that understood Britain's balanced and mixed constitution as the product of a contextualized social compact blending elements of custom, history, and prescription with inherent natural law obligations. The moral and political implications of this Pufendorfian formulation of compact and natural law were antithetical both to divine right monarchy and to the doctrine of popular sovereignty. The moderate Whig architects of the Glorious Revolution settlement of 1689 such as James Tyrrell, William Atwood, and Gilbert Burnet would set a deeply conservative stamp on British constitutional thought for the coming century by their rejection of the radical principles of popular sovereignty, the dissolution of government, and the right of revolution in favor of the more conservative principles flowing from their natural law-based idea of constitutional sovereignty. They understood sovereignty in terms of the Pufendorfian dictum that the essence of law is to be the command of a superior, and as such they rejected popular sovereignty, or the extra-constitutional supreme power of the people, turning instead to the idea of sovereign power as the product of compact and law. In the moderate Whig conception of liberty so deeply influenced by Pufendorf, political liberty and civil order could be secured only by the complex and balanced set of institutions enshrined in the British Constitution.

Sidney offered a modern republican version of radical Whig thought. In contrast to Tyrrell and the moderate Whigs, he held popular sovereignty to be the logical and moral implication of natural liberty and equality. Sidney's commitment to republicanism derived from a populist conception of the proper form of government for securing liberty. He criticized England's mixed monarchical system as an obsolete legacy of the country's feudal past, and favored rather a constitutional reordering based on the goal of establishing the radical legislative supremacy of a democratized parliamentary system marked by more equal and numerous representation, frequent elections, and the rotation of delegates. Sidney argued for what we will call a "reflection theory" of sovereignty, whereby the sovereign power in any constitutional order must reside in the representative legislative body, which alone among institutions can mirror or reflect the popular will. Sidney advanced classical republican notions of virtue and hostility to monarchy and heredity, but he incorporated the ideals of the old republicanism in the language and logic of modern natural jurisprudence. The conceptual model that best helps us understand Sidney's new republicanism is that provided by the Dutch republican theorist Benedict Spinoza. The heart of Sidney's republicanism is, as it was for Spinoza, an attempted synthesis of Machiavellian republicanism and Hobbesian natural rights theory on the basis of the quintessentially Spinozist reflections on the natural order of power relations. In a sense, Sidney employs a Spinozist understanding of power and the naturalness of democracy in order to republicanize Hobbes with elements from Machiavelli and liberalize Machiavelli with Hobbesion natural rights theory. The final product of Sidney's republicanism is a complex mixture of philosophical elements that breaks radically from the tradition of classical republicanism and moves in the direction of a distinctly modern democratic understanding of republicanism.

One goal of this study is to help us understand what is distinctively Lockean in the Anglo-American political tradition. Locke's radical Whiggism rests on a liberal individualist theory of government and natural rights. He, like Sidney and in contrast to Tyrrell, is a partisan of popular sovereignty. Locke's liberalism, however, derives from the individualist core of his philosophy. For Locke, government is a product of consent directed to the securing of certain individual natural rights, most significantly property. While the Lockean theory of rights is not opposed to republicanism as a legitimate form of government, the individualist core of Lockean-liberal philosophy is consistent with a variety of models of limited government. Lockean constitutionalism was consistent with mixed constitutionalism, including mixed monarchy, and went far in developing a sophisticated theory of the separation of powers that included a crucial role for executive prerogative. Moreover, Locke's principle of sovereignty did not necessarily share Sidney's populist premises. Sidney propounded a view of sovereignty that stressed the need for government to reflect the public will and popular consent directly and continuously through democratic institutions. For Locke, on the other hand, the derivation of political power from the people logically means that the people can delegate their authority to a number of constitutional bodies, including the kind of dispersed and balanced system of sovereignty typical in mixed and compound governments. The theoretical core of Lockean-liberal constitutionalism represents his most important innovation of the seventeenth-century natural liberty tradition, namely, his argument for political individualism that maintained that all political power originates in the natural executive power of individuals and can return or devolve to this original source in the event of a dissolution of government. Locke thus supplied the individualist basis of liberal constitutionalism.

The radical Whig assertion of popular sovereignty in the people's right to alter or abolish their form of government was anathema to the Pufendorfian moderate Whig philosophy of Tyrrell and the moderate Whigs who helped

craft the Glorious Revolution settlement and came to dominate British political and constitutional thought in the eighteenth century. In the last two
chapters in Part Two, we will examine the development of British constitutionalism from the Glorious Revolution to the middle of the eighteenth century, paying particular attention to the gradual consolidation of the moderate
Whig interpretation of the constitution and the marginalization of radical
Whig arguments in Britain. In 1680 there was a very wide variety of opinions on the British political spectrum ranging from divine right monarchists
on the right to radical republicans on the left. Through the course of the
century following the Glorious Revolution, however, Britain experienced a
process of ideological convergence toward the conservative moderate Whig
understanding of sovereignty and rights. Republican and liberal ideas were
soon marginalized in Britain after 1689, while hard-core divine right royalists after 1714 gradually accepted the principles of a balanced constitution
and absolute legal sovereignty residing in king-in-Parliament. In my analysis of eighteenth-century British constitutional thought, I demonstrate that
the British regime eulogized by Bolingbroke, Montesquieu, and even the
skeptic David Hume was the compound balanced government rooted in the
principles of seventeenth-century conservative natural law. So complete was
this moderate Whig intellectual hegemony in the second half of the eighteenth century that when Britain's preeminent authority on the constitution,
William Blackstone, affirmed the "supreme, irresistible, absolute, uncontrolled" sovereignty of a Parliament that can make or alter any law it chooses,
scarce a voice in Britain demurred. Thus, when the British public and political leaders confronted colonial resistance to parliamentary sovereignty in the
1760s and 1770s, they understood the dispute in terms of the conservative
philosophical principles of rights and sovereignty derived from Pufendorf a
century earlier.

   Part Three of this study will trace the development of Whig thought in the
context of the British Empire, and analyze the role of Whig philosophy in
the American Revolution and the first experience of constitution making in
the early American Republic. The central argument in Part Three is that the
philosophical origins of the American Revolution lay in the unraveling of the
complex fabric of seventeenth- and eighteenth-century Anglo-American natural jurisprudence that pitted American radical Whigs against their British
moderate Whig cousins. The legacy of the Whig politics of liberty was inherently multifarious, complex, and characterized by internal ideological tensions between not only, or even primarily, a liberal and a republican strain,
but also between radical principles, on the one hand, and the more conservative principles of the moderate Whigs, on the other. The defining feature
of Anglo-American thought in the eighteenth century was the gradual coa-
lescing of the various elements of radical and moderate Whiggism into two
competing interpretations of the meaning of liberty and constitutionalism.
The philosophical origins of the imperial crisis that produced the American

Revolution lay in the mirror image of parallel processes of ideological convergence on either side of the Atlantic as moderate Whig philosophy and the doctrine of parliamentary sovereignty gradually became the dominant constitutional philosophy of eighteenth-century Britain, whereas radical Whig principles and the doctrine of popular sovereignty emerged as the central political creed in the American colonies. During the imperial crisis of 1763–76 leading up to American independence, the cultural, historical, and intellectual bonds of unity between American and British Whigs frayed fatally in the face not only of political events but, more importantly, with the increasing awareness of the fundamental philosophical differences within the broader parameters of Anglo-American Whig political philosophy.

While republican and liberal ideas about popular sovereignty may have been out of step with the conservative temper of eighteenth-century Britain, these ideas took deep root in the American colonies. There the long experience of self-government and benign neglect from the mother country encouraged Americans to see their colonial assemblies as a reflection of popular sovereignty rather than merely subordinate legislatures governed by the supreme authority in Britain. The colonists read voraciously Locke and Sidney, and the radical Whig classic Trenchard and Gordon's *Cato's Letter's* – books that had become pretty much déclassé in eighteenth-century Britain. This produced a remarkable paradox during the imperial crisis whereby British and American Whigs interpreted the same events and institutions in Anglo-American political history in substantially different terms. For example, the colonists held traditional British liberties like habeas corpus and jury trials not as products of custom and prescription but as individual natural rights, and saw the Glorious Revolution of 1688 as a popular revolution against tyranny. These interpretations had been thoroughly rejected in Britain by the second half of the eighteenth century. Thus, Americans and British Whigs were talking past each other throughout much of the imperial crisis, using similar terms and concepts from the common Whig political lexicon and often citing the same historical and legal precedents, but supplying them with different meanings rooted in competing philosophical ideas about the political, constitutional, and moral implications of natural liberty.

The imperial crisis of 1763–76 was primarily a dispute among Anglo-American Whigs over the early modern idea of rights and sovereignty. The British position rested on the idea of absolute legal sovereignty in Parliament. Even the colonies' biggest supporters in Westminster, such as the Pittite and Rockhamite Whigs including the conservative Edmund Burke, affirmed the principle, if not the prudence, of parliamentary sovereignty over the colonies. For their part, the colonists were committed to popular sovereignty and insisted that the only legitimate legislative power lay in their own assemblies. I argue that the major event in this period was the gradual radicalization of the philosophical premises of the colonial position. Early colonial spokesmen like James Otis and John Dickinson qualified their case for popular sovereignty with both an emotional desire to keep the colonies in the British Empire and an intellectual commitment to many of the conservative philosophical principles underlying the moderate Whig interpretation of the British Constitution. However, in three successive chapters of Part Three, I demonstrate how the American position become radicalized throughout the course of the imperial crisis as colonial spokesmen such as Jefferson and Paine rejected practically the last traces of this moderate Whig philosophy in America and reconceptualized both the empire and the right of colonial self-government almost entirely in terms of radical Whig philosophy.

By 1776 the idea of popular sovereignty that Americans had inherited from the radical fringe in early-seventeenth-century England was in the process of becoming virtually the sole legitimate philosophy of government in the colonies. The final chapter of this study will conclude with an analysis of the philosophical and ideological impact of radical Whig ideas on the process of constitution making in the American states in the period following independence. The first state constitutions were to some extent the laboratories of radical Whig philosophy in which the drafters experimented and innovated with liberal and modern republican principles of representation, separation of powers, and popular sovereignty. In the first wave of constitution making in 1776 many states, most notably Pennsylvania, adopted radical republican systems characterized by strong, even unicameral, legislatures regulated by annual elections and broad representation and a very weak executive and judiciary. In this respect, the first revolutionary constitutional framers demonstrated their philosophical indebtedness to Sidney and his understanding of Whig modern republicanism. The second wave of state constitution making in America saw a shift toward the Lockean-liberal model of government, with New York and Massachusetts institutionalizing a clear separation of powers with a bicameral legislature, an independent executive with veto power, and more formidable judiciaries. This parceling out of constituent power and the innovation of popular ratifying conventions was, I contend, a demonstration of the modified Lockean philosophy underlying the American idea of divided sovereignty. The framers of the first state constitutions thus began the perhaps definitively American long-term process of blending and harmonizing the liberal and republican elements of their Whig philosophical inheritance.

This picture of the distinct and interpenetrating strands of thought characterizing early modern Anglo-American thought belies the Kuhnian paradigms too often constructed in contemporary work on the history of early modern political thought. I believe this study can illustrate that English and American Whigs in the formative seventeenth and eighteenth centuries sang a common song of liberty with several different voices and parts.

PART ONE

THE DIVINE RIGHT CHALLENGE
TO NATURAL LIBERTY

Robert Filmer is usually remembered by posterity, if at all, as the ideological and philosophical nemesis of early English Whigs, most notably James Tyrrell, Algernon Sidney, and John Locke. There is, however, much more to Filmer's thought than what is suggested by the charred remains left to history by his polemical mauling at the hands of the Whigs. On one level, Filmer is conspicuous as the direct target of attack for the Whigs. In the minds of many Whigs, Filmer's work embodied all too clearly everything that was mistaken and dangerous in English royalism. For this reason alone, Filmer is an important figure in the development of early modern political thought. In order to understand the first Whigs and their intellectual descendants, the serious student of the period must pay careful attention to Filmer. However, Filmer should be regarded as more than just a hapless polemical foil for his more talented Whig antagonists. As we shall see, Filmer's arguments for divine right monarchy and political absolutism in the turbulent years from the 1630s to the 1650s provided the intellectual nerve of the mainstream royalist and Tory position in England well into the eighteenth century. Filmer's passionate and articulate defense of the principles of passive obedience, indefeasible hereditary right, and royal supremacy echoed through much of the Tory literature at the time of Exclusion and well beyond.

In order to understand Filmer's importance as a political thinker, it is important to consider both the substance of his argument and the historical context in which he wrote. Born in 1588 under the shadow of a looming Spanish invasion, Filmer grew up in a victorious England seemingly assured of its national independence, hopeful for the end of religious controversy with the broad acceptance of the Elizabethan church settlement, and confident in its monarchy after the successful and peaceful accession of James Stuart to Elizabeth's throne in 1603.[1] As a promising scion of the

---

[1] For a good biographical treatment of Filmer, see Johann Somerville's introduction to his edition of Robert Filmer, *Patriarcha and Other Works* (Cambridge: Cambridge University Press, 1991): pp. ix–xxiv.

Kentshire gentry, young Robert Filmer established strong connections to the higher Anglican clergy and to the court, marrying Anne Heton, the daughter of the bishop of Ely, in 1618 and receiving a knighthood the following year. No doubt Filmer's arch-royalist sympathies were securely planted in his formative years in association with the court and clergy. However, the optimism of the later Elizabethan age would not last, and Filmer's lifelong commitment to the sanctity of throne and altar would be the cause of great anxiety, disappointment, and even persecution throughout the course of his later life. He witnessed the disintegration of the tenuous Elizabethan church settlement, lived through decades of bitter conflict between crown and Parliament that culminated in rebellion, civil war, and regicide, and died a bitter old royalist under the rule of the Commonwealth in 1653. Filmer's works were written in response to the dramatic events of this period and stand, at least in his view, as a painful chronicle of England's political, constitutional, and religious woes in the first half of the seventeenth century.

The causes of the deep political instability in Filmer's age were twofold: religious and constitutional.[2] First, a bitter religious and theological controversy plagued the reign of the first two Stuart kings. This controversy primarily took two forms. On the one hand, seventeenth-century Englishmen feared the specter of Catholic power. In the context of Counter-Reformation Europe, English national independence, tied since the Tudor era to the idea of a national Protestant Church, seemed under threat both from foreign invasion by or interference by Spain and later France, and from domestic Catholic opponents to the crown. The memory of the Spanish Armada and later the failed Gunpowder plot of 1605 seared into the English political consciousness. The bitter controversy over the Oath of Allegiance for Catholic subjects between James and the supporters of papal power, both foreign and domestic, only confirmed the suspicion about Catholicism for many Englishmen, including Filmer, who came to see in Catholic natural law doctrines the principle of anarchy itself. As Filmer put it: "the only point of Popery is the alienating and withdrawing of subjects from their obedience to their prince, to raise sedition and rebellion."[3] On the other hand, the most intractable source of religious division in Filmer's England was the failure of the Elizabethan church settlement to produce religious uniformity among Protestants. The deep cleavages within English Protestantism over the correct form of church government and the right of individual conscience that widened throughout the reign of Charles I would prove even more dangerous

---

[2] For good general overviews of the ideological and historical context of the period in which Filmer lived and wrote, see Jonathan Scott, *England's Troubles: Seventeenth Century English Political Instability in European Context* (Cambridge: Cambridge University Press, 2000); Johann P. Somerville, *Politics and Ideology in England, 1603–1640* (London: Longman, 1986) and Austin Woolrych, *Britain in Revolution, 1625–1660* (Oxford: Oxford University Press, 2002).

[3] Filmer, *Patriarcha and Other Writings*, pp. 132–3.

to political order than the Protestant–Catholic controversies during James' rule. Politically active dissenters exercised significant influence in Parliament and the wider society. The Calvinists of various hues in England and Scotland consistently frustrated and opposed royal efforts to impose religious uniformity through such measures as the Laudian reforms of the 1630s. Moreover, among the dissenters or Puritans, English royalists perceived dangerous arguments supporting the principle of resistance to monarchical power taking root and proliferating at an alarming rate. During Filmer's lifetime, the Elizabethan ideals of the essential unity between church and state and royal supremacy in the constitution disintegrated under the pressure of bitter theological disputes that would in time contribute greatly to the causes of the civil war.

The constitutional parallel to the religious divisions in Filmer's England was the bitter and durable struggle for power between the crown and Parliament. For the most part, during James' reign, the wily Scot tempered his public pronouncements advancing claims of divine right and royal supremacy with a prudent dose of political pragmatism, rarely pushing his contests with Parliament to the constitutional point of no return. Charles, his less politic son, did, however, invite serious and bitter disputes with Parliament. His decision to rule without calling Parliament for eleven years, the attempt to circumvent the parliamentary power of supply through excise and customs measures, and his failed effort to impose religious uniformity on the prickly and combative Scots represented to many in the nation an intolerable exercise and extension of royal prerogative. Parliament's measures to curtail executive power and to assert its own constitutional muscle culminated in a series of measures intended to limit the crown's authority in the turbulent years immediately preceding the outbreak of war in 1642. To most English royalists like Filmer, the bitter constitutional disputes of Charles' reign signified nothing less than an attempt by Parliament to subvert the crown's position as governor. In the theoretical arguments for mixed regime theory and the notion of ancient constitutionalism used to support Parliament's claims, Filmer and his royalist compatriots saw a danger not only to the power and sanctity of the crown, but also to the hierarchical social, political, and religious fabric binding the entirety of English society.

The true source of these various religious and constitutional challenges to monarchical power in England was, according to Filmer, a single pernicious principle: the doctrine of the natural liberty of humankind. In Filmer's view, this single proposition resting on the idea that all human beings are naturally free and equal, and thus that consent to form government was the unifying thread, the philosophical core, of the various arguments challenging monarchical authority. Catholic conspirators, Puritan resisters, and parliamentary demagogues were all inspired by numerous versions of the doctrine of natural liberty then extent, and indeed flourishing, in England and the rest of Europe. The grand aim then of Filmer's project was nothing less than to refute this idea that had produced such dangerous consequences not only for the English monarchy, but more importantly for the principle of monarchy itself. In Part One, we will analyze Filmer's assault on the three most important strains of the natural liberty doctrine in his time: the later scholastic natural law theory of the Jesuit Cardinals Francisco Suarez and Roberto Bellarmine, the mixed regime and Calvinist resistance theories of the parliamentary contractarians of the civil war period, and finally, the natural jurisprudence of Hugo Grotius and Thomas Hobbes. Each of these distinct schools of thought served, in Filmer's view, to obscure the proper understanding of the individual's due submission and obligation to obey political, especially monarchical, authority. It was, as we shall see in Part Two, the first Whigs' critique of Filmer's systematic animadversions against the natural liberty theories of the first half of the seventeenth century that inaugurated a new, distinctly Whiggish, form of political and constitutional theory. In defending the principle of natural liberty against Filmer's attacks, the Whigs modified this principle in significant and in some cases radical ways. Filmer unwittingly (and presumably much to his eternal chagrin) became the critical conduit through which the Whigs would establish the distinctly modern form of the doctrine of natural liberty that would come to define the Anglo-American tradition for the next century.

With respect to the substance of Filmer's argument, much more will be said in the following discussion. However, at this point, it would be helpful to introduce briefly the main feature of Filmer's political thought. Filmer's response to the various versions of the natural liberty doctrine was essentially a form of political theology rooted in the tradition of Martin Luther. Filmer's approach to political issues may be stated simply: the Bible, not nature or unassisted human reason, is the only authoritative guide for political and moral matters. This extreme *sola scriptura* position informed Filmer's deep political conservatism and his support for the supremacy of the monarch in religious affairs. The Bible, in his view, not only failed to support the idea of natural liberty, but any uncorrupted reading of Scripture clearly demonstrated the natural and fundamental human subjection to political and patriarchal authority. In Filmer's interpretation of Adam's creation in Genesis, the divine establishment of absolute monarchy was unmistakably apparent. It was the essentially theological bases of Filmer's argument that distinguished his position from that of the *politique* Bodin or his fellow English royalist Hobbes. It was, moreover, Filmer's theological foundation that directed and animated his assault on the proponents of natural liberty. In a particularly striking way, Filmer proposed that the only means to counteract what he took to be the prevailing libertarian trend in intellectual fashion in his day and to remedy England's political and constitutional woes was by recourse back to the first things simply.

I

The Attack on the Catholic Natural Law

In 1613 a book was officially condemned and ceremonially burned in London. An English king and a Spanish cardinal were the chief actors in the latest installment of a by now protracted dispute at the highest levels of civil and ecclesiastical government. James I's dramatic denunciation of Francisco Suarez's *Defensio Fidei Catholicae* framed the momentous struggle over competing claims of authority. On the one side was a king who claimed that his power derived originally and directly from God. And on the other side was a Jesuit scholastic defending the pope's claim to a divinely ordained right to depose heretical civil rulers. This dispute brought to a head a long-simmering controversy over the English Oath of Allegiance, which required English Catholics to renounce papal pretensions in temporal politics.[1] For the better part of a decade following the enactment of the oath by Parliament in 1606, Jesuit thinkers including Suarez, Roberto Bellarmine, and the Englishman Robert Parsons had criticized James' claim to rule by divine right, even as James and his supporters, such as John Hayward and William Barclay, just as vehemently affirmed the king's right against the claims of papal supremacy.

While it is a long way from the Jesuit College at Coimbra to the streets of Revolution-era America, this inauspicious Counter-Reformation backdrop is a fitting point of departure for the study of the philosophical foundations and historical development of the modern politics of liberty. The dispute over regal and papal authority in early-seventeenth-century England had implications extending far beyond the acrid smell of burning pages in London. As we shall see, this theologico–political controversy raised important questions about the fundamental issues of our understanding of political life such

---

[1] See Francis Oakley, *The Politics of Eternity: Studies in the History of Medieval and Early-Modern Political Thought* (Leiden: Brill, 1999): pp. 193–4) for a discussion that puts the English controversy in the broader European context of disputes between the papacy and political authority such as the contemporaneous Venetian Interdict.

as the principle of consent, the legitimacy of popular resistance to political authority, and the philosophical underpinnings of the doctrine of natural liberty. In important respects, Robert Filmer, the divine right opponent of the Whigs at the end of the seventeenth century, would reintroduce a conflict first engaged many years before.

Filmer's account of his own activity in the opening section of his classic *Patriarcha* provides an unusually candid glimpse into his motivation and aims in this book. He presents this work as a refutation of the "new, plausible and dangerous" tenet of the natural liberty of humankind.[2] He ascribes this doctrine primarily to the Catholic scholastics denounced by James I. Concerning these opponents, he speculates whether their ideas "be more erroneous in divinity or dangerous in policy." Filmer's observation here points to the central theme of *Patriarcha*.[3] It is Filmer's contention that there is a direct and palpable connection between theology and politics, between a notion "first hatched in the schools" and the political doctrine of natural liberty and legitimate resistance to monarchical authority. It is from the writings of one such "schoolman," the Jesuit Cardinal Bellarmine, that Filmer draws what he calls "the strength of all that I ever read or heard produced for the natural liberty of the subject."[4] The passages that attract Filmer's fire contain Bellarmine's argument that civil power

[i]s immediately in the whole multitude, as in the subject of it. For this power is by the divine law, but the divine law hath given this power to no particular man. If the positive law be taken away, there is left no reason why amongst a multitude (who are equal) one rather than another should bear rule over the rest. . . . It depends upon the consent of the multitude to ordain over themselves a king, or consul, or other magistrate; and if there be a lawful cause, the multitude may change the kingdom into an aristocracy or democracy.[5]

Thus, the central propositions of the Catholic doctrine of natural liberty that Filmer identified with the Jesuits Bellarmine and Suarez are: (1) the natural condition of humanity is one of equality and liberty, (2) political authority in general derives from the ordination of divine law, but the particular form of government for a people is the product of consent, (3) government as such may be understood as a form of contract, and (4) the "multitude" may alter or rescind the political contract under certain conditions so as to reconstitute the regime or replace the rulers as they deem fit. It is in the light of Filmer's professed horror about the theological and political consequences of this

---

[2] Robert Filmer, *Patriarcha and Other Writings*, Johann Somerville, ed. (Cambridge: Cambridge University Press, 1991): p. 2.

[3] Ibid., p. 3.

[4] Ibid., p. 5.

[5] Ibid., p. 5 and Roberto Bellarmine, *De Laicis*, Kathleen Murphy, trans. (New York: Fordham University Press, 1928), III, IV: 25–7.

doctrine of natural liberty that the Adam of Genesis emerges as the central figure in the divine right drama.

The Adamite Thesis

Filmer's response to the Catholic natural law doctrine of natural liberty was rooted in the Genesis account of the creation of Adam. The characteristic elements of Filmer's political teaching, the arguments that would come to constitute the core of English Toryism – such as the divine ordination of political power, the doctrine of passive obedience, and indefeasible hereditary right – derived from his contention that "the lordship which Adam by creation had over the whole world, was as large and ample as the absolutest dominion of any monarch which hath been since the creation."[6] Filmer grounds this claim on his interpretation of the broader scriptural teaching regarding creation: just as God has dominion over all earthly creatures as their source, so Adam has dominion over his progeny as their source.[7] This source-based logic and its tendency to collapse the supernatural and the mundane pervades Filmer's reading of Scripture and provides the basis for his tracing the subordination of children to parents down to the first parent, Adam, the surrogate begetter of the human world. In Adam's creation, Filmer found the origin of government in the first exercise of power demonstrated over his offspring. The crucial twist in Filmer's argument, however, is that Adam's sovereignty did not in any real sense depend on the recognition or even the existence of his progeny but rather in the simple revealed truth of his sole creation.[8] Political rule does not, according to Filmer, derive from consent. In God's creation of Adam, He established the paradigmatic pattern for rule by indicating that "neither Eve nor her children could either limit Adam's power or join others with him in the government."[9] By this creation of one man alone and the generation of all humankind from this one source, Filmer argues, the biblical teaching on the origin of political power is immediately apparent. The subjection of Adam to God and the derivation of every human being from Adam as the primal source reveal the two signal facts about political power – hierarchy is imprinted in the structure of the created order, and this hierarchy denotes the natural subjection of all human beings, a subjection that is impervious to human initiative or alteration.

The argument that to have a source is to be under subjection and obligation to that source forms the guiding hermeneutical principle of Filmer's scriptural exegesis. From the primal demonstration and example of rule in

---

[6] Filmer, *Patriarcha*, p. 7.
[7] Michael Zuckert, *Natural Rights and the New Republicanism* (Princeton: Princeton University Press, 1994): p. 44.
[8] Filmer, *Patriarcha*, pp. 187–8.
[9] Ibid. p. 192.

the first father, Adam, Filmer derives the teaching that the Israelite patriarchs and indeed all biblical rulers had by right of fatherhood a royal authority over their children, inasmuch as by his birth everyone "becomes a subject to him that begets him."[10] Filmer proceeds to employ the patriarchal principle both to trace the lineage of the political authority of all the biblical rulers back to the original source in Adam and to discover the very nature of authority and subjection in the character of creation itself. For example, from Paul's injunction in Romans 13 that "every power be subject to the higher powers," Filmer draws two specific implications about the divine ordination of politics: the general doctrine of passive obedience to political rulers and the particular scriptural support for absolute monarchy.[11] In Scripture old and new, Filmer draws divine sanction for the same absolutist teaching.

The argument from Adam's creation exposes two distinct but related dimensions of Filmer's thought. On the one hand, it possesses a genetic dynamic whereby Filmer suggests that authority is a type of being intelligible in linear terms inasmuch as the individual can trace his or her subjection back to Adam and ultimately to God. In this light, any rejection of the inherent political subjection such as that posited by Catholic natural law is tantamount to atheism, a denial of God as the supreme source.[12] However, Filmer's divine right also manifests what might be called an "existential dynamic" concerning an exposition of the origin of political power per se. In this sense, Filmer's interpretation of creation in Genesis rests on the premise that the existence of rule and subjection in the world is intelligible only in terms of the revealed truth of Scripture. The existential aspect of Filmer's logic does not rely so much on the individual's relation to a particular paterfamilias as on a recognition of the utterly extrinsic character of political power vis-à-vis humanity. It is not merely the legal codification of patriarchal principles that is the operating factor in Filmer's theory; rather, he identifies the patriarchal perspective as the only one from which to distinguish the origin of *all* law and political authority. This aspect of Filmer's argument radically minimizes human participation in the generation of rule and thus serves his central theoretical concern to combine the genetic and existential aspects of patriarchalism in a single account of the fundamental human stance toward political authority as well as the whole of creation.

---

[10] Ibid., p. 282.

[11] Ibid., pp. 236, 238. The use of the singular form in St. Paul's query "Wilt thou not be afraid of the power?" is the foundation of Filmer's argument for the New Testament support for monarchy.

[12] As his critics were quick to point out, however, the consequence of Filmer's doctrine of natural subjection is to radically reinterpret the traditional Augustinian position that political life, and hence subjection, is a product of the Fall and sin. See St. Augustine, *The City of God* (New York: Penguin, 1984): bk. XIX, ch. 15 and Ernest Fortin, "St. Augustine," in *The History of Political Philosophy*, Leo Strauss and Joseph Cropsey, eds. (Chicago: University of Chicago Press, 1987): p. 183.

The unifying thread in Filmer's account of creation, the guiding principle that combines the genetic and existential dynamics in his argument, is the formulation of an ontology of obedience. This position rested on the premise that all human beings are defined and constrained by the source of their being, whether by God and Adam as the source of all or by the particular fathers of families as the source of each. The chief political implication Filmer draws from this premise is that the natural obligation each individual has to obey his or her father means that individuals are never sufficiently free to be the authors of their own political obligation.[13] The difference between paternal and regal power is simply one of degree, not a difference in kind. Filmer claims: "If we compare the natural duties of a father with those of a king, we find them to be all one, without any difference at all but only in the latitude or extent of them."[14] Filmer's reflections on the account of creation in Genesis constitute the core of his thoughts on the essence of being and human being. The full expression of the creatureliness of all creatures – but especially the humanity of the human – is found in loving obedience to the source of one's being and the authority inhering in a superior.

For Filmer, the patriarchal family signifies the human participation in God's perpetual creation, but it does so in a way that both minimizes human initiative in the project and culminates in the production of naturally subject beings. Just as obedience is the law of creation, so is rebellion the root of all sin. In the broad frame of Filmer's ontology of obedience, human beings stand as created beings. They are thus under obligation to a superior, and are most fully engaged in their essential nature when they are submitting to some authority. Filmer reminds his readers that "the desire for liberty was the cause of the fall of Adam."[15]

The creation of Adam recounted in Scripture and the ubiquity of the patriarchal family through history and across cultures stand as the twin pillars of Filmer's political teaching on obedience. Adam's creation supplied the basis for Filmer's contention for the divine ordination of political rule. From the absolute rule of Adam held by creation, Filmer argues, it "follows that civil power not only in general is by divine institution, but even the assignment of it specifically to the eldest parent."[16] This combination of a theological and a more naturalistic form of argumentation marks Filmer's approach to the question of the relation of regal and paternal authority. The argument that the father who begets and engenders rightfully rules and commands his children meshes with Filmer's chronology from Genesis of the transferal of the lordship of Adam. According to Filmer, this sovereignty passed to Noah after

---

[13] Filmer, *Patriarcha*, pp. 7, 185 and Gordon Schochet, *Patriarchalism in Political Thought* (Oxford: Oxford University Press, 1975): p. 13.

[14] Filmer, *Patriacha*, p. 12.

[15] Ibid., p. 2.

[16] Ibid., p. 7.

the Flood and to "the distinct families, which had fathers ruling over them" following the confusion at Babel and finally "by right descending from him [Adam] the patriarchs did enjoy."[17] A particularly striking feature of this account is Filmer's effort to harmonize the complex politics and cataclysmic events of Genesis with his profession of God's approval for the patriarchal family structure. Despite the Fall from grace, an earth-ravaging flood, and the dispersion of the peoples at Babel, God, Filmer argues, was careful to preserve paternal, and hence monarchical, rule.

Filmer's Theology

Having identified the theological basis of Filmer's political teaching in the account of the creation of Adam in Genesis, we are still left with a question regarding the source of Filmer's political theology. What were the intellectual and authoritative theological influences on Filmer's ideas? Despite Filmer's robust claims of originality, we can uncover two underlying influences on his brand of divine right thinking. One source is the general approach to religious and political issues introduced by Martin Luther, and the other is the distinctive development of English royalist thought among the higher clergy in England during Filmer's formative years.

The reformation orientation toward political questions articulated by Luther provides the general historical and theological context necessary for any full understanding of Filmer's political thought. As Quentin Skinner has demonstrated, "the main influence of Lutheran political theory in early modern Europe lay in the direction of encouraging and legitimating the emergence of unified and absolutist monarchies."[18] In many ways the Kentshire squire was a product of Luther's political, social, and religious worldview. First, as we have seen, Filmer was deeply influenced by the *sola scriptura* theological orientation instituted by the Lutheran Reformation. Filmer inherited Luther's deep conviction that the Bible unalloyed with church tradition

---

[17] Ibid., pp. 7–8. Filmer's account of the transferal of rule in the Bible parallels what Schochet has termed "anthropological patriarchalism" (Schochet, *Patriarchalism*, p. 11). In this view, Filmer treats Genesis as the earliest historical record of human association and thus employs it to explain the transformation of primitive familial association into a wider, more complex society. While I believe that Filmer did look to something akin to anthropological history, I emphasize the more fundamental theological basis of the Adamite thesis. Figgis, for example, greatly exaggerates the anthropological dimension in Filmer when he argues that he turned to Scripture primarily to provide "authentic information as to the nature of primitive society" (J. N. Figgis, *The Divine Right of Kings* [New York: Harper, 1965]: p. 159). In contrast to Schochet and Figgis, I maintain that Filmer's treatment of Adam is more normative than descriptive and more theological than anthropological.

[18] Quentin Skinner, *The Foundations of Modern Political Thought, Volume II* (Cambridge: Cambridge University Press, 1978): p. 113. Cf. John Clement Rager, *The Political Philosophy of Blessed Cardinal Bellarmine* (Washington, DC: Catholic University of America Press, 1926): pp. 44–56, 61–2.

or clerical authority is the only proper guide for political, moral, and religious matters. Luther's hostility to the humanist and scholastic claims for the power of human reason to intuit the ways of God through observation of nature produced a clear echo in Filmer's rejection of reason and nature as authoritative guides for political life. Luther's profound suspicion of "this beast... Reason" and his vitriolic diatribes against the pervasive influence in the schools of the "damned, conceited, rascally heathen" Aristotle provide an important element of the context for Filmer's own assertion of the impotence of reason and his general dismissal of the authority of the classical political tradition.[19] By elevating the claims of what Luther called the "holy and sacred certain doctrine of Scripture" over and against appeals to human reason, virtue, and capacities, Filmer followed Luther's decisive break from the humanist and scholastic tradition advancing the essential harmony between reason and revelation.[20] For Filmer, as for his German predecessor and intellectual light, all politics and morality was Bible politics.

The second major element of Filmer's inheritance from Luther had to do with his view of human nature. Underlying Filmer's rejection of the claims of reason regarding intuition and speculation about the ways of God is an abiding certainty of the utter depravity of human nature. Filmer's political teaching rests on the Lutheran principle that "the whole world is evil" and that human nature, at least since the Fall, is fundamentally perverse and alienated from God.[21] The central Reformation doctrine of justification by faith, resting on the notion that the only righteousness that matters is "passive righteousness" that is endowed by God's grace but cannot be earned, provides the theological foundation for Filmer's divine right theory.[22] Luther's assertion of humanity's total incapacity to advance our salvation through our own rational efforts, tradition, or clerical intermediaries establishes the moral grounding for Filmer's principle of natural subjection. The Filmerian proposition of natural subjection, with its emphasis on the moral incapacity of human beings to constitute sovereign political power, is a direct political corollary of Lutheran theology. While Filmer generally eschewed the ultra-Augustinian distinction between the temporal realm and the community of

---

[19] See, for example, Luther's "Commentary on Galatians" in *Martin Luther: Selections from His Writings,* John Dillenberger, ed. (Garden City, NY: Doubleday, 1961): pp. 128, 131 and "An Open Letter to the Christian Nobility" in *The Works of Martin Luther,* C. M. Jacobs, trans. (Philadelphia: Muehlenberg Press, 1915–32), Vol. II: pp. 146–7 (hereafter *Works*).

[20] Luther, "An Open Letter to the Christian Nobility," *Works,* Vol. II: pp. 150–1. Cf. Skinner, *Foundations,* p. 4.

[21] See Luther, "On Secular Authority, to What Extent It Should Be Obeyed," *Works,* J. J. Schindel, trans., Vol. III: p. 236; compare this with Filmer's identification of the cause of Adam's fall in "the desire of liberty" (Filmer, *Patriarcha,* p. 2). Cf. W. D. J. Cargill Thompson, *The Political Thought of Martin Luther* (Brighton, MA: Harvester, 1984): pp. 19–21.

[22] For Luther's doctrine of justification by faith, see "A Treatise on Christian Liberty," *Works,* W. A. Lambert, trans., Vol. II: pp. 316–17, 322–3, 329–34.

Christians that is central for Luther, the Englishman did frame his characterization of human nature and the status of the human vis-à-vis the divine on
the basis of theological categories and existential principles traceable back
to Luther.

The third feature of Luther's influence on Filmer had to do with the
deep political conservatism identified with the Lutheran version of reformed
theology. It is not surprising that the author of the virulent anti-populist
tract *Against the Robbing and Murdering hordes of Peasants* (1525) would find
no more enthusiastic protégé than the dutiful Sir Robert. Filmer followed
Luther in repeatedly asserting the Pauline doctrine of submission to political authority. In this key respect regarding the divine institution of secular
authority, Filmerian and Lutheran divine right arguments are practically
indistinguishable: for both Luther and Filmer, political power flows from
God. Luther's fear that his call for religious change would be associated
with political radicalism, and thus discredited among the German nobility,
led him to formulate a rigorous theological doctrine of political obedience
rooted in Scripture.[23] By adopting Luther's principle of unyielding nonresistance, Filmer located himself in the deeply rooted English Erastian tradition
of Tyndale, Cranmer, and the earliest followers of Luther in England in the
first half of the sixteenth century.[24] Filmer's Scripture-based argument for
human subjection and political obedience derived from the central Lutheran
theological premise that the entire existing social and political order is a
direct reflection of God's inscrutable will.[25] The God who reveals His will
to radically imperfect human faculties through revelation is omnipotent and
governs everything in the world through divine providence.

In a few respects, Filmer's adoption of the Lutheran Scripture-based principle of political obedience extended in even more authoritarian directions
than that of Luther himself. For example, Filmer does not entertain Luther's
idea that "if all the world were composed of real Christians, that is true
believers, no prince, king, lord, sword or law would be needed. . . . For what
were the use of them, since Christians . . . of themselves they do more than its
laws and doctrines can demand."[26] Despite Luther's immediate qualification
that Christians are very few and far between, considering that "the world and
the masses are and always will be unchristian, although they are baptized and
nominally Christian," the incipient utilitarianism in Luther's view of secular
government does not comport with Filmer's more rigorous assertion of natural human subjection to both political and patriarchal authority. For Filmer,
piety does not exempt the individual from the ontological state of obedience

---

[23] For Luther's affirmation of the Pauline doctrine of political obedience, see "On Secular
   Authority," *Works*, Vol. III: pp. 231–4, 255–7. Cf. Thompson, *Martin Luther*, p. 94.
[24] Thompson, *Martin Luther*, pp. 92–4.
[25] Skinner, *Foundations*, p. 18.
[26] Luther, "On Secular Authority," *Works*, Vol. III: p. 234.

and subjection. Moreover, while Filmer strongly adhered to Luther's principle that no active resistance to political authority is ever justified, he did not follow his German master in identifying the binding moral duties of princes such as maintaining civil order and true religious worship.[27] From the strict Lutheran perspective, Filmer's idea of monarchy runs the risk of confusing the agent of divine omnipotent power with the actual divine source of that power. Despite these few noteworthy differences between Filmer and Luther's teaching on government, there is a clear sympathy between them on the more fundamental aspect of obedience and nonresistance. Luther's contention that political rulers had to be obeyed for conscience's sake, and his rejection of forcible resistance to rulers as sinful, both produced, in the words of one Luther scholar, a decisive break from "late Medieval Catholics" and made the issue of political obedience "the central and critical question confronting European political thinkers."[28] The profound influence of Luther's teaching regarding obedience and the divine ordination of political authority provided the theological foundation for Filmer's conception of the sacred character of monarchy.

While one aspect of Filmer's political theology derived from the European context of the Lutheran Reformation, the other major theological, and indeed ideological, component of Filmer's theory of monarchy was the political doctrine of the higher clergy in England in the formative years of his life in the opening decades of the seventeenth century. Luther provided Filmer with a model of the absolute authority of Scripture, the idea of the omnipotence of God and moral incapacity of humanity, and the sacred principle of nonresistance. The central role of Adam in Filmer's argument, however, had a more emphatically English source. It is in the context of seventeenth-century England's perennial conflicts over the extent and origin of royal power that Filmer's essentially Lutheran theology assumes its distinctive mantle of defending royal supremacy. Luther's support for monarchy as the best regime was never as central to his thoughts on government as it was for Filmer and his brand of English royalism. Moreover, Luther did not actually root the origin of government in Adam's creation in Genesis or attach anything like the significance given to this particular scriptural passage by Filmer. To identify the source of the prominence of Adam in Filmer's thought, we have to look to England.

---

[27] Sheldon Wolin emphasizes Luther's limits on the power of princes and links this with what he takes to be the democratic implications of Luther's plan for church reform (see *Politics and Vision: Continuity and Innovation in Western Political Thought* [London: Methuen, 1969]: pp. 153, 155, 163–4). Wolin's democratic interpretation of Luther belies the more fundamental authoritarian tendencies in Lutheranism that had a profound influence on English royalism.

[28] Francis Oakley, "Christian Obedience and Authority, 1520–1550," in *The Cambridge History of Political Thought, 1450–1700*, J. H. Burns and Mark Goldie, eds. (Cambridge: Cambridge University Press, 1991): p. 171.

The patriarchalist and Adamite arguments popularized by Filmer had their precursors in the theological and constitutional controversies of early-seventeenth-century England. The Adamite interpretation of Genesis, which would assume such importance for Filmer, first appeared in England in authoritative circles in the Convocation of 1606 under the leadership of Bishop John Overall. This convocation of bishops organized at the height of James' controversy with the Jesuit scholastics and English Catholics made a particular reading of Genesis the scriptural basis for a patriarchal account of the origin of government. The Convocation also proposed a highly politicized interpretation of the Fifth Commandment as a scriptural support for divine right monarchy.[29] It is hardly surprising that Filmer would be profoundly influenced by the formulation of patriarchal monarchy proposed as an addition to the canon of the Church of England by the leading men of the church. Filmer did not, however, simply duplicate the argument of the Convocation, but rather made some significant modifications in the basic scriptural theory propounded by the bishops. For example, whereas Filmer based his own scriptural account of the origin of government on the account of Adam's creation, the Convocation emphasized Noah's role and example as the epitome of "patriarchal [and] ... regal government." Filmer did not follow the Convocation's interpretation that "there is more expressed in the Scriptures" about Noah "than there was before the Flood, of the power and authority of Adam."[30] While the direct centrality of Adam in Filmer's political theology was paradoxically suggested by his Jesuit opponents, nonetheless it is obvious that Filmer's political reasoning was informed by the spirit of scripturalism and the view of a patriarchal-monarchical nexus prevalent among the higher clergy in the England of his day.

Another important influence on Filmer was the celebrated writings and sermons of key clerical supporters of the crown in the Jacobean and early Carolinian periods. It is remarkable how naturally, almost effortlessly, clerical supporters of the crown in early-seventeenth-century England appealed to the authority of divine right to undergird their conception of royal prerogative in the king's disputes with Parliament. To cite just a few instances, in *A Sermon Preached Before the King's Most Excellent Majestie* in 1614, the Anglican divine William Goodwin asserted the divine anointing of the English king and the prohibition on all resistance to royal authority flowing from this theological premise. Of the divinely instituted office of kings, Goodwin intoned, "they cannot be deposed by the sentence, they may not bee deprived by the force of any Mortall Man."[31] Not only did Filmer imbibe

---

[29] For a fuller discussion of the patriarchalist teaching of the Convocation of 1606, see Schochet, *Patriarchalism*, pp. 92–5.

[30] Convocation of 1606, chapter vi, p. 7 (quoted in Schochet, *Patriarchalism*, p. 93).

[31] William Goodwin, "A Sermon Preached Before the Kings most Excellent Majestie" (1614), *The Struggle for Sovereignty: Seventeenth Century English Political Tracts*, Joyce Lee Malcolm, ed.

the central notions of divine right and nonresistance from the vocal Anglican leadership of his day, he also adopted, quite naturally, many of the constitutional and legal positions advanced by the crown's clerical supporters in the periodic disputes with Parliament. For example, Roger Maynwaring's argument in two sermons entitled *Religion and Allegiance* (1627) that the king, being the Lord's anointed, can raise taxes without the consent of Parliament would be incorporated into Filmer's constitutional arguments in the 1630s.[32] And Filmer's old friend Peter Heylyn offered an argument for royal supremacy over the legislative body based on an understanding of law as deriving from the king's personal will that would also become part of Filmer's argument.[33] Filmer's political theology, then, clearly did not develop in an intellectual and ideological vacuum. Important elements of Luther's reformed theology and the authoritative pronouncement of high church leaders in England combined to produce the fertile philosophical and theological soil that nourished Filmerian divine right politics. Both the general historical context of Reformation Europe and the specific constitutional controversies in England in his day provided the ideological assumptions informing Filmer's view of human nature, the characteristics of God's rule over the world, and the origin and structure of the English Constitution.

The Assault on the Scholastics

The Jesuit scholastics Cardinals Bellarmine and Suarez were, as we noted earlier, Filmer's most conspicuous adversaries in *Patriarcha*. The two cornerstones of the scholastic argument on which Filmer trains his attack are the proposition of natural liberty and equality and the argument that particular forms of government are the product of consent. Bellarmine describes the original human condition as one of a "multitude of equals," while Suarez affirms: "from the nature of the subject all men are born free, and therefore none has political jurisdiction over another, just as no dominion."[34] The Catholic position, moreover, rested on the premise of the divine ordination of political power insofar as God is the "prime and principal Author" of

(Indianapolis: Liberty Fund, 1999): p. 39; cf. pp. 37–40 for Goodwin's statement on the general principle of divine ordination.

[32] Roger Maynwaring, "Religion and Allegiance" (1627), in Malcolm, *Struggle for Sovereignty*, pp. 67, 70.

[33] Peter Heylyn, "A Briefe and Moderate Answer" (1637), in Malcolm, *Struggle for Sovereignty*, p. 82.

[34] Bellarmine, *De Laicis*, p. 25 and Francisco Suarez, *De Legibus, Ac Deo Legislatore* (1612, Coimbra), in *Selections from Three Works of Francisco Suarez, S. J.*, Vol. I photographic reproduction of selections from original editions. Volume II, English version of text prepared by Gwladys L. Williams et al. (Oxford: Clarendon Press, 1944): Book III, ch. 2, sec. 3: pp. 373 (hereafter *De Leg.*, bk., ch., sec., and page number).

political life.[35] While the Catholic natural lawyers and Filmer agreed that political power in general comes directly from God alone, for the Jesuits the particular political forms under which human beings live – monarchy, aristocracy, and democracy – depend upon consent.[36] It is this distinction between a general and a particular, or direct and mediated, species of divine ordination of political authority that Filmer sought to refute with the Adamite account of the source of political power.

Filmer frames a fundamental dichotomy between his position and that of Bellarmine: either natural subjection is the truth of the human condition or natural liberty is. In this light, Filmer and Bellarmine's agreement on the divine ordination of political power becomes crucial inasmuch as they agree that Scripture can, and in fact must, decide the matter regarding the origin of political right. For Filmer, only a theologically premised argument can be decisive on the question of sovereignty. This is the major source of Filmer's break with the naturalistic absolute sovereignty argument of Bodin. While Filmer maintains that Bodin's attack on the mixed regime theories of Machiavelli and Contarini is sufficient to refute a secular argument for mixed or limited sovereignty, he suggests that secular absolutists like Bodin, as well as Hobbes, misunderstand the foundations of political rule.[37] The real debate over sovereignty, he suggests, must be about the political teaching of Scripture and the character of the divine ordination of political authority. For Filmer, the great danger and appeal in the Catholic natural law position is its attempt to harmonize the divine ordination of politics with the principle of consent. The aim of Filmer's Adamite thesis is, then, to prove that the doctrine of natural liberty is inconsistent with any plausible interpretation of Scripture.

The procedure Filmer adopts in this refutation of the scholastic account of the origin of political society depends on two central premises. First, Filmer

---

[35] Suarez, *De Leg.*: III. 3.2.378.
[36] Bellarmine, *De Laicis*, p. 24. Cf. Rager, *Blessed Cardinal Bellarmine*, pp. 42–3.
[37] Filmer, *Patriarcha*, pp. 134, 184–5. For Bodin's argument for absolute and indivisible sovereignty, see Jean Bodin, *The Six Books of the Republic* (1606), trans. by Richard Knolles from the original *Les six livres de la république* (Paris, 1580), K. D. McRae, ed. (Cambridge: Harvard University Press, 1962): pp. 86, 91, 98. It is also important to note that although Filmer generally approved of Bodin's theory of absolute sovereignty, there were many points on which Filmer's conception of absolutism was far more arbitrary than Bodin's. See, for example, the limits Bodin placed on sovereign power relating to the family (p. 13), property rights (pp. 109–11), and fundamental laws like the Salic Law (p. 95) and Bodin's general reliance on the classical regime types rejected by Filmer (pp. 193–5 and 218 for the right to slay a tyrant). Cf. James Daly, *Sir Robert Filmer and English Political Thought* (Toronto: University of Toronto Press, 1979): p. 22 for a thoughtful caution not to exaggerate the connection between Bodin and Filmer. It is ironic that Filmer criticizes the *politique* Bodin, scourge of the Huguenots, for not paying enough attention to religion, but it may be fair to say that Bodin conceived of absolute sovereignty as a political solution to what he takes to be a theological problem, while Filmer posited a theological solution to a political problem.

aims to demonstrate that the core of the scholastic argument for natural liberty is classical thought, not Scripture. Second, he attempts to dismantle systematically the logic of scholastic contract theory in order to demonstrate the incompatibility of the doctrine of natural liberty not only with Scripture, but also with any form of organized political existence.

Filmer emphasizes the classical or naturalistic basis of the scholastic argument for consent. All of the passages that Filmer gleans to represent "the strength of all that I ever read or heard produced" for natural liberty are taken from Chapter VI of *De Laicis*, which provides Bellarmine's proof of political magistracy "drawn from the efficient cause."[38] However, this chapter offers only one of five of Bellarmine's proofs for natural liberty. Filmer implicitly draws our attention to the fact that the two most fully developed and most radical proofs of magistracy Bellarmine offers relate to the Aristotelian logical categories of efficient and final causality, with only one discussion or proof drawn directly from Scripture.[39] Filmer castigates the scholastics for trying to harmonize the idea of divine ordination with the classical justification of the ends of political rule. Filmer is correct to point to the essential role of classical thought in the scholastic political teaching. For example, Bellarmine justifies political power in terms of the social requirements needed to fulfill human beings' rational nature. In a direct reference to Aristotle, Bellarmine cites the gift of speech as an indication of the character and proper end of political society.[40] It is the end and not the source that guides Bellarmine's understanding of political life.

This classical dimension in the scholastic argument reflects the general Catholic theological concern in the context of the Counter-Reformation to rebut the twin heresies of the Lutheran political teaching, namely, *sola scriptura* and the direct divine ordination of temporal power.[41] However, one effect of Filmer's emphasis on the role of consent and efficient causality in Bellarmine's position makes it appear "more radically constitutionalist" than the Jesuit scholastic intended it to be. As Bellarmine himself notes: "The liberty in which we were created does not conflict with political authority, but with despotic, that is, with true and real slavery."[42] Contrary to what we

---

[38] Daly, *Sir Robert Filmer*, p. 24 and Filmer, *Patriarcha*, 5.

[39] Bellarmine's other two proofs of the purpose of political society relate to the authority of the saints and of antiquity; of course, neither of these sources have much authority for Filmer (Bellarmine, *De Laicis*, chs. 3–7). Cf. Rager, *Blessed Cardinal Bellarmine*, pp. 53–4.

[40] Bellarmine, *De Laicis*, p. 20 and Suarez, *De Leg.*, III.1.3, 11, pp. 364–5, 370 (cf. Aristotle *Politics*, I:2).

[41] For a good discussion of the larger polemical aim of the Jesuit scholastics to refute primarily the Lutheran teaching, but also Erasmian humanism and Machiavelllianism, see Skinner, *Foundations*, pp. 137–46.

[42] Bellarmine, *De Laicis*, pp. 26, 33. Though there is some ground for Somerville's claim that the late scholastics were "far more radically constitutionalist than is usually supposed," this suggestion runs the risk of exaggerating the extent of their populism (J. P. Somerville, "From Suarez to Filmer: A Reappraisal," *The Historical Journal* 25, 3 [1982]: p. 525 and

would expect given Filmer's emphasis on Bellarmine's argument for the consensual origins of government, the Jesuit does not understand despotism as a violation of consent so much as a violation of the classical and Thomistic injunction in support of rule directed to the right end, namely, the common good.[43] Thus, for the Jesuit scholastics, popular sovereignty cannot be understood as a reflection of individual natural rights, but rather as a principle of legitimacy flowing from the organic nature of political community.

With respect to Filmer's aim to undermine scriptural support for the scholastic idea of natural liberty, his tactic is to exploit the patriarchal implications of Suarez and Bellarmine's interpretations of Genesis in order to demonstrate the irremediable conflict between Scripture and the Catholic natural law, which claimed to contain the biblical teaching. He does this by attempting to show the discrepancy between Bellarmine's assertion of natural freedom and equality and his reflections on the significance of creation. For instance, Bellarmine argued: "from creation itself; ... God made woman from man, and did not create many men at the same time, but only one, from whom all others were to be born; so that He might show the order and supremacy which He wished to exist among men."[44] From this observation, Bellarmine proceeds to make the quintessentially Filmerian arguments that sexual generation immediately produced the subjection of the young to their elders and the subjection of Adam's sons and grandsons to him in particular.[45] Bellarmine's apparent concurrence with St. John of Antioch as to the implications of Adam's creation allows Filmer to pit Bellarmine against Suarez, who had offered his own refutation of St. John's crypto-Filmerism. In response to the Church Father's argument in his *34 Homily on I Corinthians* "that from one Adam were formed and procreated all men in order that the subordination to one prince might be signified," Suarez maintains that Adam's creation denoted only economic power over his offspring, not political authority. This economic power, Suarez suggests, related exclusively to the rule proper to a family, and hence extended over children only until

Rager, *Blessed Cardinal Bellarmine*, pp. 43, 107], who draws a far too direct connection between scholastic political theology and American political theory). I argue that the "radical" reading of Jesuit constitutionalism actually shows the coloring traces of Filmer's critique, especially his emphasis on their account of the efficient cause of political power at the expense of their more fundamental argument from final causality. For other useful cautions about Jesuit radicalism, see Skinner, *Foundations*, pp. 182–4 and Annabel Brett, "Individual and Community in the 'Second Scholastic': Subjective Rights in Domingo de Soto and Francisco Suarez," *Philosophy in the Sixteenth and Seventeenth Centuries: Conversations with Aristotle*, Constance Blackwell and Sachiko Kusukawa, eds. (Aldershot: Ashgate, 1999): pp. 167–8.

[43] St. Thomas Aquinas, *Summae Theologica*, trans. by the Fathers of the English Dominican Province, 3 vols. (New York: Benziger Brothers, 1947): ST I–II q. 90, a. 4. Cf. Suarez (1944), *De Leg.*: I.7.1–16. pp. 90–101 and Rager, *Blessed Cardinal Bellarmine*, pp. 47–51.

[44] Bellarmine, *De Laicis*, pp. 31–2 (cf. Filmer, *Patriarcha*, p. 14 and Suarez, *De Leg.* II.8.8–9. 222–3). See also Skinner, *Foundations*, pp. 150–1.

[45] Bellarmine, *De Laicis*, pp. 32, 35.

their maturity, and never at any time included the power of life and death over a wife and children. Political power, in Suarez's view, "did not begin until several families began to be gathered into one perfected community."[46] Politics was not a result of Adam's creation, but rather of the consent of the assembled family heads to the creation of a more complex association befitting the needs and rational potential of human nature.

Filmer rebuts Suarez's argument with the assertion that the distinction between economic and political power is nonsensical given the perfect agreement of regal and paternal power. He complains: "I see no reason but that we may call Adam's family a commonwealth, except we will wrangle about words."[47] Filmer reduces Suarez's treatment of the differentiated forms of rule based on the composition and proper end of the particular species of association to mere semantics. But it is Bellarmine that Filmer turns to in the hope of delivering the hammer blow to the edifice of Suarez's argument. From Bellarmine's attribution of political subjection to Adam's offspring – "the first parents ought to have been princes of their posterity" – Filmer draws the memorable conclusion: "Until Suarez bring some reason for what he saith, I shall trust more to Bellarmine's proofs than to his bare denials."[48] Filmer hopes to prove that this division in the Catholic natural law camp, particularly over the significance of Adam's creation and the extent of paternal power, fatally undermines the cause of scriptural support for the doctrine of natural liberty.

Both Bellarmine and Suarez affirms the naturalness of paternal power but typically deny, in contrast to Filmer, that it extends to the power over life and death. In contrast to later radical Whig arguments such as that of Locke, the scholastics denied the rightful power of punishment with death to any individual, arguing instead that only the political community as such possesses this right.[49] In attacking the Jesuits, Filmer is not only defending paternal right but also extending it into the realm of political power by making that right absolute. Moreover, pitting Bellarmine against Suarez served the useful rhetorical purpose of displaying (or exaggerating) contradictory opinions within the schools, as well as suggesting Suarez's heterodoxy in his opposition to such a prominent Church Father as St. John of Antioch.

It is not surprising that of the two Jesuits, Suarez is Filmer's deadlier opponent, for it is Suarez who anticipates an argument not unlike Filmer's. Suarez criticizes "the opinion of some of the canonists . . . who say that this power from the nature of the subject is in some supreme prince, on whom

---

[46] Suarez (1944), *De Leg.* III.2.3. 374. Cf. Tierney, *Natural Rights*, pp. 308, 310.

[47] Filmer, *Patriarcha*, p. 16.

[48] Ibid., p. 19.

[49] For example, see Suarez, *De Leg.* III.3,6. 378–80; cf. Tierney, *Natural Rights*, pp. 308, 310, 314.

by God it has been conferred, and by succession it ought to remain always in someone."[50] It is in reference to this opinion that Suarez raises his objections to St. John of Antioch's homily on I Corinthians. In a stunning inversion of Filmerian logic, Suarez points to Adam's creation as the source of a very egalitarian interpretation of the distribution and origin of political power. On the political import of creation, Suarez argues: "It should be said that this power from the nature alone of the matter exists in no single person, but in the collectivity of men."[51] Rather than Filmer's absolutist model of the Adamite thesis, Suarez draws out the more democratic implications of his own interpretation of Genesis. The effort to divide and conquer the twin pillars of seventeenth-century Jesuit scholasticism depended on Filmer's exposing possible contradictions in their accounts of creation in order to discredit the scriptural foundation of the Catholic natural law alternative to divine right monarchy. Filmer's fundamentally Lutheran *sola scriptura* orientation pervades his treatment of these Catholic divines. His intention is to expose these Christian Aristotelians as all Aristotle and no Christian or all nature and no Scripture.[52] All the while, of course, he operates on the presumption that nature, understood apart from generation, is a poor or defective guide to the truth.

The problem of nature in Filmer's thought comes to light most clearly when one compares his stance on the question of reason and revelation to that of his Catholic opponents and to their philosophical inspiration Aristotle. He prefaces his consideration of Aristotle with a clarion call for the absolute necessity of analyzing political phenomena through the prism of Scripture. He condemns the attempt to find the ground of natural liberty in ancient philosophers and poets as "the great scandal of Christianity" and then proceeds to restate the Adamite thesis of *Patriarcha*.[53] Though Filmer expresses his disdain for those who appeal to ancient pagan philosophers as champions of natural liberty, he does not preclude the possibility of deriving some utility in examining ancient authors. In fact, Filmer identifies Aristotle as "the profoundest scholar ... in natural philosophy."[54] Filmer's point in examining Aristotle is to reveal both the possibilities and limits of natural reason. Ignorance of the manner of the creation of the world, Filmer cautions, "occasioned several errors amongst heathen philosophers."[55] Nonetheless, many pagan thinkers could see the truth of the patriarchal origins of political power, even if their ignorance of Scripture ensured they could only grasp

---

[50] Suarez, *De Leg.* III.2.2. 373.

[51] Ibid., III.2.3. 373.

[52] It is interesting to note how Filmer's treatment of Suarez and Bellarmine recalls the parallel between Filmer's condemnation of Polybius (*Patriarcha*, p. 14) and Bellarmine's criticism of Cicero (p. 22). In both cases, Filmer and Bellarmine emphasize the limits of unassisted reason.

[53] Filmer, *Patriarcha*, p. 237.

[54] Ibid., p. 4.

[55] Ibid., pp. 14, 236.

this truth incompletely. Filmer suggests that Aristotle's argument that "at the beginning cities were under the government of kings, for the eldest in every house is king," indicates that the power of government, in Filmer's words, "did originally arise from the right of fatherhood, which cannot possibly consist with that natural equality which men dream of."[56] Moreover, Filmer draws on Aristotle's identification of monarchy as the "first and divinest sort of government" to prove the ancient philosopher's support of absolute monarchy.[57]

Filmer's understanding of the limits of natural reason emerges in his sharp criticism of Aristotelian classical republicanism. The scholastic argument that the people may consent to form a variety of regimes (e.g., monarchy, aristocracy, and democracy) reflected their agreement with the fundamental premises of Aristotelian regime analysis.[58] Filmer's assertion that absolute monarchy is the natural and divinely inscribed form of rule departs radically from the classical tradition of political science. To the extent that Suarez and Bellarmine affirm the possibility of a multiplicity of regimes types that may be directed toward the common good, the Catholic natural law teaching on politics may be said to be a form of classical republicanism, albeit a form with serious theological dimensions. Thus, Filmer's attack on classical republicanism is an effort to knock the classical legs out from under the Christian edifice of the scholastic political teaching. One way to do this is to deny that Aristotle, the classical founder of mixed and balanced constitutionalism, was a proponent of mixed government at all.[59] Filmer even goes so far as to present Aristotle as a champion of patriarchal monarchy. His treatment of this great classical authority on regimes deserves our attention.

One of the most striking aspects of Filmer's analysis of Aristotle is his emphasis on the latter's preoccupation with the issue of force. Filmer condenses Aristotle's entire complex constitutional teaching into the simple formula that

[t]he Grecians, when they left to be governed by Kings, fell to be governed by an army. Their monarchy was changed into a stratocracy, and not into an aristocracy or democracy. For if unity in government, which is only found in monarchy, be once broken, there is no stay or bounds, until it come to a constant standing army.[60]

---

[56] Aristotle, *The Politics*, Carnes Lord, trans. (Chicago: University of Chicago Press, 1984): 1252b15–21 and Filmer, *Patriarcha*, p. 14. Filmer also approvingly cites Plato's view of the city as a "large family."

[57] Aristotle, *Politics*, 1289a39–41. Filmer also turns to ancient legal practice, particularly Roman patriarchalism, to support his contention that it is futile to look to the ancients for a defense of natural liberty (Filmer, *Patriarcha*, pp. 18, 26; cf. Daly, *Sir Robert Filmer*, p. 19).

[58] Aristotle, *Politics*, 1278b6–1284b20. Rager does a good job of illuminating the essentially Aristotelian character of late scholastic regime analysis (*Blessed Cardinal Bellarmine*, pp. 35–9).

[59] Aristotle, *Politics*, 1295a25–1296b12.

[60] Filmer, *Patriarcha*, p. 247. Filmer reaches this conclusion from Aristotle's argument "that the first commonweals among Grecians after kingdoms, [were] made of those that waged war"

Filmer's skewed approach to interpreting Aristotle reflects his own deep dissatisfaction with the ancient understanding of political life. At one point Filmer confesses that the "one benefit I have found by reading Aristotle" is to show the consequences of allowing "any man or multitude of men either by cunning or force to set up what government they please."[61] The larger effect of Filmer's distorting presentation of Aristotle's political thought is to make a very specific point. Filmer's emphasis on ancient militarism – of the ancients, he concludes that it was "in their power who manage arms to continue or not the form of government" – leads to the conclusion that, in Filmer's view, the problem that Aristotle is attempting to solve is the legitimization and classification of armed power and acts of force.[62] According to Filmer, the Aristotelian regime typology reflects little more than a rationalization of civil discord, an attempt to reify the slings and arrows of political fortune in a discrete constitutional category. The divine right argument simply could not accept either the internal integrity of Aristotle's regime forms or the composite elements of the one, the few, and the many that comprised Aristotle's mixed regime theory. For Filmer, the clarity of Aristotle's discovery of the patriarchal and monarchical origins of government ultimately succumbed to the bloody spectacle of war and chaos.

Filmer suggests that without the sustaining logic of patriarchalism and a full-blown scriptural account of the workings of the world, natural reason can never penetrate the cacophony and clamor of political life to reach a core of intelligibility. The problem of natural reason, then, is that it is trapped at the level of phenomena and lacks the access to being provided by revelation. Of Aristotle's classification of the five sorts of monarchies, Filmer argues that they "are at most but different and accidental means of the first obtaining or holding of monarchies, and not real or essential differences of the manner of government."[63] The problem of the ancient phenomenology of politics was its inability to distinguish accident from essence. In absence of Scripture, Filmer holds, there is no firm foundation for a comprehensive understanding of politics. For Filmer, "nature" is constantly acted upon by an energetic God, not by human beings. By positing revelation as offering the comprehensive truth about politic life, Filmer allows little room for politics as traditionally understood. Gone are Aristotle's reflections on distributive justice. If all that is required for a full understanding of the human role in creation can be known by revelation, then in Filmer's view, there is no place

(Aristotle, *Politics*, 1297b16–17). Of course, Aristotle never suggests that these early political forms preclude the possibility of aristocracy, democracy, or mixed regimes in the more fully developed city. This use (and abuse) of Aristotle may reflect Filmer's own concern about the possibility, and eventual realization, of military rule in England following soon after the abolition of the monarchy in 1649.

[61] Filmer, *Patriarcha*, p. 252.
[62] Ibid. (cf. Aristotle, *Politics*, 1329a11–12).
[63] Filmer, *Patriarcha*, p. 160.

for the deliberation and rational discourse of civic life: there is only room for obedience.

Contract and Consent

The second main thrust of Filmer's attack on the scholastics was directed against their contract theory. One of the chief bones of contention for Filmer against the Catholic natural law is the scholastic justification for rebellion. For Filmer, the popular sovereignty notion that grounded the Jesuits' theory of the consensual origins of government had two serious implications. First, Suarez and Bellarmine's argument that the relationship between the subjects and the secular ruler is the result of human arrangements bore the clear implication that the civil ruler owns no divine right to his power.[64] The second consequence of the scholastic consent theory is that "with lawful cause" the people may change the form of regime from a monarchy to an aristocracy or a democracy.[65] Suarez argues that there are two grounds upon which revolution could be justified: either when a tyrant has seized civil power without the just title acquired through popular consent (*tyrannus in titulo*) or when a ruler who gained power through a just title misuses that power by injuring the common good (*tyrannus in regimine*).[66] The contract that creates government is binding on both the people and the rulers, but Suarez holds that the subjects may sever their allegiance to the ruler "according to the conditions which have either been expressly stated in the first contract between the king and the kingdom or which are intimately included in it by natural law."[67] In answer to the question of who decides when rulers have broken the social contract, both Suarez and Bellarmine clearly indicate that the people will decide. Predictably, Filmer finds this a "pestilent and dangerous conclusion."[68]

In the context of the complex world of Counter-Reformation theological and political controversy, Filmer views the Catholic apologists' patronization of contractual theories of the origin of political power and the grounds of legitimate popular resistance to civil authority as a means to lower the status of civil government in relation to the direct divine ordination of papal power. To some extent this is true, insofar as Suarez attempts to demonstrate the largely human origin of political power by contrasting it with the direct

[64] Reijo Wilenius, *The Social and Political Theory of Francisco Suarez* (Helsinki: Suomalaisen Kirjallisuuden Kirjapaino, 1963): p. 81.

[65] Bellarmine, *De Laicis*, p. 27 (Filmer, *Patriarcha*, p. 6). Cf. Rager, *Blessed Cardinal Bellarmine*, pp. 112–18.

[66] Wilenius, *Social and Political Theory of Suarez*, p. 83 and Suarez, "Defensio Fidei Catholicae" in *Selections*, VI. 4. 1–3. 705–8.

[67] Wilenius, *Social and Political Theory of Suarez*, p. 81 and Suarez, "Defensio,": VI. 4. 11.714.

[68] Filmer, *Patriarcha*, p. 6.

divine conferral of papal authority.[69] What is not so apparent, though, are some of the profound similarities between Filmer and his Catholic opponents. One of the many direct and explicit adversaries targeted by the Jesuits were the various antinomian Protestant sects, which argued that any and all civil government is incompatible with Christianity.[70] Far from being the pseudoanarchists Filmer charged them to be, Suarez and Bellarmine operate from the presumption of the naturalness and intrinsic goodness of political authority, even if they reject the more stringently Aristotelian understanding of the natural city. Bellarmine says of the relation between the civil and divine law: "civil law is just, that it is always either the conclusion or the moral determination of the Divine law; therefore they have the same end."[71] As to the democratic character of the origins of civil power, Suarez qualifies the implications of these origins with the observation that the natural law does not prescribe that the institutions of government reflect this natural democracy. He explains: "Therefore this power, as far as it is given directly by God to the community...does not absolutely order that it ever remain in it, nor through it this power be directly exercised."[72] Therefore, consent, for Suarez, does not denote or necessarily even support democracy. Both the presumption of the naturalness of politics and the possibility of, if not preference for, monarchy are common strains in Filmer and his Catholic antagonists.

One implication of Bellarmine and Suarez's version of the original democracy is their rejection of the argument that the origin of political power lies in individuals or in the multitude understood in universal terms. Suarez in particular calls attention to the circumstance that the divine conferral of civil power presupposes a "perfect community" that is not a mere aggregation of individuals "without a physical or moral union" but rather a community formed by "common consent."[73] This act of popular consent transforms

---

[69] See Suarez, *De Leg.* III.iii.8. 381–2 and Tierney, *Natural Rights*, p. 311.

[70] Bellarmine, *De Laicis*, p. 6. Cf. Rager, *Blessed Cardinal Bellarmine*, pp. 103–6.

[71] Bellarmine, *De Laicis*, p. 47. Brett ("Individual and Community," pp. 167–8; cf. pp. 164–5) observes that Suarez was less Aristotelian than de Soto with regard to Suarez's emphasis on the distinction between the categories of the moral and the natural, and between the social community and the contrivance of political government. For a fuller treatment of the development of the Spanish Thomist thought of the "Salamanca School" that preceded Suarez, see Brett, *Liberty, Right and Nature* (Cambridge: Cambridge University Press, 1997). Cf. Skinner, *Foundations*, pp. 156–63.

[72] Francisco Suarez, *Extracts on Politics and Government*, George Moore, trans. (Chevy Chase, MD: Country Dollar Press, 1950); *Defenio Fidei Cathlicae*: III.ii.9.14. (cf. Suarez, *De Leg.* III.3.7–8.380–82). Cf. Wilenius (*Social and Political Theory of Suarez*, p. 79) and Tierney (*Natural Rights*, p. 312), who demonstrates that Suarez did not endorse the radical Whig idea of popular sovereignty as a delegated power. However, see Bellarmine's description of the relationship between natural freedom and equality and the formation of government in these terms: "by the same natural law, this power is delegated by the multitude to one or several, for the State cannot of itself exercise this power" (*De Laicis*, p. 26).

[73] Suarez, *De Leg.*: III.2.4.375.

a particular collectivity of people into a "mystical body" infused with the divine gift of civil authority. Suarez agrees with Filmer as to the inability of individuals qua individuals to constitute sovereign political authority when he asserts that "the force of natural law alone is ... not in individuals." Furthermore, they agree that "this power is not ... in the species as a whole, or in the total collection of men living in the whole world." Filmer, in fact, makes much of Suarez's admission that it "was hardly possible, and much less expedient" that all humanity be congregated into one political community.[74]

Filmer's intention in pointing to this statement is to show the incompatibility of the argument for natural liberty with *any* account of the origins of particular political communities. The natural liberty of the multitude would, Filmer argues, require the consent of the entire multitude (all of humanity) in order to break it into distinct communities. The natural liberty of the people and the contractual origins of government are, in this view, incompatible; thus, the Catholic natural law argument fails on its own terms. Filmer illustrates this alleged internal inconsistency of Bellarmine and Suarez's argument:

> Can they show or prove ever the whole multitude met and divided this power, which God gave them in gross, by breaking it into parcels and by apportioning a distinct power to each several commonwealth? Without such a compact, I cannot see, according to their own principles, how there can be any election of a magistrate by a commonwealth, but by a mere usurpation upon the privilege of the whole world.[75]

It is typical of Filmer's dichotomous approach to theologico–political disputation – natural liberty versus natural subjection, with little room for play in the middle – that the suggestion of a supposed contradiction in the argument for natural liberty, in effect, proves the argument for natural subjection.

Filmer's assertion of the incompatibility of natural liberty with the formation of particular political communities derives from the logical and moral premises of an argument that denies the unique human capacity to form or participate in government. Though Filmer offers his own almost perfunctory assurance "not to question or quarrel at the rights of this or any other nation," it is clear from his Adamite thesis of the origins of political power that he deprives the law of nations of the moral status and rational content presupposed by Bellarmine and Suarez.[76] For Filmer, the laws of distinct communities are not the products of consent and rational deduction from certain natural laws; rather, they are rooted in natural subjection and the

---

[74] Ibid., 375.

[75] Filmer, *Patriarcha*, p. 20.

[76] Ibid., p. 4. For the Thomist account of the relation of the law of nature and the law of nations, see Bellarmine, *De Laicis*, p. 27 and Aquinas, *Summa*, I–II, q. 95, a. 4.1. See Skinner, *Foundations*, pp. 152–3 for the late scholastic modification of Thomistic understanding of the relation of the law of nature and the law of nations.

incapacity of human beings to freely form governments. Thus, these laws simply reflect the will of a particular ruler. With Filmer's argument that the general law of creation is strict obedience to authority and that the determination of rule is existentially beyond the purview of the subject, we can see how the Christian Aristotelian notion of nature almost disappears altogether in the theologico–political calculus of Filmer's divine right.

The divine right phenomenology of politics articulated by Filmer was grounded on a complex understanding of divine providence. Such serious political and constitutional issues as usurpation, succession disputes, and popular elections provided obvious logical problems for Filmer's argument regarding the uninterrupted transfer of political authority from Adam to his successor monarchs in the modern age. Clearly in the distant past, as well as in England's turbulent present, rulers had emerged through such irregular means as usurpation and election. How could Filmer make the manifest contingency of politics in the world consistent with his doctrine of natural subjection? His answer was to suppress the role of autonomous human agency in political life by explaining such events as usurpation, election, and succession disputes in terms of divine providence. Filmer's providentialist argument is twofold. First, he claims that the usurpation of power is a reflection of God's will, not of any natural right for the people to replace their rulers. Although God may "use and turn men's unrighteous acts to the performance of His righteous decrees," Filmer makes no attempt to justify God's actions in terms amenable to natural reason.[77] Even the example of a group of electors selecting a monarch upon an escheat of power through want of an heir does not signify a natural constitutive power inhering in all or even some of the people. In this event, Filmer claims, the electors simply assume the natural paternal power of Adam on a temporary and limited basis. Second, Filmer denies that the manifest interruptions to rule signify any qualification on the obedience of the subject. In this view, God can replace or select rulers, and it is simply the people's duty to await the result of this mysterious process of providential politics. Filmer claims that the obedience due to existing rulers does not depend on "the difference of obtaining the supreme power – whether by conquest, election, succession or by any other way."[78] Subjects must wait as spectators to see who will be their new master. Thus, Filmer's conception of divine providence includes a notion of God's

---

[77] Filmer, *Patriarcha*, p. 11. Cf. Daly, *Sir Robert Filmer*, p. 86; Schochet, *Patriarchalism*, pp. 150–1; and Nathan Tarcov, *Locke's Education for Liberty* (Chicago: University of Chicago Press, 1984): p. 14.

[78] Filmer, *Patriarcha*, p. 132. Of course, as events in English history following the civil war would demonstrate to Filmer, obedience to usurpers becomes a more difficult position to explain when the "rightful heir" is still alive. To understand Filmer's difficulty in the Engagement Controversy in dealing with the issues of loyalty and the extent of obedience due from the subject in "dangerous and doubtful times," see Filmer's "Directions for Obedience" in *Patriarcha*, pp. 281–6.

willingness both to remove and supply rulers for His naturally subject creatures. That we must have rulers is an ontological necessity, but who they will be and how they will come to power is a matter for the wide and ultimately mysterious scope of divine providence.

The deeper thrust of Filmer's providentialist argument is meant to undermine the Catholic natural law principles of contract and consent. This attempt to refute several of the key premises of the contractual theory of government places Filmer in the uncharacteristic position of assuming the doctrine of the natural liberty of the people, at least for the sake of demonstrating its inability to generate a plausible account of the creation of political authority. The doctrine of natural liberty, Filmer argues, is an inherently anarchical principle. His aim in examining the problems of election, majority rule, and tacit consent is to demonstrate, as Gordon Schochet observes, "the moral and logical impossibility of deriving government, private property, and the hierarchical arrangements that exist in society from the conditions of original natural freedom and equality predicated by contractual thinkers."[79] For Filmer, the insuperable practical and theoretical chasm between natural freedom and the hierarchical order required for political society may be demonstrated on several grounds.

First, he argues that the formation of particular communities would require the universal consent of all humankind, or else the election of a ruler by one group would constitute a usurpation of the rights of humanity generally. Even conceding the theoretical possibility of such a consensual division of the universal multitude into distinct communities, Filmer makes a second, more practical, argument that there are no actual historical examples of an entire people electing a ruler. He charges: "Was a general meeting of a whole kingdom ever known for the election of a prince? Was there any example of it found in the whole world?"[80] Some kings in Poland, Sweden, and Denmark, Filmer admits, have been chosen "by some small part of a people.... But by the whole or major part in a kingdom not any at all."[81] It is important to recognize that Filmer does not intend here to dispute the custom of electing monarchs seen in some kingdoms. Rather, his aim is to demonstrate that such elections are all practical violations of natural freedom and equality inasmuch as they all involve only a minority of electors, not the vast multitude of subjects. More importantly, however, Filmer's intention is to demonstrate that contemporary elective monarchies in Europe reflect only the existing, and in Filmer's view highly flawed, arrangements set by the ruling power in those countries and do not indicate the inherent right of a people to select their rulers. These elective monarchies disprove rather than affirm the liberty of the people.

[79] Schochet, *Patriarchalism*, p. 122.
[80] Filmer, *Patriarcha*, p. 20.
[81] Ibid., p. 143.

In addition to stating the practical and moral impossibility of popular elections, Filmer argues that the principle of majority rule is itself antithetical to natural freedom and equality. Even if an entire people were to gather for the election of their rulers, Filmer denies that dissenters would be morally bound to accept the will of the majority. He claims that "the acts of multitudes not entire are not binding to all but only to such as consent to them."[82] A particularly interesting feature of Filmer's criticism of contract theory is how seriously he takes the individualist implications of natural freedom and equality. As he argues, if the assent of one man can be excluded in any election or in any assembly vote, "the same reason that excludes that one man may exclude many hundreds, and many thousands, yea, and the major part itself."[83] The principle of unanimity, Filmer argues, is embedded in the logic of natural freedom, and the doctrine of natural freedom is the theoretical foundation of every attempt to defend the people's right or power to constitute political authority. At the heart of Filmer's contention for the inalienability of natural freedom is the supposition that if natural freedom were the fundamental human condition – which Filmer denies – then he assumes it must be inalienable because "the law of nature is unchangeable, and howsoever one man may hinder another in the use or exercise of his natural right, yet thereby no man loseth the right itself."[84] With this supposition in the background, Filmer defies his opponents to prove how any theory of natural liberty can eventuate in anything but anarchy.

The problem of natural liberty is also a theme in Filmer's treatment of the notion of tacit consent. The proposition that merely obeying or enjoying the protection of an existing government (in a sense, simply not rebelling against it) signifies the election of the ruler through "silent acceptation" leads, in Filmer's opinion, to the logical conclusion that

[e]very prince that comes to a crown, either by succession, conquest or usurpation, may be said to be elected by the people. Which inference is too ridiculous, for in such cases the people are so far from the liberty of specification that they want even that of contradiction.[85]

Apart from the charge that the principle of tacit consent reduces the active principle of consent to a veritable nullity, Filmer levels two additional criticisms against it. He implicitly denies that any consistent natural rights theory could countenance the power of one generation to bind the political allegiance of their descendants. Filmer charges that if each generation or even every individual does not have the right to alter the inherited political order, then natural freedom is irrelevant to political discourse.[86] If natural rights

[82] Ibid., p. 21.
[83] Ibid., p. 261.
[84] Ibid., p. 21.
[85] Ibid., p. 21.
[86] Schochet, *Patriarchalism*, p. 130.

are taken seriously, in Filmer's view, the natural ebb and flow of humanity, as some individuals die and others are born, ensures that any existing government will degenerate into chaos before the perpetual stream of new life. A second implication of Filmer's rejection of tacit consent is that the unanimity required to establish political society must be precisely that: unanimity. The removal of the possibility of tacit consent removes the possibility of virtual unanimity or government being derived from the actions of some and the acceptance of others. To Filmer, the impossibility of the ever-changing multitude's agreeing even on the process of majority rule itself marks the futility and incoherence of populist theories of government.

Filmer's notion of consent is both active and retractable. Though individuals may agree to establish government or rules of private property, Filmer denies that this consent, in principle at least, need be perpetual.[87] Filmer's attack on the populist dimensions of contract theory aims to reinforce a crucial Filmerian premise, namely, that contract theory assumes the very social machinery necessary for the operation of government and society that is precluded by the doctrine of natural liberty. Political communities can never be formed without universal consent, and majorities cannot act for the whole without direct reference to a primary and unanimous social contract establishing the process of majority rule. It is a contract, however, that Filmer argues can never be made.

Filmer's attack on scholastic natural law populism signifies his bold attempt to dismantle contract theories from within by carrying their core assumptions and deepest commitments to natural liberty and equality to their logical extremes. In every instance, Filmer contends that the doctrine of natural liberty results in chaos and anarchy. One commentator even suggests that Filmer's attack on the fundamental notions and presuppositions of popular sovereignty was "a concise statement of the traditional political beliefs that had to be overcome before constitutional liberalism could become a dominant ideology."[88] Filmer's challenge to the Catholic natural lawyers, as well as to any proponent of consent and contract theory, was for them to prove that natural liberty need not eventuate in anarchy.

---

[87] Daly, *Sir Robert Filmer*, pp. 90–1.
[88] Schochet, *Patriarchalism*, p. 121.

2

Calvinism and Parliamentary Resistance Theory

In the early 1640s England exploded into civil war. The decades'-long conflict between the supporters of Parliament and the supporters of the crown came to a dramatic test of arms. In the pamphlet war that preceded and accompanied the military contest, the disputants dealt with fundamental questions about the nature and origin of political power and the status of the monarchy in the English system of government. Filmer joined this controversy about first political principles with characteristic aplomb. In *The Anarchy of a Limited Monarchy* he offered a comprehensive critique of the theoretical foundations of the parliamentary position propounded in the influential works of Philip Hunton and Henry Parker. It is in this attack on the parliamentary contractarianism of the civil war era that Filmer presented his fullest articulation of the divine right theory of absolute sovereignty.

Filmer joined the fray not only to defend the rights and privileges of his sovereign, Charles I, but also to counter what he took to be the noxious doctrine of mixed monarchy that underpinned the parliamentary cause in the war. He identified the intellectual foundations of the parliamentary position in the potent combination of Calvinist resistance theory and the English notion of ancient constitutionalism. In the mixture of theological and secular arguments that animated the apologists of Parliament, Filmer perceived dangerous doctrines that justified resistance to the crown and denied the legal and constitutional supremacy of the monarch. The two preeminent statements of parliamentary resistance theory were Philip Hunton's *A Treatise of Monarchie* (1643) and Henry Parker's *Observations upon some of his Majesties late Answers and Expresses* (1642). Hunton and Parker argued that political society is a form of contract produced by the consent of the people. In this variant of the natural liberty tradition, popular resistance to monarchical authority was justified by the people's natural constitutive power to order political society and to establish legal limitations on the crown. Philip Hunton, Filmer's chief opponent in the *Anarchy*, argued that the English government was a mixed monarchy in which sovereignty is distributed more or less equally among the three coordinate powers in the king, the Lords, and the Commons. The Puritan divine Hunton affirmed that political authority is ordained by God, but he emphatically argued that the character of the political contract was the product of the popular will. He maintained that in the event of a serious constitutional conflict between the various elements of the government, such as the situation in England in 1642, the matter could only be decided by recourse to the judgment of the entire community. Whereas Hunton represented a relatively moderate version of the parliamentary position that afforded a large share of sovereign power to the monarchy, Parker articulated a more radical stance. He argued not only that all political power derived from the people, but also that the ultimate legal and constitutional authority in England lay in the two houses of Parliament. In Parker's populist notion of the political contract, the representative institutions of the English government, especially the Commons, expressed popular sovereignty, and the crown simply did not.

Filmer's response to the parliamentary contractarians constitutes his most comprehensive reflections on the issue of sovereignty. He systematically critiqued the ancient constitutionalist principle of mixed monarchy and the Calvinist argument for justified resistance to the crown. In doing so, Filmer put divine right theory firmly and predictably in the service of political absolutism. He argued that God's ordination of political power extends "not only [to] the constitution of power in general, but the limitation of it to one kind (that is, monarchy, or the government of one alone) and the determination of it to the individual person and line of Adam."[1] In the Filmerian version of divine right, the power of a monarch is not only divinely ordained, it is also inherently unlimited and illimitable. Before we examine Filmer's attack on the parliamentary position advanced by Hunton and Parker, it will be useful to consider the theological and constitutional context produced by the ideas underlying their arguments.

The Problem of Calvinist Politics

Filmer recognized a number of conduits for the transmission of the doctrine of natural liberty in England. One, as we have seen, was the amorphous but still palpable threat to political stability posed by the late scholastic natural law theory. But Filmer also identified a more emphatically English support for the notion of natural liberty "first hatched in the schools." These

---

[1] W. J. Allen points to Filmer's sovereignty thesis as one of his most innovative arguments (*A History of Political Thought in the Sixteenth Century* [London: Methuen, 1977]: p. 434). James Daly agrees (*Sir Robert Filmer and English Political Thought* [Toronto: University of Toronto Press, 1979]: pp. 151–3) and even goes so far as to suggest that Filmer's divine right Adamite thesis was "relatively unimportant" to Filmer, inasmuch as his "core lay in the doctrine of sovereignty." In contrast, I shall argue that Filmer's sovereignty argument is fundamentally derivative from his theological foundation.

more dangerous political foes were the "overzealous favorers of the Geneva discipline."[2] English and to a lesser extent Scottish Calvinism was Filmer's most direct ideological opponent in the years preceding the civil war.

The source of this key conflict lay in English political and ecclesiastical history. One of the most significant developments in early-seventeenth-century England was the failure of the Elizabethan Church settlement to produce religious uniformity. Even as the Catholic threat to national independence became more abstract, increasingly in the early 1600s internal divisions within the ranks of English Protestantism acquired greater political significance. The late Tudor settlement championed by the great English scholastic Richard Hooker rested on the idea of the fundamental harmony between church and state and the establishment of royal supremacy over both. In Hooker's complex formulation of Christian Aristotelianism, humankind's two substantive ends, secular and spiritual, were distinct but connected in a comprehensive theological and political system.[3] Hooker responded to the calls for church reform by the early Calvinist forerunners of the Puritans, who sought a return to a "pure" form of Christian church discipline rooted in Scripture, by contending that Scripture does not provide absolute guidance on all matters moral, political, and ecclesiastical.[4] As a proponent of the Christian-Aristotelian tradition extending back to Thomas Aquinas, Hooker sought to defend what he maintained was the proper, and by no means insubstantial, sphere of human reason against the extreme scripturalism of the Calvinists. Filmer, then, was correct to identify a major source of the constitutional struggles of the 1630s and 1640s in the internal quarrel over the structure and doctrine of the Church of England between Calvinists and the orthodox religious establishment. Where Filmer would depart from his predecessor Hooker, however, was that Filmer would not try to temper Calvinist scripturalism with the authority of reason; he would try to out-Scripture the scripturalists.

Filmer's condemnation of the "Geneva discipline" drew its animus from a long history of political and religious division in England. As far back as the late Tudor period, English Calvinists had challenged not only the political role of the bishops in the House of Lords, but in the most extreme cases even the existence of the bishops in the church structure. The English royalists' conception of the underlying connection between the power of the monarchy

---

[2] Filmer, *Patriarcha and Other Writings*, Johann Somerville, ed. (Cambridge: Cambridge University Press, 1991): p. 3. Frances Oakley's argument (*The Politics and Eternity: Studies in the History of Medieval and Early-Modern Political Thought* [Leiden: Brill, 1999]: p. 178) illustrating the indebtedness of English and French Calvinists to scholastic resistance theory suggests that Filmer may not have been so far off the mark!

[3] See Richard Hooker, *Of the Laws of Ecclesiastical Polity* (1593), George Edelen, W. Speed Hill, and P. G. Stanwood, eds. (Cambridge, MA: Harvard University Press, 1977–81) 3.11.16; 8.2.3 (cf. 8.1.5). Hereafter *Laws*.

[4] Hooker, *Laws*: 2.8.5.

and the status of the episcopacy was given clear expression in James I's famous royal dictum "No bishop, no king" dating from his earliest arrival in England.[5] While the split within English Protestantism was somewhat muted during James I's long controversy with the Catholic Church, continued Calvinist dissent and the enduring problem of an obstinate Presbyterian majority in Scotland greatly contributed to the major crisis in the reign of Charles I.[6] This crisis simmered ominously throughout the period of church reforms instituted by Archbishop Laud in the 1630s. Laud's efforts to excise the Calvinist theological principles of grace and predestination from the Church of England through endorsement of Arminian orthodoxy and a new emphasis on forms, ceremony, and sacramentalism sparked a bitter reaction from English Calvinists.[7] The crown's support for Laud's effort to eradicate "Puritanism" inevitably reignited the politically charged dispute over church government and doctrine. In the context of Counter-Reformation Europe, Laud's intention to restore "papist" practices in the church and the contemporaneous bold assertion and extension of royal prerogative by Charles produced a highly combustible situation. In this context open defiance of the crown was predictable.

Filmer voiced the opinion of many English royalists when he associated Calvinism with political instability and opposition to monarchy. He identified a deep connection between Calvinist resistance to Laudian reform and parliamentary opposition to the crown. The parliamentary leaders in the late 1630s and early 1640s most likely to oppose the crown were Calvinists who bitterly opposed royal support for Laudian reform and who sought to exclude the bishops from their political role in Parliament in the House of Lords. By the time of the civil war English Calvinists, especially Presbyterians, were committed to the twin goals of reforming the national church and

---

5 For an excellent treatment of the ongoing dispute between English and Scottish Presbyterians, on the one hand, and the Elizabethan and Stuart commitment to episcopacy, on the other, see Michael Mendle, *Dangerous Positions: Mixed Government, the Estates of the Realm, and the Answer to the XIX Propositions* (University, AL: University of Alabama Press, 1985): chs. 3–5.

6 Johann Somerville notes that there were many important Calvinist supporters of James in his quarrel with the Catholics (*Politics and Ideology in England, 1603–1640* [London: Longman, 1986]: pp. 44–5). The alienation of Calvinists from the crown is one of the central features of Charles' reign, although Mendle points out that the more extreme elements of English Calvinism had linked the theological problem of episcopacy with the political question of whether the bishops were one of the "estates" of the realm at least since the late Tudor period (*Dangerous Positions*, pp. 63–5, 77–96). Cf. Austin Woolrych, *Britain in Revolution, 1625–1660* (Oxford: Oxford University Press, 2002): pp. 85–148.

7 For analysis of the impact of arminianism on English Calvinists, see R. T Kendall, *Calvin and English Calvinism to 1649* (Oxford: Oxford University Press, 1979): esp. ch. 10. For an account that downplays the significance of Laud's reforms as a catalyst for civil war, see William Lamont, "Arminianism: The Controversy That Never Was," in *Political Discourse in Early Modern Britain*, Nicholas Phillipson and Quentin Skinner, eds. (Cambridge: Cambridge University Press, 1993): pp. 45–66.

permanently limiting the powers of the king.[8] However, Filmer perceived a more fundamental fault line in the doctrines of reformed theology that produced the intrinsic causal relation between Calvinist principles and opposition to monarchy. Filmer audaciously reversed the Puritan charge associating Stuart absolutism and Laudian crypto-papism by uncovering what he took to be the common philosophical heritage of Calvinist and Catholic resistance theory in the natural liberty tradition. It was the Puritan and parliamentary resisters who were the crypto-papists, not the king and his archbishop. For Filmer, the ideological and theological context of England's religious and political troubles was indelibly linked to a seminal cleavage within reformed theology represented by the distinctive political teachings of Luther and Calvin, or more properly between their followers and successors.

For Filmer, the problem of the English adherents of the Geneva discipline had to do with their mistaken understanding of God's design for human government. While Calvin followed Luther in advocating the divine ordination of political authority, a general Christian duty of obedience to temporal power, and a commitment to scripturalism, Filmer pointed to a number of fateful differences between Luther's and Calvin's political teachings.[9] First, whereas Luther's approving presentation of government as the "great engine of repression" warmed the cockles of Filmer's royalist heart and supplied theological support for his authoritarian interpretation of Scripture,

---

[8] Mendle, *Dangerous Positions*, pp. 8, 136–7, 155–62; Somerville, *Politics and Ideology*, p. 219 and David Wootton, "Leveller Democracy and the Puritan Revolution," in *The Cambridge History of Political Thought, 1450–1700*, J. H. Burns and Mark Goldie, eds. (Cambridge: Cambridge University Press, 1991): p. 417. For a good discussion of the appeal of Calvinism to the English gentry in the early seventeenth century and its role in the development of antimonarchical sentiment in England, see Hiram Caton, *The Politics of Progress: The Origins and Development of the Commercial Republic, 1600–1835* (Gainesville: University of Florida Press, 1988): pp. 175–6.

[9] See Jean Calvin, *Institutio of the Christianae religionis*, Ford Lewis Battles, trans, trans. from the 1559 Latin edition (Library of Christian Classics, Vols. 20, 1, John T. McNeill, ed. [Philadelphia: Westminster Press, 1967], hereafter *Institutes*) for divine ordination of temporal authority (4.20.4), for the duty of obedience (4.20.29), and for the supremacy of Scripture over philosophy (4.20.8). Cf. Michael Zuckert, *Natural Rights and the New Republicanism* (Princeton: Princeton University Press, 1994): p. 49. The debate over the character of Calvin's political teaching covers the full range of possibilities. For a conservative reading of Calvin that places him closer to Luther than I do, see Perez Zagorin, *A History of Political Thought in the English Revolution* (London: Routledge & Kegan Paul, 1954): pp. 72–4 and John Clement Rager, *The Political Philosophy of Blessed Cardinal Bellarmine* (Washington, DC: Catholic University of America Press, 1926): pp. 111–12. For the opposite view of Calvin's thought as laying the ideological groundwork for modern radical politics, see Michael Walzer, *The Revolution of the Saints: A Study in the Origins of Radical Politics* (Cambridge, MA: Harvard University Press, 1965). For more balanced readings of Calvin that identify the radical dimensions of his thought but also recognize its distance from modern secular arguments about government, see Ralph Hancock, *Calvin and the Foundations of Modern Politics* (Ithaca: Cornell University Press, 1989), and Harro Hopfl, *The Christian Polity of John Calvin* (Cambridge: Cambridge University Press, 1982).

Calvin's view of government was less reassuring. While Calvin was as much of a scripturalist as Luther, the humanist-trained legal scholar presented a conception of the moral possibilities for political life that were potentially a good deal more elevated than those permitted by Luther. In the exhortation for magistrates to ensure that piety and "due honor [have] been prepared for virtue" among the citizens, Calvin assumed a role in moral education in virtue for government that was largely absent in Luther.[10] Filmer certainly denied the complex classical conception of citizenship in favor of the single comprehensive virtue of humble obedience.

Moreover, Calvin's studious attention to the reform of the structure of the church government reflected an interest in institutional design that, in Filmer's view, indicated a dangerous propensity toward the classical under-standing of politics. For example, in the 1543 edition of the *Institutes*, Calvin argued that as a pure matter of speculation "aristocracy, or a system com-pounded of aristocracy and democracy far excels all others."[11] In the later edition of 1559, Calvin added to this section a more precise endorsement of polity or mixed government, contending that "men's faults or failings causes it to be safer and more bearable for a number to exercise government, so that they may help one another, teach and admonish one another; and, if one asserts himself unfairly, there should be a number of censors and teachers to restrain his willfulness."[12] This could hardly be construed as any kind of approval for absolute monarchy. To make matters worse from Filmer's perspective, Calvin had the temerity to base his argument for mixed govern-ment on the scriptural authority of the Israelite model of government prior to the kings. While the political teachings of both Luther and Calvin operated from the reformed theological premise of human corruption, Calvin drew less authoritarian implications from this premise than does Luther.[13] Calvin reached a distinctly classical republican conclusion that human frailty justi-fies and necessitates institutional checks and balances to remedy the magis-trate's presumed lack of control. From Calvin's statements about the moral economy of human nature and the importance of institutional safeguards

---

[10] Calvin *Institutes*: 4.20.9. Cf. Paul Rahe, *Republics Ancient and Modern: Classical Republicanism and the American Revolution* (Chapel Hill: University of North Carolina Press, 1992): p. 354 and Sheldon Wolin, *Politics and Vision: Continuity and Innovation in Western Political Thought* (London: Methuen, 1969): pp. 170, 182–4.

[11] Calvin, *Institutes*: 4.20.8.

[12] Calvin, *Institutes*: 4.20.8. Cf. Hopfl, *Christian Polity*, pp. 124–6, for a good discussion of this passage.

[13] Of course, it was this aspect of Calvinist theology – the combination of a theological doctrine of fundamental human depravity and a political commitment to austere republicanism – that caught the attention of later commentators such as Mill, Tocqueville, and Weber (see John Stuart Mill, *On Liberty* [New York: Penguin, 1985]: pp. 126–30; Alexis de Tocqueville, *Democracy in America*, George Lawrence, trans. [NewYork: Harper, 1966]: pp. 31–49; Max Weber, *The Protestant Ethic and the Spirit of Capitalism*, Talcott Parsons, trans. [New York: Vintage, 1958]).

on magisterial power, his English followers could and did derive theological and scriptural support for a regime type unmistakably resembling the parliamentary formulation of the English Constitution in the years leading up to and during the civil war.

The second aspect of Calvinist thought that gravely concerned Filmer had to do with the idea of legitimate resistance to magisterial power. In castigating Bellarmine's argument for the right to depose rulers, Filmer indicated that Calvin also looked "asquint this way."[14] Calvin's teaching paralleled that of Luther insofar as both maintained that private individuals are never justified in actively resisting their ruler. However, Calvin included a portentous modification to the Protestant teaching on resistance when he added that certain subordinate "magistrates of the people, appointed to restrain the willfulness of kings," have not so much a right as a positive duty to resist a tyrannical sovereign.[15] Calvin adduced the ephors of Sparta, the tribunate in Rome, and the Estates General in France as examples of inferior magistrates who are justified in resisting wayward monarchs. Calvin was not endorsing popular sovereignty – all power still derived from God – but rather stating that in any constitutional order including institutional checks on royal power, the members of these institutions are exempt from the general duty of obedience incumbent on all private individuals. For English royalists like Filmer this was tantamount to asserting a divinely ordained resistance right against monarchy, and thus was totally antithetical to the proper Protestant position regarding the subject's absolute obedience to temporal rulers. In the particular context of England, the potential for justifying parliamentary resistance on the grounds of Calvin's theory of subordinate magistrates was not lost on Filmer. In looking "asquint" at the dangerous Catholic teaching, Calvin was, in Filmer's view, not being true to the politics of reformation. Thus, the unique historical and political circumstances in England of the 1640s produced a violent clash between Luther's and Calvin's visions of reformation politics, between a theory of Protestant absolutism and obedience and a Protestant ideal of mixed government and legitimate resistance that would bloody England's green fields in a form of intra-Protestant warfare for the most part unseen on the Continent.

Filmer was correct to observe that when English Calvinists developed the parliamentary resistance theory in the 1640s, they were building on an established legacy of resistance ideas rooted in Calvin's teaching and modified and radicalized by his successors and followers.[16] The idea of divinely ordained

---

[14] Filmer, *Patriarcha*, p. 3.

[15] Calvin, *Institutes*: 4.20.31.

[16] As several scholars have illuminated, Lutheran resistance theory predated and significantly influenced Calvinist ideas about resistance (e.g., W. D. J. Cargill Thompson, *The Political Thought of Martin Luther* (Brighton, MA: Harvester Press, 1984): pp. 92–4; Quentin Skinner: *The Foundations of Modern Political Thought*, Vol. 2 (Cambridge: Cambridge University Press, 1978): pp. 192–224 and Robert Kingdon, "Calvinism and Resistance Theory, 1550–1580"

institutional checks on monarchy that legitimize resistance resonated in both the Huguenot and Scottish traditions of Calvinist thought. The Huguenots represent an important modification and radicalization of Calvin's position on justified active resistance to rulers. However, it is important to observe that even the most radical expressions of Huguenot contract and resistance theory were a far cry from the natural rights–based arguments of the Whigs a century later. For the Huguenots the constituent elements of the social contract were groups, estates, and congregations, not individuals possessing pre-civil rights.[17] The Huguenots held a special place in the political consciousness of sixteenth- and seventeenth-century England. The image of a persecuted Protestant minority, victims of the traditional Catholic nemesis and its brutal centralized monarchy, as waves of pitiful refugees yearning for the safety of England's shores struck deep chords of sympathy among many Englishmen.[18] The theoretical innovations that Huguenot polemicists developed in the principle of resistance, however, alarmed English royalists like Filmer. In the religious wars in France prior to the massacres of 1572, Huguenots efforts to secure official toleration for Protestant worship had been framed in terms of professed loyalty to the crown and opposition to the ultra-Catholic advisors surrounding the king.[19] Following the catastrophe of 1572 in which the Huguenot leadership was decimated by the forces of the crown, the Huguenot champions François Hotman, Theodore Beza, and the anonymous author of *Vindicae Contra Tyrranos* took Calvinist resistance theory in new and radical directions.

Hotman's *Francogallia* was a landmark work in the development of Calvinist resistance theory.[20] In this sweeping constitutional history of France,

---

in *Cambridge History of Political Thought*, pp. 203–5). Luther grudgingly advocated a theory of resistance to support the Protestant princes of the Schmalkaldic League against imperial attempts to crush the reformation in Germany in the 1530s and 1540s. Filmer and other English royalists, however, identified Calvin as the source of the Protestant analogue to Catholic resistance theory, suggesting that the classical elements in Calvin's thought, and his more clearly formulated principles of institutional resistance to monarchy, signified a much more serious departure from the true path of Scripture-based reformed politics than that of Luther's justification of resistance *ex tempore*.

[17] For an insightful analysis of the Calvinist theological and emphatically anti-individualist basis of Huguenot contract theory, see Harro Hopfl and Martyn Thompson, "The History of Contract as a Motif in Political Thought," *American Historical Review*, vol. 84, no. 4 (October 1979): pp. 929–34.

[18] For a demonstration of the degree to which the idea of the Huguenots still evoked the sympathy of English radicals even in the seventeenth century, see Locke's somewhat macabre fascination with the declining French Protestant population (Maurice Cranston, *John Locke: A Biography* [New York: Macmillan, 1957]: 163).

[19] Skinner, *Foundations*, p. 254. For a comprehensive treatment of the Huguenots' position prior to 1572, see Robert Kingdon, *Geneva and the Consolidation of the French Protestant Movement, 1564–1572* (Geneva: Librarie Droz, 1967).

[20] For excellent treatments of Hotman, see Kingdon, "Calvinism and Resistance Theory," pp. 208–10 and Skinner, *Foundations*, pp. 306–7. W. J. Allen denies that *Francogallia* had

Hotman advanced several radical claims. He argued that the early Frankish monarchy was elective and maintained the claim that some form of public council had always played an integral role representing the whole French population. For Hotman, the national Estates General rather than the local *parlements* was the modern version of this ancient popular assembly. Most significantly, Hotman avowed that this public council held the ultimate power in the state as the custodian of the immutable fundamental laws limiting the power of the French king.[21] He presented the Estates as the French equivalent of Calvin's "ephoral" power, a divinely instituted constitutional check on the monarchy, and consequently defended the legitimate right of resistance to the crown by the leaders of this representative assembly. In this way Hotman established the pattern for other Huguenot theorists to adapt Calvin's teaching on inferior magistrates to a populist reading of French constitutional history. Calvin's successor in Geneva, Theodore Beza, expanded Hotman's idea of resistance even further in his *Of the Right of Magistrates*. Beza accounted for the resistance right of two types of subordinate magistrates, officials of local government and constitutionally established leaders of the national government. Among the examples of national institutions that derive their authority from a reciprocal contract with the king Beza included not only the Estates General but also, significantly, the English Parliament.[22] In the later *Vindicae Contra Tyrranos*, Huguenot resistance theory reached a zenith of populism. Whereas Hotman and Beza had, in keeping with Calvin, never extended the right of resistance to individuals, but rather reserved this power to legally established inferior magistrates, the author of *Vindicae* argued that a tyrant holding office by usurpation may be resisted by every individual and even sanctioned assassination.[23] While Huguenot thinkers were careful not to equate a right of resistance with a claim of popular sovereignty – as Calvinists they adhered to the principle of divine ordination of all political power – the clear trajectory of the Huguenot argument for resistance was radical and potentially populist. This incipient populism would manifest itself in the later arguments of the Calvinist apologists for Parliament in England such as Hunton and Parker.

---

a lasting influence outside of Huguenot circles (*History of Political Thought*, pp. 310–11). However, Tyrrell and Sidney make reference to it in their own critique of Filmer in Exclusion era England.

[21] For François Hotman's *Francogallia* (1573) as well as Beza and the anonymous author of *Vindicae contra tyrannos*, see Julian Franklin's translations of the original editions in *Constitutionalism and Resistance in the Sixteenth Century: Three Treatises by Hotman, Beza and Mornay* (New York: Pegasus, 1969): pp. 57–8, 90 (hereafter *Three Treatises*).

[22] For Theodore Beza, *Of the Right of Magistrates* (1573), see Franklin, *Three Treatises*, pp. 97–135, esp. pp. 110–15, 118–19. Cf. Kingdon, "Calvinism and Resistance Theory," pp. 210–11.

[23] For *Vindicae contra Tyrranos* (1579), see Franklin, *Three Treatises*, pp. 142–99, esp. 187–97. Cf. excellent treatments of this seminal Huguenot tract in Hopfl and Thompson, "History as Contract," pp. 929–33 and Kingdon, "Calvinism and Resistance Theory," pp. 212–14.

For their part, Scottish Calvinists provided not only a consistent irritant to Charles I in the religious struggle of the 1630s over the status of the bishops in their relation to the kirk, they also supplied their English coreligionists with a rich heritage of political resistance theories. The most important of the Scottish monarchomachs, and the one Filmer singled out for abuse, was the humanist scholar George Buchanan.[24] Buchanan's *De jure regni apud Scotos* was written as a defense of the Protestant nobles who ousted Queen Mary Stuart. It was in the context of justifying Mary's expulsion that Buchanan, drawing heavily on classical sources, established the crucial classical distinction between kingship and tyranny. Kings, he argued, derive their power from popular consent, and rule by and are subject to law. In addition, Buchanan argued that laws may be changed by the estates of the realm and the public council that a king must assemble to help him govern. Tyrants, on the other hand, seize power illegitimately and aspire to rule unbound by law. Political obedience, in Buchanan's view, applied only to kings, whereas tyrants may be deposed by legal action, military force, or assassination.[25] In this respect Buchanan drew Filmer's ire as another populist incendiary produced by the Geneva discipline.

The Calvinist supporters of Parliament inherited a rich legacy of resistance theories drawn from the Huguenot, the Scots, and the writings of Calvin himself. The logic of the argument for parliamentary resistance is fully intelligible only in the context of the development and modification of Calvin's theory of inferior magistrates. The danger for English royalism that Filmer identified lay in the volatile combination or fusion of Calvinist resistance theory and the arguments for mixed government and ancient constitutionalism that he complained were gaining increasing currency in England prior to the civil war. In order to complete our discussion of the unique historical and political context in which Filmer and his parliamentary opponents found themselves, we must briefly consider the emergence and development of ancient constitutionalism in England.

Divine Right and the Ancient Constitution

In *The Anarchy of Limited Monarchy* Filmer set out to dismantle the theory of mixed and limited monarchy propounded by the parliamentary apologists Hunton and Parker. However, Filmer also indicated that any successful defense of absolute monarchy would require overcoming a deeply ingrained feature of English political culture. He suggested that by the time of the civil war, the theory of mixed and limited monarchy had become the standard

---

[24] Filmer, *Patriarcha*, p. 3. For good discussions of Buchanan, see Kingdon, "Calvinism and Resistance Theory," pp. 216–18 and J. H. Burns, "George Buchanan and the Anti-Monarchomachs," in *Political Discourse in Early Modern Britain*, pp. 3–22.

[25] Kingdon, "Calvinism and Reistance Theory," p. 218.

coin of the realm in English political discourse. He complained: "There is scarce the meanest man of the multitude but can now in these days tell us that the government of the kingdom of England is a limited and mixed monarchy."[26] In order to understand the complex theoretical and constitutional backdrop to Filmer's argument, it is useful to present a brief account of the historical and intellectual climate that brought limited and mixed monarchy theories to such prominence in mid-seventeenth-century England.

The historical origins and political context that produced such widespread acceptance of mixed and limited monarchy theories may be understood as a response to the divine right pretensions of James I at the beginning of the seventeenth century.[27] James conceived of the kingship as "the office given him by God" over England. His divine right theory had certain superficial similarities to that of Filmer, such as the analogy of the king to the father's rule of a family and the exhortation to unquestioned obedience on the part of the subjects.[28] James's theory, however, rested on a kind of modified Aristotelianism that melded divine right with a conception of the organic character of political society and the natural principle of rule inhering in composite bodies. As we have seen, Filmer's argument extends beyond James's use of the general notion that all associations require a ruling element to the proposition that the truth about political rule can be derived from the details of Scripture. Even without the strong scriptural foundation of Filmerism, however, James's argument had serious constitutional implications. In one celebrated passage, James compared monarchy to the head's rule of the body and declared that just as it is best to remove a diseased member before it affects the whole body, "even so is it betwixt the prince and the people," and as such the prince may remove a diseased member of the polity in order to preserve the common good.[29] Presumably, under certain circumstances, one or both of the houses of Parliament could be conceived as such a diseased member of the polity.

The main response to James's pretensions from his parliamentary and judicial opponents was another sort of Aristotelianism. The ancient constitution theory of James's opponents shared the Aristotelian assumption that

---

[26] Filmer, *Patriarcha*, p. 133.

[27] The following discussion owes a great deal to Michael Zuckert's excellent account of the origins of ancient and balanced constitution theories in English political thought (*Natural Rights*, pp. 49–66), as well as to Mendle, *Dangerous Positions* and to Corinne Weston, "Theory of Mixed Monarchy under Charles I and after," *English Historical Review*, vol. 75 (July 1960): pp. 426–43.

[28] James I, "Trew Law of a Free Monarchie," in *Divine Right and Democracy*, David Wootton, ed. (Hammondsworth, Middlesex: Penguin Classics, 1986): pp. 103, 99, 105. Oakley (*Politics of Eternity*, p. 325) sees James following Lutheran theology with respect to the distinction between God's absolute and ordained power. However, with respect to monarchy I argue that James is much more Aristotelian than Filmer.

[29] James I, "Trew Law," p. 99.

the English Constitution was natural and, though an organic composition, was a whole irreducible to its parts. It also contained, however, theoretical elements inimical to divine right ambitions. For example, the ancient constitutionalist position that the preconstitutional origins of the English regime have no bearing on its actual operation attenuated the divine rightists' claims to royal supremacy on the grounds that the rights and privileges of the estates originally derived from and are ultimately subject to retraction by the king. The ancient constitutionalism propounded by many parliamentarians and jurists in the first half of the 1600s defended the English regime on the basis of both its antiquity and its utility. The English Constitution, they argued, with its emphasis on the structural relation of the parts – the Commons, the Lords spiritual and temporal, the bench, and the king – to the whole worked well and had worked well for a very long time. Ancient constitutionalism made no appeal to pre-civil individual rights, but rather held the English model of divided sovereignty as the embodiment of the structural arrangement most consistent with the natural purpose of political society.

Filmer's confrontation with the parliamentary contractarians marks the dramatic shift that occurred in English political discourse in the decade or so preceding the civil war. Just as Filmer's divine right theory signifies a radicalization of James's similitudes of the father to the king and the head to the body, so does the civil war era theory of mixed and limited monarchy indicate a significant departure from ancient constitutionalism. While the immediate issues that produced intense friction between the king and Parliament related to matters of taxation and the ecclesiastical dispute over episcopacy and Presbyterianism, the heart of the conflict that precipitated the shift from ancient constitutional to mixed regime arguments sprang from the constitutional dilemma raised by competing claims for royal prerogative and the extension of parliamentary power. The court's judgment in favor of Charles I in the Ship Money case of 1638, which recognized the king as the supreme arbiter in determining national emergencies, as well as his long period of rule without a sitting Parliament from 1629 to 1640, were seen by his opponents as brazen attempts to extend the royal prerogative beyond traditional limits.[30] The parliamentary response to these actions included the Triennial Act legislating regular parliaments every three years with or without royal assent; the Grand Remonstrance, which would have required the king to employ only ministers acceptable to Parliament; the act excluding bishops from the House of Lords; and the Nineteen Propositions, which would have legislated parliamentary control over the militia, church reform,

---

[30] J. P. Kenyon, *The Stuart Constitution: 1603–1688* (Cambridge: Cambridge University Press, 1966): pp. 109–11. Notice also the Filmerian arguments made by Sir John Finch, lord chief justice of common pleas, who maintained that the king's power historically precedes that of Parliament and that Parliament cannot bar a succession. Compare Kenyon, pp. 114–16 with Filmer, *Patriarcha*, III: 5, 6, 9.

and the education of the royal children.[31] These measures were intended to transform radically the English conception of the Constitution and the relation of church and state. Clearly, by the early 1640s, many in Parliament were no longer willing to accept the traditional premise that the king was the head of the three estates composing Parliament – the Commons and Lords spiritual and temporal. Amid the tumultuous climate and spiraling events of this period, ancient constitutionalist arguments were drowned out by the mutual recriminations and charges of executive tyranny and legislative usurpation. Clearly, in the minds of the English political class, even if the English regime had operated smoothly in the past, it was not doing so now and would not do so in the foreseeable future until the constitutional crisis had been resolved. The mixed constitutional theory emerged as an argument with appeal on both sides of the constitutional divide.

Mixed government theory, then, was essentially an innovation in English constitutional thought flowing from both the political quarrel between crown and Parliament and the religious battle over episcopacy and the presbytery. It was more theoretical than ancient constitutionalism in that it emphasized the need to balance and calibrate the distinct elements in the English polity, rather than appealing primarily to its antiquity.[32] Ironically, the classic expression of the mixed constitution was contained in Charles I's *Answer to the Nineteen Propositions*. It is here that Charles and his advisors, who had bitterly opposed the idea only a year before, now made the case that England was a mixed regime:

There being three kinds of government among men (absolute monarchy, aristocracy, and democracy), and all these having their particular conveniences and inconveniences, the experience and wisdom of your ancestors has so moulded this out of a mixture of these as to give this kingdom (as far as human prudence can provide) the conveniences of all three, ... as long as the balance hangs even between these three states, and they run jointly on in their proper channel.[33]

Mixed regime theory is at once palpably Aristotelian and yet uniquely attuned to the particular circumstances in England circa 1642.[34] The idea of

---

[31] For the Triennial Act, see Kenyon, *Stuart Constitution*, pp. 219–22; for the Grand Remonstrance, see pp. 228–40 (esp. p. 230), and for the Nineteen Propositions see pp. 244–7. A curious feature of those turbulent and confused times is the similarity between Filmer's crusade against Catholic scholasticism and the particular animus of his parliamentary opponents toward "the Jesuits and other engineers and factors for Rome" (*Grand Remonstrance*, in Kenyon, *Stuart Constitution*, pp. 229, 231) – proof, I suppose, that you can't always choose your friends. Cf. Weston, "Theory," p. 428.

[32] Zuckert, *Natural Rights*, p. 60.

[33] Charles I, "His Majesties Answer to the Nineteen Propositions of Both Houses of Parliament" (1642) in Wootton, *Divine Right and Democracy*, p. 171.

[34] Aristotle, *Politics*, IV: 11. For two diverging approaches to the development of classical regime typology in England and its bearing on the King's *Answer*, see Weston, "Theory," pp. 426, 436–7 and Mendle, *Dangerous Positions*, pp. 2–3, 38–40 and 111–13. Cf. Woolrych, *Britain in Revolution*, pp. 223–4.

mixed government was sufficiently protean to allow for its appropriation by both sides in the constitutional struggle. The king employed it to stigmatize Parliament's actions of the previous year as unjustifiable invasions of legitimate royal prerogative. Parliamentary radicals saw Charles's acceptance of mixed regime theory as a victory on two counts. It reversed, or at least attenuated, the traditional claim of royal supremacy maintained since the time of Elizabeth and James by including the monarchy as one of the estates of the realm. Moreover, with the exclusion of the bishops from the schema of estates, the *Answer* also satisfied the desire of many English Calvinists to reduce the political power of the bishops, if not destroy the episcopacy entirely.[35] Despite the particular partisan claims of victory resulting from the king's *Answer*, the emphasis on balance and respect for the position of the part in the order of the whole held both intellectual and rhetorical attractions to royalists and parliamentary radicals alike.

Mixed regime theory did not, however, appeal to Filmer. His sarcastic reference to the ubiquity of mixed constitution theory in English political circles was as critical of many of his fellow royalists as it was of the king's opponents. Filmer rejected the inclusion of the king as one of the three estates and detested the malleability of mixed regime theory and the wide range of interpretations it allowed.[36] Filmer's attempt to ground a theory of absolute monarchy in Scripture is as much a correction of civil war era English royalism as a refutation of English parliamentarianism and popular sovereignty theories. One such errant royalist is Henry Ferne. This moderate royalist was castigated by Filmer for accepting the central tenets of mixed regime theory, even though Ferne argued that the king retained supreme power within the mix and that Parliament's rights derived from the king.[37] In admitting the practical superiority of England's mixed regime, Ferne insisted that rejecting resistance to royal authority did not constitute a defense of absolutism.[38] In his dispute with the parliamentary contractarians Filmer had few, if any, true soul mates even on the royalist end of the political spectrum.

---

[35] Cf. Mendle, *Dangerous Positions*, pp. 171–85.

[36] Filmer (*Patriarcha*, pp. 88–9) saw the three estates in more traditional terms as the Commons, the Lords Spiritual, and the Lords Temporal. In adopting this formulation of the Constitution, Filmer perhaps followed the lead of some of Charles' many royalist critics such as Sir Matthew Hale and Thomas Hobbes, who believed the Crown conceded far too much to Parliament in the king's *Answers* (cf. Corinne Weston, "England: Ancient Constitution and Common Law," in *Cambridge History of Political Thought*, pp. 396–7).

[37] Henry Ferne, "The Resolving of Conscience" (Cambridge: 1642). See also Zuckert, *Natural Rights*, p. 66. Compare with Filmer's criticism of "Dr. Ferne" in Filmer, *Patriarcha*, p. 134.

[38] See Ferne cited in J. W. Allen, *English Political Thought 1603–1644* (London: Archon, 1967): p. 495. Ferne's position regarding the legislative power was also very different from that of Filmer. Whereas Filmer considered the legislative power to be, following Bodin, the first mark of sovereignty and thus entirely belonging to the monarch, Ferne allowed only that there could be no law without royal assent, i.e., the concurrence of all three branches of government.

Hunton and the Mixed Regime

Two of the most articulate and effective defenders of Parliament in its open struggle with the crown during the civil war were the Puritan divine Phillip Hunton and the parliamentary lawyer Henry Parker. The core idea of Hunton's *A Treatise of Monarchie* is that the king is one of the three estates of the English constitutional order. England is, in Hunton's view, a "mixed monarchy" because within the balance of the three coordinated branches, sovereignty is shared but the "primity (sic) of share in the supreme power" is in the king.[39] Despite the king's "primity of share" in the supreme power, the king does not have supreme power in toto; rather, in the event of conflict between the monarch and one or both of the houses of Parliament, there is no internal judge to such disputes. The underlying premise of Hunton's mixed monarchy theory is the idea of contract. For Hunton, all government is derived from consent and must be understood as a contract between the rulers and the people.[40] Hunton's emphasis on the contractual arrangement that forms the fundamental laws of a particular regime indicates two important features of his thought. First, it signifies his departure from the ancient constitution model inasmuch as he looks for the legitimacy of the English regime in its preconstitutional origins. Furthermore, Hunton emphasizes that political subjection is primarily a moral act "because man, being a voluntary agent, and subjection being a moral act, it does essentially depend on consent."[41]

Where the Calvinist Hunton, the Lutheran Filmer, and the Jesuits Suarez and Bellarmine all agree is about the divine ordination of political authority. The moral character of political obligation is ultimately derived from this central theological fact. Hunton's schema of the four levels of political authority illustrates important parallels between English Calvinist thought and that of the Jesuits. On the most fundamental level, the power of government derives from God, but this divine grant specifies that no particular form of government is required.[42] The next level relates to the presovereign power of the people from which derives the consent to form a government. The third level involves the establishment of a particular constitution by the people. The fourth and most immediate level of political authority comprises those who actually exercise power in a given constitution. It is Hunton's contention, in contrast to Filmer, that the divine ordination of politics allows wide possibilities for the variety of regimes human beings can produce. In England in particular, the four levels of authority signify "the rule of God, the people of England, and, for the final two, the mix of King and

[39] Philip Hunton, "A Treatise of Monarchy" (1642), in Wootton, *Divine Right and Democracy*, p. 192.
[40] Hunton, "Treatise," pp. 177, 183, 191.
[41] Ibid., p. 189.
[42] For the four levels in general, see Hunton, "Treatise," pp. 175–7. Cf. Calvin, *Institutes* 4.20.8.

Parliament."[43] Hunton's precise account of the theological premises underlying the legitimacy of England's contractual mixed monarchy demonstrates
the significant departure of English Calvinist supporters of Parliament from
the earlier understanding of ancient constitutionalism.

Hunton's theory of mixed monarchy was a compelling target for Filmer's
attacks due both to its appeal to divine sanction and to the use of contract.
Though Hunton's powerful injection of consent into the Aristotelian frame
of mixed constitutionalism bears strong links to the arguments of Filmer's
Catholic enemies, there is at least one significant difference. While Suarez
and Bellarmine propounded the consensual origins of government, the moral
power exercised through consent was mainly a device to explain the legitimate acceptance of existing authority. Hunton, on the other hand, more
strongly emphasized the creative role of the moral power expressed through
consent and the right of resistance that flowed from this understanding of
consent.[44] This difference in emphasis was no doubt partly influenced by
the context of the civil war conditions under which Hunton wrote, when the
claims of competing existing authorities were so manifestly at issue.

However, another explanation for Hunton's emphasis on the active moral
agency of consent is his reliance on the idea of "subordinate magistrates"
so central to Calvinist resistance theory. Hunton's theory of coordinate
sovereignty represents an English argument similar to the radicalization of
the principle of resistance by institutions and political leaders participat-
ing in, although not exercising exclusively or even primarily, the right of
sovereignty. In the context of mid-seventeenth-century England, in which
the notion of mixed sovereignty had already taken root somewhat with the
spread of ancient constitutionalism, it was not a major theoretical or theological leap to transfer the idea of a justifiable resistance right in "subordinate
magistrates" to a right of resistance against the crown by the two houses of
Parliament as almost coequal sovereigns.[45] Hunton, however, takes Calvinist
resistance theory even further in the radical direction than the Huguenot
position in *Vindicae Contra Tyrannos* by arguing that in the event of a constitutional conflict between the various branches of government, judgment
regarding the validity of these institutional claims devolves to "the sentence
in every man's conscience."[46] While Hunton recognized the act of resistance
as a moral power inhering in individuals, he also firmly contends that it
does not denote a "civil" right of resistance. Hunton clearly limits the individualist implications of his notion of devolution. Consent, he argued, is

---

[43] Hunton, "Treatise," pp. 195–211. The quote is from Zuckert, *Natural Rights*, p. 68.
[44] Zuckert, *Natural Rights*, p. 332.
[45] It is typical of Hunton's contractualist argument that he distinguishes the general theological
and moral justification of resistance ("Treatise," pp. 185–8) from his discussion of the particular scope of resistance in England ("Treatise," pp. 202–9). Cf. Calvin, *Institutes* 4.20.31.
[46] Hunton, "Treatise," pp. 187–8.

required to form government and to choose a constitutional structure, but coercive power properly derives from God. Following the Calvinist political teaching, Hunton argues that only governments or institutions ordained by divine sanction can exercise coercive authority, not individuals.[47] Thus, while Hunton granted that individuals may possess a moral power to resist civil authority, such resistance must be understood by reference to the community. The individual may pass judgment on his own safety and the safety of the entire community of which he is a member, but Hunton grounded this right of resistance in the good of the whole community rather than in the pre-political rights of the individual. For Hunton, the ultimate end of the individual's power to resist is the verdict of the whole community decided in war.[48] In this way Hunton stops far short of the radical theory of the dissolution of government.

Filmer and Hunton agree that government involves a moral subjection. Hunton, however, argues that this subjection is not natural, but rather originates in contract. Filmer's own account, of course, denied human beings the capacity to form obligations on their own terms. In attacking another theory rooted in a divine grant of political power, Filmer is actually condemning Hunton's attempt to mix divine right with the coactive power of human beings.[49] For Filmer, God's general and specific ordinances arising from Adam's creation allow no moral space for human participation in the formation of rule; there is only subjection. There is, however, an important ambiguity in Filmer's rejection of Hunton's argument for the mixed character of sovereignty in England. On the one hand, like Ferne, he accepts the practical existence of the estates in England – though not including the king as one of them – and he argues that the king alone has supreme power.[50] On the other hand, Filmer, unlike Ferne, rejects the mixed regime motif as not being even practically beneficial to the good order of the realm. Filmer's emphatic insistence on the supremacy of the monarch alone is born from his broader doctrine of obedience. Though the Lords and Commons may assist the king in ruling – and Filmer admits that they do – the implicit suggestion

---

[47] Julian Franklin, *John Locke and the Theory of Sovereignty*, (Cambridge: Cambridge University Press, 1978): p. 39. In this respect, Hunton's Calvinist argument shares the Christian-Aristotelian premises of the Catholic natural lawyers. Cf. Calvin, *Institutes* 4.20.4 and Francisco Suarez, *Ac Deo Legislatore* (1612, Coimbra), in *Selections from Three Works of Francisco Suarez, S. J.* (Oxford: Clarendon Press, 1944): III.3.3.378. Cf. Oakley, *Politics of Eternity*, p. 178.

[48] Franklin, *John Locke*, p. 42.

[49] Zuckert, *Natural Rights*, p. 69. However, note the inherently conservative character of Hunton's idea of contract (e.g. "Treatise," pp. 177, 182, 186) by which he allows that a people may legitimately subject themselves and their posterity to absolute government. In this respect, Hunton not only recoils from the idea of a general right of rebellion, he also falls short of the scholastic argument that delegitimated tyranny prima facie on the basis of the natural law.

[50] Filmer, *Patriarcha*, pp. 99, 145.

of Filmer's teaching is that even the appearance of mixture in the sovereign power confuses the operation of the obedience principle and tends to divide the subject's loyalty.[51] Filmer's repeated emphasis is on the unity necessary for sovereign power, a unity in its deepest sense antithetical to Hunton's or Aristotle's notion of mixture. As Filmer argues: "Neither his primity of share in the supreme power, nor his authority being last, no, nor having the greatest authority, doth make him a monarch unless he have that authority *alone.*"[52] Mixture, moreover, opens the possibility of internal disputes within the sovereign power – the very situation prompting Hunton's writing – and Filmer sees no way to resolve these disputes if no organ of rule possessed supreme power in its entirety. To Filmer, this incapacity to settle disputes and provide for a final arbiter or judge makes mixed regime theories the very embodiment of the principle of anarchy itself. As Filmer cautions, "farewell all government if there be no judge."

The other important element in Hunton's theory is the notion of legal limits. In addition to being a mixed regime, England is also, in Hunton's view, a limited monarchy in which the supreme sovereign power – the king – is regulated by certain fundamental laws and principles. Hunton lists the five "principal and most apparent limitations of this monarchy" as involving a wide range of issues relevant to the operation of government.[53] These limits reflect both the mixed character of the English Constitution and the contractual origins of government in general. The first limit has to do with the "nomothetical power" and forbids the kings to make laws "solely and by themselves, but together with the concurrent authority of the two other estates in parliament." The second limit prohibits the monarch from contravening the "fundamental common laws," which appear to include the common law precedents and such fundamental constitutional laws as the Magna Carta. Third, though the king reserves the right of judicial appointment, Hunton argues that he is prohibited from exercising the "power of constituting officers and means of governing" such as courts of judicature. The fourth limit relates to the crucial matter of succession, as a "successive monarch is so far limited in his power that he cannot leave it to whom he pleases, but to whom the fundamental law concerning that succession has designed it." The fifth and final "principal limitation" on the English

---

[51] For Filmer's admission that kings first created written laws and called parliaments to assist them in ruling large and diverse realms, see Filmer, *Patriarcha*, III: pp. 5, 12.

[52] Filmer, *Patriarcha*, p. 156 (emphasis in the original).

[53] For the five limits, see Hunton, "Treatise," pp. 199–201. Goldsworthy argues that Filmer displays a crucial misunderstanding of Hunton's point about fundamental laws in seeing them only as limits on the king alone and failing to see the absolute authority of king-in-Parliament (Jeffrey Goldsworthy, *The Sovereignty of Parliament: History and Philosophy* [Oxford: Clarendon Press, 1999]: p. 134). This argument does not, however, take full account of Hunton's concern to place certain limits on sovereignty per se through the medium of quasi-Aristotelian statements about the inherent character of political life.

monarchy is the prohibition on taxing the subjects without the assent of Parliament or "to make an alienation of any lands or other revenues annexed by law to the crown." Though Hunton's account of the chief limits on monarchical power is not radical or innovative in itself – Hunton's limits are nowhere near as intrusive as those proposed by Parliament in the measures of 1641 – it inflamed Filmer's deepest fears of the dark populist implications of the mixed monarchy theory.

Apart from the limitations placed on regal power by the fundamental constitution, the original contract, Hunton identifies a second source of legal limitation that he terms "after condescent." Hunton maintains that after condescent occurs "when a lord who, by conquest or other right, has an arbitrary power but, not liking to hold by such a right, does either formally or virtually desert it and take a legal right."[54] Filmer condemns this argument as a veil for populism. Who decides whether a ruler has "virtually" deserted one of his prerogatives? Predictably, he charges, most likely the people! The limits instituted by such a development, Hunton argues, amount to a "secondary original constitution." Filmer attacks this notion of the self-limiting character of regal power both on its own terms and in relation to Hunton's professed originalism. On its own terms, Filmer argues that a self-limitation of regal power depends entirely on the will of the monarch and hence is no limit on sovereign will at all. For Filmer, a will can only be limited by a greater will. He proposes that after condescent is merely an "act of grace" that is fully retractable with no diminution of sovereign power.[55] Filmer's second criticism of after condescent is that it signifies a noncontractual form of limitation that does not require the consent of the people. In this way, Filmer maintains that after condescent represents an erosion of the primacy of the fundamental or original constitution. Filmer even suggests that after condescent reflects Hunton's more sober second thoughts on the matter of consent. He explains:

Howsoever our author speak big of the radical, fundamental and original power of the people as the root of all sovereignty, yet in a better mood he will take up and be contented with a monarchy limited by an after condescent and act of grace from the monarch himself.[56]

Filmer does not deny that monarchs may choose not to exercise fully their power or may change the laws as they please, but he does deny that such actions assume a legal character that binds sovereign power. For Filmer, even if every English king since William the Conqueror has ruled by certain standing laws, these developments, such as the calling of parliaments and the incorporation of the Magna Carta, do not form constitutional limitations

[54] Hunton, "Treatise," pp. 183–4.
[55] Filmer, *Patriarcha*, pp. 149–50. Cf. Hunton, "Treatise," p. 184.
[56] Filmer, *Patriarcha*, p. 150.

extrinsic to the particular will of the current monarch. Filmer's theory of sovereignty denies the very possibility of any meaningful treatment of constitutional development.

Filmer's response to Hunton's notion of legal limits on the crown is that a king, being the source of all law, cannot govern by fixed constitutional laws. The very arbitrariness of law, in Filmer's view, militates against a sovereign setting his own rules and promising to keep them. The supreme power cannot be restrained by law because if it is "restrained by some law, is not the power of that law, and of them that made that law, above his supreme power?"[57] The power to make laws is arbitrary, and thus laws cannot be made in a legal way. Filmer also criticizes Hunton's caution that subjects should obey the monarch, even if he passes certain limits, unless the king's actions endanger the survival of the realm. As Filmer observes, any breaking of the law by the king destroys the limited monarchy: "if there be illegality in the act, it strikes at the very being of limited monarchy, which is to be legal."[58] It is the particular character of Filmerian divine right that law and arbitrary will, usually seen as opposites, are integrated in a theory of absolute sovereignty.

Parker and Parliamentary Supremacy

Henry Parker's *Observations* was one of several parliamentary responses to Charles's thesis concerning English mixed monarchy. Charles, we recall, sought to affirm the integral position of the crown in the Constitution as one of the three major elements of the government and to defend his exclusive rights and prerogatives. Parker, already a celebrated opponent of the crown for his brilliant tract against the decision in the Ship Money case and his criticism of the Laudian church reforms, advanced the most sweeping claims for parliamentary authority in the civil war period. His argument for legislative supremacy also signified the most radical extension of parliamentary resistance theory. For example, whereas William Prynne argued in *the Soveraigne Power of Parliament* (1643) that the two houses together held greater authority than the crown alone, and whereas Hunton, as we have seen, maintained a primity of share for the crown in supreme power, Parker argued that Parliament was the supreme constitutional power because it alone represented the nation as a whole.[59] Parker did not deny the role of the monarch

57 Ibid., pp. 148, 136. Cf. Zagorin, *English Revolution*, p. 197.
58 Filmer, *Patriarcha*, p. 152 and Hunton, "Treatise," p. 188.
59 Caton even goes so far as to identify Parker with a "version of republicanism" (Caton, *Politics of Progress*, p. 135). Richard Tuck, on the other hand, argues (*Philosophy and Government, 1572–1651* [Cambridge: Cambridge University Press, 1993]: p. 229) that Parker's defense of parliamentary authority is largely pragmatic (cf. Goldsworthy, *Sovereignty of Parliament*, pp. 86, 88, 97–9, 103). For arguments that, I believe correctly, observe the naturalistic basis of Parker's argument, see Alan Craig Houston, "Republicanism, the Politics of Necessity and the Rule of Law," in *A Nation Transformed: England after the Restoration*, Alan Houston and

in the English government, but he did confine it to a clearly subordinate status vis-à-vis the absolute legislative power of Parliament. While Filmer paid less attention to Parker than to Hunton, his response to the parliamentary apologist he called the "Observator" was indicative of his divine right opposition to civil war era resistance theories.

Parker maintained that the laws of society are dictates of reason "ratified by common consent." To this extent he, like Hunton, operated from the Aristotelian premise of natural human sociality. However, Parker also grounded his populist account of the origins of government in an interpretation of constitutional history characteristic of the radical Huguenot resistance theorists. According to Parker, the human need for law meant that in the early stages of human civilization people conferred supreme power on monarchs. In time, however, they saw the dangers of "unbounded prerogative" and realized the need to establish "laws for the limiting of supreme governors."[60] While Parker affirmed that by the law of nature "the body of the people" may rise against abusive magistrates and "redress all public grievances," he also maintained that in the course of their constitutional development nations instituted "public assemblies, whereby the people may assume its own power to do itself right." Parker's central contention is that in England the people established the houses of Parliament so that "by virtue of election and representation a few shall act for the many."[61] For Parker, the representative institutions of Parliament play a similar role in England that the Estates General did in the Hugenot interpretation of French constitutional history. These institutions express popular sovereignty, and as such the crown, properly speaking, has no share in the sovereign power. Thus, Parker defended parliamentary resistance to the crown in the civil war on the grounds that it was in Parliament that the "whole community in its underived majesty shall convene to do justice." As such, he granted Parliament sweeping powers "to create new forms and precedents" and to have "jurisdiction over itself."[62] With this assertion of absolute legislative power, Parker ascribed to Parliament the right to assume the executive function in the event of a national crisis.

In the heated atmosphere of civil war era England, Parker's argument was attractive to the more radical defenders of the parliamentary cause, even as Hunton's position was more suited for the many moderates still committed to some royal share in sovereignty. Huntonian moderates in the parliamentary

Steve Pincus, eds. (Cambridge: Cambridge University Press, 2001): pp. 248–9 and Michael Mendle's "Parliamentary Sovereignty: A very English absolutism" *Political Discourse in Early Modern Britain*, in Phillipson and Skinner, eds., pp. 116–17 and his *Henry Parker and the English Civil War* (Cambridge: Cambridge University Press, 1995).

[60] Parker, *Observations*, p. 13 (quoted in Filmer, *Patriarcha*, p. 163).

[61] Ibid., pp. 13–14 (in Filmer, *Patriarcha*, pp. 164–5).

[62] Ibid., pp. 14–15 (in Filmer, *Patriarcha*, p. 165). Cf. Houston, "Republicanism," pp. 250–1 and Mendle, *Henry Parker*, p. 183.

camp could only be deeply concerned by the populist implications of Parker's tendency to elide the power of the people and the sovereignty of Parliament. For Hunton and the moderates, the ultimate appeal to the judgment of the "community" in time of constitutional crisis was meant to ensure, not derogate from, the crown's pivotal role as the primary organ of sovereign power. Only the community could seriously restrict the crown, not Parliament. For Parker, on the other hand, Parliament's conflict with the crown did not need to be explained and justified by recourse to the uncertain judgment of the community because, in a fundamental sense, Parliament was the community.

Filmer's brief critique of Parker rested on two major objections. First, he countered Parker's claim that Parliament had jurisdiction over itself by observing that Parker had no way to explain this jurisdiction in cases of "divisions" arising between the Commons and the Lords.[63] Filmer reiterated his opposition to the logic of divided sovereignty and applied this objection to Parker's claims regarding sovereignty in any composite body. Who would or could resolve a dispute between the Lords and Commons? Filmer responded that clearly Parker's argument for parliamentary sovereignty is simply another recipe for anarchy. Only the unified and unlimited system of command embodied by an absolute monarch could avoid the anarchic possibilities inhering in any theory of mixed government.

Filmer's other major objection to Parker's theory of mixed government was his claim that Parker could not point to a single historical example of a nation governed by a system of limited monarchy. Filmer claimed that insofar as the legislative power inheres solely in a monarch, it is absurd to propose that any king could be restrained by a legal superior. Moreover, he charged that Parker could not identify any regime operating on the principles of limited monarchy. According to Filmer, limited monarchy did not occur to the ancient Greeks or to any of the modern states such as Sweden, Poland, or Denmark that were often cited as exemplars of it. Filmer charged:

Now let the Observator bethink himself, whether all or any of these three countries have found out any art whereby the people or community may assume its own power. If neither these countries have, most countries have not, nay none have. The people or community in these realms are as absolute as any in the world.[64]

With an argument echoing his assault on the populist implications of the scholastic contract theory, Filmer challenged Parker to provide any example of a nation "where the community in its underived majesty did ever come to do justice."[65] In Filmer's view, insofar as neither England nor any country could point to such a radically populist origin of government, no argument

[63] Filmer, *Patriarcha*, p. 166.
[64] Ibid., p. 170.
[65] Ibid., p. 167.

for mixed or limited sovereignty or for popular resistance to monarchical authority could be justified.

The divine right attack on the parliamentary contractarians pointed beyond the immediate issues of the English constitutional controversy in the civil war era. Filmer saw in the parliamentary resistance theories of Hunton and Parker another variant of the dangerous doctrine of natural liberty. Filmer perceptively traced the origin of these arguments to two confluent sources: the tradition of Calvinist resistance theory and the English idea of mixed monarchy that had developed from ancient constitutionalism. With his articulation of a divine right theory of unlimited sovereignty, Filmer buttressed the cause of English royalism with the theological support of Lutheran absolutism. In so doing, he framed the constitutional dispute in England in terms of the general context of a fundamental quarrel within Protestantism over the nature of political obligation and the proper form of government. For England in particular, the exchange between Filmer and his parliamentary opponents foreshadowed the constitutional upheavals that would take place during the 1640s and 1650s. Hunton's appeal to the "conscience of every man" would indeed result in a long and bitter contest of arms. In Parker's radical argument for legislative supremacy we see the seeds of the Commonwealth and the full absorption of all constitutional powers into a single legislative body.[66] Even further down the road, however, loomed Cromwell, the collapse of the Commonwealth, the restoration of the Stuart monarchy, and the dark prospect of further constitutional travails in the future. Filmer, then, was correct in one crucial respect. The mixed regime proposed by Hunton and the principle of legislative supremacy advocated by Parker signally failed to achieve their direct aim: to establish the theoretical grounds for a permanent settlement of the jurisdiction of the various elements of the English Constitution. The challenge of establishing such a comprehensive settlement would confront Filmer's new Whig antagonists nearly forty years later.

---

[66] For a good treatment of Interregnum republican thought, see Blair Worden, "Marchmount Nedham and the Beginnings of English Republicanism, 1649–1656," in *Republicanism, Liberty, and Commercial Society 1649–1776*, David Wootton, ed. (Stanford: Stanford University Press, 1994): pp. 45–81. Cf. Woolrych, *Britain in Revolution*, pp. 432–56.

3

The Problem of Grotius and Hobbes

The two civil wars from 1642 to 1648 proved to be calamitous for the cause of divine right monarchy in England. Filmer's greatest fears about the parliamentary radicalism in the mixed regime theories of Hunton and Parker, the latter eventually becoming a secretary of state under Cromwell, were realized in the regicide and the establishment of the Commonwealth in 1649. Filmer lived to see not only the triumph of Calvinist and Independent resisters over crown and church, but also the utter implosion of Charles and the moderate royalists' argument for mixed monarchy when a radicalized Parliament assumed the full right of sovereignty as the sole representative of the nation. The postwar period also, however, saw the publication in 1652 of the nothing if not resilient Filmer's *Observations concerning the Originall of Government*, the greatest portion of which composed an extended critique of Hugo Grotius' *De Jure Belli ac Pacis* and Thomas Hobbes' *Leviathan*. With this substantial offering in the closing years of his life, Filmer's work took on a somewhat new direction. Whereas his prior efforts had focused primarily on the Catholic natural law and the Calvinist-influenced parliamentary resisters, now near the end of his career Filmer trained his sights on the two most prominent natural law and natural rights theorists of the period.

Unlike his Catholic and Calvinist theological opponents of years past, Filmer's new antagonists in the natural liberty school did not fuse their arguments for consent with the principle of divine ordination of political power. Grotian and Hobbesian natural jurisprudence represented, although to decidedly varying degrees, the process of secularization in the natural liberty tradition in the seventeenth century. While Hobbes was more emphatically modern than Grotius, a greater secularist and a more rigorous and logically consistent proponent of individual natural rights, Filmer recognized in both a new dimension in the natural liberty tradition "first hatch'd in the schools." This, he believed, marked, again to varying degrees, a significant modification, and indeed a departure from, the classical and Christian premises of the schoolmen and the favorers of the Geneva discipline.

Hugo Grotius and Thomas Hobbes cast a long and complex shadow over the philosophical foundations of the Whig politics of liberty. As we shall see in Part Two, the Whig argument for natural liberty and limited government also rested on the philosophical foundation of modern natural jurisprudence. In this respect, Grotius and Hobbes were the thinkers most similar to the Whigs out of all of Filmer's opponents in the natural liberty school. Yet Hobbes and Grotius advanced theories of right affording no necessary or even easy connection between natural rights and limited government. The politics of Filmer's Whig critics was of an emphatically anti-absolutist character, and as such, their adoption of natural rights theory had to involve significant modifications of the inherited notions in order to avoid the authoritarian or absolutist implications of Grotian and Hobbesian natural law and natural rights theory.[1] Prior to the Whig theorists of the 1680s, natural law and natural rights held only a limited and deeply suspect utility in promoting limited constitutionalism. In order to understand the modification of modern natural jurisprudence that occurred in England in the early 1680s, we will have to examine Filmer's critique of Grotian and Hobbesian theory and assess the possibilities and limitations for harmonizing these theories with a defense of limited government. Insofar as Grotius and Hobbes provided the Whigs with the basic theoretical and conceptual materials necessary to produce theories of right and government more liberal and republican than Hobbes or Grotius intended or envisioned, an examination of Filmer's critique of these two thinkers will help us understand how the Whigs managed to square the natural rights circle.

Filmer and Grotius

Hugo Grotius' *De Jure Belli ac Pacis* was first published in 1625 and was soon recognized as a seminal work in modern natural jurisprudence. As the title suggests, Grotius' explicit aim and most of the argument in the work was directed to finding a natural law basis for legitimate relations between nations, rather than among individuals, both in war and in peace.[2]

---

[1] While I recognize the authoritarian or even absolutist possibilities in Grotius, I do not go as far as Tully, who argues that Grotius (and Pufendorf) set out to establish an absolutist theory of sovereignty (James Tully, *A Discourse on Property: Locke and His Adversaries* [Cambridge: Cambridge University Press, 1980]: pp. 157, 172). Rather, the glaring difference between Grotius and Filmer's Whig critics was the latter's rejection of even the *possibility* of legitimate absolute rule.

[2] For Grotius' role in the development of the international relations theory, see Peter Ahrensdorf and Thomas Pangle, *Justice Among Nations: On the Moral Basis of War and Peace* (Lawrence: University Press of Kansas, 1999): pp. 162–77, in which they identify Grotius as the "last great representative of the Medieval Christian just war tradition" (p. 162). For a similar assessment of Grotius' thought as rooted in the late medieval tradition, see Charles Edwards, *Hugo Grotius, the Miracle of Holland: A Study in Political and Legal Thought* (Chicago: Nelson-Hall, 1981): esp. chs. 4 and 5.

However, it was primarily through his reflections on the contractual basis of government and property and his naturalistic theory of sovereignty that Grotius acquired his prominence in the natural liberty tradition. In England, the impact of Grotius' work was considerable, being widely respected by Englishmen of all political stripes. Supporters and opponents of royal power in the mid-seventeenth century drew theoretical support for their arguments from Grotius. Thus, as James Daly observes, Filmer was unusually anti-Grotian for an English royalist.[3] Grotius' aim in formulating his law of nature theory was to identify universally valid minimalist moral and ethical principles that could counter the relativism of late-sixteenth-century skeptics such as Montaigne and Charron, on the one hand, and provide a more rigorous empirical and scientific approach to moral and political questions than that of orthodox sixteenth-century Christian Aristotelianism, on the other.[4] In response to skepticism, Grotius provided an argument for a set of albeit minimalist moral principles underlying and operative in every human society. As a corrective to what he took to be the rigid categories and excessively dogmatic tenets of orthodox Aristotelianism, Grotius offered an empirical analysis producing a nonsectarian law of nature rooted in a rationalist conception of human nature and the proper ends of human society.

In contrast to both the Catholic and Calvinist variants of Christian Aristotelianism, Grotius rejected the idea of the divine ordination of political authority. He even went so far in the direction of secularism as to argue that his natural law theory would be intelligible "even if we should concede, that which cannot be conceded without the utmost wickedness, that there is no God, or that the affairs of men are of no concern to him."[5] With this celebrated *etiamsi daremus* statement Grotius did not, of course, mean that a

---

3 James Daly, *Sir Robert Filmer and English Political Thought* (Toronto: University of Toronto Press): p. 142; cf. p. 24 for Grotius' royalist sympathies. Michal Zuckert (*Natural Rights and the New Republicanism* [Princeton: Princeton University Press, 1994]: ch. 4) and Richard Tuck (*Natural Rights Theories* [Cambridge: Cambridge University Press, 1979]: ch. 3) have shown the wide range of interpretations of Grotius at the time, with Tuck observing: "Grotius was both the first conservative rights theorist in Protestant Europe, and also, in a sense, the first radical rights theorist" (p. 71).

4 Richard Tuck, "Grotius and Selden," in *Cambridge History of Political Thought, 1450–1700*, J. H. Burn and Mark Goldie, eds. (Cambridge: Cambridge University Press, 1991): pp. 516, 518 and J. B. Schneewind, *The Invention of Autonomy: A History of Modern Moral Philosophy* (Cambridge: Cambridge University Press, 1998): pp. 66–7. Zagorin argues that Grotius showed little concern with refuting skepticism, and rather was following the lead of Bacon's empiricism (Perez Zagorin, "Hobbes without Grotius," *History of Political Thought*, vol. 21, no. 1 [Spring 2000]: pp. 24–5). Although Grotius does not identify or deal with the modern skeptics at length, I think the thrust of his argument suggests that the ancient conventionalist Carneades is a proxy for the modern skeptics.

5 Hugo Grotius, *De Jure Belli ac Pacis Libre Tres*, Vol. I, photographic reproduction of the 1646 Amsterdam edition, and Vol. II, translation of the text by Francis Kelsey (Oxford: Clarendon Press, 1925): prolegomena, sec. 11 (hereafter DJB book, chapter, section, page number or prol. sec.).

comprehensive system of morality could be established on a purely secular foundation. What he meant to suggest was that there was an empirically discoverable law of nature with identifiable minimalist moral principles that existed independently of the divine positive law in Scripture.[6] Grotius' concern to establish a nonsectarian natural law was rooted in the context of his own formative political and intellectual experience as a participant in the bitter intra-Protestant theological controversies in the United Provinces in the early seventeenth century.[7] As a supporter of the ill-fated Oldenbarnevelt regime's policy of religious toleration and by virtue of his criticism of the orthodox Calvinist doctrines in theology and politics during the Arminian controversy, Grotius suffered imprisonment and a twenty-three-year exile spent largely in Paris as a pensioner of the French and Swedish courts. Grotius' effort to establish a naturalistic basis for a universal system of morality did not, however, produce the distinctly modern natural rights theory of Hobbes with its rigorous secularism and a fully developed principle of individual natural rights. Grotius blended classical and Christian ideas of natural sociability and intrinsic moral knowledge with the modern ideas of consent and contract to produce a version of natural law theory that modified significantly, but ultimately did not sever its connection to, the Aristotelian tradition.

The law of nature, for Grotius, is a "dictate of right reason, which points out that an act, according as it is or is not in conformity with rational nature, has in it a quality of moral baseness or a moral necessity."[8] The natural law relates to the general principles supporting the requirements for human society. It reflects both human physical needs and the social conditions required to develop human rational and moral potential. In his response to the ancient conventionalist Carneades, Grotius maintains that justice and society cannot be simply reduced to a standard of utility. Rather, the distinctly human capacity for law and society is rooted in a "desire for society ... according to the measure of his intelligence."[9] It is the possession of this "impelling desire for society, for the gratification of which he alone among animals, possesses a special instrument, speech" that makes it reasonable to assume that human beings have "a faculty of knowing and of acting in accordance with general

---

[6] In fact, far from being a great secularist, Grotius ascribed a great deal of importance to God. See, for example, DJB prolegomena, sec. 12 for Grotius' assurance that the rational faculties were planted in humans by God; see also DJB prol., sec. 20 for his invocation of divine support for justice. For Grotius' reliance on religion, see Schneewind, *Invention of Autonomy*, pp. 68–70, 73–5; Edwards, *Miracle of Holland*, pp. 47–66 and Zagorin, "Hobbes," pp. 29–30.

[7] For Grotius' biographical and historical context, see Tuck, "Grotius," pp. 509–14, 521–2 and Edwards, *Miracle of Holland*, pp. 1–8.

[8] DJB, 1.1.10.1. Barbeyrac adds rational "*and social*" nature of man. For a good discussion of the important classical elements in Grotius' natural law theory such as the argument for natural human sociality and the naturalness of a ruling element in any composite body, see Richard Cox, "Hugo Grotius," *History of Political Philosophy*, 3rd ed., Leo Strauss and Joseph Cropsey, eds. (Chicago: University of Chicago Press, 1987): pp. 390–2.

[9] DJB, prol., sec. 6.

principles."[10] In the context of the law of nature, the natural freedom of individuals includes the freedom to choose the form of government under which one lives. Grotius explains: "But as there are many ways of living, one better than another, and each man is free to choose which of them he pleases; so each nation may choose what form of government it will." Government is a product "not of Divine Precept" but of human will, reflecting human necessity and the natural impulse toward society.[11] In addition to the formative power of contract, Grotius maintains that all legitimate political power is exercised through the terms of the original contract. The central tension in Grotian thought rests on the double source of society both in physical necessity and in human rational nature. The "first principles of nature," such as self-preservation, Grotius admits, "commends us to Right Reason; but Right Reason ought to be more dear to us than those things through whose instrumentality we have been brought to it." Although the status of political society is determined mainly by reference to the social character of human rationality, Grotius does not deny that it originates in necessity. He claims: "Society has in view this object, that through community of resources and effort each individual be safeguarded in the possession of what belongs to him."[12]

Connected to this argument is Grotius' understanding of the natural right of individuals to punish transgressors of the law of nature. Grotius justifies this particular example of force on the grounds that "it is not then contrary to the nature of society to look out for oneself, . . . and consequently the use of force which does not violate the rights of others, is not unjust." Though this natural right to repel injury by forceful means does not disappear in society, Grotius asserts "that the license which was prevalent before the establishment of courts has been greatly restricted."[13] It is precisely the transferal of this punishment power to the public authority that constitutes civil government. In contrast to Suarez and Bellarmine, who deny this natural punishing power in individuals, Grotius makes this right of punishment one of the core features of the moral power of individuals to create government.[14] At its source, then, Grotius sees government emerging as much from the conflict of rights bearers and the improper exercise of those rights as from the requirements of human moral and intellectual development.

How are we to understand Grotius' apparent insistence both on subjective individual rights and on the classical notion of natural sociability? Grotius scholars are divided between those who emphasize his role as an individual rights thinker and forerunner to Hobbes and those who contend

[10] Ibid., sec. 7.
[11] Ibid., 1.3.8.2; 1.4.7.3.
[12] Ibid., 1.2.1.5. Cf. 1.4.2.1.
[13] Ibid., 1.2.1.6; 1.3.2.1; see also 1.4.2.1.
[14] Zuckert, *Natural Rights*, p. 126.

that Grotian rights are entirely derivative from directives of the substantive moral principles inhering in the law of nature.[15] There are two aspects of Grotius' teaching that cast serious doubt on the subjective individual rights interpretation. First, Grotius does not articulate a pre-political state of nature on which we can ground the moral claims of the individual independently of society.[16] While he does ascribe considerable importance to preservationist considerations of necessity impelling individuals into society, Grotius is careful to remind us that "Right reason ought to be more dear to us than those things [like the "first principles of nature" involving self-preservation] through whose instrumentality we have been brought to it."[17] By identifying the law of nature as intrinsic moral rules drawn from human rationality, Grotius subordinates the universalistic and appetitive principle of self-preservation to a more elevated standard of right reason, which contains but is not limited to subjective preservationist morality. The second and related aspect of Grotius' law of nature teaching that belies the subjective rights interpretation is his formulation of political society as the "complete" or "perfect association" in some sense ontologically prior to the individual.[18] By positing the formal political order complete with laws as the "perfect association," rather than simply validating the social entity of community, Grotius adopts a more rigorous Aristotelian teleology than even the Calvinist Hunton. Grotius, nonetheless, does not Christianize civil society in the manner of Suarez's "mysical union." In the modified Aristotelianism of Grotian natural law theory, political society is both natural to human beings and yet emphatically a human construction.

Thus the role of rights in Grotian natural law theory is fully intelligible only in the context of the moral rules derived from the law of nature that

---

[15] The most famous statement of the subjective rights school is Tuck, *Natural Rights Theories* (for Grotius' formative impact on Hobbes see also Tuck, "Grotius, Carneades and Hobbes," *Grotiana*, vol. 4 [1983]: pp. 59, 61). Other proponents of the subjective rights school include Knud Haakonssen, "Hugo Grotius and the History of Political Thought," *Political Theory*, vol. 13, no. 2 (May 1985): pp. 239–65 and Schneewind, *Invention of Autonomy*. For the clearest rejections of this view, see Edwards, *Miracle of Holland*, ch. 3; Zagorin, "Hobbes without Grotius"; and Zuckert, *Natural Rights*, ch. 5.

[16] Contra Tuck, "Grotius and Selden," p. 515. Cf. Zuckert, *Natural Rights*, p. 137 and DJB 1.2.1 and 2.5.9, 15 for Grotius' only uses of the term "state of nature," neither of which bear any relation to a pre-civil condition. Cf. Edwards, *Miracle of Holland*, pp. 51–4 for Grotius' rejection of the possibility of there ever being a presocial existence for human beings.

[17] DJB 1.2.1.2. Cf. prol., secs. 8, 9.

[18] Ibid., 1.3.7.1. Cf. Suarez, *Extracts on Politics and Government*, George Moore, trans. (Chevy Chase, MD: Country Dollar Press, 1950): p. 101. Edwards, for example, goes too far to connect Grotius and Suarez because they both may have a similar argument about God's role as proximate efficient cause for the natural law. Grotius is much more insistent than Suarez that political society must be understood as an emphatically human creation, i.e., the source of obligation is our natural revulsion to injuring the cause of "right reason," not a suprarational "mystical union" (Edwards, *Miracle of Holland*, pp. 55–6).

facilitate social life. Individual rights and duties such as those relating to property are meant by Grotius to be seen as means to maintain the civil peace and order necessary for human flourishing. While Grotius roundly criticized Aristotle's prudential understanding of justice and virtue, he did so not to affirm pre-political individual rights, but rather to enhance the normative status of these ideas by connecting them to an enforceable and rigorous conception of law.[19] It is this aspect of Grotius' teaching that caused particular concern for the Whigs toward the end of the seventeenth-century. For Grotius, the moral status of subjective natural rights is so contingent on law that not only individuals, but also entire peoples, are capable of completely alienating their liberty through contractual slavery. The implications of this theoretical possibility of complete alienability with respect to the right of resistance and the settlement of property were obviously disconcerting to Filmer's Whig opponents in the 1680s.[20] In a fundamental sense, it is contract rather than consent that dominates Grotian natural law theory because it is the binding character of contract that Grotius cites as the decisive factor preventing natural liberty from endangering society. As such, he emphasizes the laws of nations – actual historical constitutions – as the primary determinant of political obligation, not pre-political rights. Thus the subjective rights dimension of Grotian natural law theory is ultimately best understood as a significant and even radical modification of essentially Christian-Aristotelian categories and assumptions.

Filmer's objections to Grotian contractualism rest on his dispute with two key ideas: the law of nations and the arguments for legitimate resistance to sovereign authority that derive from Grotius' notion of contract. The importance of the law of nations in Grotius' thought is due both to his reliance on the classical Roman legal distinctions between natural, national, and civil law and to his own method of procedure. In the Roman law typology of the distinct species of law, the law of nations had an even more elevated status than the law of nature, as witnessed in the natural law proposition of natural equality giving way to the conventional national laws codifying slavery.[21] Grotius justifies his use of the law of nature classification on the grounds that there are two ways to prove the existence of the law of nature.

---

[19] Zagorin, "Hobbes without Grotius," pp. 31–4 and Zuckert, *Natural Rights*, p. 145. Cf. DJB prol. secs. 42–5 for Grotius' criticism of Aristotle's position on virtue and justice.

[20] DJB 1.3.8.1; 1.3.8.14; 1.3.12.1. Tuck attenuates the absolutist tendencies in Grotius' idea of contract by pointing to Grotius' expectation of what Tuck calls "interpretive charity"; that is, people are logically free to enslave themselves, though we may assume almost no one would be so foolish to do so (Tuck, *Natural Rights Theories*, p. 155–6). Haakonssen ("History of Political Thought," p. 245) takes this argument I believe too far in the direction of Hobbes claiming that Grotius may see that an absolutist regime may be the best guarantor of individual rights in some cases. The protection of rights is not Grotius' primary goal, although it may be an important ancillary one.

[21] Zuckert, *Natural Rights*, p. 133.

The first is by the a priori method, which deduces the natural law from "the necessary agreement or disagreement of anything with a rational and social nature." The empirical a posteriori method, on the other hand, which constitutes the lion's share of the book, involves "every probability that that is according to the law of nature which is believed to be such among all nations, or among all those that are more advanced in civilization."[22] The laws of nations, then, are a means to apprehend the law of nature.

Filmer's argument is that Grotius' law of nations obscures the divine will that grounds political life. He condemns the Roman law distinction between the law of nature and the law of nations as spurious, reflecting the pagan ignorance of revelation. Filmer returns to the theological premises of his own argument:

If we will allow Adam to have been lord of the world, there will need no such distinctions of the law of nature and of nations. For the truth will be that whatsoever the heathens comprehended under these two laws, is comprised in the moral law.[23]

In Filmer's view, Grotius' reliance on Roman law produced "an error which the heathen taught that 'all things at first were common' and that 'all men are equal.'" Predictably, he charges that falling into these pagan errors is a "fault scarce pardonable for any Christian."[24] While accepting Grotius' position that each nation must have the power within itself to bind its subjects to its particular laws, Filmer denies that the ubiquity of certain legal practices proves the natural law in the Grotian sense. Filmer holds that Grotius' law of nations is really aimed at promoting the "mutual society of nations among themselves" and cannot be seen to point to a higher, more natural, standard of law beyond the legislative will of particular sovereigns.[25] For Filmer, all law requires a supreme power, and the active agency of divine will is the only common power that can bind all nations. Any conception of a law of nature that does not directly depend on divine sanction or sees God only as an "obliger of last resort" distorts the profound role of divine providence in human affairs.[26] Filmer's point here is not to deny the naturalness of such practices as patriarchalism, for example, which may indeed be ubiquitous; rather, he aims to reveal the obscuring effect Grotius' law of nations idea has on our broader understanding of the "moral law" that reflects God's active agency in politics.

---

[22] DJB 1.1.12.1.

[23] Robert Filmer, *Patriarcha and Other Writings*, Johann Somerville, ed. (Cambridge: Cambridge University Press, 1991): p. 200.

[24] Ibid., p. 210.

[25] Ibid., pp. 215–16. See also DJB 1.1.14.1 and 2.8.1.2.

[26] DJB 1.4.7.3; 1.1.10.2 and prol. 6. The quote is from Haakonssen, "History of Political Thought," p. 252. Even though Grotius identifies the two sources of *jus* as nature and the "free will of God," he attributes this view as much to Jupiter as to the biblical God, thus showing it to be an a posteriori position (DJB prol. 12).

Filmer's most serious objections to Grotian contractualism, however, have to do with the question of resistance. For his part, Grotius went far to deny the purportedly seditious implications of his theory. Though human beings are endowed with certain rights and form civil societies, at least in part, to secure those rights, this does not extend to a general natural right of rebellion. As Grotius argues:

> By nature all men have the right of resisting in order to ward off injury. But as civil society was instituted to maintain public tranquillity, the State forthwith acquires over us and our possessions a greater right, to the extent necessary to accomplish this end. The State therefore in the interest of public peace and order can limit that common right of resistance. That such was the purpose of the state we cannot doubt, since it could not in any other way achieve its end.[27]

The justification of resistance is deduced from the terms of the original contract that formed society and not from any claim of pre-political right. Grotius explicitly rejects the position that "everywhere and without exception sovereignty resides in the people so that it is permissible for the people to restrain and punish kings whenever they make a bad use of their power."[28] This opinion, Grotius continues, has given rise to "many evils." Moreover, Grotius rejects the Calvinist "subordinate magistrate" argument, and he very narrowly construes the possibility of legitimate resistance being offered by private individuals or only a minority of the people.[29] Filmer holds these restrictions on the right of resistance to be neither sufficient nor entirely sincere. With respect to the authority of "the will of those men who at first joined themselves in a civil society," Filmer argues that the submissive character of this appeal to original intent is utterly undermined by Grotius' later admission that if the will of the founders of the contract is unknown, then it may be interpreted and expounded by the present generation.[30] In addition to this obvious loophole in the construction of Grotius' strict originalism, Filmer deduces a further right of resistance from within the logic of Grotius' own theory. Even if there is a contractual obligation of nonresistance, Filmer argues, it is a human law of not resisting superiors and can thus be superseded by the implied conditions of the contract itself. The chief implied condition Filmer cites is that even if a people "made an absolute grant of their liberty . . . it must necessarily be implied that it was upon condition to be well governed."[31] In contrast to his own theologically premised doctrine of obedience, a purely human law, Filmer argues, lacks the normative power to compel absolute non-resistance.

---

[27] DJB 1.4.21.
[28] Ibid., 1.3.8.1 and 1.4.3–5.
[29] Ibid., 1.4.7.4 and 1.4.6.1.
[30] Ibid.; cf. 1.4.7.2 and 2.7.27.2.
[31] Filmer, *Patriarcha*, p. 223.

This problem is evident in Grotius' own admission of the possibility of explicitly reserved powers on the part of the people. He claims: "It may happen that a people when choosing a king, may reserve to itself certain powers, but may confer the others to the king, *absolutely*." From this reservation of power in the people, Filmer concludes that Grotius' lawful kings do not have "property in their kingdoms, but an usufructuary right only as if the people were the lords and the kings but their tenants."[32] All of Filmer's particular objections to the seditious implications of Grotian contractualism center on what he takes to be Grotius' fundamental premise that "the empire which is exercised by kings doth not cease to be the empire of the people." From this Filmer draws the contention that "the very effect of the constitution of kings by the people depends upon the will of them that constitute, and upon no other necessity."[33] The inability to ground a consistent theory of nonresistance on Grotian contractualism is due to the proposition that in some sense government is a creature of those who created it. The very power of government to command obedience points to a deeper power in the constitutive right of the people. Filmer's stance on Grotius' restrictions on resistance recalls his treatment of the English royalist Ferne's account of mixed monarchy. In rejecting a general right of rebellion, yet drawing a lengthy list of cases in which resistance to the king was justifiable, Grotius, like Ferne, provides an example of Filmer's suspicion that a halfhearted defense of royal power is as bad as or worse than its complete rejection.

The critique of Grotius' account of the origin of private property reveals Filmer's most fully developed thoughts on the relationship between property and government. For Grotius, both private property and government derive from human compact. The core of Grotius' account of the origin of private property is his adoption of the Roman law proposition of natural community. Grotius argues that at the Creation and after the Flood, all things were common and "each man could at once take whatever he wished for his own needs, and could consume whatever was capable of being consumed."[34] This condition continued while human beings lived in a "primitive state," but became untenable with the invention of the arts and the inequality of possessions that developed. The original grant that all individuals may use whatever they seized then became the ground for widespread violence and bloodshed. It was for this reason that human beings compacted to establish propriety in goods in order to distinguish the claims of individuals. Filmer observed the apparent contradiction between Grotius' inclusion of "the rule of abstaining from that which belongs to other persons" in the natural law requirements of society and his notion of the disappearance of the original common through the widespread violation of rights in that condition.[35] The

[32] DJB 1.3.17.1 and Filmer, *Patriarcha*, p. 222.
[33] DJB 2.16.16.1 and Filmer, *Patriarcha*, pp. 221, 224
[34] DJB 2.2.2.1.
[35] Ibid., prol. 8 and Filmer, *Patriarcha*, pp. 212–13.

key mistake in Filmer's understanding of Grotius' natural community is to see it as a positive common rather than a negative one.[36] The original common was not owned by everyone but by no one in particular. It was precisely the vacant character of the original common that justified the original seizure right of individuals: "thus the use of things in common was in accordance with the law of nature so long as ownership by individuals was not introduced; and the right to use force in obtaining one's own existed before laws were promulgated."[37] Filmer is struck both by the assertion that human will can negate God's original law of community and by Grotius' further contention that God is powerless to alter these enactments. Of the Dutchman, Filmer says, "He gives a double ability to man: first, to make that no law of nature, which God made to be the law of nature; and next, to make that a law of nature which God made not."[38] Grotius' idea, Filmer charges, goes beyond human *participation* in the divine will and extends to a power of absolute *negation*. It is in reference to this aspect of Grotius' argument that Filmer injects the celebrated English legal scholar John Selden into the discussion.

Grotius and Selden shared similar positions with respect to the mutability of the original common, but the Englishman dated this alteration to the period following the Flood in Scripture. Filmer explicitly employs Selden, however, to draw Scripture into the conflict against Grotius, for it is Selden's argument that Adam "by donation from God was made the general lord of all things" that Filmer employs to prove how repugnant Grotius' doctrine is to "the truth of Holy Scripture."[39] Selden accepts the original donation of the world to Adam, hence denying the natural common, but he asserts that the primitive community of which Grotius speaks did emerge a few generations after the Flood. What makes Selden such an interesting ingredient in the argument is his intermediary role between Filmer and Grotius. On the one hand, he agrees with Grotius that the institution of private property followed an earlier period of community, but he prefaces this argument

---

[36] Tully, *Discourse on Property*, p. 97 and Zuckert, *Natural Rights*, p. 250.

[37] DJB 1.1.10.4, 7. Grotius uses Cicero's celebrated example of a seat in a theater to illustrate the character of the ownerless original common (DJB 2.2.2.1).

[38] Filmer, *Patriarcha*, p. 215. Filmer also adopts his familiar anti-populist arguments about the universality and retractibility of consent (pp. 219, 234).

[39] Ibid., pp. 216–17. Tuck (*Natural Rights Theories*, pp. 82–100) identifies Selden as a precursor to Hobbes because, for Tuck, Selden's argument that God promulgated the natural law at a specific point in history following the Flood, before which there was no morally obligatory natural law, foreshadows the Hobbesian concept of a state of nature. For a persuasive account that challenges Tuck's claim for the "historicity" of the natural law in Selden, and tends to locate Selden more clearly in the Christian-Aristotelian camp along with Suarez and Hooker, see J. P. Somerville, "John Selden, the Law of Nature, and the Origins of Government," *Historical Journal*, vol. 27, no. 2 (June 1984): pp. 439–41, 443–5. For his part, Filmer is more in keeping with Somerville's reading of Selden inasmuch as Filmer appropriates Selden to the cause of divine right precisely because of the *theological* basis of his argument for the law of nature rather than Tuck's historical interpretation.

with the admission of the divine donation to Adam, a position central to Filmer's thesis. In response to Selden, Filmer argues that the donation to Adam in Genesis 1:28 was the unalterable source of propriety and that the supposition of community between Noah and his sons in Genesis 9:2 is not warranted by the text.[40] Noah inherited Adam's right alone and entire.

In response to both Grotius and Selden, Filmer claims that the very notion of the mutability of the original condition by human compact diminishes the power of divine providence. He queries: "Doth it not derogate from the providence of God Almighty to ordain a community which could not continue?" Moreover, Filmer argues that the affirmation of the institution of propriety by human will suggests that the duties contained in the second table of the Decalogue, concerning the right of property, are themselves of human creation. "But if property be brought in by a human law," Filmer observes, "then the moral law dependeth upon the will of man."[41] Filmer concludes with the familiar assertion that the theoretical and theological problems of Grotius' treatment of property – error and atheism – are solved in the impenetrable core of his Adamite thesis. In the beginning the whole world was given to Adam, and all claims to rule and title to property derive from that one irrefutable source.

Another major source of dispute between Grotius and Filmer has to do with the question of the means of acquiring supreme power. Filmer does not explicitly take issue with Grotius' understanding of sovereignty as such, inasmuch as the Dutchman maintained that the sovereign power is by definition subject to no higher human power and is itself indivisible.[42] The object of Filmer's attacks rather is Grotius' view of the means of acquiring supreme power and the terms upon which it is exercised. Filmer articulates three ways "Grotius propoundeth, whereby supreme power may be had: First, by full right of propriety. Secondly, by an usufructuary right. Thirdly, by a temporary right."[43] In contrast to Filmer's tendency to conceptualize political rule in terms of proprietary right, Grotius' schema of the different kinds of supreme power separates the character of supreme power from the full possession of it. The particular character of Grotian contractualism presupposes both the possibility of forming a variety of regime types and the capacity to constitute and regulate the supreme power in any given regime by an assortment of contractual arrangements.

Filmer disputes the features of the three means of acquiring supreme power, but more importantly, he denies the contractual premises of Grotius'

---

[40] Filmer, *Patriarcha*, p. 218.

[41] Ibid., p. 218.

[42] Filmer notes this at p. 233. For Grotius' statement on the indivisibility of sovereignty, see DJB 1.3.7.1 but note the historical examples of mixed sovereignty in antiquity – Rome, Athens, and Macedon – that Grotius cites at DJB 1.3.20.4–7.

[43] Filmer, *Patriarcha*, p. 229.

argument. For Filmer, supreme power is absolute, illimitable, and not of human origin. He dismisses out of hand Grotius' category of the temporary right of supreme power, the chief example of which is the Roman dictators.[44] Any grant of power with an expiration date is, to Filmer, just democracy by another name. Grotius argues that usufructuary right holds when a ruler holds title as a kind of "tenant for life," and he adds that "most kings, both elected and hereditary, (rule) by usufructuary right."[45] The clear implication for Filmer is that Grotius allows the possibility that supreme power remains inviolate in the people. The king – the majority of kings, in fact – become like hired managers and ultimately the servants of the people. As Filmer complains, the usufructuary right "is to make a kingdom all one with a farm, as if it had no other use but to be let out to him that can make most of it."[46]

If Filmer's criticism of Grotius' usufructuary right argument can be seen as a fairly cut-and-dried example of his anti-populism, the same cannot be said of his critique of Grotius' understanding of full right. Grotius' *jure pleno* results from an absolute cession of liberty by the subjects to the ruler. A king by full right exercises rule with no restrictions and is bound by no contractual obligations. This king by full right seems to be the classic Filmerian monarch, yet Filmer takes issue with the origins of such rule. Grotius argues that full right is acquired either through conquest in a just war or by the original consent, or donation, of the subjects. Filmer immediately raises the problem of an exiled ruler returning to conquer his former kingdom. In this case, Filmer argues, the conquest, be it ever so just, does not produce a full right but simply restores the conqueror/former exile to his original title. He explains:

For if originally he and his ancestors had but an usufructuary right... yet shall not the conqueror in this case gain any full right of property, but must be remitted to his usufructuary right only.[47]

Even in the case of war between kingdoms, Filmer argues, Grotius' full right by just war unravels on the grounds of natural freedom and the original title of the conquered people. He charges: "if they have no governor, then they are a free people, and so the war will be unjust to conquer those that are free.... But if the people have a governor, that governor hath either a title or not. If he have a title, it is an unjust war that takes the kingdom

---

44 Filmer ignored this argument in Bodin also. See Jean Bodin, *The Six Books of the Republic* (1606), trans. by Richard Knolles from the original *Les six livres de la republique* (Paris, 1580), K. D. McRae, ed. (Cambridge, MA: Harvard University Press, 1962): pp. 85–6.

45 DJB 1.3.11.1.

46 Filmer, *Patriarcha*, p. 232. One aspect of this usufructuary right Filmer does not address is Grotius' argument that such a king does not possess the power to alienate or sell any territory of the kingdom. At times Filmer's exhortations about the duty of kings "to feed, clothe, instruct and defend the *whole* commonwealth" suggest his agreement with at least this one limit on supreme power (cf. Filmer, *Patriarcha*, p. 12 [emphasis mine] and DJB 1.3.13.1).

47 Filmer, *Patriarcha*, p. 229.

from him."[48] Filmer here ignores the possibility that an aggressor power or the leaders in an aggressive war lose the protection and legitimacy of their natural freedom and original title.[49] Filmer is less interested in the subtleties of just war theory than in revealing the purely formal character of Grotius' full right by conquest argument. To Filmer the formalism of this argument is exposed by the core Grotian teaching that "public subjection is that condition in which a people is that surrenders itself to some man, or to several men, or even to another people."[50] Filmer advances the impossibility of harmonizing the just war as title to rule with the theoretical origins of political authority as such: "If subjection be the gift of the people, how can supreme power *pleno jure*, in full right, be got by a just war?" Despite Grotius' official pronouncements, Filmer concludes: "I cannot find in Grotius' book *De Jure* how that any case can be put wherein by a just war a man may become a king *pleno jure proprietis*."[51]

It is with regard to Grotius' argument for the consensual origins of full right that Filmer delivers his *coup de main*. Grotius explains full right by donation of the people as emerging "through the submission of a people, to avoid greater disaster, subjected itself without any reservation."[52] The "greater dangers" Grotius suggests are extreme poverty and the threat of destruction in war. But in these cases, Filmer observes, it is war and poverty that cause the cession of power, not a free gift of the people. Filmer denies that it even makes sense to speak of a freedom for contract in the face of the kind of crushing necessity that would cause a people to alienate their freedom totally.[53] What is remarkable in Grotius' presentation of full right by donation is the extreme lengths to which he goes to justify even total subjection in terms of contract. Grotius, in Filmer's view, sacrifices the claims of full proprietary right of rule on the altar of contractualism and natural freedom. He accuses Grotius of surreptitiously undermining the very possibility of the full right of property in rule: "Howsoever Grotius in words acknowledge that kings may have full right of property, yet by consequence he denies it by such circular suppositions as by coincidence destroy each other."[54] Filmer's use of a hermeneutic of suspicion tends, it is true, to uncover a "plebist" under every rock, but in this case he does reveal some of the crucial tensions and ambiguities in Grotius' account of supreme power. The English royalist's critique of the Dutchman served an important theoretical function by

---

[48] Ibid., p. 230.
[49] As for example in Locke, *Two Treatises*, Chapter Sixteen, especially sections 176–80.
[50] DJB 2.5.31.
[51] Filmer, *Patriarcha*, p. 230.
[52] DJB 1.3.11.1.
[53] Filmer, *Patriarcha*, p. 231. Tyrrell cites the example of the Dutch submitting to the French and Joseph to the Egyptians (James Tyrrell, *Patriarcha, Non Monarcha* [London, 1681) pp. 120–1* (second pagination).
[54] Filmer, *Patriarcha*, p. 231.

indicating the difficulty, if not impossibility, of articulating a contractual basis of sovereignty that could satisfy the obedience requirements of Filmerian divine right. Filmer set the bar for contractual absolutism very high. Enter Mr. Hobbes.

Filmer and Hobbes

At first glance, the difference between Filmer's treatment of Hobbes and his use of Grotius could not be more starkly drawn. While both Hobbes and Grotius posit natural rights arguments that supplied mid-seventeenth-century Europeans with a theoretical alternative to divine right, Filmer shows a gentleness with Hobbes that is distinctly lacking in his use of Grotius. Hobbes' pronounced royalism and his castigation of Calvinist and Catholic resistance theories in the years preceding and following the civil war in England signified an important affinity between Filmer and Hobbes.[55] Filmer by and large approves of Hobbes' theory regarding the extent and character of sovereignty, and he never really questions his fellow countryman's dedication to the royalist cause, as he does with the Dutchman. Indeed Filmer chimes: "With no small content I read Mr. Hobbes' book *De Cive*, and his *Leviathan*, about the rights of sovereignty, which no man, that I know, hath so amply and judiciously handled."[56] Despite his opening expression of a few kind words for his subject, however (a rarity for Filmer), Sir Robert's brief treatment of Hobbes comprises a series of specific criticisms that amount to a variation on two themes: the rejection of Hobbesian natural right and of Hobbes' account of the contractual origin of government. Filmer grumbles: "His *jus naturae* (right of nature) and his *regnum institutiuum* (kingdom by institution) will not down with me, they appear full of contradiction and impossibilities."[57] He then proceeds to show how Hobbes' theory of absolute and indivisible sovereignty would be better and more solidly grounded on paternal right.

Filmer's rejection of Hobbesian natural right is drawn out of his statement that "I wonder how the right of nature can be imagined by Mr. Hobbes, which, he saith is a liberty for 'each man to use his own power as he will himself for preservation of his own life'; 'a condition of war everyone against everyone'; 'a right of every man to every thing, even to one another's

---

[55] But as Goldie observes, royalists and Tories were often Hobbes' most severe critics, primarily because they, like Filmer, detected the radical potential in Hobbes' natural rights theory and his heterodox position on church–state relations (Mark Goldie "The Reception of Hobbes," in *Cambridge History of Political Thought*, pp. 595, 610–15; see also pp. 596, 598, and 604 for Filmer's criticism of Hobbes). Cf. Quentin Skinner, "The Ideological Context of Hobbes' Political Thought," *Historical Journal*, vol. 9 (1966): pp. 286–317.

[56] Filmer, *Patriarcha*, p. 184.

[57] Ibid., p. 185.

body'."[58] Filmer's own conception of the origin of political power runs contrary to each of the three central tenets he identifies in Hobbes, namely, the primacy of self-preservation, the natural state of war, and the absolute liberty marking the natural human condition. It is in response to this presentation of Hobbesian natural right that Filmer offers his most complete and succinct statement of the Adamite thesis in his entire corpus:

> If God created only Adam and of a piece of him made the woman, and if by generation from them all mankind be propagated; if also God gave to Adam not only the dominion over the woman and the children that should issue from them, but also over the whole earth to subdue it, and over all the creatures on it, so that as long as Adam lived no man could claim or enjoy anything but by donation, assignation or permission from him.[59]

The two seminal aspects of Filmer's theory, Adam's right of dominion by creation and his full right of property by donation, are the bedrock of his refutation of Hobbesian natural right. With the scriptural support of Genesis for the natural subjection of humankind in the background, Filmer proceeds to attack the Hobbesian formulation of the state of nature on the grounds of the naturalness of the family and the pervasive operation of divine providence.

Filmer's strategy to refute the state of nature theory by reference to the ubiquity and naturalness of the family takes two tacks. First, he draws as many concessions as he can out of Hobbes regarding the naturalness of the family and of paternal power in particular. His second method is to cast the general thrust of Hobbes' theory in the unfavorable light cast by Scripture. A good example of Filmer's first method is his illustration of the implication of Hobbes' admission that while the state of nature "was never generally so . . . there are many places where they live so now. For the savage people in many places of America (except the government of small families, the concord whereof dependeth on natural lust) have no government at all."[60] Filmer concludes from this single example of familial rule in America that "one exception bars all." The existence of families, even in the most uncivilized conditions, precludes the possibility of the state of nature.[61] Moreover, the specific character of "the government of small families" conforms perfectly with Filmer's patriarchalism inasmuch as Hobbes asserts that "originally the father of every man was also his sovereign lord with power over him of life and death."[62] Hobbes' apparent admission of the naturalness of the

---

[58] Ibid., p. 187 and Thomas Hobbes, *Leviathan*, Edwin Curley, ed. (Indianapolis: Hackett, 1994): pp. 79–80.

[59] Filmer, *Patriarcha*, p. 187.

[60] Hobbes, *Leviathan*, p. 77.

[61] Filmer, *Patriarcha*, p. 187 and Gordon Schochet, *Patriarchalism in Political Thought* (Oxford: Oxford University Press, 1975): pp. 225–6. In this respect, Schochet argues, Filmer was typical of Hobbes' seventeenth-century critics.

[62] Hobbes, *Leviathan*, p. 224.

patriarchal family is grist for Filmer's mill, for in Sir Robert's view it admits of only two interpretations. Either the state of nature is a moral and historical nullity or the condition of perfect freedom Hobbes describes is enjoyed solely by the male heads of independent families. The latter alternative offers an account of the origins of government not far removed from that of Filmer himself. Hobbes' reference to the "Fathers of families" who "when by instituting a Common-wealth, they resigned that absolute power" over the life and death of their children/subjects, echoes Filmer's statement that "By the uniting of great families or petty Princedoms, we find the greater monarchies were at first erected."[63] In exposing what he takes to be the incompatibility of Hobbes' historical account of the origins of political society in absolute paternal power and the theoretical propositions of contract and consent, Filmer implicitly calls attention to his own postulation of the perfect consistency of his Adamite patriarchal thesis.

Despite Hobbes' allusion to something approximating a patriarchalist account of early societies, he suggests that the comprehension of his natural rights theory requires a theoretical abstraction from the family per se; human beings must be conceived as "mushrooms (*fungorum more*) they all on a sudden were sprung out of the earth without any obligation one to another."[64] A more clear antithesis to Filmer's source-based argument is scarcely imaginable, and he responds predictably that "the Scripture teacheth us otherwise, that all men came by succession and generation from one man." The denial of natural dependency and subjection contained in Hobbes' mushroom metaphor constitutes, in Filmerian terms, either a rejection of the moral implications of human generation and the family that it produces or a conjecture of the multiple creation of men by God in the beginning. In the full range of Filmer's Adamite thesis both arguments amount to atheism, inasmuch as, according to Filmer, Scripture clearly relates the original creation of one man alone and authorizes the subjection of his progeny to him. Beneath Filmer's charge against the ahistorical character of the state of nature lies a deeper condemnation of its atheism. He warns: "We must not deny the truth of the history of creation."[65]

Filmer's charge against the inherent atheism of Hobbes' state of nature raises the problem of scriptural interpretation as a whole. Much as Hobbes' conjectural multiple creation offends Filmer's religious sense, he also ponders the implications of Hobbes' mushroom theory of moral individualism for the Fifth Commandment. In *De Cive* Hobbes responded to an anonymous questioner that the obedience of children to their parents demanded by divine law is not affected by his argument for natural liberty inasmuch as "no son

---

[63] Filmer, *Patriarcha*, p. 11 and Schochet, *Patriarchalism*, p. 239.
[64] Thomas Hobbes, *Man and Citizen*, Bernard Gert, ed. (Indianapolis: Hackett, 1991): p. 205 and Filmer, *Patriarcha*, p. 187.
[65] Filmer, *Patriarcha*, pp. 187, 188.

can be understood to be in the state of nature." This admission that no son is naturally free because he has parents requiring obedience, Filmer explains, "is all one with denying his (Hobbes') own principle."[66] Hobbes defended this position on the grounds that children must recognize the *power* that protects them, whether that power be in a father, a mother, or any surrogate who nourished them.

Hobbes' reinterpretation of the Fifth Commandment in terms of power – a parent is simply a recognized power – retains the logic of consent even in this primal relation of parent or provider to child. The obligation of children to parents is not a part of the recognition of the obedience due to the original source of one's being, but is rather a feature of the obedience promised to one's protector in the here and now. Filmer utterly denies Hobbes' inference that when this parental protection ceases or ceases to be necessary, so too does the ground of this obligation. Natural freedom, if it is to have any plausibility at all, must be an irreducible aspect of human nature, not subject to the exigencies of rational development or the increase of physical strength. The subjection of children to parents is the natural condition of humankind, not Hobbes' theoretical postulation of the state of nature. Filmer challenges Hobbes: "For if men be not free-born, it is not possible for him to assign and prove any other time for them to claim a right of nature to liberty, if not at their birth."[67] Filmerian source anticipates and subsumes Hobbesian force.

Hobbes' state of nature theory rejects Filmer's notion of providence at its core. It is a condition without governors, order, or even the most basic advantages of communal life. In such a condition:

There is not place for industry, . . . no culture of the earth, no navigation, . . . no knowledge of the face of the earth, no account of time, no arts, no letters, no society, and which is worst of all, continual fear and danger of violent death, and the life of man solitary, poor, nasty, brutish and short.[68]

Neither the hand of God nor human beings can secure justice and prosperity in this state. Filmer argues that even if we were to assume a condition wherein no "common power" prevailed, this would not result in an anarchic state of war. It is scarcity that would cause primeval war, not the absence of recognized rule. Filmer charges:

But God was no such niggard in the creation, and there being plenty of sustenance and room for all men, there is no cause or use of war till men be hindered in the preservation of life, so that there is no absolute necessity of war in the state of pure nature.[69]

[66] Hobbes, *Citizen*, p. 117 and Filmer, *Patriarcha*, p. 188.
[67] Filmer, *Patriarcha*, p. 188.
[68] Hobbes, *Leviathan*, p. 76.
[69] Filmer, *Patriarcha*, p. 188.

This statement goes beyond a mere rejection of the historical possibility of the state of nature. Filmer's argument, rather, is that the institution of natural bounty by creation combined with God's perpetual providence remedies the only conceivable situation that would produce universal warfare. Filmer attempts to superimpose divine providence on Hobbes' preservationist argument in order to confound the state of nature on its own terms. The "artificial providence" supplied by the Hobbesian state is a cipher because of the continual stream of divine providence.[70] Though Hobbes and the Whig thinkers of a later generation agree with respect to human power being the animating principle of politics rather than divine power, there is a striking parallel between Filmer and the liberals with regard to the identification of scarcity as the fundamental cause of war. In this sense, at least, Filmer's critique of Hobbes anticipates the liberalization of natural rights theory.[71] Filmer's postulations of natural bounty and divine providence constitutes a denial of Hobbes' treatment of the psychological causes of war, including those lodged deep in human psychology, such as diffidence and a love of glory. Both the insecurity caused by relative equality and the presence of some that take "pleasure in contemplating their own power in the acts of conquest" are psychological factors operating in the Hobbesian state of war.[72] The Leviathan is primarily "King of the Proud," not of the hungry.

Filmer contends that Hobbes' law of nature, which is "a rule found out by reason" forbidding a man "to do that which is destructive to his life, and to omit that by which he thinks it may be preserved," cannot secure the peace it intends.[73] For the law of nature to be effective, "in the first place nature must teach him that life is to be preserved," but in this event, Filmer concludes, "the right of nature and the law of nature will be all one."[74] If nature teaches human beings the importance of self-preservation, then this natural guidance acts more like a command or duty to preserve life than Hobbes' formulation of a prohibition against doing things that are self-destructive. The major issue between Filmer and Hobbes here has to do with the distinction between right and law. Hobbes explicitly directes his argument against those who "confound *jus* and *lex* (right and law)."[75] The Hobbesian argument for the primacy of rights over law reduces these dictates of reason to an instrument to serve the most fundamental passion for self-preservation. Filmer, in contrast,

---

[70] Pierre Manent, *An Intellectual History of Liberalism*, Rebecca Balinski, trans. (Princeton: Princeton University Press, 1994): pp. 30–1.

[71] See Locke, *Two Treatises*, ch. 5, Tyrrell, *Patriarcha, Non Monarcha*, pp. 118–21, and Algernon Sidney, *The Discourses Concerning Government*, Thomas West, ed. (Indianapolis: Liberty Fund Classics, 1996): ch. 1., sec. 10. Cf. Leo Strauss, *Natural Right and History* (Chicago: University of Chicago Press, 1953): p. 235.

[72] Hobbes, *Leviathan*, p. 75.

[73] Ibid., p. 79.

[74] Filmer, *Patriarcha*, p. 189.

[75] Hobbes, *Leviathan*, p. 79 and Tuck, *Philosophy and Government*, p. 307.

presumes the primacy of law with its obligatory character over the supposed natural freedom contained in Hobbes' notion of rights. Filmer is heavy on law but very sparing with rights. For Filmer, the law of nature cannot simply be a deduction from reason; rather, to be a law, it must have an obligatory and commanding quality in itself. As Hobbes suggests, it was typical of political thinkers to confound or conflate natural law and natural right. Even Grotius, while distinguishing right and law, still defines *jus naturale* in a way that makes it a command.[76] Filmer goes beyond Grotius, though, in the sense that his notion of law completely subsumes right. Right for Filmer is always the right of rulers. While both Hobbes and Filmer hold law and right as contradictory, the scriptural premises of the latter's Adamite thesis make Hobbesian natural right a moral and ontological impossibility.

We recall that Filmer agreed with Hobbes' account of the exercise of sovereign power but not with his means of acquiring it. Filmer's critique of Hobbes' contract theory rested on his argument for paternal right, the problem of regimes, and the even bigger problem of resistance. First, regarding paternal right. The contractualism of Hobbes' *regnum institutium* drew Filmer's appeal for the *regnum patrimoniale*. Filmer's method in refuting contract theory is to point out what he takes to be Hobbes' own admissions that paternal rule of the family is the primal core and model of political authority. He gleefully cites Hobbes' statements that "the 'father being before the institution of a commonwealth' was originally an 'absolute sovereign' 'with power of life and death', and that 'a great family, as to the rights of sovereignty is a little monarchy.'"[77] This does not signify a criticism of Hobbes' view of sovereignty, however, as both he and Filmer agree that sovereign civil power can and usually does place limits on the power of fathers in families.[78] Filmer's aim is to attack Hobbesian contractualism at its source. If paternal rule is such an undeniable feature of human life, Filmer argues, then there is little freedom left in individuals to consent to the institution of government. Hobbes, however, explicitly argues that paternal dominion, despite its appearance and ubiquity, is not the result of generation but actually is a product of contract. He cautions that paternal dominion "is not so derived from the generation as if therefore the parent had dominion over his child because he begat him, but from the child's consent, either express or by other sufficient arguments declared."[79] Filmer responds incredulously: "How a child can express consent, or by other sufficient arguments declare it before it comes to the age of discretion I understand

---

[76] DJB 1.1.10.12 and see Curley's note in Hobbes, *Leviathan*, p. 79. Zagorin ("Hobbes without Grotius," pp. 37–8) makes a persuasive case that with this argument Hobbes may be targeting Grotius in particular as a thinker who fails to distinguish right (*jus*) and law (*lex*).

[77] Filmer, *Patriarcha*, p. 185 and Hobbes, *Leviathan*, pp. 153, 132, 107.

[78] Compare Filmer, *Patriarcha*, p. 12 and Hobbes, *Leviathan*, p. 153.

[79] Hobbes, *Leviathan*, p. 128.

not."[80] The issue between Filmer and Hobbes is not, however, the character of reason but the primacy of the source.

There is a profound antipatriarchalism in Hobbes' theory. As Tarcov relates of Hobbes, the only "generation that is truly the work of man by way of art is the generation of artificial man, the body politic."[81] In contrast to Filmer's scriptural argument that by creation God made man the "nobler and principal agent in generation," Hobbes claims in *De Cive* that the "mother originally hath the government of her children, and from her the father derives his right, because she brings forth and first nourishes them."[82] Hobbes explains the prevalence of patriarchy by a woman's need to submit to a man in order to secure her children in the state of nature and by the fact that "for the most part commonwealths have been erected by the fathers, not by the mothers of families."[83] These arguments are clearly anathema to Filmerian scripturalism. The decidedly tortured logic of Hobbes' treatment of the origins of the subjection of women and children amounts ultimately to an attempt to ground all legitimate authority in contract.[84] For Filmer, these species of subjection reflect the natural subjection of all human beings. The individual, however understood, lacks the moral power to create moral obligation.

Another aspect of Filmer's critique of Hobbesian contractualism relates to the issue of regimes and representation. In this respect alone, Hobbes' monarchist credentials come under Filmer's microscope much as had Grotius'. Like the Dutchman, though to a lesser degree, Hobbes' blue blood is found wanting. Hobbes and Grotius both maintain the possibility of instituting three distinct regime types: monarchy, aristocracy, and democracy.[85] But whereas Filmer finds that the Grotian typology formally includes the possibility of absolute monarchy yet undermines it by implication, he finds that Hobbes' typology admits of aristocracy and democracy but always reduces, by the logic of his argument, to absolute monarchy. Of Hobbesian aristocracy and democracy, Filmer remarks, "he affirm in words, yet by consequence he

---

[80] Filmer, *Patriarcha*, p. 192.

[81] For example, Richard Allen Chapman, "*Leviathan* Writ Small: Thomas Hobbes on the Family," *American Political Science Review*, vol. 69, no. 1 (March 1975): p. 89; Ingrid Makus, *Women, Politics, and Reproduction* (Toronto: University of Toronto Press, 1996): ch. 1; Nathan Tarcov, *Locke's Education for Liberty* (Chicago: University of Chicago Press, 1984): p. 37 and John Zvesper, "Hobbes' Individualistic Analysis of the Family," *Politics*, vol. 5 (October 1985): p. 3. For a contrary view that identifies Hobbes as a patriarchalist, see Carole Pateman, "'God hath ordained Man a Helper': Hobbes, Patriarchy, and Conjugal Right," in *Feminist Interpretations of Political Theory*, Carole Pateman and Mary Shanley, eds. (University Park: University of Pennsylvania Press, 1991): pp. 64–5.

[82] Hobbes, *Citizen*, p. 215 and Filmer, *Patriarcha*, p. 192.

[83] Hobbes, *Leviathan*, p. 129.

[84] Schochet, *Patriarchalism*, pp. 232–3.

[85] Hobbes, *Citizen*, ch. 7 and Hobbes, *Leviathan*, ch. 18.

denies."[86] Democracy by institution fails because "if every man covenant with every man, who shall be left to be the representative? If all must be representatives, who will remain to covenant?"[87] Democracy by institution falls on the ground that the sovereign, in Hobbes' theory, cannot be a party to a covenant. If all individuals covenant, there is no sovereign; if all individuals are sovereign, it is the state of nature. The democratic character of the state of nature militates against democratic government. Aristocracy faces similar problems. If a commonwealth were ruled by an aristocratic assembly, any member of that body could kill any subject freely, not being himself party to a covenant with them, and every member would be in an identical state of nature with every other.[88] Filmer maintains that within the strict context of Hobbesian natural rights theory any representative body would be plagued with violence toward the subjects and strife within the body itself. With respect to the possibility of contract between conquerors and the conquered, Filmer muses: "I would know how the liberty of the vanquished can be allowed if the victor have the use of it at pleasure."[89] His attack on the more practical aspects of Hobbesian contractualism results in his affirmation that Hobbes' theory of sovereignty is only consistent with absolute monarchy, which, Filmer adds, does not have a contractual but a paternal origin. The striking feature of Filmer's treatment of Hobbesian regime types is his unique criticism of Hobbes as a closet Aristotelian.[90] Though he suggests that in most respects Hobbes made a much more decisive break from Aristotle than Grotius, Filmer charges that they both cling to the Aristotelian regime typology. In his rejection of the three distinct regime types, Filmer's anticlassicism outstrips them both.

Filmer's most involved attack on Hobbesian contractualism has to do with the question of resistance. To Hobbes' principle that "if other men will not lay down their right as well as he, then there is no reason for any one to divest himself of his," Filmer offers his characteristic retort: "if all the men in the world will not agree, no commonwealth can be established." This standard of universal consent could never be attained "though all men should

---

[86] Filmer, *Patriarcha*, p. 185.
[87] Ibid., p. 185. Filmer uses the same logic to refute democracy by acquisition. If all are conquerors, who covenants? If all are not conquerors, how can it be a democracy by conquest?
[88] Ibid., p. 187.
[89] Ibid., p. 186.
[90] Paul Rahe also identifies a "partially concealed teleology" in Hobbes' thought (*Republics Ancient and Modern: Classical Republicanism and the American Revolution* [Chapel Hill: University of North Carolina Press, 1992]: p. 397). While Rahe is correct to point out that Hobbes' "concealed" teleology shares a rationalistic core with that of the classics – i.e., for Hobbes irrational behavior that endangers self-preservation is immoral – it is still important to observe that Hobbes' quasi-teleology lacks the normative component of moral education so crucial to the classic thinkers such as Aristotle and was still a prominent feature in Grotius' thought.

spend their whole lives in nothing but running up and down to covenant."[91] Filmer's peculiarly active and catholic understanding of consent permeates his view of assemblies as well. In contrast to Hobbes, who admits that "the only way to erect a common power" is to cause individuals to "reduce all their wills by plurality of voices to one will, which is to appoint one man or assembly to bear their person," Filmer cautions, "it is not a plurality but a totality of voices which makes an assembly be of one will."[92] Filmer implies that Hobbes sets a standard for the unity of political action that is impossible except in absolute monarchy: "It seems Mr. Hobbes is of the mind that there is but one kind of government, and that is monarchy. For he defines a commonwealth to be one person."[93]

However, the deeper strand of Filmer's argument relates to the significance of the covenant itself. Filmer attacks Hobbes' statement that "the consent of a subject to sovereign power is contained in these words, 'I authorize and do take upon me all of his actions', in which there is no restriction at all of his own former liberty."[94] The argument that sovereign authorization does not alienate natural liberty holds individualist implications that Filmer rejects. For example, according to Hobbes, the authorization I give a sovereign to punish criminals, potentially including myself, does not negate my or anyone else's natural right of self-defense. An individual's chances in any contest with the sovereign may be pitifully slight, but no one can deny the legitimacy of whatever resistance or flight is offered.[95] The seditious consequences of this theory are undeniable to Filmer. Hobbes' postulation of inalienable rights subverts the very idea of absolute sovereignty he is trying to defend inasmuch as the proposition that "a covenant not to defend myself from force by force is always void" encourages rebellion and disobedience.[96] To Hobbes' qualification that the individual can disobey any "dangerous or dishonorable" command unless "our refusal frustrates the end for which sovereignty was ordained" Filmer queries: who decides this important question? Ultimately, he suspects it can only be the individual (and hence the people), and thus he reaches the conclusion that Hobbes' natural right undermines the sovereign's capacity to execute war or maintain national defense.[97] For Filmer, the logic of resistance is embedded in the very fabric of Hobbes' theory.

The heart of Filmer's critique of Hobbes' contractualism is his argument that the mere laying down of individual rights is not enough to secure the ends of the commonwealth. For Filmer, the essence of sovereignty should be

---

[91] Hobbes, *Leviathan*, p. 80 and Filmer, *Patriarcha*, p. 189.
[92] Hobbes, *Leviathan*, p. 109 and Filmer, *Patriarcha*, p. 190.
[93] Filmer, *Patriarcha*, p. 193.
[94] Hobbes, *Leviathan*, p. 142 and Filmer, *Patriarcha*, p. 193.
[95] Hobbes, *Leviathan*, pp. 142, 141–2, 87.
[96] Ibid., p. 87.
[97] Filmer, *Patriarcha*, p. 194. See also Strauss, *Natural Right and History*, pp. 197–8 and Schochet, *Patriarchalism*, p. 129.

nonresistance, but instead Hobbes places significant limitations on political obligation.[98] Moreover, Filmer contends that Hobbes signally fails to create in the subject a positive obligation directly to obey the sovereign. If the subject is to be bound actively to obey the sovereign's commands, the contract must be to *obey*, not simply to *refrain* from doing as one wishes.[99] Hobbes was clearly aware of this problem. He rejected the idea that active obedience could arise from a contract between the sovereign and the subject because this would impose obligations and limitations on the sovereign incompatible with absoluteness. Hobbes proposes two possible solutions: the principle of authorization and the natural freedom of the sovereign. As we have seen, the first involved the idea that the individual creates his or her obligation to obey by authorizing all the sovereign's actions.[100] The other explanation Hobbes offers for the obligation to obey the sovereign is the natural freedom of the sovereign as the one uncontracted agent in the commonwealth. In this account, the sovereign's undiminished freedom includes the natural right to the use of anything, including his subjects' bodies, to exercise rule. The problem, from Filmer's point of view, is that simply promising not to interfere with the sovereign's exercise of rule is not morally compelling, especially given the subject's inalienable natural right to employ any means to secure self-preservation. If subjects are not bound to absolute obedience and nonresistance, Filmer contends, then Hobbes' sovereignty rests on a bed of sand.

Filmer's most powerful criticism of Hobbes is that the preservationist justification of his absolute sovereignty argument undermines this very idea of sovereignty. The inalienability of the preservation right makes government, which is instituted to secure that right, a cipher. Auto-interpretation of obligation, Filmer cautions, is the very problem of the state of nature.[101] Filmer extends this problem to the issue of property. He argues that if it could be inferred from Hobbes' argument that the *means* of preservation can never be fully renounced, then no contract is possible given the circumstance that any contract could be broken to restore one's goods, or to take anyone else's goods, if one feels the need.[102] In this respect, Filmer anticipates one of the major theoretical difficulties in natural rights theory that his Whig critics would later have to work through. Filmer's often friendly advice to Hobbes, from one good monarchist to another, is to recognize patriarchy and the scriptural account of creation as the only starting point from

---

[98] Filmer (190) argues that rights must be completely alienable or else it will frustrate the ends of sovereignty. Cf. Schochet, *Patriarchalism*, pp. 128–9.

[99] Clifford Orwin, "On the Sovereign Authorization," *Political Theory*, vol. 3, no. 1 (February 1975): p. 29.

[100] As Orwin illustrates, there is good reason to suspect that Hobbes' use of the authorization principle was largely rhetorical. See Orwin, "Sovereign Authorization," esp. p. 32.

[101] Schochet, *Patriachalism*, p. 129.

[102] Filmer, *Patriarcha*, p. 195.

which to proceed in order to reach Hobbes' goal of an absolute, indivisible sovereignty.

The Problem of Grotius and Hobbes

The legacy of Hobbessian and Grotian natural jurisprudence presented a serious problem for later English constitutionalists. On the one hand, the Whigs were attracted to their ideas about contract and the secularizing direction in their notions of natural rights. But on the other hand, both Hobbes and Grotius proposed theories of contract and sovereignty that inclined toward absolutism.[103] With respect to Grotius, the Whig constitutionalists of the 1680s would by and large reject him as a model for their political theory. They did so primarily for two reasons. First, Grotius' idea of natural rights was, in their view, far too liable to the dangers of contractual absolutism. Radical and moderate Whigs alike sought to avoid any notion of rights that allowed the theoretical possibility of complete alienation. Admitting this possibility would have left the battle between the Whigs and Tories as simply an interpretive one fought over the nature and history of the English Constitution. While Whig authorities such as James Tyrrell and William Petyt were quite prepared to fight Tory historians like Robert Brady in the primeval forests of Saxon history, the Whigs did not want to put all their polemical or logical eggs in the antiquarian basket. Second, Grotius retained important Aristotelian and even late medieval elements in his argument that comported poorly with the scientific bent of the Whig mind. For Grotius, the principle of consent still retained strong traces of the scholastic and Calvinist arguments that understood it as the human acceptance of nature or God's rational purposes. In the context of an England ravaged by past religious wars and dreading the prospect of renewed war, the Whigs desperately sought to excise any substantive theological elements from their constitutional theory. Moreover, they no longer accepted the classical teleology animating Grotian natural jurisprudence, seeing in this teleology little more than another fertile ground for philosophical and theological controversy over the "proper" end for humanity. A minimalist political morality of rights protection was precisely what the Whigs felt England's situation warranted.

Hobbes, of course, offered such a minimalist preservationist political morality. However, the uncompromising movement of Hobbes' individualistic preservationist thesis actually grounds his theory of absolute sovereignty.[104] In many ways, Hobbes' theory of sovereignty is the antithesis of Whig constitutionalism. For Hobbes, sovereign power is by its very nature absolute. In *Leviathan* he states: "So that it appeareth plainly, to my

---

[103] Tuck, *Natural Rights Theories*, p. 53 and Zuckert, *Natural Rights*, p. 244.
[104] Manent, *Intellectual History*, p. 28.

understanding, both from reason and Scripture, that the sovereign power . . . is as great as possibly men can be imagined to make it."[105] In response to those who fear such a concentration of power, Hobbes replies that "there happeneth in no commonwealth any great inconvenience, but what proceeds from the subject's disobedience and breach of those covenants from which the commonwealth hath its being."[106] In keeping with Hobbes' fear of the natural state of war, it is the breaking of promises that threatens self-preservation, not the unlimited power of the one who enforces covenants. Furthermore, Hobbes' sovereign power is indivisible. He maintains that the powers required for sovereignty, such as control of the militia and the power to make war and peace, are "incommunicable and inseparable."[107] To divide sovereign power is to create rival sovereigns and, thus, inevitably to initiate the kind of strife that civil society is supposed to remedy and prevent. Hobbes' argument for the indivisibility of sovereignty extends to an utter rejection of any notion of a mixed regime. To Hobbes "such government is not government, but division of the commonwealth into three factions."[108] Filmer and Hobbes were almost unique among mid-seventeenth-century Englishmen in their steadfast opposition to mixed regime theory. Like Filmer, Hobbes blames Charles I's councilors for legitimating the principle of mixed government in the pre–civil war period.[109] Moreover, neither criticizes the mixed regime as simply a bad or defective form of government; rather, in the Hobbesian and Filmerian theory of sovereignty, a mixed government is no government at all.

Hobbes' natural rights theory also contains an explicit denial of the logic of resistance. In contrast to the varying degrees of this right asserted by the Whig constitutionalists, Hobbes' preservationist thesis militates against the logic of resistance.[110] The ancillary effect of Hobbes' hostility to resistance theories is his rejection of tyranny as an intelligible species of political rule. Hobbes calls tyranny monarchy "misliked" and accounts for its persistence as a recognized regime type on the grounds that "they that are discontented under monarchy call it tyranny."[111] The essence of sovereignty, for Hobbes, is power simply. Whereas the possibility of tyranny is central to Filmer's Whig critics' understanding of legitimacy – they refer legitimate rule at least partly to its antithesis in illegitimate rule – Hobbes

---

[105] Hobbes, *Leviathan*, p. 135 and Hobbes, *Citizen*, pp. 180–3. Filmer praised Hobbes' claim regarding "the rights of sovereignty, . . . no man that I know hath so amply and judiciously handled" (*Patriarcha*, p. 184).

[106] Hobbes, *Leviathan*, p. 135.

[107] Ibid., p. 115.

[108] Ibid., p. 216 and Strauss, *Natural Right and History*, p. 192.

[109] Corinne Weston, "Theory of Mixed Monarchy under Charles I and after," *English Historical Review*, vol. 75 (July 1960): p. 437.

[110] Hobbes, *Leviathan*, pp. 112–13.

[111] Ibid., pp. 118–19.

refers government simply to its antithesis, namely, anarchy. In response to the influential Aristotelian argument that monarchy is one-man rule directed to the common good, while tyranny is directed to the private advantage of the ruler, Hobbes concludes that it is in the absolute prince's good to see the kingdom thrive. To those who object that the condition of a subject of an absolute ruler is miserable, Hobbes replies: "the greatest pressure of sovereign governors proceedeth not from any delight or profit they can expect in the damage or weakening of their subjects (in whose vigour consisteth their own strength and glory)."[112] It is somewhat surprising to see such an innovative thinker as Hobbes employ this very pedestrian royalist argument, virtually replicated in Filmer and James I.[113] Yet Hobbes, Filmer, and James I, despite their other differences, agreed on the need to erase, or at least blur, the classical distinction between monarchy and tyranny. For their part, Filmer's Whig critics maintained that absolute power and moderation simply do not cohere. It is central to their understanding of human nature and the fragility of liberty and rights that no individual can be trusted with absolute power.

For his part, Hobbes denies the very possibility of fundamental or constitutional laws. Law cannot restrain sovereign power because the former is purely an expression of the latter. In *De Cive* Hobbes defined civil laws as "nothing else but the commands of him who hath the chief authority in the city, for direction of the future action of the citizens."[114] For Hobbes, even custom becomes law only by the authority of the sovereign's will.[115] Together Hobbes and Filmer stripped of any meaning the moral claims of ancient constitutionalism and popular consent by common practice. As such, they denied the antiquity of Parliament in the English constitutional order and any moral authority for representative institutions that these arguments suggest.[116] What Filmer liked about Hobbes' theory of law was its hostility to the logic of constitutionalism. Hobbes articulates a conception of sovereign power that resists constitutional limits.[117] Quite simply, for Hobbes, as for Filmer, laws are not made in a legal way. Inasmuch as law originates in the sovereign's will, Hobbes argues: "Neither is he bound to the civil laws, for

---

[112] Ibid., pp. 117–18 and Aristotle, *Politics*, 1279a32–b10.

[113] Filmer, *Patriarcha*, p. 31 and James I, "Trew Law of a Free Monarchy," in *Divine Right and Democracy*, David Wootton, ed. (Hammondsworth: Penguin, 1986): p. 101.

[114] Hobbes, *Citizen*, p. 178. In *Leviathan*, Hobbes' radically voluntaristic conception of law included a rejection of prior law restraining the sovereign with respect to the issue of succession: "It is manifest that by the institution of monarchy the disposing of the successor is always left to the judgment and will of the present possessor" (p. 138; cf. 173, 125). Clearly Hobbes was a particularly inapposite authority for Whigs in the Exclusion Crisis!

[115] Hobbes, *Leviathan*, p. 174 and Filmer, *Patriarcha*, pp. 279–80, 45.

[116] J. G. A. Pocock, *The Ancient Constitution and the Feudal Law* (Cambridge: Cambridge University Press, 1987): pp. 151–6.

[117] Strauss, *Natural Right and History*, pp. 193–4. For Filmer's own hostility to constitutional limits on sovereign power, see Filmer, *Patriarcha*, ch. III: 1, 6, 7–9.

this is to be bound to himself."[118] Hobbes holds law to be, at its core, a restraint on popular freedom, thus being a reflection of that freedom only in a highly problematic way. The problem of freedom produces the need for absolute sovereignty.

When the Whigs attempted to formulate their political and constitutional theory in the context of late-seventeenth-century England, they were forced to grapple with the difficulty presented by Grotius and Hobbes. The problematic relation of Hobbes and Grotius to their predecessors in the natural liberty tradition encapsulated the dilemma facing English Whigs in the 1680s. These leading lights of early modern natural jurisprudence offered secularizing and, in Hobbes' case, emphatically individualistic models of political theory, but these models also contained dangerous absolutist tendencies. The anti-absolutist traditions of Calvinist and Catholic political and constitutional thought, however, carried heavy theological and classical baggage that the Whigs sought to shed. Each of the important strains of Whig thought we will now consider represented a distinctive effort to synthesize the secularist and anti-absolutist dimensions of the natural liberty tradition in a new politics of liberty.

---

[118] Hobbes, *Citizen*, pp. 183–4 and Hobbes, *Leviathan*, p. 174.

PART TWO

THE WHIG POLITICS OF LIBERTY IN ENGLAND

In 1660 the eighteen-year nightmare for English royalists of rebellion, regicide, and republicanism finally and dramatically came to a close. Soon after the arrival of General George Monck's army in London, events moved rapidly toward the disintegration of the Commonwealth. While the diehard republican John Milton would offer posterity a plaintive cry against "this noxious humour of returning to bondage," most Englishmen welcomed the Convention's invitation to Charles II to return to rule his dead father's kingdom.[1] The general public and political elites alike expressed great support for and confidence in the restored Stuart monarchy. The Cavalier Parliament elected in 1661 in the immediate euphoria following the restoration imprinted a decidedly pro-royalist stamp on the Restoration Settlement. Despite renewing the Triennial Act in 1664 declaring that the king should summon Parliament at least every three years, in other respects Parliament strengthened the power of the crown through a series of measures securing royal authority over the military, affirming the principle of nonresistance, and establishing strict treason laws. In some respects, the Cavalier Parliament acted more strenuously to efface the memory of the Commonwealth than even the new king himself. In spite of court support for limited toleration, Parliament passed a series of harsh laws, known as the Clarendon Code, to enforce religious uniformity and penalize the dissenters held by

[1] John Milton, "Readie and Easie Way," in *Areopagitica and Other Political Writings of John Milton*, John Alvis, ed. (Indianapolis: Liberty Fund Press, 1999): p. 415. The varied interpretations of Milton's thought cover a wide range of possibilities. For the argument that Milton represents a radicalization of Christian humanism, see Joan Bennett, *Reviving Liberty: Radical Christian Humanism in Milton's Great Poems* (Cambridge, MA: Harvard University Press, 1989) and Michael Zuckert, *Natural Rights and the New Republicanism* (Princeton: Princeton University Press, 1994): ch. 3. For interpretations that emphasize the classical republican elements of Milton's thought, see Paul Dowling, *Polite Wisdom: Heathen Rhetoric in Milton's Areopagitica* (Lanham, MD: Rowman & Littlefield, 1996) and Zagorin, *A History of Thought in the English Revolution* (London: Routledge & Kegan Paul, 1954): pp. 113–20.

many English royalists to have been the chief instigators of the "late unhappy rebellion."

However, within twenty years of Charles' return, events would expose the underlying fragility of the Restoration Settlement. The long-simmering constitutional dispute in this period between crown and Parliament revealed that many of the issues raised by the civil war had been temporarily deferred but by no means entirely resolved. It is in the context of these unresolved fundamental questions regarding the nature, character, and limits on royal and parliamentary authority that the Exclusion crisis acquired major significance. The immediate issue in question during the crisis was whether Parliament could alter the line of succession with the aim of barring the heirless Charles' Catholic brother James, the Duke of York, from the throne. What was at stake in the controversy, however, went beyond the immediate political or constitutional issues raised by James' possible succession. At the core of the debate lay fundamental questions regarding the principle of indefeasible hereditary right, the distribution of powers in the English constitutional order, and the nature of representative government. In three successive Parliaments in 1679, 1680, and 1681, a group of exclusionist parliamentarians advanced a bill to exclude James, only to see Parliament prorogued and finally dissolved in 1681 by Charles, who, in violation of the Triennial Act, refused to call another for the remaining four years of his reign. In this bitter contest between the claims of parliamentary authority and the exercise of royal prerogative, the king and his supporters won the day.

The Whig thinkers and tracts we will examine forthwith wrote in support of the abortive effort to exclude James from the succession. This pro-Exclusion group known as Whigs was led by the Earl of Shaftesbury, and its position in support of Exclusion rested on two main grounds. First, the Whigs were deeply concerned that the accession of the militantly Catholic James Stuart would endanger the Protestant religious establishment deemed by many as a vital element in the English ideal of national independence and free government. Could a zealous Catholic be trusted as head of church and state? This was a dilemma English Protestants had not had to face directly since Mary's brief reign from 1553 to 1558. Besides the constitutional problem posed by a Catholic sovereign, many Whigs feared that James' sympathies for Catholic France would further compromise English national security. The second main ground for the Whig position was fear of the extension of royal power. At least since the time of the unpopular policies of the Cabal period in 1670–3, many in Parliament and in the country suspected Stuart ambitions for absolutism. In the Whigs' view, the open distaste for parliamentary "interference" expressed by the Stuarts could plausibly signify their long-term goal of eroding parliamentary authority and privilege and installing an absolute monarchy. For their part, the Tory supporters of the crown rested their position on an assertion of monarchical authority, the sanctity of hereditary succession, and the doctrine of nonresistance to the sovereign. It was in support of these principles that the Tories republished the largely forgotten works of Robert Filmer. Despite his vociferous support for absolutism, Filmer's arguments resonated deeply among supporters of the court in the higher clergy, in Parliament, and in much of the country at large.

While it is outside the purpose of this study to provide a detailed analysis of the complex issues and events surrounding the Exclusion crisis, an awareness of the general political and ideological context of the period is important for understanding the motives, arguments, and rhetorical strategy of the major Whig pamphleteers.[2] Tyrrell, Sidney, and Locke were sophisticated theoreticians operating in an ideologically charged context that required that attention be paid to important practical considerations. The Whig tracts we will analyze are each to some extent *pieces d'occasion* set in the clear context of specific political and constitutional issues. Moreover, given the overriding practical aim of the Whig apologists, namely, to garner and solidify popular and institutional support for the policy of Exclusion, deeply rooted conventional assumptions and political and cultural commitments could not fail to shape the rhetorical strategy of the Whig writers. Three features of the historical and ideological context of the Exclusion crisis are worthy of special notice.

The first relates to the English tradition of anti-Catholicism. This was by far the most lethal weapon in the Whig propaganda arsenal against the Stuarts. As we have seen, the Whigs held James' vociferous Catholicism to be a sufficient justification for his exclusion from the line of succession. The long-standing association of Catholicism with foreign threats to national independence had been a touchstone in English political culture since the Elizabethan and Jacobean ages. The popular suspicion of Catholics had only intensified since the days of the failed Gunpowder Plot, which was still ritually and boisterously celebrated annually on November 5. In addition to the strong cultural suspicion of Catholics, the Whigs capitalized on the English perception of Louis XIV's France. By the late seventeenth century, Catholic France had replaced Spain as the dominant European power, and Louis' centralized monarchy was seen by most Englishmen as an axiomatic demonstration of the irremediable connection between Catholicism and arbitrary government. Besides exemplifying the incompatibility of Catholicism and constitutional government, Louis XIV's aggressive foreign policy and persecution of the Huguenots suggested to many Englishmen a threat to the

---

[2] For good general treatments of the events of the Exclusion crisis, see J. R. Jones, *The First Whigs: The Politics of the Exclusion Crisis, 1678–1683* (London: Oxford University Press, 1961); Mark Kishlansky, *A Monarchy Transformed* (London: Oxford University Press, 1996); Howard Nenner, *The Right to Be King: The Succession to the Crown of England, 1603–1714* (Chapel Hill: University of North Carolina Press, 1995): pp. 100–46; and J. R. Western, *Monarchy and Revolution: The English State in the 1680's* (Totowa, NJ: Rowman & Littlefield, 1972): pp. 35–45.

very survival of Protestantism, not only on the Continent but also in England itself.

Perhaps the most cynical, but politically advantageous, example of the Whig manipulation of anti-Catholic feeling in England was the disclosure of the Popish Plot in 1678, which helped bring down the king's detested chief minister, the earl of Danby, and pressured Charles into calling the first Exclusion Parliament. The public outcry caused by Titus Oates' utterly baseless claim about a Jesuit plot to assassinate the king and install James on the throne with the aid of an invading French army allowed the Whigs under the earl of Shaftesbury to ride a wave of popular support into a parliamentary majority.[3] The anti-Catholic furor produced by the Popish Plot was, however, a mixed blessing for the Whigs. On the one hand, it made James a very unpopular figure at the time and ensured solid Whig support in Parliament. But on the other hand, it left Whig polemicists such as Tyrrell, Sidney, and Locke in the tricky position of having to attack the arguments of Filmer – himself the mortal enemy of all things Jesuitical – while preventing the Tories from associating Whig natural liberty arguments with those of the Catholic natural lawyers. At least one obvious interpretation of the Whig assault on Filmerian divine right was that the Catholic natural law argument of the later scholastics was part of the natural liberty tradition the Whigs were defending against the Tory champion Filmer. At least one Tory opponent of Exclusion made this point declaring in Parliament that with the Whigs "Jesuitical principles [have been] brought upon the stage again."[4] The Whigs strenuously attempted to refute this interpretation of their position. As we shall see, Tyrrell, Sidney, and Locke each tried to maintain a prudent distance from their Catholic predecessors in the natural liberty tradition. Thus, at least one aspect of the rhetorical strategy of the Whig theorists was to avoid a boomerang effect from the anti-Catholic furor the Whig political leaders and organizers had done so much to encourage.

The second important feature of the historical context of the Exclusion period was the widespread revulsion toward the idea of republicanism in England. If the Whigs capitalized on the aura of the anti-Catholic celebrations every November 5, it was the Tories who took enormous political advantage from January 30, the anniversary of the execution of Charles I by Parliament. Only the regicides of 1649 rivaled the fabled Jesuit Plotters in the rogues gallery of the English political imagination. In the potent political symbolism of Restoration England, the executed king assumed the status of a patriotic martyr sacrificed on the wicked altar of radical republicanism. Every January 30 clerical voices from nearly every pulpit in the land decried the evil lessons of rebellion. In the cultural memory of the English people,

[3] For a full account of the Popish Plot, see the classic J. P. Kenyon, *The Popish Plot* (New York: St. Martin's, 1972).
[4] Quoted in Nenner, *Right to Be King*, p. 105.

the civil war and the Commonwealth evoked the painful experience of military rule by a politicized army, threats of social and economic leveling, and the dismantling of the church establishment. In large measure the failed experiment of the Commonwealth inoculated English political society against the lure of republicanism for generations.[5] In the context of this profound revulsion toward republicanism, the Tory strategy in the crisis was simply to paint all Whigs as dangerous crypto-republicans by presenting the legislative effort to control royal succession as the ideological descendant of mid-century parliamentary radicalism.[6] The Whig response to this charge generally took on a number of characteristics. First, as we shall see most clearly in Tyrrell, nearly all of the Whigs were careful to disavow republicanism in the strongest possible terms.[7] Most Whigs presented themselves as staunch defenders of the traditional form of the English monarchy conceived within established legal limits and in terms consistent with the tradition of the national commitment to Protestantism.[8] The Whigs charged that it was the Catholicism of James and the excessive use of prerogative by Charles II that constituted the radical and dangerous innovation in the constitutional order. Tyrell, Sidney, and Locke repeatedly attempted to drive home the idea that the Tory endorsement of Filmerian divine right theory demonstrated the radical and absolutist tendencies in English royalism. To achieve this aim, however, the Whig apologists had to demonstrate that parliamentary control over succession was a traditionally acceptable form of legislative authority.[9] Only by proving that altering the line of succession was not a radical innovation could the Whigs hope to present their position as a defense of, as opposed to an attack on, the English monarchy as an institution.

The final major element of the historical context of the exclusion period is the widespread fear of civil war in later Stuart England. To some extent this fear was rooted in the memory of the long and bloody period of political instability unleashed by the constitutional struggle of a generation earlier. Ultimately it was this fear of renewed civil strife that, more than any other factor, undermined the Whigs' position in their quarrel with the king. Charles' defense of the principle of indefeasible hereditary right had

---

[5] For an account of the revulsion toward republicanism during the Restoration period, see Blair Worden "Republicanism and the Restoration, 1660–1683," in *Republicanism, Liberty, and Commercial Society, 1649–1776*, David Wootton, ed. (Stanford: Stanford University Press, 1994): pp. 139–40.

[6] Cf. Nenner, *Right to Be King*, pp. 124–6.

[7] For his part Locke, included an approving discussion of prerogative in the *Second Treatise*. It is Sidney's open admiration for republicanism that most firmly cast him outside mainstream English Whiggery of the 1680s.

[8] O. W. Furley, "The Whig Exclusionists: Pamphlet Literature in the Exclusion Crisis, 1679–81," *Cambridge Historical Journal*, vol. 13, issue 1 (1957): p. 35.

[9] Nenner, *Right to Be King*, pp. 56–7.

at least the plausible claim of ensuring a stable succession.[10] Sensing that the English people, and even the majority of Whigs, had no appetite for civil war, Charles gambled successfully that his decision to dissolve the third Exclusion Parliament would be perceived as an acceptable resolution to the crisis in the eyes of most of his countrymen. Popular support for the Whigs eroded as the crisis appeared to be lurching toward war. By dissolving Parliament, Charles removed the Whig platform and broke up the Whigs as a serious opposition group. Once again we will see most clearly in Tyrrell the abiding concern to demonstrate the principled moderation animating most Whigs. The typical Whig supporters of exclusion were deeply conservative men in many respects, from some of the oldest and most respectable families in the country. They were not predisposed to political radicalism either by temperament or by ideology. The desire of most Whigs to resist the drift to absolutism, on the one hand, and social upheaval and populism, on the other, was rooted in their attachment to the principles of limited monarchy that they believed supported the stable, hierarchical political order that protected property, established privileges, and traditional liberties.[11] Indeed, the radical Whigs Sidney and Locke are identifiable as radicals in large part precisely because of their openness to the idea of popular revolt against monarchical rule. Given the fact that even most Whigs in 1681 did not wish to see the dispute between crown and Parliament explode into a contest of arms, it is perhaps not surprising that of the three major Whig tracts composed during the Exclusion years, only Tyrrell's moderate offering saw the light of day during the crisis.

The first Whigs were political failures but philosophical victors. Their actions and arguments failed to exclude James from the line of succession, but the writings of the Exclusion Whigs changed the English political landscape permanently and made a formative impact on the Anglo-American tradition of political and constitutional thought. English and American Whigs for at least the next century would approach issues of political obligation, resistance, and the nature of government in terms first conceived largely in the turbulent years of the Exclusion crisis. In the following analysis of the major Whig writings of the period, we must bear in mind the historical context of this seminal time. The general lines of development in the Whig arguments of the period can, in part, be traced back to the specific constitutional, legal, and religious issues brought to the fore by the crisis. Only by paying careful attention to this complex historical context are we in a position to understand why the Whigs made the arguments they did in the manner they did and perhaps even why they deemed some things better left unsaid.

---

[10] Ibid., p. 122.
[11] For an excellent discussion of the conservative ideology of the majority of Whigs, see H. T. Dickinson, *Liberty and Property: Political Ideology in Eighteenth Century Britain* (London: Weidenfeld & Nicolson, 1977): pp. 57–70.

4

James Tyrrell

The Voice of Moderate Whiggism

The publication of James Tyrrell's *Patriarcha, Non Monarcha* in 1681 was the first major Whig shot fired in the polemical dispute raised by the issue of Exclusion. It was at once a *piece d'occasion* devoted to advancing the Whig position in the Exclusion crisis and a major work of political philosophy dealing with such issues as the nature of political society, the origin of property, the principle of consent, and the main features of late-seventeenth-century natural jurisprudence. One commentator has observed that *Patriarcha, Non Monarcha* is "perhaps the most interesting work of political theory published in England between 1660 and 1689."[1] At its core, this work is the classic moderate Whig defense of limited government against what Tyrrell calls Filmer's "Absolute Monarchy *Jure Divino*." In contrast, Tyrrell presents himself as a defender of the rule of law and rejects all of Filmer's attempts to deny the validity of the legal limits on monarchical power that require rulers to abstain from the "Lives, Liberties or Properties of their Subjects."[2]

Tyrrell's moderate political credentials were impeccable. He was born in 1642 at the outbreak of England's turbulent civil war period.[3] As the son of a prominent Buckinghamshire gentleman in royal service, Sir Timothy Tyrrell, and grandson on his maternal side of the celebrated champion of the divine right of kings, Archbishop Ussher of Armagh, James Tyrrell's familial political legacy was decidedly Cavalier. Indeed, his first literary

---

[1] Richard Tuck, *Natural Rights Theories* (Cambridge: Cambridge University Press, 1979): p. 154.

[2] James Tyrrell, *Patriarcha, Non Monarcha* (London, 1681): Preface, p. 1 (hereafter PNM and page number).

[3] For useful biographical accounts of James Tyrrell, see John Gough, "James Tyrrell, Whig Historian and Friend of John Locke," *The Historical Journal*, vol. 19, no. 3 (1976): pp. 581–610; Julia Rudolph, *Revolution by Degrees: James Tyrrell and Whig Political Thought in the Late Seventeenth Century* (New York: Palgrave, 2002): pp. 24–8 and *The Dictionary of National Biography*, Leslie Stephen and Sidney Lee, eds. (London: Oxford University Press, 1921–2), Vol. XIX: pp. 1368–9 (hereafter DNB).

venture in 1661 was a dedication to Charles II of a republished edition of his grandfather's famous sermon *The Power Communicated by God to the Prince*.[4] While Tyrrell perhaps inherited his native abhorrence of political radicalism from his family background, the formative experience in his intellectual development, and the event that would eventually set him on the Whig course, was his time at Oxford.

Tyrrell entered Queen's College, Oxford, in 1657 near the end of the Interregnum and graduated with an M.A. in 1663. He studied law and was called to the bar three years later, although he never practiced law, preferring to retire to one of his family estates at Oakley in Buckinghamshire. The most important development in Tyrrell's Oxford years did not, however, involve directly his studies, but rather his meeting and befriending the man who would in many respects shape the course of his life: John Locke. In Locke, who was ten years his senior and at the time a promising young lecturer, Tyrrell found an intellectual companion with whom he discussed all the major political, scientific, philosophical, and religious issues of the day. It was Locke who invited Tyrrell to join the Exeter House circle of intellectuals that met regularly under Shaftesbury's mentorship in the late 1660s and early 1670s, thus introducing him to the informal web of relations that would in time form the nascent Whig opposition. The lifelong, but in later years often rocky, friendship between Tyrrell and Locke represents one of the most fascinating and touching personal stories in the Whig high political drama.

Tyrrell moved in Whig circles and knew most of the important public figures of the day, but he was not particularly politically active, at least on the national stage. His experience in public life was limited to local administration in his home county, where he served as a justice of the peace and as deputy lieutenant. He never sat in Parliament and by most accounts was not directly involved in Shaftesbury's activities during the Exclusion crisis in 1679–81.[5] However, it was in this period that he offered his polemical skills in the service of the Whig cause, publishing anonymously *Patriarcha*,

---

[4] It is important to note that the decidedly low church Ussher (1581–1656) was never a Filmerian divine rightist. Although he strongly affirmed the principle of divine right in 1648 at the time of Parliament's debate over how to handle the fate of the imprisoned Charles I, Ussher also held strongly Calvinist views on church government that frequently set him at odds with high churchmen and made him one of Cromwell's favorite antiepiscopal divines. As one biographer described this complex man: "His Augustinian theology commended him to the puritans, his veneration for antiquity to the high churchmen; no royalist surpassed him in deference to the divine right of kings" (DNB, Vol. XX: pp. 96–7). For Ussher's attempts to mediate between episcopacy and presbytery, see Austin Woolrych, *Britain in Revolution, 1625–1660* (Oxford: Oxford University Press, 2002): pp. 48, 162, 676 and Michael Mendle, *Dangerous Positions: Mixed Government, the Estates of the Realm, and the Answer to the XIX Propositions* (University, AL: University of Alabama Press, 1985): pp. 141–2.

[5] Richard Ashcraft suggests otherwise (*Revolutionary Politics and Locke's Two Treatises of Government* [Princeton: Princeton University Press, 1986]: pp. 387–8).

Non Monarcha and perhaps even collaborating with Locke, who was then a frequent visitor to Tyrrell's Shotover estate near Oxford, on a pamphlet on toleration.

He survived unscathed the Tory backlash that followed the collapse of the Whig parliamentary opposition, despite his Whiggish associations. Unlike Sidney or his friend Locke, the crown does not appear to have considered Tyrrell to be a threat, in part because he was not seen as a radical activist and in part out of deference to his lineage, with one government spy assuring his superiors that James "is the son of a very good [i.e., royalist] man, Sir Timothy Tyrrell."[6] The crown's treatment of Tyrrell in this period displays poignantly the extent to which the civil war loyalties of one's forebears still mattered in late Stuart England. During the Whig years in the political wilderness from 1683 to 1688, Tyrrell was never arrested or forced into exile. He also does not appear to have had any real contact with the "Council of Six," including Sidney, Essex, Russell, Hampden, Howard, and Monmouth, who briefly and disastrously assumed leadership of the Whig movement after Shaftesbury's flight to Holland and subsequent death in early 1683. For most of the half decade before the Glorious Revolution Tyrrell stayed put at his estates, performing local administrative duties and keeping Locke, now in Dutch exile, informed of political events at home. To Locke's great annoyance, Tyrrell pressed for a royal pardon for his friend and regularly pleaded with him in letters to return to England. Tyrrell was initially favorably disposed to James' Declaration of Indulgence extending toleration, as were many Whigs, but he soon changed his mind (possibly under the influence of Locke's vehement opposition to it) and was eventually stripped of his offices by James in early 1688 for refusing to support the Declaration.[7] Although he played no direct part in the dramatic events of 1688–9 and never held high office, Tyrrell did become celebrated as one of the chief moderate Whig apologists for the Glorious Revolution settlement, especially through the influence of his massive *Bibliotheca Politica* and his emphatically Whiggish and unfinished *History of England*.

It is clearly impossible to understand Tyrrell's role as a Whig theorist without recognizing the profound effect of his relationship with Locke. The typical interpretation of their friendship emphasizes the minor dramas of domestic intercourse involving disputes over money loaned and owed, confidences exposed to strangers, and new acquaintances interrupting old affections. To many historians the Locke–Tyrrell connection presents a relatively uncomplicated picture, with Locke as the towering figure who becomes progressively more detached from the sycophantic, cloying, insecure, and

---

[6] Gough, "James Tyrrell," p. 589.

[7] In this regard he cannot be mistaken for one of what Goldie calls "James' Whigs." See Mark Goldie, "John Locke's Circle and James II," *Historical Journal*, vol. 35, no. 3 (September 1992): pp. 568–9. Cf. Rudolph, *Revolution by Degrees*, p. 27.

obviously less talented Tyrrell.[8] While there is some truth to this account, it misses the mark on the most important aspect of their relation. Locke and Tyrrell's friendship was rooted in the liberating experience of intellectual discourse and the mutual exchange of ideas. Tyrrell admired Locke deeply, but this admiration should not occlude our understanding of the important philosophical disagreements between the two. Tyrrell was not one to hide his light under a bushel, and when they enjoyed close relations, as they did at the time of the Exclusion crisis, it is likely that Locke and Tyrrell would have some influence on each other, even if primarily in the form of critiques.[9] After the publication of Locke's *Essay Concerning Human Understanding* in 1690, Tyrrell chided Locke in a letter for not distinguishing his teaching on the law of nature sufficiently from the vile "Epicureanism of Hobbes." As Julia Rudolph perceptively observes, "Locke finally decided to retrieve all of his possessions from Oakley – setting in motion the final round of accusation and bargaining between them – soon after he defended his position on the natural law against Tyrrell's critique."[10] The suggestion is that they were intellectual rivals harboring serious disagreements on important political and philosophical questions. As we shall see, the disagreements between Locke and Tyrrell on these issues can be traced as far back as *Patriarcha, Non Monarcha*.

The moderate Whiggism in this early writing emerged as a distinct form of thought with the infusion of the philosophical categories and premises of late-seventeenth-century natural jurisprudence into the English constitutional controversies of the Exclusion era. Tyrrell's moderate Whig version of the natural liberty doctrine departed from that of its predecessors by following the philosphical authority of Samuel Pufendorf. Many of the key elements of moderate Whig thought such as the rejection of popular sovereignty, the seriously qualified right of rebellion, and the denial of the theory of the dissolution of government derived from a fundamentally Pufendorfian understanding of the natural law and the contractual origins of government. In order to defend the principle of legal limits on the monarchy against Filmer and his Tory supporters, Tyrrell addressed the fundamental questions regarding the nature of political society, the origin of property rights, and the constitutional limits on sovereign authority. In this chapter we will examine the main features of Tyrrell's moderate Whig position, paying particular attention to his essentially Pufendorfian natural law theory, his account of property, and the character of constitutional sovereignty. For Tyrrell and the moderate Whigs, resisting absolutism did not require advocating radical natural rights or a dramatic increase in popular control of the government.

[8] This view has been persuasively challenged recently by Rudolph, *Revolution by Degrees*, pp. 26–7.

[9] Ibid., pp. 161–7.

[10] Ibid., p. 26.

Yet even as the moderate Whigs tried to defend the traditions of England's complex and balanced Constitution, they introduced new principles of natural jurisprudence to undergird their conception of limited monarchy. Thus, Tyrrell's critique of Filmer produced a defense of the old England that required an articulation of a new England.

Pufendorf and Whig Philosophy

Before we examine the substance of Tyrrell's moderate Whig argument for Exclusion, it is important to understand the intellectual context informing his and the mainstream Whig position. Samuel Pufendorf was, as we shall see, the most influential philosophical authority for moderate Whigs in the 1680s. But who was Pufendorf and why was he so influential among his contempories? It is one of the great ironies in the history of political thought that this largely neglected figure was once one of the leading philosophic voices for educated Europeans.[11] Born in Saxony in 1632, the same year as Spinoza and Locke, Pufendorf has had the misfortune for centuries to be overshadowed by his more illustrious cohorts. Yet to uncover the roots of the moderate Whig position in the 1680s and beyond, we must briefly consider the sources, assumptions, and arguments of this complex thinker. From his early days in Saxony during the tumultuous Thirty Years War, Pufendorf carried with him a burning desire to explicate, rationalize, and demystify political and moral phenomena. As a student and later as a lecturer at the universities of Leipzig and Jena, Pufendorf began a rigorous study of politics that continued through the several incarnations of a colorful career that included lengthy tenures as the court historian to the king of Sweden and later to the elector of Brandenburg in Berlin.

Pufendorf's voluminous and diverse body of work comprised many celebrated works of philosophy, history, theology, and jurisprudence, but it was his massive compendium of legal and political philosophy *De Jure Naturae et Gentium* (1672) that left the deepest imprint on the English political mind. The most fundamental principles of the Pufendorfian teaching on politics in *De Jure Naturae et Gentium* reflect the maturation of ideas conceived during

---

[11] A clear sign of the neglect that Pufendorf has suffered in recent times is the fact that there is, to my knowledge, only one full-length modern treatment of him in English: Leonard Krieger, *The Politics of Discretion: Pufendorf and the Acceptance of Natural Law* (Chicago: University of Chicago Press, 1965). But see also Craig Carr and Michael Seidler, "Pufendorf, Sociality and the Modern State," *History of Political Thought*, vol. 13, no. 3 (Autumn 1996): pp. 352–78; Alfred Dufour, "Pufendorf," in *The Cambridge History of Political Thought, 1450–1700*, J. H. Burns and Mark Goldie, eds. (Cambridge: Cambridge University Press, 1991): pp. 561–88; and Istvan Hont "The Language of Sociability and Commerce: Samuel Pufendorf and the Theoretical Foundations of the 'Four-Stages Theory,'" in *The Languages of Political Theory in Early-Modern Europe*, Anthony Pagden, ed. (Cambridge: Cambridge University Press, 1987): pp. 253–76. These works were very helpful to me in the following discussion.

Pufendorf's formative political experiences while growing up and studying in the German lands deeply scarred by sectarian conflict in the Thirty Years War. The two guiding principles of Pufendorfian political theory were a horror of theologically charged politics and a visceral concern for the political and constitutional instability caused by poorly designed governing institutions and, more particularly, what he took to be the fundamentally defective conception of sovereignty then regnant in the Holy Roman Empire. Thus, Pufendorf set himself the daunting task of establishing a secular foundation for moral and political science and reconstituting viable political orders through the articulation of a theoretically rigorous and logically consistent conception of sovereignty.

Pufendorf's reputation as one of the great synthesizers in the modern natural law tradition is certainly apposite. Indeed, his conciliating spirit and his efforts to harmonize diverse intellectual influences comported well with the intellectual temperament of most English Whigs, themselves avid blenders of philosophical principles, historical custom, and legal precedent. However, it is important to recognize that Pufendorf's chief political authorities in the natural liberty tradition were emphatically secular. Pufendorf represents perhaps the most ambitious voice among the generation of conservative natural law thinkers who followed in the wake of Hobbes' groundbreaking critique of the central principles of Christian Aristotelianism. Repulsed by the Hobbesian rejection of natural justice, Pufendorf sought to incorporate fundamentally Hobbesian insights about the character of natural rights into a comprehensive natural law theory that would provide a moral grounding for political life. Thus, he generally rejected the arguments of Catholic scholastic and reformed divine apologists for the divine ordination of political power, favoring rather the solid rationalist foundations of Hobbes and Grotius.[12] While Pufendorf's eclectic style drew in an enormous variety of sources both sacred and profane, the political teaching of *De Jure Naturae et Gentium* is best understood primarily as a synthesis of the ideas of Hobbes and Grotius. From Hobbes, Pufendorf borrowed the idea of political society originating in a pre-political state of nature. However, he blended the idea of the state of nature with an identifiably Grotian conception of a relative sociability inherent in human nature. By fusing the individualist premises of Hobbes with the anthropological observations of natural human sociability expounded by Grotius, Pufendorf established a conception of the natural human condition that rejected the amoral atomism and mechanical materialism of Hobbes while also eschewing the teleological Aristotelian assumptions still integral

---

[12] See Samuel Pufendorf, *De Jure Naturae et Gentium Libri Octo*, Vol. I, a photographic reproduction of the Amsterdam edition of 1688, and Vol. II, a translation of the text by W. A. Oldfather and C. H. Oldfather (Oxford: Clarendon Press, 1934): bk 7, ch 3, secs. 1–2, pp. 683–4 (hereafter in notes DJNG bk., ch., sec., and page number where applicable). Cf. Dufour, "Pufendorf," pp. 574–5.

for Grotius.[13] The Pufendorfian individual who contracted to form political society possessed not only Hobbesian natural rights, but also natural duties and obligations flowing from the dictates of the natural law, which directs rational beings toward peace and a viable social existence.

Pufendorf's account of the origin of political society also reflected this effort to moderate and fuse the Grotian and Hobbesian elements in the natural liberty tradition. In contrast to the Hobbesian pattern of collapsing the contract of association and the contract of subjection through the act of recognizing a sovereign power, Pufendorf separated these stages in the formation of political society into two distinct forms of voluntary agreement. In addition, Pufendorf added a third, decidedly Grotian, stage in the process, a pact established in the time between the contract of association, which forms one people, and the contract of subjection, which completes the formation of the political state. This intervening pact establishes the type of government that will lead the state.[14] It not only parallels the Grotian notion of the contractual agreement underlying any particular form of government, but also provides logical and theoretical support for the consensual and legal source of particular institutions such as the English Parliament and situates the creation of these institutions in the very origins of the state. Operating in tandem with this innovative conceptual space between the pre-civil social existence of voluntary association and the morally binding character of political subjection is Pufendorf's assertion of the moral reality inhering in the corporate entities he calls "composite moral persons" that are both voluntary in origin and can, theoretically, predate the formation of sovereign power.[15] By including the formation of corporate bodies and a system of property ownership within the range of contractual possibilities available to pre-civil society through the dictates of the law of nature, Pufendorf provides a theoretical account of the complex, multilayered, and potentially hierarchical web of relations forming and underlying political society.

In one vital respect, it may appear odd to argue for Pufendorf's role as the philosophical authority for the Whigs. Pufendorf has come down to posterity as one of the strongest proponents of an absolutist conception of sovereignty, the kind of argument the Whigs would be expected to reject out of hand. Whig thinkers did typically reject Bodinian, Hobbesian, and even Grotian notions of sovereignty precisely because of the absolutist tendencies or potentialities of these positions, but they viewed Pufendorf in a different light from his predecessors on this issue. The Whigs recognized that Pufendorf's

13 For Pufendorf's attempt to synthesis Hobbes and Grotius, see Carr and Seidler, "Sociality and the Modern State," pp. 355–6, 363; Dufour, "Pufendorf," pp. 567–9; and Hont, "Sociability and Commerce," pp. 253, 256, 258–9, and 263–5. Cf. DJNG 2.3.15.
14 DJNG 2.6.5–6.120. Cf. Krieger, *Politics of Discretion*, p. 121 and Dufour, "Pufendorf," p. 573.
15 DJNG 7.2.13. Cf. Carr and Seidler, "Sociality and the Modern State," p. 374; Dufour, "Pufendorf," p. 567; and Hont, "Sociability and Commerce," pp. 256–7, 263–5.

teaching on sovereignty was far from being a principled defense of absolute monarchy. Rather, the thrust of Pufendorf's sovereignty argument was
that whatever form of government a people constituted must be guided by
an indivisible and absolute supreme power that is subject to no limitations
from any other institution or external moral force.[16] Pufendorf's argument
for sovereignty, then, appealed to Whigs for several reasons.

First, Pufendorf's emphasis on the indivisibility of sovereign power included an emphatic rejection of any form of mixed regime theory resting on
the idea of coordinate sovereign powers. This kind of argument, as we have
seen, was very influential among civil war era parliamentary resistance theorists such as Hunton and Parker and bore the strong approbation of Grotius.
More importantly mixed regime theory was identified by most Whigs as one
of the chief causes of political and constitutional instability in the civil war
period. Pufendorf's dismissal of mixed constitutionalism as productive of
"irregular," and hence radically defective, forms of government (like the
Holy Roman Empire) conformed admirably to the Whig understanding of
English political history.[17] Second, Pufendorf supplemented his condemnation of mixed regime theory with an articulate and theoretically sophisticated
argument in support of limited monarchy. He claimed that a people may
choose at the time of the formation of the state to establish fundamental laws
and representative institutions to limit royal power.[18] This argument not only
provided a rationalized and theoretically attractive support for the Whig view
of the historical English Constitution, with its institutional checks on monarchical authority, but also located the authority of Parliament *within* a unified and absolute sovereign power. Pufendorf made the sovereignty of king-
in-Parliament a plausible and theoretically consistent possibility. Finally,
the Whigs were attracted to the very narrow, but significant, Pufendorfian
formulation of the right of resistance. In keeping with the conservative mindset of most Whigs, Pufendorf maintained a general prohibition against resistance, especially of the popular variety.[19] Like most Whigs, Pufendorf was
deeply hostile to the idea of social upheaval and threats to civil order and
the security of property. However, Pufendorf did sanction a limited right
of resistance framed in terms of a legitimate self-defense right that would
allow legally established institutions to repel tyrannous actions against the
entire people.[20] This limited right of self-defense was not an endorsement of
popular sovereignty or a right of radical constitutional change, but rather
was legitimated by the more conservative goal of restoring the original

---

[16] DJNG 7.4.11.695–6 and 7,6,7.
[17] For good discussions of Pufendorf's teaching on "irregular" regimes, see Dufour,
    "Pufendorf," pp. 581–3 and Krieger, *Politics of Discretion*, pp. 156–64.
[18] Cf. DJNG 7.6.7,9,11.
[19] DJNG 7.8.5.
[20] DJNG 7.8.6.

constitution. To the Whigs who were seeking justification for their own resistance to the crown during the Exclusion crisis and the Glorious Revolution, but were also profoundly suspicious and fearful of the populist or even republican implications of radical resistance theory, Pufendorf's formulation of a limited, primarily restorative, right of resistance in emergencies was the ideal theoretical support for Whig claims to being the defenders of traditional constitutional liberties.

It is not surprising that Pufendorf's political project to anchor the idea of sovereignty in firm and logically consistent grounds appealed to a generation of Englishmen whose formative political experiences of theological–political controversy and constitutional instability so clearly paralleled his own. Pufendorf's account of the origins and ends of government with its articulate rejection of popular sovereignty, on the one hand, and unbridled absolute monarchy, on the other, fit perfectly with the moderate and in many respects deeply conservative temper of most English Whigs. In Pufendorf's argument for the threefold contract establishing civil society, he supplied logical support for Whig historical claims about the antiquity and centrality of Parliament at a time when royalists appealed to Filmer and Brady to deny both its historical pedigree and its legal autonomy. His account of the nature of government and sovereignty seemed to provide a theoretical reflection of the Whigs' instinctive view of the complex, hierarchical whole that was the English Constitution and society. In his repudiation of mixed regime theory, an idea inauspiciously associated in the Whig mind with the radicalism of the 1640s, and his defense of limited monarchy checked by fundamental laws and representative institutions, Pufendorf appeared to be the philosophical champion of the English Constitution as Whigs like Tyrrell conceived of it.

Moderate Whig Natural Law and Natural Rights

Tyrrell's opening salvo against Filmer aims to defend the principle of natural liberty. He observes that Filmer's "first Argument against the natural Freedom of Mankinde is drawn from Scripture." In Filmer's Adamite thesis Tyrrell finds "the substance and strength of all that the Author had to say in defense" of the "Divine Right of Absolute Monarchy."[21] The objections Tyrrell raises to Filmer rest on the interpretation of two key passages in Genesis that Filmer had appropriated from John Selden and Philip Hunton. The argument that "Children are tyed to an Absolute Subjection or Servitude to their Parents," Tyrrell detects, is rooted in Filmer's attribution of the absolute "dominion of Adam over the Earth and all the Creatures therein, on Gen. 1.28." This point Filmer draws from "Mr. Selden in his *Mare Clausum.*" The second key scriptural passage that Tyrrell singles out by which Filmer "seems to found this Power of Adam upon" is "Mr. Hunton's

[21] PNM: 9.

concession.... That it is God's ordinance that there should be Civil Government, because Gen. 3.16 God ordained Adam to rule over his wife."[22] Tyrrell's strategy is to develop a comprehensive design to sever Filmer's argument from the authority of Scripture. Tyrrell attempts to prove that Scripture does not afford Adam an exclusive or despotic dominion over creation.[23] Moreover, whatever right Adam may have enjoyed, it was not transferable to his heirs. Tyrrell admits that even if Scripture did grant this sweeping power to Adam's heirs, the holy text provides no promise that Adam's heirs can be known contemporaneously. Tyrrell employs Scripture's obscurity regarding the extent of Adam's power and the possibility of its transferability to prove that different forms of subjection, for example filial and conjugal, cannot be traced back to a single patriarchal authority in Adam.

Tyrrell argues that the Bible recognized different forms of subjection both political and familial. For his part, Filmer had cited the subjection of Eve at Genesis 3:16 as proof of "God's Ordinance that there should be Civil Government." Tyrrell counters Filmer with the position that "all Expositors look upon these words *thy desire shall be to thy husband* as respecting only a Conjugal and not a Filial Subjection."[24] The key element in Tyrrell's interpretation of this passage is his insistence that whatever power Adam "or any other Husband" acquired by this divine grant, it did not extend to "an Absolute Authority over the Life of his Wife." The justification for this limit on conjugal power is its basis in compact. Tyrrell affirms that Eve, or any wife, has that "right left to her to defend herself from the unjust violence or rage of her Husband."[25] This self-defense right also appears, in a somewhat muted form, in Tyrrell's treatment of the power of eldest sons. He interprets the Bible's promise that Cain "shalt rule over his brother Abel" as falling far short of political subjection. Tyrrell claims that this promise may have been given only to Cain personally and thus does not "give a Right to all Eldest Sons." Moreover, even if it did, "the words do not signifie an absolute Despotick Power, but a ruling or governing by persuasion or fair means."[26] Tyrrell reduces the promise to Cain to a sadly ironic endorsement of the importance of warm brotherly advice. Jacob and Esau, in Tyrrell's

[22] PNM: 10, 13.
[23] James Daly, *Sir Robert Filmer and English Political Thought* (Toronto: University of Toronto Press, 1979): p. 65 and Alan Craig Houston, *Algernon Sidney and the Republican Heritage in England and America* (Princeton: Princeton University Press, 1991): p. 104.
[24] PNM: 13.
[25] PNM: 13. Tyrrell follows Grotius and Pufendorf in emphasizing the contractual basis of conjugal right. However, Shanley and Rudolph are correct to observe that by stressing the voluntary origins of women's secondary position in marriage rather than assumptions about natural subjection, Tyrrell more closely follows Pufendorf than Grotius (Rudolph, *Revolution by Degrees*, pp. 39–45 and Mary Shanley, "Marriage Contract and Social Contract in Seventeenth Century England," *Western Political Quarterly*, vol. 32, no. 1 [March 1979]: p. 86). Compare PNM: 109 with Grotius, DJB 2.5.1 and Pufendorf, DJNG 6.1.9.
[26] PNM: 39 and Daly, *Sir Robert Filmer*, p. 75.

view, exemplify this relation inasmuch as even the inheriting of his father Isaac's blessing did not make Jacob "Lord over Esau," his brother. With these biblical examples, Tyrrell drives home his contention that Scripture's understanding of the relations of husband and wife, and of elder son to younger siblings, do not conform to Filmer's Adamite thesis.

Tyrrell never denies that fatherhood determines a kind of filial subjection. His aim rather is to show that this authority arises from the general character and end of the relation and not from any specific right of Adam. Of the rule the biblical patriarchs exercised over their children, Tyrrell argues that it "must belong to them either as Fathers, or else as Masters, or Heads of their particular Families; and not as Heirs to Adam."[27] Where, then, does Tyrrell find the "true original" of paternal right, if not in Adam? He grounds it in the "Laws of Nature, or Reason" governing the state of nature, or the condition "separate from any Commonwealth." These laws, Tyrrell states, "are intended for one end or effect, viz. the common good and preservation of Mankinde." As such, parental power over children "extends no farther than it conduces to this end."[28] Tyrrell's law of nature does not endorse despotic paternal or parental power because such a right is antithetical to the stated end of this law: the common good and preservation of humankind. Tyrrell understands legitimate paternal right as the power deriving from the education of children. The source of this right, however, is a duty, the "great Duty of Education." Tyrrell's God of the natural law who imposes duties on parents replaces Filmer's God, who is the giver of power simply. The rational law governing human relations in the natural condition determines that "the highest Right which Parents can have in their Children, is not meerly natural, from generation; but acquir'd by their performance of that nobler part of their Duty."[29] One effect of Tyrrell's reinterpretation of paternal right in terms of a duty is to alter the claims on filial obedience. Obedience now becomes a product of gratitude, and obligation is transformed into a much more self-determined and self-generated phenomenon than Filmer would allow. Tyrrell argues that the duty of children rests on "that Gratitude and Sense they ought to have of the great obligation they owe their Parents, for the trouble and care they put them to in their Education."[30] This "great obligation" is conditional in two senses. It requires performance of a duty by parents, and it may repose in a nongenerative caregiver. Tyrrell's aim here is not merely to sever paternal right from its allegedly generative source, but also to stipulate the terms of the natural law that governs human relations

---

[27] PNM: 12. See PNM: 27 for Tyrrell's radical reinterpretation of the meaning of the binding of Isaac.

[28] PNM: 15, 17. For Tyrrell's appeals to the claims of mothers as possessors of parental right, see PNM: 14, as well as Gough, "James Tyrrell," p. 587.

[29] PNM: 16.

[30] PNM: 16–17.

apart from civil society and that indeed must be implicit and reflected in any legitimate civil law.

Tyrrell explains the limits on paternal power as the product of the natural law directive toward peaceful human coexistence. He argues that a son may restrain a mad or drunken father out of "that love and charity which all men in the state of nature ought to shew toward each other." If the uncontrollable rage of such a violent fellow were to endanger the lives of his children, then preventive action would be justified by the requirements of the natural law:

The evils which an Aggressor, or Wrong-doer, suffers from him he injured, though in respect of God the Supreme Lawgiver they may be natural punishments ordained by him, to deter men from violating the Laws of Nature, yet they are not so in regard of the Person who inflicts them.[31]

Notably Tyrrell posits God as the "Supreme Lawgiver." While he does not suggest that both the knowledge and obligatoriness of the natural law are absolutely dependent on the rational knowledge of the existence and will of the transcendent God, Tyrrell does indicate that human beings are somehow dependent on both God and society for their existence and flourishing.[32] Tyrrell implies that the natural punishments offered by the lawgiving God are identical to the primary punishing power of individuals in the state of nature.

The core of this punishment power is a natural right of self-preservation. Tyrrell argues that a wife, for example, may resist her husband's "ungovernable rage" in order to save the lives of her children and herself.[33] Moreover, Tyrrell emphatically asserts that this right does not denote any superiority on the part of the resister. Quite the contrary, it signifies a profound natural equality. As Tyrrell explains, when a son defends himself or others from the unjust violence of a father

[h]e doth not act as his superior, but in this case as his Equal, as he is indeed in all the Rights of Nature, considered only as a Man; such as a Right to live, and to preserve himself, and to use all lawful means for that end.[34]

Moreover, Tyrrell extends this right of self-defense even to the point of justifying the taking of human life: "Since the first law of Nature is Self-Preservation, it is lawful for a man to use all means conducing to this

---

[31] PNM: 26.

[32] Michael P. Zuckert, *Natural Rights and the New Republicanism* (Princeton: Princeton University Press, 1994): p. 207 and James Tully, *A Discourse on Property: Locke and His Adversaries* (Cambridge: Cambridge University Press, 1980): p. 49. By Zuckert's suggestion, this would make Tyrrellian natural law much closer to that of Pufendorf than Locke's presentation in the *Questions on the Law of Nature*.

[33] PNM: 10–11, 25–6, 109–13 and Daly, *Sir Robert Filmer*, p. 66.

[34] PNM: 26.

end...so that if any Man assault me in the State of Nature, I may defend myself, and consequently kill the assailant."[35] This is both a statement of natural equality and a further reminder that all power is restricted by the ends it serves. Tyrrell both breaks from the scholastic prohibition on the natural punishment right and extends the principle of resistance to arbitrary rule far beyond the strictly political or constitutional limits of the earlier parliamentary contractarianism of Philip Hunton. For his part, Tyrrell takes seriously Filmer's assertion that absolutist politics has a familial root. Yet it is important to note that the moderate Whig Tyrrell attempts to place certain restrictions on this resistance right. For example, a son resisting a violent father may "use all lawful means" toward the end of self-preservation and the safety of others. At one point, Tyrrell restricts this right to a practical nullity, advising: "Patience is the only lawful means to make the Father see his Errour."[36] While Tyrrell is prepared to break from the more conservative scholastic position on the individual punishment right, he is clearly uncomfortable with some of the radical implications of his natural rights teaching. He argues, for example, that this right of resistance does not operate for frivolous reasons and should not extend to revenge for past actions. The "lawful means" Tyrrell supports seem to have safety as the aim. Once safety is achieved the use of force should end, "otherwise quarrels would be perpetual."[37] Tyrrell's conception of individual natural rights, then, reflects a more primary concern with the social ends authorized by the natural law.

Tyrrell extends his account of the natural law to an analysis of the way in which it regulates other relations in addition to those specifically involving paternal and conjugal power. The first such relation with which he deals is that of master and slave. Tyrrell follows Pufendorf and Grotius in assuming that slavery and servitude more generally falls into two varieties: that by contract and by conquest. Slavery by conquest arises as a punishment for aggressors who are defeated by a defensive power waging a just war. As this relation has no basis in compact, both master and slave are still in a state of war, and as such, the master's right imposes no obligation on the slave to serve. Tyrrell affirms that "there is no sober Planter in Barbadoes (who are most of them Assignees of Slaves taken in War) but will grant such a Slave may lawfully run away if he can."[38] The law of nature, which incorporates a primary natural right of self-preservation, determines that even a slave taken

35 PNM: 115. Compare with Roberto Bellarmine, *De Laicis*, Kathleen Murphy, trans. (New York: Fordham University Press, 1928): pp. 25–6 and Francisco Suarez, *Extracts on Government and Politics*, George Moore, trans. (Chevy Chase, MD: Country Dollar Press, 1950): *Defensio* 3.2.1–4. pp. 372–5.
36 PNM: 29.
37 PNM: 28. Tyrrell's emphasis on the proportionality between crime and punishment resembles that of Grotius, but his prohibition of revenge is more akin to Pufendorf. Compare Grotius DJB 2.20.28, 2.20.1, 4 and Pufendorf, DJGN 2.5.3.
38 PNM: 105. Cf. Grotius, DJB 3.7, 8.

in a just war cannot be presumed to have surrendered this right. Tyrrell also limits the legitimate exercise of despotic power in this case. In answer to "what Mr. Hobbes says, That no injury can be done to a Slave," he offers the idea that by the laws of nature no slave is "so absolutely at his Masters dispose, as that because he hath him in his Power, he hath therefore a Right to use him as he will."[39] Whereas Hobbes intended by this to argue that injury can only arise in a condition already normalized by contract, Tyrrell asserts that the subjection of even the "worst of slaves" means no more than that such a slave "hath no just reason of complaint though his Master give him Victuals that does not suit his palate, or prescribe him Work which may not please his humour." This almost comical formulation of the natural law restrictions on despotic power has serious implications for Tyrrell's broader argument against Filmer.

In addition to asserting basic natural law limits on despotic power, Tyrrell makes a characteristically Pufendorfian argument for the co-relativity of rights and duties. He asserts that no "rational man will affirm, that this slave [by conquest] hath given up the natural rights of living."[40] As such, the persistence of this right produces a duty in the master to observe certain limits in his treatment of the slave. It is this Pufendorfian aspect of Tyrrell's account that makes his version of natural rights more robust than that of Grotius, for example. The "natural Rights of living" inhering in "a rational Creature" place not a positive duty on the master, but a negative duty to refrain from abusing the slave or giving commands obviously beyond the slave's capacity. By this means, Tyrrell incorporates something like Hobbesian natural rights into a law of nature directed toward social life and ultimately sanctioned by God. Tyrrell does not, however, anchor this natural right in a form of natural proprietorship or in an explicit statement of the indefeasible character of the primary human passion for self-preservation.[41] As we saw in his criticism of Hobbes' view of the rights of masters, the Tyrrellian individual is a more social animal than Hobbes' and more clearly subject to the rational and divinely sanctioned directive of the natural law.

A useful way to approach this problem is to examine Tyrrell's discussion of contractual slavery. Tyrrell affirms that this form of slavery arises when individuals "submit themselves to the will and disposal of another" regarding such things as their diet, clothes, productive labor, and leisure time. In addition, such an individual accepts that "the Master may beat or correct him if he do amiss."[42] Self-enslavement, for Tyrrell, seems to be a real moral possibility in the state of nature and in some civil societies. While affirming this possibility, Tyrrell also, however, denies that this condition need be

---

[39] PNM: 105–6 and Thomas Hobbes, *Man and Citizen*, Bernard Gert, ed. (Indianapolis, Hackett, 1991): p. 208.
[40] PNM: 106. Cf. Pufendorf, DJNG 3.5.3 and Tuck, *Natural Rights Theories*, pp. 159–60.
[41] Hobbes, of course, roots natural rights in the latter.
[42] PNM: 102.

absolute or perpetual. Reciprocal obligation, he argues, accompanies the very act of contract, such that if a master does not fulfill his obligations to the slave – whatever the terms of the contract stipulate these obligations to be – then the contract is void. Beyond the legal strictures of the contract, Tyrrell finds a deeper argument for the limits placed on despotic power by contract. He proposes that

[n]o man can be supposed so void of common sense (unless an absolute Fool, and then he is not capable of making any Bargain) to yield himself so absolutely up to anothers disposal, as to renounce all hopes of safety or satisfaction in this life, or of future happiness in that to come.[43]

Tyrrell, then, follows the Grotian argument that individual freedom is in principle totally alienable, although it is scarcely imaginable that anyone would do such a foolish thing. There seems to be nothing inherent in the notion of natural rights that makes them inalienable.

While conceding the legitimacy of contractual slavery, Tyrrell also attempts to mute its despotic character.[44] The logic of Tyrrell's presentation of a kinder, gentler understanding of slavery is rooted in the law of nature and its duties of humanity. Tyrrell asserts that no matter how sweeping the power granted to a master by contract, the natural law prohibits absolute power. As he explains: "the Laws of Humanity do not permit, that however a man hath carried himself towards us, all Remains of that Primitive Equality between men should be quite extinguished towards him."[45] Tyrrell includes a direct moral obligation, however minimal, on the wielder of despotic power. For a master to behave as though the slave retains no trace of that "Primitive Equality" among human beings is to act against the law of nature. In a bold move, Tyrrell affirms that no "Slave hath given up the natural Rights of Living."[46] Thus, Tyrrell's natural rights teaching on contractual absolutism differs from Grotius' inasmuch it places greater normative power in the reciprocity of duties and rights and, in effect, unearths the theoretical materials out of which to construct a refutation of contractual absolutism.

Tyrrell's moderate Whig understanding of the law of nature regulating familial relations indicates that society, in a sense, is natural to human beings.[47] The moderate Whig idea of natural law expressed by Tyrrell in some respects departs considerably from the more radical natural rights theories of his fellow Exclusionists Locke and Sidney. Tyrrell followed Pufendorf in articulating a natural law directed toward establishing the grounds for the

---

[43] Ibid., 103.

[44] For example, he repeatedly asserts that Scripture offers no support for slavery (PNM: 104). Likewise, he rejects the notion of an Old Testament defense of slavery by arguing that the English word "slavery" has no counterpart in Hebrew (PNM: 108–9). Cf. Tyrrell's treatment of the prediction of Canaanite servitude (PNM: 48).

[45] PNM: 107.

[46] PNM: 106.

[47] Tully, *Discourse on Property*, p. 73.

common good of society. In the moderate Whig conception of natural jurisprudence, individual natural rights are neither nugatory nor primary. In keeping with Pufendorf, the moderate Whigs argued that individual rights are in fact subordinate to the more fundamental duties human beings have to ensure and encourage the social good of the community. Tyrrell argues that we do not form societies out of primarily selfish calculations. The right of self-preservation is subsumed in and in effect given its normative content only as the particular expression of a general duty and an obligation toward society. Thus, Filmer's extreme patriarchalism violates not only Tyrrell's understanding of the right of self-preservation, but also the extent of power and authority legitimately required to further the natural law requirements of human sociality. In moderate Whig natural law theory, absolute power is incompatible with the ends or purposes of the various layers of association – parental, conjugal, and perhaps even quasi-despotic – required for the good of society.

Property and Government: Moderate Whig Consent Theory

In the course of dismantling Filmer's divine right theory of monarchy, Tyrrell advances his own moderate Whig account of the origin of government and property. This involves him in exposing many serious practical and theoretical flaws in Filmer's attack on the principle of consent. Tyrrell's attempt to rehabilitate consent theory in the face of Filmer's anti-populist attacks includes both a conservative and a radical dimension. In response to Filmer's charges of the anarchic implications of consent theory, Tyrrell presents a more moderate and conservative reading of the principle of natural liberty than Filmer would ever allow. This involves refuting Filmer's position that individual consent is fundamentally unrepresentable, as well as his charge that the revocability of individual consent undermines and endangers every government and property settlement. With respect to the issue of representation, Tyrrell assures his readers that when he speaks of consent, he must not be supposed to mean the consent of the whole "promiscuous Rabble of Women and Children." They may be understood to be represented by their male family heads. In Tyrrell's estimation, the principle of representation precludes the dark and revolutionary implications of consent theory that Filmer ruthlessly sought to exploit. In a passage meant to comfort the moderate Whig and Tory alike, Tyrrell affirms:

Civil Government does not owe its Original to the consent of the People, since the Fathers of Families, or Freemen at their own dispose, were really and indeed all the People that needed to have Votes; since Women, as being concluded by their Husbands, and being commonly unfit for civil business, and Children in their Fathers Families being under the notion of servants, and without any Property in Goods or Land, had no reason to have Votes in the Institution of Government.[48]

[48] PNM: 83–4.

Here Tyrrell affirms that the direct operation of individual consent results from a particular status, as father or propertied man, and not from the bare possession of a human nature. The same paternal status that confers direct consent to government also produces a capacity to represent one's dependents in the formation of civil power.

Although Tyrrell's appeal to the principle of representation seems to fend off many of Filmer's charges about the revolutionary implications of consent theory, it leaves us with a number of serious questions. By what means do married men acquire this right of representing their family members if, as Tyrrell claims, human beings are marked by a "Primitive Equality"? If this sole right of male family heads to consent to government does not derive from a natural superiority, how then can it be justified? Even keeping in mind Tyrrell's argument that male rule in the family most clearly conforms to the utilitarian considerations of the natural law, does this principle of utility extend even to the very formation of civil society?

Tyrrell's responses to these questions are at the core of moderate Whig consent theory. Tyrrell asserts that men are generally superior to women with respect to "civil business." The key moral implication of the natural "Primitive Equality" of all human beings is that absolute or despotic power is never justified on natural grounds. As such, the natural law injunction to preserve the common good of humankind is, in Tyrrell's view, in no way injured by male family heads representing their dependents in matters of civil government. The profoundly utilitarian considerations inhering in the natural law support such a principle of representation even in the very foundation of society. The conservative ramifications of Tyrrell's treatment of the practical aspects of consent theory extend beyond the political status of women and children into the areas of obligation and property.

One particularly vexing question for Filmer had been the status of individuals or groups who simply withdraw their consent to an original compact, whether that compact is governmental or relates to property. Tyrrell argues that people generally are loath to undo the solemn bonds of social union "and reduce all things to the state of Nature again." The state of nature clearly contains its own inconveniences that would make it deeply unattractive. Even so, Tyrrell concludes, any individuals or groups that withdraw their consent from an existing society enter a "state of War" and become "Enemies to the Government." This obligation to existing authority extends also to those, such as women, children, and servants, who did not consent directly to the institution of government but nevertheless owe a high "obligation in Conscience and Gratitude to this Government" that protects and nourishes them.[49] This subordination of individual rights to the demands of the common good also operates in Tyrrell's assessment of the issue of

[49] PNM: 76–7.

property. In contrast to Filmer, who asserted that the notion of individual natural rights endangers the right of private property, Tyrrell counters that "every Possessor of a propriety in Lands or Goods, in any Government" accepts the maintenance of this right on the same terms as those "that first instituted the Government." The enjoyment and use of property implies and confirms consent to the existing distribution of property. Tyrrell also affirms that even those "possessing no state in the Lands or Goods of a Kingdom" enjoy the protection of the government and hence are morally bound to uphold the existing system of property.[50] Tyrrell's point is that even while the propertyless may find it inconvenient to obey a government that upholds a system of property contrary to their direct private interest, they must obey it in order to prevent violation of the natural law by introducing conditions tending toward anarchy and violence.[51] Thus, in many crucial respects relating to the representation of women and children by male family heads and to the distribution of property, Tyrrell advances a natural law argument that supports a very conservative reading of consent theory – a reading bound to appeal to the broad center of the political spectrum in seventeenth-century England.

The other, more muted, dimension of Tyrrell's rehabilitation of consent theory has more radical aspects. Even in the course of his argument for the deep moral obligation accruing from compact, Tyrrell affirms that people are not always "directly or expressly bound by the Acts or Consents of their Ancestors."[52] If, for example, an existing system of government or property has come to be disastrous to the interests of a large body of the people, an alteration of the system may be justified. The sanctity of compact need not signify the complete ossification of the social and political order. The significance of this conceptual opening to the idea of contractual revision, however, relates more to the possibility of organic constitutional change than radical revolution. The one concession Tyrrell makes to a more radical individualist understanding of natural rights relates to the natural right of emigration. This is a right Tyrrell identifies with nature and uses to reveal the limits of civil law. As he reflects: "I cannot think that the positive Laws of any Government do oblige any man in Conscience...never to go out of the Country where he was born." Positive laws may legitimately entail loss of property for emigration but, Tyrrell affirms, they cannot "bind the Conscience" in this important matter.[53] Although Tyrrell strives to reduce the revolutionary implications of natural rights as they relate to civil order and property, these individual rights never entirely disappear as factors in his reflections on political life and the principle of consent.

---

[50] PNM: 86–7.
[51] Ashcraft, *Revolutionary Politics*, p. 236.
[52] PNM: 76.
[53] PNM: 87.

Perhaps the most striking aspect of Tyrrell's treatment of the problems arising in consent theory is his open disagreement with Catholic scholasticism. In the course of critiquing Filmer's contention that sovereignty could not possibly arise from the people, Tyrrell makes reference to the position of Bellarmine and Suarez, particularly their opinion that sovereignty originally resided in the whole body of the people prior to any compact. In this instance, Tyrrell at least partially takes Filmer's side. He states: "I conceive the Jesuit hath gone too far, in asserting an undivided Soveraignty in the whole Multitude collected together before any Civil Government instituted."[54] Tyrrell agrees with Filmer that originally there was no undivided sovereignty in the multitude. Rather, in contrast to the Jesuits, Tyrrell asserts that the rule existing prior to any express social or political compact was the rule of independent family heads.[55] By holding the family as the basic unit of association, Tyrrell counters the charges of radical individualism that Filmer made against natural rights. In the view Tyrrell advances, "the people" is not meant to express atomistic individualism but rather an articulated whole composed of parts that are related to each other through agreement and the natural laws regulating human association.[56] In this way, Tyrrell locates the origins of government in an identifiable and ubiquitous form of association rather than a theoretical abstraction of the isolated self. While this effort may go far toward countering English royalist charges of radical individualism, it does not fully explain Tyrrell's position vis-à-vis the Catholic natural law theorists Suarez and Bellarmine. As we have seen, they are hardly radical individualists either. For them, the consent forming government was of a profoundly communal character.

It appears that Tyrrell's primary aim in confronting the Jesuits is to disclose the particular features of his own moderate Whig version of contract theory. In emphasizing the familial, as opposed to the communal, origin of the political compact, Tyrrell aims to illustrate the multiple compacts that produce government. Tyrrell's schema emphasizes the layers of compact operative in the family, in society, and in political rule. The family represents only a pseudocompact inasmuch as Tyrrell maintains that while it is for the most part a natural relation, it does operate on the principle of tacit consent. So, even if the family may be more natural and less conventional than government, it still bears witness to the primal equality that grounds individual consent. In the state of nature individuals exist "under the conduct or Government of distinct Heads of Fathers of Families." It is on the basis of this social arrangement that these family heads take the further step to form governing political institutions.[57] Thus, Tyrrell's position with respect

---

54 PNM: 81.
55 Tyrrell ignores Suarez's argument, which is identical to this position. See Suarez, *Extracts: Defensio*, p. 103.
56 Ashcraft, *Revolutionary Politics*, pp. 298–9 and Daly, *Sir Robert Filmer*, p. 92.
57 PNM: 82–3.

to Filmer and the Jesuits is complex. On the one hand, he wants to show English royalists that Whig consent theory is not as atomistic as Filmer's Tory apologists would like to present it. The central importance of the family in Tyrrell's consent theory goes far in this direction. On the other hand, Tyrrell's emphasis on the multiple compacts culminating in political society suggests that his other, perhaps more theoretical, concern is to show his decisive break from the central tenets of Christian Aristotelianism. Tyrrell's assessment of the need to view political society in terms of the progression of compacts that form it denies the Aristotelian claim for the naturalness of political society. In contrast to Bellarmine, Suarez, or even Grotius, Tyrrell never refers to political society as a "perfect association" or "mystical union." By maintaining the multiplicity of compacts, he reinforces the notion of the contractual character of politics while simultaneously defending the family as the basic unit of association. In Tyrrell's moderate Whig version of natural law, human beings appear to be naturally social – in the sense of being familial – but citizenship is definitely contrived.

What, then, is political society? And what precisely is the character of the compact that produces it? Tyrrell indicates that the compact that forms political society differs from the other layers of association in that it is only the political compact that can form a duly recognized sovereign power. Tyrrell argues that the participants in the political compact engage in "the submission of the Wills that institute it to the Will of him on whom they confer it" in order to make use of "all their Powers for the common good."[58] Although the same natural law principle of concern for the common good operates in the political compact as in the familial and social compacts, the former differs from the latter two in that only the political compact can generate legislation in the proper sense.

The political compact differs from the other compacts in that it alone is capable of creating a sovereign political authority capable of making and enforcing civil legislation. Neither the father nor the clan leader can exercise sovereignty in the full sense. In order to confront Filmer's providentialist account of the operation of political sovereignty, Tyrrell articulates the profoundly conventional and hence decidedly human character of sovereignty. His major criticism of Filmer is that his divine right treatment of sovereign power is at once highly abstract and yet strangely somatic. Tyrrell states that sovereignty is not included among human beings' natural powers or faculties, as it is "not any physical but a moral Quality." As such, it can be produced in another human being only through compact. As a purely conventional thing, it is "absurd to alledge, that Soveraignty is not derived from men."[59] Tyrrell discloses the absurdity of Filmer's position in the following terms: Filmer conceives of sovereignty "as an abstracted

[58] PNM: 117.
[59] Ibid.

Ems, or Physical Quality, which is immediately produced by God, and conferred upon the Soveraign at his Election or Declaration."[60] In response, Tyrrell proffers a number of searching queries. Where does this "abstracted Soveraignty" exist before it finds a "King to settle upon"? Is this abstracted sovereignty "a Substance or an Accident"? If the latter, can it "subsist without its Subject"? And when was it created? Perhaps most importantly, he asks, is there "one single Soul of Soveraignty diffused all over" the world to animate kings?

Tyrrell's central aim is to flesh out an understanding of the relationship between the law of nature and the unique human capacity to generate sovereign political institutions through compact. The question this relationship inevitably reintroduces is that of God's relation to human beings. Although Tyrrell maintains unequivocally the proposition that political sovereignty has a human source, he concedes:

> I will not deny that God is properly the original and efficient Cause of Soveraignty as of all good things, and particularly of that Power whereby every individual Freeman in the state of Nature, hath a power to dispose of his actions for his own preservation and the common good of mankind.[61]

Tyrrell immediately checks the theological tenor of this statement with his reaffirmation that "the particular powers of many men being put together, constitute that which we call a Politick or Civil Power." Nonetheless, Tyrrell leaves unclear the precise role of God, "the Supreme Lawgiver," in the formation of political society. While Tyrrell argues that human beings were given reason by God principally for "the constitution of Civil Government," he also maintains that "God hath not imposed upon any People an absolute Obligation of constituting any Civil Government at all, if they can live without it."[62] In one fell swoop, Tyrrell reaffirms the divine sanction behind the natural law while simultaneously carving out a field for free human choice in the institution of government, especially given the possibilities that arise "if they can live without it." This is, of course, a portentous "if" that requires further examination.

Tyrrell's response to this dilemma is that curious mixture of political theory and amateur anthropology that characterizes the Pufendorfian notion of the state of nature.[63] He suggests the possibility of society without sovereignty – the notion that individual natural rights need not necessitate

---

[60] See PNM: 118–19 for this and the following passage. It is interesting to note that Tyrrell lifts this critique of Filmer almost verbatim from Pufendorf's critique of the German divine rightist Friedrich Horn, who made an argument very similar to that of Filmer (see DJNG 7.3.4).

[61] PNM: 119.

[62] PNM: 119–20.

[63] For the important historical dimension in Pufendorf's state of nature account, see Hont, "Sociability and Commerce," pp. 256–7, 263–5.

the dichotomy of anarchy or political society – by pointing to the example of "the West Indians, in several parts of America," who live socially but not politically. Of these "Carribes," Tyrrell says, "they have lived many Ages without any common Power to keep them at peace amongst themselves; . . . and so they could live together without any other Government than that of the Fathers of Families over their Wives and Children." Despite lacking any common power to check the excesses occasioned by glory-seeking individuals or even the simple fear of one's fellow human beings, Tyrrell states that these Caribbes "have much fewer Crimes committed amongst them than us."[64] The key to the possibility of society without sovereignty is property, or rather the lack of substantial property holdings.

Though Tyrrell's treatment of the Caribbes serves the purpose of illustrating his theory of multiple compacts and layers of association that compose political society, its deeper purpose has to do with an elaboration of the complex connection between property and government. The Caribbes lack recognized civil power but they also coexist with "no distinct propriety in Land." As such, Tyrrell continues, "one of the main ends of a supreme power among us, *viz.* to decide Controversies about Property, and punish Thieves, are there of no use."[65] Tyrrell's understanding of the state of nature, then, reflects a central agreement with Grotius as to the origin of political society. Like Grotius, Tyrrell considers that the simple needs and tastes of a people little developed in the arts obviates the need for civil rule.[66] What small holdings the Caribbes possess, such as "their little Gardens, and Cabins," they enjoy "by a tacite consent." Lacking the need to generate the formal political institutions required to secure the mine–thine distinction in more advanced and prosperous societies marked by increasingly large property holdings, this tacit consent can accommodate a minimal level of social existence and cooperation. In contradistinction to Grotius, however, Tyrrell never identifies political society as a "perfect association" having its origins in the protection of property but pointing beyond this to a higher end in the development of human rationality and virtue. Tyrrell quite explicitly contends that God gave human beings reason in order to decide when and whether to form political societies. As such, Tyrrell's moderate Whig articulation of the possibility of a social state of nature both rejects Hobbes' sharp distinction between the state of nature and political society and resists Grotius' tendency to justify civil government on grounds more elevated than the protection of property.

---

[64] PNM: 121. Cf. Julia Rudolph, *Revolution by Degrees: James Tyrrell and Whig Political Thought in the Late Seventeenth Century* (New York: Palgrave, 2002): pp. 35–8 and Martyn P. Thompson, *Ideas of Contract in English Political Thought in the Age of John Locke* (New York: Garland, 1987): pp. 240–1, 251–2.

[65] PNM: 120–1.

[66] Tyrrell (PNM: 120) emphasizes the simplicity of Caribbe life – "they never have any superfluities" – and in this sense agrees with Grotius that the small holdings of these people reduce the need for political society.

Tyrrell leaves little doubt as to the profound connection between the security of property and the purpose of government.

The most conspicuous feature of Tyrrell's account of the origin of property is his argument for the original common. In rejecting the Filmerian logic of Adam's unique title to property, Tyrrell maintains that Eve and her children "had as much right to their lives as Adam had himself."[67] Their right to property was natural and did not rely on the generosity or consent of Adam. But how, then, did they actually acquire a title to the property that they had a natural right to use for their preservation? Tyrrell's answer is twofold. First, he insists that the original community was one in a negative rather than a positive sense. It was a condition in which no one owned anything; rather than everyone had a title in everything. The latter Tyrrell calls "a sociable community of all things." In this Tyrrell explicitly corrects Filmer's misreading of Grotius' version of original community.[68] Tyrrell even iterates Grotius' use of Cicero's celebrated example of the seat in the public theater to illustrate the sensible and respected character of the negative community teaching. Second, Tyrrell's addition to the traditional teaching is his emphasis on both labor and occupancy as the means to remove something from the original common. The key problem he identifies with the positive community teaching is the principle that acquisition depends on the consent of all the others who use the vast, ordered natural whole. For Tyrrell, it is sensible to assume that by nature no one owned anything in particular, but it would be sheer madness to infer that "no man could have eat anything which another might not have pulled out of his mouth, pretending he could not eat without his leave, because he had a share in it."[69] The requirement of the consent of all commoners for the use right of any individual would have resulted in mass starvation. Tyrrell's aim here is to demonstrate that the original claim to property emphatically did not rely on consent because such a condition would both frustrate "Gods first command to man [which] was, encrease and multiply" and constitute a denial of the individual's natural "right to the means of his preservation."[70] Hence, positive community would be impious as well as irrational and unnatural.

In Tyrrell's understanding of negative community, occupancy and labor replace consent or express divine donation as the original basis of property. He argues that a "Propriety of occupancy or the personal possession of things and applying to the needs of one or more men while they have need of it" is perfectly consistent with and indeed is "absolutely necessary to the preservation of Mankind." By labor too, Tyrrell asserts, an individual can have

[67] PNM: 102*.
[68] PNM: 99*. For this reason I believe Tully (*Discourse on Property*, p. 178) has mistakenly construed Tyrrell to mean community in the positive sense. See PNM: 108–9*.
[69] PNM: 109*.
[70] PNM: 100*.

"acquired such a proportion of either as would serve the necessities of him-self, and family, they become so much his own, as that no man could without manifest injustice rob him of these necessities of life."[71] The principal feature of Tyrrell's negative community, and that which makes it consistent with his larger natural law teaching, is the duty of abstention. Like Grotius before him, Tyrrell includes a negative duty to abstain from taking the goods of others as the "first principle of natural Justice."[72] To this extent, Tyrrell characterizes the sociableness commanded by the natural law essentially by the negative duty of respecting what belongs to others, not by a positive duty to give what one has of one's own.[73] Yet despite this appeal to a natural duty of abstaining, the signal element of Tyrrell's teaching on property is his insistence that while labor or occupancy can generate, however tenuously, the mine–thine distinction that ought to be respected, it is primarily through compact that the right to property produces a moral effect on all parties.

Tyrrell's defense of the Grotian account of the origin of property against Filmer's attack veils his own modification of Grotian natural law theory. While Tyrrell openly endorses Grotius' notion of the original negative com-munity in opposition to Filmer's donation thesis, he also introduces an anthropo-historical approach to the state of nature, which is alien to Grotius' thought. After having defended the possibility of negative community, Tyrrell declares that neither community nor propriety is simply natural or unnatural. He explains:

I will not take upon me to maintain what Grotius asserts, that after property was once introduced, it was against the law of nature to use community, since neither community, nor property are by the absolute law of nature.[74]

Tyrrell's reasoning here requires some further elucidation. As we recall, Grotius maintained that after the institution of private property, this ar-rangement became an unalterable feature of the natural law and anyone who failed to respect the established proprietary right of another was in violation of that law. This argument predictably had driven Filmer into a veritable frenzy.

Tyrrell's positing of an "absolute law of nature," in contrast to the law of nature simply, introduces a deeply pragmatic or circumstantial element into his natural law teaching. For example, he argues that the natives in America exist in a state of negative community, whereas the European "planters" have introduced a proprietary right that must be respected by all. The thrust of Tyrrell's natural law teaching on property is the proposition that God has

---

[71] PNM: 99–100*.
[72] PNM: 110*.
[73] As Tully (*Discourse on Property*, p. 86) points out, this is also a feature of Pufendorf, DJGN 2.3.15.
[74] PNM: 113*.

"left it to the discretions of those several parcels of Mankind who agreed to live in civil society" whether or not to introduce property rights in land, depending on "their particular way of living, or common safety and interest."[75] The logic behind Tyrrell's argument reflects the much more utilitarian considerations in his view of natural law than in that of Grotius. The basis for the introduction of property, in Tyrrell's view, is not the unimpeachable character of the law of nature, but rather the socioeconomic circumstances of a people. In a "thinly peopled" country, where all the necessities of life are provided "by the Labour of the Inhabitants," there is no need for distinct propriety, while "where the People are more than the Country can well maintain from its own Products," private property rights become necessary to allow and encourage trade and commerce. Tyrrell confides "this is the true reason why there is an absolute necessity for a division of lands in Holland, but not so in Surinam."[76]

Tyrrell's modified Grotianism and the more utilitarian character of his law of nature reflect the profound theoretical influence of Pufendorf. Tyrrell's great debt to Pufendorf is seen in his use of the multiple compact theory. Tyrrell's argument that the natural law allows different peoples to use property or community – and indeed, the same people may alter their arrangement because of population change or natural disaster – allows greater scope for human agreement and decision than does the argument of Grotius. Just as Tyrrell's reliance on the notion of tacit consent to establish the contractual character of familial and nonpolitical communal life reveals a more Pufendorfian than Grotian influence, so too does Tyrrell's heavy emphasis on the contractual and hence alterable character of the property right.[77] Tyrrell's understanding of the multiple compacts that form the layers of association culminating in political society is closely connected to his teaching on property. What separates the political compact from the others is its explicit end, namely, the preservation of property. Although property exists prior to government by a right of occupancy or labor, Tyrrell insists that its effective security depends on "Government, one main aim of which is to maintain the Dominion or Property before agreed upon."[78] As we saw in Tyrrell's earlier example of the Caribbes, he envisions government principally as the institution devised by human beings to settle the disputes that inevitably arise with the expansion of holdings.

The final aspect of Tyrrell's modification of Grotius' teaching on property has to do with the issue of labor. Previously, we saw that Tyrrell held both labor and occupancy as means to separate a thing from the common.

---

[75] PNM: 112–13*. Cf. DJGN 4.4.1.

[76] PNM: 113–14*.

[77] Tully, *Discourse on Property*, pp. 88–9 and Zuckert, *Natural Rights*, pp. 251–2. Cf. Rudolph, *Revolution by Degrees*, pp. 46–50 for Tyrrell's indebtedness to Pufendorf for his ideas on property.

[78] PNM: 116*.

Yet his heavy emphasis on the need for compact to establish property on a secure moral plane suggests that while Tyrrell views both labor and occupancy as ways to refute the idea of positive community, neither alone can establish property right in the full sense. Tyrrell never denies the profound negative duty of individuals to abstain from taking the goods produced or the land improved by another's labor, but the precise role labor plays in the formation of property for Tyrrell is left ambiguous. This ambiguity has caused considerable debate among scholars.[79] While it is correct to observe the ambiguous character of Tyrrell's position on labor, this ambiguity is not one Tyrrell, at least intentionally, leaves unresolved. It appears that Tyrrell's connecting labor with occupancy may amount to something like a use right. It is undeniable that Tyrrell extends labor to the possession of land, but for him labor only confirms an individual's property in what he may rightfully possess: "since the owner hath possessed himself of this land, and bestowed his Labor and Industry upon it," no other individual can claim it.[80] We must resist the temptation to exaggerate the Lockean undertones in Tyrrell's view of labor. One way to assess the genuine role of labor in Tyrrell's account of property is to locate it in the context of his broader natural rights and natural law teaching. Despite the professed importance of labor in the formation of property rights, Tyrrell adds the significant qualification that the "natural Propriety in things much less, that which is introduced by Law, or common consent, cannot exclude the natural right every man hath to his own preservation, and the means thereof." Thus, Tyrrell's natural law commands that each individual proprietor leave as much and as good for others.

In contrast to Locke, Tyrrell does not overturn this limitation on appropriation with the introduction of money and political society. On the contrary, Tyrrell affirms explicitly that all human compacts assume this natural right: "therefore this right of self preservation is still supposed in all humane compacts, or laws about the division, and distribution of things."[81] In this sense, Tyrrell follows Pufendorf and Grotius in stressing that human agreement must embody the social imperative animating the natural law that designates the assignment of things for the common advantage of human society.[82] Yet Tyrrell also follows Pufendorf's critique of Grotius on the issue

---

[79] For example, Tuck (*Natural Rights Theories*, p. 171) argues that Tyrrell's position here in what he calls "the Lockean subsection" of the book is practically identical to that of Locke. Ashcraft, on the other hand, argues that Tyrrell's reliance on both a Lockean-type labor argument and a Pufendorfian or Grotian idea of occupancy as the source of property rights reflects a theoretical incoherence that Tyrrell never fully works out. I agree with Ashcraft that Tyrrell's moderate Whig property account uses both a labor and an occupancy argument (and thus is not thoroughly Lockean), although I do not believe he is incoherent.

[80] PNM: 112*. See also Laslett's very helpful footnote at II:32 of his edition of Locke's *Two Treatises*.

[81] PNM: 110–11*.

[82] Zuckert, *Natural Rights*, p. 254. Cf. Pufendorf, DJNG 4.4.4.

of the relation of natural rights to property. Pufendorf's famous criticism of Grotius was that the proposition of the first seizure right of things violated the principle of natural equality.[83] Pufendorf and Tyrrell argue that all individuals have an equal right to necessary goods, but the seizure right offers no natural principle of distribution consistent with this natural right. Thus, before the institution of government individuals could conceivably starve, being excluded from the goods seized by others. This, of course, would violate the natural law principle enjoining the preservation of humanity. This presumption seems to animate Tyrrell's admission of something very nearly approaching a natural theft right in extreme circumstances. Ultimately, it is only compact that promises some principle of distribution that does not prejudice natural equality.

How, then, does Tyrrell harmonize his assertion of a right to take another's goods "without the owners consent" with the broader aims of his natural law teaching directed to social peace?[84] The persistence of natural rights in any human compact holds anarchic possibilities that are not difficult to imagine. We should keep in mind that Tyrrell has no intention of advancing "leveling notions" concerning property. In fact, one clear intention of his work is to show that the divine right idea that all property is subject to the crown is more dangerous to property rights than constitutionalism.[85] The moderating element in Tyrrell's justification of a theft right is his stipulation that it be respected only "in case of extream necessity" and if the taker intends to restore the goods later.[86] In this way, Tyrrell suppresses the radical potential of this idea by locating it in the broader framework of his natural law teaching. The law of nature may sanction subsistence for all, but Tyrrell does not envision it as a threat to property or as a justification for leveling.

For all practical purposes, Tyrrell's insistence on an extreme necessity provision in the law of nature reflects something more akin to Pufendorf's concept of the duties of humanity than any radical confiscation right.[87] These duties, which we saw Tyrrell employ earlier to moderate despotic power over slaves, are defined by Pufendorf as reflecting a kind of imperfect as opposed to a perfect right. In Pufendorf's understanding, the difference between these two forms of rights is one of degree rather than of kind. Whereas perfect rights relate to the "very being" of society seen in such things as the protection of property, imperfect rights relate to a society's "well-being." The latter refer to what one is due by stipulation of the natural law and not to what is one's

---

[83] Two good discussions of Pufendorf's critique of Grotius are Tully, *Discourse on Property*, pp. 86–8 and Zuckert, *Natural Rights*, pp. 250–4. Tyrrell does not, however, offer a detailed treatment of the three levels of compact. Compare this with Pufendorf, DJNG 4.4.5–8.

[84] PNM: 111*.

[85] PNM: Preface 1 and Ashcraft, *Revolutionary Politics*, p. 251.

[86] PNM: 111*.

[87] See DJNG Book II, ch. 6, "On the Right and Privilege of Necessity." See especially secs. 1, 2, and 4 dealing with the extreme necessity theft right.

own; as such, they indicate but do not require the performance of a duty.[88] Although Tyrrell never denies a universal "right to the necessities of life," he does not make the satisfaction of this right an absolute duty on the part of others or even of government; rather, he indicates that this aim would be one of any well-ordered society. Moreover, Tyrrell never appeals to Scripture or the tenets of Christianity to justify charity. Scripture is conspicuously absent in this account of the origin of property. Once again, it appears that utility rather than piety, and a combination of natural rights and certain natural law duties and obligations, animate Tyrrell's discussion of the political and moral implications of the deep underlying connection between government and property.

---

[88] Tully, *Discourse on Property*, p. 90 and Pufendorf, DJNG 2.6.6.

5

The Pufendorfian Moment

Moderate Whig Sovereignty Theory

Although he was a committed Whig and an ardent opponent of Stuart pretensions to arbitrary rule, Tyrrell's philosophical and constitutional position displays an abiding moderation. Moderate Whigs like Tyrrell did not advocate dramatic constitutional reform in England. He is careful to emphasize that a rejection of divine right absolutism does not amount to an endorsement of popular sovereignty or democracy. He openly professes his admiration for monarchy, calling it "that Government which tempered by known Laws, I take to be the best in the world."[1] Tyrrell distances himself from the radical parliamentary position in "the late unhappy times" of the English civil war, and even concedes that Filmer's arguments may have been defensible in the cause of preserving the "then Majesties lawful and just Rights" against the "domineering faction" that seized rule and the "divers levelling notions then too much in fashion."[2] Tyrrell suggests that Filmer's extreme arguments were a typical feature of a turbulent time. He presents his own moderate Whig argument as a mean between the two extremes of lawlessness reflected in the Scylla and Charibdes represented by divine right absolutism and unchecked parliamentary democracy. As a defender of "Government establisht by law," Tyrrell pits himself against the common desire of both divine rightists and extreme parliamentarians "to alter that Government, and give up those Privileges which their Ancestors were so careful to preserve and deliver down to Posterity."[3] Tyrrell suggests that whatever may have

---

[1] James Tyrrell, *Patriarcha, Non Monarcha* (London, 1681): Preface, p. 1 (hereafter PNM and page number). The moderate character of Tyrrell's Whiggism has been noted before. See James Daly, *Sir Robert Filmer and English Political Thought* (Toronto: University of Toronto Press, 1979): p. 9; Caroline Robbins, *The Eighteenth Century Commonwealthmen* (New York: Atheneum, 1968): p. 73; and Julia Rudolph, *Revolution by Degrees: James Tyrrell and Whig Political Thought in the Late Seventeenth Century* (New York: Palgrave, 2002). To this effect, the frontispiece of the 1681 edition of PNM bore a flattering likeness of Charles II.

[2] PNM: Preface 1.

[3] PNM: Preface 3.

been the vast theoretical and philosophical differences between the commonwealthmen and the divine rightists, they shared one central premise: the argument that the English Constitution understood as a constitutional monarchy framed by legal limits must be rejected.[4]

Tyrrell's explicit aim, then, in *Patriarcha, Non Monarcha* was to defend England's "Ancient Government," which he calls "the best in its kind," from two opponents; the divine rightists like Filmer, who want to remove "all Limits between Prerogative and Law," and the commonwealthmen, who want "to set up a Democracy amongst us."[5] The root of Tyrrell's argument in this defense of limited government is the notion of natural liberty. He is one of the first English thinkers to appeal to a modern notion of natural rights and natural law to *defend*, rather than criticize, the basic structures and institutions of the English regime. Prior to Tyrrell, the most conspicuous English proponents of natural rights had been among the English Constitution's most conspicuous opponents.[6] Tyrrell defends the "Ancient Government" of England in an emphatically new way, on the novel ground of individual rights and a secularized law of nature. In this way, Tyrrell aims to provide a rational foundation for the English regime that can resist the claims of absolute monarchy and extreme democracy more successfully than arguments drawn from history, classical philosophy, Christian Aristotelianism, or the parliamentary theories of the civil war era.

The final piece, then, of Tyrrell's moderate Whig puzzle, after his statement of the character of the natural law and the origins of property and government, is his idea of sovereignty. Here, as in the rest of his argument, Tyrrell is deeply influenced by Pufendorf. The moderate Whig understanding of the constitutional sovereignty of the king-in-Parliament rested on the

---

[4] While an in-depth treatment of the philosophical arguments of the Commonwealthmen is beyond the scope of the present study, it should be noted that many of the more democratic elements in the civil war era expressed deep dissatisfaction with the English Constitution as historically understood. At the Putney Debates, Captain John Clarke expressed the need for England to alter the "principal fundamental constitution that it now has" (see Clarke in *The English Levellers*, Andrew Sharp, ed. [Cambridge: Cambridge University Press, 1998]: p. 128). John Wildman went further, remonstrating that "our very laws were made by our conquerors" (see Wildman, quoted in H. N. Brailsford, *The Levellers and the English Revolution* [Stanford, CA: Stanford University Press, 1961]: p. 282).

[5] Tyrrell frames this dichotomy with the memorable statement "I know not which is worst, to be knawn to death by Rats, or devoured by a Lion" (PNM: Preface 5).

[6] As we have seen in chapter 3 Hobbes rejected the mixed or limited Constitution on emphatically natural rights grounds. At the opposite end of the political spectrum, the Leveller Richard Overton appealed to something very much like the natural rights of the individual as the root of all government, but drew from this a radical supremacy in the Commons that is antithetical to Tyrrell's understanding of the English Constitution (see "An Arrow against all Tyrants" in Sharp, *English Levellers*, pp. 55, 57, 62). See also *The Leveller Tracts: 1647–1653*, William Haller and Godfrey Davis, eds. (New York: Columbia University Press, 1944): pp. 35–7 and Theodore Calvin Pease, *The Leveller Movement* (Gloucester, MA: Peter Smith, 1965): pp. 23–7.

Pufendorfian argument for the necessity of one legally constituted supreme power in a regularized constitutional order. The moderate Whig conception of the English Constitution advanced by Tyrrell would be in essence an adaptation of Pufendorfian philosophical principles to the historical conditions of English constitutional development in the seventeenth century.

Defending Grotius and Hunton

Tyrrell begins his account of sovereignty with the observation that he hopes to prove the existence of "such a kind of Government as a limited Kingdom."[7] To support this claim, he draws heavily on the arguments of Filmer's main opponents on the issue of sovereignty, Grotius and Hunton. Tyrrell argues that Grotius' account of the "three ways whereby Supreme Power may be had" can be very well defended against Filmer "in most things..., though not in all."[8] Like Filmer himself, Tyrrell largely ignores Grotius' argument for a temporary right of supreme power and focuses on the means of acquiring supreme power with full right and with a usufructuary right. The thrust of Tyrrell's defense of Grotius on this issue is to refute Filmer's contention that Grotius ostensibly holds out the possibility of a full right of supreme power in the monarch while actually undermining any such possibility. Tyrrell states that the cause of Filmer's confusion is his desire to claim for "all Usurpers whatever to have a right, whether by Conquest or otherwise, which Grotius will not."[9] Tyrrell thus adduces Grotius as the defender of legitimacy in contrast to Filmer, the patron of usurpers and rebels. With regard to the full right by just war, Tyrrell follows Grotius' lead in asserting that if a just conqueror had only "limited Power" before losing power, he cannot return to gain absolute power. In this oblique reference to the restoration of Charles II, whose return in 1661 could be construed as a very mild form of conquest and who was the ruling monarch at the time, Tyrrell affirms that such a just conqueror "could be restored to no more than the Constitution of the Government will allow him."[10]

Tyrrell's defense of Grotius' notion of the usufructuary right of supreme power is more spirited than his treatment of full right. As we recall, Filmer detested this notion of sovereign right because it signaled a people's right to establish a constitutional order by which a monarch ruled supreme but was limited by certain fundamental prescriptions.[11] Noting that Filmer held the

---

7 PNM: 128*.
8 PNM: 117*.
9 PNM: 118*.
10 PNM: 117*.
11 Filmer scornfully argued that this arrangement, which made the people the owners and the king the tenant of the kingdom's ruling office, was to make "a kingdom all one with a farm" (Robert Filmer, *Patriarcha and Other Writings*, Johann Somerville, ed. [Cambridge: Cambridge University Press, 1991]: p. 232).

usage usufructuary right "too base to express the Right of Kings," Tyrrell
counters that "the French are not so scrupulous"; even in the "absolutest
Monarchy in Europe," they understand their monarch's title in these terms.
In holding his title by usufructuary right, the French king cannot charge his
territories "with his debts, or alienate, or dispose of them... without the
consent of the States of France." Moreover, this understanding of monarchical title extends also to England, for as Tyrrell asserts, King John had
"no Power to make this Kingdom feudatory, and tributary to the Pope."[12]
Nor could he "have made over his Kingdom to the Emperor of Morocco."
Tyrrell's intention here is to reinforce his argument that no fundamental constitutional changes may be made in a limited monarchy without the assent
of the people's representatives in the estates and assemblies.

Of particular interest in the context of the Exclusion crisis is Tyrrell's extension of the principle of usufructuary right to the issue of succession. The
argument that the people may devise a constitutional arrangement whereby
a monarch exercises supreme power without absolute propriety holds serious implications for the English succession dispute. Tyrrell argues that the
succession laws agreed to by the people and estates cannot be changed without their consent. As such, a king's testament does not bear the power to
ensure a claimant's inheritance. As evidence, Tyrrell cites the testaments of
Henry VIII and Edward VI, which disinherited "the line of Scotland" and
Edward's sisters, respectively, but were invalid because "the Loyal Subjects
of England believed that neither of those Kings could disinherit the right Heir
to the Crown by their Testaments alone." The succession of Queen Mary
and King James occurred despite "those pretended wills."[13] It is important to
note two things in Tyrrell's argument. First, in denying monarchs a unilateral
right of determining succession, Tyrrell does not advance one for the great
popular assemblies either. Second, Tyrrell implies that kings who do rule by
absolute proprietary right would be able to name anyone heir on their own
volition.

In denying the capacity of one element of a multiple-bodied constitutional
order to unilaterally determine succession, Tyrrell is, on the one hand, simply offering a realistic appraisal of the English situation in terms consistent
with moderate Whiggism. Very few people in the England of 1679 wanted a
return to the days of 1649. But Tyrrell also uses this opportunity to express
his disagreement with Grotius. Tyrrell refers to the succession issue, at least
partly, in order to express the position that "I will not affirm with Grotius
*That the Empire which is exercised by Kings, doth not cease to be the Empire of
the People.*"[14] In contrast to Grotius, Tyrrell argues that once a people have

---

[12] PNM: 122*, 124*.
[13] PNM: 125*.
[14] PNM: 126*. See also Hugo Grotius, *De Jure Belli ac Pacis Libri Tres* (Oxford: Clarendon Press,
1925): 2.16.16.1 (hereafter DJB) and Filmer, *Patriarcha*, p. 233.

consented to monarchical rule, they agree to obey it and cannot alter the succession "as long as there is a lawful Heir remaining and succeeding in his right." Tyrrell's Pufendorfian understanding of the natural law obligations informing human sociality produces a highly conservative notion of consent that commits the individual to support the continuation of the Constitution in its existing form. Thus, Tyrrell can affirm with Grotius that a king by full right holds sovereignty and hence cannot be punished by a higher power while simultaneously rejecting Grotius' argument that a usufructuary right remains the "Empire of the People." Tyrrell accepts that sovereignty is required to secure the political compact, but in a constitutional order the purpose of such sovereignty is to secure the constitutional process.[15] As such, not the people but rather the institutions of government may reclaim the power over succession when the king dies without an heir. Moreover, even Parliament can exercise this power only to restore the existing constitutional order. In this respect, Tyrrell's moderate Whiggism is even more conservative than that of Grotius.

Tyrrell's moderate Whiggism also draws important parallels with the parliamentary argument of the civil war period. He agrees with these earlier proponents of the natural liberty doctrine regarding the legal limits that may be placed on royal power. In such things as an original contract, the act of after condescent, and even in the coronation oath, Tyrrell identifies legal and institutional devices consistent with Hunton's idea of restraints on monarchical power.[16] Both Tyrrell and Hunton, for example, agree that political society is the product of a compact originally instituted by the people. What separates them, however, is Tyrrell's insistence that limited monarchy is superior both to absolute rule and to mixed monarchy. Hunton, of course, had endorsed the validity of mixed monarchy particularly in relation to England.[17] In contrast to the parliamentary contractarianism of an earlier generation, Tyrrell's preference for limited monarchy shows the profound influence of continental natural law theory. It is primarily Tyrrell's understanding of the Pufendorfian distinction between regular and irregular regimes that informs his defense of a monarchy resting on legal limits. For Pufendorf, the two major sources of irregularity in a constitution – the two elements most likely to produce instability and to frustrate the ends of government – are absolute

---

[15] PNM: 126*.

[16] PNM: 139–41 for after condescent and 159–60 for oaths. Tyrrell's treatment of the importance of oaths closely follows Pufendorf's account in Samuel Pufendorf, *De Jure Naturae et Gentium Libri Octo* (Oxford: Clarendon Press, 1934): bk. 7, ch. 6, sec. 10 (hereafter DJNG bk., ch., sec., and page number where applicable).

[17] Despite Tyrrell's objections to mixed regime theory in *Patriarcha, Non Monarcha*, he seems more open to viewing England as having a mixed Constitution in his later *Bibliotheca Politica*. See James Tyrrell, *Bibliotheca Politica* (London, 1718): dialogue 7 and John Gough, "James Tyrrell, Whig Historian and Friend of John Locke." *The Historical Journal*, vol. 19, no. 3, (1976): 602.

power and mixed power.[18] Both of these elements of irregularity are foci of criticism for Tyrrell. He maintains that a mixed body of sovereign power obscures the legitimate need for supremacy, hence inviting disorder and turmoil, while absolute power subjects the government to the vagaries of an individual's or group's passions, with equally destructive consequences. Tyrrell maintains that both the principle of mixture and the principle of absoluteness make it impossible to preserve the formal structures of rule and to restrain the abuse of power.

Tyrrell's concern with the problem of absolute power is a theme running through the moderate Whig account of sovereignty. One of Tyrrell's purposes in *Patriarcha, Non Monarcha* was to counteract Filmer's attempt to take "away all distinction between Kings and Tyrants, and between Slaves and Subjects." In fact, the primary intention of Tyrrell's critique of Filmer's observations on Aristotle is to reassert the traditional distinction between tyranny and monarchy.[19] Yet Tyrrell does not do this to endorse the classical Aristotelian regime typology. Rather, he reveals the innovative element of his thought by criticizing ancient republican Rome not in terms of the classical categories but in terms of its "irregularity," a term employed by Pufendorf and alien to the Aristotelian schema of regimes.[20] The key problem Tyrrell identifies with absolute power is the vagaries of the human passions. Tyrrell counts himself a "defender of the Government establisht by Law" because the subjection of all people to the will of one inevitably leads to the abuse of power. Absolute monarchy, Tyrrell proclaims, would be an admirable form of rule "could humane nature long be trusted with it." On this basis, Tyrrell reaches a remarkable conclusion:

The fault is not in the Government as absolute, but in humane Nature, which is not often found sufficient, at least for above one or two Successions, to support and manage so unlimited a Power in one single person as it ought to be.[21]

Thus, to some extent, Tyrrell grounds his defense of limited monarchy and constitutional government on the unreliability of securing rule by virtuous kings. This suspicion of the human possibility of acquiring virtue and controlling the passions firmly locates Tyrrell's moderate Whig thought in the larger school of modern constitutionalism identified with Montesquieu or the authors of the *Federalist Papers*. For Tyrrell, the legal structures produced by compact are the chief safeguards to liberty.

---

[18] For a succinct statement of Pufendorf's concern with constitutional irregularity, see Samuel Pufendorf, *On the Duty of Man and Citizen*, James Tully, ed. (Cambridge: Cambridge University Press, 1991): p. 144.

[19] PNM: Preface p. 2, and pp. 129–30.

[20] Tyrrell shows his departure from conventional Aristotelian regime analysis by calling ancient Rome "the most unequal and irregular" commonwealth in history (PNM: 135).

[21] PNM: Preface p. 3. See also, Tyrrell's quotation from Juvenal on Preface p. 4.

The rejection of absolute monarchical power as the ordering principle of government does not, however, constitute a denial of the validity of supremacy per se. Tyrrell maintains that supremacy is required in any constitutional order because of the need for one recognized power to secure the terms of the political compact. The contractual origins of government in the consent of individuals, even if only of family heads, requires such a ruling common power to bind the disparate elements of the polity to the terms of the original agreement.[22] In a limited monarchy such supremacy would obviously rest with the monarch. Tyrrell's aim is to harmonize the notion of supremacy with the principle of legal limitation. Filmer and Hobbes had denounced this possibility as antithetical to the very essence of political power. In his attempt to defend the proposition that a political compact formed by individuals could indeed establish a monarchy with legal limits, Tyrrell makes a crucial concession to Filmer and Hobbes. In open disagreement with Hunton, Tyrrell confesses that a constitution may limit a sovereign's power but cannot actually restrain it.[23] In this the moderate Whigs followed the authority of Pufendorf, who famously argued that because "sovereignty is supreme, that is, not dependent upon an superior man on earth, its acts cannot, for that reason be made void at the discretion of any other human being's will."[24] By this Tyrrell means that in a constitutional monarchy there can be no body with a coercive power over a king. Any body with such a coercive power would be in effect the supreme power in the constitutional order. What, then, does Tyrrell mean by legal limits if they do not signify a superior coercive power?

Tyrrell offers two suggestions. The first is that not a king, but rather his ministers, may be punished by the right of another legally constituted body.[25] This reliance on the distinction between royal infallibility and ministerial responsibility is augmented by the further argument that a people may compel a king to execute a law.[26] Noticeably, Tyrrell's examples of the actual operation of legal limits on supreme power do not result in his affirmation of a popular right of deposition. Tyrrell is more inclined to emphasize the moderate character of legal limits rather than their revolutionary potential. In keeping with the moderate tone of the discussion, Tyrrell moves to assuage the fears of royalists by denying Filmer's charge that legal limits on a king reduce him to a mere executive agent of a legislative principal. Tyrrell counters that from the principle of legal limitation, "it does not follow that in all laws where the Law governs the Monarch, he hath therefore but a Gubernative Power."[27] He insists that the constitutional monarch's source of power is

---

[22] PNM: 127–8*.
[23] PNM: 129*.
[24] Pufendorf, DJNG 7.6.1.
[25] PNM: 129*.
[26] PNM: 129–30*. Cf. Daniel XIII.
[27] PNM: 130*.

independent of the legislature, and by so doing he rejects the principle of parliamentary supremacy in England.[28] Tyrrell maintains that "the King in a Limited Monarchy is he who alone gives the Essence and Authority to the Laws." This is true, Tyrrell continues, even if the king can make no other laws "than what are offered him in the Assembly of his Estates."[29] Thus, in Tyrrell's view, it is the constitutional provision requiring royal assent that guarantees monarchical supremacy, not the sole possession of the executive *and* legislative functions. Nonetheless, despite the diminished majesty of Tyrrell's conception of a limited monarch, it should be noted that he is also at pains to distance such a ruler from the direct supervision of the legislative body. The argument for monarchical independence, at least in principle, acts as a limit on the power of the more popular forces in the constitutional order. This reflects Tyrrell's moderate Whig concern to limit the destabilizing and irregularizing tendency of absolute power in both its regal and popular forms.

Tyrrell's indebtedness to Pufendorf is most pronounced in his rejection of the principle of mixed sovereignty. Tyrrell raises his objections to mixed regime theory by explicitly criticizing Hunton. He reveals: "I shall not defend Mr. H's opinion, when he saith that in a mixed Monarchy, the Soveraign Power must be originally in all the three Estates, or that the three Estates are all sharers of the Supream Power." To defend his rejection of the mixed regime theory of Hunton and Charles I, Tyrrell appeals to the authority of "what Mr. Pufendorf hath said in that excellent work *de Jure nature et Gentium.*" It is on the basis of this authority that Tyrrell expresses his opinion that

[t]he Supream Power cannot well be divided into several shares, since there is so great a conjunction between all the parts of Soveraign power, that one part cannot be separated from the other, but it will spoil the regular form of the Government; and set up an Irregular Commonwealth, which will scarce be able to hold well together.[30]

The source of this irregularity is the inability to locate the supreme punishing power within the constitutional system. This was a theoretical difficulty that civil war era thinkers were unable to resolve except by recourse to the contest of arms and the judgment of the community expressed through civil war. Inasmuch as Tyrrell affirms that a right of punishment can only proceed from a superior, then, by the logic of his argument, this right cannot reside in the people or their assembled representatives.

---

[28] Julian Franklin, *John Locke and the Theory of Sovereignty* (Cambridge: Cambridge University Press, 1978): pp. 90–1.

[29] PNM: 133*.

[30] PNM: 130–1*. Although Tyrrell also expresses his agreement with "Grotius' mind" on the evils of divided sovereignty, the passage he cites and the direction of his argument are taken from Pufendorf. Compare Pufendorf DJNG 4.7.9–13 and Grotius DJB 1.3.9.17.

The moderate Whig theoretical objection to the principle of mixed sovereignty reflects and is rooted in the Pufendorfian notion of compact. For Tyrrell, as for Pufendorf, the claim to sovereign right derives from the moral act of submission to a government constituted by contract and consent. The moral effect of political obligation can only arise from compact. As such, Tyrrell distinguishes the moral right of compulsion inhering in sovereign power from the physical act of compulsion evinced in war: "All compulsion is performed two ways, either morally, or Physically, that is by way of Soveraign Authority, or by force of Arms, or War."[31] The major theoretical implication of Tyrrell's distinction is his concern about the instability produced by the parliamentary contractarian idea of ascribing sovereign power to coequal branches of government. Moral compulsion proceeds from a superior confirmed by compact, whereas force of arms denotes equality. While Tyrrell denies that England is simply a mixed monarchy, he affirms the possibility, however undesirable, of establishing such a form of government. This must be read in light of Tyrrell's observation that Hunton's mixed regime theory was in fact typical of "the Opinions held during the late Wars."[32] By explicitly connecting Hunton's mixed regime theory with the turmoil of the civil war, Tyrrell implicitly points to a serious problem in the prevailing interpretation of the historical English Constitution. The failure of past generations of theorists to ground England's constitutional monarchy on a foundation of natural law, Tyrrell implies, has left it open to interpretations that introduce and justify elements of irregularity and instability in English constitutional theory and practice.

Tyrrell's effort to advance the principle of compact is seen most clearly in his treatment of the legal limitation produced by the original contract establishing a particular constitutional order. He attempts to prove that constitutional monarchy is the product of human agreement and not of simple antiquity or organic development.[33] In such a regime the monarch may be understood to rule as the supreme "fountain of Power in all his Dominions," though "obliged either by original contract, or by after promise, or condescent not to make any laws, or to levy any money, or taxes from his Subjects, but what they shall offer him in the Assembly of his Estates."[34] Tyrrell understands this limitation produced by original contract as more than

---

[31] PNM: 131–2*.

[32] PNM: 236 and Franklin, *John Locke*, p. 92.

[33] Although, as Pocock and Colbourn have observed, Tyrrell did make an effort, albeit an ancillary one, to defend the historical validity of limited monarchy against Filmer's charges (H. Trevor Colbourn, *The Lamp of Experience: Whig History and the Intellectual Origins of the American Revolution* [Chapel Hill: University of North Carolina Press, 1965]: p. 30 and Pocock, *The Ancient Constitution and the Feudal Law* [Cambridge: Cambridge University Press, 1987]: pp. 206, 213), he left most of the historical heavy lifting to his friend William Petyt.

[34] PNM: 133*.

merely procedural. He understands the compact producing a constitutional monarchy in these terms: "There must be some form, or rule agreed upon, both of making, and promulgating Laws." Tyrrell's statement that such an arrangement is "absolutely the best both for the Prince and People" implies his deeper natural law teaching that government must be conceived as more than simply an instrument to secure rights.[35] Moreover, this concern with defending the validity of legal processes and political forms also reflects Tyrrell's effort to refute Filmer's principle of natural subjection, which marked a denial of the human capacity to generate political institutions and conventions. For Tyrrell, a monarch may have an independent position of authority in a constitutional order, but he or she is not the ultimate source of that authority.

Tyrrell makes this point directly in his articulation of the importance of constitutional forms for the well-being of a legally established government. As he explains:

Though Forms are not essential to the declaring of the will of a private man in the state of nature, yet they must be in respect of . . . a Prince, since the power of the former is natural and can only influence those that hear him, but that of a Prince is artificial, or political as proceeding from compact.[36]

This passage once again demonstrates Tyrrell's indebtedness to Pufendorf. Tyrrell's understanding of the importance of political forms is derived from Pufendorf's theory of the fundamentally legal, as opposed to natural, character of political authority. It is the artificiality of political life that produces and validates constitutional processes and forms. The "private man in the state of nature" does not require a legal form to express his will because, not being party to a compact, his will can in no sense be legally binding on anyone else. Tyrrell's concern with political forms amounts to a defense of representation. The preservation of the principle of representation in the legislative process requires, in Tyrrell's view, that the supreme executive power not also possess the legislative power in toto. In Tyrrell's view, the very operation of representative government requires an articulation of powers best settled in the "original and fundamental constitution of the Government." Tyrrell's chief concern in this discussion is to expound the stabilizing and regularizing effects of constitutional forms on political society. As such, Tyrrell emphasizes the normative effect of the original contract by asserting that the principle of constitutionalism ensures that these vital political forms cannot be altered without the assent of all the duly constituted bodies established by the consent of the people. For moderate Whigs, history had decisively

---

[35] PNM: 134*. See also Richard Ashcraft (*Revolutionary Politics and Locke's Two Treatises of Government* [Princeton: Princeton University Press, 1986]: pp. 206, 213), who draws from this that Tyrrell sees absolute, unlimited monarchy as antithetical to civil society.

[36] PNM: 134*.

shown that parliamentary usurpation, no less than royal absolutism, was far from unimaginable in the English constitutional system.

Resistance and Prerogative

Lying in the background throughout much of the discussion of legal limits is the vexing question of resistance. The question of who decides when a king has broken the law and what measure of resistance is justified in this situation had plagued English constitutional theorists since even before the civil war. We have seen that the parliamentary radicals of the 1640s had not resolved the issue at any level of theoretical satisfaction. Tyrrell, the Cavalier Whig, tried to fashion a theory of resistance consistent with the moderate tenor of his natural law teaching. His discussion of justifiable resistance begins with a concession to the royalist argument that "no coactive power" can judge or punish a ruling sovereign.[37] In affirming that there can be no compulsory power operating over and above a king, Tyrrell rejects the principle of parliamentary supremacy in the Parkerian sense. The memory of the English public's rejection of that principle in the Restoration of 1660 fueled the caution of most Whigs on this matter. In large measure, Tyrrell's treatment of the delicate issue of resistance reflected a desire to avoid the revolutionary consequences of 1649 that grew out of the logic of parliamentary resistance in 1642.[38] Before we can fully grasp the moderate Whig position on resistance, it may be useful to briefly consider Tyrrell's view of prerogative.

Although Tyrrell frames the issue of resistance in terms of the distinction between prerogative and law, his strong support for legal limits does not result in a simple rejection of royal prerogative. The monarch is not a mere creature of the legislative assembly. Tyrrell sees the limiting character of law in its capacity to demarcate the areas in which a sovereign may freely act from those in which he or she may not. He describes the legal relation between king and subject as being characterized by "those Laws that are the boundaries between his Prerogatives, and the Peoples just Rights."[39] Tyrrell affirms that it may be good for a king "to dispense with" some laws, "yet only for the publick good, in cases of extreme necessity."[40] Although all prerogative is properly the king's alone, Tyrrell affirms that he is bound to exercise this power in accord with certain fundamental laws.[41] The question

---

[37] PNM: 153*.
[38] Franklin, *John Locke*, p. 90.
[39] PNM: Preface p. 1.
[40] Tyrrell's examples of manifestly unjust acts of prerogative would be a royal pardon for all murderers, the maintenance of a standing army, the confiscation of property, and a refusal to take the coronation oath (PNM: 138*, 155–6*).
[41] Franklin, *John Locke*, p. 92. Alan Craig Houston (*Algernon Sidney and the Republican Heritage in England and America* [Princeton University Press, 1991]: p. 194) points out that Tyrrell's acceptance of rather wide latitude for prerogative signals a serious disagreement with Sidney.

of who judges a king's actions and, perhaps more importantly, who is in the legal position to punish unjust acts of prerogative is central to the moderate Whig treatment of resistance. Tyrrell's theory of resistance hinges on two concepts: his understanding of fundamental laws and his notion of natural rights. He considered fundamental laws as those with portentous bearing on the operation of free government. Unlike normal statute laws, Tyrrell asserts that fundamental laws are emphatically outside the scope of legitimate prerogative. Tyrrell repeats that these laws "can never be altered without the Consent of the King and the Estates."[42] Tyrrell's examples of the fundamental laws, whose transgression would threaten the integrity of the constitutional order, are succession laws, property rights, and the right of representative assemblies. In response to Filmer's challenge to Hunton to produce one example of a fundamental law, Tyrrell states that "the Crown upon the death of the King should descend to the next Heir, and so we have one Fundamental Law." Throughout the course of the discussion Tyrrell also points to the right in "Propriety in Goods and Lands and Estates of Inheritance" and the constitutional provision "ordering all publick affairs in General Councils or Assemblies of the Men of Note" as additional illustrations of the kinds of fundamental laws a people may devise and agree to.[43] It is noticeable that at least the latter two of these fundamental laws are explicitly related to the security of the subject's rights.

When Tyrrell turns to an examination of the fundamental laws particular to the historical English Constitution, there is a subtle shift in his catalog of conceivable fundamental laws. He identifies the "three great Liberties of the Subjects" of England as

[t]rial by a Mans equals, and absolute Propriety in Lands and Goods which the Kings could not justly take from them; and a Right to joyne in the making of all Laws, and raising Public Taxes, or Contributions for War.[44]

While the two more directly rights-securing laws regarding property and representative assemblies are present in both the hypothetical and the historically English list of fundamental laws, it is important to note Tyrrell's substitution of the English right of jury trial for the hypothetical succession law.[45] In so doing, Tyrrell emphasizes the individual rights-securing orientation of the English Constitution, as witnessed in his concern to highlight the importance of the jury trial. Moreover, Tyrrell suggests that one significant feature, and possible defect, of the historical English Constitution was its failure to clearly stipulate the acceptable means for the transmission of royal power through succession. At the very least, Tyrrell implies that the

---

[42] PNM: 230, 134-6*.
[43] PNM: 219, 221.
[44] PNM: 227.
[45] Franklin, *John Locke*, p. 114.

traditional understanding of the "great Liberties of the Subject" in England do not exhaust the possibilities for the establishment of fundamental laws.

Tyrrell's clearest statement of the connection between fundamental laws and justifiable resistance emerges in his defense of Hunton's position that if petitions fail to move a transgressing monarch,

> [t]hen the Fundamental Laws of that Monarchy must judge and pronounce sentence in every mans Conscience, and every man...must follow the Evidence of Truth and his own Sense, to oppose or not oppose according as he can in Conscience acquit or Condemn the Act of the Governour or Monarch.[46]

This appeal to individual conscience as the final arbiter pertaining to resistance reflects what Tyrrell calls a "moral power" inhering in individuals, which in turn grounds the right to refuse royal commands. As Tyrrell relates, "it would be our Crime, and we alone were punishable" for obeying a vicious or absurd royal command.[47] But how are we to understand this individual "moral power" and its relation to natural rights?

On the one hand, Tyrrell wants to demonstrate that the moral power that grounds his theory of resistance is a power and capacity natural to human beings. In contrast to the origin of sovereignty, this particular moral power is not the product of compact or the exclusive purview of a civil sovereign. In effect, Tyrrell attempts to inject a specific moral content into Hobbesian natural right by making it derivative from a natural law stipulating the requirements for peaceful association. For Tyrrell, unlike Hobbes, a right can be a right in the proper sense only if it is accompanied by a correlative moral duty. Herein lies Tyrrell's attempt to follow Pufendorf by synthesizing Hobbesian natural rights and Grotian natural law. Tyrrell aims to make the subjective right to self-preservation compatible with an objective law of nature governing human relations. Moreover, the moral content of this law is not derived from this right; rather, the right must be understood in terms of the duty the individual has to uphold the good of society.[48] By this means Tyrrell tries to assure moderate Whigs that an individual natural right to judge moral actions is not antithetical to the morally binding character of compact. He wants to preserve the importance of contract but still retain a fundamental layer of pre-civil individual natural rights. The means Tyrrell uses to avoid the absolutist implications of Hobbesian rights theory is to incorporate something very similar to Hobbesian natural rights into a law of nature denoting even a minimal moral order governing the state of nature.

---

[46] PNM: 217.

[47] PNM: 214–15. In this regard, I believe Rudolph is mistaken to suggest that Tyrrell does not have a teaching on resistance in PNM (*Revolution by Degrees*, p. 166). Rather, even in PNM he offers veiled threats to the king that the nation (i.e., the Parliament) can counter prerogative with a more fundamental power.

[48] Cf. Pufendorf, DJNG 3.5.3 and Richard Tuck, *Natural Rights Theories* (Cambridge: Cambridge University Press, 1979): pp. 156–60.

The Rejection of Popular Sovereignty

The moderate Whig compact theory of sovereignty follows Pufendorf in rejecting the doctrine of popular sovereignty, that is, the argument that sovereignty rests naturally in the people. The sovereign for Tyrrell is made by the people, who unanimously recognize one ruler or body as the supreme political power. They all agree to obey, or at least not obstruct, the sovereign in the execution of his, her, or its office. This is the Hobbesian core of Tyrrell's Pufendorfian moment. For Tyrrell, the sovereign power in the English Constitution is the king-in-Parliament. Tyrrell's concern to derive natural rights in some significant sense from a natural law governing human social existence has the consequence of making his theory much less radical than it might have been; in a sense, it has less radical implications even than that of Hobbes. For example, while Hobbes never holds individual resistance to civil authority morally blameworthy (at least on the ground of self-preservation), Tyrrell quite emphatically argues, à la Grotius, that the moral good reflected in civil peace should not be endangered by the unjust actions affecting individuals per se. Individuals are still, despite their claims to certain natural rights, in some sense fundamentally restricted in the exercise of those rights by the requirements of society as a whole.

Although Tyrrell defends an individual natural right to resist civil authority, he never directly affirms a general right of rebellion. He says: "The People though they do not argue so subtilly as our Author [Filmer] does, yet in their Sense of Feeling, when wrong'd or hurt, are seldome mistaken."[49] Although the general feeling of being wronged or treated unjustly by civil authority may serve to validate widespread popular resistance, Tyrrell rejects the idea that this act of rebellion leads to a dissolution of government. The prevailing tenor of Tyrrell's natural law theory and his concern to preserve the importance of compact signify the moderate Whigs' deep distrust of the radical notion of the dissolution of government.

Tyrrell's Pufendorfian moment culminates in his offering up to his readers an extended passage translated verbatim from Pufendorf's *De Jure Naturae et Gentium* as a kind of conclusion to his own work. Tyrrell prefaces this passage with a rehearsal of the main elements of Pufendorf's theoretical distinction between irregular and regular regimes. He appeals to the authority of "that eminent Civil Lawyer Mr. Pufendorf" to expose the kinds of "Disease" that affect "irregular Forms" of regime.[50] The theme of

---

[49] PNM: 219 (parentheses mine).

[50] PNM: 236–37. While Pufendorf has been identified by some as an absolutist (e.g., James Tully, *A Discourse on Property: Locke and His Adversaries* [Cambridge: Cambridge University Press, 1980]: pp. 55, 157, 171), the key to my argument is not the plain meaning of Pufendorf, but rather Tyrrell's use of him. The extended passage from Pufendorf that Tyrrell employs to enlighten those English readers who "cannot easily procure the Latine Original" highlights Pufendorf's insistence on the salutary consequences of placing legal limits on sovereign power.

constitutional regularization in the historically identifiable principle of king-in-Parliament peaks in Tyrrell's account of Pufendorf's treatment of sovereignty.

Pufendorf's fundamental argument in the passage Tyrrell quotes is that supremacy in a political order does not necessarily denote absolute power. Pufendorf aims to demonstrate that supremacy or sovereignty is not incompatible with constitutionalism. He maintains that sovereignty may be "absolute or restricted to a certain manner of procedure."[51] The reason Pufendorf cites for the need for supreme power in any proper or regular constitutional order is the character of natural liberty. The state of absolute liberty that characterizes the state of nature requires a supreme civil power to secure the obedience needed to achieve "the end of established states."[52] The end of civil society is, of course, the securing of civil peace mandated by the natural law. Although, in contrast to Hobbes, Pufendorf argues that this supreme power can be absolute or limited, he does not deny that it can be legitimately absolute.

Pufendorf defended the need for supreme sovereign power on the natural law grounds of the requirement to harmonize natural liberty with social order. Yet he immediately indicates two problems or qualifications to the supreme sovereignty argument: the problem of democracy and the problem of absolute monarchy. In this manner, Pufendorf identifies the two dangerous tendencies Tyrrell ascribed to the historical English Constitution: those that he hoped to alleviate with his formula of naturalization and regularization. First, we should consider Pufendorf's (and implicitly Tyrrell's) understanding of the problem of democracy.

Pufendorf's presentation of the necessity for a recognized supreme power in a constitutional order is a stinging indictment of both democracy and mixed regime theory. By democracy Pufendorf means a regime governed solely by the people's will expressed through a broadly popular legislative assembly. The major problem Pufendorf identifies is the impossibility to preserve written laws when there is no distinction between the circumscribed and absolute sovereignty of the people. As Pufendorf's examples of Caesar in Rome and Solon's successors in Athens illustrate, in a democracy the

Even if Pufendorf is not a bona fide champion of limited government, which is debatable, the Pufendorf Tyrrell delivers up for English consumption most certainly is sympathetic to it. Perhaps the one major flaw in Rudolph's otherwise very worthy study of Tyrrell is her failure to recognize the role of Pufendorf's theory of sovereignty in the development of Tyrrell's arguments about the legally constituted nation embodying "the people" (*Revolution by Degrees*, pp. 55–7; but see also pp. 126–7).

[51] For purposes of clarity, I shall note the passage both as to its page number in Tyrrell's PNM and to its book, chapter, and section numbers in Pufendorf's DJNG. The direct quotations will be from Oldfather's authoritative translation. I shall note where Tyrrell's translation differs substantially from this edition. See PNM, 239 and DJNG 7.6.7.

[52] PNM: 238 and DJNG 7.6.7.

people can abrogate any law or custom they wish.[53] Legal limits on sovereign power cannot be enforced when the sole legislative power rests with the people. Thus, Pufendorf points to the necessity for a supreme power to secure the legal limits created by the original compact forming political society. Democracy, for Pufendorf, is antithetical to legal and political forms. A constitutional provision institutionalizing bicameralism and/or granting the executive power a role in the formation of law provide checks on unbridled popular sovereignty. For Pufendorf these structural checks on popular will protect both individual rights and the common good. Tyrrell's use of this passage reflects his own moderate Whig fear of the radical consequences of the doctrine of parliamentary supremacy for England. Tyrrell expresses this concern in his antipathy to the radical Rump Parliament and his sympathy for Charles I. Pufendorf assists Tyrrell in confirming the latter's status as a Whig with Cavalier sympathies.

Regarding the problem of absolute monarchy, Pufendorf identifies this as a highly unstable ordering principle for any regime and advises that it is wise to prescribe certain legal forms to limit such a power. Pufendorf declares that "it has appeared advisable to many people not to commit in so absolute a fashion such power as this to a single man,... but to prescribe for him a definite manner of holding office."[54] In addition to the practical or utilitarian advantages of circumscribing sovereign power, Pufendorf points to another problem particular to absolute monarchs, namely, the tendency of such rulers to rely on divine right as a source of legitimacy to replace the lack of a popular foundation. Pufendorf emphatically rejects the "trite and banal" arguments of those defenders of divine right who claim that "Kings are constituted by God, and He has enjoined upon them the proper conduct of their office, which is impossible without the exercise of supreme authority" illimitable by any law.[55] Pufendorf, like Tyrrell, argues that all human government is a product of consent. In order to deflate the divine right argument, Pufendorf offers his remarkable reinterpretation of the crucial scriptural passage I Samuel 8.

Filmer, of course, had used Samuel's illustration to the Israelites of the sweeping powers of kings in order to support his argument that Scripture endorsed absolute monarchy.[56] Pufendorf rejects both the divine right interpretation of this passage and Grotius' interpretation, which held it to be a scriptural support for the principle of nonresistance to established authority. As Pufendorf presents it, Grotius was mistaken to refer to the authority of I Samuel 8 to give scriptural credence to contractual absolutism. For his part,

---

[53] DJNG 7.6.8 and PNM: 241. Tyrrell leaves the dramatic examples of Caesar and Solon out of his version.

[54] DJNG 7.6.9 and PNM: 242.

[55] DJNG 7.6.9 and PNM: 243.

[56] Filmer, *Patriarcha*, pp. 35–8.

Pufendorf interprets Samuel's dire predictions of monarchical power as evidence of the particular consequences of the establishment of the warrior king desired by the citizens of the Hebrew democracy. As such, it is not meant as a "protection to wicked princes, nor dictates any set measure, as it were, of kingly sovereignty, as by a law of God"; rather, it is a cautionary tale of the care a people should take in determining the legal limits they impose on sovereign power.[57] Noticeably, Pufendorf both defends the people's right to make terrible errors and affirms the necessity of maintaining the constitutional order originally produced by compact. However, Pufendorf also offers Scripture as testimony to the natural liberty of human beings to devise political orders as they see fit. Moreover, he does so even as he articulates the dangers of democracy and absolute monarchy.

While Pufendorf advocates the necessity of one supreme power in any constitutional order, he also suggests certain limits that can be set on sovereignty. One structural way to ensure limited sovereignty is for a people to "establish a council without whose consent those acts which had been excepted cannot be exercised."[58] While the creation of such a body does, in Pufendorf's view, act as a check on monarchical power, he also suggests that the existence of two or more autonomous branches of government operating without clearly circumscribed powers can lead to the problem of mixture. Pufendorf does not envision limited constitutionalism as a pitched battle between the claims of royal and popular sovereignty. It is Pufendorf's deep theoretical objection to the mixed regime model that leads him to modify the concept of council limitations by offering the principle of councils with the additional limitation of certain basic constitutional laws. These "basic laws" place limits on both royal and popular sovereignty by registering the supremacy of the principle of legal and formal process over the expressions of raw power from above or below.

Pufendorf's argument for the supremacy of fundamental laws does not, however, negate the importance of popular representation. Rather, he affirms that the existence of "an assembly of the people or council of nobles" that is enshrined in law makes these bodies "an absolute necessary condition" for the exercise of sovereign power. The way in which Pufendorf envisions this limited sovereignty operating in practice is revealed in his treatment of the two kinds of matters he argues are issues for "the nature of limited monarchies." These are "those decided in advance" and those in which a judgment can be "reached only at the time they arise."[59] An example of the former sort of pressing political issue would be the religious settlement of a nation. Pufendorf maintains that "a People satisfied of the truth of its religion...could lay down a law for the king, when they crowned him,

---

[57] DJGN 7.6.9 and PNM: 244–6.
[58] DJNG 7.6.10 and PNM: 248. Tyrrell calls this assembly a "Great Council."
[59] DJNG 7.6.11 and PNM: 251.

that he would not on his own authority make any change in the matters of the religion of the land."[60] Pufendorf offers this both as an example of a political device that could reduce theological controversy in a kingdom – a concern shared by many English Whigs – and as the kind of fundamental provision that can regularize sovereign power with preestablished legal limits.

As to the kinds of issues that must be decided contemporaneously with events, Pufendorf adduces the questions of war and peace. Since these largely prudential matters are impossible to address fully in the original contract or even properly by after condescent, Pufendorf suggests that it is best to require the monarch to consult with the established noble council and/or popular assembly. This provision is particularly well advised, in Pufendorf's view, given the tendency of monarchs to use war as a means of satisfying their "ambition and luxury."[61] Once again, Pufendorf's central thesis in this passage is that structural and legal provisions in the constitution can produce stability and regularity in the vital operations of sovereign power. For moderate Whigs such as Tyrrell, Pufendorf's insights regarding sovereign power were comforting. Pufendorf's argument that supreme, and indeed irresistible, constitutional power could be moderated by internal structural designs such as that characterizing the king's relation to Parliament conformed perfectly with the moderate Whigs' deep commitment to the natural law principles of social order, as well as their attachment to the historical tradition of England's political institutions. That there could be a supreme legal power above any claims for popular sovereignty soothed moderate Whig fears about radical democracy. That this supreme power could be limited by the interaction of the representative institutions of England's complex and balanced Constitution allayed moderate Whig concerns about the dangers of absolute monarchy.

Tyrrell's Pufendorfian moment culminates in a theoretical outline of an England governed by parliamentary sovereignty including the three historic parts of the balanced Constitution. Pufendorfian natural jurisprudence and constitutional theory provided moderate Whigs with the intellectual and conceptual materials necessary to articulate a vision of the English government that avoided and resisted what they perceived to be the twin pitfalls of royal absolutism and radical popular sovereignty. By denying the principles of dissolution and general right of rebellion, moderate Whigs asserted the contractual, and hence legal, character of sovereign political power. Sovereignty in England rested in the king-in-Parliament, not in the people understood independently of the institutions of government. And yet the capacity of the people in their original constitutive role to create representative institutions

---

[60] DJNG 7.6.11 and PNM: 251–2. Tyrrell adds the example of Sweden to Pufendorf's treatment.
[61] DJNG 7.6.11 and PNM: 253.

also provided moderate Whigs with the means to defend the identifiable legal and constitutional limits on the power of the crown established by the houses of Parliament. For moderate Whigs such as James Tyrrell, somewhere between the radical democracy of the "promiscuous rabble" and the tyranny of "Absolute Monarchy *Jure Divino*" lay the promised land of government by the rule of law.

6

Algernon Sidney and the Old Republicanisms

Algernon Sidney and his *Discourses Concerning Government* cut a striking figure even among the colorful cast of characters in English Whiggery. Whereas the Cavalier country squire Tyrrell was self-consciously moderate and measured in tone, Sidney's argument is bellicose, incendiary, and defiantly republican. He was born in 1622, the scion of two illustrious aristocratic families, the Sidneys and the Percys.[1] His father was the second earl of Leicester and his mother was the daughter of the ninth earl of Northumberland. His ancestors included the famed Elizabethan courtier, warrior, and poet Sir Philip Sidney and the proud, warlike, aristocratic rebel Hotspur, immortalized in Shakespeare's history plays. His youth was spent divided between the family estate in Kentshire at Penshurst and living with his diplomat father on assignments in Denmark and France in the 1630s, where the second earl met and came to know Grotius and other leading continental thinkers.

As was true of most Englishmen of his generation, the formative experience of Sidney's life was the civil war. Ironically, the man who would become so clearly identified with the "old cause" of the Commonwealth actually began the war in royal service in Ireland but took up the parliamentary cause upon his return to England in 1643. By all accounts, he served gallantly as an officer in the earl of Manchester's Horse Regiment and was seriously wounded in a charge at Marston Moor in 1644. It was in the period of

---

[1] For biographical accounts of Sidney's life and times, see *Dictionary of National Biography*, 24 vols., Leslie Stephen and Sidney Lee, eds. (London: Oxford University Press, 1921–2): Vol. XVIII, pp. 202–9 (hereafter DNB); J. G. A. Pocock, "England's Cato: The Virtues and Fortunes of Algernon Sidney," *Historical Journal*, vol. 37, no. 4 (December 1994): pp. 915–35; Jonathan Scott, *Algernon Sidney and the English Republic, 1623–1677* (Cambridge: Cambridge University Press, 1988) and *Algernon Sidney and the Restoration Crisis, 1677–1683* (Cambridge: Cambridge University Press, 1991); Thomas West, "Introduction" to *The Discourses Concerning Government* (Indianapolis: Liberty Fund Press, 1996); and Blair Worden, *Roundhead Reputations: The English Civil Wars and the Passions of Posterity* (London: Penguin Press, 2001): esp. chs. 5, 6.

recuperation from his wounds that the twenty-four-year-old Sidney entered parliamentary politics, being returned to the Long Parliament in 1646 from Cardiff. The young aristocrat served in a variety of functions in the Long Parliament and acquired an intimate knowledge of the workings of the institution after the war. He was self-admittedly a difficult person to work with and probably would not have quarreled with Burnet's account of him as a learned and courageous man, but of a "rough and boisterous temper" that "could not bear contradiction."[2] Appointed as a commissioner for the court created to try Charles I, Sidney angered Cromwell by publicly questioning the legality of the proceedings on the grounds that "first, the king could be tried by no court; secondly, that no man could be tried by that court." Sidney resolutely refused to take part in the proceedings of the court. He also ran afoul of Cromwell by opposing the Act of Engagement, although more on prudential than doctrinal grounds.

However, for the most part, his time in the Rump Parliament was the high point of Sidney's life. In his glory days in the final year before its demise in 1653, Sidney was elected to the Council of State and served on the foreign affairs committee then busily engaged in conducting the First Anglo-Dutch War. Sidney drew from his experience of this period a deep commitment to republicanism and a conviction that the Rump, a unicameral legislature with executive committees, was the best government England ever had.[3] When Cromwell and the army dissolved the Rump in 1653, legend has it that Sidney, sitting to the right of the speaker, was the last member of Parliament to leave, and only after being threatened with forcible removal by army troopers.

Predictably, Sidney chafed under the Protectorate and loathed the military dictator Cromwell. Again legend has it that Sidney signaled his feelings toward the Protector by putting on a performance of Shakespeare's *Julius Caesar* at Penshurst, pointedly casting himself in the role of Brutus.[4] When the army restored the Long Parliament in 1659 after Cromwell's death, Sidney returned to the House of Commons and was again elected to the Council of State, dealing primarily with foreign relations. It was while on a diplomatic mission in Denmark to mediate a dispute between the kings of Sweden and Denmark that he first learned about the plans for the Restoration and was in Scandinavia when the dramatic events of 1660 unfolded. In contrast to his colleague John Milton, and even in contrast to his reaction to the dissolution of the Rump seven years earlier, Sidney's initial response to the Restoration was not immediate hostility. As a matter of principle, he was willing to defer to the authority of the Parliament that installed Charles II. Moreover, he personally was not on Charles' list of proscribed regicides. Sidney did not, however, return to England.

[2] Worden, *Roundhead Reputations*, p. 124.
[3] Pocock, "England's Cato," p. 919.
[4] DNB, Vol. XVIII, p. 205.

His reasoning appears to have been twofold. First, as a matter of personal honor, he was not willing to renounce his actions in the Commonwealth government and was unwilling to live in England under a cloud of suspicion. In a letter to his father, who had pleaded with the new king to allow his son's return, Sidney proudly declared: "When I call to remembrance all my actions relating to our civil distempers, I cannot find one that I can look upon as a breach of the rules of justice or honor."[5] Second, Sidney's political principles were still unrepentantly republican. He created a stir among English royalists when he famously autographed the visitor's album at the University of Copenhagen with the monarchomach motto "Manus haec inimical tyrannis" – "This hand inimical to tyrants."

For Sidney, the Restoration meant a seventeen-year-long career in exile on the Continent. In this time he traveled widely throughout Europe, studied, wrote, survived assassination attempts by Charles' men, and periodically plotted an English republican exile invasion of their homeland. During the Second Anglo-Dutch War in 1665–6 he lived in Holland, fruitlessly petitioning the Dutch republican leaders, and later even France's Louis XIV, to support the English republican cause. Dispirited by his failure to mobilize support for a republican return at home or abroad, Sidney bemoaned his fate as a "broken limb of a shipwrecked faction," eventually settling in the south of France in dignified retirement as "le comte de Sidney."[6] However, Sidney's European exile was not totally consumed by personal frustration and inevitable political fatalism. It was during his long exile that Sidney contemplated the primary theoretical principles that would become the foundation for his political teaching in the *Discourses*. He reflected deeply on the painful lessons of the English Commonwealth's failure to establish secure republican government as well as on the resilience of the English monarchy. Sidney spent his forced retirement from politics thinking through the philosophical foundations of modern republicanism by assimilating the English experience of 1649–53 into the lessons provided by the example of Dutch republican government and, more importantly, of Dutch republican philosophy.[7] The *Discourses* would be the product of these reflections on English political history in light of the broader context of European Enlightenment philosophy.

Sidney's long-awaited return to England in 1677 occurred not at the head of a republican invasion, but rather as the result of royal permission to return to settle mundane private family matters. He expected to stay only briefly, but the death of his father and an unseemly quarrel with his parsimonious

---

[5] Ibid., p. 205.
[6] West, "Introduction," xxxi and Pocock, "England's Cato," p. 921.
[7] This reading runs counter to that of Pocock ("England's Cato," pp. 917–18 and 929–31), who sees Sidney's republicanism as decidedly unphilosophical, more a matter of aristocratic temperament than egalitarian principles.

elder brother over Sidney's patrimony compelled him to extend his stay. Sidney was drawn irresistibly back into political activity by the fall of Danby and the ensuing Exclusion controversy. He was frustrated by several unsuccessful attempts to win a seat in Parliament, but despite these electoral failures he established himself in Whig circles. Sidney did not, however, have any real contact with the Shaftesbury circle Locke and Tyrrell moved in, partly because Sidney and Shaftesbury loathed each other personally and partly because Sidney's political aims were more emphatically anti-royalist than the Exclusion program designed by Shaftesbury. Sidney feared and distrusted the Orange interest as much as the Stuarts, and saw the crisis more as a way to severely circumscribe the power of the crown (or, ideally, establish a republic) than as a way merely to ensure a pliant Protestant successor to Charles.[8] With the collapse of the Whig parliamentary opposition in 1681, Sidney began writing the *Discourses* and plotting more extreme measures. After Shaftesbury's flight to Holland and subsequent death, Sidney and the rest of the "Council of Six," including Monmouth, Essex, Russell, Hampden, and Howard, assumed leadership of the Whig movement and tirelessly sought French support for a broad-based Whig insurrection in England and Scotland. He was arrested and sent to the Tower along with other top Whig leaders in June 1683 after the discovery of the Rye House Plot to kidnap the king and the duke of York.

Sidney's political career did not, however, end with his arrest. In a sense, it really began to assume legendary proportions only with his trial for treason in the autumn of 1683. The hagiography of Sidney the martyr for the cause of freedom drew its inspiration from the manifest irregularities and outright illegalities orchestrated by Sidney's prosecutor, Chief Justice Jeffreys. It was established in English law that two witnesses were required to prove treason. Jeffreys, having only the well-known scoundrel Howard as a witness against Sidney, used portions of the unpublished manuscript of the *Discourses* found in Sidney's rooms to demonstrate the defendant's treasonous state of mind. With a packed Tory jury and given the public mood at the time, Sidney's fate was sealed, and he was executed after being refused the chance to resume exile in December 1683, by all accounts going to the scaffold with courage and dignity. Among Whigs the obvious travesty of the trial, and especially the violation of an individual's private chambers and even more private thoughts, assumed great significance as a symbol of Stuart tyranny.

Immediately upon his death Sidney entered the pantheon of Whig martyrs, but the manuscript that had assumed such significance at this trial would not be published until 1698, fifteen years after his death and nearly a decade after the Glorious Revolution. The *Discourses* as they have come down to history under the editorial guidance of the Whig publicist John Toland are a

[8] Scott, *Restoration Crisis*, pp. 24–5, 106–7. Cf. Worden, *Roundhead Reputations*, pp. 135–6.

remarkable piece of work.⁹ They are by far the longest of the Exclusion era Whig responses to Filmer. Their three enormous chapters and their presentation as a point-by-point refutation of Filmer make them a notoriously dense and voluminous offering. Despite the general recognition of the *Discourses* in the eighteenth century as one of the seminal texts in republican constitutionalism, this density and opacity have produced widespread neglect of Sidney's work over the past 200 years.¹⁰ However, the *Discourses* are the foundational writing in the radical Whig republican tradition. The defining features of Sidney's radical Whiggism were his endorsement of the principle of popular sovereignty, the general right of revolution, and his emphatic defense of republicanism. In one sense, Sidney was in fundamental agreement with Tyrrell and the other moderate Exclusion Whigs. They concurred that Parliament is sovereign in England, but they disagreed about the meaning and character of Parliament. In contrast to the moderate Whigs, Sidney's brand of modern republicanism did not conceive of sovereignty residing in the balanced Constitution embodied in the notion of king-in-Parliament. Where Sidney most clearly departed from his moderate Whig colleagues was in his harsh criticism of mixed regime theory and his insistence that political sovereignty must reside in popular institutions marked by numerous representation, rotating delegates, and frequent elections, which can reflect the general will of the people and the collected power of the multitude of individuals in society. As such, Sidney founded a strain of Whiggism that was deeply opposed to the principle of prerogative and an independent executive. In the course of defending the doctrine of natural liberty against Filmer's divine right attacks, Sidney advocated a distinctly modern form of republicanism infused with the principles of radical natural rights theory associated with Benedict Spinoza. The republican strain of Whig thought originating in Sidney incorporated important elements of classical and Machiavellian republicanism into the rubric of Spinoza's radical natural rights teaching, producing an egalitarian and democratic version of modern republicanism that

---

⁹ For an account of Toland's relatively minor editorial license with the *Discourses*, see Worden, *Roundhead Reputations*, pp. 131–3.

¹⁰ Sidney's work was well known to eighteenth-century European, English, and American thinkers. For Sidney's influence on Montesquieu, see *The Spirit of the Laws*, Anne Cohler, ed. (Cambridge: Cambridge University Press, 1989): bk. 11, ch. 6, pp. 159–60. For good discussions of Sidney's influence on the early American Republic, see Peter Karsten, *Patriot Heroes in England and America* (Madison: University of Wisconsin Press, 1978) and Alan Carig Houston, *Algernon Sidney and the Republican Heritage in England and America* (Princeton: Princeton University Press, 1991): esp. ch. 6. Also note John Adams' letter to Thomas Jefferson of September 17, 1823, in Lester J. Capon, ed., *The Adams–Jefferson Letters* (Chapel Hill, NC: University of North Carolina Press, 1959): p. 598 and Jefferson's praise of Sidney as one of the leading sources for the American understanding of the principles of political liberty in "From the Minutes of the Board of Visitors, University of Virginia," March 4, 1825, in Thomas Jefferson, *Thomas Jefferson Writings* (New York: Viking Press, 1984): p. 479.

would provide the theoretical inspiration for generations of radical Whigs in England and America.

In this chapter, we will examine Sidney's defense of the earlier natural liberty arguments associated with the Catholic natural lawyers, and the classical and Machiavellian forms of republicanism against divine right royalism. We will also consider the way in which Sidney modified these older forms of republicanism by synthesizing them with the modern natural rights theories of Hobbes and Spinoza to produce a distinctly modern vision of radical Whig republicanism for a dramatically reformed English Constitution. In the following chapter, we will consider Sidney's effort to limn the features of a modern republican political science modeled on Spinoza's articulation of the natural order of power relations and the naturalness of democracy. With his emphatically modern version of republicanism, Sidney paradoxically both located himself on the extreme fringe of Whig opinion at the time and also planted the seed for a vibrant strain of Anglo-American republicanism that would resonate far beyond England's shores.

Sidney and the Old Republicanisms

Sidney's defense of the doctrine of natural liberty began as a critical response to Filmerian divine right but gradually expanded into a treatise on the nature of republicanism. Sidney's response to Filmer is multilayered. First, he denies that any consistent reading of Scripture supports Adam's "natural and private dominion" over creation.[11] Sidney disputes Filmer's claim that Adam's unique creation directly by God is a sign of Adam's sovereignty. Rather, Sidney contends that whether the creation had been of a single man or a multiplicity, "they had all been equal, unless God had given preference to one."[12] Fatherhood, Sidney claims, signified no such preference. The bare fact that "every man should be chief of his family" does not in any degree "signify an absolute power." Sidney maintains that far from elevating Adam above the rest of humankind, Scripture actually suggests a primal equality: "the same law that gave to my father a power over me, gives me the like over my children, and if I had a thousand brothers each of them would have the same over their children."[13] Sidney maintains that Scripture's Adam differs greatly from that of Filmer.

Sidney claims that even if Adam had an absolute right, his heirs did not. For example, Scripture never suggests that the fratricide Cain "had any dominion over his brethren, or their posterity." Scripture, moreover, affords

---

[11] Houston, *Algernon Sidney*, pp. 104–5.
[12] Algernon Sidney, *The Discourses Concerning Government*, Thomas West, ed. (Indianapolis: Liberty Fund Classics, 1996): ch.1, sec. 7, p. 24 (hereafter in notes as D, ch., sec., and, where appropriate, page number).
[13] D 1.6.22, 2.2.89.

little help in determining the political status of Adam's heirs. The Bible's obscurity about what passed between the Creation and the Flood means that it is "not easy to determine, whether Shem or Japheth were the elder." Sidney contends that if Scripture had intended to teach the absolute right of Adam's heirs it would have said so plainly rather than "leave us in a dark labyrinth, full of precipices."[14] The uncertainty in tracing the descent of Adam's line, he charges, ensures that even if Scripture did intend to teach the supreme right of Adam's heirs to rule, they cannot be known in any reliable way in the present.[15] In this opening salvo against Filmer, Sidney demonstrates both that Scripture offers no political right to Adam and his heirs and that paternal power does not contradict natural liberty.

Sidney aims to prove that Scripture explicitly distinguishes between paternal and regal power. For example, Abraham may have enjoyed a form of rule over his wife, children, and servants, but he was equal to all other men, including his nephew Lot.[16] His sons likewise had a legitimate power over their families but were also rulers "void of all worldly splendor." Moreover, Moses and the judges who succeeded him were not hereditary monarchs, but rather were magistrates chosen from different tribes and whose children did not succeed them. As Sidney wryly remarks, if Moses and the judges had ruled by Adam's supreme right, then "Saul, David and Solomon could never have been kings."[17] More importantly, Sidney suggests that the Bible is unenthusiastic regarding regal power. Of the first king, Nimrod, "Scripture testifies to it as a usurpation," and through the Babel story shows "the pride, cruelty, injustice and madness of this first kingdom."[18] In addition to highlighting Samuel's warning to the Hebrews before the accession of Saul, Sidney is at pains to display the turbulent history of the Israelite kings, which he observes is chronicled in grim detail in Scripture.

Sidney also tries to prove that Scripture does not even fully support Filmer's conception of the patriarchal family. First, he argues that while it endorsed patriarchal rule in the family, it did not extend this into a model legitimating absolute monarchy.[19] By the very fact that the Bible chronicles the establishment of the Hebrew regime under Moses and the later monarchy under Saul, Scripture relegated patriarchal government to a very distant and primitive past. Sidney claims: "We may reasonably affirm, that mankind is forever obliged to use no other clothes than leather breeches, like

---

[14] D 2.2.89, 1.8.25–6, 1.6.23.

[15] D 1.12.33–4.

[16] D 1.7.24–5.

[17] D 1.13.37.

[18] D 1.8.26–7.

[19] Unlike Locke and to a lesser degree Tyrrell, Sidney explicitly separates the issue of sexual equality from his general defense of natural liberty. Sidney approves of patriarchalism and the exclusion of women from political life but wonders whether it provides a model for political society (D 2.9.130; 1.18.159–60).

Adam; ... as to think all nations forever obliged to be governed as they govern their families."[20] Second, Sidney excoriates Filmer's attempt to ground the practice of primogeniture in Scripture. Sidney points to the many obvious deviations from this rule in Scripture, such as God's election of Moses before his elder brother, Aaron, and Jacob's surpassing of Esau. The evidence in Scripture generally contradicts Filmer's model, but even if it were only a rare instance, Sidney affirms: "If one deviation from it were lawful, another might be, and so to infinity."[21] If primogeniture were sacrosanct, Moses, Aaron, David, and Solomon would never have ruled. Sidney strongly suggests that most of the Bible's great figures came to prominence not by their status as the eldest heirs, but on some other basis of selection to rule.

According to Sidney, Filmer's refusal to ground political rule on the principle of consent logically leads to the most destructive consequences for political life. The only two ways to come "to command many" are through consent or by force. In delegitimating consent, Filmer encourages force. By the principle of consent Sidney argues, "every man be free, till he enter into such a society as he chuseth for his own good." Consent includes the power to comprehend one's own good in the "common stock" of the community and the right both to elevate one to rule over the community and to limit the power of these rulers.[22] For Sidney, consent proves compatible with society. Force, on the other hand, produces slavery. Sidney reveals that "by the name of slave we understand a man, who can neither dispose of his person or his goods, but enjoys all at the will of his master." He draws from this that "there is no such thing in nature as a slave."[23] Sidney posits force or usurpation as the antipode of consent and slavery as the antithesis of rightful political subjection. His general rhetorical strategy in this discussion is not unlike that of Bellarmine and Suarez. Like them, Sidney wants to demonstrate that natural liberty is not an anarchic doctrine; rather, it is the violation of the principle of consent that introduces confusion and misery.[24] In contrast to the moderating effect of consent theory, Sidney charges that by Filmer's doctrine no European monarch is legitimate, because none can demonstrate direct descent from Adam's line and none are as absolute as Filmer requires.[25] Sidney

---

[20] D 1.6.22–3.

[21] D 1.13.37. See also Sidney's claim that primogeniture is merely a civil law in some nations, like England, but not a divine or natural law (D 2.4.93).

[22] D 1.12.35–6, 1.11.32.

[23] D 1.5.17.

[24] The Christian Aristotelians whom Sidney seems to support in Chapter One of the *Discourses* were concerned to assert the compatibility of natural liberty with society in an attempt to refute the Antinomian Christian sects of the period. Cf. Roberto Bellarmine, *De Laicis*, Kathleen Murphy, trans. (New York: Fordham University Press, 1928): ch. 1, p. 9.

[25] D 1.18.52, 1.19.67; see also 1.16.50 for Sidney's treatment of the tumultuous succession struggles in the Roman imperial period. The abuses of the Roman emperors are also a prominent theme in Chapter Two of the *Discourses*.

proposes that regimes founded on consent, whether monarchical or otherwise, contain an internal stability rooted in the support of the community.
Divine right, on the other hand, Sidney presents as a recipe for confusion
that "goes directly against the letter and spirit of the Scripture."

Sidney allies with Bellarmine and Suarez to counter Filmer's claim that
arbitrary government, and absolute monarchy in particular, represents the
uniform and immutable form of rule ordained by God. Sidney claims that
"the best and wisest of men" having constituted "aristocratical, democrat-
ical, or mixed governments" would thus have produced regimes in opposition to that monarchy "from which we are not to swerve."[26] Sidney joins the
Catholic natural lawyers in affirming that natural liberty implies a people's
rational capacity to devise political institutions to satisfy their needs. Thus,
the natural freedom to consent to government makes monarchy only one of
a variety of regimes available to human beings and sanctioned by God.

Sidney attempts to demonstrate natural liberty in two ways.[27] First, and
primarily, he uses an a priori method in which he argues that the principle of
consent is one no rational being can deny without doing violence to his own
nature. To demonstrate the self-evidence of natural liberty, Sidney indicates
that even such bitter theological and political foes as the Jesuit scholastics
and the English Calvinist divines agree on this fundamental proposition.[28]
The second method Sidney employs is a posteriori, by which he argues that
natural liberty is an idea almost universally accepted among the nations.
Sidney claims that people from all ages "in love with liberty, and desirous to
maintain their own privileges," have created a variety of regimes, not only
monarchy.[29] Natural liberty can be proven by demonstrating that nations
have always made their own laws and constitutions.

Sidney's main effort is dedicated to the proof of natural liberty a priori.
He claims that the "principle of liberty in which God created us . . . is written
in the hearts of every man." Although liberty consists "in an independency
upon the will of another," Sidney insists that it is not "a licentiousness of
doing what is pleasing to everyone against the command of God; but an exemption from all human laws, to which they have not given their assent."[30]
He thus locates his doctrine of natural liberty in an appeal to the Christian-
Aristotelian understanding of a natural law with a force binding on "the
conscience."[31] He defends natural liberty as a moral or practical truth as

---

[26] D 1.1.5–6.
[27] The general structure of Sidney's argument in Chapter One of the *Discourses* follows a pattern
employing the a priori and a posteriori methods of demonstration. In this way, Sidney appears
to follow a pattern similar to that of Grotius. Cf. Hugo Grotius, *De Jure Belli ac Pacis Libri
Tres* (Oxford: Clarendon Press, 1925): 1.1.12.1. (hereafter DJB).
[28] D 1.2.8–10.
[29] D 1.1.7.
[30] D 1.2.8, 1.5.17, 1.2.9.
[31] D 1.1.7.

demonstrable as the speculative truths of mathematics such as "the whole is greater than a part, that two halfs make a whole, or that a straight line is the shortest way from point to point." These are truths as evident to pagan as to Christian, Euclid as to Bellarmine, like the "principles of geometry which no sober man can deny."[32] Sidney's discussion of natural liberty aims to display the perversity of Filmer's position, a position that Sidney claims to be contrary to the universal human experience. Moreover, while he is careful not to endorse Bellarmine's argument for papal pretensions in temporal affairs,[33] Sidney nonetheless successfully places his own position in the context of the respectable Christian-Aristotelian tradition of Catholic and Anglican scholasticism.

Sidney also displays a careful and muted use of the state of nature concept in the first chapter of the *Discourses*. Like the Catholic natural lawyers, he affirms the condition of natural liberty only to demonstrate its fundamental compatibility with society. The "equal right to everything" typical of man's condition outside of civil society produces inconveniences so great "that mankind cannot bear them." The natural condition unimproved by human art is not a viable state for human beings. However, Sidney uses the state of nature image primarily to show that no rational person would persist in it.[34] What Sidney achieves by his use of the pre-civil condition is to establish the origins of government in the "common consent" of people joining into one body. The theoretical implication of natural liberty is the conventional variety of regimes, not the natural war of all against all. Sidney emphasizes that a naturally free people may create a democracy, aristocracy, monarchy, or "mixed governments composed of the three."[35] In each case, however, men resign their private right into the community only "in such measure as they think fit for the constituting of societies for their own good."[36] The varying degrees of subjection and the variety of regimes do not follow a uniform pattern inhering in the human condition but rather are the products of the contractual arrangements of human beings. Thus, Sidney tries to prove that the fact that human beings typically are in society and not born exempt from civil law does not mean that they are not naturally free.

---

[32] D 1.2.8. Cf. St. Thomas Aquinas, *Summa Theologica*, 3 vols. (New York: Benziger Brothers, 1947): q. 79, a. 12 and I–II, q. 94, a. 2 and Francisco Suarez, *Extracts on Politics and Government*, George Moore, trans. (Chevy Chase, MD: Country Dollar Press, 1950): *Defensio*, bk. III, ch. 2, p. 100.

[33] Compare D 2.1.77–8 and 1.2.8, where Sidney argues: "Tho' the Schoolmen were corrupt, they were neither stupid nor unlearned." See also D 1.5.18, where Sidney appeals to the authority of Aristotle and the great Anglican scholastic Richard Hooker.

[34] D 1.10.30. Cf. Scott Nelson, *The Discourses of Algeron Sidney* (Cranbury, NJ: Associated University Presses, 1993): pp. 36, 58 and Bellarmine, *De Laicis*, p. 20.

[35] D 1.10.31. Cf. Aristotle, *The Politics*, Carnes Lord, trans. (Chicago: University of Chicago Press, 1984): 1288b10–1290a30.

[36] D 1.12.35–6, 1.10.31, 1.11.32.

A striking feature of the natural liberty doctrine Sidney presents in Chapter One of the *Discourses* is his close association of liberty with human rationality. For Sidney, the human capacity to form and to participate in political society reflects the endowment of reason. He argues that men form political societies for two related purposes. The first is to secure the material advantages of society. Sidney muses: "It cannot be believed that rational creatures would advance one or a few of their equal above themselves, unless in consideration of their own good."[37] Society secures the bodily necessities by establishing general rules of justice. Outside of political society, "the liberty of one is thwarted by another" and none can reliably enjoy their property with security.[38] Sidney further testifies to humankind's essentially social nature by his argument for the central role of the family in the origins of political society. In essence, Sidney agrees with Suarez's presentation of political society as a product of the increasing complexity of social relations produced by the extended family.[39] Political society originates in, but transcends, the needs of the family.

The second purpose for the creation of political society is the satisfaction of the human rational nature. Sidney echoes the Aristotelian dictum "homo est animal rationale." Politics stands, for Sidney, as the expression of reason. Reason "cannot be in beasts, for they know not what government is."[40] Sidney asserts that "nature, which is reason," clearly inclines people to society, inasmuch as they have "understanding to provide for themselves, and by the invention of arts and sciences, to be beneficial to each other." Most importantly, people "ought to make use of that understanding in forming governments according to their own convenience." Sidney offers a privileged position for the practical wisdom denied by divine right: "Every people is by God and nature left to the liberty of regulating these matters relating to themselves according to their own prudence." The importance of prudence in constitution making reflects the architectonic character of politics, the activity that Sidney claims comprehends "all that in this world deserves to be cared for."[41] Sidney charges that if there is a uniform rule in nature, it is not hereditary absolute monarchy; rather, Scripture and classical thought indicate that the uniform rule is the government of the best men. He claims that "*detur digniori* is the voice of nature" calling nations to elevate those "who are most fit to perform the duties belonging to their stations, in order to the publick good."[42] Insofar as the end of government is to secure and

---

[37] D 1.6.21.

[38] D 1.10.30.

[39] D 2.1.78. Cf. Aristotle, *Politics*, 1252b10–1253a1 and Suarez, *Extracts: Defensio*, III.2.100.

[40] D 1.18.60, 2.8.22. Cf. Aristotle, *Politics*, 1253a2; Bellarmine, *De Laicis*, p. 20; and Suarez, *Extracts: Defensio*, III.2.105.

[41] D 2.8.121, 1.18.61, 1.1.5. Cf. Aristotle, *The Nicomachean Ethics*, H. H. Rackham, trans. (Cambridge, MA: Harvard Univesity Press, 1934): 1094a30–1094b12.

[42] D 1.16.49. West translates *detur digniori* as "Let it be given to the worthier."

promote the common good, virtue as a claim to rule is entirely consistent with the principle of consent. Sidney presents republican rule of the virtuous as the antidote to divine right absolutism.

Sidney's rhetorical strategy in his defense of republicanism is complex.[43] In his effort to present a unified front in the natural liberty school against divine right, he blurs significant distinctions between the Catholic, classical, and Machiavellian forms of consent theory and republicanism. In the process, Sidney incorporates classical notions of virtue and government into his own very modern republican theory. First, he demonstrates the fundamental harmony between Catholic natural law and classical republicanism. In revealing this essential harmony, he reinforces his claim that monarchy is only one of several regimes available to human beings. Second, Sidney defends classical republics against Filmer's charge that they were the home of demagogues and regimes inimical to moral virtue and patriotism.[44] In response, Sidney proposes the superiority of republics over monarchies. He argues that only the mixed governments typical of classical republics successfully imposed restraints on magistratical power, and promoted a notion of civic equality and the rule of law consistent with natural liberty. The unified republican front against divine right, however, ultimately gives way to Sidney's endorsement of Machiavellian republicanism rather than classical republicanism or Christian Aristotelianism. Sidney reinterprets republican virtue in terms of a lupine foreign policy and the capacity for military expansion, and thus concludes his defense of republicanism with an account of human nature more reflective of Machiavelli and Hobbes than of Aristotle and the other major classical and Christian thinkers.

In the course of his defense of republicanism, Sidney asserts that liberty is a "truth planted in the hearts of men," and is thus accessible to Christian and pagan alike. Both the Christian-Aristotelian theory of government, seen in Bellarmine and Suarez, and the classical republicanism, which Sidney associates with Aristotle and Plato, share the core teaching that "magistrates are chosen by societies, seeking their own good, and that the best men ought to be chosen for the attaining of it."[45] Sidney claims that these traditions share two common assumptions about government. First, the purpose of government is to promote the common good and to educate virtuous rulers and citizens dedicated to it. The end of government is both to provide for material security and to develop the rational faculties of the members of the community. Second, Sidney claims that all previous serious thinkers endorsed

---

[43] For a fuller treatment of Sidney's complex rhetorical strategy and design in the *Discourses*, see Lee Ward, "Rhetoric and Natural Rights in Algernon Sidney's *Discourses Concerning Government*," *Interpretation*, vol. 28, n. 2 (Winter 2000–1): pp. 119–45.

[44] For a representative sample of Filmer's antipathy toward the classical republics, see Robert Filmer, *Patriarcha and Other Writings*, Johann Somerville, ed. (Cambridge: Cambridge University Press, 1991): pp. 25–6.

[45] D 2.1.78, 82.

the mixed regime: "the wisest, best and far the greatest part of mankind, rejecting these simple species [monarchy, aristocracy, democracy], did form governments mixed or composed of the three."[46] Thus, the connection between virtue and mixed government lay at the heart of Sidney's conception of classical republicanism.

Sidney argues that only regimes informed by republican principles reward virtue with rule and encourage civic virtue among the people. Virtue in this understanding is inseparable from concern for the common good. Like Aristotle, who defined the deviant forms of the three simple species of regimes by their service to the private advantage of the ruling group at the expense of the common good, Sidney is concerned to demonstrate the connection between virtue and the proper end of government. Echoing Plato, Sidney even proposes that political power properly understood is a burden to rulers inasmuch as it binds them inextricably to the service of others.[47] Unmixed monarchy fails, in Sidney's view, to promote virtue for several reasons. First, monarchs historically have tended to hate and fear "all those that excelled in virtue," and typically saw the slaughter of these best men as a security for the throne.[48] Second, Sidney not only criticizes the abuses of power coincident with absolute monarchy but also contrasts the meritocratic tendencies of republics with any species of monarchy, even a limited one, based on hereditary right. Sidney presents the unthinking custom of heredity as the antithesis of selection due to virtue.[49] Third, Sidney lauds the capacity of republics to encourage public spirit. He calls them the "nurse of virtue," in which the private interests of individuals were successfully comprehended in the common good. The classical republics recognized the need to institute rewards and honors as inducements to virtuous activity among the citizenry.[50] Their legislators managed to combine public service with the individual's natural love of liberty.

Sidney contends that the citizens of ancient republics were more patriotic than royal subjects because the citizens had a genuine stake in the regime's

---

[46] While Sidney makes this statement at 1.10.31, he claims that he will prove this assertion "hereafter," presumably in Chapter Two.

[47] D 2.1.78–80. Cf. Aristotle, *Politics*, 1279b5–10 and *Ethics*, 1160b; and Plato, *The Republic*, Allan Bloom, trans. (New York: Basic Books, 1968), 345b–347a. Sidney does, however, confront the questions raised by Aristotle's celebrated praise for the supremely virtuous man by suggesting that Aristotle may have set the bar for monarchy so high – with almost godlike virtue – in order to prove its impossibility in practice (D 2.1.85 and 3.23.453). For a contemporary interpretation of Aristotle's treatment of the problem of kingship that is similar to that of Sidney, see Mary Nichols, *Citizens and Statesmen: A Study of Aristotle's Politics* (Savage, MD: Rowman & Littlefield, 1992): pp. 77–81.

[48] D 2.11.136, 2.12.144, 2.25.256.

[49] D 2.6.109–12, 2.11.135. Cf. Fink, who demonstrates how important the critique of heredity was for Sidney's defense of classical republicanism. See Zera Fink, *The Classical Republicans* (Chicago: Northwestern University Press, 1962): p. 152.

[50] D 2.1.78, 2.19.190, 2.12.146. Cf. Aristotle, *Ethics*, 1109b30–1110a1.

survival and success. The popular voice in public affairs produced a citizenry committed to the defense of the commonwealth. By contrast, in absolute monarchies, individuals lack the power to help their friends or to prevent injuries, and therefore they neglect "the affairs in which they had no part." In absolute regimes, the subjects are too insecure to defend it enthusiastically and are too apathetic to fear a change in government. Sidney presents numerous examples, ancient and modern, of small public-spirited republics defeating the armies of much larger absolute monarchies. He claims: "I think no example can be alleged of a free people that has ever been conquer'd by an absolute monarch."[51] If the unique genius of republican government, for Sidney, was its ability to combine concern for the public good with great military strength in an armed citizenry, then absolute monarchy emerges as the personification of the idea of using public force for private advantage.

Sidney's account of the importance of virtue to the classical republics is closely connected to his treatment of the structural aspects of the mixed governments typical of those regimes. The two major features of the mixed regime, which Sidney contrasts favorably with monarchy, are the popular element and the limits on magistratical power.[52] First, regarding the popular element, Sidney praises mixed regimes like the Mosaic and Roman republics for embodying the principle of civic equality, for instituting popular assemblies, and for their emphasis on the rule of law. Sidney argues that the popular voice given institutional expression in mixed regimes encouraged an ethos of civic equality consistent with natural equality. His concern to demonstrate the importance of this popular voice is reflected in his opposition to the notion of tacit consent, whereby a people are thought to express their sanction for a government by simply obeying its laws and not rebelling. Sidney charges that the "bare sufferance of a government" does not imply consent; rather, consent requires "an explicit act of approbation, when men have ability and courage to resist or deny."[53] Sidney strongly suggests that the explicit consent to rule is available only through popular assemblies where citizens can participate as members or at least in the election of those members. The principle of civic equality embodied in the popular element of government

---

[51] Bourbon France is Sidney's chief example of a great power unable to exert its natural strength because of the apathy of its subject people (D 2.21.196, 2.28.277). His major examples of small republics defeating large monarchies are the English Commonwealth in its struggles with the European powers and the ancient Greek city-states in their defeat of the mighty Persian Empire (D 2.11.134–5, 43–4). Cf. Aristotle, *Politics*, 1283a20 for the classical republican claim to citizenship based on military service.

[52] Sidney treats what he calls "the magistracy" as something like the modern executive, i.e., any supreme officer who administers the laws, not necessarily a king. Thus, the Israelite judges or the Roman consuls could play this traditionally monarchical part in the mixed regime (D 2.8.126). Throughout this chapter dedicated to Sidney, we will retain his use of "magistratical" rather than the more contemporary "magisterial."

[53] D 2.6.108–9.

found expression in the classical republican emphasis on the rule of law. For Sidney, law-abidingness is a republican virtue.[54] This virtue recognizes that while government requires a restraint on natural liberty, this restraint must be general. Only in a regime governed by law can the structures of the state preserve a measure of civic equality. Moreover, the rule of law allows the redress of injury without recourse to force. Sidney argues that the rule of law secures justice among citizens and allows the state to restrain and punish the ambition of private citizens seeking to usurp power. In absolute monarchy, which he poses as antithetical to the rule of law, "every man has recourse to force" in pursuit of justice and the defense of liberty.[55]

One key aim of the rule of law, in Sidney's view, is to limit magistratical power. He appeals in this respect to the philosophical authority of Hugo Grotius, who maintained that the law gives and measures the power of magistrates. As we have seen, even Grotius maintained that the people have a right to resist a magistrate bent on the destruction of the community.[56] As a creature of law, Sidney asserts that magistratical power is of an inherently limited character. The elevation of private interest that marks absolutism runs directly contrary to the republican practice of applying law to direct and restrain magistrates. Absolute monarchy repudiates the civic equality so central to the preservation of republics and, by extension, constitutes a rejection of natural liberty. Tyrants, Sidney charges, resist all law and "desire an unrestrained liberty of doing that which is evil."[57] Indeed, Sidney locates the symptom of the Roman republic's decline into empire in the elevation of its magistrates above the law. These were men like Pompey, "the author and destroyer of his own laws," rulers who "could no longer content themselves with that equality which is necessary among citizens."[58] Sidney argues that if one individual or group is above the law, then no one is safe. This condition undermines the general restraint on natural liberty implicit in the social contract.

The final thrust of Sidney's defense of classical republicanism expands beyond the particular criticism of divine right absolute monarchy to identify a problem inherent in monarchy per se. He reduces his opposition to the principle of monarchy to the formula: "Whatever is done by force or fraud to set up the interests and lusts of one man in opposition to the laws of his country, is purely and absolutely monarchical."[59] In this curious play on the meaning of the words "purely" and "absolutely," Sidney classifies monarchy as an idea, a regime pointing to a deeper principle of corruption in

---

[54] See, for example, Aristotle, *Ethics*, 1129a31–5, 1129b12–5.
[55] D 2.13.151, 2.30.297.
[56] Compare D 2.7.115., 2.27.265, 2.17.171 and Grotius, DJB, 1.3.14, 16 and 1.4.11.
[57] D 2.14.153, 2.20.195.
[58] D 2.18.179–80, 2.26.263, 2.19.184.
[59] D 2.24.250.

human nature. While Sidney admits that the corrupt use of public power for private interest is a possibility in any government, he insists that monarchy is *rooted* in it. Monarchy is natural only in the sense that "our depraved nature is most inclined to it."[60] The purest expression of monarchy is a form of lawlessness. This is the tendency of one-man rule of any kind, and this is why republics were so careful to restrain magistrates. Even mixed monarchies, Sidney suggests, find it difficult to resist the slide into absolutism.

Machiavellian Republicanism

At a point roughly two-thirds through the second chapter of the *Discourses*, Sidney's defense of classical republicanism takes a dramatic Machiavellian turn. He explicitly jettisons some of the central elements of classical republican thought. Instead of defending traditional republican moderation and anti-imperialism, Sidney praises wars of territorial expansion; rather than lauding the classical republican concern for civic unity, he commends the salutary consequences of popular tumults. In praising the imperialistic and turbulent Roman Republic at the expense of Sparta, the classical exemplar of moderation and civic unity, he follows Machiavelli rather than respected ancient commentators like Plutarch and Polybius.[61] Sidney's broad defense of the idea of republicanism ultimately narrows into a specific theory of republicanism rooted in a Machiavellian conception of human nature rather than that of the ancients.

The classical republican argument for citizen armies rested on a concern to ensure communal self-government. While Sidney praises both Sparta and Rome as regimes dedicated to war, he presents a distinction between the ends these republics pursued through war. He relates: "some of those that

---

[60] See D 2.19.189 and 2.24. 234, where Sidney describes the passions in these terms: "Every man has passions, few can moderate and none can wholly extinguish them."

[61] Plutarch, "Life of Lycurgus" in *The Lives of the Noble Grecians and Romans*, John Dryden, trans. (New York: Everyman, 1952): pp. 49–74 and Polybius, *The Histories*, Evelyn Shuckburgh, trans. (Lake Bluff, IL: Regnery Gateway, 1987): VI 10–11, 48. Cf. Cicero's criticism of the Roman tumults in Cicero, *Republic*, II: 33 (Cicero, *The Republic and The Laws*, Niall Rudd, trans. [Oxford: Oxford University Press, 1988]). For good treatments of Machiavelli,'s decisive break from the classical republican view of human rationality, civic concord, and political moderation, see Harvey Mansfield, *New Modes and Orders: A Study of the Discourse on Livy* (Ithaca: Cornell University Press, 1979); Paul Rahe, "Situating Machiavelli," in *Renaissance Civic Humanism*, James Hankins, ed. (Cambridge: Cambridge University Press, 2000): pp. 270–308 (esp. pp. 293–308); and Vickie B. Sullivan, *Machiavelli's Three Romes: Religion, Human Liberty, and Politics Reformed* (DeKalb: Northern Illinois University Press, 1996). For the contrary view, which associates Machiavelli with classical republicanism broadly understood, see Pocock, *The Machiavellian Moment: Florentine Political Thought and the Atlantic Republican Tradition* (Princeton: Princeton University Press, 1975): pp. 183–218 and Quentin Skinner, "Machiavelli's *Discorsi* and the Pre-Humanist Origins of Republican Ideas," in *Machiavelli and Republicanism*, Gisela Bock, Quentin Skinner, and Maurizio Viroli, eds. (Cambridge: Cambridge University Press, 1990): pp. 121–41.

intended war desir'd to enlarge their territories by conquest; others only to preserve their own, and to live with freedom and safety upon them. Rome was of the first sort; ... On the other side the Spartans." A few pages later, Sidney implicitly refers to Machiavelli to decide the contest between Sparta and Rome: " the best judges of these matters have always given the preference to those constitutions that ... think it better to aim at conquest, rather than simply to stand upon their own defense."[62]

What is perhaps most striking in Sidney's choice of Rome over Sparta is that he bases this decision on an understanding of politics alien to the classical republican tradition that these two regimes represent. Sidney justifies Roman imperial expansion by reference to a theory of the natural process of growth and decay. As he states, if a nation does not grow, "it must pine and perish; for in this world nothing is permanent; that which does not grow better will grow worse." Sidney reveals that by "better" he means *stronger*:

That government is evidently the best, which, not relying upon what it does at first enjoy, seeks to increase the number, strength, and riches of the people; and by the best discipline to bring the power so improved into such order as may be of most use to the publick.[63]

The inevitable process of expansion and demise is rooted in the natural state of hostility between peoples. Sidney's preference for Roman imperialism over Spartan moderation depends on his reflections on the brutal character of nature. In their concern for virtue and decent political life, the classical republican theorists who praised Sparta did not, he suggests, adequately appreciate that the natural state of international relations is a brutal struggle and competition for scarce resources.

With this presentation of an essentially Machiavellian view of the natural state of war, Sidney indicates the dramatic shift from his earlier position. God and nature are no longer assumed to be hospitable to and providing for human needs. Classical republican and Catholic natural law theorists assumed a greater beneficence in nature than there actually is. In praising war as good in itself, because it reflects the natural necessity of power, Sidney registers his increasing distance from Aristotle.[64] One of the prominent features of Sidney's Machiavellian turn is the reduction of reason to an instrument of the passions. Sidney's presentation of reason's inability to secure justice in a violent world reveals that the moral and intellectual benefits of association

[62] D 2.22.203, 205. Cf. Niccolo Machiavelli, *Discourses on Livy*, Harvey Mansfield and Nathan Tarcov, trans. (Chicago: University of Chicago Press, 1996): bk. 1, chs. 2, 6.
[63] D 2.23.209.
[64] See Aristotle, *Politics*, 1271b1–2, 1333b4–15. Cf. Vickie B. Sullivan, "Muted and Manifest English Machiavellianism: The Reconciliation of Machiavellian Republicanism with Liberalism in Sidney's *Discourses Concerning Government* and Trenchard and Gordon's *Cato's Letters*," in *Machiavelli's Republican Legacy*, Paul Rahe, ed. (in press), pp. 14–15 of currently unpublished manuscript.

are not a truth immediately apparent to human beings. Rome surpassed its classical republican contemporaries not because of the genius of its founders or the carefully crafted reason behind its institutions, but rather because the regime unleashed the passions of its citizens in brazen, lupine wars of expansion.

Whereas classical republicans emphasized civic unity, Sidney argues that the Roman popular tumults were a salutary device that corrected defects in the original constitution. Even the best-laid constitutions contain defects and "Rome in its foundations was subject to these defects," but the problems "were by degrees discover'd and remedi'd."[65] Opening the magistracies to the plebs was one such correction. Sidney follows Machiavelli in arguing that the genius of Rome was its appreciation of the positive benefits of mutability in constitutional orders. Popular discontent acted as a vehicle for change. Sidney goes so far as to practically equate the legislative power in Rome with the popular will expressed through tumults. These disturbances, he argues, "were composed without blood; and those that seemed to be the most dangerous produced the best laws."[66] Like Machiavelli, Sidney praises the Roman tumults and contrasts these largely bloodless disturbances with the periodic spasms of terrible civil violence seen in monarchies.[67] He thus defends the Roman Republic against its monarchist detractors. Yet in contrast to the classical republican tradition of Plato and Aristotle, Sidney does not posit perfect domestic harmony or even civic concord as the proper goal of political life. Sidney defends the passionate self-interest expressed in the class warfare of the Roman tumults as the animating principle in a republic of liberty.

Sidney's defense of republicanism includes the characteristically Machiavellian argument for the benefits derived from periodically reducing nations to their "first principles." Like Machiavelli, Sidney's understanding of these first principles relates to a nation's military capacity. He admits that "the wisdom of man is imperfect, and unable to foresee the effects that may proceed from an infinite variety of accidents." Thus, regarding the "superstructure" of government, "changes are therefore unavoidable," though the "foundations" of good government remain "unchangeable." Sidney points to Moses

---

[65] D 2.13.150. Cf. Machiavelli, *Discourses*, I: 4–6.

[66] D 2.14.153–54. Wood gives a good account of the manner in which Sidney sees popular tumults as indicative of a regime that recognizes popular freedom as one of its constituent elements (Neal Wood, "The Value of Asocial Sociability: Contributions of Machiavelli, Sidney, and Montesquieu," in *Machiavelli and the Nature of Political Thought*, Martin Fleisher, ed. [New York: Atheneum, 1972]: pp. 290, 296). I argue, however, that in Chapter Three of the *Discourses*, where Sidney deals more particularly with England, he exposes the fundamental flaw in Machiavellian republicanism to be its inability to properly ground the expression of popular freedom in institutions, such as the parliament. This grounding is connected to his greater emphasis in this chapter on fleshing out the character of his natural rights teaching.

[67] D 2.24.235–6.

as the one who laid "the foundation of the laws given to the Israelites."[68] While he does not immediately disappoint the traditional or pious expectation that the foundation of the Israelite regime was fidelity to God's revealed laws, Sidney eventually reveals that Moses provided for "the government given by God to the Hebrews, which chiefly fitted them for war, and to make conquests."[69] Sidney offers a thoroughly Machiavellianized reading of Scripture in order to propose the argument that the capacity to wage and win wars is inseparable from the very foundations of political society. War is the natural human condition, and any regime not directed to military success will not endure in the brutal and unforgiving arena of international affairs.

At one point in the discussion in Chapter Two of the *Discourses* Sidney uncharacteristically collapses the distinction between republics and absolute monarchies. War, Sidney contends, does not "less concern monarchies than commonwealths; nor the absolute less than the mixed: All of them have been prosperous or miserable, glorious or contemptible, as they were better or worse arm'd, disciplin'd or conducted." Despite his general approbation of republics vis-à-vis monarchies, he then proceeds to laud "the Assyrian valour" under Nebuchadnezzar and "the Persians who under Cyrus conquer'd Asia."[70] These examples of powerful despots raising obscure peoples to the heights of conquest cast a troubling shadow over Sidney's Machiavellian turn. If military success is the only standard by which to judge regimes, then on what basis can Sidney condemn the absolute monarchies of Nebuchadnezzar, Cyrus, or any modern despot who might emerge with their virtù? Sidney's rather tepid response is that absolute monarchy may allow exceptional leaders wide scope for their talents, but it does not generally produce them. Poor and unknown nations have been carried to military glory "by the bravery of their princes," but there is no reliable guarantee that their virtues will be transmitted to their successors.[71] Sidney claims: "The impossibility of this is a breach never to be repaired."

In the harsh light of Sidney's treatment of war, the biggest problem of absolute monarchy appears to be not its violation of the principle of consent, but rather the very practical problem of its inability to vouchsafe a perpetual stream of great military leaders. It appears that utility, rather than legitimacy, is the central problem of despotism. In the closing sections of the second chapter of the *Discourses*, Sidney subtly acknowledges the growing uneasiness of even his most sympathetic readers. The partisans of natural liberty can only be chilled by Sidney's praise of the kingcraft of two ancient

---

[68] See 2.17 (chapter title) and 2.17.173–4.

[69] D 2.22.205.

[70] D 2.23.210–11. Cyrus, of course, was praised by Machiavelli as one his great "armed prophets," along with Moses, Theseus, and Romulus, in Chapter 6 of *The Prince*. See Niccolo Machiavelli, *The Prince*, Harvey C. Mansfield, trans. (Chicago: University of Chicago Press, 1985).

[71] D 2.23.211.

despots. The argument for consent returns as a major theme after a short but painful absence. Sidney's position toward democracy becomes more conciliatory than hitherto, and he reaffirms the contractual origins of government.[72] He even registers an implicit criticism of Machiavelli by citing two of the Florentine's "armed prophets," Romulus and Theseus, to prove that no single man, regardless of his extraordinary courage and strength, "was ever able to subdue many."[73] In the final chapter, Sidney will try to purge Machiavellian republicanism of its crypto-monarchical tendencies by planting it on a firm foundation of natural rights. From Sidney's reformed and popularized English Constitution, the idea of a radical Whig modern republic is born.

---

[72] D 2.30.298–302, 2.32. It is interesting to note that at 2.30.293 Sidney refers to François Hotman's argument in Chapter 6 of *Francogallia*, where the Huguenot theorist claims that tyrannical or abusive magistrates are subject to removal by the people because the power of the rulers is originally conferred by the people. Sidney's gesture toward Hotman near the end of Chapter Two clearly prepares the way for Sidney's more involved reflections on the Gothic Polity in Chapter Three. While Sidney employs Gothic constitutionalism to refute Filmer's contention that all government is monarchical in origin, he differs from a thinker like Hotman inasmuch as he ultimately consigns the Gothic Polity to a particular historical period. Moreover, Sidney reveals that the mixed governments of the Gothic Polities of the "Northern Kingdoms" were grounded on inherently unstable social relations rather than on the theoretical postulation of popular sovereignty expressed institutionally. Contrast Sidney's use of Hotman near the end of Chapter Two (D 2.30.292–3, 295) with his later account of the collapse of England's ancient constitution (D 3.28, 3.37.527).

[73] D 2.31.305.

7

A New Republican England

Sidney's broad defense of republican principles culminated in the articulation of a distinctly modern form of radical Whig republicanism. In his synthesis of Machiavellian republicanism and the modern natural rights theories of Hobbes, and especially of Spinoza, Sidney presents a vision of a new English republic grounded on radical Enlightenment philosophy. This new radical Whig English republic would be ruled by broadly based popular representative institutions that would immediately and directly reflect the sovereign power of the people. Sidney's republican idea of sovereignty is in a sense as absolutist as the moderate Whig idea of parliamentary sovereignty of king-in-Parliament; however, with the republican Sidney, the sovereign power is emphatically popular, even democratic. As such, Sidney offers a stinging critique of executive prerogative, and of the mixed and limited monarchical models of constitutionalism prevalent in England in the seventeenth century. In this respect, Sidney's vision of a democratic English republic broke new and uncharted ground in the Anglo-American constitutional and political tradition.

Republican Natural Rights

The core of Sidney's radical Whig republicanism is the idea of natural rights. These are the rights and liberties of individuals, which are "innate, inherent, and enjoy'd time out of mind."[1] The character of these rights "subsists as arising from the nature and being of man." They derive from a source independent of their particular civil or historical context. The ground for Sidney's version of rights is the natural equality existing "in a multitude that is not entered into any society." This natural equality, however, is more reminiscent

---

[1] Algernon Sidney, *Discourses Concerning Government*, Thomas West, ed. (Indianapolis: Liberty Fund Classics, 1996) (hereafter as D, ch., sec., and, where appropriate page): D 3.9.366, 3.14.394, 3.29.495.

of Hobbes than of Bellarmine or Suarez. Sidney claims: "One man can justly demand nothing...where there is no society, one man is not bound by the actions of another."[2] Moral obligation arises only when individuals offer "a publick declaration of their assent" to resign their natural liberty.

Natural rights are the underlying premise of Sidney's treatment of the origin and ends of government. He states: "the only ends for which governments are constituted, and obedience rendered to them, are the obtaining of justice and protection." As with Hobbes, the core of Sidney's natural rights teaching is the universal right of self-preservation. The state of natural liberty, for Sidney, is one of great insecurity in which "a private man from knowledge of his own weakness and inability to defend himself, must come under the protection of a greater power than his own."[3] But what do natural rights imply for the origin of government? First, Sidney's natural rights argument establishes the security of property as one of the main motives for the formation of political society. Commentators on Sidney typically observe that he does not treat the issue of property with nearly the same degree of attention as many of his Whig contemporaries. While this is certainly true, this should not blind us to its importance for Sidney.[4] Sidney evinces the individualistic character of natural rights in his assertion that "liberty consists only in being subject to no man's will." But, he adds, a necessary component of this idea of liberty is the means to self-preservation:

Property also is an appendage to liberty; and 'tis as impossible for a man to have a right to lands or goods, if he has no liberty, and enjoys his life only at the pleasure of another, as it is to enjoy either when he is deprived of them.[5]

As such, Sidney charges that one of the duties of political rulers is "to preserve the lands, goods and liberties of their subjects." By identifying one of the primary ends of government to be the protection of the individual "in the peaceful enjoyment and innocent use of what I possess," Sidney denies the moral and psychic telos posited in classical philosophy and Christian thought.

---

[2] D 3.29.495, 3.33.510–11.

[3] D 3.33.512, 3.41.548–9.

[4] Contrast Sidney's sporadic treatment of property with John Locke, *Two Treatises of Government*, Peter Laslett, ed. (Cambridge: Cambridge University Press, 1988), II: ch. 5 and James Tyrrell, *Patriarcha, Non Monarcha* (1681): pp. 109–13* (second pagination) (hereafter PNM). One major exception to the general neglect of the property issue among Sidney scholars is Houston, who does treat Sidney's notion of property in the context of its relation to the more celebrated theory of Locke (Houston, *Algernon Sidney*, pp. 111–14).

[5] D 3.16.402–3. Sidney repeats the formula in the following sentence, later at 3.42.557 and 3.43.558. Cf. Neal Wood ("The Value of Asocial Sociablity: Contributions of Machiavelli, Sidney and Montesquieu, in *Machiavelli and the Nature of Political Thought*, Martin Fleisher, ed. [New York: Atheneum, 1972]: p. 292) where he identifies Sidneyan civil society as a contractual arrangement intended to secure rights like property in land and goods.

In presenting property rights as an appendage of liberty, Sidney follows a broadly Grotian reading of the origin of private property. He maintains that the original title to property derived from a kind of seizure right. The original negative community – no one owning anything in particular – soon gave way, in Sidney's view, to the claims of occupancy. Sidney relates:

> If every man take upon him to seize what he could, a certain method of making the distribution was necessarily to be fixed; and it was fit, that every man should have something in his own hands to justify his title to what he possessed, according to which controversies should be determined.[6]

While Sidney does not indicate that the creation of private property *required* the approval of the entire community, he does maintain that individual property rights are not the result of feudalism but were always derivative of membership in the larger society.[7] Thus, while political society may raise the normative status of property rights from an insecure natural seizure right to a mutually recognized civil right, it is the claim of natural rights, rather than membership in the community, that is the primary source of property for Sidney.

However, the most fundamental aspect of Sidney's treatment of the origins of political society is his attempt to mediate between the positions of Hobbes and Machiavelli. As we have seen, Sidney suggested that Machiavelli's republicanism was prejudiced by his indiscriminate praise of men like Cyrus, the founder of the Persian autocracy.[8] In Chapter Six of *The Prince* Machiavelli exalts Cyrus in addition to Moses, Romulus, and Theseus as "armed prophets" who founded great empires. Machiavelli presents these men as extraordinary individuals who gained command of a relatively small armed force capable of dominating an obscure and distressed people and then transforming them into a conquering nation. Though Theseus, Romulus, and Moses were, in contrast to Cyrus, founders of republics, this founding was not an expression of popular consent, but rather showed the effective and calculated use of terrifying force. In Machiavelli's view, only the simulation of the anxiety and insecurity of a state of natural

---

[6] D 3.29.496.

[7] Conniff observes that Sidney ties property rights to membership in the community but nevertheless roots this right in the natural self-preservation right of the individual rather than in the consent of the community (see James Conniff, "Reason and History in Early Whig Thought: The Case of Algernon Sidney," *The Journal of the History of Ideas*, vol. 23 [July 1982]: p. 409).

[8] In this respect, Sidney differs from the pattern of Spinoza and Rousseau. They expressed the view that Machiavelli's study of kingcraft in the *Prince* was actually a satire of princes intended to educate a republican audience. See Benedict Spinoza, *A Theologico-Political Treatise and A Political Treatise*, R. H. M. Elwes, trans. (New York: Dover, 1951): V, 7, p. 315 and Jean-Jacques Rousseau, *On Social Contract*, in *Rousseau's Political Writings*, Alan Ritter and Julia Conaway Bondanella, eds., (New York: Norton, 1988): III, 6, p. 129. In contrast, Sidney treats Machiavelli's monarchical tendencies as a problem inherent in the latter's conception of the origins of political society.

liberty can produce the proper conditions for founding any well-ordered political society, whether republican or monarchical.[9] And Machiavelli implies that the power to do this, at least initially, is generally not popular.

One of the ironies in Sidney's thought is that he employed an essentially Hobbesian natural rights teaching to expunge the crypto-monarchical tendencies he saw in Machiavelli. The antipathy of the arch-royalist Hobbes to the republican school associated with Machiavelli is a prominent feature in the former's work.[10] In order to understand Sidney's complex position regarding these two giants of early modern political thought, it is necessary to identify an important element in Hobbes' treatment of the origin of government. Hobbes understood the origin of political society in terms of two distinct processes: the "Commonwealth by Institution" and the "Commonwealth by Acquisition." While the rights of the sovereign are the same in both, they differ inasmuch as in the former individuals choose their sovereign "for fear of one another," whereas in the latter they "subject themselves to him they are afraid of."[11] Hobbes' Commonwealth by Acquisition is but another version of the regimes founded by Machiavelli's "armed prophets." Sidney's method is to defend the popular and freely given consent of the Commonwealth by Institution against the coercive models offered by Machiavelli and Hobbes. Although Hobbes was open to the possibility of violent foundings, he was less taken by its furious charms than the famous Florentine.

It is the latent populism of Hobbesian natural rights theory to which Sidney appeals. Even in the midst of his defense of classical republicanism Sidney offered circumspect praise of Hobbes. He observed that "Hobbes fearing the advantage" taken by bold and violent men

[h]as no regard at all to him who comes in without title or consent;...and allows all things to be lawful against him, that may be done to a publick enemy or pirate: which is as much as to say, any man may destroy him who can.[12]

---

9 Sullivan, "Muted and Manifest English Machiavellianism: The Reconciliation of Machiavellian Republicanism with Liberalism in Sidney's *Discourses Concerning Government* and Trenchard and Gordon's *Cato's Letters*," ed. Paul Rahe (Lanham, MD: Rowman and Littlefield, in press): pp. 6–7. See also Harvey Mansfield, *Machiavelli's Virtue* (Chicago: University of Chicago Press, 1996), ch. 2 and Leo Strauss, *Thoughts on Machiavelli* (Glencoe, IL: Free Press, 1958): pp. 25, 70–1. In viewing the difference between Machiavelli and Sidney regarding first principles as one of populism versus violent foundings, rather than a difference relating to historical progress, my argument differs from that of Worden (see Blair Worden, "The Commonwealth Kidney of Algernon Sidney," *Journal of British Studies*, vol. 24, no. 1 [January 1985]: 1–40, esp. 19).

10 For Hobbes' harsh criticism of republicanism, see Thomas Hobbes, *Leviathan*, Edwin Curley, ed. (Indianapolis: Hackett, 1994): 21.8–9, pp. 139–41 and *De Cive* in *Man and Citizen* (Indianapolis: Hackett, 1991): 10.8–15, pp. 228–33.

11 Hobbes, *Leviathan*, 20.2–3. pp. 127–8.

12 D 2.24.221.

Sidney wryly notes that whatever Hobbes "may be guilty of in other respects, he does in this follow the voice of mankind." While Sidney never goes so far as to call Romulus, Theseus, et al. public enemies or pirates, he does consciously diminish their importance as founders in favor of the more popular notion of consent. For example, Sidney finds the origin of Rome not in the "armed prophet" Romulus, but rather in the meeting of "a company of Latins, Sabines and Tuscans" on the banks of the Tiber. These men, Sidney continues, "carried their liberty in their own breasts.... This was their charter; and Romulus could confer no more upon them."[13] When Machiavelli speaks of the need periodically to return states to their "first principles," it often means to a state of nearly universal fear like that produced by its founder-conquerors. When Sidney speaks of returning to first principles, it *always* means popular freedom. Sidney's Rome was clearly a commonwealth by institution.

Despite Sidney's reliance on an essentially Hobbesian understanding of natural rights, radical Whig republican politics is more akin to that of Machiavelli. Sidney tried to purge the monarchical undertones in Machiavelli's thought precisely to purify the latter's conception of republican government. According to Sidney, Machiavelli recognized the dangers magistratical power posed for republican self-rule, but he failed to provide the theoretical foundation necessary to assess and limit this danger properly. Sidney employs the individualist logic of Hobbes' consent theory against Machiavelli's violent foundations in order to correct a fundamentally Machiavellian position. Indeed, as we shall see, the great majority of Sidney's argument expressed serious disagreement with Hobbes over the character of sovereignty.

The Problem of Executive Power

Radical Whig republicanism expressed a deep distrust of executive power. In Sidney's treatment of England's mixed Constitution, executive power is identified as one of the principal dangers to popular liberty. In contrast to Hobbes, Sidney argued that any free people must establish "the moderate government of a legal and just magistracy."[14] Sidney emphasizes that the popular foundation of regimes precedes the magistracy and thus can limit and direct it through law. The three most important limitations Sidney identifies that inform a "legal and just magistracy" are the separation of powers, certain prescribed fundamental laws, and the natural limits of the power of any single human being. Consent implies the power to limit the power created by the people.

---

[13] D 3.25.462, 3.33.511.
[14] D 3.10.370.

The primary aim of Sidney's discussion of the separation of powers is to distinguish magistracy from sovereignty. The first phase of Sidney's argument is his assertion that kings or other magistrates are created by the people, not vice versa. Rather than the monarch or executive officer, Sidney claims that the legislative body is the primal expression of political power in any civil society. In the specific case of England, Sidney claims to prove "the essence of parliaments to be as ancient as our nation." With this claim, Sidney aims to make two points. First, he offers a standard Whig response to the royalist charge that Parliament originated in and continues by virtue of royal grace. In positing Parliament as antecedent to the institution of monarchy, Sidney presents royal power as one delegated from the legislature: "All magistratical power ... receives its being and measure from the legislative power in every nation."[15] Thus, by definition, nations are legally constituted bodies. The second point Sidney makes, in contrast to Machiavelli, is that founding is an essentially legislative process. Sidney's presentation of the inherent limits on magistratical power expresses his concern to demonstrate that the first and most fundamental active agency in regime formation is the agreement of many individuals to unite into one legislative body; it is not the awesome exercise of brute force.

Sidney defines the "two swords" of government as the sword of justice and the sword of war. These swords represent the powers of government that Sidney emphasizes must be located in separate bodies if mixed government is to survive and flourish. Moreover, he claims that historically in good governments the magistrates have been given partial but not total power over both swords. The sword of justice, in Sidney's view, includes the legislative and executive power, and the sword of war relates exclusively to military command.[16] While Sidney never offers a detailed treatment of the latter, he goes to considerable lengths to show that mixed regimes in the past have given their magistrates only partial control over the legislative and executive functions. For example, Sidney refers to the Hebrew regime as one in which the king could make no law and could only judge controversies in conjunction with the Sanhedrin council of nobles. In Sparta, Sidney claims, the kings had no role in the legislative or judicial functions but were restricted purely to military command.[17] In both cases, the power of the kings was limited by a legislative body of some kind.

The second major source of limitation Sidney identifies for magistratical power is that of prescribed legal limits. These limits both inhere in the

---

[15] D 3.9.366, 3.12.386.
[16] D 3.10.374. The sword of justice seems to include the judicial function or, as Sidney terms it, the power of "judging controversies." It is important to note that Sidney's "two swords" appear to replace the Christian-Aristotelian notion of the swords spiritual and temporal. Cf. D 2.24.219.
[17] D 3.10.374–5.

legislative process and represent basic fundamental laws directing and restraining magistratical action. Sidney claims that mixed government establishes the powers in such a way that the legislative body formulates the public
good that a king, for example, must pursue. However, Sidney also turns to
fundamental laws as means to bind the actions of magistrates. For example,
he argues that in England the Magna Carta commands the kings never to
"sell, delay, nor deny justice to any man, according to the laws of the land."
Likewise, Sidney claims that in republican Rome "there was a reservation
of the supreme power in the people, notwithstanding the creation of the
magistrates without appeal."[18] Thus, Sidney defends the possibility of creating laws unalterable by magistratical action. These laws support the formal
separation of powers by providing the people with a means to measure the
rectitude of the executive's actions.

Sidney's treatment of the issue of legal limits on magistratical power
closely relates to his opposition to the principle of prerogative. The idea
of prerogative so dear to English royalists held that magistrates are justified
in acting above, beyond, or even against the law if the public good requires
such action. Sidney is unique, even among Whig theorists, inasmuch as he
utterly rejects the idea of prerogative power. He does so on a number of
grounds. First, Sidney maintains that regardless of the public good that may
be served by prerogative power in particular instances, in the general scheme
of political affairs it destroys the liberty it intends to protect. Sidney's chief
concern is that prerogative power sets a dangerous constitutional precedent,
inasmuch as while good rulers may act for the public good, bad rulers may
appeal to the precedent of their virtuous predecessors in order to do ill.[19]
Second, Sidney maintains that the traditional royalist argument for prerogative in cases of equity and in the pardon power was unjustified given that
royal exercise of this right did no genuine good for protecting the liberty of
the subjects and only excused royal interference in the legal process. Instead
he advances the position that the rights of the accused are best protected by
the institution of grand and petty juries composed of the accused's peers.
Sidney both endorses and extends the claims for the popular element in the
judicial process by maintaining that juries may act as triers both of fact and
of law. He claims that "grand and petty juries, are not only judges of matters
of fact, as whether a man be kill'd, but whether he be kill'd criminally."[20]
Sidney argues that unlike powerful magistrates, whose interference in judicial cases would be hard to resist if prerogative were widely accepted, the
malfeasance of individual jurors may be deterred or at least punished by the
threat of an indictment for perjury.

---

[18] D 3.14.394–5.
[19] D 3.21.442. Despite their differences over the issue of prerogative, Locke also feared this
problem. See John Locke, *Two Treatises of Government* (1690), Peter Laslett, ed. (Cambridge:
Cambridge University Press, 1988): II:166.
[20] D 3.22.447.

Sidney is also ambivalent toward the traditional royalist argument that prerogative is necessary as an emergency power. He does not completely reject this argument; rather, he defines this power narrowly and then extends its application far beyond the unique purview of magistrates. Sidney accepts the emergency power as a central ingredient of magistratical duty. However, he restricts this power to that of calling the popular assembly at times "when the law does not exact it."[21] While the magistrate remains in office when the popular assembly is not in session, his only discretionary power, according to Sidney, is to assess the threat of an emergency and then do his duty to reconvene the assembly. To this narrow definition of magistratical prerogative, Sidney adds the important proviso that this power is not the exclusive preserve of the magistrate. As he relates of the Romans, "when Hannibal was at the gates . . . no wise man can think that formalities were to have been observed. In such cases every man is a magistrate."[22] Thus, Sidney radicalizes and popularizes this emergency power element of prerogative by extending it to any member of the assembly or to the public. In Sidney's view, popular or legislative bodies contain within themselves a right of convening, regardless of the exact stipulations of law.

On one level, Sidney's opposition to prerogative is very practical. The potential advantages of such a magistratical right are severely outweighed by the palpable dangers. Moreover, these advantages may be gained more safely and reliably by extending discretionary power to the other, more popular elements of the government. Prerogative is, by and large, antithetical to the public good and individual liberty. Yet, Sidney also poses a more theoretical objection to prerogative. He explicitly connects the practice of prerogative with the principle of divine right. He relegates the practice of unlimited prerogative to a time of greater "simplicity" in the distant past, when men were unschooled in the abuses of power it introduces.[23] He implies that it begins a dangerous process of encouraging popular acceptance of arbitrary acts, a process that almost inevitably eventuates in the divinization of politics. Even the worldly-wise Romans, in Sidney's view, succumbed to this tendency. Sidney adduces the case of Augustus, who came to power through the support of a "mad corrupted soldiery" and ruled the people arbitrarily, but who came in time to be "the object of their religion."[24] For Sidney, prerogative power undermines the principle of consent by affirming a right of political action independent of the popular will expressed through law.

Another, more fundamental limit on magistratical power that Sidney identified is the natural limit of any individual's physical power. In his discussion about the difference between the coactive and directive power of law he

[21] D 3.39.538.
[22] D 3.38.528.
[23] D 3.21.443.
[24] D 3.24.455.

equates right and power: one has the right to do, what one has the power to do, and by nature a magistrate's power is very limited. Sidney's reflections on the relation between the right to command and the power to command are at the core of his theory of radical Whig republicanism. Sidney denies that the "coactive" (or coercive) power of law is inherent in the magistratical office. For example, although Nero formally exercised the coercive power of the Roman Empire for a time, when the legions overthrew him it became apparent that Nero, as an individual, had little or no coercive power over a multitude of people.[25] The unifying thread in Sidney's observations on the directive and coactive power of law is his concern to show the natural foundations of democracy. It is only in popular regimes that these two aspects of law, right and power, can be made compatible. The tendency to equate power and right in Sidney's treatment of law rests on a deeper metaphysical reflection on the natural order of power. It is in this respect that the influence of Spinoza emerges as a key element in Sidney's thought. While accepting the Hobbesian premise of the origin of government in consent and the natural rights of individuals, Sidney follows Spinoza in advancing a harsh criticism of the absolutist implications Hobbes drew from this premise. Sidney associates strength, and thus right, with popular government because it alone among regimes actively engages the collected power of the multitude of individuals.[26] The right to rule is coextensive with the power to rule. Thus, Sidney responds to Hobbes that democracy is stronger than autocracy. The weakness of the individual Nero is indicative of the weakness of the individual per se. The government that best secures the liberty of the individual is that which most effectively augments the power of the individual with the collected power of the multitude of individuals.

Sidney's defense of popular sovereignty against Hobbes' absolutism mirrors that of Spinoza little more than a decade earlier. In the *Theologico-Political Treatise*, Spinoza implicitly responded to Hobbes:

Men have never so far ceded their power as to cease to be an object of fear to the rulers who received such power and right; . . . If it were really the case that men could

---

[25] D 3.11.382. Winston Churchill succinctly described the phenomenon of military rule in England, a situation all too familiar to Sidney, as follows: "The story of the Second Civil War is short and simple. King, Lords, and Commons, landlords and merchants, the City and the countryside, bishops and presbyters, the Scottish army, the Welsh people, and the English Fleet, all now turned against the New Model Army. The Army beat the lot" (Winston Churchill, *A History of the English Speaking Peoples: The New World, Volume II* [New York: Dodd, Mead, 1956], p. 274). Cf. Austin Woolrych, *Britain in Revolution, 1625–1660* (Oxford: Oxford University Press, 2002), pp. 402–33, for a more comprehensive, though less dramatic, treatment of the war.

[26] See Benedict Spinoza, *A Theologico-Political Treatise and A Political Treatise*, R. H. M. Elwes, trans. (New York: Dover, 1951): TPT 16. 205 and PT 4.1.309, 8.3–4.347 (here and hereafter TPT and PT, respectively, followed by chapter, page number, and section for PT). Spinoza's understanding of the relation between power and right explains his shared concern with Sidney regarding the dangers of a corrupted military. See Spinoza, PT 7.12.333.

be deprived of their natural rights so utterly as never to have any further influence on affairs...it would then be possible to maintain with impunity the most violent tyranny, which, I suppose, no one would for an instant admit.[27]

As Sidney argues repeatedly in the last chapter of the *Discourses*, echoing Spinoza, democracy is the most natural, and thus the best, regime because it is physically impossible for an individual or even an unarmed but substantial minority to govern a multitude without their consent. From this Spinozist modification of Hobbesian natural rights theory, Sidney offers a defense of popular republicanism against Hobbesian absolutism. By linking the doctrine of natural liberty to the contention that all legitimate rule rests on popular sovereignty and is directed to the security of rights, Sidney establishes the theoretical foundations of radical Whig republicanism.

It is with regard to the issue of revolution that the difference between Sidney's popular sovereignty theory and Hobbes' theory of sovereignty is most apparent. Sidney refers directly to Hobbes to disprove the latter's claim that insofar as the people give all their power to the sovereign, the sovereign can use this power to absolve himself of the crime of perjury. While Sidney agrees with Hobbes' minor premise – the sovereign derives all his power from the people – he disputes the absolutist implications of this premise. Echoing Spinoza, Sidney responds that the people have not "conferred upon him all, but only a part of their power."[28] With this reservation of power in the people as a collectivity over and against that power granted to the political ruler, Sidney expands the notion of inalienable rights far beyond the limits set by Hobbes.[29] It amounts to a general right of revolution. What is particularly striking in Sidney's treatment of this reservation of power in the people is the emphasis on the collective right of the people to rebel against the institutions of their own creation. Within this logic of rebellion, there is a further subset of assumptions validating the legitimate rights and power of the legislative assembly over those of the magistrate or monarch. Sidney assumes that if government is created by naturally free and equal beings in pursuit of their security and advantage, then any formal structure of government or any particular ruler is subject to replacement by the sovereign people. Sidney maintains that political obligation only extends to a government demonstrably pursuing the public interest.

Sidney's position on the right of revolution signals his profound differences from Hobbes. Although he advances a theory of natural rights and the contractual origins of government that reflects some central Hobbesian

---

[27] Spinoza, TPT 17.214–15. While primarily directed against Hobbes, I believe this statement would also constitute one of Spinoza and Sidney's objections against the possibility of contractual absolutism in Grotius.

[28] D 3.17.409. Cf. Hobbes, *Citizen*, 6.14, 7.11, 12.4.

[29] Sidney argues that vis-à-vis government "the people continue as free as the internal thoughts of a man" (D 3.36.521). For Hobbes' limits on inalienable rights, see *Leviathan*, 21.8–9.141–5.

premises, Sidney repudiates Hobbes by validating revolution as a reflection of the popular foundations of any regime. The "extrajudicial" power expressed in revolution is merely the exertion of the collected power of individuals, which underlies the actions of government. For Sidney, only the collected power of individuals can ensure the end of government, the protection of rights, and the preservation of free and popular institutions. Sidney marks a sharp distinction between the political obligation of the individual and the constitutive power of the community as a whole. He argues that the obedience due to government from "private men is grounded upon and measured by the general law; . . . the whole body therefore of a nation cannot be tied to any obedience that is inconsistent with the common good, according to their own judgment."[30] By this Sidney does not, of course, deny the individual's right of resistance; rather, he emphasizes that only an entire community acting as a collectivity can legitimately alter the system of government. Indeed, he defines the "general revolt of a nation" as nothing less than such a radical constitutional reordering. His response, then, to Hobbesian natural rights absolutism includes the argument that autocracy is too weak to secure even the individual right of self-preservation. Sidney opines that "the best constitutions are of no value, if there be not a power to support them." The animating force of all legitimate constitutional orders, Sidney continues, is "the power of the whole."[31] Autocratic regimes, he contends, are isolated from popular support and thus are vulnerable to internal and external threats.

England Old and New

Sidney's argument for popular sovereignty underlies his entire treatment of the English Constitution. He defends the popular origins of the English Constitution against the royalist position rejecting the independence of Parliament.[32] In Sidney's presentation of his country's government, the theoretical "ought" is popular sovereignty expressed through parliamentary supremacy. However, the practical and historical reality differs substantially from this principle of legitimacy. Sidney's reflections on the historically unresolved problem of royal pretensions to supremacy and the uncertain future of England's hereditary nobility cast serious doubt on the future success or even survival of the English Constitution. It is only in his account of English constitutional development that Sidney discloses the full extent of his departure from traditional English mixed regime theory. Sidney suggests that

---

[30] D 3.36.519.

[31] D 3.36.524.

[32] See, for example, Filmer's argument that Parliament originates in and continues by royal grace and the plenitude of royal power (Robert Filmer, *Patriarcha and Other Writings*, Johann Somerville, ed. (Cambridge: Cambridge University Press, 1991): ch. 3, secs. 12–14).

the English experiment in mixed government has failed and can only be corrected by a radical reordering culminating in an unshakable legislative supremacy. From Sidney's defense of the ancient mixed constitution against the divine right challenge, a new, more democratic and republican England emerges.

Sidney asserts that the popular origin of the English regime lies with those "lovers of liberty," the Saxons. He claims that "the Saxons in their own country had their councils, where *all* were present," and they carried this practice with them to England.[33] These radically democratic councils pre-existed and actually created the monarchy: "tho our ancestors had their councils and magistrates...they had no kings." It was by these "general councils and assemblies" that "kings were made." Sidney emphasizes that the legislative power inhering in the people and expressed through their universal participation in the general assemblies is not only the source of the monarchy, but also signifies the popular foundation of the English nobility. The important role of the nobility in the creation of England's mixed government is central for Sidney. He claims: "In all the legal kingdoms of the North, the strength of the government has always been placed in the nobility; and no better defense has been found against the encroachment of ill kings."[34] However, the Saxon nobility in Sidney's account is not the exclusive hereditary aristocracy of the later England; rather, the nobility itself was originally inseparable from England's democratic foundation. Sidney claims "that those called noblemen...are often by the historians said to be...an infinite multitude." Sidney's democratic interpretation of the term "nobility" rests on his association of noble titles with military service. Among a people like the Saxons, "perpetually in arms," military service as a claim to title provides for a highly egalitarian understanding of nobility.[35] In principle, the Saxon popular assembly and their council of nobles could have been virtually identical.

With this claim that England's mixed constitution originated in a popular foundation – an elective monarchy and a highly democratic council of

---

[33] D 3.28.479 (emphasis mine), 481. In contrast to Conniff ("Reason and History," pp. 399, 404, 412) and J. G. A. Pocock (*The Ancient Constitution and the Feudal Law* [Cambridge: Cambridge University Press, 1987]: pp. 46, 188, 238), I do not believe Sidney appealed to history as a legitimate or determinative source of political right. Rather I agree with Scott Nelson (*The Discourses* of Algernon Sidney [Cranbury, NJ: Associated University Presses, 1993]: p. 43) that Sidney dealt with historical claims to right largely in order to show their limitations in this regard. However, I believe Sidney appealed to English constitutional history primarily to criticize the historical understanding of the English Constitution. In this sense, the need to respond to Filmer afforded Sidney the opportunity to level his criticisms at one of England's most revered legal and political traditions.

[34] D 3.28.484.

[35] D 3.28.487, 490–2. Conniff ("Reason and History," p. 406) notes that Sidney was unique among Whig theorists inasmuch as his notion of popular sovereignty contains no clearly formulated idea of property qualifications.

nobles – Sidney goes some distance in harmonizing the historical origin of the regime with his theoretical account of natural rights and popular sovereignty. For Sidney, Saxon history stands as a plausible conceptual tool to delineate natural democracy. The strength of the Saxon regime lay literally in the body of the people. However, Sidney acknowledges that English constitutional development has obscured this popular foundation. The recurring theme in English history, he argues, has been the profound difficulty in preserving the balance of power in the mixed Constitution. In fact, Sidney's stance toward the Constitution becomes increasingly critical throughout the course of the final chapter. His earlier praise of the Magna Carta sours when he accuses it of failing to ensure that the law "for annual parliaments was observed." Sidney's distance from the ancient Constitution becomes gradually more palpable:

In England our ancestors who seem to have had some such thing in their eye as balancing the powers, by a fatal mistake placed usually so much in the hands of the king, that . . . his extravagances could not be repressed without great danger.[36]

These two major departures from the government's popular foundation – the failure to secure annual Parliaments and the delegation of sweeping powers to the crown – combined to deal a serious blow to England's balanced Constitution. These seeds of royal supremacy came to fruition, Sidney relates, in the "horrid series of the most destructive mischiefs" known as the War of the Roses.[37] The Constitution's incapacity to restrain regal power encouraged ambitious nobles backed by armed factions in their struggle for the crown. Sidney strongly implies that, despite his earlier protestations to the contrary, Parliament has not always settled the succession in England.[38] The balance of power has historically failed.

The problem lay in both the structural and the sociopolitical dimension of the English constitutional balance of power. The English attempt to balance the powers of government structurally by assigning the monarch a role in the legislative and judicial functions produced, in Sidney's view, a strong public impression that all the proceedings of government and the legal system depend on the will and judgment of the king and his ministers. Sidney systematically examines the historical royal powers of calling and proroguing Parliament, vetoing legislation, pardoning criminals, and presiding in the courts of law in order to reveal Parliament's superior claim in these matters.[39] In their effort to produce an effective executive power to check the popular

[36] D 3.27.475, 477.

[37] D 3.35.517.

[38] See D 3.18.430 for Sidney's earlier insistence that Parliament has always possessed a historic right to determine the succession.

[39] For the power to call Parliament, sec D 3.31, 38; the veto, 3.27.476, 3.34, 3.36: the pardon power, 3.22, 3.45.555; and the courts, 3.26 and 3.42.

assembly, the English produced a constitutional order that consistently and gradually eroded the legitimate claims of the popular branch.

The sociopolitical dimension of the problem of constitutional balance relates to the collapse of the feudal nobility. Sidney suggests that the nobility successfully checked royal power when noble title was rooted in military service and large property holdings. With their independent source of arms and wealth, these feudal lords had the wherewithal to resist monarchical pretensions.[40] However, this reliance on social bases of institutional power proved mistaken, for the feudal nobility was unable to prevent or even survive the vicious succession disputes of the later Middle Ages. Sidney claims that the War of the Roses "was the first step towards the dissolution of our ancient government."[41] The great losses sustained by the old nobility destroyed their standing in relation to the new nobility created by the victorious contenders for the crown. These new nobles were not independent of the king, but rather were his creatures. The centralization of power in the monarchy, especially regarding the distribution of titles and land, made nugatory the nobility's capacity to resist the king. Sidney implicitly contrasts the democratic character of the Saxon nobility with the increasingly narrow and dependent position of their successors.

The primary consequence of the collapse of the feudal nobility is the stark division of the nation into two camps. Sidney claims: "all things have been brought into the hands of the king and the commoners, and there is nothing left to cement them, and to maintain the union."[42] In the dissolution of the "ancient" English Constitution, Sidney finds the formation of, or devolution to, a civil society of increasingly autonomous individual rights bearers. Unforeseen developments have shattered the illusion of England as an organic whole composed of different social classes with competing and mutually limiting claims to rule. History has put to the sword the classical assumptions of English mixed regime theory. For Sidney, England is returning to its first principles: the balance cannot hold.

The argument for a radical Whig republic in England rests on Sidney's view of the legislative supremacy necessary for any legitimate and stable constitutional order. He does not endorse a return to the pristine Saxon democracy of the past or advocate the restoration of the mixed Gothic

---

[40] D 3.28.484. Cf. James Harrington, *The Commonwealth of Oceana*, J. G. A. Pocock, ed. (Cambridge: Cambridge University Press, 1992): pp. 52, 54–6.

[41] D 2.24.248.

[42] D 3.37.527. In arguing that Sidney rejects the classical republican notion of mixed government, my view differs from that of Zera Fink (*The Classical Republicans* [Chicago: Northwestern University Press, 1962]: pp. 163–5). I agree more with Conniff ("Reason and History," pp. 413–16), who maintains that Sidney seriously attempts to incorporate a progressive theory of history into his natural rights teaching. Unlike Conniff, however, I see Sidney's theory of history as closely linked to his critique of the English Constitution as traditionally understood.

Constitution. He cautions that it is best to make "new constitutions to repair the breaches made upon the old." The solution to England's constitutional problem, the problem of mixed government, is the institutionalization of the popular will through parliamentary supremacy.[43] Sidney agrees with absolutists such as Filmer, Hobbes, and Bodin that supreme power must be located somewhere in any proper constitutional order.[44] Indeed, he agrees with the moderate Whig Tyrrell that the inability to locate the supreme power has been the cause of England's constitutional woes. In Sidney's reformed republican England, supremacy rests unmistakably in Parliament. Parliamentary supremacy, in turn, points to a radical popular sovereignty, which stipulates that legislative supremacy is incompatible with an independent executive. He denies the executive practically any role in the legislative process: "The legislative power that is exercised by the parliament, cannot be conferred by writ of summons, but must be essentially and radically in the people." In Sidney's new England, Parliaments will be regular, democratic, and irresistible. He asserts that "the Legislative Power is always Arbitrary."[45] By this Sidney does not mean that it is unrestrained or not responsible, but rather that by nature it can assume the executive and judicial functions of the government at its own discretion. These functions are essentially delegated powers. Indeed, by its capacity to express the collected power of individuals, Sidney finds the coercive power of law proceeding from the authority of Parliament.

The distinction Sidney draws between the sovereign right of Parliament, essentially the Commons, and the subordinate or delegated powers of the executive and judiciary rests on the radical Whig "reflection theory" of republican sovereignty. Sidney maintains that popular sovereignty must translate into the constitutional supremacy of the popular legislative body. Sidney's defense of popular sovereignty is a product of a Spinozist natural rights philosophy of power. In Sidney's Saxon democracy we have the exemplar of Spinoza's teaching that "the right of the commonwealth is determined by the common power of the multitude."[46] Only the lawmaking body with broad popular representation can reflect both the power and interests of the

---

[43] D 3.37.526–7. Cf. Alan Houston, "Republicanism, the Politics of Necessity and the Rule of Law," *A Nation Transformed: England after the Restoration*, Alan Craig Houston and Steve Pincus, eds. (Cambridge: Cambridge University Press, 2001): pp. 258–9.

[44] In this respect, Sidney differs greatly from the strand of parliamentary contractarianism of the English civil war period typified by Philip Hunton's "A Treatise of Monarchie" (1643), in *Divine Right and Democracy*, David Wootton, ed. (Hammondsworth: Middlesex: Penguin Classics, 1986): Hunton maintained that the English Constitution was composed of three coequal branches, each with some share of the supreme power. Cf. Bodin, *Six Books*, (1606) 1:10 and 2:1; Hobbes, *Leviathan*, 29.16.216–17; and Filmer, *Patriarcha*, pp. 155–6.

[45] D 3.44.564, 3.45.569. Cf. Houston (*Algernon Sidney*, p. 195), who observes that by rejecting prerogative, Sidney virtually abolishes the monarchy.

[46] Spinoza PT 3.9.305.

collected power of all the individuals composing society. Sidney's defense of parliamentary supremacy in England, and his antimonarchism more broadly, follow Spinoza's reasoning that the individual in society "should be no more conditioned by the force and desire of individuals, but by the power and will of the whole body."[47] In Sidney's adaptation of Spinoza for the context of England, only Parliament can be sovereign because only Parliament, more particularly the Commons, can be understood to reflect "the power and will" of the whole body of the nation.

The reflection theory of sovereignty rests on Sidney's identification of power and right. From his understanding of the spectacular weakness of the individual as an individual, seen dramatically in the examples of Nero and of any number of ill-fated tyrants described in the *Discourses*, Sidney draws the conclusion that the supreme political power in any commonwealth coincides with the body or institution most closely reflecting or approximating the greatest power, namely, the people as a whole.[48] While Sidney and the moderate Whigs agreed on the need for supreme sovereign power, in this respect Sidney's natural rights and constitutional theory departs considerably from the moderate Whig position associated with Tyrrell and Pufendorf. The latter two, modifying Hobbes and Grotius, retained a compact theory of sovereignty whereby the determination of constitutional supremacy was essentially a matter to be settled by contract and agreement. In this theory, sovereignty could rest in the monarch or in some combination of the executive and legislative power. Sidney, following Spinoza, looks not to the explicit terms of the social compact to determine sovereignty, but rather to the character of the institution assuming this power. For the modern republican Sidney, only a popular legislative body can retain sovereign power, because this is the only kind of institution capable of harmonizing the fullest right with the greatest power. As Sidney's reinterpretation of the English Constitution clearly indicates, he holds any compact that locates sovereignty in anything other than a popular institution, for example the English effort to divide sovereignty in a mixed regime model, as a distortion of the essence of sovereignty and the nature of power.

At the core of Sidney's reflection theory of sovereignty is his insistence that there must be a homogeneity of interests between the governors and the governed. Legislative supremacy is defensible both because it reflects something like the general will of society, at least as long as the legislature is marked by frequent elections and numerous representation, and because the lawmakers are subject to the laws they make, just like every other citizen. Of course, Sidney indicates that the people may delegate powers to the executive or to judicial bodies, but this delegation occurs entirely to perform functions strictly defined and limited by the people or their representatives

---

[47] Spinoza TPT 16.202–3.
[48] Cf. D 3.11.

in the legislature. The homogeneity of interests between the people and the legislators ensures, in Sidney's view, that magistrates will not govern and act in pursuit of their particular interest. Once again, Sidney's version of democratic republicanism and the reflection theory of sovereignty on which it is based echo Spinoza's warning that "[if] a few are deciding everything in conformity with their own passions only, liberty and the general good are lost."[49] Sidney's fundamentally Spinozist conception of the reflection theory of sovereign right shapes his understanding of the character and scope of the institutions operating in a democratic republic like his envisioned new and improved England.

Although in some important respects Sidney's argument for legislative supremacy resembles the position of radical parliamentary contractarians of the civil war period like Henry Parker, it is crucial to recognize Sidney's deeper differences with his parliamentarian predecessors. Both Sidney and Parker concur that Parliament best represents the interests of the nation as a whole. Thus, they agree that Parliament can assume the executive functions of the crown in the event of an emergency or a serious dispute between the branches of government.[50] In addition, Parker and Sidney share a deep distrust of the principle of balanced government as an end in itself; rather, both look to the consideration of the efficient cause of government as the ground of sovereignty. Inasmuch as government derives from the consent of the people and aims at the public good, then, Parliament as the representative of the popular will must be supreme in the English constitutional order.[51] The popular character of Parliament more or less ensures that it can have no private interest separate from the public good.

Where Sidney and the parliamentary radicals of the 1640s most clearly diverge is over the character of rights. Parker identifies consent as a communal phenomenon. In viewing consent in terms of the rights of the community as opposed to the rights of the individual, Parker offers a more restricted notion of resistance than does Sidney.[52] Parker closely follows Grotius in maintaining that a community may rebel against its rulers only to enforce the terms of the original contract that established the constitutional order. Sidney, as we have seen, supports the popular right to alter the terms of political rule

---

[49] Spinoza PT 15.14.376.

[50] Corinne Weston, "Theory of Mixed Monarchy Under Charles I and After," *English Historical Review*, vol. 75 (July 1960): pp. 435–6 and Henry Parker, "Observations upon some of his Majesties late Answers and Expresses": pp. 16, 21–2, 45.

[51] Houston, "Republicanism," pp. 250–1 and Michael Mendle, *Henry Parker and the English Civil War* (Cambridge: Cambridge University Press, 1995): p. 183 (see Parker, "Observations," 181, 188, 194, 200, 202, 211–12). Cf. Michael P. Zuckert, *Natural Rights and the New Republicanism* (Princeton: Princeton University Press, 1994): pp. 73–5 for Parker's relation to later Whig natural rights thinkers.

[52] Richard Tuck, *Natural Rights Theories* (Cambridge: Cambridge University Press, 1979): pp. 147, 150–1 and Zuckert, *Natural Rights*, p. 75.

unilaterally, on any ground determined by the people. Whereas both Parker and Sidney reject the Grotian notion of contractual absolutism, they differ inasmuch as Parker's notion of resistance and supremacy is constitutionally conservative – to restore the original construction of powers – while Sidney's advocacy of legislative supremacy is inextricably linked to his argument for the salutary consequences of periodic political change and constitutional reordering. Moreover, while Parker opposes absolutism as contrary to the final causality of government, promoting the public good, Sidney eschews Aristotelian categories altogether and rejects absolute monarchy as antithetical to the modern scientific understanding of the natural order of power relations. Thus, Sidney's anti-absolutism is rooted in a conception of nature substantially different from that of the Calvinist parliamentary radicals of the English civil war era.

For Sidney, the arbitrariness of Parliament is qualitatively different from the arbitrary commands of a monarch. The only irresistible sovereign is the general will of the people understood as the collected will of the multitude of individuals. Sidney claims: "No nation that has a sovereign power within itself, does want this king."[53] Here Sidney both reconceptualizes the understanding of popular sovereignty in terms of freedom from foreign domination and affirms the equal abridgment of natural liberty that grounds political society and subjects all to the general rule but subjects none to any particular will. While Sidney's version of natural rights republicanism places a heavy emphasis on free institutions – indeed, popular institutions are more central to Sidney's account of government than are individual rights – nonetheless, he is concerned to demonstrate that the will of the people as a collectivity holds greater moral and political significance than any particular institutional arrangement. Sidney makes the point that even Parliament is not sacrosanct: "This being under God, the best anchor we have, it deserves to be preserved with all care, till one of a more unquestionable strength be framed by the consent of the nation."[54] In Sidney's radical Whig republicanism, the people are the source and purest expression of sovereign power.

Democratic republicanism emerges for Sidney, and his republican forbear Spinoza, as the most stable and most rational system of government. This is true primarily because it sufficiently suppresses the dangerous human passions and thus allows the collected wisdom of the people to be expressed through the institutions of government. As we have seen from Sidney's critique of monarchy, he views the strength of the passions as the salient feature of human life. He charges that "man is of an aspiring nature" and is marked by "a strange propensity to run into all manner of excesses when plenty of means invite, and there is no power to deter." On another occasion he confessed: "Every man has passions; few know how to moderate, and no

[53] D 3.42.555. Cf. D 3.41.548.
[54] D 3.45.572.

one can wholly extinguish them."[55] Political society, then, is chiefly a device to limit the passions and to bring them under the control of reason. Sidney affirms that liberty without restraint is inconsistent with any government; therefore, the good people seek is only found in society, which restrains liberty. Sidney formulates this:

Everyone sees they cannot well live asunder, nor many together, without some rule to which all submit. This submission is a restraint of liberty, but would be of no effect as to the good intended, unless it were general; nor general, unless it were natural.[56]

It is on this basis that Sidney posits law-abidingness as the quintessential republican virtue. By this argument he also expresses his disagreement with Hobbes' sharp distinction between nature and society. The construction of society is not for Sidney and Spinoza the radical exit from nature that it is for Hobbes.

Political society, in Sidney's view, originates in the need to control the human passions. The passions are brought under the control of reason in two ways. The first way is by the encouragement of the rational autonomy of the republican citizen who dedicates himself to the strict observance of the society's general laws. For Sidney, the citizen's dedication to the public good expressed through law does not indicate the nullification of the individual's concern for his private good. Rather, the application of general laws acts as a constant check on the excesses of unrestrained self-interest and desire. The second way the passions are brought under the control of reason is by the institutions of government. It is on the issue of institutional rationality that Sidney sees democracy's greatest advantage over monarchy or aristocracy. His deep suspicion of the capacity of one man or a small group of governors to control their self-interest in favor of the public good grounds his defense of democracy. Democracy is the wisest and most stable of regimes. Even a well-intentioned monarch or ruling class will not provide the stability and wisdom of a popular assembly. Sidney states:

Many eyes see more than one: the collected wisdom of a people much surpasses that of a single person, and tho he should truly seek that which is best, 'tis not probable he would so easily find it, as the body of a nation, or the principal men chosen to represent the whole.[57]

The irregular appetites endemic to the individual of the species are ameliorated in the collected wisdom and interest of the whole.

The superiority of popular governments rests on their capacity to provide institutional expression for the collected wisdom of the people. Moreover, popular legislative assemblies comprehend the interest of the legislators into

[55] D 2.19.184, 187; 2.24.234.
[56] D 2.20.192.
[57] D 3.16.403.

the common interest more reliably than any alternative system of government. Sidney realistically argues that the question is not whether Parliament is infallible, but rather whether "a house of commons composed of those who are best esteemed by their neighbours in all the towns and counties in England, are more or less subject to error" than a monarch or small group of rulers.[58] As such, he affirms that the most important political matters "ought to be placed where there is most wisdom and stability." Of course, for Sidney this is Parliament:

[w]hich being the representative body of the people, and the collected wisdom of the nation, is least subject to error, most exempted from passion, and most free from corruption.... They cannot do anything that is ill without damage to themselves and their posterity; which being all that can be done by human understanding, our lives, liberties and properties are by our laws directed to depend upon them.[59]

The logical conclusion of Sidney's argument for the inherent wisdom and stability of popular institutions is a sovereign power that is in practical terms as absolute as the Pufendorfian ideal underlying the moderate Whig view of parliamentary sovereignty: "the power of altering, mitigating, explaining or correcting the laws of England, is only in the Parliament, because none but the Parliament can make them."[60] Sidney grants Parliament sweeping powers of judicial review of its own legislation and control over the strict construction of the execution of law, all in addition to and deriving from the lawmaking power itself. In doing so, his modern republican theory leaves the separation of powers in tatters. Sidney assumes that the legislative body maintains the government's strength and stability by anchoring its actions and legitimacy in the popular will. Thus, the concentration of power is not Sidney's real concern; rather, it is where the awesome power of government is located. When it is located without question in the popular branch, the combined power and wisdom of that body, and not the separation of powers, will produce good government.

Sidney is careful, however, to recommend several vital reforms to ensure that the popular assembly is truly representative of the general will. First, he advocates the institutionalization of annual Parliaments to keep the body informed of the public mood and responsible to the public interest. In this way, he registers his opposition both to the corruption of the lengthy Cavalier Parliament of 1661–79 and to the very short Parliaments of the Exclusion period, which were prorogued and later dissolved by the king after a matter of weeks. Sidney suggests that regular and annual elections will keep Parliament close to the public interest and will allow for the circulation of membership to counteract the corrupting effects of long-term incumbency. Moreover, the

[58] D 3.38.532 and *Proverbs* 11:14.
[59] D 3.42.557.
[60] D 3.22.451.

institutionalization of annual Parliaments practically removes the possibility of executive caprice in the area of calling and dissolving the popular assembly. The arbitrary character of the legislative power need not be incompatible with responsible government. Sidney argues, "what defects soever may be in any statute, no great inconvenience could probably ensue, if that for annual parliaments was observed."[61]

Second, Sidney offers a mild endorsement of the practice of instructing members of Parliament. He affirms : "We always may, and often do give instructions to our delegates." Though he asserts the public's right to instruct their members on how to vote on specific issues, Sidney recommends giving these elected officials the freedom to vote their conscience on issues of national concern. To oblige members to follow particular orders from the electors on every vote "would make the decision of the most important affairs to depend upon the judgment of those who know nothing of the matters in question, and by that means would cast the nation into the utmost danger."[62] Moreover, Sidney assures that frequent elections would allow electors to punish unpopular members of Parliament and would actually increase the capacity of deputies to act in the public interest, given that they only need fear electoral defeat, not death or disgrace. In his discussion of the instruction issue, Sidney shows that the arbitrary or discretionary power in his constitutional system ultimately rests with the people, not Parliament. As Sidney cautions: "The less we fetter them [the delegates], the more we manifest our rights."[63] The electors have the right or power to bind their delegates' decisions, though he suggests on prudential grounds that they should consider not doing so as a matter of course.

The final justification for arbitrary legislative power rests on Sidney's support for increasing the size of the popular assembly. We should recall that when Sidney speaks of "Great Assemblies" and the power of bodies "consisting of many men, and several orders of men," he never repudiates the Saxon model of direct democracy in principle. The practice of representation arose in England only due to the "inconveniences" of calling assemblies of large numbers scattered over great distances.[64] The recognition of the practical difficulties in assembling large popular bodies does not preclude the possibility of expanding the membership of the legislature. Given the logic of Sidney's argument, an expanded Parliament would presumably be a further check on corruption and would be more representative of the popular will than the historical House of Commons. A larger, more representative Parliament subject to annual elections would help ensure that the popular foundations of the English republic would not become too narrow over time. With these

---

[61] D 3.27.475. Cf. Houston, *Algernon Sidney*, p. 201.
[62] D 3.44.567, 69.
[63] D 3.44.567.
[64] D 2.5.102–3, 3.16.404. Cf. Houston, *Algernon Sidney*, p. 197.

structural reforms in Parliament, England would go some distance toward embodying Sidney's vision of a democratic republic directed to the security of individual rights and free institutions.

Whig Republican Political Science of Liberty: Amsterdam-on-Thames

The recurring theme of the *Discourses* is Sidney's attempt to demonstrate the defective character of practically all prior modes of political thought. He systematically treats and then shows the limitations of Christian Aristotelianism, classical republicanism, Machiavellian republicanism, and Hobbesian natural rights theory, all in addition to his originally stated aim of refuting Filmer's account of divine right monarchy. In his treatment of the English Constitution, Sidney registers his criticism of traditional English mixed regime theory and proposes in its stead a democratic republic founded on popular sovereignty and directed toward the security of free institutions and individual rights. In Sidney's new England, radical legislative supremacy is the sine qua non of political legitimacy as well as the primary device allowing for constitutional change. This radical Whig English republic is both the product of and the model for Sidney's political alternative to the earlier natural liberty theories of government he considers in the book. He incorporated various elements of these other natural liberty theories into his own notion of "political science."[65] He identified this branch of knowledge as "that which of all others is the most abstruse and variable according to accidents and circumstances." Sidney presents this study of politics both as scientific and prudential, resting on demonstrable, if abstruse, principles of causality, while also being subject to the many exigencies and contingencies attending human life and political society. But on what does Sidney base his political science?

The key to understanding Sidney's republican political science of liberty is determining his relation to Spinoza. Sidney's understanding of the limits and possibilities of modern republican government was profoundly influenced by the theory and practice of the Dutch Republic in the 1660s and early 1670s. Both in his early unpublished and only recently discovered work, the *Court Maxims*, and in the *Discourses*, Sidney expressed a deep admiration for the Dutch Republic. In his time in exile in Holland in the mid-1660s Sidney was exposed to the work of the most influential republican theorists in that most notable of European republics. His work shows the pervading influence of a number of Dutch thinkers, most particularly Benedict Spinoza.[66]

---

[65] D 2.8.121.
[66] Other Dutch republican thinkers who undoubtedly influenced Sidney were the De La Court brothers, Jean and Pieter, authors of the *Political Discourses* and *The Political Maxims of the State of Holland*, respectively (both published in 1662). The influence of the De La Courts is most apparent in Sidney's *Court Maxims*, Hans Blom, Eco Haitsma, and Donald Janse,

Sidney moved in circles in which Spinoza was a celebrated, indeed dominant, figure. Their shared commitment to the principles of modern republicanism established their common association with men like Jan DeWitt,
the Dutch republican leader, and Benjamin Furly, the influential Rotterdam
Quaker leader.[67] Sidney's relation to Spinoza went beyond their mutual dedication to the cause of popular government. Indeed, the stamp of Spinozism
is particularly strong in the final chapter of the *Discourses*, in which Sidney
presents his reformed English Constitution. They both defend democracy on
a similar assessment of the character of the human passions. Sidney rejects
the Hobbesian theory of sovereignty precisely on the Spinozist ground that
democracy, rather than absolute monarchy, is the form of government best
able to restrain the destructive passions and to bring the government and the
people under the control of reason.[68] Spinoza's theoretical defense of Dutch
republicanism so unmistakably influenced Sidney that the Englishman's
recent biographer Jonathan Scott claims that what distinguished Sidney from
his English contemporaries was the "location of his political perspective in
the world of the European cities, with an accent on Amsterdam."[69]

eds. (Cambridge: Cambridge University Press, 1996), probably written in 1665, whereas I
suggest that Spinoza's influence is most significant in the later *Discourses*, written at around
the time of the Exclusion crisis. Cf. Hiram Caton, *The Politics of Progress: The Origins and
Development of the Commercial Republic, 1600–1835* (Gainesville: University of Florida Press,
1988): pp. 230–3 and Jonathan Scott, *Algernon Sidney and the English Republic, 1623–1677*
(Cambridge: Cambridge University Press, 1988), p. 211 for the important role of the De La
Courts in shaping the commercial republican ideology of the Dutch Republic. For Spinoza's
impact on Dutch republican thought, see Jonathan I. Israel, *The Dutch Republic: Its Rise,
Greatness, and Fall 1477–1806* (Oxford: Clarendon Press, 1998): pp. 917–21. For a treatment
of Spinoza's influence in the broader context of European thought, and an interpretation the
general thrust of which supports my claims for the connection between Sidney and Spinoza,
see Jonathan I. Israel, *Radical Enlightenment: Philosophy and the Making of Modernity, 1650–
1750* (Oxford: Oxford University Press, 2001): Parts III–V, esp. ch. 33 on England, which
relates more to English deism than to republicanism per se.
[67] Scott, *English Republic*, pp. 216–17. The fact that Spinoza's entire corpus was published by
1677 and Sidney wrote the *Discourses* in the early 1680s makes it possible for Sidney to have
read Spinoza. Moreover, the fact that Sidney had spent time in exile in Holland in the 1660s
and shared acquaintances with Spinoza, men like the republican leader Jan DeWitt, and the
Rotterdam Quaker leader Benjamin Furly suggests that it is more than likely that Sidney
was familiar with Spinoza's work. Given the great controversy Spinoza provoked at the time
(see Caton, *Politics of Progress*, pp. 237–9), it is not surprising that Sidney did not refer to
him directly in the *Discourses*, even as he made characteristically Spinozist arguments. For
evidence of Sidney's connection to Spinoza and the Dutch republican theorists of the 1670s,
see Scott, *English Republic*, ch. 13 and Lewis Samuel Feuer, *Spinoza and the Rise of Liberalism*
(Boston: Beacon Press, 1958): pp. 50, 271, 289.
[68] For Sidney and Spinoza's similar treatment of the passions, compare D 2.19, 2.24, 3.41
with Spinoza, TPT 17. 230. Also, to see the way in which both Sidney and Spinoza envision
government as a device for the control of the passions, compare D 3.16.404 and Spinoza,
TPT 17.206.
[69] Scott, *English Republic*, p. 210.

In addition to the deep theoretical influence Spinoza had on Sidney, there was also a great similarity between Sidney's political project and that of his Dutch colleague. For example, Spinoza's project in defense of Dutch republicanism is analogous to Sidney's defense of parliamentary constitutionalism in England. The parallels between Holland in the 1670s and Exclusion era England are striking. Spinoza wrote his great political works, the *Theologico-Political Treatise* and the *Political Treatise*, in large part in order to defend Holland's republican institutions against the personal ambitions of the House of Orange, much as Sidney aimed to efface the personal rule of the Stuarts in England.[70] Moreover, the problematic relation of religion and politics played a large part in both Sidney's and Spinoza's projects. The conservative Calvinist ministers who supported the Orangist faction were to Spinoza what the Anglican establishment of Heylyn and his associates were to Sidney: the clerical agents of monarchy. In order to defuse the political influence of orthodox or established religion, these republican thinkers proposed interpretations of Scripture that were compatible with, or even sympathetic to, republican government.

It may, nevertheless, appear odd to connect Sidney with Spinoza, one of the great system builders of the Enlightenment project. Certainly, Sidney showed little relish in his work for elaborate metaphysical speculation. There is nothing approaching Spinoza's *Ethics* in Sidney's corpus. The more obvious parallels between Sidney and Spinoza come to light primarily from the latter's more emphatically political writings. Yet are there signs of a Spinozist metaphysic underlying Sidney's political science? Or to put it differently, does Sidney's defense of democracy on modern natural rights grounds presuppose such a metaphysic?

In order to understand the seminal relation between Sidney's argument in the *Discourses* and Spinoza's modern republicanism, it is useful to compare some of the key elements in their arguments. Spinoza's political naturalism follows Machiavelli's decisive break from the classic writers who, he argues, "conceive of men, not as they are, but as they themselves would like them to be." Just as Sidney assumes that "every man has passions; few know how to moderate," Spinoza contends that "men are more led by blind desire than reason." The most important passion for both Spinoza and Sidney grounds the natural right whereby humans "strive to seek their preservation."[71] The preservationist Hobbesian core of Spinozist–Sidneyan republicanism is subject to a number of important qualifications, however.

[70] For a good treatment of the political context and character of Spinoza's writings, see Etienne Balibar, *Spinoza and Politics*, Peter Snowdon, trans. (New York: Verso, 1998), esp. ch. 1. Cf. Caton, *Politics of Progress*, pp. 237–9, 241 and Israel, *The Dutch Republic*, pp. 796–806.

[71] Spinoza, PT 287, 292 (cf. TPT 230) and Sidney, D 2.24.234, 2.23.210,14 and 3.41.547. Cf. Spinoza, TPT 16.200 and Benedict Spinoza, *Ethics*, Edwin Curley, trans. (Amherst, NY: Prometheus Books, 1989): part IV, def. viii, p. 191; and part IV, prop. xviii, p. 202.

First, while Spinoza agrees with Hobbes that the state of nature is a violent condition in which "men are naturally enemies," he, like Sidney, does not concur with the Hobbesian emphasis on the profound artificiality of government. Spinoza claims that since "no one in solitude is strong enough to defend himself, and procure the necessaries of life; it follows that men naturally aspire to the civil state." Sidney employs practically identical language in asserting the quasi-natural status of political society: "a private man from the knowledge of his own weakness and inability to defend himself, must come under the protection of a greater power than his own."[72] The second way in which Spinoza and Sidney depart from Hobbes has to do with their assessment of the political implications of natural liberty. They both advance a case for the naturalness and superiority of democracy as a regime. Spinoza declares that "of all forms of government" democracy is "the most natural, and most consonant with individual liberty. In it no one transfers his natural right so absolutely that he has no further voice in affairs." Sidney opines similarly that "of all governments, democracy, in which every man's liberty is least restrained" is the best regime "because every man hath an equal part, would certainly prove to be most just, rational and natural."[73]

Sovereignty, then, for Sidney and Spinoza has a much more emphatically popular foundation than is the case either with Hobbes or the Pufendorfian moderate Whigs. Sidney advances the opposition of one-man rule to the principle of natural power relations: "No man comes to command many, unless by Consent or Force." Spinoza knocks the metaphysical legs supporting monarchy even more forcefully: "they are much mistaken, who suppose that one man can by himself hold the supreme right of a commonwealth. For the limit of right ... is power. But the power of one man is very inadequate to support so great a load." For both Sidney and Spinoza, the only firm basis of supreme authority is the collected power of "the multitude."[74] The sovereign power in Sidney and Spinoza's modern republican theory must express this natural power, preferably through a large, popularly elected general assembly. Not only is such a body strong, but it is also more rational than a monarch or ruling elite. As Spinoza says in praise of popular assemblies: "so large a council cannot be so much determined by lust as by reason." Sidney concurs in almost identical terms: "the collected wisdom of a people much surpasses that of a single person."[75] However, it is the alliance of popular strength and wisdom that Spinoza and Sidney identify as the basis of sovereign right. In one crucial respect the Spinozist–Sidneyan modern republican idea of sovereignty parallels the Hobbesian absolutist and Pufendorfian

---

[72] Spinoza, PT 296, 316 and Sidney, D 3.41.549. Cf. D 3.33.512.

[73] Spinoza, TPT 207 and Sidney, D 2.20.192. Cf. D 3.28.481, 487, and 490.

[74] See Spinoza, PT 317 (cf. 346) and Sidney, D 1.11.32 and 3.11, as well as Spinoza, PT 301, 297 and Sidney, D 3.28.487.

[75] Spinoza, PT 348 and Sidney, D 3.16.403. Cf. D 3.42.557.

moderate Whig position. In both the modern republican and the Hobbesian and Pufendorfian arguments political sovereignty is practically absolute, although for the modern republicans sovereignty is also necessarily popular. Spinoza argues that since a popular assembly "needs no counsellors, its every explicit will ought to be law. And hence we conclude that dominion conferred upon a large enough council is absolute. . . . For if there be any absolute dominion, it is, in fact that which is held by the entire multitude." Sidney captures the essence of this Spinozist teaching in his formulation of the sovereign power of a radically popularized Parliament in which "the Legislative power is always Arbitrary," and, foreshadowing Blackstone, alone has "the power of altering, mitigating, explaining or correcting the laws of England, . . . because none but the Parliament can make them."[76] Sidney's defense of popular institutions and their practically unlimited power reflects the underlying influence of the Spinozist metaphysic of nature and power. The central promise of both Spinozist and Sidneyan republicanism is the possibility of supplying a modern political science that can improve human political reasoning in light of an understanding of this natural order.

The first pillar of Sidney's republican political science is his notion of the predictable character of the human passions. As we have seen, Sidney identified the self-interested passions as the primary agents and springs of human action.[77] He claims that this universal cause of action produces regular and measurable effects. For example, Sidney does not attribute the mischiefs witnessed in monarchies primarily to the personal qualities of this or that particular ruler. He charges rather that the problems of monarchy "proceed not from accidents, but from the power of a permanent cause that always produces the same or like effect."[78] Although Sidney affirms that the precise measures necessary to ameliorate the problems of monarchy may vary from case to case, depending on the particular constitutional order of a given nation – an elective mixed monarchy will need a remedy different from that of a hereditary one. Nevertheless, he ascribes the cause of these problems to the universal character of the human passions.

Sidney's political science is not, however, relegated simply to diagnosing the problems of monarchy. He employs this scientific understanding of the principles of natural causality primarily in order to formulate the theoretical grounding for efforts to strengthen and preserve popular governments, as well as to reform non-popular regimes. Sidney's political science is deduced from and attempts to replicate the rigor of modern natural science. He offers certain institutional arrangements, such as popular general assemblies, which will, within variations open to different political and historical

---

[76] Spinoza, PT 347 and Sidney, D 3.45.569, 3.22.451. For Blackstone's essentially Pufendorfian view of sovereignty, see my discussion in Chapter 11.

[77] D 2.19, 2.24, 3.41. Cf. Spinoza, PT 3.3.302.

[78] D 2.24.240.

circumstances, be able to provide the most reliable foundations for securing individual rights and communal self-government. Monarchy and aristocracy distort the natural order of power relations by asserting the right of one or a few to rule many, despite the fact that these rulers lack the natural power to coerce a multitude. Democracy, in contrast, operates on principles consistent with the objective and scientific observation of nature. Democracies locate the supreme right to govern in the one body possessing the actual power to govern in a supreme or irresistible fashion, namely, the people. The central tenet of Sidney's political science is the principle that only popular institutions reflecting the natural power of the people can guarantee political liberty. This, too, is an axiom for Sidney, as manifestly proceeding "from the power of a permanent cause" as any of the demonstrable failings of monarchy. The core of Sidney's political science is the idea that democracy is the most natural and thus the most rational system of government. To understand Sidney's claim for the superior rationality of democracy vis-à-vis the other regimes, we must look at two issues: his understanding of virtue and his suggestions for practical political reform.

Modern Republican Virtues

The conception of virtue embedded in Sidney's version of modern republicanism is a nuanced and complex formulation that belies the stark distinction between the language of virtue and the logic of rights often espoused by the contemporary proponents of the liberal and republican theses. Sidney incorporates classical republican virtues, such as self-sacrifice, patriotism, and dedication to the common good, into a modern republican teaching consistent with the principles of individual rights, enlightened self-interest, and the importance of observing contracts. Sidney's understanding of virtue, as with so much of his thought, parallels the thought of Spinoza. For both, law-abidingness emerges as the cardinal virtue in their reflections on ethics. They rejected the aristocratic presuppositions of classical republicanism in favor of a notion of virtue based on republican liberty and the rule of law. The virtues Sidney associates with natural rights republicanism draw their moral and theoretical source from his natural rights philosophy: "The equality in which men are born is so perfect, that . . . I cannot reasonably expect to be defended from wrong, unless I oblige my self to do none; or to suffer the punishment prescribed by the Law, if I perform not my engagement."[79] The virtue of law-abidingness, then, is rooted in the natural equality of the individuals composing society. The core conceptual device for understanding this virtue, as for understanding Sidney's view of virtue more generally, is the rule of reason over the passions. Sidney's assessment of the role of reason in

[79] D 3.41.548. Cf. Houston, *Algernon Sidney*, p. 133.

the virtues forms the fulcrum in his thought regarding the characteristically republican concepts of virtue and corruption.

Reason is the guiding principle for Sidney's view of political life. He followed Spinoza in defending democracy and attacking absolute monarchy precisely because popular regimes were able to bring rulers and ruled under the control of reason.[80] Given the universal character of the human passions, no individual could be trusted with absolute power. For Sidney and Spinoza, a nation governed by a system of laws passed by a freely consenting public was one with an enhanced capacity to act rationally.[81] By positing obedience to laws at least indirectly of one's own making as the key republican virtue, Sidney redirects the issue of morality away from the antithesis of rights and duties, and instead posits the chief opposition as that between reason and passion. Sidney clearly indicates that the virtue he associates with republican liberty is not licentiousness or a freedom to do whatever one wishes.[82] Such licentiousness would be a function of the rule of the passions rather than of reason. In Sidney's view, reason informs the individual that peace and security – the goals of political life – are best maintained when a people remain united in one body under law. For Sidney and Spinoza, liberty and virtue are linked because virtue must be understood as action in accordance with the law of human nature. The foundation of virtue is the natural right of self-preservation.[83] Self-interest, in this sense, cannot be conceived as conceptually distinct from virtue because the ethos of law-abidingness that links individual interest to the public interest is a function of this natural right.

Sidney recognizes this self-regarding core of republican virtue in these terms: "Virtuous actions that are profitable to the commonwealth ought to be made, as far as it is possible, safe, easy, and advantageous."[84] Virtuous action must be made as compatible with self-interest as possible. One way to achieve this aim is to define virtue in terms of obedience to law produced under conditions allowing a public voice in legislation. In this light, Sidney reevaluates virtue not in terms of the renunciation of private interest, the view typically associated with classical republicanism, but rather in the recognition that the private interests both bound by and expressed through law made in popular institutions are the composite elements of the public interest.[85] Whereas the passions unchecked by reason encourage the advance

---

[80] See D 3.13.387, 389; 3.15.401; 3.43.558 and Spinoza, PT 3.7.303–4.

[81] Compare D 3.1.323, 3.14.396, 3.40.543–4 and Spinoza, PT 5.2.313, 6.3.317, 7.27.341, 7.29.342. Cf. Houston's good discussion (*Algernon Sidney*, p. 135) of Sidney's view of the connection between rationality and legislation.

[82] D 1.2.8–9.

[83] Spinoza sums up this connection between virtue and self-interest in these terms: "The endeavor after self-preservation is the primary and only foundation of virtue" (*Ethics*, part IV, prop. 22, cor., p. 202).

[84] D 3.43.559.

[85] Houston, *Algernon Sidney*, p. 166.

of private interests at the expense of the public good, Sidney argues that an informed and rational assessment of the character of political association and its benefits for the individual will preserve the importance of law. Moreover, Sidney maintains that the corruption derived from the human passions is actually a condition of slavery directly contrary to republican liberty. He sees the slavish effects of the unchecked passions both as a kind of moral weakness, or in Spinozist terms an "impotence" of mind, and as a feature of the kind of life experienced under arbitrary government, whereby the individual cannot truly be master over his or her own actions and thoughts.[86] The inherent lawlessness of absolute monarchy mirrors the passionate and irrational behavior of the individual lawbreaker who seeks to injure the public good for purely private advantage. Thus, virtue, in Sidney's view, is instrumental in its service to the self-interest of individuals and is simply good in the sense of representing the most rational human response to the challenges facing political association and its central goals: peace and security.

If Sidney's reflections on virtue are intended to indicate how an individual may be brought from the slavery of the passions to the liberty experienced under the rule of law, then his observations on regimes may be said to demonstrate how unfree regimes may be more free and popular. In the *Discourses* Sidney demonstrates that regimes are improved by the degree to which their popular element is strengthened.[87] Indeed, Sidney's political science is directed to the preservation of popular governments and the reform of non-popular regimes. Part of this teaching is that strong institutions are strong because they are anchored in popular legitimacy. The political science of liberty encourages both monarchies and aristocracies to expand the popular voice in public affairs through the institution of general councils and assemblies that would participate in the legislative process. This element of Sidney's teaching is most pronounced in his frequent appeal to the leaders of the successor states to the gothic polities. He strongly advocates the revitalization of the assemblies, *cortes*, *diets*, and *parlements* of the great European monarchies.[88] These measures are especially urgent given the

---

[86] Spinoza, PT 2.20.298, 2.7–11.294–5; TPT 16.206 and *Ethics*, pt. IV, prop. 18, p. 202; and pt. IV, prop. 37, p. 215. I disagree with Houston (*Algernon Sidney*, p. 147) regarding the importance of the biblical Fall in Sidney's understanding of corruption and the passions. While Sidney does speak of humanity's fallen nature early in the *Discourses*, this biblical language falls away entirely by the later chapters. Rather than focusing on Sidney's early and almost perfunctory references to the Fall, it might be more useful to compare Sidney and Spinoza's use of Tacitus' observations on the servility, i.e. slavery, produced by absolute monarchy. For example, compare D 2.15.160 and Spinoza, PT 5.4.314.

[87] This is also the pattern and methodology of Spinoza's treatment of monarchy and aristocracy in *A Political Treatise*. In this work Spinoza invariably advocates the establishment of large popular assemblies and general councils in order to improve (i.e., strengthen) nondemocratic regimes. Cf. Balibar, *Spinoza and Politics*, pp. 71–5.

[88] This can be seen, for example, at D 3.27.477, 3.28.488, 3.31.504–5.

collapse of the feudal nobility "in all the legal kingdoms of the North." The concomitant to Sidney's frequent appeal to the legitimate right of revolution of a people against aspiring autocrats is an implicit warning to European monarchs. He encourages them to assess their situation realistically, or rather scientifically, and to reform the institutions of government in the direction of greater popular control in order to forestall or preclude such explosive and revolutionary possibilities.

While Sidney's lesson for the political leaders in mixed or limited monarchies was to begin or continue the democratization process of reform, he also had a warning for the supporters of republicanism. As we saw in Sidney's treatment of early Saxon England, he presented democracy less as a formal system of government than as an actuality of power relations.[89] With the narrowing of the popular foundations of the English Constitution, the legal and institutional devices intended to preserve some measure of popular sovereignty became obsolete. In stressing the mutability of formal structures, Sidney identifies the power of the multitude as the core of any healthy regime. To preserve popular regimes, he cautions, this power must be expressed institutionally, even if it means reforming or replacing existing institutions. Sidney reminds popular leaders not to cling to outdated institutions and political structures.

This reasoning lay behind Sidney's call for several measures to ensure that Parliament would be responsible to the people. In this sense, Sidney's political science aims as much to enlighten England's parliamentarians as to challenge the monarchists. He reminds popular leaders that their right to rule diminishes as the strength of their opposition grows.[90] The collapse of the Dutch Republic in 1672 and the grisly fate of its leader, Sidney's friend DeWitt, at the hands of an Orangist mob forms an important backdrop for Sidney's discussion of the uncertain future of parliamentary rule in Exclusion era England. Sidney's dramatic appeal for the saliency of military strength is a warning to England's parliamentary leaders not to trust in empty legalities. Despite democracy's natural claim to legitimacy, as opposed to monarchy's divine claim, the specter of monarcho-military rule looms over England as much as it threatens the Continent. In this light, the revolutionary dimension of Sidney's teaching forms part of a political science directed toward the mobilization of mass movements in defense of free institutions. Popular

---

[89] D 3.27. My understanding of the dangers Sidney and Spinoza saw for republican leaders who might cling to formalities and empty legalities while ignoring the balance of forces vis-à-vis the opponents of republicanism in their nations is indebted to Balibar (*Spinoza and Politics*, pp. xvii, 31–5). However, note Spinoza's caution about the "terrible example" furnished by English civil war radicals who tried and failed to install a republic without broad popular support (TPT 18.243).

[90] In this respect, Sidney's fears about popular government in England recall Spinoza's assessment of the demise of the Dutch Republic on account of its narrow popular foundation or simply "the fewness of its rulers" (PT 15.14.376).

regimes and their leaders must understand the source of their strength if they are to preserve it.

The central paradox of Sidney's political science is what might be called the "problem of democracy." Democracy, for Sidney, is at once the best regime and a reflection of the immanent causality of all regimes. Certainly all governments are not popular but, he insists, they all originate in the power of the people. As we have seen, the major element of political reform Sidney suggests for existing political societies is to expand the popular voice in government through popular institutions such as general legislative assemblies. Sidney is aware that affirming the consensual origins of political society does not preclude the ubiquity of autocracies, oligarchies, and military dictatorships. Rather, he posits these regimes as a product of the corruption of the popular foundation of government. Indeed, Sidney offers his own regime analysis of the English Constitution as a model for democratic reform. The political science of liberty aims to strengthen the tendency toward democracy inherent in any social order. In order to produce Amsterdam-on-Thames or sur-Seine, Sidney appeals to the popular elements already existing in Europe's monarchical regimes.

In his claim that the multitude will not bear violent or irrational rule if they are capable of opposing it, Sidney suggests that the universal passion for self-preservation is served well by an openness to science and philosophy. Indeed, the premise of Sidney's political science of liberty is that philosophy – the scientific understanding of nature and its application to politics – is the surest guarantor of self-preservation for the multitude of individuals.[91] Thus, a people acting rationally will see the benefits of Sidney's political science and presumably will be open to the free investigation of nature. Sidney claims that it is not democracy, but rather nondemocratic regimes, that are hostile to political philosophy. This is his repeated charge against Filmer's theologically based divine right theory. Defenders of democracy, the natural regime, will have little to fear and much to gain from the objective study of nature. Sidney implies that scientists and philosophers will see the salutary consequences of their support for popular government. He assumes that they will be drawn to the study of politics in order to strengthen and preserve systems of government friendly to their investigations. Sidney claims that "The wisest and best have ever employed their studies in forming kingdoms and commonwealths, or in adding to the perfections of such as were already constituted."[92] For Sidney, of course, the "perfection" of the kingdoms founded by the "wisest and best" requires movement in the direction of democracy.

---

[91] In this fundamental respect, I believe Sidney's political science and Spinoza's conception of the relation between politics and philosophy are practically the same. For a good discussion of Spinoza's understanding of the relation between philosophy and politics, see Stanley Rosen, "Benedict Spinoza," in *The History of Political Philosophy*, 3rd ed., Leo Strauss and Joseph Cropsey, eds. (Chicago: University of Chicago Press, 1987): pp. 456–74, esp. p. 459.

[92] D 2.6.112.

The key to Sidney's republican political science is the promise of general enlightenment. While all political society originates in consent, Sidney suggests that the peoples of earlier, prescientific times failed to understand properly the implications of this democratic origin of their regimes. As we recall, Sidney mildly rebuked England's Saxon ancestors for failing to see the potential dangers of mixed constitutionalism. He repeatedly contrasts past ignorance with present enlightenment and, as such, he casts his own political science in a distinctly modern light. He affirms emphatically that the present generation is not bound to continue the errors of the past. Sidney claims:

Men were sent into the world rude and ignorant and if they might not have used their natural faculties to find out that which is good for themselves, all must have been condemn'd to continue in the ignorance of our first fathers, and to make no use of their understanding to the ends for which it was given.[93]

Filmer's theory of divine right monarchy is, for Sidney, representative of this political primitivism. Sidney identifies the two hallmarks of Filmer's system of monarchy, unlimited prerogative and the principle of heredity, as indicative of and suitable only for very primitive and ignorant peoples. Sidney concedes that even if "all nations were at first governed by kings, and that no law were imposed upon those kings," nonetheless, succeeding generations "could no more be obliged to continue in so pernicious a folly, than we are to live in that wretched barbarity in which the Romans found our ancestors, when they first entered this island."[94] It is important to notice that Sidney's statement here is conditional; he does not affirm monarchy as the primal regime, but rather denies that there would be a morally binding character to monarchies simply because they were of ancient pedigree. Rather, Sidney sees the simplicity and ignorance reflected in prerogative and heredity as antithetical to political right because these practices suggest sources of legitimacy independent of human law and consent. Neither prerogative nor heredity, Sidney argues, is consistent with a scientific understanding of nature.

In asserting the progressive character of human knowledge throughout history, Sidney implicitly connects his political science with the methodology and animating spirit of modern natural science. By associating monarchy with a primitive state of social and intellectual development, Sidney places his own political science of liberty in stark opposition to any theory of government that mystifies political institutions and thus obscures their human origins. This mystification of political life manipulates the fears and superstition of prescientific peoples. The chief culprits in this manipulation, Sidney charges, are the clergy; men like those in the Anglican Church hierarchy who support Filmer's vision of an unlimited and divinely vouchsafed monarchy in England. Sidney charges that Filmer and his clerical supporters maintain that God set "a Law . . . to all mankind which none might

[93] D 3.7.357. Cf. 1.6.22 and 2.8.121–2.
[94] D 3.13.388. Cf. 3.21.

transgress, and which put the examination of all those matters out of their power."[95] Sidney identifies this process of political mystification, however, not only with the claims of the divine rightists, but also with England's common law tradition.

Sidney argues that the common law is at once too dense and complex for common understanding, and yet displays a much greater reliance on custom and historical practice than it does on reason. He charges that in England "the laws are so many, that the number of them has introduced an uncertainty and confusion which is both dangerous and troublesome."[96] Significantly, Sidney eschews confronting the divine rightists with the common law tradition, a major source of opposition to the absolutist pretensions in England in the seventeenth century during the ascendancy of the great jurists Coke and Halles; rather, he pits the tenets of his political science against common law as well as divine right. Sidney associates England's common law heritage with a persistent antiquarianism and advocates in its stead rationally and scientifically grounded principles of jurisprudence. He contends:

Axioms are not rightly grounded upon judged cases, but cases are to be judged according to axioms: the certain is not proved by the uncertain, but the uncertain by the certain; and everything is to be esteemed uncertain till it be proved to be certain. Axioms in law are, as in mathematics, evident to common sense; and nothing is to be taken for an axiom, that is not so.

Slyly Sidney implies his agreement with the attempt of the Nominated Parliament to codify the common law during the Interregnum period.[97] While he does not explicitly go this far in his reevaluation of England's common law tradition, Sidney strongly suggests that serious legal reform in England would be an additional step toward a rationalized society.

In addition to Sidney's skepticism toward the English legal heritage and historical custom, another important target for his modern republican political science is the religious orthodoxy that he finds generally supportive of monarchy. In this respect, Sidney's project reflects concerns about the theologico–political problem similar to those advanced by his Dutch republican comrades. For instance, Sidney's opposition to the Anglican Church hierarchy mirrors Spinoza's effort to refute the charges of the Dutch Calvinist ministers who maintained that Scripture was antithetical to republicanism.[98]

---

[95] D 1.1.7.

[96] D 3.26.465.

[97] D 3.26.466. By legal principles adhering to "common sense," Sidney does not mean ideas that are simplistic but rather those apprehensible to reason or rationally deduced from general principles. For a discussion of the actions of the Nominated Parliament, see J. P. Kenyon, *The Stuart Constitution, 1603–1688* (Cambridge: Cambridge University Press, 1966): p. 333.

[98] For Spinoza's opposition to the Calvinist ministers in Holland, see Spinoza, TPT, "The Preface," pp. 3–11. Cf. Balibar, *Spinoza and Politics*, pp. 3–5 and Caton, *Politics of Progress*, pp. 237–9.

In order to refute the political claims of religious orthodoxy, Sidney employed a hermeneutical principle of scriptural exegesis pioneered by Spinoza. Sidney's primary aim in his treatment of Scripture was to deny the orthodox interpretation of biblical texts, which emphasized the privileged status of the human things in the order of nature. He saw this presentation of a uniquely human moral order, vouchsafed by revelation, as the cause of the general hostility to science among the people and as the source of clerical strength. Sidney offers his modern natural rights – based republicanism as an antidote to the superstition and primitivism encouraged by the traditional understanding of the relation between politics and religion.[99] For example, he identifies the source of success for the Hebrew republic not in the mystery of divine election, but rather in natural causes. In asserting the foundation of the Mosaic law to be the nation's capacity for war, Sidney follows Machiavelli and Spinoza in tying the notion of Jewish election to the regime's political and military success, resulting from its internal structures, rather than to the divine providence of a God active in human affairs.[100] More importantly, however, Sidney divests revealed religion of its claim as a support for certain forms of political rule. By calibrating the goals of political life to the universal passion for self-preservation, Sidney denies the tangible political relevance of the spiritual end for human life posited by religious authorities. In this way, he sets his political science against the distortion of natural power relations advanced in divine right theory. The perspective claimed by the orthodox interpreters of Scripture gratifies human vanity but distorts our proper place in the whole of nature.

Sidney's radically secularized political science of liberty aims to encourage progress in the advance of scientific and political knowledge. An important element in this project is the separation of religion and politics. What one commentator observed of Spinoza could be said of Sidney: he presents his critique of orthodoxy as "a critique of the 'prejudice' that reason must subject itself to the supra-rational revelation laid down in Scripture. Its task is to liberate men's minds, held fast in that prejudice, so that they may philosophize freely."[101] While Sidney does not make toleration a sustained theme in the *Discourses*, the assumption favoring freedom of conscience and religious

---

[99] Significantly, unlike Spinoza, Sidney does not make the critique of miracles a feature of his attack on religious orthodoxy. However, Sidney's generally agnostic tone and his quite obvious contempt for divinized politics suggest an acute sympathy with Spinoza's rigorous rationalist project. Cf. Leo Strauss, *Spinoza's Critique of Religion* (New York: Schocken Books, 1965): pp. 123–36.

[100] D 2.17.174 and 2.22.205. This may be due to Sidney's skepticism about the talk of English "election" among Puritans in the civil war period. Cf. Spinoza, TPT 3. 48, and Steven Smith, *Spinoza, Liberalism and the Question of Jewish Identity* (New Haven: Yale University Press, 1997), p. 99.

[101] Strauss, *Spinoza's Critique of Religion*, p. 144.

freedom underlies Sidney's larger argument for popular sovereignty.[102] Indeed, the issues surrounding freedom of conscience do emerge in the book. For example, he attributes "the persecution for religion" in the time of England's Henry V to "the ignorance of that age, [rather] than to any evil in his own nature."[103] The whole tenor of Sidney's discussion of a modern democratic England in the final chapter of the *Discourses* suggests that prescribed religious belief and practice is not a precondition of citizenship. The arbitrary power of Parliament does not extend to religious uniformity because Sidney denies that it is possible by force or fear to make any man believe any doctrine. In some sense, no political order can control completely "the internal thoughts of a man."[104] Sidney's defense of religious toleration is connected at least in part to his concern for freedom of speech. It is perhaps no surprise that Sidney, the great Whig martyr to the cause of free speech, should contrast his own openness to debate with that of the rigid censorship indicative of absolutist regimes. At one point in the *Discourses*, he reminds his divine right opponent Robert Filmer that regarding the freedom to investigate political and religious questions, Filmer "ought to have considered, that in asserting that right to himself, he allows it to all mankind."[105] While freedom of conscience and freedom of speech never develop into sustained themes in the work, Sidney does suggest that these freedoms are a sign of the moral and intellectual improvement of enlightened societies over that of their prescientific forbears.

One final feature of Sidney's radical Whig republicanism worth noting is his openness to the ideal of commercial republicanism epitomized in the seventeenth century by Holland. Sidney presents the Dutch commercial republic as a model for enlightened, tolerant modern republicanism. In this respect, Sidney's argument broke decisively from the agrarian classical model and the militaristic imperialist Machiavellian form of republicanism.[106] While it is true that Sidney praised Plato early in Chapter Two for not intending "to teach us how to erect manufactures, and to increase trade or riches," we have noted that later in the *Discourses* Sidney largely disposes of the classical tradition he associates with Plato and Aristotle. From the perspective of Sidney's later criticism of classical thought, Plato's scorn of commerce seems typical of what Sidney identifies as the excessive faith in the beneficence

---

[102] Houston (*Algernon Sidney*, p. 124) suggests that "the key for understanding Sidney's defense of toleration is the *Court Maxims*, not the *Discourses*." My reading of Sidney's thought on toleration follows Houston's excellent discussion (*Algernon Sidney*, pp. 122–30).

[103] D 3.46.575.

[104] D 3.36.521.

[105] D 1.5.18.

[106] I agree with Houston that the "heroic character" of Sidney's imperial vision is undermined by his more preservationist position in the later portions of the book. However, I go beyond Houston's speculation that "the depth of Sidney's commitment to 'Constitutions that Principally intend War' is unclear" (*Algernon Sidney*, pp. 160–1). Rather, I believe that Sidney modifies this position considerably and methodically by the end of the work.

of nature witnessed in classical philosophy.[107] On the other hand, Sidney's praise of Machiavellian militarism near the end of Chapter Two is seriously muted in Chapter Three, where Sidney limns the features of a modern commercial republic in England. Sidney's earlier praise of unlimited militarism was intended more to indicate his break from classical republicanism than to reflect his final position on the character of modern republicanism. Even at his warmongering best in Chapter Two, Sidney still offers remarkable praise for the military capacity of the commercial republics of Holland and Venice. While Sidney cautions against regimes directed solely to commercial activity, he does not view such activity as antithetical to military strength. In fact, Sidney lauds the military achievement of the English republic, in which he affirms "neither the Romans nor the Grecians in their time of liberty ever performed any actions more glorious," principally for the English success against the "formidable power of the Hollanders," their chief commercial rivals.[108]

For his part, the Dutch theorist Spinoza appeared to find little conflict between commercial activity and the military requirements of republican self-government and military dominance. Spinoza and his Dutch colleagues shared Sidney's concern to establish the importance of citizen armies and his deep hostility to and distrust of mercenary troops and professional armies.[109] Neither Sidney nor Spinoza held commerce to be simply incompatible with military strength. Their primary concern vis-à-vis the army was to elucidate the dangers of the kind of monarcho-military rule evinced by the House of Orange in Holland and Cromwell or potentially the Stuarts in England. Possibly a vibrant commercial society would undermine the military ambitions of such political leaders. Sidney implies that if the technological advance promised by free scientific inquiry allowed military strength and commercial prosperity to conjoin reliably, he would support commercial republicanism.[110] From his praise of the English Commonwealth and the Dutch and Venetian commercial regimes, as well as his general openness to intellectual, scientific, and economic progress, it appears that Sidney already foresaw such a possibility in the more advanced nations and commercial cities of late-seventeenth-century Europe.

The *Discourses* heralded a new era in the long history of republicanism. Sidney's decisive break not only from the prevailing paradigms in English constitutional thought, but also from both the classical and Machiavellian

---

[107] D 2.1.83.
[108] D 2.28.276. For Sidney's praise of the commercial Dutch and the Venetians, see 2.22.206–8, 2.23.216, 2.28.275. Sidney does criticize the Venetians at 2.22.203, but he retracts this criticism at 2.28.275.
[109] See, for example, Spinoza, TPT 17. 220–7; PT 6.10.319, 7.12.333, 7.17.335, and 7.22.338.
[110] Conniff's argument suggests such a possibility of linking Sidney's progressive approach to history with a potential openness to commercial society ("Reason and History," pp. 413–16).

strains of republicanism, introduced a radically populist strain of modern natural rights – based republicanism into Whig constitutional and political thought. With the infusion of Spinozist philosophy into the conceptual frame of the constitutional debate in Exclusion era England, Sidney presented a more emphatic and theoretically sophisticated argument for its popular government than had hitherto been witnessed in England. The Sidneyan form of Whig republicanism with its call for radical legislative supremacy, its popular control of government, and its distrust of executive power and the balanced constitutional model embedded in English history presented a blueprint for later variations of Anglo-American republicanism. Sidney's heroic vision of a modern republic grounded on natural rights and open to the liberating power of science, commerce, and general enlightenment would become a touchstone for many radicals in England and America in the century to come.

8

Natural Rights in Locke's Two Treatises

John Locke's *Two Treatises of Government* is by far the most celebrated work among those of Filmer's three major Whig critics and is generally recognized as a classic of early modern thought. Although it was written more or less contemporaneously with Tyrrell's *Patriarcha, Non Monarcha* and Sidney's *Discourses Concerning Government*, the fame and influence of the *Two Treatises* as one of the seminal texts of liberal thought has far outlasted those of these other Whig works. But before he was a philosophical legend, Locke was a relatively unknown partisan Whig. John Locke was born in 1632 into a West Country gentry family with small but prosperous estates in Somerset near Bristol.[1] In contrast to his friend James Tyrrell, Locke's family loyalties were decidedly parliamentarian in the civil war, with his father, a successful attorney, serving as a captain in a parliamentary regiment of horse commanded by a local notable, Alexander Popham. Popham was elected to the Long Parliament in 1646, the same year as Algernon Sidney, and it was through Popham's patronage that Locke was admitted to the prestigious Westminster School that same year. In 1652 he entered Christ Church, Oxford, graduating with an M.A. in 1658, the same year Tyrrell began his matriculation.

Locke thus began a long but often troubled relation with Oxford University that would span over three decades. In his student days Locke acquired a keen interest in science and philosophy and shed much of the dogmatism of his Puritan background. After graduation he took on a variety of limited-term appointment lectureships in Greek, rhetoric, and moral philosophy. His academic career was stymied considerably by the fact that most of the senior studentships then offered were available only to candidates planning to enter

---

[1] For biographical accounts of Locke, see *Dictionary of National Biography*, 24 vols., Leslie Stephen and Sidney Lee, eds. (London: Oxford University Press, 1921–22): Vol. XII: 27–36 (hereafter DNB); Maurice Cranston, *John Locke: A Biography* (London: Macmillan, 1957); and Peter Laslett's introduction to Locke, *Two Treatises of Government* (Cambridge: Cambridge University Press, 1988): esp. pp. 16–79.

the ministry. However, the free-thinking and scientifically inclined Locke determined to remain a layman and eventually settled on the study of medicine, which he later practiced, although he never graduated with a medical degree. Like nearly all of his colleagues at Oxford, Locke welcomed the Restoration in 1660, seeing in it the possible end of many years of religious discord in the country. In some early political tracts written at around this time, Locke vehemently supported religious uniformity and strong monarchical rule as an antidote to England's chronic instability. It was only several years later, when he was acting as secretary to Sir Walter Vane on a diplomatic mission to Cleves, that Locke began to reconsider the question of toleration after seeing in the small German duchy Catholics and Protestants living in peace and equality.[2]

The major turning point in Locke's life occurred at Oxford in 1666, when he first met and successfully treated a medical ailment plaguing Ashley Cooper, the future earl of Shaftesbury. The Oxford academic and the rising political star hit it off almost immediately, and within a year Locke moved into rooms in Shaftesbury's Exeter House on the Strand in London. Locke acted as the family physician and as private secretary to Shaftesbury. For the next several years Locke would preside over gatherings of intellectuals and personages including Tyrrell, Sydenham, and Shaftesbury himself, who would meet regularly at Exeter House to discuss matters philosophical, scientific, political, and religious. In this role Locke played an important part in helping to form the nucleus of the future Whig movement. Shaftesbury came to admire not only Locke's healing powers but also his political acumen, and he was soon employed in a variety of public functions relating to Shaftesbury's duties as lord chancellor, including a stint as secretary of presentations, dealing with religious matters, and as secretary of trade and plantations, responsible for colonial affairs. It was in this capacity that Locke penned the proposed constitution for the Carolinas colony, in which Shaftesbury was a major shareholder. However, Locke's career in public service was inextricably connected to Shaftesbury's political fortunes, and when he lost the chancellorship in 1673, Locke's political activities appeared for all intents and purposes to be over. Between 1673 and 1679 Locke took a leave from Oxford and passed most of his time traveling through France, where he enjoyed the company of many of the leading scientific minds on the Continent.

In the late 1670s Locke's political career, like that of Sidney, appeared to be a thing of the past. Locke's patron, Shaftesbury, had fallen from grace and was cooling his heels in the Tower. The philosopher seemed more interested in travel and science than in his nation's political life. However, it was the fall of Danby and the ensuing Exclusion crisis that drew Locke, as it did Sidney, back into England's political troubles. Locke's return to England in

[2] Cranston, *Biography*, pp. 57–67, 82.

1679 coincided, not by accident, with Shaftesbury's return to prominence in the Exclusion Parliaments. Locke's activities during 1679–83 are a subject of considerable historical debate.[3] It is probably fair to say that Locke was neither a hard-core agitator and revolutionary nor a purely disengaged philosopher. He certainly worked closely with Shaftesbury in this period, perhaps collaborating with him on some Exclusion pamphlets generally attributed to the earl. He split his time in these years between Shaftesbury's new residence in Thanet House and Oxford, where he regularly visited Tyrrell's nearby estate at Shotover. It was during this period of intimate contact with Shaftesbury and Tyrrell that Locke began writing the *Two Treatises*.

After the collapse of the Whig parliamentary opposition to the crown, Locke began a very uneasy existence in England. He perhaps knew as well as anyone that Shaftesbury's promised Whig insurrection in 1682 manned by "ten thousand brisk boys from Wapping" would never materialize, and as a well-known confidante of the earl, Locke was under constant surveillance by government spies at Oxford. But the notoriously cautious Locke was never one to show his hand unadvisedly. As one Oxford informer reported at this time: "John Locke lives a very cunning unintelligible life.... Certainly there is some Whig intrigue amanaging [sic], but here not a word of politics comes from him, nothing new or anything else concerning our present affairs, as if he were not at all concerned with them."[4] Of course, Locke was closely following events, and after Shaftesbury's death in Holland and particularly following the arrest of Sidney and the other Whig leaders in 1683, Locke grew alarmed and made for refuge on the Continent, settling in Holland for the next five years.[5] In his Dutch exile Locke did go underground for a while, assuming the pseudonym "Dr. Van der Linden" to avoid extradition back to England. He also lost his position at Oxford and resolutely rejected the efforts of his friends, including Tyrrell, to secure him a royal pardon. Locke spent most of his time in Holland writing and making contacts with other Whig exiles in the Dutch provinces. He probably played no role in the failed Monmouth rising in 1685, but did become thereafter a trusted friend and adviser to William and Mary. He also lived for a time with Sidney's dear old friend Benjamin Furly in Rotterdam, and it was from there that Locke watched the dramatic events unfolding in England in late 1688, finally

[3] Richard Ashcraft tends to see Locke as a highly active revolutionary (*Revolutionary Politics and Locke's Two Treatises of Government* [Princeton: Princeton University Press, 1986]: esp. chs. 10–11), whereas Cranston's Locke is considerably more disengaged from conspiratorial politics (*Biography*).
[4] Cranston, *Biography*, p. 221. For a discussion of Locke's notorious caution, see Richard Cox, *Locke on War and Peace* (Oxford: Clarendon Press, 1960): pp. 1–44.
[5] Cranston argues that Locke probably had no direct contact with Sidney's group (*Biography*, p. 228), but Jonathan Scott suggests that they may have had common connections such as Essex (*Algernm Sidney and the English Republic, 1623–1677* [Cambridge: Cambridge University Press, 1988]: p. 219).

returning to England with Queen Mary in February 1689, just in time to witness Parliament's offer of the crown to the Oranges.

After the Glorious Revolution, Locke published the many works that had been germinating during and prior to his exile, including anonymously the *Two Treatises* (1690), as well as his publicly attributed works the *Essay Concerning Human Understanding* (1690), the *Letters on Toleration* (1690 and 1692), and the *Treatise on Education* (1693). With the publication of the *Essay* in particular, Locke became practically overnight one of the most celebrated philosophers in Europe. For the last decade or so of his life Locke held some public offices, most notably as a member of the Board of Trade, in which capacity he consulted with Isaac Newton, among others, on the issue of currency reform.[6] Retiring from public life in 1700, Locke spent his last years at Oates in Essex, frequently visited by a host of friends and admirers from all over Europe, finally dying in 1704 one of the most widely recognized leading minds of his age.

Locke's major contribution to the formation and development of Whig political philosophy was undoubtedly the *Two Treatises of Government*. Locke's version of Whig political thought was, as we have seen, only one strain in the complex, heterogeneous body of ideas included in the Whig politics of liberty. Locke was a radical Whig and a defender of the doctrine of natural liberty. He rejected Tyrrell's moderate Whig notions of political and contractual sovereignty, as well as the fundamentally Pufendorfian idea of the natural law underlying the moderate Whig view of nature and government. Instead, Locke championed the principles of individual natural rights, popular sovereignty, and the dissolution of government.

However, Locke's liberal strain of radical Whiggism also departed in important respects from the republicanism advocated by the radical Whig, Sidney. Locke was a radical Whig, but his principles of individual natural rights and popular sovereignty did not eventuate in a defense of republicanism and popular government. Lockean Whiggism placed greater emphasis on the role of property in the purpose of the government and in the individualist logic of natural rights than did Sidney. The individualistic and acquisitive premises of Lockean natural rights theory rested on fundamentally different reflections on the character of nature than we saw in Sidney's Whig republican thought. Moreover, the republican emphasis on the institutionalization of popular sovereignty through the constitutional supremacy of popular legislative assemblies runs counter to Locke's support for the separation of powers and his assertion that sovereignty is a product of the delegated natural power of individuals. In Locke's delegation theory of sovereignty, the various powers of government, being originally derived from individuals in society, may be constituted and structured in a variety of ways, including forms of government more akin to mixed constitutionalism than to

[6] Cranston, *Biography*, pp. 345–7.

republicanism. Lockean liberal Whigs, for example, were much more open to the idea of an independent executive and the principle of prerogative than the republican Whigs. Lockean liberalism and republican freedom, while deriving from a common origin in the defense of the natural liberty doctrine against the absolutist claims of Filmerian divine right theory, would traverse separate but interconnecting paths in Anglo-American and early modern thought.

In this chapter, we will examine the major elements of Locke's argument for radical Whig liberalism. First, we will analyze the radical premises underlying Locke's long-neglected *First Treatise* and consider the important ways in which he departed from his scholastic, parliamentary contractarian, and Grotian and Hobbesian predecessors in the natural liberty tradition. We will also examine Locke's theory of natural rights and his account of property in order to illustrate his rejection of the principles of moderate Whiggism articulated by Tyrrell. In the following chapter, we will consider the main elements of Lockean liberal constitutionalism in order to illuminate Locke's liberal and individualistic alternative to the moderate Whig and radical republican constitutional thought of Tyrrell and Sidney.

Reconsidering the *First Treatise*

It is common to observe that Locke's *First Treatise* has historically received much less attention than its more illustrious sequel. This neglect is understandable but not warranted. Whereas in the *Second Treatise* Locke defines and outlines such characteristic concepts as the state of nature, the law of nature, and his theory of property, the *First Treatise* is generally regarded as a tedious and uninspiring refutation of Filmer. In viewing the one mainly as a defense of the doctrine of natural liberty against Filmer's claims and the other as the work in which Locke presents his own innovative use and understanding of natural jurisprudence, Locke scholars have traditionally maintained the conservatism of the *First Treatise* and the radicalism of the *Second Treatise*.[7]

While Locke presents the *First Treatise* in a conservative light, I believe this posture obscures the radical character of his argument in this work. Locke's moderate tone conforms to his claim to be a defender of the notion

---

[7] For examples of the tendency to underestimate the radicalism of the *First Treatise*, see John Dunn, *The Political Thought of John Locke* (Cambridge: Cambridge University Press, 1969): esp. chs. 5 and 6 and Martin Seliger, *The Liberal Politics of John Locke* (New York: Praeger, 1969): esp. pp. 188–90 and 203–5. The most important exceptions to this trend include Richard Ashcraft, *Locke's Two Treatises of Government* (London: Allen & Unwin, 1987): pp. 60–96; Thomas Pangle, *The Spirit of Modern Republicanism* (Chicago: University of Chicago Press, 1988): pp. 133–51; Paul Rahe, "John Locke's Philosophical Partisanship," *Political Science Reviewer*, vol. 20 (1991): pp. 29–30; and Michael Zuckert, "An Introduction to Locke's First Treatise," *Interpretation*, vol. 8 (1979): pp. 58–74.

of natural liberty against the radicalism of divine right theory. By defending the principle of consent, Locke counters Filmer's claim that human beings are not morally capable of creating, and thus limiting the power of, political and social institutions. Locke ostensibly sides in this quarrel with other natural liberty theorists like Bellarmine and Grotius. Locke's apparent conservatism in this treatise operates on two levels. First, he offers an indirect defense of the legitimacy of the English Constitution against the claims of the divine rightists. Locke claims that peoples, including the English, have always made constitutions and that these fundamental laws determine legitimate rule. Second, Locke offers a combination of natural and scriptural arguments in order to demonstrate their fundamental compatibility and their common hostility to the doctrine of divine right. God has left human beings free to choose the form of government they think best for themselves. As Locke presents it in the *First Treatise*, revelation and reason speak with one voice in their opposition to Filmer.

The conservative posture Locke assumes in this treatise, however, is only part of the story. In the title of the work, Locke calls the reader's attention to the fact that the *First Treatise* is a refutation of "the False Principles and Foundation of Sir Robert Filmer," but it is only in the *Second Treatise* that Locke offers an account of the "True Original, Extent, and End of Civil Government."[8] Thus, by Locke's admission, the "True Original, Extent and End" of political society is not the proper subject of the *First Treatise*. He proposes that a mere refutation of Filmer, and more importantly even the defense of traditional notions of natural liberty, do not constitute in themselves an adequate account of the nature and character of political society. But, as we shall see, the *First Treatise* operates from more radical premises than Locke initially led the reader to assume. Indeed, when we reexamine Locke's treatment of property, paternal power, and the political importance of Scripture, it becomes clear that Locke's most important aim in the *First Treatise* is not to refute Filmer, but rather to deliver a powerful, if often implicit, criticism of extant variations of the doctrine of natural liberty. The radicalism of the *First Treatise* presupposes Locke's assessment of the inadequacy of his predecessors in the natural liberty tradition.

In the Preface to the *Two Treatises*, Locke offers the work as a defense of the "People of England" in "their Just and Natural Rights" against the teaching of Robert Filmer. He continues to assert that "the King, and Body of the Nation," following the Glorious Revolution and the accession of William III, have so clearly shown their support for constitutional monarchy and the principle of natural liberty that any refutation of Filmer would have been unnecessary "had not the Pulpit, of late years, publickly owned his Doctrine,

---

[8] This is the full title of the 1698 version used on p. 135 of Laslett's edition. All references to Locke's *Two Treatises* in notes and in the text are from the Laslett edition and signify Treatise I or II and the section number.

and made it the Currant [sic] Divinity of the Times."[9] Of Filmer's doctrine, Locke judges: "His System lies in a little compass, 'tis no more but this, *That all Government is absolute Monarchy*. And the Ground he builds on, is this, *That no Man is Born free*" (I:2). As Locke presents it, so great is the support of the English people and their leaders for the legitimacy of their constitutional order and the principle of natural liberty on which it is grounded that only a fanatical group of Tory clergymen remain obstinate in their defense of the divine right claims of the Stuarts. To combat these religious leaders and the many people influenced by them, Locke offers his treatises.

Locke's strategy in the initial phase of the treatise is twofold. First, he claims that he will refute the "Scripture proofs" Filmer "pretends wholly to build on" in his argument for Adamic supreme paternal right. Second, Locke adopts an "enemy of my enemy is my friend" approach whereby he defends several of the targets of Filmer's attacks. In this way, Locke indirectly aligns himself with such notable natural liberty theorists as Bellarmine, Grotius, Hobbes, and Philip Hunton. Indeed, it is in a passage from Filmer's *Observations on Mr. Hob's Leviathan* that Locke draws "the Sum of all his Arguments, for *Adam's Sovereignty*, and against *Natural Freedom*." The passage is as follows:

If God Created only Adam, and of a piece of him made the Woman, and if by Generation from them two, as parts of them all Mankind be propagated: If also God gave to Adam not only Dominion over the Woman and the Children that should arise from them, but also over the whole Earth to subdue it, and over all the Creatures on it, so that as long as Adam lived, no Man could claim or enjoy any thing but by Donation, Assignation, or Permission from him. (I:14)

Using this statement as a framework, Locke proceeds to examine Filmer's claims for Adam's title to sovereignty by creation, as well as by donation, Eve's subjection, and by title of fatherhood. Locke's strategy develops as follows. In Chapters Three through Six, Locke confronts Filmer with a series of descending hypothetical counterarguments and alternative interpretations of Scripture intended to obstruct Filmer's thesis at every turn. Locke first examines Filmer's claim for Adam's title to sovereignty by creation. Initially Locke argues that it could not be the bare act of Adam's creation or his coming to be "without the Intervention of parents or the pre-existence of any of the same species to beget him" that established his title to rule, because by this reasoning the lion would "have as good a Title to it as he, and certainly the Ancienter" (I:15). Locke observes that Filmer relies ultimately on some form of unique divine appointment in order to assign any special sovereignty claim in Adam, rather than in the lion or any other created being. By this inevitable recourse to divine appointment, Locke claims, Filmer obviates the need for asserting the extraordinary moral standing of the process

---

[9] Locke, *Two Treatises*, "Preface," pp. 137–8.

of Adam's creation. Moreover, even if Adam derived a unique title to political sovereignty on the basis of divine appointment, Filmer would have to
identify when this appointment occurred in Scripture. Logically, it could not
have occurred simultaneously with Adam's creation, Locke claims, because
then Adam would have been a king with no subjects, a mockery of Filmer's
Adamic "Governor in Habit, and not in Act" (I:18). Locke concludes that
having a title to rule in potential, or independently of the possibility of exercising that right, is "no Title at all."

In his brief examination of Adam's right by creation in Chapter Three,
Locke makes two major points. First, he denies that any title to rule, can
exist independently of the consent of the governed. For Adam to be a ruler
he must have subjects to rule, and these subjects must recognize the exercise of this rule. Second, through his treatment of the importance of divine
appointment for Filmer's claims for Adam, Locke establishes that it is not
Adam's rule of humankind that Scripture expresses in the creation story, but
rather God's rule of all humankind, including Adam. Presumably, God could
have appointed whomever He wished to rule.

In Chapter Four, Locke examines Filmer's claim for Adam's title to rule by
God's donation of power over all the creatures of the Earth. In this discussion
Locke deals with Genesis 1:28, in which God commands human beings to
"be Fruitful and Multiply and Replenish the Earth and subdue it, and have
Dominion over the Fish of the Sea" (1:23). It is important to recall, however,
that Filmer did not present the donation thesis – that Genesis 1:28 gave Adam
sovereignty over all human beings – as his own, but rather acknowledged
that it was part of Selden's critique of the Grotian account of the origin of
private property. Thus, in attacking Filmer's purported use of this argument,
Locke implicitly defends Grotius' idea of the original negative community. To
support this original community, Locke combines scriptural and naturalistic
argumentation. For example, he argues that the plain meaning of the biblical
text, the presentation of God's gift of the world to "them," signifies God's
authorization of the use of the world at least to both Adam and Eve, but
most likely to all humankind to satisfy their wants and needs (1:24, 29,
30). Locke charges that even if Scripture did intend by this some special
rights for Adam, these could not extend to a property right in human beings;
otherwise, "Princes might eat their Subjects too, since God gave as full power
to Noah and his heirs, Chap. 9.2, *to eat every living thing that moveth*" (1:27).
Locke contends that even if Adam did derive unique rights, these rights
were severely limited. Locke claims that far from being the proud lord of all
creation, Adam, by the terms of his grant, "could not make bold with a Lark
or a Rabbet [sic] to satisfy his hunger, and had the herbs but in common
with the Beasts" (1:39). Locke calls our attention to the fact that the divine
prohibition on meat eating was not rescinded until after the Flood, long after
Adam's time. Most importantly, however, Locke argues that irrespective of
any alleged property right in Adam or any one else, this divine donation did

not extend to political sovereignty (1: 40–41, 43). As Locke presents it, God, the maker and owner of the world, could give or withhold the goods of the Earth freely, but He left determinations of political rule up to the people to decide for themselves.

In Chapter Five, Locke examines Adam's presumed title to sovereignty by right of the subjection of Eve in Genesis 3:16. As we have seen, Filmer used this passage to rebut Hunton's case for natural liberty. Locke charges that the subjection of Eve does not contradict the doctrine of natural liberty because by this act God gave no special privilege to Adam. Indeed, Locke states that Adam "too had a share in the fall, as well as sin." Adam was also punished by "his offended Maker," who commanded him to toil and labor and "seems rather to give him a Spade into his hand, to subdue the Earth, than a Scepter to Rule over its inhabitants" (1:44, 45). For Locke, Scripture is more concerned with identifying the scope of God's rule over creation than any particular human being's title to sovereign authority. Locke concedes, however, that even if any grant of rule can be derived from Genesis 3:16, it suggests only the male rule over women in conjugal society, what Locke calls "that Subjection they (the Female Sex) should ordinarily be in to their Husbands" (1:47). He clarifies that this authority extends only to "things of private concernment" in the family and never sanctions "a Political Power of Life and Death over her, much less over any body else" (1:48). Locke concludes that, by any reasonable interpretation of Genesis 3:16, it is apparent that Scripture does not contradict Hunton's principle of natural liberty.

The final element in Locke's series of counterarguments against Filmer relates to Adam's purported title to sovereignty by right of fatherhood. This both involves Locke in an indirect defense of Grotius and Bellarmine and allows him to examine the moral and political implications of the Fifth Commandment. From the admission of these two heavyweights in the natural liberty school that paternal right is a natural power, Filmer concluded that the subjection of children to their parents nullified the doctrine of natural freedom and all the political implications, like consent, that flow from it.[10] Locke defends Grotius and Bellarmine on several grounds. First, he radicalizes the underlying premise of his position in the earlier chapters by arguing that Scripture is concerned to show God's rule over human beings. But now he reveals that Filmer's patriarchalist argument actually diminishes God's role as the actual and direct source of life for every human being. Locke

---

[10] Locke also raises the issue of Bellarmine's admission of paternal right at I:12. Robert Filmer quotes Bellarmine to this effect at 1:3 of *Patriarcha and Other Writings*, Johann Somerville, ed. (Cambridge: Cambridge University Press, 1991). Locke deals with Filmer's use of Grotius' statement of paternal generative rights at I:50. The phrase under discussion is Grotius' statement that "by generation a right over children is acquired by parents" (Hugo Grotius, *De Jure Belli ac Pacis Libri Tres* [Oxford, Clarendon Press, 1925]): 2.5.1 (hereafter DJB). Filmer used this statement with great aplomb in his observations on Grotius. See Filmer, *Patriarcha*, p. 226.

claims that all humans are the "Workmanship" of God, the "All-wise Contriver" who is the "Author and Giver of Life" (1:52–54). Human fathers, Locke claims, cannot even begin to understand the complexity involved in creating a single human being, and as such, the primary obligation is to the divine maker, not the human parent. Locke simply pushes the logic of Filmer's patriachalism to the final degree: all human beings are born subject, but only to God and not to any other human being. With similar antipatriarchal reasoning, Locke claims that the obedience and honor enjoined by the Fifth Commandment explicitly include that due to the mother as well as the father.[11] Filmer, of course, had repeatedly dropped the mother from the rubric of the commandment. Locke concludes his reflections on this scriptural teaching by charging that the commandment does not indicate political obedience of any kind (1:65, 68). For Locke, the honor due parents in no way affects the origins and claims of political sovereignty.

The final movement of Locke's argument in Chapter Six involves his claim that Scripture clearly distinguishes political from paternal rule; otherwise, no father could be subordinate to political authority and any claimant to rule could base his claim on paternal right. Filmerian logic leads, in Locke's view, to what might be called the "sometimes problem." Locke tries to demonstrate the complete incoherence of Filmer's theory, and the anarchic consequences if such a teaching were to be taken seriously, by cataloging a detailed list of the circumstances in which Filmer identified the supreme paternal right. Here is just a sample of what Locke offers: "Sometimes Parents have it, . . . Sometimes Children during their Fathers lifetime . . . , Sometimes the posterity of Adam . . . , Sometimes all Kings . . . , Sometimes he that can catch it, an Usurper" (1:72). The clear thrust of Locke's argument is that in rooting political right in fatherhood, a biological possibility for practically half of the human race, Filmer has delivered an invitation for sedition and usurpation to every (male) rascal with a notion to rule. Locke leaves the obvious implication that Filmer's opponents, Grotius and Bellarmine, made no such error.

The second half of the *First Treatise* is a detailed analysis of the problems attending Filmer's account of the transmission of Adam's supreme paternal right through biblical times up to the present day. Much of this discussion is simply an amplification of the implications of the sometimes problem. Locke argues that the dark, anarchic core of Filmer's teaching rests on his inability to identify who, given Adam's original right, should rule in the present in the many nations of the world. He concludes that by the logic of Filmer's argument there are two possibilities: either there is one sole descendant or heir of Adam to whom we all owe obedience or every man has as much claim

---

[11] I:60–2. See also Locke's claim that with respect to generation, a mother would derive even more honor than a father inasmuch as she nourished "the Child a long time in her body out of her Substance" (I:55).

to this title as anyone else. Both possibilities, Locke cautions, undermine the legitimacy of every sovereign in the world.[12] Locke argues that Filmer offers no middle course between these extremes. The *First Treatise* concludes with the skillfully crafted portrait of Filmer as the half-ridiculous, half-villainous (or half-comic, half-tragic) perpetrator of many wild philosophical and theological innovations, all tending to the unsettling of peace, order, and good government.

The Radicalism of the *First Treatise*

Beneath the conservative rhetoric of the *First Treatise* lies a much more radical core than Locke originally suggests. This radical character comes to light when we examine the complex relation between the two treatises. This relation bears several important features. First, Locke presents the *First Treatise* as a refutation of Filmer's argument, but he indicates in the full title of the work that it is the *Second Treatise* that contains his account of the "True Original, Extent, and End of Civil Government." Thus, the act of refuting Filmer on natural and scriptural grounds, as well as deflecting his attacks on other natural liberty thinkers, does not constitute, for Locke, an account of the true nature of government. The apparent conservatism of the *First Treatise* is emphatically in the service of Locke's own argument in the *Second* and is in contradistinction to other natural liberty theorists.[13] Second, Locke's characterization of Filmer's influence presents a startling ambiguity. While Locke confirms that divine right theory has been almost universally rejected by the English people and their leaders, he affirms that Filmer's argument holds great currency among the "Drum Ecclesiastick." These supporters of Filmer, then, are the Anglican clergy, a group one might reasonably assume to be one of the more conservative and traditional elements in English society. Locke's sleight of hand on this issue is remarkable. He presents himself as a defender of the respectable and traditional notions of natural liberty and limited monarchy, as opposed to the "radical" clergymen of the established church. One suspects that traditional English Christianity has come under much more skeptical and critical scrutiny in the *First Treatise* than one might originally suppose.

Third, while Locke presents himself as the defender of the natural liberty tradition, he implicitly reminds the reader of the distinct variations

---

[12] I:104–5. Locke refers obliquely to Tyrrell as "the Ingenious and Learned Author of *Patriarcha Non Monarcha*," who has demonstrated the incoherence of Filmer's account of the transmission of Adamic paternal right by carefully detailing the enormous variety and complexity among the succession laws and practices of the European monarchies (I:124; cf. James Tyrrell, *Patriarcha, Non Monarcha* (London, 1681): pp. 57–61 (hereafter PNM and page number).

[13] Locke twice cross-references the *First* and *Second Treatises* more or less directly at I:90 and I:100. The former relates to the issue of property and the latter to paternal power.

within this school of thought. Locke nudges us to consider whether Grotius, Bellarmine, and Hunton, while in common opposition to Filmer, make arguments compatible with each other. This question assumes even greater poignancy when we recall that Hobbes appears as a shadowy but crucial figure in this treatise. Indeed, it was Filmer's response to Hobbes that provided Locke with the "sum of all" Filmer's arguments for Adam's supreme right. Locke implicitly suggests that the vindication of Hobbesian natural rights theory against Filmer is his primary concern in the work.[14] It would be difficult to find stranger bedfellows than the radical individualist Hobbes and the Christian-Aristotelian Bellarmine, but this is the intellectual context Locke frames for his audience. Locke subtly and cautiously directs the reader to reexamine his professed endorsement of the univocity in the natural liberty tradition.

When we return to Locke's discussion in the *First Treatise* with more suspicious eyes, we begin to see ambiguities and movements in his argument that were not apparent previously. For example, the first thing that strikes the careful reader about Locke's treatment of property in this treatise is the extent to which he exaggerates its importance for Filmer. As we have noted, Filmer did not present the donation argument from Genesis 1:28 in *Patriarcha*. Rather, he employed it as a minor element in his critique of Grotius. Locke slyly points to his own role in giving prominence to the property issue when he omits it from his list of the important arguments upon which Filmer built his theory (1:14). It is Locke, more than Filmer, who is concerned to compare Grotius' account of the origin of property with the Genesis account. The Bible, Locke argues, presents the world as the gift of God to all humankind for the satisfaction of their wants and needs. In the Grotian account of the origin of property, the Dutchman presented an original negative community in which no one owned anything in particular but individuals had the right to seize what they needed. For Grotius, this right of seizure produced a reciprocal duty on others to abstain from taking the goods another has claimed. Upon closer examination, it is clear that Locke, despite his rhetoric of harmony, actually sees a deep tension between these two conceptions of the origin of property.

This comes to light near the end of Chapter Four when Locke argues that irrespective of any seizure claim or individual property right, "God the Lord and Father of all, has given no one of his Children such a Property, in his peculiar Portion of the things of this World, but that he has given his needy Brother a Right to the Surplasage of his Goods; so that it cannot be justly denied him, when his pressing Wants call for it" (1:42). This argument opposes Filmer's claim for the peculiar property rights of Adam, but it also operates as a critique of the Grotian seizure right. Locke follows Pufendorf in advancing a necessity right to another's surplus goods as a means to

---

[14] See I:14; cf. Michael P. Zuckert, "Introduction to Locke's First Treatise," p. 69.

correct the Grotian model, by which individuals could conceivably starve if all the available goods and land have been seized already by others.[15] Most importantly, Locke appeals to God and Genesis to support his claim that the goods of the world were intended for all humankind, irrespective of any prior individual claim. Locke suggests that in this crucial respect regarding the origin of property, the author of Genesis was not a Grotian.

The tension between the Bible and the Grotian theory of property becomes even more pronounced when Locke deals with the meat-eating prohibition. The Grotian seizure right gives no account of such a divine prohibition. The logic of Grotius' argument, rooted in a primal right of self-preservation, would actually make any such prohibition a cruel and inhumane restriction on the human capacity to satisfy physical needs. The difference between Grotius and the Bible that Locke illuminates has to do with their views of the proper human stance toward the world. Locke echoes Genesis by stating that human beings are created in "the Image of God," who is our "Maker" (1:30, 40). In viewing human beings as what Locke later calls the "Workmanship" of God (1:53), he suggests that the Bible and Grotius profoundly disagree about the character of human freedom. Whereas Grotius defended the possibility of contractual absolutism as an unfortunate product of natural freedom, Locke suggests that the Bible's teaching precludes such a possibility because it bases human political freedom on the deeper theological premise of our natural subjection to God.

Locke's radical purpose in this discussion relates to two major issues. First, he continues his theme of distinguishing the right of property and the right of political rule, but he does so now with Grotius, not Filmer, as his primary target. As we have seen, Grotius' theory left open the possibility, however unattractive, of absolute rule resting on contract and consent.[16] Locke reminds his readers that not only Filmer and the divine rightists but also natural rights theorists like Grotius failed to distinguish the proper ends of government and property. When Locke argues that title to rule cannot be transferred or inherited in the way property can, his opponent is as much Grotius as Filmer. The second major issue raised in Locke's treatment of property relates to the biblical conception of the rights of individuals vis-à-vis the physical world. While God's claim over human beings as his "Workmanship" may logically resist the absolute claims of human sovereignty, Locke

---

[15] This is the thrust of Tyrrell at PNM, 109–13* (second pagination) and of Samuel Pufendorf, *De Jure Naturae et Gentium Libri Octo* (Oxford: Clarendon Press, 1934): bk. 4, ch. 4, pp. 5–8 (hereafter DJNG bk., ch., sec., and page number where applicable). However, for the tension between the Lockean and the Pufendorfian–Tyrrellian view of property, see Ruth Grant, *John Locke's Liberalism* (Chicago: University of Chicago Press, 1987): p. 59 and John Marshall, *John Locke: Resistance, Religion and Responsibility* (Cambridge: Cambridge University Press, 1994): p. 235; Seliger, *Liberal Politics*, p. 175; and James Tully, *A Discourse on Property: Locke and His Adversaries* (Cambridge: Cambridge University Press, 1980): pp. 131–2, 137–8.

[16] For the "Full Property Right in Government," see Grotius, DJB 1.3.11.1.

implies that the Bible's emphasis on human stewardship and the promise of divine provision does not cohere with the true human experience of the world. Hungry individuals should be free to eat anything edible, regardless of specific divine prohibitions. In the celebrated fifth chapter of the *Second Treatise*, the question of the proper human stance toward the physical world will become an explicit and seminal theme in Locke's natural rights theory, but the first glimmerings of Locke's theory of property appear here in the *First*.

The underlying radicalism of the *First Treatise* can also be seen in Locke's discussion of the family. Locke's stated concern in Chapters Five and Six was to refute Filmer's claims for Adam's title by the subjection of Eve and by the right of fatherhood. With respect to Hunton's argument regarding the moral status of the subjection of Eve, Locke offers a number of observations meant to demonstrate that the Bible's endorsement of the subjection of wives to their husbands conferred at most a conjugal rather than a political power.[17] We recall that the Puritan divine and parliamentary radical Hunton had argued from the premise of the divine ordination of political power.[18] While Hunton defended the principle of natural liberty, he denied that individuals as individuals have the moral capacity to constitute sovereign political institutions. Rather, for the Calvinist Hunton, communal consent to a form of rule merely placed sovereignty in particular institutions or individuals; consent did not produce sovereign right. Insofar as Hunton's argument rested ultimately on the divine ordination of political power, then, Locke's treatment of Scripture, and Genesis 3:16 in particular, is significant for determining his stance toward this predecessor in the natural liberty tradition. Locke argues that not only does the subjection of Eve *not* denote Adam's sovereign right, in

---

[17] For a fuller treatment of the way in which Locke went much further than any of his Whig colleagues in extending his individualist principles to women and children in the family, see Melissa Butler, "Early Liberal Roots of Feminism: John Locke and the Attack on Patriarchy," *American Political Science Review*, vol. 72, no. 1 (March 1978): pp. 135–50; David Foster, "Taming the Father: John Locke's Critique of Patriarchal Fatherhood," *Review of Politics*, vol. 56, no. 4 (Fall 1994): pp. 641–70; Mary Walsh, "Locke and Feminism on Private and Public Realms of Activity," *Review of Politics*, vol. 57, no. 2 (Spring 1995): pp. 251–77; and Lee Ward, "The Natural Rights Family: Locke on Women, Nature, and the Problem of Patriarchy," in *Nature, Woman, and the Art of Politics*, Eduardo Velasquez, ed. (Lanham, MD: Rowman & Littlefield, 2000): pp. 149–79. For the classic study portraying Locke as a patriachalist, albeit of a liberal persuasion, see Carole Pateman, *The Sexual Contract: Aspects of Patriarchal Liberalism* (Stanford: Stanford University Press, 1988): pp. 3, 22, 92–3. For a recent study that not only demonstrates the diversity of opinion among the Whigs with respect to the family but also disputes the importance of patriachalism in Filmer's argument for divine right monarchy, see Rachel Weil, "The Family in the Exclusion Crisis: Locke versus Filmer Revisited," in *A Nation Transformed: England after the Restoration*, Alan Houston and Steve Pincus, eds. (Cambridge: Cambride University Press, 2001): pp. 101, 103,107, 109, 111, 121, 124.

[18] Philip Hunton, "A Treatise of Monarchy," in *Divine Right and Democracy*, David Wootton, ed. (Hammondsworth: Middlesex: Penguin Classics, 1986): pp. 176–7.

contrast to Filmer, he also suggests that, in contrast to Hunton, Scripture's injunction to Eve may possess no obligatory moral status whatsoever. Locke charges that in the Bible's command

[t]here is here no more Law to oblige a Woman to such a Subjection, if the Circumstances either of her Condition or Contract with her Husband should exempt her from it, then there is, that she should bring forth her Children in Sorrow and Pain, if there could be found a Remedy for it. (1:47)

In his putative defense of Hunton, Locke offers two startlingly secular arguments that Hunton would surely have contested: the contractual character of conjugal society and the capacity of human initiative to overcome divine injunction.

If Locke's professed conservatism in defense of the natural liberty tradition is not all that it appears to be, then we are entitled to ask whether Locke's stance toward Scripture is equally deceiving. In the early sections of the *First Treatise* Locke presented himself as the defender of the plain meaning of Scripture against "so much glib Nonsense" and transparent manipulations of the biblical text proffered by Filmer. This is a particularly pressing issue, Locke indicates, because Filmer "pretends wholly to build on Scripture-proofs."[19] By demonstrating that Filmer's argument is incompatible with the scriptural passages upon which he attempts to build, Locke promises to undermine the entire edifice of Filmerian divine right theory. Yet, Locke frequently employs both scriptural and natural forms of argumentation. Locke's refutation of Filmer is not even putatively based wholly on "Scripture-proofs." Does Locke's effort to demonstrate that Filmer fails to build his system of government on Scripture also imply Locke's own skepticism that a decent system of government could be built upon the principles in Scripture?[20]

Here it may be useful to examine briefly Locke's own observations on the art of political and philosophical writing. As the dispute between Filmer and Locke reveals, the charge of theological innovation, or even more so atheism, was a powerful weapon in seventeenth-century English polemics. Locke both directly and indirectly accuses Filmer of these heresies, as had Filmer against his opponents a generation or so earlier. It is precisely because of the sensitive nature of theologico–political disputes that Locke accuses Filmer of attempting to conceal the radical character of his divine right theory by means of skillful rhetoric and esoteric writing. Locke charges that Filmer, fearing that a clear statement of his teaching would shock the religious sensibilities of his audience, resorted to crafty writing in order to conceal the

---

[19] Locke, *Two Treatises*, "Preface" and I:1–2.
[20] Cf. Nathan Tarcov, *Locke's Education for Liberty* (Chicago: University of Chicago Press, 1984): pp. 64–5.

radical character of his teaching from all but the most discerning reader. Locke claims:

> Like a wary Physician, when he would have his Patient swallow some harsh or Corrosive Liquor, he mingles it with a large quantity of that, which may dilute it; that the scatter'd Parts may go down with less feeling, and cause less Aversion. (1:7)

We can assume that Locke's caution to the reader applies as much, and probably more, to himself than to the irrepressible and brutally candid Robert Filmer.[21] In fact, I shall argue that Locke, a former medical student himself, was the very picture of a "wary Physician."

Although the status of Scripture as a guide for political life is a consistent theme of the *First Treatise*, Locke rarely in this work offers his own view of the proper approach one should take in reading biblical texts. In Chapter Five he states: "God, I believe, speaks differently from Men, because he speaks with more Truth, more Certainty: but when he vouchsafes to speak to Men, I do not think, he speaks differently from them, in crossing the Rules of language in use amongst them" (1:46). Thus, Locke boldly claims that God, and perforce Scripture, speak in clear and understandable language to human beings, and only charlatans and partisans would seek to exploit fabricated ambiguities or inconsistencies in the holy text for their own ends. However, just a few sections later, Locke muddies this picture of the pristine and perfectly clear language of Scripture when he argues that God's words in Genesis 3:16, "Thy desire shall be to thy Husband" – the core passage for the subjection of Eve – "is too doubtful an expression, of whose signification Interpreters are not agreed, to build so confidently on, and in a Matter of such Moment" (1:49). Later Locke disputes Filmer's claim for Cain's rule over his younger brother, Abel, by offering the remarkable judgment that the phrase in Genesis "his desire shall be subject to thee, and thou shalt Rule" is "so doubtful and obscure a place in Scripture, which may be well, nay better, understood in a quite different Sense" (1:112). Further on, Locke suggests that regarding the status of Cain's right as the elder, nothing "can convincingly be conferr'd from so doubtful a Text" (1:118). Scripture, originially presented as so clear and unambiguous, soon appears for Locke to be impenetrably doubtful and obscure on matters of great importance for political life.

---

[21] For good discussions of Locke's famous caution, see Butler, "Early Liberalism Roots of Feminism," p. 147; Cox, *Locke on War and Peace*, pp. 1–44; Jean B. Elshtain, *Public Man, Private Woman* (Princeton: Princeton Press, 1981): pp. 121–2; Pangle, *Spirit*, pp. 132–8; Leo Strauss, *Natural Right and History* (Chicago: University of Chicago Press, 1953): pp. 200, 206–9, 246 and Michael Zuckert, "Fools and Knaves: Reflections on Locke's Theory of Philosophical Discourse," *Review of Politics*, vol. 36, no. 2 (1974): pp. 544–64 and his "Of Wary Physicians and Weary Readers: The Debate on Locke's Way of Writing," *Independent Journal of Philosophy*, vol. 2 (1977): pp. 55–66.

The trajectory of Locke's critical approach to biblical hermeneutics leads ultimately to an implicit denial that Scripture provides authoritative guidance for politics and the character of natural rights. Locke claims late in the *First Treatise* that with respect to the condition of the people following the dispersion at Babel, "Scripture says not a word of their Rulers or Forms of Government" (1:145).[22] While this pattern of rejecting Scripture's role as a positive guide for political life becomes more pronounced in the closing sections of the treatise, evidence of Locke's skepticism toward the political authority of the Bible appears throughout the *First Treatise*. For example, Locke's first direct quotation from Scripture was buried in the midst of his claim that if Filmer's system of monarchy was overturned, then "Governments must be left again to the old way of being made by contrivance, and the consent of Men (*anthropine ktisis*)" (1:6). The scriptural passage Locke refers to in the original Greek is 1 Peter 2:13, in which the apostle articulated a principle of government rather different from the one Locke suggests. Indeed, when we look at the scriptural passage as rendered in the King James version of the Bible, we can see that Locke takes considerable liberties with the original Greek. The full passage in the King James version runs as follows: "Submit yourselves to every ordinance of man [*anthropine ktisis*] for the Lord's sake: whether it be to the king, as supreme, Or unto governors." At the very least, Locke subtly suggests his own departure from the common authoritarian interpretation of this passage in traditional English Christianity. By rendering this celebrated and politically potent passage in Peter in a more populist vein than is generally accepted, Locke forces his reader to reexamine the authentic biblical position toward politics.[23] Locke interprets this famous scriptural passage to suggest that the biblical teaching on the origin and character of political society may not conform to the principles of right deduced from reason. Articulating, defining, and defending these principles of political sovereignty and natural rights, however, was Locke's focus of the *Second Treatise*.

The Law of Nature

The *Second Treatise* begins very much where the *First* left off. It begins ostensibly as an elaboration of the Christian-Aristotelian strain of the natural

---

[22] Cf. Tarcov, *Locke's Education*, p. 62.

[23] While I agree with Thomas Pangle that Locke uses his gloss on this passage to show his disagreement with Scripture, I would not go so far as to argue that "it would be difficult to imagine a clearer endorsement, *prima facie*, of the divine right of kings" than the King James version of 1 Peter 2:13 (Pangle, *Spirit*, p. 138). However, it is fair to say that the apostle's words are hardly a ringing endorsement of the principle of consent and limited government either. I believe that in its proper context 1 Peter 2:13 is more about the political moderation required of a minority religious community in the Roman Empire than a celebration of the divine origins of monarchy.

liberty tradition. However, throughout the course of the first five chapters of this work, Locke's argument heads off in new and uncharted directions. In his treatment of the state of nature and the origin of property rights, Locke cautiously but firmly leads us to a more radical account of natural liberty emphasizing the primacy of individual natural rights over moral duties and the dictates of natural law.

After recounting the main features of his refutation of Robert Filmer in the *First Treatise* as a kind of introduction to the *Second*, Locke proceeds in Chapter Two to offer his own assessment of the "True Original, Extent, and End of Civil Government." Locke claims that "to understand Political Power aright, and derive it from its Original, we must consider what State all Men are naturally in" (II:4). Locke's state of nature has two central features. First, for individuals it is "a *State of Perfect Freedom* to order their Actions, and dispose of their Possessions, and Persons as they think fit, . . . without asking leave, or depending upon the Will of any other Man" (II:4). Moreover, the state of nature is "a *State* also *of Equality*, wherein all the Power and Jurisdiction is reciprocal, no one having more than any other" (II:4). In this opening presentation of the state of nature, Locke firmly locates his position in the natural liberty tradition, inasmuch as

[t]here being nothing more evident, than that Creatures of the same species and rank promiscuously born to all the same advantages of Nature, and the use of the same faculties, should also be equals one amongst another without Subordination or Subjection. (II:4)

Locke initially associates his state of nature with the Christian-Aristotelian tradition represented in this case by the great English scholastic Richard Hooker. He argues that the principle of natural equality was held by "the Judicious Hooker" to be "so evident in it self, and beyond all question, that he makes it the Foundation of that Obligation to mutual Love amongst Men" (II:5; cf. II:15).[24] The precise character of this "Obligation to mutual Love," Locke suggests, can only be ascertained by reference to the "Law of Nature."

While Locke indicates that God and nature have not provided a natural order of political rule for human beings, he does argue that individuals have been provided with a natural rule to measure their actions. The state of liberty is not a "State of Licence" because "the State of Nature has a Law of Nature to govern it, which obliges everyone" (II:6). Locke indicates that "Reason, which is that Law," teaches that all human beings are "the Workmanship of one Omnipotent, and infinitely wise Maker." As we recall

---

[24] Simmons astutely observes that Locke does not include the portion of this passage in the *Ecclesiatical Polity*, Book I, Chapter viii, in which Hooker acknowledges the right to rule for those individuals who are most rational. See John Simmons, *The Lockean Theory of Rights* (Princeton: Princeton University Press, 1992): p. 30.

from the *First Treatise*, there Locke employed this modification of an essentially Filmerian concept in order to counter both Filmer and Grotius. Here in the *Second Treatise*, Locke develops this argument even further. By virtue of God's claim on humanity arising from his status as our source or "Maker," Locke affirms, in contrast to Filmer, the primal and fundamental equality that characterizes human relations. All human beings, no less than Adam, are the "Workmanship" of God and are bound to follow divine laws as they are expressed through revelation and the operation of our rational nature. In contrast to Grotius, Locke argues that the law of nature stipulates that the individual "has not Liberty to destroy himself" (II:6). Though every human being is naturally free and equal vis-à-vis other human beings, they are not therefore logically free to kill themselves or alienate their liberty entirely, through contractual absolutism, because of their obligation to serve God's "business" rather than "one anothers Pleasure." The natural law suicide prohibition rooted in humanity's status as God's property appears to form the bedrock of Locke's opposition to Grotian contractual absolutism.

From the premise of God's ownership of human beings, Locke derives a transcendent natural law depending entirely on the human relation to God, who is the guarantor of that law. The key principles of the natural law are what may be termed the "no-harm" commands. Locke contends that people are not only not at liberty to harm themselves, but also "no one ought to harm another in his Life, Health, Liberty or Possessions" (II:6). Significantly, Locke frames the moral order derived from the natural law in terms of duties rather than rights. Even self-preservation is presented as a duty an individual owes to God the maker. Locke claims that by the law of nature "Everyone is *bound to preserve himself*, and...when his own Preservation comes not in competition, ought he, as much as he can, *to preserve the rest of Mankind*" (II:6). At this point, Locke's natural law appears similar to that of the Pufendorfian Tyrrell. For both, the right of self-preservation appears to be derived from a deeper duty to serve the natural law by ensuring the common good of society. Even Locke's admission that the right of self-preservation can only be overridden when one's preservation "comes not in competition with others" appears not as an endorsement of the primacy of rights over duties, but rather as a statement of the status of the right of self-preservation as a means to perform the duty to preserve others.[25] Overzealous defenders of others may, it seems, contravene the claims of their divine owner by recklessly exposing themselves to harm and thus, as a corollary, doing little to help others.

But what dangers do human beings pose for each other if the natural law is apparent to all individuals "who will but consult it"? Locke responds that

[25] James Tully, *An Approach to Political Philosophy: Locke in Contexts* (Cambridge: Cambridge University Press, 1993), p. 26 and Michael P. Zuckert, *Natural Rights and the New Republicanism* (Princeton: Princeton University Press, 1994): pp. 218–19.

there will always be some individuals who do not apprehend the natural law. He does not offer much guidance for determining who would not follow this law and why; presumably they are governed by passion rather than "Reason, which is that Law." But he indicates that the natural law contains a crucial provision allowing for individuals to protect themselves and others from these flouters of the natural law. This is every individual's "right to punish the transgressors of that Law to such a Degree, as may hinder its Violation" (II:7). Once again, Locke does not present this punishment power as a right independent of a more fundamental duty; rather, Locke identifies this right as "a Power to Execute" the natural law. As Locke presents it, human beings serve God by punishing violators of the natural law. Indeed, he claims that the natural law would "be in vain" without this human participation in the natural injunction against the destruction of God's property. By this reasoning, Locke argues that the only exemption to the no-harm principle of the natural law would be in the service of that very principle.

There are two important features of Locke's initial presentation of the executive power of the law of nature. First, he locates this power in the right of individuals in the state of nature. By doing so, he rejects the Catholic natural law argument that the right to punish malefactors of the natural law belongs exclusively to established political authority.[26] This right preexists the establishment of political society and, Locke claims, persists within it to some extent. Locke goes further, however, to argue that the power of government, its right to punish offenders against both the natural law and its own civil laws, derives from this natural power of individuals. Locke defends the "very strange Doctrine" that every individual can punish offenders of the natural law by reference to that "Right any Prince or State can put to death, or *punish an Alien*, for any Crime he commits in their Country" (II:9). In answer to the traditionally vexing question "From where does government derive the right to punish criminals and execute its laws?" Locke offers the startling suggestion that government can ensure the preservation of its members, and presumably all of humanity, by virtue of the same power any individual has independently of membership in political society.

---

[26] In this respect, Figgis exaggerates the connection between the Whigs and the Catholic natural lawyers when he argues that the Whigs learned their ideas and arguments for natural rights and resistance from "the Society of Jesus" (Figgis, "On Some Political Theories of the Early Jesuits," *Transactions of the Royal Historical Society*, new ser., vol. XI [London, 1897]: pp. 89–112). In locating Locke's natural law in the medieval voluntarist tradition of Ockham and d'Ailly, Francis Oakley (*The Politics of Eternity: Studies in the History of Medieval and Early-Modern Political Thought* [Leiden: Brill, 1999]: pp. 242–5) makes a similar mistake by not recognizing the radical individualism underlying Locke's law of nature. Two thoughtful accounts of Locke's executive power of the law of nature that rely on a theistic interpretation, but draw political implications from Locke's argument that are decidedly radical and individualistic, are Kirstie M. McClure, *Judging Rights: Lockean Politics and the Limits of Consent* (Ithaca: Cornell University Press, 1996): pp. 127–32, 141–55 and Tully, *Locke in Contexts*, pp. 315–23.

The second important feature of Locke's initial presentation of the executive power of the law of nature is his consideration of the extent of that power. Locke makes it clear that the punishment power of individuals extends to a natural right of capital punishment.[27] He reveals that in the course of executing the law of nature, individuals "may restrain, or where it is necessary, destroy things noxious to them" (II:8). While it is apparent that the natural executive right allows the ultimate violation of the no-harm principle, namely, killing, Locke is also careful to soften the implications of this right. For example, Locke argues that the natural punishment power does not afford an individual an "Absolute or Arbitrary Power, to use a Criminal when he has got him in his hands, according to the passionate heats, or boundless extravagancy of his own Will" (II:8). By clarifying that the workmanship of God can never rightfully become the playthings of sadistic individuals, Locke appears to include a prohibition on torture or slavery in his natural law. Retribution may require swift and lethal punishment, but it does not sanction despotism and cruelty. Moreover, Locke is careful to stipulate that the ends of this punishment right should be reparation and restraint. He emphasizes this measured and moderate dimension of the natural punishment right throughout much of his early discussion in Chapter Two. Proportionality must be the primary consideration for any act of punishment. Thus, while capital punishment may be required for particularly dangerous individuals or for purposes of deterrence, Locke leaves the impression that such severe punishment will be the exception rather than the rule in the state of nature.

Locke's response to the "mighty Objection, Where are, or ever were, there any Men in such a State of Nature?" is twofold. First, he replies that "all Governors of Independent Communities" are in a state of nature with respect to each other (II:14). Second, he points to "a Swiss and an Indian, in the woods of America" as another example of "Men living together according to reason, without a common Superior on Earth, with Authority to judge between them" (II:14, 19). From these examples, Locke makes the case that not all agreements and compacts form political society, "for Truth and keeping of Faith belongs to Men, as Men, and not as Members of Society" (II:14). With this assertion, Locke begins to develop more fully the artful process of distinguishing his state of nature from that of Hobbes. Locke's initial

---

[27] Locke refers to Scripture in order to support this natural right of capital punishment. He offers the example of Cain to demonstrate Scripture's agreement with "the great Law of Nature, *Who so sheddeth Mans Blood, by Man shall his Blood be shed*" (II:11). From Cain's plea to God that "Everyone that findeth me, shall slay me" Locke deduces two things: that this natural right of capital punishment is "writ in the Hearts of Mankind" and that the injury done by one individual to another affords everyone a "Right to destroy such a Criminal" (II:11). Thus, Locke's natural executive power is both lethal and universal, allowing all individuals to participate in the punishment of an injury not directly related to themselves. For two different interpretations of Locke's use of the story of Cain, see Seliger, *Liberal Politics*, pp. 56–7 and Strauss, *Natural Right and History*, p. 223, note 84.

presentation of the state of nature differs from that of Hobbes. Whereas for Hobbes the original moral fact is a natural liberty to do what each considers necessary for survival – including the "right to everything, even to one another's body" – Locke's natural law orientation emphasizes the natural moral limits on human action.[28] Inasmuch as human beings are the natural property of God, Locke denies individuals even a right over their own bodies and lives (II:6). Moreover, while Locke concedes a few exceptions to the no-harm principle of the natural law, he does so only in furtherance of individuals' natural law obligations to "preserve Mankind." Locke leaves the reader with the distinct impression that his state of nature is much more peaceful and orderly than that of Hobbes.

In the following chapter Locke makes the contrast with Hobbes even more explicit. He announces, with an oblique reference to Hobbes and his followers, that "the State of Nature, and the State of War, which however some Men have confounded, are as far distant, as a State of Peace, Good Will, Mutual Assistance, and Preservation, and a State of Enmity, Malice, Violence, and Mutual Destruction are from one another" (II:19). By equating nature and war, Locke suggests, Hobbes made a fundamental error. The state of war, for Locke, is not the scene of hit-and-run raids and irregular warfare Hobbes presented in his state of nature; rather, Locke defines the state of war as "declaring by Word or Action, not a passionate and hasty, but a sedate settled Design, upon another Mans Life" (II:16). Locke suggests that not all human beings are naturally warlike, but that a few incorrigible characters will systematically attempt to invade the rights of others. Against these villains, all individuals may exercise their punishment power. To this extent, Locke's state of nature appears more like Pufendorf's and Tyrrell's than that of Hobbes. Like Tyrrell, Locke suggests that a minimalist social order, albeit below the sophistication and extent of political society, will be relatively peaceful and secure. Indeed, in a clever but indirect reference to Hobbes' sovereign, Locke turns the table on Hobbes by arguing that anyone "who attempts to get another Man into his Absolute Power, does thereby *put himself into a State of War* with him."[29] The "sedate settled Design" Locke associates with the state of war appears more characteristic of one who would aspire to being captain of the *Leviathan* than the sensible individuals Locke presents in his state of nature.

Locke's attempt to distance himself from Hobbes revolves around his distinction between the state of nature and the state of war. Locke defines the state of nature as one characterizing human beings "living together according to reason, without a common Superior on Earth, with Authority to judge between them" (II:19). The state of war, on the other hand, occurs as a result

---

[28] Zuckert, *Natural Rights*, p. 219.
[29] II:17. Here Locke claims that freedom is "the Fence" to the individual's preservation, and in so doing, in one fell swoop, he disqualifies any preservationist argument for absolutism, whether Grotian or Hobbesian.

of the use of force without right (any use of force that is not in execution of the law of nature), either in the state of nature or "against an aggressor, though he be in Society and a fellow Subject" (II:19). In this way, Locke both extends the executive power of the law of nature to civil society and severs the Hobbesian argument for the exclusive connection between war and the natural condition.[30] Locke suggests that in principle, at least, the state of nature may be no more violent than political society. Given this fact and Locke's picture of the relatively peaceful and orderly character of the state of nature, we are left to wonder why anyone would want to leave the state of nature as Locke presents it.[31] If the state of perfect freedom and political society, which requires a considerable restraint of that freedom, provide a comparable degree of security, there seems to be little reason to do so. Moreover, given the logic of Locke's argument that an individual's freedom is a "Fence" to his or her preservation, it would presumably follow that the state of perfect freedom would provide greater security for one's preservation than civil government, especially strong and autocratic governments in the Hobbesian mold.

Lockean Natural Rights

From an initial reading of Chapters Two and Three of the *Second Treatise* the reader is led to believe that Locke, for the most part, sees government as a greater threat to life and liberty than that "State all Men are naturally in" (II:4). It is thus with considerable surprise that we encounter Locke's statement in the last section of Chapter Three, where he reveals: "To avoid this State of War (wherein there is no appeal but to Heaven, and wherein every the least difference is apt to end, where there is no Authority to decide between the Contenders) is one great *reason of Mens putting themselves into Society*, and quitting the State of Nature" (II:21). With this, Locke pulls the rug out from under our feet; he undermines the very premise of his transcendent natural law, the operation of which we had been assured would ensure the relative peace and security of the natural condition. To understand how Locke could have led us unwittingly to this point, we must reexamine his state of nature and especially his account of the executive power of the law of nature.

---

[30] Of course, Hobbes also found support for the state of nature in the latent possibilities of civil society. We recall Hobbes' response to the skeptical reader in *Leviathan*, Chapter 13: "Let him therefore consider with himself, when taking a journey, he arms himself, and seeks to go well accompanied; when going to sleep, he locks his doors; when even in his house he locks his chests; and this when he knows there bee Laws, and publicke Officers, armed, to revenge all injuries shall be done him" (p. 77).

[31] Hans Aarsleff, "The State of Nature and the Nature of Man in Locke," in *John Locke: Problems and Perspectives*, John Yolton, ed. (Cambridge: Cambridge University Press, 1969): pp. 99–136, esp. p. 101.

Let us take stock of what we already know (or think we know) about Locke's state of nature. It appears to include, but is not limited to, an original pre-political condition. As was the case with Tyrrell, the state of nature describes a form or forms of human society that exist without reference to the degree of political experience of the individuals in it.[32] A Swiss trader and an Indian brave meeting in "the woods of America" are as truly in the state of nature as Napoleon Bonaparte and Tsar Alexander meeting on a raft in the Niemen River. Locke indicates that there are perfect forms of the state of nature (II:14) – suggesting less perfect or imperfect forms – but does not in these early stages of the treatise account for the degrees of perfection.[33] All Locke has left us for guidance as to the precise character of the state of nature is his formal definition presented earlier. But it is perhaps a little puzzling that Locke's definition of the state of nature, "Men living together according to Reason, without a common Superior on Earth," appears not in Chapter Two, entitled "Of the State of Nature," but in Chapter Three, "Of the State of War." The distinction between Locke's account of the state of nature and the state of war may not be as great as we originally assumed.

Locke was careful to demonstrate that the executive power of the law of nature was not a license for war, but rather a use of force *with right* needed to punish offenders against the law of nature. These malefactors were irrational and violent individuals who endangered the peace in the state of nature. Locke went so far as to call them "wild Savage Beasts" who "may be destroyed as a Lyon or a Tyger" (II:11). He admitted that the no-harm principle of the law of nature could be contravened for the sake of preserving the general peace and safety of all the individuals in the state of nature. Indeed, Locke affirmed that an individual executing the law of nature may legitimately employ great force to the point of causing death. While Locke was careful to make the deterrent value of such lethal force harmonize with his concern to preserve proportionality as a measure of this punishment power in the state of nature (a plausible argument in the case of murder), he also slipped in the possibility of punishing "the lesser breaches" of the law of nature with capital punishment.[34] Clearly, there is no necessary or easy connection between Locke's argument for deterrence and his emphasis on the principle of proportionality.

Two arguments serve to extend Locke's defense of lethal force in the state of nature far beyond the measure of proportionality he originally offered. Both of these arguments emerge in Locke's account of the state of war. First, Locke states that an individual in the state of nature is entitled to view an

---

[32] Tyrrell, PNM 62. Cf. Richard Goldwin, "John Locke," in *The History of Political Philosophy*, 3rd ed., Leo Strauss and Joseph Cropsey, eds. (Chicago: University of Chicago Press, 1987), p. 479 and Strauss, *Natural Right and History*, p. 230.

[33] Pangle, *Spirit*, p. 247.

[34] II:12. Cf. Zuckert, *Natural Rights*, p. 235.

aggressor against himself or herself as an enemy to all humankind, "a Wolf or a Lyon," and is right to destroy such an enemy.[35] Here Locke makes the remarkable argument that an injury in the state of nature against a single person makes the aggressor a rightful object of force, even lethal force, for the *entire* human race. This at the very least suggests some very large posses in the state of nature and many individuals not unaccustomed to blood on their hands. Second, and more importantly, Locke extends the right of punishment beyond aggressive action to mere hostile intent. Locke argues: "one may destroy a man who makes war upon him, or has discovered an enmity to his being" (II:16). He soon reveals that the enmity defense for lethal force "makes it Lawful for a Man to kill a Thief, who has not in the least hurt him, nor declared any design upon his Life, any further than by use of Force, so as to get him in his Power, as to take away his Money" (II:18). Thus, in the logic of Locke's enmity doctrine, any interference with an individual's liberty, in action or in plan, entitles that individual to kill the interferer or aggressor.[36] Given the manifold possibilities for interference with individual liberty in the state of nature, where there is no common superior to appeal to for aid and the inscrutability of determining human intentions, the potential for endemic violence is very real.

Locke suggests that there are many rational reasons for the use of force in the state of nature. Retaliating against individuals who interfere with one's liberty is the rational response of a sensible being to this condition. The implications of this rational and defensible action, however, are not particularly conducive to the peaceful coexistence of "men living together according to Reason, without a common Superior on Earth." Human beings, Locke admits, are passionate creatures, often "partial to themselves and their Friends" (II:13). It is because of their "Self-love" that "it is unreasonable for Men to be Judges in their own Cases" (II:13). Yet it was precisely the Christian-Aristotelian assumption of human rationality that appeared to make the peaceful state of nature conceivable at all. We realize that the right to use lethal force against any enemy, real or perceived, lies not only with rational individuals but with all human beings per se. Locke concedes that it is the problematic character of the human passions and the weakness of reason that makes "*Civil Government*... the proper Remedy for the Inconveniencies of the State of Nature" (II:13). Locke admits that these "Inconveniencies" must "certainly be Great, where Men may be Judges in their own Case."

Two important arguments emerge from Locke's discussion of the problematic character of the human passions. First, he reveals that the law of nature may be apprehensible to all "who will but consult it," but he also

---

[35] II:16. Cf. Goldwin, "Locke," p. 482.
[36] Zuckert, *Natural Rights*, pp. 235–6 and John Simmons, *On the Edge of Anarchy* (Princeton: Princeton University Press, 1993): pp. 40–2.

suggests that human partiality ensures that people will not admit that this law applies to them. Even if we are all the workmanship of God, Locke suggests, the human passions will resist the moral prohibitions flowing from this central theological and natural fact.[37] Moreover, given the strength of the human passions, most notably for self-preservation, Locke implies that even if people apprehend the rational dictates of the natural law, those not immediately threatened will not reliably enforce a sentence when the guilty party resists and makes punishment dangerous and frequently destructive.[38] Thus, the executive power of the law of nature inhering in individuals, far from promoting the peace and preservation of all humankind, which is the end of that law, actually generates potentially chaotic conditions antithetical to the intention of the law of nature.

Second, while Locke quietly affirms the destructive possibilities intrinsic to the natural punishment right in the state of nature, he also emphatically denies the argument that absolute monarchy is the solution to the problem of the natural condition. Locke argues that it is precisely because of the chaotic potential of the self-regarding passions that absolutism is the worst possible regime. Locke rejects Hobbes' "terrible misstep" with the following argument:

I desire to know what kind of Government that is, and how much better it is than the State of Nature, where one Man commanding a multitude, has the Liberty to be Judge in his own Case, and may do to all his Subjects whatever he pleases, without the least liberty to any one to question or controle those who execute his Pleasure? And whatsoever he doth, whether led by Reason, Mistake or Passion, must be submitted to.[39]

In this passage, so reminiscent of Sidney's and Spinoza's attack on absolutism, Locke argues that, perhaps paradoxically, the same disorderly and self-regarding passions that habitually upset the peace in the state of nature also ensure that the state of nature is a better condition for the preservation of life and liberty than absolute monarchy.

When we retrace our steps through the twists and turns of Locke's argument, we come to the conclusion that the state of nature, for Locke, is or is always potentially a state of war. This conclusion is puzzling considering that Locke's executive power of the law of nature ends up looking suspiciously like Hobbes' right of nature, but Locke emphatically rejects Hobbes' theory of absolute sovereignty devised to solve the grave problems

---

[37] Ian Shapiro, *The Evolution of Rights Theory* (Cambridge: Cambridge University Press, 1986): p. 113. For a good discussion of Locke's assessment of the serious difficulty in determining the substance of the law of nature, see Peter Josephson, *The Great Art of Government: Locke's Use of Consent* (Lawrence: University Press of Kansas, 2002): ch. 3.

[38] II:13, 136. Cf. Tully, *Locke in Contexts*, p. 35.

[39] II:13. The phrase Hobbes' "terrible misstep" is from Pangle, *Spirit*, p. 245.

produced by this conception of natural rights.[40] In Locke's crucial example of an individual's right to kill a thief, he reveals that war is a condition possible in civil society only when and where "the Law, which was made for my Preservation... cannot interpose to secure my Life from present force" (II:19). Facing a robber on a lonely highway, miles from any police station, one is in a state of nature with respect to that criminal because the civil law can be of no assistance. Where one can appeal to a common superior to settle any controversies or disputes with others, the threat of war is generally defused by the overwhelming force available to the civil authorities. Contrary to our first impression, Locke concludes that the state of war is possible only in the state of nature or something approximating it in civil society.[41] Approximations of the state of nature may not only include facing the robber on the highway but may also occur in civil society when an individual is denied justice or assistance by corrupt magistrates: "where an appeal to the Law, and constituted Judges lies open, but the remedy is deny'd by a manifest perverting of Justice, and a barefaced wresting of the Laws" (II:20). Although there is the possibility of corruption in the civil administration of justice, Locke indicates that generally in civil society, in contrast to the state of nature, war ceases when the actual use of force is over because "continuance of the State of War is excluded, and the Controversy is decided by that Power" (II:21). War or the threat of war is a constant feature of the state of nature.

When Locke considers the issue of slavery in Chapter Four, the picture of the state of nature worsens even more dramatically. In this crucial chapter, Locke's workmanship thesis disintegrates as a meaningful model for human relations and his transcendent natural law is left in tatters. Four important developments emerge in this chapter. First, Locke demonstrates that by the executive power of the law of nature, humans are not only often in conflict and punish for the sake of deterrence, but they actually can gain a despotic right over one another. While Locke reaffirms that no one may by "his own Consent, enslave himself to any one else," he does insist that an aggressor in the state of nature may be held as a slave by his victim. Of this aggressor, Locke claims: "having, by his fault, forfeited his own Life, by some Act that deserves Death; he, to whom he has forfeited it, may (when he has him in his Power) delay to take it, and make use of him to his own Service, and he

---

[40] I agree with Shapiro (*Evolution*, p. 124) that Locke adopts the Hobbesian "tactic" of separating rights from obligations. But I believe that Locke's aim is more than just tactical. That Shapiro does not view it this way is probably due to his insistence on Locke's workmanship model as the underlying premise of his natural law teaching (pp. 103–7).

[41] See Goldwin's excellent treatment of the distinction between the state of nature, the state of war, and civil society ("Locke," p. 481). Cf. also Simmons, *Anarchy*, pp. 42–4 and Nathan Tarcov, "Locke's Second Treatise and 'The Best Fence Against Rebellion,'" *Review of Politics*, vol. 43 (April 1981): pp. 203–4.

does him no injury by it."[42] This contradicts Locke's earlier prohibition of cruel and despotic practices in the exercise of the executive power of the law of nature (II:8). Moreover, it clearly contravenes the central tenet of the workmanship thesis, which affirmed that God sent human beings "into the World by his order and about his business, they are his Property...made to last during his, not one anothers Pleasure."[43] Even Locke's argument that the aggressor has forfeited his life does not explain and account for how the actions of individuals could exempt them from the duty they ultimately owe God, not other human beings, to preserve their lives. Only the potter can destroy his product, not the other pots.

Second, Locke's admission of slavery as a legitimate natural law practice accentuates the chaotic and brutal character of the state of nature. His argument that slavery is "the State of War continued, between a Lawful Conqueror, and a Captive" adds a new sense of permanence to the warlike potential of the state of nature. Conflict in the state of nature no longer appears as a series of isolated incidents. Now we have a picture of sadistic slaveholders systematically torturing suspected thieves. With this admission of a natural law basis for despotic rule, Locke presents the possibility of a distorting and dangerous model of rule antithetical to legitimate government by consent.

Third, Locke more or less overturns the suicide prohibition, which seemed to underlie the entire workmanship thesis. Locke admits that the slave, "whenever he finds the hardship of his Slavery out-weigh the value of his Life, 'tis in his Power, by resisting the Will of his Master, to draw on himself the Death he desires" (II:23). The direct agency Locke identifies in the "Power" of the slave to cause his own death belies the argument that the slave is only indirectly responsible for his death and therefore has not broken the suicide prohibition. Thus, Locke reveals that fundamental preservation rights are not only forfeitable but also in a sense alienable.[44] In this light, Locke's contention that each individual lacks complete moral power

---

[42] II:23. Contrast this with Tyrrell, PNM 107, 113, where Tyrrell criticizes Hobbes' argument in *De Cive* 2.8 that no injury can be done a slave. In this passage Locke seems to be following Hobbes rather than Tyrrell, demonstrating his own greater affinity with Hobbes' natural rights teaching than with Pufendorfian–Tyrrellian natural law.

[43] II:6. Simmons (*Anarchy*, pp. 52–4) distinguishes between two senses of absolute power: moral and physical. Simmons argues that Locke means (or should mean) primarily the latter sense in his discussion of the state of war. However, the confusion between these two ideas of absolute power is not Locke's; rather, I believe his point is that in the state of nature these two species of despotic reasoning tend to collapse by virtue of the self-regarding character of private judgment.

[44] For good accounts of how Locke's suicide prohibition shows the limits of inalienability, see Simmons, *Anarchy*, pp. 102, 118–19 and Zuckert, *Natural Rights*, pp. 242–5. For the contrary position, see Gary Glenn, "Inalienable Rights and Locke's Argument for Limited Government: Political Implications of a Right of Suicide," *Journal of Politics*, vol. 46, no. 1. February (1984): pp. 80–105.

over his or her life stands less as a divine prohibition on suicide than as a statement that by the natural faculties and properties of human beings, they cannot legislate themselves into slavery. In other words, Locke repeats that no individual is under a moral obligation to honor an absolute contract.

The fourth feature of Locke's account of slavery is his denial of any natural law limits on the treatment of slaves. In this respect, Locke clearly signals his distance from the moderate Whig Tyrrell. As we recall, Tyrrell had argued that while slaves taken in war are under no moral obligation to serve their masters (they are free to escape if they can), he also affirmed that the holder of any slave, either by war or by contract, was bound by certain natural law limits in his treatment of his slaves.[45] Tyrrell had maintained that there is a basic self-preservation right that has to be respected as part of the larger natural law duty to supply, or at least not hinder, the requirements of peaceful social existence. Ominously, Locke places no such restrictions on the right of a master who may put the slave "to his own Service" (II:23). For Locke, whatever is left of his transcendent natural law teaching, it does not bind the actions of despotic rulers in this case. Actually, the executive right of Locke's law of nature seems to ground this despotic right.

The complexity in Locke's state of nature also pervades his account of the executive power of the law of nature. The execution of this natural right or power gives Locke's natural law teaching a unique point of departure from prior natural liberty theories. Throughout the first four chapters of the *Second Treatise* Locke's natural rights teaching presents a central dilemma. On the one hand, Locke boldly states that the power of government is derived from and grounded in the natural power of individuals (II:9). Political society is conventional, a product of contract and consent, but Locke contends that the animating principle of this convention is a natural power reducible to the individual. On the other hand, Locke also indicates that the unregulated and uncontrolled exercise of this individual natural right is, if not antithetical to, at least in deep tension with the peace and order of society. Filmer's dire predictions of the theoretical and practical difficulties produced by natural liberty theory seem vindicated in the early chapters of this treatise. However, Filmer is not Locke's only opponent or target here. Locke uses this early discussion to signify his own clear break from many of the central tenets of the natural liberty school. To understand the radical implications of Locke's natural rights teaching, we will briefly compare and contrast it with that of the Christian Aristotelians, particularly Hooker, and the other natural liberty theorists, Grotius, Pufendorf, and Hobbes.

Locke's conspicuous appeal to Hooker in his account of the state of nature is more or less indicative of his differences with the Christian-Aristotelian

[45] Tyrrell, PNM, 107, 119*.

natural liberty tradition as a whole.[46] What makes Hooker so important for our understanding of Locke, however, is the former's modification of the Thomist and Suarezian accounts of the origin of government. Hooker, in the passages Locke cites, affirms a pre-political condition and a kind of natural right of self-defense inhering in individuals.[47] Locke skillfully employs carefully selected and edited passages from Hooker ostensibly to demonstrate their fundamental agreement that civil society is produced by consent. However, by placing Hooker's arguments back in their proper context and by comparing these contextualized arguments with Locke's position, we can appreciate how radically Locke departs from this respectable Anglican scholastic. For instance, while Hooker claims that individuals can defend themselves from injury by the provision of the natural law, he also, unlike Locke, explicitly blames the inadequacy of the natural law alone to provide for human security given the corruption of human nature caused by the Fall.[48] In the *First Treatise*, Locke radically reinterprets the meaning of the Fall, especially with respect to Eve and the status of women, and generally suppressed its political and moral import. Inasmuch as Hooker considers the natural self-defense right only to illustrate its deficiency and the intrinsic need for political society, Hooker expresses his fundamental agreement with St. Thomas and Suarez that political power inheres in the community and is not grounded on the natural power of individuals. In this crucial regard Locke breaks from Hooker.

Locke's natural rights theory also breaks from the more secular accounts of Grotius, Pufendorf, Sidney, and Hobbes. In contrast to Locke, Grotius maintained a form of natural self-preservation right, but he did not make it the ground of political power. For Grotius, the ground of political power was the compact forming society. In effect, the source of political authority is the agreement of subjection supported by the natural law.[49] While Grotius allowed the possibility of a people to rebel against a vicious tyrant, he did not ascribe this to a natural punishment power, but rather to the violation of the compact any rational people would have made to empower their rulers. Pufendorf and his moderate Whig follower Tyrrell come closer to Locke than

---

[46] Clearly, I disagree with Simmons' (*Lockean Theory of Rights*, p. 16) and Ashcraft's (*Locke's Two Treatises*, pp. 35–80) argument that Locke's natural law theory falls largely within the Christian-Aristotelian tradition. Cf. Rahe's ("Locke's Philosophical Partisanship," pp. 32–6) critical response to Ashcraft.

[47] Cf. St. Thomas Aquinas, *Summa Theologica*, 3 vols. (New York: Benziger Brothers, 1947): II-II 64.3, ST I 96.4 and Francisco Suarez, *De Legibus, Ac Deo Legislatore* (1612, Coimbra), *in Selections from Three Works of Francisco Suarez, S. J.* (Oxford: Clarendon Press, 1944): ch. 3, sec. 3, pp. 3, 6. See also Zuckert, *Natural Rights*, pp. 222–33.

[48] Richard Hooker, *Of the Laws of Ecclesiastical Polity* (1593). George Edelen, W. Speed Hill, and P. G. Stanwood, eds. (Cambridge, MA: Harvard University Press, 1977–81): bk 1, ch. 10, sect. 4.

[49] Grotius, DJB 2.20.40.

does Grotius. They allow an unlimited right of self-defense but, in contrast to Locke, Pufendorf, and Tyrrell, maintain that punishment in the proper sense can only be exercised by a superior over an inferior; thus punishment, strictly speaking, has no place in the state of nature.[50] Insofar as the right of punishment does not inhere naturally in individuals, it cannot perforce derive from individuals. Furthermore, Pufendorf and Tyrrell defuse the potentially serious political implications of this universal right of self-defense by giving it a much more conservative bent than does Locke. They argue that the right of self-defense must be understood as derivative from the more comprehensive natural law duties establishing the requirements of peaceful social existence.

The contrast between Locke, on the one hand, and Sidney and Hobbes, on the other, is somewhat more complex. For his part, Sidney based his political teaching on a natural right of self-preservation but, in contrast to Locke, he was not concerned to develop a state of nature concept because the central aim of Sidney's natural rights theory was to show that the individual, monarch or otherwise, was not the primary unit of political analysis. In Sidney's fundamentally Spinozist system of natural power relations, political authority derives its right of punishment from the collected power of individuals, but the great difference in the degree of power between government and the individual produces a qualitative difference in the exercise of that power.[51] The right of the individual to defend himself against injury rests on that individual's power, but the right of government to punish individuals rests on its much greater power vis-à-vis any particular individual. For Sidney, attempting to ground the power of government in the power of the individual qua individual is like mistaking the forest for the trees.

Locke's departure from Hobbes has serious implications for radical Whig liberal constitutional theory. Hobbes derived the power to punish from individuals, particularly a sovereign free of contract and a people contracted to assist that sovereign in the execution of the civil law.[52] But for Hobbes, in contrast to Locke, the natural power of the individuals composing political society cannot be understood as political power in the full sense, because this natural power, as opposed to the civil power employed by the sovereign, is not a jurisdictional power to judge any controversy over right or to execute the judgment and impose sanctions of the natural law. Thus, for Hobbes, individual natural power may provide the material cause of a political punishing power but it does not, except in the strict formulations of an absolutist theory of sovereignty, provide any meaningful dimension of formal causality. In his curious manner of discussing the natural executive power, by

---

[50] Tyrrell, PNM 153,232 and Pufendorf, DJNG 8.3.7, 10.

[51] See, for example, Algernon Sidney, *The Discourses Concerning Government*, Thomas West, ed. (Indianapolis: Liberty Fund Classic, 1996): ch. 3, sec. 11 (hereafter D, ch., sec.).

[52] Thomas Hobbes, *Leviathan*, Edward Curley, ed. (Indianapolis: Hackett, 1994): ch. 28. Cf. Tully, *Locke in Contexts*, p. 20.

associating himself with thinkers with whom he seriously disagrees and criticizing thinkers whose arguments closely parallel his own, Locke invites us to ponder the radical character of his break with the natural liberty tradition.

By the end of Chapter Four of the *Second Treatise*, Locke's original presentation of the transcendent natural law is in shambles. The power of every individual to execute that law, in the absence of any natural or divine provision of government, leads to dangerous and potentially chaotic consequences. Moreover, Locke insists that the power of individuals precludes the possibility of a Hobbesian solution to this problem. Given the disorderly structure of the human passions and the ineradicable right of individuals to punish aggressors, real or perceived, absolute monarchy, in Locke's view, is worse than the problem it intends to solve. In Locke's famous discussion of property in Chapter Five, he begins the difficult process of putting his natural law Humpty-Dumpty back together again.

Locke on Property

A veritable ocean of ink has been spilled and an Amazon of trees felled in recent years in examining Locke's account of the origin of private property. It has been by far the most frequently scrutinized aspect of Locke's political teaching.[53] I do not promise here to add a great deal of new and original analysis regarding Locke's theory of property. Rather, I intend to locate Locke's theory of property in the larger context of his argument for political

[53] The main source of contention among scholars regarding the issue of property in Locke is the extent to which he justifies unlimited acquisition. One school maintains that Locke imposes strict natural law limitations on individual appropriation derived from certain moral duties the individual has toward society (e.g., Ashcraft, *Locke's Two Treatises*, pp. 124–35; Dunn, *Political Thought of John Locke*; and Tully, *Discourse on Property*), while the other school tends to emphasize Locke's aim to justify unlimited acquisition as a natural individual right (e.g., C. B. MacPherson, *The Political Theory of Possessive Individualism* [Oxford: Oxford University Press, 1962]; Pangle, *Spirit*, esp. chs. 14, 19; Strauss, *Natural Right and History*, esp. pp. 236–46; Ross Zucker, "Unequal Property and Its Premise in Liberal Theory," *History of Philosophy Quarterly*, vol. 17, no. 1 (January 2000): pp. 29–49; and Zuckert, *Natural Rights*, esp. ch. 9). Another aspect of the Lockean property debate pits those who see Locke's defense of unlimited acquisition as a feature of a conservative argument for "historical entitlement" or the "agrarian capitalism" of England's landed interest (e.g., Jeremy Waldron, *The Right to Private Property* [Oxford: Oxford University Press, 1988]: esp. cf. pp. 137–41 and 207–18 and Neal Wood, *John Locke and Agrarian Capitalism* [Berkeley: University of California Press, 1984]: pp. 49–92) against those who see Locke's property teaching as politically radical and subversive of traditional economic elites (e.g., Harvey Mansfield, "On the Political Character of Property in Locke," in *Powers, Possessions and Freedoms: Essays in Honor of C. B. MacPherson* Alkis Kontos, ed. [Toronto: University of Toronto Press, 1979]: pp. 24, 34–7 and Rahe, "Locke's Philosophical Partisanship," pp. 18–22). Given my reading of the rigorous individualism in Locke's natural rights theory, my examination of Locke's notion of property rights in the following discussion will owe much to the many insights of the scholars in the unlimited accumulation and political radicalism schools.

individualism. To do this, I will focus on the way Locke uses his account of property to provide a new conceptual model for natural rights to replace the divine workmanship model that has proved so problematic. This new model is Locke's theory of self-ownership.

Locke begins his treatment of property in this treatise with the same line of argument he offered in his response to Filmer's argument for Adam's title by donation in the *First Treatise*. Indeed, given Locke's rather detailed discussion of property in the latter, his ensuing account initially promises to be superfluous at best. Locke echoes the earlier account by beginning with the assertion that both "natural Reason" and "Revelation" confirm that the goods of the Earth were given "to Mankind in common."[54] But if the original condition was a negative community of goods, meaning that no one had an exclusive right to anything, it is unclear how any individual could appropriate the goods and acquire the exclusive right to these goods necessary for preservation. Locke responds that there are two things that are not in common: the individual's body and the actions of that body. Locke claims:

Though the Earth, and all inferior Creatures be common to all Men, yet every Man has a *Property* in his own *Person*. This no Body has any Right to but himself. The Labour of his Body, and the *Work* of his Hands, we may say, are properly his. (II:27)

The implications of Locke's self-ownership argument are twofold. First, it changes the entire fabric of Locke's proposed law of nature. The central moral and political fact is not God's ownership of human beings, but rather each individual's ownership of himself or herself. This development in Locke's argument opens a gap in the conceptual space between God's governance of the world and the legitimate ground of human action, which Locke will expand to dramatic effect in his treatment of property. Second, the self-ownership model of natural rights provides Locke with a way to explain how a private right of property can emerge from an original common. He argues that it is the "labour" of the individual that appropriates goods and puts "a distinction between them and common" (II:28). In answer to the question of why the labor of an individual produces exclusive title to a natural good, as opposed to, say, eating or digesting it, Locke replies that without human labor – even so little as picking up apples from the ground – the natural plenty would be worthless for human beings.[55] Locke indicates that the forest may be full of game, but this is of little use to human beings until these creatures can be caught and killed. As such, "this Law of Reason makes the Deer, that Indian's who hath killed it" (II:30). As Locke presents it here, labor is the human participation in the production of the great abundance provided by God and nature for the satisfaction of human needs.

---

[54] II:25. Note Locke's use of 1 Timothy 6:7 in II:31. Cf. II:26, II:28.
[55] Goldwin, "Locke," p. 487.

A second implication of the self-ownership model relates to the problems Locke identified in Grotius' notion of the original negative community. Importantly, Locke does not take the Tyrrellian–Pufendorfian path of directly affirming a natural theft or dire necessity right.[56] Rather, Locke places a few natural law limits on the appropriative right of individuals in the state of nature. Locke presents these limits as an extension of the no-harm principle he articulated in Chapter Two. By the command of the natural law, people are not morally free to harm each other indirectly by appropriating more than their fair share of the external world. The law of nature governs not only human relations vis-à-vis other human beings but also their relation to the physical world.

The first of these natural law limits on appropriation is the requirement to leave "enough, and as good" for others (II:27). Locke suggests that this natural law limit is essentially a moral restraint acting directly on the actions (he does not say the conscience) of the individual appropriator. By the logic of this first limitation, Locke implies that the Indian who kills a deer for his own needs or those of people close to him must be fully conscious that killing every deer in the forest for his private use would be wrong and morally blameworthy. Locke also, however, suggests that the original natural bounty made this limitation more or less superfluous inasmuch as given "the plenty of natural Provisions there was a long time in the World, and the few spenders," there was little or no possibility that "the industry of one Man could extend itself, and ingross it to the prejudice of others."[57] Locke's second natural law limit on appropriation is the spoilage limit. Whereas the "enough, and as good" for others limit had both a natural and a moral component – there naturally being many provisions and few spenders, as well as a moral obligation to leave plenty for others – the spoilage limit is purely a result of the operation of the laws of natural necessity. Locke claims that nature and God have given human beings "as much as any one can make use of to any advantage of life before it spoils; . . . Whatever is beyond this, is more than his share, and belongs to others" (II:31). He implies that nature has a safeguard against the moral failings of human beings; it is not only morally wrong to appropriate more than one needs or can use, it is also stupid and perverse given that most edibles eventually spoil. Locke suggests that this is a particularly effective limitation on human appropriation

---

[56] Although Locke comes close to it at I:42, it is significant that he never hints at this possibility in the *Second Treatise*, where he lays out his argument for property rights in much greater detail.

[57] II:31. It is interesting to note that in Chapter Five, the state of nature is more closely associated with primitive society à la Pufendorf and Tyrrell than in the earlier treatment of the state of nature proper in Chapter Two, where some of the prime examples of rights based relations are often emphatically political (e.g., II:14). Locke's reliance on primitive material conditions as a basis for his natural law limitations on appropriation will shift the emphasis of his natural rights teaching dramatically in Chapter Five.

because "the greatest part of *things really useful* to the Life of Man...are generally things of *short duration*" (II:46). As such, nature, in Locke's view, nudges human beings into primitive forms of economic association like the barter system. The barter system also has the salutary effect of allowing one individual to pick the plums before they rot on the ground and trade the surplus for more durable nuts. As Locke initially presents it, far from being a tremendous hardship, the spoilage limitation actually generates a form of a natural division of labor.

There is, however, a central contradiction in Locke's initial account of the original common. If God and nature provide the great abundance Locke indicates, why is there any need for natural law limits on appropriation at all? Is God's bounty, the natural common, actually a ticking time bomb threatening human preservation? Locke begins to address this complex issue in his treatment of land. He baldly states that the main matter for understanding the natural common is not the goods of the Earth, but the Earth itself: "The *chief matter of Property* being now not the Fruits of the Earth, and the Beasts that subsist on it, but the Earth itself, as that which takes in and carries with it all the rest" (II:32). Locke now admits that God's original provision to humankind had a major catch; He commanded humans to labor "and the penury of his Condition required it of him" (II:36). God supported his commandment – as though His command was not good enough in itself – by making the original condition one of "penury." The reader has not been left entirely unprepared for this shift in Locke's argument. A little earlier, he admitted that human "Wants forces him to Labour" (II:35). This labor, Locke indicates, would extend beyond merely harvesting the goods offered by the "spontaneous Hand of Nature." Land is the "*chief matter of Property*" because agriculture is the only hope for redemption from this state of natural penury.

To illustrate, then, how human beings came to cultivate the vast natural common, Locke presents his theory of labor value. Locke initially defended labor as the source of private property on the grounds that the natural goods of the Earth are worthless unless they are acquired for human use through labor. The apples on the ground or on the branches are of no use to anyone unless they are gathered. Later Locke extends this logic to the act of cultivation and claims that "the provisions serving to the support of humane life, produced by one acre of inclosed and cultivated land, are...ten times more than those, which are yielded by an acre of Land, of an equal richnesse, lyeing wast in common" (II:37). When human beings apply their labor to the cultivation of the Earth, they add to its value by tenfold. Over the course of the next six sections, Locke radicalizes this principle of labor value to one thousand times the value of uncultivated land (cf. II: 37, 40, 43).

In this way Locke makes two significant points. First, he underscores the incredible service agriculture offers for human preservation. If gathering the fruits of one acre of uncultivated land can support only 1 individual and the harvest from one acre of cultivated land can nourish 1,000, then clearly preagricultural society would face severe natural limitations on population growth. Second, and more importantly, Locke uses this discussion of the value of labor to make the point that the penury of nature should not be underestimated. Locke boldly states that "Nature and the Earth furnished only the almost worthless Materials, as in themselves" (II:43; cf. II:40). The benefit derived from the uncultivated "waste" is "little more than nothing" (II:42). Locke reveals that the massive scale of waste under the rule of nature dwarfs any spoilage that could be produced by the selfish accumulation of human beings.[58] With this argument for the almost unimaginable poverty and harshness of nature, Locke delivers the final hammer blow to the naive and reassuring assumptions underlying the transcendent law of nature embodied in the divine workmanship model. The lack of material provision for human needs from God and nature parallels Locke's contention that the divine or natural failure to provide human beings with reliable and structured passions conducive to social life has left human beings in the state of nature in a very dangerous and fragile condition. Indeed, Locke's discussion of property caps his earlier treatment of the natural executive power by drawing the clear inference that perhaps the chief factor contributing to conflict in the natural, pre-political condition is the brutal competition among human beings for scarce resources.[59] For Locke, it is natural rights, the universal right of self-preservation, rather than a natural duty to conform to transcendent laws that is the fundamental moral fact. The only natural duty is to oneself. This is true, for Locke, because the right of self-preservation both conforms to our deepest natural passions and reflects a realistic assessment of the great hostility of nature toward human preservation. In Locke, Hobbes' war of all against all becomes the war of each against everything.

Locke's presentation of the barrenness of unassisted nature lays the groundwork for his overturning of his initial natural law limitations on acquisition and appropriation. In the process, he both justifies the principle of unlimited acquisition and defends the proposition that human labor, especially the labor of the mind, must and should work to overcome the natural obstacles to abundance and comfortable self-preservation. The "enough, and as good" for others limitation is steamrolled by Locke's defense of agriculture and the value of labor. Locke contends that through the act of appropriating land an individual does not, in principle, deny the goods of the Earth to others, but rather increases "the common stock of mankind" (II:37). As proof of this statement, Locke offers the contrast between a preagricultural society like precolonial America and a modern European state. The universal poverty of people living in the conditions offered by unassisted nature in wild America means that "a King of a large and fruitful Territory there feeds,

[58] Goldwin, "Locke," p. 491.
[59] Strauss, *Natural Right and History*, p. 235.

lodges, and is clad worse than a day Labourer in *England*" (II:41). With this statement Locke does two major things.

First, he suggests that the inequality of property introduced by agriculture does not in itself produce political inequality.[60] Despite the universal poverty in America and the great abundance in England, there are still kings in America and day laborers in England. But the Englishman lives better and is more secure, and in this crucial sense *freer*, than the American monarch. Second, Locke uses this discussion to introduce his doctrine of increase. He argues that the recognition of the natural right to acquire unlimited amounts of property serves the common interest of humanity by encouraging the industry necessary for material and technological advance. The key to the doctrine of increase is the invention of money. The invention of money, according to Locke, overturns both the "enough, and as good" limit and the spoilage prohibition. With the invention of money, "Men had *agreed, that a little piece of yellow Metal*," a durable but scarce resource of some kind "which would keep without wasting or decay, should be worth a great piece of Flesh, or a whole heap of Corn" (II:37). Locke explains that the implications of this invention were enormous. Money gave individuals a rational incentive to produce far beyond their need by facilitating a system of exchange much more dynamic than the barter system (II:48). Insofar as the invention of money encouraged a potential for the inequality of property, it actually benefited the whole of humanity, or at least those in commercial, monetarized societies.

Locke insists that the institutions of money and commerce were products of consent. He claims that money derives from "the consent of Men, where of Labour yet makes, in great part, *the measure*, it is plain, that Men have agreed to disproportionate and unequal Possessions of the Earth, they having by a tacit and voluntary consent found a way, how a man may fairly possess more land than himself can use the product of" (II:50). Locke also contends that the institution of money occurred in pre-political society. By this argument, Locke demonstrates that there are many forms of contract and agreement that serve the cause of human association but fall short of political society.[61] He reveals that the rational capacity demonstrated in the invention of money indicates a latent potential in human reason that operates independently of political society. Thus, Locke posits the economic foundations of political life. Furthermore, by insisting that money predates and operates independently of civil society, Locke claims that individuals could leave the state of

---

[60] Indeed, Locke suggests that hierarchical social and political institutions are more characteristic of primitive and subsistence conditions than they are of advanced capitalist societies (II:107, II:111). I believe this would be part of Locke's response to the thesis of Rousseau's *Discourse on the Origin of Inequality*.

[61] By separating the institution of money from political society, Locke disputes one of the traditional absolutist claims for the right of sovereignty. As we noted in Chapter 2, this position was shared by the secularist Bodin and the divine rightist Filmer.

nature not only with some property, but potentially with a great deal of it. Locke hereby lays the groundwork for the central argument of his theory of political individualism, namely, that individual natural rights, particularly to property, exist before political society and, in fact, that political society exists and is created by human beings for the purpose of protecting these natural, pre-civil rights.

Locke's doctrine of increase and his insistence on the political implications of the natural right to property are unique among natural rights theorists of the seventeenth century. While Grotius, for example, affirmed a natural occupancy right to property, he did not emphasize the importance of labor. This was because while he made the settlement of property rights a key reason for forming civil society, he did not want to enhance natural claims to property that would interfere with the supremacy of contract. Grotius made contract the key to the obligation to respect property rights, not the natural claims derived from labor. In contrast to Tyrrell and Pufendorf, who present a much less harsh picture of nature, Locke did not rely on a series of multiple compacts in order to establish the property right. Rather, his clear intention was to establish the core right of property, and the right to expanded holdings made possible by money, semi-independently of the consent of others. In this way, Locke ensured that property rights would be freer of communal or governmental interference than did Tyrrell or Pufendorf.[62] With respect to Filmer's other Whig critic, while Sidney suggested that individuals create political societies in order to secure their lives and goods, he was generally not concerned to develop a state of nature concept that would account for the origin of private property rights as such.[63] The difference between Locke's liberal individualism and Sidney's republican treatment of individual rights was not, however, simply a matter of emphasis. For Sidney, the solution to the fundamental human problem of tyranny, both political and intellectual, was available essentially at the political level with the creation of popular regimes. Locke, on the other hand, saw the solution operating both on the economic level, with the need to secure the material conditions necessary for comfortable self-preservation, and on the political level, with free governments devised to secure rights. Liberal constitutionalism was the necessary concomitant of Lockean property rights.

---

[62] Marshall, *John Locke*, pp. 234–5.
[63] Sidney, D 1.10.

9

Lockean Liberal Constitutionalism

Lockean constitutionalism represents an important dimension of his critique of Filmer's divine right absolutism. In response to Filmer's charge that communities and/or individuals lack the moral capacity to generate sovereign political power, Locke maintains that the principle of natural liberty indicates not only that the people can institute sovereign power, but that the people are the only true repository of sovereignty. The chief postulations that flow from Locke's argument are the delegation theory of sovereignty and the notion of the dissolution of government. Together these principles affirm that inasmuch as all political power derives from the natural power of individuals, political power can and does, in the event of abuse of power, devolve to the people. Moreover, Locke affirms that the people may delegate their natural sovereign power to whichever arrangement of institutions they wish. In order to understand the main features of Lockean constitutionalism, we will first have to examine Locke's treatment of the origins of political society.

The Origins of Political Society

Locke's discussion of the origins of political society logically follows from his account of the state of nature. This is a state of perfect freedom and equality, but because of the individual natural right to execute the law of nature, the state of nature always either is or hovers dangerously close to the state of war. In order to solve the "Inconveniencies" of the state of nature, especially the lack of "settled Standing Rules" and an impartial common "Umpire" to settle disputes, particularly those relating to property, Locke indicates that individuals consent to form political society:

Those who are united into one Body, and have a common established Law and Judicature to appeal to, with Authority to decide Controversies between them, and punish Offenders, *are in Civil Society* one with another. (II:87)

Locke indicates that the chief end of government is "the preservation of the property of all the Members of Society, as far as possible" (II:88), but the primary institutional means of attaining this end is the creation of a common legislative power that will "make laws . . . as the public good of Society shall require" (II:89). In arguing that the political society originates in the creation of a legislative power, Locke agrees with Sidney that founding is essentially a legislative process.[1] For Locke, political society emerges, at its moral core, as a community of laws. He defends the postulation of the legislative character of the political compact on the grounds that no other formulation of the contract would resolve the problems he identifies with the state of nature. Locke argues that given the partiality and self-regarding character of the human passions, especially in the state of nature, where every individual is the "Judge in his own Case," the Hobbesian solution of absolute monarchy must be "inconsistent with Civil Society, and can be no Form of Civil Government at all" (II:90). By placing one individual above the law as a means to enforce the law for everyone else, Hobbes exposes the property and lives of the subjects to the unlimited passions of the monarch. Locke indicates that it is precisely because society is created by the consent of discrete individuals that the prospect of unrestrained sovereign power is so contrary to the logic informing civil society. He also suggests that the simplicity of Hobbes' theory of absolute monarchy belies the power of human reason to escape the dangers of the state of nature. Locke claims that absolutism is so contrary to the manifest experience of the human rational enterprise, and the sensations of fear and hope for future security that drive individuals into civil society, that it "is to think that Men are so foolish that they take care to avoid what Mischiefs may be done to them by Pole-Cats, or Foxes, but are content, nay think it Safety, to be devoured by Lions" (II:93).

For Locke, majority rule, rather than absolutism, is the animating principle of civil society. The consensual origins of political society require that unanimity be the condition for consolidation into one people, and that majority rule be the condition for the construction of political institutions. Locke states: "When any number of Men have *consented to make one Community* or Government, they are thereby presently incorporated, and make *one Body Politick*, wherein the *Majority* have a Right to act and conclude the rest" (II:95). Locke gives two reasons for the operation of majority rule in the construction of political society. The first is the practical impossibility of achieving perfect agreement on any decision other than the agreement to unite into one society (II:98). The general desire to escape the "Inconveniencies" of the state of nature and the need to secure the consent of each individual to lay down the full exercise of his or her natural liberty makes unanimity

---

[1] Cf. Pierre Manent, *An Intellectual History of Liberalism*, Rebecca Balinski, trans. (Princeton: Princeton University Press, 1994): p. 48.

the precondition for the creation of society. But with the introduction of a majority rule argument, Locke sharpens the distinction between society and government and in so doing reveals that the unanimity underlying society differs from the majoritarianism animating the construction of governing authority.

There are two strands of Locke's majority rule argument that stand in considerable tension with each other. The first strand relates to what Locke identifies as the law of "greater force." He employs a kind of institutional physics to defend the proposition that the contract to form society includes an irreducible claim for majority decision regarding the political structures that society adopts. Locke claims: "It is necessary the Body should move that way whither the greater force carries it, which is the *consent of the majority*: or else it is impossible it should act or continue one Body, one Community" (II:96). Locke presents majority rule as a form of the natural law of political society; political society properly construed cannot be formed in any other way.[2] He also, however, emphasizes the consensual principles underlying majority rule. Locke's admission that majority rule must be informed by a deeper layer of unanimous consent gives majoritarianism a dubious status as a principle of natural law.[3] Clearly, Locke sets limits to what the majority may decide. They cannot, for example, create an absolute monarchy because such an action would undermine the principle of legitimacy by which the majority is empowered to act. In a crucial sense, society reflects rather than creates or defines the rights of individuals.[4] In fact, Locke more or less concedes the conventionality of the majority rule principle when he affirms that society may have "expressly agreed in any number greater than the majority" (II:99). Of course, Locke's suggestion of the legitimacy of supermajority rule does not efface the law of greater force simply, but rather indicates that the core of Locke's majoritarianism is the belief that anything less than a majority would be illegitimate for the construction of political society, not that majorities are omnipotent. Individuals in society may specify supermajority regulations, but in so doing they point to the bedrock of individual rights – supermajorities protect minorities – that give moral legitimacy to the law of greater force.

However, Locke maintained that there were several forms of human association that did not produce civil society or end the state of nature. Locke

[2] Robert Goldwin, "John Locke," in *The History of Political Philosophy*, 3rd ed., Leo Strauss and Joseph Cropsey, eds. (Chicago: University of Chicago Press, 1987): p. 498.
[3] John Finnis, *Natural Law and Natural Rights* (Oxford: Oxford University Press, 1980) pp. 256–7.
[4] I believe Locke's concern to demonstrate the individualistic core of governmental power and his argument for the possibility of supermajorities proves Kendall's presentation of Locke as a radical majority rule democrat (à la Rousseau) to be overdrawn. See Willmore Kendall, *John Locke and the Doctrine of Majority Rule* (Urbana: University of Illinois Press, 1965): esp. pp. 66, 101.

speculated that wherever any number of individuals *"however associated"* have no common legislature to appeal to, "they are still in the state of nature."[5] The patriarchal family and the government of fathers constituted such a form of association. Locke identifies an additional form of quasi-natural rule in the election of war leaders to conduct the military affairs of the loosely assembled tribes of primitive society. The two parallel tracks of primitive monarchy were the habituation to one-man rule in the family and the requirements of military necessity in the precarious state of nature.[6] Locke's presentation of primitive peoples loosely assembled along blood lines of the extended family could not be further from his theoretical account of the origins of political society in contract and majority rule. How then does this historico–anthropological account of primitive societies relate to Locke's more theoretical account? He admits that his intention is to justify the principle of consent against the historical claims of patriarchy and monarchy (II:112). Locke also indicates that primitive societies were natural, as opposed to political, societies precisely because, though products of consent, they registered faulty attempts to respond to natural necessity. These early patriarchal–monarchical societies reflected the weakness of undeveloped human reason, the lack of self-conscious awareness of the true gravity of the human condition, and the enormous economic and psychological causes of conflict.[7] By demonstrating that the primitive forms of human association evinced in paternal government and tribal war leaders do not constitute political society or satisfy the proper ends of such a society, Locke offers a theoretical template by which the improvement of societies may be measured and formulated. Locke's deeply ironic appeal to the "Golden Age" of virtue and simplicity in early societies (II:110, II:111) suggests that what has historically been understood as political society appears, to Locke, as something much less secure or rational.

Locke's theoretical account of the origins of political society suggests two central features of his argument for political individualism. First, the theoretical criteria for legitimate political society provide the standard for

---

[5] II:89 (emphasis mine).

[6] II:108 and Locke's rather impious example of the biblical judges as the sort of one-man rule typical in primitive societies (II:109). Ironically, Locke calls the elevation of military leaders an example of the "peaceful beginnings" of political society (II:112). These "peaceful beginnings" rooted in military necessity foreshadow Locke's later admission that the most common historical origin of political societies was in conquest (cf. II:175). This admission demonstrates even more clearly the distinction between Locke's theoretical criteria for political legitimacy and the faulty governments displayed in history.

[7] Note II:101, where Locke argues that the origins of historical societies usually predated the development of the arts, letters, and recorded history. Cf. Thomas Pangle, *The Spirit of Modern Republicanism* (Chicago: University of Chicago Press, 1988): p. 245 and Geraint Parry, "Locke on Representation in Politics," *History of Political Thought*, vol. 3, no. 4 (1982): pp. 409–10.

understanding Locke's conception of the relation of the individual to civil government. The close-knit and trusting communities of early society based on ethnic and familial ties stand in stark contrast to the fully self-conscious form of political obligation Locke identifies with full citizenship in political society. Locke contends that nothing can make any individual a member of a political society "but his actually entering into it by positive Engagement, and express Promise and Compact." It is this express consent of a rational being, rather than the tacit or presumed consent of natural societies, that Locke argues marks "the beginning of Political Societies" (II:122). It is for this reason that Locke rejects the Grotian assumption that the compact reached by one generation binds their posterity. Locke boldly charges that no compact any individual may agree to can "bind his Children or posterity" (II:116). Political obligation must always be reducible to the express consent of the individual.

Second, the chief difference between political societies and natural societies, such as the family or the tribe, is that, for Locke, political societies are constituted by representative institutions, such as a common legislature, whereas natural societies signify the direct, personal, and noninstitutional practices of the paternal ruler and temporary war leader.[8] The representative character of political society derives from its status as the edifice intended to protect the right of self-preservation of all its members. Locke states: "The great and chief end therefore, of Mens uniting into Commonwealths, and putting themselves under Government, is *the Preservation of their Property*" (II:124).[9] It is important to note that Locke's emphasis on property as the end of government must be understood in light of the expanded notion of property he develops throughout the *Second Treatise*. Locke reveals that property extends beyond simply ownership of physical goods to the "Lives, Liberties, and Estates, which I call by the general Name, *Property*" (II:123; cf. II:87, II:131). The full scope of the protective and preservationist duties of civil society includes the recognition of the individual's property in the right to life and liberty, which are, Locke claims, as vital to self-preservation as shelter and food. In affirming not only a right to property but also a property in rights, Locke rejects the notion that political power may be understood as the property of the government. In making the protection of property, and by derivation the natural rights grounding the property right, the chief end of government, Locke once again signals his departure from the absolutist possibilities of contract theory posited by earlier figures such as Grotius, Hobbes, and even the moderate Whig authority Pufendorf.

---

[8] II:87. Cf. James Tully, *An approach to political philosophy: Locke in Contexts* (Cambridge: Cambridge University Press, 1993): pp. 20–2.

[9] See also II:88, 94–5, and 127.

The Powers of Government

The limited character of governmental power, for Locke, derives from the natural foundation of the two principal powers of government: the legislative and the executive powers. As we saw earlier in Locke's state of nature, he was concerned to demonstrate that these traditional and characteristic powers of government have their basis in the natural powers of individuals existing independently of political society. In defining these powers as they operate on the political level, Locke also signals their inherent, indeed natural, limits. The executive and legislative powers of government emerge from the uncertainty and dangers of the state of nature as the product of an agreement among all the members of society to "willingly give up every one his single power of punishing to be exercised by such alone as shall be appointed to it amongst them; and by such Rules as the Community, or those authorised by the purpose, shall agree on."[10]

For Locke, the executive and legislative powers of government derive from different aspects of the individual's natural power, and the transfer of these powers occurs in different ways and to differing degrees. The legislative power, which marks the crucial step from natural to political society, involves the right of the individual to do *"whatsoever he thought fit for the preservation of himself,* and the rest of Mankind." This natural self-defense right, which is at the core of the natural law, the individual "gives up to be regulated by Laws made by the Society." The individual, however, gives up this power only "so far forth as the preservation of himself, and the rest of Society shall require" (II:129). The legislative power in nature is only partially surrendered to civil government because it is the direct extension of the individual's desire for self-preservation. It is supreme because it directly expresses the universal desire for preserving property, which is the chief end of government.[11] Thus, Locke indicates that the surrender of natural liberty required for the creation of civil government is limited by the end or purpose of the contract and not by the origin of government in the act of contracting. He emphasizes that the power of civil legislation derives from and must ultimately conform to some principle of natural legislation rooted in the right of self-preservation.

Locke indicates that the legislative power is "first and fundamental positive Law of all Commonwealths," inasmuch as it sets the structure and form of the entire constitutional order and is logically prior to any other aspect of political authority (II:134). He nevertheless establishes four distinct natural limits on the extent of legislative power. First, "it is not, nor can possibly

---

[10] II:127. As we noted earlier, this marks one of Locke's big breaks from the Christian-Aristotelian tradition associated with Hooker and Bellarmine.

[11] Manent, *Intellectual History*, p. 50. Thus, I disagree with Kendall (*Majority Rule*, pp. 103–4), inasmuch as Locke is clear that the surrender of this power to society is limited by the universal concern for individual self-preservation.

be absolutely Arbitrary over the Lives and Fortunes of the People."[12] To support this claim, Locke refers back to the power of individuals in the state of nature. Just as in this condition no one could willingly consent to a legal despotic subjection, so too is civil law prohibited from enjoining a complete and arbitrary subjection to political authority. Second, Locke contends that civil legislation cannot assume the character of "Arbitrary Decrees," but rather must issue in *"promulgated standing Laws"* (II:136). Here Locke uses "arbitrary" in the more technical sense of the partial administration of justice. The natural equality underlying the formation of civil government must find expression in the operation of legislation. Third, Locke claims that the supreme legislative power cannot take the property of the people without their consent. Locke emphasizes the connection between individual liberty and self-preservation: "For I have truly no *Property* in that, which another can by right take from me, when he pleases, against my consent" (II:138–39). Thus, taxation, for Locke, can be legitimate only if it is levied by "the Consent of the Majority . . . or their Representatives chosen by them" (II:140).[13] Finally, Locke claims that the "Legislative cannot transfer the Power of Making Laws to any other hands" (II:141). Inasmuch as the legislative power reflects "a positive voluntary Grant and Institution" by the people, this condition precludes its alteration by any power other than the people.

Locke's treatment of the executive power differs considerably from that of the legislative power. First of all, Locke states that the natural executive power of the law of nature, from which the civil executive derives its power, is a power the individual "wholly *gives up*" (II:130). Whereas the natural legislative power to do whatever is necessary for self-preservation is surrendered only in part to society, the natural executive or punishment right is given up entire, "to be so far disposed of by the Legislative, as the good of Society shall require" (II:131). Locke hereby establishes the ground of legislative supremacy in the capacity of the legislature to organize the "natural force" of the members of society for the good of the entire community. The executive power reflects the need to create a "Power always in Being, which

---

[12] II:135. Contrast this with Algernon Sidney's treatment of the arbitrary power of the legislature in *Discourses Concerning Government*, Thomas West, ed. (indianapolis: Libery Fund Press, 1996): ch. 3, sec. 45 (hereafter D, ch., sec.), where Sidney means by "arbitrary" having no higher political authority.

[13] The famous Lockean rallying cry of American Whigs "No Taxation without Representation" is, surprisingly, Locke's only indication that the legislative power must, in principle, reside at least in part in some sort of representative body. Yet given the seminal importance of the preservation of property to the end of government, Locke quietly but unmistakably makes the representative principle central to his constitutional theory. For a decidedly populist reading of Lockean constitutionalism, see Robert Faulkner, "The First Liberal Democrat: Locke's Popular Government," *Review of Politics*, vol. 63 Fall (2001): pp. 17–19, 28, 36.

should see to the execution of the Laws that are made."[14] That this necessity extends beyond the practical difficulty of enforcing civil legislation is demonstrated by Locke's concern to associate the executive power with the power over foreign affairs, which he calls the "Federative" power. Whereas the executive power relates to the provision of a perpetual enforcement mechanism for existing laws, the federative power employs the natural force of the community in the sphere of foreign relations, a sphere independent of the operation of civil jurisdiction. They are distinct powers, but Locke considers that given their similarities – both employ the whole force of the community and require perpetual maintenance – "they are always almost united" (II:147).

Two important features of liberal constitutionalism emerge from this discussion. First, while Locke states that the federative and executive powers are typically, almost naturally, united, he emphatically cautions that the legislative and executive power should be divided. Given that it is "too great a temptation to humane frailty apt to grasp at power," Locke cautions that it is best that those who have the power to make the laws not be given the power to execute them (II:143). If these two powers are not separated, Locke implies that civil society will experience and replicate the problems of the state of nature, only on a much larger scale. The self-regarding nature of the human passions ensures that individuals will not apply the law equally to themselves and others unless the legislative power resides in an impartial and common judge for society as a whole. The second and related feature of Locke's discussion is his association of the executive and federative powers. This association is somewhat ambiguous given the fact that the executive power is, at least in theory, limited to performing the functions assigned by antecedent and standing laws, whereas Locke baldly states that the federative power that operates in the state of nature conditions of foreign relations relies ultimately on the "Prudence and Wisdom of those whose hands it is in" (II:147). As Locke presents it, the same person may be asked to perform very different tasks, the one delimited by law and the other largely discretionary. Locke's endorsement of discretionary power eventually seeps into his treatment of the executive in the form of prerogative. The necessity underlying the preservation of society in the lion's den of foreign relations does not in fact differ so greatly from the necessity informing domestic politics.

The argument that the legislative power is the supreme constitutional power because it is the "first given by the Majority" to a distinct political authority has serious implications for Locke's treatment of government in

---

[14] II:144. The secondary but ineradicable character of the executive power draws our attention back to the disorderly structure of the human passions (II:3). The dangerous tendencies of the state of nature remind us that in Locke's view, individuals must be forced to obey the law.

general and England in particular. Locke shows his fundamental disagreement with traditional Aristotelian regime analysis by emphasizing the importance of the *powers* of government rather than the *forms* of regime. Powers replace forms as the primary consideration in Lockean constitutionalism. Democracy, oligarchy, monarchy – elective and hereditary – and mixed or compound regimes are, in Locke's view, simply the product of the community's choice regarding where to locate the supreme legislative power.[15] Thus, for Locke, the form of a particular government derives entirely from the disposal of the individual power of the members of the community. The natural power of individuals contains the capacity to produce political forms. One important implication of Locke's argument about powers and forms is his radical reconceptualization of the theoretical underpinnings of the English mixed regime. Rather than viewing the English regime as a composite of three distinct forms of regime representing unique interests or claims to rule, Locke justifies the principle of constitutional balance on the grounds of an original societal disposition meant to reflect the universal concerns of the preservation of property and, ultimately, of self-preservation.[16] The primacy of powers over forms in Lockean constitutionalism removes the veil of traditional Aristotelian authority from England's ancient Constitution and thus exposes the individualistic underpinnings of what to moderate Whigs like Tyrrell was better understood as an organic political whole.

The issue of the status of the English constitutional system recurs throughout Locke's treatment of the complex relation between the legislative and executive powers of government. His theoretical account of the origins of political society asserts the priniciple of legislative supremacy; however, this principle is seriously qualified by Locke's argument for the fiduciary character of all political power. Locke claims that in any existing government or "Constituted Commonwealth" there can be but "*one Supreme Power*, which is the *Legislative*, to which all the rest are and must be subordinate" (II:149). However, Locke qualifies this institutional supremacy with a more fundamental popular supremacy: "yet the Legislative being only a Fiduciary Power to act for certain ends, there remains still *in the People a Supreme Power* to remove or *alter the Legislative*, when they find the Legislative act contrary to the trust reposed in them" (II:149). If the legislative power fails in its task of

---

[15] II:132. Cf. Faulkner, "First Liberal Democrat," pp. 11–12.

[16] See ibid., pp. 24–6. I disagree with the thrust of Peter Myers' argument ("Equality, Property, and the Problem of Partisanship: Lockean Constitution as Mixed Regime," *Interpretation*, vol. 22, no. 1 [Fall 1994:]: pp. 39–64). Although Aristotelian regime analysis may provide useful insights into a Lockean state, it is pivotal to recognize that Locke himself abandons this approach in his reflections on constitutionalism. For an excellent treatment of the difference between Lockean constitutionalism, with its emphasis on natural powers, and the Aristotelian regime analysis directed to particular forms representing claims to justice and the best kind of life, see Harvey Mansfield, *Taming the Prince: The Ambivalence of Modern Executive Power* (New York: Free Press, 1989), pp. 184–7.

preserving society, it may be subject to a more fundamental and sovereign power in the people.

Locke's notion of popular sovereignty anchors what we will call his "delegation theory of sovereignty." The logical implication of Locke's argument that the power of government derives from the natural power of the individual is that all the powers of government are essentially delegated powers. Even the legislative power, in this view, is a delegated power. As a result, Locke maintains both that the power of the legislature cannot be truly supreme, being a creature of the people, and that the people may locate the legislative function in a wide variety of institutional structures and forms. In this respect, Locke's understanding of legislative supremacy differs from that of Sidney, for example. Whereas the modern republican Sidney defended legislative supremacy on the grounds that large representative assemblies embody the will of the sovereign people, and thus cannot do real harm to the people without harming themselves, Locke's separation of society and government reduces all political institutions to instruments designed to protect society's interests. This institutional instrumentality derives from Locke's premise of political individualism.[17] Thus, for Locke, even though the legislative power reflects both the act of its creation in the consent of the individuals in society and its proper end, the preservation of its members' property, the principle of legitimation in the former process does not, and cannot, preclude a divestiture of right for failure to provide the latter service.

The second major proviso Locke makes to the argument for legislative supremacy relates to his crucial discussion of the subordination of powers in Chapter Thirteen. Here Locke's theoretical reflections on the origin and nature of political society most closely intersect with his considerations of the actual condition of the English constitutional system. Although Locke does not refer to England directly in this chapter, he presents a hypothetical constitutional model identical to that of his native land. It is also here that Locke demonstrates a central tenet of his delegation theory of sovereignty: The people may legitimately divide the legislative power among a number of constitutional actors. Locke qualifies his earlier defense of legislative supremacy by turning to examine "some Commonwealths where the Legislative is not always in being, and the Executive is vested in a single Person, who has also a share in the Legislative; there that single Person in a very tolerable sense may also be called Supream" (II:151). In this virtual England, the executive may "in a very tolerable sense" be identified as supreme not because "he has in himself all the Supream Power, which is that of Law-Making," but rather by virtue of the fact that this executive has no legislative power above him. This is true both in the sense that no law can be made without his or her consent and in the sense that all inferior magistrates derive their subordinate

---

[17] Sidney, for example, generally saw the executive as an office of trust but not, strictly speaking, the legislative power, which he argued should be by definition representative of society.

power from the "Supream Executive" (II:151). Locke is careful to indicate that the powers of the "Supream Executive," most notably the power of convoking and dismissing the legislature, are also fiduciary powers and thus do not denote a superiority over the legislature (II:152, II:156).

Two important arguments emerge from Locke's treatment of the subordination of powers. First, he employs this discussion to affirm indirectly his position that the English monarch is independent of Parliament. The king properly derives his authority from the community, not from the positive grant of the legislative. In contrast to Tyrrell and Pufendorf, Locke insists that the ideal English Constitution is a mixture of coordinate authorities with no manifest supremacy within the constitutional order itself.[18] Moreover, by arguing that Parliament has no more inherently valid claim to represent the national interest than does the king, Locke rejects both the resistance theories of the civil war radicals and the ideas of the republican Whig Sidney. Second, Locke reveals that the powers of government may be divided among the governing institutions. Thus, the executive may be a person who is not necessarily in a position subordinate to the legislature.[19] The introduction of the personalistic character of the executive power into the societal formulations of the legislative power implies Locke's recognition of a deep ambiguity in the notion of constitutional supremacy. The community may not only trump the authority of existing institutions with a more fundamental claim to supremacy, it may also design and ascribe the powers of those institutional actors in such a way as to locate constitutional supremacy in an authority other than the legislature.[20] The subordination of powers introduces the notion of personalism into an otherwise abstract account. Locke admits that the supreme executive in England will "be subordinate and accountable to" the legislature no "farther than he himself shall joyn and consent," which Locke suggests "one may certainly conclude will be but very little" (II:152). Locke's assessment of the self-regarding character of the human passions practically precludes the plausibility of the voluntary submission to fundamental law, which anchors Tyrrell's theory of limited, as opposed to mixed, monarchy.

[18] Julian Franklin, *John Locke and the Theory of Sovereignty* (Cambridge: Cambridge University Press, 1978): pp. 91–2. Whereas Faulkner ("First Liberal Democrat," pp. 26–7) takes Locke to be critical of the idea of an independent executive, I believe Locke sees such an executive as a salutary counterforce to the dangerous concentration of power even in a representative legislature.

[19] Mansfield (*Taming the Prince*, pp. 201, 211) argues that Locke's teaching on the legislative and executive power built "a divided mind into constitutional government." Cf. Manent, *Intellectual History*, p. 51.

[20] Locke does admit, however, that the legislature may resume the executive power it has given up and punish maladministration (II:153), but how it can do this effectively when the executive has a share in the legislative power is not so clear. Presumably, the legislature would have no such power with respect to an independent executive unless this power was stipulated in a written constitution.

The third major proviso Locke proposes to the idea of legislative supremacy has to do with prerogative. Here too Locke relies on the delegation theory of sovereignty to demonstrate that the people may delegate even discretionary power to the executive. Locke defines prerogative as the "power to act according to discretion, *for the publick good*, without the prescription of the Law, and sometimes even against it."[21] The connection between discretionary power and the public good (practically antipodes for Sidney) rests on Locke's fundamental premise that the authority of government must be informed by the natural law command to preserve the whole of society. Locke states: "'Tis fit that the Laws themselves should in some Cases give way to the Executive Power, or rather to this Fundamental Law of Nature and Government, viz. That as much as may be, all the Members of Society are to be preserved" (II:159). A seminal feature of Lockean constitutionalism is his effort to incorporate discretion, one of the major causes of disorder in the state of nature, into government through prerogative.

The exactness and predictability Locke identifies with the rule of the lawmaking body appears in tension with his justification of discretionary power. Clearly, Locke qualifies his original position that the natural executive power is given up wholly upon the formation of political society. He admits that the individual retains the natural executive power insofar as the law can never be completely effective – for example, when one faces a robber on a lonely highway (II:130–1). But Locke similarly suggests that society retains the executive power of government through prerogative when the law is either ineffective or injurious to the good of society.[22] Remarkably, Locke offers very standard royalist arguments for the regal pardon power and equity claims as justification for prerogative (II:159). However, he makes these arguments while operating from much more radical premises than his royalist opponents in England. For example, he employs the radical parliamentarian slogan "Salus populi, Suprema Lex" as a vindication of regal prerogative. Locke justifies prerogative much less in terms of sovereign majesty than by the constant flux and change in the natural order of things (II:157, II:160).[23] Locke's practical objection to the principle of absolute legislative supremacy

---

[21] II:160 (emphasis mine). Faulkner ("First Liberal Democrat," pp. 33–4) interprets Locke to be hostile to the idea of prerogative and concerned to place legal and institutional limits on it. However, by my reading, Locke offers no legal or institutional limits, but rather only the extralegal limit of public opinion, which, of course, is no necessary endorsement of legislative supremacy.

[22] Manent, *Intellectual History*, p. 50.

[23] Mansfield (*Taming the Prince*, p. 203) identifies this as a sign of Locke's break from Aristotelian regime analysis in favor of a Machiavellian conception of the flux and change in nature. See Peter Josephson, *The Great Art of Government: Locke's Use of Consent* (Lawrence: University Press of Kansas, 2002): pp. 23–43 for an interpretation of Locke's use of prerogative that emphasizes the distinction between rationality and consent.

reflects a deep tension in his thought between the notions of legitimacy and utility. Locke argues, on the one hand, that the legislature is supreme because it most emphatically represents the community, being itself the product of the majority in society. Yet Locke also indicates that the harsh realities of political necessity may require some qualification of the representative principle embodied in the legislature by recognizing the great service discretionary, as opposed to legislative, power can do for society.[24] In this respect, Locke and Sidney are mirror images.

Republican Whigs detested the principle of prerogative. Sidney argued that by the logic of individual natural rights and the principle of representation it supports, the claim to constitutional supremacy of large popular assemblies rests on their capacity to reflect the general will of society. In this view, the executive power is a delegated power inasmuch as it derives its source from and its scope is defined by the legislature. Locke, however, indicates that an independent executive derives legitimacy from the power delegated by the people. The people may choose to make the executive and the members of the legislative assembly equal partners in the exercise of sovereign constitutional authority. For Locke, every branch of the government exercises power delegated by society. In this respect, Locke points to the existence of a sovereign constitutional will of the people expressed in the original compact forming political institutions, which is distinct from, and superior to, the will of the people expressed in normal legislation. It is this crucial theoretical distinction that informs Locke's understanding of the relation between the legislative and executive power. Whereas Sidney saw the subjection of the executive power to the legislative as the sine qua non of constitutional legitimacy and the survival of liberty, Locke suggests that the delegatory character of sovereignty, and nature in all its complexity and stubborn resistance to human flourishing, offer the individual and society two diverging though not necessarily antithetical means of securing preservation.

---

[24] Two major examples Locke adduces for the salutary benefits of prerogative relate to the issues of representation and toleration. Locke appeals to the flux and change in population as justification for an executive's redrawing electoral districts in order to preserve the "true proportion" necessary for any representative body (II:158). In granting this sweeping power to the executive, Locke suggests certain inherent limits on the legislature's capacity to effect reform. I disagree with Richard Ashcraft (*Revolutionary Politics and Locke's Two Treatises of Government* [Princeton: Princeton University Press, 1986]: p. 238) that Locke's argument here is a tactical ploy meant to push the burden of reform on the king. However, I maintain that it suggests the great theoretical and practical import Locke ascribes to the executive power. The connection between prerogative and religious toleration is not a major theme in the *Two Treatises*, but given Locke's work with Shaftesbury in the 1670s, it would seem to suggest that toleration is more likely to be established by the executive than by a legislature controlled by members of the established church. For Locke on prerogative and toleration, see Ashcraft, *Revolutionary Politics*, p. 111 and Maurice Cranston, *John Locke: A Biography* (London: Macmillan, 1957): pp. 129, 144.

The executive power is manifestly a central feature of Locke's reflections on constitutionalism. His account of prerogative is not restricted simply to the practical issue of the operation of the English system. Indeed, Locke's caution that the legislature should not be in perpetual session effectively precludes the possibility of locating the executive power within the structure of the legislature.[25] The executive, we recall, must be a "Power always in being" (II:144). Moreover, Locke admits that the executive may have some share in the legislative power, but he offers no operational guidance for the reverse. However, Locke admits that there are dangers to the practice of prerogative. As we saw earlier, Locke identified prerogative with the early age of society when "Commonwealths differed little from Families in number of People" (II:107, II:111). Given the lack of political sophistication of these primitive peoples and the inability of uncultured reason to devise institutions capable of producing the rule of law, Locke admits that these early patriarchal governments were "almost all Prerogative" (II:161). In this light, prerogative appears at least in part as a residual practice from a distant and unlamented past.

However, Locke affirms that the personalistic and discretionary nature of the executive power persists in any constitutional order. He presents this as a natural condition out of which society cannot progress. Insofar as Locke defines prerogative as a "power to do good," there appears to be no inherent limits on how far this power may legitimately extend. The deeply personalistic character of prerogative means that this practice can in principle extend as far as the executive chooses to exercise it. Locke reduces the difference between the legitimate and illegitimate use of prerogative down to the psychological and moral traits of the executive himself. The good prince "is mindful of the trust put into his hands," whereas the bad prince views prerogative as "belonging to him by Right of the Office" (II:164). Given Locke's discussion, it appears that these two conditions or perspectives are not mutually exclusive. It is rather the end to which the executive aims – the good or harm of society – that determines the legitimacy of the action. Locke suggests that the reigns of good princes "have always been most dangerous to the Liberties of their People" because they set extralegal precedents that may disguise the ill intentions of their lesser successors.

Locke and Sidney agree that a people used to the exercise of executive prerogative is one dangerously close to losing a sense of the true grounds of political legitimacy.[26] Locke's only safeguard against executive abuse of

---

[25] Faulkner, on the contrary, argues ("First Liberal Democrat," p. 30) that Locke envisages something like modern cabinet government, although even in the cabinet system there is always some, even if largely formal, permanent executive, whether an Israeli president, a British monarch, or a Canadian governor-general.

[26] Locke perhaps echoes Sidney's concern for the quasi-religious character of prerogative when he refers to "God-like Princes" at II:166.

the prerogative right is the right of the people to reassert their primal extra-constitutional supremacy. In answer to the question of who decides when prerogative does or does not intend the public good, Locke baldly states: "The good or hurt of the People, will easily decide the Question" (II:161). It is important to notice that Locke does not reserve this judgment to the legislature. With respect to the relations of the English monarch and Parliament, "between an Executive Power in Being, with such a Prerogative, and a Legislative that depends upon his will for their convening, there can be no Judge on Earth" (II:168). The independence of the monarchy in Locke's interpretation of the English Constitution suggests two things: that prerogative will be an essential component of this system and that the people or society, understood independently of any existing political authority, will be the final arbiter in any constitutional dispute.

Resistance and Dissolution

The heart of Locke's constitutional theory is the principle that governmental power derives from the natural power of individuals and is held by the governors as a form of trust. By this logic, if the government breaks its trust to pursue the public good, then power devolves back to the individuals who compose society. This in itself constitutes a radical break from traditional justifications of resistance in the natural liberty school, but Locke goes even further to radicalize this notion of the devolution of power into a theory of the dissolution of government. The issue of trust provides the intrinsic connection between Locke's accounts of legislative and executive power. He affirms that the natural status of the legislature as the supreme constitutional power is severely qualified by its basis in a fiduciary power delegated by and ultimately responsible to the community (II:150). He also introduces the concept of trust as a limitation to the notion of executive power inasmuch as he maintains that even prerogative reflects a societal power held in trust (II:156). Locke treats at some length the most important element of trust in the English system – the king's power to call and dissolve Parliament – and finds this power more worthy of attention on the part of society than any other.[27] He relates that political power derives from "that Power which every Man having in the state of Nature" then gives to society and "therein to the Governours, whom the Society hath set over itself, with this express or tacit Trust, That it shall be imployed for their good, and the preservation of their Property."[28] This is Locke's clearest statement about the concept

---

[27] II:154–6. Cf. Ashcraft, *Revolutionary Politics*, p. 230.

[28] II:171. In Chapter fifteen of the *Second Treatise*, where Locke recaps his view of the character of paternal, despotic, and political power, only the last is presented as a form of rule based on trust. Compare II:170 and II:172 with II:171.

of trust inasmuch as he makes trust and the devolution of power features of all political compacts. Whether this fiduciary relationship is expressly stated or not, it is implicit in the very fabric of the compact forming political society.

The concept of trust has serious implications for Lockean liberal constitutionalism. On a general and theoretical level, Locke employs this concept to reformulate the relations of the governors and the governed in terms consistent with his individualistic account of the origin of political power. In contrast to the absolutist tendencies and possibilities in Hobbes, Grotius, Pufendorf, and the moderate Whigs, Locke not only argues that sovereignty rests outside the strict confines of contract, but he also asserts the community's right to reassert supremacy irrespective of the explicit terms of the political contract.[29] On a more immediate and practical level, Locke's use of the concept of trust suggests his dissatisfaction with the ability of the English constitutional order to prevent the abuse of power. For Locke, trust replaces faith in checks and balances by offering a justification of popular sovereignty that can solve what he takes to be the problem of the moderate Whig idea of the conjoint sovereignty of the king-in-Parliament.[30] One crucial reason for Locke's rejection of the English mixed regime theory and its praise of the balance of parliamentary and monarchical power is his skepticism of this theory's capacity to account for and resist the tendency of political institutions, legislative or executive, to slide into corruption and tyranny over time.

A central feature of Locke's theory of the dissolution of government is his concern to demonstrate that the principle of lawful resistance to unlawful government action is not inherently anarchic. In the last chapter of the *Second Treatise*, however, Locke shifts the emphasis away from trying to counter royalist charges against the dangers of resistance theory toward his effort to develop a unique theory of the devolution of power, which justifies such resistance. This theory departs from all prior accounts of resistance inasmuch as it confirms the people's right to resist a monarch and to restore a legislative assembly. However, Locke also extends this right of the people to a legitimate power to alter or replace the legislative power in any manner they see fit.[31] The dissolution of government extends far beyond a communal self-defense right of restoration, restoring the terms of the original compact. Locke claims that "when *the Government is dissolved*, the people are at Liberty to provide for themselves, by erecting a new Legislative, differing from the other, by

[29] Tully, *Locke in Contexts*, p. 30.

[30] Ibid., pp. 36, 38.

[31] Although Franklin (*Theory of Sovereignty*) offers an interesting study showing Locke's relation to George Lawson's account of dissolution, I believe that by basing his theory on the devolution of power to individuals in society, as opposed to certain communal institutions, Locke shows his great difference from Lawson.

the change of Persons, or Forms, or both as they shall find it most for their safety and good" (II:220).[32] It is perhaps because of the radical implications of dissolution, the possibility of creating a new government *ex nihilo* from the preexisting soil of society, that Locke makes no reference to the authority of Parliament as a justification for popular resistance. Such authority would, it seems, be utterly superfluous.

The dissolution of government, according to Locke, occurs by virtue of executive or legislative action. However, he distinguishes the dissolution of government that occurs through domestic forces and the dissolution of society that can apparently result only from foreign conquest. When a foreign conqueror makes it impossible for a people "to maintain and support themselves, as one *intire* and *independent* Body," through the scattering of the population and the destruction or confiscation of their material resources, then Locke argues that the social union "is dissolved" and every individual returns "to the state he was in before, with a liberty to shift for himself, and provide for his own Safety as he think fit in some other Society" (II:211).[33] The dissolution of government, on the other hand, has different causes and consequences.

The fundamental cause of the dissolution of government is the alteration of the legislature without the consent of the people. From this premise, Locke immediately draws the reader's attention to the particular case of the conditions for the dissolution of government in England. Locke suggests that it is hard to construe properly how governments dissolve "without knowing the Form of Government in which it happens" (II:213). He then proceeds to sketch an exact, if supposedly fictitious, duplicate of the English constitutional system. While Locke asserts that, at least in principle, the executive or the legislature may be responsible for the dissolution of government if either submits the nation to foreign subjection or acts contrary to the trust established by the people, it also becomes clear in this discussion that the most typical culprit in the dissolution of a mixed monarchy will be the executive. There are three ways Locke considers that a monarch can commonly dissolve the government.

[32] Locke's account of the dissolution right strangely parallels the language of his earlier treatment of the divine workmanship right. Now, however, the property is government rather than individuals, and the owners or workmen are the individuals composing society rather than God.

[33] For the complexity in distinguishing these two kinds of dissolution in Locke, see John Simmons, *On the Edge of Anarchy: Locke, Consent, and the Limits of Society* (Princeton: Princeton University Press, 1993): pp. 161–63; Leo Strauss, *Natural Right and History*, (Chicago: University of Chicago Press, 1953): p. 232; and Nathan Tarcov, "Locke's Second Treatise and the 'Best Review of Politics,* vol. 43 (April 1981): Fence Against Rebellion,'" pp. 207–10. Locke's discussion of the natural law limits on the rights of conquerors in Chapter sixteen went some distance to reduce, if not preclude, the awful destruction Locke describes in the dissolution of an entire society. Cf. II:177–82.

The first is when "a single Person or Prince sets up his own Arbitrary Will in place of the Laws, which are the Will of the Society" (II:214). Locke claims that when any "Rules [are] pretended, and inforced" other than those enacted by the legislature, then the "Legislative is changed" and the government is dissolved. A second way the monarch in such a system can dissolve the government is when "the Prince hinders the Legislative from assembling in its due time, or from acting freely, pursuant to those ends, for which it was Constituted" (II:215). Executive interference with the legislative process and the freedom of parliamentary debate cuts to the heart of the rule of law: "For it is not Names, that Constitute Governments, but the use and exercise of those Powers that were intended to accompany them" (II:215). The third way a government like England's is typically dissolved occurs when "the Supream Executive Power, neglects and abandons that charge, so that the Laws already made can no longer be put in execution" (II:219). Locke claims that the failure to perform the executive duty is equivalent "to reduc[ing] all to Anarchy." Moreover, the English king has the power of dissolving the legislature and thus making the representatives of the people in Parliament private persons.[34] Simply put, the legislators in Parliament cannot alter the legislative power without the monarch's approval anyway.

To those royalists and others who would invoke the radical ghosts of 1649, Locke is deeply concerned to demonstrate that the theory of dissolution does not produce anarchic consequences. However, Locke largely conceals, rather than denies, the radical implications of his dissolution theory – implications Tyrrell, for example, was not prepared to accept – beneath a veil of conservative rhetoric. Locke dismisses the charge that dissolution theory will produce frequent rebellions on several grounds. First, he claims that people will revolt when oppressed irrespective of the form of government or any particular ideological justification of obedience (II:224). In this respect, Locke clearly obviates discussion of the ubiquity of tyrannies in the world both historically and contemporaneously, and as such he self-consciously and self-servingly diminishes the importance of his own role as political philosopher and educator of a citizenry conscious and suspicious of guarding their liberty.[35] Locke also concludes that recognition of the popular right to make a new legislature acts as "the best fence against Rebellion" by encouraging caution and political moderation in rulers (II:226).[36]

---

[34] II:218. I disagree with Tully regarding his view that Locke held England to be the best regime (*Locke in Contexts*, p. 38). Rather, I believe that the political implications of his natural rights theory are considerably more radical than the traditional English Constitution.

[35] Pangle, *Spirit*, p. 258.

[36] Tarcov, "Best Fence Against Rebellion," pp. 212–17. Locke premises this contention on his argument that the real rebels in the event of a dissolution of government are not the people but the putative rulers. Note the similarity in Locke's use of the notion of *rebellare* at II:226 and Sidney's use of it at D 3.36.

Locke is also careful, however, to temper this line of argument by appealing to the natural conservatism of the people. He charges that the people will allow the dissolution of government only when the oppression affects the majority of the population, and even then they will act not after isolated examples of "mismanagement in publick affairs," but rather when they perceive "a long train of Abuses, Prevarications, and Artifices, all tending the same way."[37] Finally, Locke claims that even in the event of a dissolution of government there is a general "Slowness and Aversion in the People to Quit their old Constitutions," as the longevity of the English Constitution testifies, despite the various concatenations in English history (II:223). In brief, as James Tully observes, "Locke plays the conservative trump card of partiality and habit against his conservative opponents, showing that these causal factors make popular sovereignty more stable than absolutism."[38] For Locke, the people are generally loath to do that which they have a perfect right to do.

The theory of dissolution is the cornerstone of Locke's account of the right of revolution. This right constitutes Locke's celebrated "Appeal to Heaven." With language identical to that in his discussion of the state of war, Locke ascribes a natural right of the people to resist oppressive government and to retain the legislative power of society in themselves in order to restore the old government or to erect a new one. It is important to recognize that Locke does not designate the community in toto as the determinant of whether government has been dissolved or not; rather, he claims that "every Man is Judge for himself, as in all other Cases, so in this, whether another has put himself into a State of War with him."[39] In contrast to Tyrrell, Locke does not place any moral prohibitions on the individual's right to resist government. Rather, Locke merely observes that an individual or even a minority group would be very unlikely to effect a change in the government without majority support (II:209, II:230). Whereas the moderate Whig Tyrrell criticized individual resistance to political authority as immoral and antithetical to the natural law requirements of peaceful social existence, Locke offers merely practical objections based on the feasibility of success. The primary reason Lockean liberal constitutional thought does not contain such a natural law moral prohibition against individual resistance is that Locke understands revolution as the exercise of the natural power of the people, a power finally reducible to individuals.[40] With this much greater emphasis on

---

[37] II:230, II:225. Cf. II:209–10.
[38] Tully, *Locke in Contexts*, p. 45.
[39] II:241. Cf. Simmons, *Anarchy*, pp. 155–6 for the distinction between breach of trust and state of war.
[40] Franklin, *Theory of Sovereignty*, p. 96; John Marshall, *John Locke: Resistance, Religion, and Responsibility* (Cambridge: Cambridge University Press, 1994): p. 236; Simmons, *Anarchy*, pp. 148–9, 173–9; and Tully, *Locke in Contexts*, p. 41.

the individual's natural right to decide the means for self-preservation and the protection of property, Lockean resistance theory slips the leash of the natural law duties of political obedience so central to Tyrrell, Pufendorf, and Grotius.

Locke's theory of dissolution is clearly a radical departure from the position of his contemporaries. His claim that the dissolution of government does not mean the dissolution of society points to his argument that a society of individuals primarily concerned with economic activity can exist independently of government for a time.[41] More particularly, Locke's position differs from that of the modern republican Sidney inasmuch as Locke does not identify the sovereign right of the people solely with the right of the legislative body. For Sidney, the right of revolution was essentially a rallying cry to support Parliament against the king. Locke, on the other hand, makes little or no reference to Parliament, or any legislative body, to justify the people's right to resist and alter the government. Lockean natural rights theory indicates that the foundation of all government in a society of individual rights bearers is emphatically democratic, although the actual forms of government may be more representative than purely popular.[42] Locke's openness to a variety of regime forms, in contrast to the modern republicans, presupposes this firmly democratic foundation for legitimacy in a social entity that transcends particular institutional arrangements. In contrast to moderate Whigs like Tyrrell and William Atwood, Locke does not restrict the right of resistance to a self-defense right or even to a purely restorative right. As Julian Franklin amply demonstrates, these moderate Whigs feared the radical implications of Lockean dissolution theory, and they hoped to show that it was Parliament's right to restore or modify the Constitution in the event of any crisis with the monarchy. Tyrrell and Atwood followed Pufendorf in maintaining that the political compact that forms society implicitly precludes dissolution and the radical democratic implications such a theory would invite.[43]

---

[41] Simmons, *Anarchy*, pp. 167–72; Strauss, *Natural Right and History*, p. 232; and Tarcov, "Best Fence Against Rebellion," pp. 205–10.

[42] Parry, "Locke on Representation," pp. 409–13; Tarcov, "Best Fence Against Rebellion," pp. 205–6; and Simmons, *Anarchy*, p. 184. By this measure, Faulkner ("First Liberal Democrat," pp. 24–39) pushes Locke too far in the democratic republican direction, while MacPherson and Wood go too far in the other direction by attributing characteristically moderate Whig arguments to Locke that were considerably more conservative than his own (C. B. MacPherson, *The Political Theory of Possessive Individualism* [Oxford: Oxford University Press, 1962]: p. 224 and Ellen Meiskins Wood, "Locke Against Democracy: Consent, Representation and Suffrage in the Two Treatises," *History of Political Thought*, vol. 13, no. 4 [Winter 1992]: pp. 671–7, 685–9).

[43] Franklin, *Theory of Sovereignty*, pp. 105–10. Samuel Cf. Pufendorf, *De Jure Naturae et Gentium Libri Octo* (Oxford: Clarendon press, 1934): bk. 7, ch. 7, sec. 9 (hereafter DJNG) for his rejection of dissolution. It is interesting to note that Atwood's *The Fundamental Constitution of the English Government* (1690) was written in part as a critical response to the dissolution theory in the *Second Treatise*.

Locke forcefully concludes that every political contract contains a unilateral popular right of dissolution. This is as true of the English Constitution as of any other; indeed, for Locke, no contract could preclude such a possibility.

The parting shot in Locke's break from traditional English constitutional theory is the assault on the Scottish arch-royalist William Barclay that practically concludes the *Two Treatises*. Locke's strategy in his treatment of Barclay is twofold. First, he attempts to exploit the radical potential in Barclay's admission of a severely limited right of a people to resist a tyrant. Second, Locke skillfully employs Barclay as a stand-in for other thinkers, like Grotius and Pufendorf, who had considerable prestige among many Whigs and had developed potentially absolutist theories of sovereignty from the premise of natural liberty. The main thrust of Locke's criticism relates to Barclay's admission that there is a limited right of resistance against tyrants. Locke quotes Barclay to the effect that "Self-defense is a part of the Law of Nature; nor can it be denied the Community, even against the King himself" (II:233). However, Barclay places two potentially serious limitations on this right of self-defense. First, it must not "exceed the bounds of due Reverence and Respect." Second, this resistance must be "without Retribution, or Punishment" because "an Inferior cannot punish a Superiour" (II:235). Predictably, Locke ridicules the first limitation, savagely charging: "He that can Reconcile Blows and Reverence, may, for ought I know, deserve for his pains, a Civil Respectful Cudgeling where-ever he can meet with it" (II:235). With respect to the second limit, Locke agrees with Barclay that punishment cannot proceed from a position of inferiority, but Locke seizes on Barclay's admission that a king "becomes no King" when he endeavors "to overturn the Government" or when he "makes himself the dependent of another, and subjects his Kingdom which his ancestors left him."[44] Locke thus radicalizes the principle of forfeiture, which was the final safety valve against tyranny traditionally held even by many royalist thinkers, and turns this rather conservative principle into the more radical proposition of dissolution. Locke is wholly disingenuous in his claim that he is simply supplying "the Principle" from which Barclay's notion of forfeiture flows (II:239). Locke's theory of dissolution operates from a premise of the derivation of political power from the natural power of individuals, a premise clearly anathema for Barclay.

This use and abuse of Barclay serves Locke's larger aim of breaking new ground in the theory of natural rights constitutionalism. While Locke tries to make Barclay's once reputable natural liberty theory of absolutism appear more populist than it is, he also establishes his own distance from Grotius, Pufendorf, and Hobbes. For instance, while Grotius admitted that

[44] II:237, 239. Here Locke attempts to capitalize on the English fear that Charles II was taking bribes from Louis XIV and threatening to subject Parliament to the crown and, by extension, subject England to France. Given the circumstances surrounding the secret Treaty of Dover, there was probably some truth to these suspicions.

the people, individually or collectively, could resist an intolerable tyrant, he did not follow Locke in asserting that the entire society could exercise political power.[45] Likewise, with respect to Pufendorf, Locke rejects the argument that the right of resistance must be construed as a self-defense right. For Pufendorf and his moderate Whig followers, political power does not revert to the people in the event of a constitutional crisis, but rather to the representative bodies or "great councils," which are entitled to settle the issue definitively.[46] Neither the Grotian nor the moderate Whig Pufendorfian strain of natural law theory would allow or countenance Locke's argument that political power derives from and ultimately devolves to a society of morally autonomous individuals. Quite the contrary, these thinkers explicitly sought to establish some ground of sovereignty, even absolute sovereignty, somewhere within the political structures and institutions of any given constitutional order.

On the other hand, both Hobbes and Locke posit a source of political right independent of any contract. Hobbes' sovereign, free of any contractual obligations, and Locke's society of individuals, bound to observe none they may not freely break, are essentially two sides of the same coin. Locke, we may say, simply turns Hobbes on his head. The moral and political implications of this inversion, however, are enormous. We need only look back to Hobbes' powerful criticism of the principle of independent judgment as a cause of civil war to recognize how far Locke takes a Hobbesian principle in a radically different direction.[47] Hobbes views resistance as a natural act, one that threatens literally to restore the state of nature. Locke, on the other hand, sees revolution itself as a political act, an expression of the natural political power of the people. For Locke and Hobbes, the primacy of natural rights and the inherent fragility of political society produce very different theories of the right of resistance.

The paradox of Lockean constitutionalism is that while it asserts the general principles of political legitimacy, it pairs these principles not with a specific form of regime, but rather with a theoretical and moral justification of the dissolution of government itself. Locke is a less doctrinaire defender of parliamentary supremacy than the republican Sidney – indeed, he upholds the independence of the monarchy in his understanding of the English Constitution – precisely because Locke views the right of dissolution, rather than the right of Parliament, as the ultimate guarantee of political liberty and natural rights. Locke's dissolution theory is not merely a theoretical contrivance designed to resolve the serious constitutional problems and

---

[45] Cf. Hugo Grotius, *De Jure Belli ac Pacis Libri Tres* (Oxford: Clarendon press, 1925): ch. 1, sec. 4, pp. 7–11 (referring directly to Barclay) and Tully, *Locke in Contexts*, pp. 18, 41–2.

[46] James Tyrrell, *Bibliotheca Politica* (London, 1718): p. 643 and Pufendorf, DJNG 7.7.9, 7.8.7.

[47] Thomas Hobbes, *Leviathan*, Edwin Curley, ed. (Indianapolis: Hackett, 1994): ch. 29 and Tully, *Locke in Contexts*, p. 44.

issues in seventeenth-century England.[48] Rather, it is essentially a product of his more fundamental natural rights theory, a direct consequence of his radical argument for the derivation of political power from the natural executive power of individuals. Constitutional government, for Locke, can be a legitimate expression of the natural political power of individuals only insofar as it contains or represents the moral justification of its own demise or dissolution. Locke presents his dissolution theory as the logical culmination of what the idea of political individualism at the heart of Lockean liberalism means for the relation of the individual to government.

The theoretical core of Lockean liberal thought is individual natural rights. In his assessment of both the character of rights and the political implications of natural rights, Locke departed from nearly all his predecessors and contemporaries. The liberal rights theory underlying Locke's political teaching provided a much more democratic foundation for the origin, end, and dissolution of government than the vast majority of moderate Whigs could countenance. With his endorsement of a delegation theory of sovereignty and a refurbished separation of powers theory, albeit based on functional instrumentality rather than historical socioeconomic interests, Lockean liberalism differed from the radically populist version of modern republicanism introduced to England by Sidney. Liberal constitutionalism, as Locke conceived it, broke from both radical republican and moderate Whig ideas by reconceptualizing government power in such a way as to make political sovereignty difficult, and perhaps impossible, to locate. Neither the moderate Whig king-in-Parliament nor the modern republican popular assembly would be sovereign in Lockean society. In a fundamental sense, society would be sovereign, not institutions.

The theoretical and practical implications of Lockean liberal thought for the English Constitution were momentous. Locke's emphasis on the societal as opposed to the institutional grounding of legitimacy reveals a subtle criticism of the historical understanding of the English Constitution. By tracing constitutional development from the powers of individuals in a state of nature, Locke undermines the sacrosanctity, if not the fundamental integrity, of the existing and cherished political institutions in England. Locke implies that granting too much reverence to political forms and structures inculcates an understanding of the end of political society as the preservation of existing institutions, rather than the true or natural end of preserving the pre-civil rights these institutions were meant to protect. In trying to resist the reification of the idea of liberty in particular institutions, Locke points to the concerns of civil society, primarily the realm of economic activity, as representing the best human response to the deep problem of natural scarcity. For Locke, it is a mistake, even if an understandable one, to view the defense of

---

[48] In this respect I disagree with Franklin (*Theory of Sovereignty*) and rather follow the main lines of Tully's argument (*Locke in Contexts*).

what is familiar to us as an end in itself.[49] In an England informed by Lockean principles, the Constitution would be an object of obligation and respect only to the extent that it protected property and facilitated the material and technological advances necessary for ensuring the comfortable self-preservation of the people and the security of their rights. Locke cautiously suggests that the government of England must undergo deep and fundamental reforms, far beyond the limited goal of Exclusion, if it is to satisfy these demands. In the early stages of the Glorious Revolution, Locke expressed his concern that if the Convention "think of themselves as a Parliament, and put themselves in a slow method of proceeding usual therein, and think of mending great faults piecemeal, or anything less than the great frame of government, they will let slip an opportunity."[50] As we shall see in what follows, few Whigs in England at the time were prepared to follow Locke's lead.

---

[49] See, for example, Locke's criticism of the natural "Slowness and Aversion" to correct constitutional "defects" (II:223). Even Locke's defense of prerogative rested on a natural rather than a historical or divine form of right.

[50] Letter to Edward Clarke, February 7, 1689 (quoted in Franklin, *Theory of Sovereignty*, p. 121).

IO

The Glorious Revolution and the Catonic Response

The themes and issues raised in the writings of the Exclusion era Whigs foreshadowed the constitutional and legal arguments supporting the Whig triumph in the Glorious Revolution less than a decade later. However, the dramatic events of 1688–9 came to represent a victory primarily for a particular strain of Whig thought. The official Whig account of the revolution rested on the theoretical premises of the moderate brand of Whiggism we saw in Tyrrell. The radical Whig positions and theories associated with Locke and Sidney were largely marginalized. In both form and substance, the actions of the Convention Parliament in replacing the errant James II with William and Mary were accounted for and defended in terms counter to the central premises of radical Whiggism. The spirit of 1689 was not the stuff of radical Whig dreams.

The Glorious Revolution and the Exclusion crisis of a decade or so earlier are linked on a number of levels. First, both situations raised many of the same issues about the extent of prerogative and parliamentary authority, the character of the English Constitution, and the very nature of the political and religious settlement in the nation. Second, the actors involved in the Glorious Revolution operated in a complex historical and ideological context that was in many respects unchanged from that of a decade earlier. Fear of civil war, popular revulsion at the idea of republicanism, and virulent anti-Catholicism once again dominated the political scene, but in the late 1680s this complex dynamic of deeply rooted social attitudes and potent political imagery produced a different outcome from that of the Exclusion period precisely because these same forces acted differently than they had in 1679–81. Whereas the ideological and historical context of the Exclusion years tended to act as a centrifugal force driving Whigs and Tories apart, in 1688–9 the fear of civil war and profound suspicion of a Catholic monarch forced many Tories to join, however reluctantly, with the Whigs in removing James from the throne.

A third connection between the Exclusion crisis and the Glorious Revolution was one of personalities and pamphlets. While some of the key figures of the Exclusion era were gone from the scene by 1688 – the enigmatic Whig leader Shaftesbury dying a broken man in exile in Holland and accumulated years of hard court living finally separating Charles II from his mortal coil – many of the key actors in the Glorious Revolution were veterans on both sides of the Exclusion battles. Moreover, the great Whig writings of the Exclusion period resurfaced during and after the revolution, with Locke's *Two Treatises* anonymously and Sidney's *Discourses* posthumously seeing the light of day only in the 1690s, and with Tyrrell riding a wave of acclaim originating in the success of *Patriarcha, Non Monarcha* on his way to becoming the "doyen among Whig intellectuals" in the decade after the Glorious Revolution.[1] The most important connection between Exclusion and revolution, however, had to do with the fact that the man targeted for exclusion from the line of succession in 1679–81 was finally removed from the throne in 1689, just four years after he ascended to it. What happened to bring most Whigs and most Tories, bitter opponents in the Exclusion period, into an unlikely union to remove James from the throne? The most obvious explanation for the cause of the revolution is the actions of James himself as king. Whether or not James consciously and in a programmatic manner aimed to subvert the Constitution and establish an absolute monarchy, his actions between 1685 and 1688 succeeded in alarming Whigs and Tories alike, and ultimately produced the alienation of all but his most steadfast supporters. Four main policies and events mark the descent of James' rule into revolution and removal.

First, James' religious policy with its assertive pro-Catholic agenda alienated many of the strongest supporters of the crown among the Anglican clergy and country gentry. The legacy of the Exclusion crisis for the victorious Tories was the intellectual inheritance of Filmerism and the hardening of the commitment to the divine right principles of indefeasible hereditary succession and the doctrine of nonresistance, which reached a peak in the Oxford Decrees of 1683 condemning all resistance to the sovereign as sinful. However, many Tories came to see James' suspension of the Test Acts with the Declaration of Indulgence and the establishment of Ecclesiastical Commissions to enforce his policies on the Church of England as a clear indication of the Catholic monarch's hostility to the established church. James' perceived depredations toward the Anglican Church climaxed with the second Declaration of Indulgence in May 1688 and the arrest and imprisonment of the seven bishops who refused to read the declaration from the pulpit. For the London crowds who cheered the "not guilty" verdict of the bishops, traditional anti-Catholic sentiment and genuine concern about James' harsh

---

[1] Mark Goldie, "The Roots of True Whiggism 1688–94," *History of Political Thought*, vol. 1, no. 2 (Summer 1980): p. 202.

treatment of the venerable church leaders undermined the Tories' ideological commitment to the principle of absolute obedience to the monarch.

Second, James' explicit efforts to maintain a standing army in a time of peace, especially one packed with Irish Catholic officers and troops, evoked vivid cultural memories in Protestant England of the massacres of 1641 and enflamed suspicions that he sought to rule without Parliament. Third, James' policy of altering the charters of local government in the boroughs and placing his own handpicked loyalists in the electorally sensitive offices of sheriff and justice of the peace raised fears among Whigs and Tories alike that James' interference in the electoral process would dangerously undermine the independence of Parliament. The calls for a newly elected "free and legal Parliament" in 1688 largely transcended the ideological differences between Tories and Whigs. The final link in the chain of events dragging the nation toward a major crisis was the birth in June 1688 of a male heir to James. At this point, even Tories who had hoped to bear patiently with James' political excesses and offensive religious policy on the grounds that the aging king's successor would be a staunchly Protestant daughter were now jarred into facing the new reality of a potentially long line of Catholic Stuart monarchs. The rumors of the mysterious circumstances surrounding the birth of the new prince only fed the growing charges that the baby boy was the product of a "suppositious" and darkly suspicious plot to fabricate a Catholic heir when nature and grace would not comply with James' long-term ambitions. To many of James' royalist supporters, the news of the birth of a Catholic heir was the last straw testing their absolute loyalty.

The players in the revolutionary drama were each in their own way motivated by the circumstances created by James' policies from 1685 to 1688. To the Whigs at home demoralized by the failure of Exclusion and the Monmouth debacle, and those like Locke watching events closely from the relative safety of exile in Holland, James' brief reign signified all the fears of the Exclusion period coming to pass. The establishment of popery and arbitrary government was, in their view, the clear trajectory of events during James' rule. Disaffected Tories painfully balanced their commitment to the principles of nonresistance and indefeasible hereditary succession with their alarm at James' obvious hostility to the Church of England and his contempt for Parliament. James' son-in-law William, the prince of Orange, saw the Dutch interest in keeping England among the Protestant powers of Europe, especially with a renewed war with Louis XIV's France on the horizon.[2] William

---

[2] For excellent discussions of the Dutch interest in William's invasion of England, see Jonathan Israel, "William III, the Glorious Revolution, and the Development of Parliamentary Democracy in Britain," in *Foundations of Democracy in the European Union: From the Genesis of Parliamentary Democracy to the European Parliament*, John Pinder, ed. (New York: St. Martin's, 1999): pp. 36–40 and Jonathan Scott, *England's Troubles: Seventeenth-Century English Political Instability in European Context* (Cambridge: Cambridge University Press, 2000): pp. 454–64.

and the Dutch Estates proved quite prepared to advance the Dutch interest, as well as William and Mary's claims to the English throne, through armed intervention. By the time William landed in England in early November 1688 with a small Dutch force, there was a broad bipartisan consensus in the nation at large that new elections for a free and legal Parliament were desperately needed to check James' ambitions and restore the constitutional balance.

Interpreting the Glorious Revolution

The rapidly unfolding series of events in the winter of 1688–9, including James' flight from the country, the request of the Assembly of Lords and Commons for William of Orange to assume temporarily the executive power in order to call the Convention, and the debates of the Convention that ultimately produced the Declaration of Rights and offered the crown to William and Mary are well known and do not need repetition here.[3] What is significant for our purposes is to examine the theoretical principles and issues raised by James' removal from office and the installation of William and Mary.

The Glorious Revolution and the settlement established by the Convention Parliament are often seen as a triumph for the partisans of extreme moderation.[4] While there is a good deal of truth in this assessment of the Convention as a contest won by the Trimmers, it is important to distinguish the practical imperatives toward compromise circa 1689 from the philosophical principles at issue in this period. Four central questions and issues emerged in the Convention debates that would have serious implications for the Whig understanding of the meaning of the Glorious Revolution. The first had to do with the question of James' status after his flight to France. By allowing (even encouraging) James to flee the country, William and the Whigs pointedly avoided any repeat of the regicide of 1649. James would not be allowed to play the role of another Stuart martyr, however unwilling, on the altar of political radicalism. But his flight left unclear how his removal from office was to be understood. Was this a case of deposition, forfeiture, or abdication? Had the nation experienced a Lockean dissolution of

---

[3] For good general treatments of the events leading up to and surrounding the Revolution, see J. R. Jones, *The Revolution of 1688 in England* (New York: Norton, 1973); W. A. Speck, *The Reluctant Revolutionaries: Englishmen and the Revolution of 1688* (Oxford: Oxford University Press, 1988): esp. chs. 4 and 5; and J. R. Western, *Monarchy and Revolution: The English State in the 1680's* (Totowa, NJ: Rowman & Littlefield, 1972): chs. 8–10.

[4] Perhaps the most famous expression of the "compromise" account of the events in 1689 is by Thomas Babbington Macaulay, who identifies the settlement produced by the Convention as the catalyst for the progressive "Whig" interpretation of history (*The History of England from the Accession of James the Second* [London: G. P. Putnam's Sons, 1898]: Vol. I, pp. 1–4 and Vol. IV, pp. 350–2).

government? The Convention adopted the rather implausible interpretation of abdication not only as a concession to Tory sensibilities about legitimacy, but also out of a very genuine concern on the part of most Whigs to avoid the populist and even republican implications of deposition and dissolution so anathema to the Tory ideology of monarchy and obedience.[5] The Tory lawyer Sir Robert Sawyer exploited the moderate Whig dilemma, incisively pointing out that if James' flight caused a dissolution of government, then power should logically devolve to the "people," including "all men under 40s a year" who were not represented in Parliament. Sawyer continued to observe that in the Lockean logic of dissolution the Convention Parliament would have no authority to settle the crown unless all the people were consulted in a process that would open the possibility of radical constitutional revision not only regarding the monarchy, but all three estates.[6] The potential for dramatic political, social, and economic change implicit in the radical idea of dissolution was as shocking to most Whigs as to the Tories. While some of the more radical Whigs at the Convention were prepared to support the idea of deposing James, most were not.

The second major constitutional issue that emerged in the Convention had to do with the notion of contract. The philosophical debate over the contractual character of government was, of course, closely related to the difficult question of James' status. If the king had been deposed or somehow forfeited his right to rule, what legal or moral grounds justified this course of events? One obvious interpretation is that James had violated the contract binding ruler and ruled. The Whig lawyers called to give expert counsel to the House of Commons, including Tyrrell's old friend William Petyt, generally concluded that there was an "original contract" underlying the English Constitution. The date at which this contract originated and its substantive features were, however, subject to widely divergent interpretations. The more radically inclined Whigs at the Convention, such as Sir Robert Howard and John Maynard, advanced the idea that James had been deposed for violating

---

[5] Alternative interpretations include Miller's argument that the idea of abdication was sufficiently ambiguous to allow Tories to interpret it one way and Whigs to interpret it in a more radical direction as a kind of deposition, and Slaughter's suggestion that the verb "to abdicate" was used in a transitive sense at the time and thus can be interpreted to mean that James was deposed for breaking the original contract and fundamental laws (see John Miller, "The Glorious Revolution: 'Contract' and 'Abdication' Reconsidered," *The Historical Journal*, vol. 25, no. 3 [September 1982]: pp. 541–5 and T. P. Slaughter, "'Abdicate' and 'Contract' in the Glorious Revolution," *Historical Journal*, vol. 24 [1981]: 323–37). Frankle argues that William's well-known opposition to a radical interpretation of the removal of James stifled Whig hopes for more serious constitutional reform in 1689 (Robert Frankle, "The Formulation of the Declaration of Rights," *The Historical Journal*, vol. 17, no. 2 [June 1974]: pp. 277–8).

[6] See the discussions of Sawyer in H. T. Dickinson, *Liberty and Property* (London: Weidenfeld and Nicolson, 1977): p. 74; Lois Schwoerer, *The Declaration of Rights, 1689* (Baltimore: Johns Hopkins University Press, 1981): pp. 178–9; and Speck, *Reluctant Revolutionaries*, p. 247.

this original contract. It is important to recognize, however, that even the Whig proponents of contract theory in the Convention were careful to frame the discussion in the moderate Whig philosophical terms of traditional constitutional practice and fundamental laws rather than the radical Whig idea of a general natural right of revolution.[7] The king, they claimed, had violated "ancient" and "undoubted rights." The Declaration of Rights and earlier resolutions made no reference to natural rights. Moreover, the formulation of contract theory in the Convention rested on the Pufendorfian idea of a contract *between* a king and the people, a version of contract theory rejected by the radical Whig Locke.[8] Most Whigs and some Tories were prepared to accept the idea of fundamental laws and monarchical obligations to protect the traditional liberties of the subject, but even then, the final resolution of the House of Commons that tentatively accused James of having "endeavoured to subvert the constitution of the kingdom, by breaking the Original Contract between king and people" did not present these actions as grounds for his rightful deposition, but rather asserted the legal fiction of abdication. Perhaps the final proof that the Convention Whigs did not make radical contract theory the centerpiece of their argument is the fact that all mention of an original contract was expunged from the final version of the Declaration of Rights presented to William and Mary by the Convention.

While the Convention Parliament generally avoided pressing the theoretical issues of deposition and contract that had very clear radical and populist implications, on the two other major issues of the day the Convention was much less cautious. Regarding the issue of succession following James' removal/abdication, Tory efforts to preserve some measure of the principle of indefeasible hereditary right through proposals to install James' Protestant daughter Mary alone as queen, and Nottingham's suggestion to establish William as temporary regent, were defeated by the combined pressure of the Whigs and by William and Mary's determination to establish joint rule. A combination of factors including fear of civil war and concern that a Catholic Stuart might eventually succeed James if his right was not extinguished forced the Tories to accept the installation of William and Mary on

---

[7] J. P. Kenyon, *Revolution Principles: The Politics of Party 1689–1720* (Cambridge: Cambridge University Press, 1977): pp. 7–8. Cf. Dickinson, *Liberty and Property*, p. 74.

[8] Jeffrey Goldsworthy (*The Sovereignty of Parliament: History and Philosophy* [Oxford: Clarendon Press, 1999]: p. 159) and Schwoerer argue that the idea of contract expressed in the first draft of the resolution is analogous to Locke's argument about political power as a form of "trust" (Lois Schwoerer, "Locke, Lockean Ideas, and the Glorious Revolution," *Journal of the History of Ideas*, vol. 51, issue 4 [October–December 1990]: pp. 538–9). For a fuller treatment of Schwoerer's argument for the Convention Parliament's radicalism, see Schwoerer, *The Declaration of Rights*. However, I argue that the idea of contract the Whigs presented at the Convention was more like the Pufendorfian idea of an original pact of subjection, including stipulations about fundamental laws and institutional forms, than the popular sovereignty argument of Locke.

Whig terms. The Whig victory on the issue of James' successor was carried even further in the Bill of Rights that enacted the Declaration of Rights into law, and that proscribed any future Catholic monarch or one married to a Catholic. The one Tory sting in the tail in this matter was the removal of the terms "rightful and lawful" from the prescribed oath of allegiance to the new rulers. Perhaps the clearest victory for the Whig philosophy coming out of the Convention was the explicit affirmations of the rights of Parliament. Seven of the thirteen declaratory statements in the Declaration had to do more or less directly with the central role of Parliament in the legislative process, such as the prohibition on the royal suspending and dispensing power, the affirmation of Parliament's control over revenue, and a statement of the importance of freely and regularly elected Parliaments.[9] The Declaration, then, stood as a vindication of the moderate Whig commitment to parliamentary authority dating back to the Exclusion period. It not only established the principle of making Parliament a more regular and permanent feature of the constitutional order, it also laid the foundation for the idea of parliamentary sovereignty that would come to characterize Whig philosophy in the eighteenth century.[10]

Who, if anyone, actually carried the day at the Convention Parliament? On many issues, Whigs and Tories reached a compromise position keenly attuned to the uncertain political context of the time. However, the marginalization of radical ideas at the Convention and the persisting Tory unease with the settlement after 1689 suggest that the moderate Whigs did more to shape the way the revolution and its settlement would be understood than any other group. The moderate Whig position in the formation of the revolution settlement was not, however, simply a product of practical compromise made to win Tory support. Most Whigs avoided radical Whig arguments for individual natural rights and popular sovereignty because they did not agree with this philosophy.[11] When the Declaration speaks of rights, it typically refers to the powers of the different estates, which formed the mixed government in England. Individual rights are understood primarily in terms

---

[9] See Articles 1, 2, 4, 6, 8, 9, and 13 of the *Declaration of Rights*. Schwoerer (*Declaration of Rights*, pp. 100–1) argues persuasively that the authors of the Declaration were innovating more than they let on. She observes that the bans on the royal dispensing power and ecclesiastical courts were not matters of "ancient" and "undoubted rights," but rather reflect Whig efforts to reform the monarchy on the quiet.

[10] George L. Cherry, "The Role of the Convention Parliament (1688–9) in Parliamentary Supremacy," *Journal of the History of Ideas*, vol. 17, no. 3 (June 1956): pp. 390–406; Goldsworthy, *Sovereignty of Parliament*, pp. 159–64; and Speck, *Reluctant Revolutionaries*, pp. 242–6.

[11] See, for example, Pocock's interesting observation that the term "dissolution" had negative Hobbesian connotations for most Glorious Revolution era Whigs (J. G. A. Pocock, "The Fourth English Civil War: Dissolution, Desertion, and Alternative Histories in the Glorious Revolution," in *The Glorious Revolution: Changing Perspectives*, Lois Schwoerer, ed. [Cambridge: Cambridge University Press, 1992]: p. 60).

of one's place in the balance of hierarchical estates in society.[12] In their defense of legal parliamentary sovereignty composed of the social class–based estates, the moderate Whigs who shaped the revolution settlement operated on the conservative premises of Pufendorf's constitutional and political philosophy.[13] The spirit of 1689 had a distinctively Pufendorfian stamp. Three examples of moderate Whig Pufendorfians are the prominent champions of the revolution and settlement Gilbert Burnet, William Atwood, and the ubiquitous James Tyrrell.

The remarkable career of the Scotsman Gilbert Burnet established him as one of the most important Whig bishops and all-round politicos in the revolution period. Burnet was one of William's closest British advisors and confidantes. His 1688 pamphlet *The Measures of Submission*, which was distributed widely upon William's landing in England, is the closest thing to an official Williamite statement on the revolution. This statement of the philosophical principles justifying resistance to James is saturated with the language and logic of Pufendorfian natural and constitutional jurisprudence. Burnet's aim in this work was to prove that the Filmerian Anglican royalist doctrine of absolute nonresistance had no basis in natural law, Scripture, or the English constitutional tradition. He begins with the proposition that "the Law of Nature has put no difference or subordination among Men."[14] This apparently Lockean or Sidneyan statement of natural liberty is, however, soon revealed to be not a radical but a Pufendorfian conception of natural liberty. For example, Burnet insists that an individual may alienate his liberty entirely by selling "himself to be a slave." The thrust of Burnet's argument

---

[12] Michael Zuckert, *The Natural Rights Republic* (Notre Dame, IN: University of Notre Dame Press, 1996): pp. 100–1. Regarding the one right identified in the British Declaration that resembles an individual natural right, namely, the right to bear arms in Article 13, Schwoerer astutely observes that the restriction of this right to Protestants suggests that it reflects more of a neo-Harringtonian concern to preserve Protestant militias against the threat of a Catholic standing army than an individual natural right (Schwoerer, *Declaration of Rights*, pp. 75–6). For a contrary reading that sees the Declaration of Rights expressing a universal right to bear arms, see Joyce Lee Malcolm "The Right of the People to Keep and Bear Arms: The Common Law Tradition," in *Gun Control and the Constitution*, Robert J. Cottrol, ed. (New York: Garland, 1994): pp. 247–56. For a fuller treatment of the historical development of the right to bear arms in England and America, see Joyce Lee Malcolm, *To Keep and Bear Arms: The Origins of an Anglo-American Right* (Cambridge, MA: Harvard University Press, 1994).

[13] In his own reflections on the Glorious Revolution, Pufendorf expressed great admiration for the results of the revolution and the moderate spirit in which it was carried out. He congratulated the English people on having "executed their rightful duty, under the pressure of necessity, of guarding the safety of the state through which their religion, liberty, life, and property are secured" (quoted in Leonard Krieger, *The Politics of Discretion: Pufendorf and the Acceptance of Natural Law* (Chicago: University of Chicago Press, 1965): pp. 197–8).

[14] Gilbert Burnet, "The Measures of Submission" (1688), in *The Struggle for Sovereignty: Seventeenth Century English Political Tracts*, Joyce Lee Malcolm, ed. (Indianapolis: Liberty Fund Press, 1999): pp. 850, 852.

is the claim that the right of resistance is not universal and unlimited, but rather is determined from "the express Laws of any State."[15] The underlying premise of Burnet's argument is the Pufendorfian dictum that the degree of submission to government is set by the terms of the compact of subjection, not by any reference to an abstract standard of radical natural rights. While Burnet, like most of the Convention Whigs, generally eschewed the authority of the ancient constitution, he did emphasize the point that the fundamental compact underlying the English Constitution established limited monarchy. Burnet argued that the king recognized by his oath constitutional and legal restraints on his power set by Parliament's role in legislation, "determined" limits on prerogative, and a public commitment to protect certain liberties of the subject.[16] Insofar as James' actions subverted the Constitution, Burnet claimed that he undermined the ground of his own authority and ceased to be a lawful ruler. With this argument Burnet foreshadowed the logic of the abdication thesis and presented resistance to James as a form of self-defense, effecting not so much a revolution as a restoration of the traditional Constitution. Moreover, Burnet's essentially conservative reading of the resistance to James presaged the Convention's rejection of the radical idea of dissolution. The corruption and subversion of the Constitution by James would be rectified, in Burnet's view, by the election of a free and legal Parliament, not by the reactivation of the supposed constituent power of the people.

William Atwood's celebrated defense of the revolution settlement in *The Fundamentals of the English Government* (1690) reiterated and in some senses clarified the Pufendorfian premises of the moderate Whig argument in Burnet's pamphlet. The argument of the Whig lawyer Atwood is particularly useful for distinguishing the moderate and radical Whig positions. As a public admirer of Locke and a veteran of the Brady Controversy (marked by his own offering to the dispute *Jus Anglorum ab Antiquo* [1681]), Atwood has been identified as a soulmate of the radical Whigs who sold out to the establishment.[17] While he did praise Locke's account of the origin of government in consent and even made the radical claim that the English monarchy is in some sense elective, Atwood was not simply a timid or politic Lockean.[18] Indeed, in the *Fundamentals* he took the opportunity to reject emphatically the Lockean idea of dissolution. His argument was not that Locke's position was theoretically sound but practically inapplicable because no dissolution of government had occurred in 1688–9. Quite the contrary, Atwood

---

[15] Ibid., p. 853.
[16] Ibid., p. 856.
[17] Mark Goldie, "The Roots of True Whigism 1688–94," *History of Political Thought*, vol. 1, no. 2 (Summer 1980): pp. 203, 225.
[18] Howard Nenner, *The Right to Be King: The Succession to the Crown of England, 1603–1714* (Chapel Hill: University of North Carolina Press, 1995): p. 196.

argued that the notion that Parliament was the organ of continuity to which authority naturally reverted upon the king's abdication/flight was rooted in the Pufendorfian argument that every compact of subjection implicitly includes a provision against dissolution. Atwood pointedly referred to the authority of Pufendorf to counter Locke:

They who once came together in a civil society and subjected themselves to a king;...cannot be presumed to have been so slothful as to be willing to have their civil society extinct upon the death of a king, and to return to their natural state and anarchy, to the hazarding of the safety now settled.[19]

The appearance of Atwood's legalistic defense of the revolution and settlement, then, is somewhat misleading. It actually involves the utilization of the principles of Pufendorfian philosophy not only, or even primarily, to supply a historically based rationale for the Convention, but rather to provide a natural law authorization for Parliament's assumption of the authority to restore the limited monarchy and settle the succession. It was the legal sovereignty of Parliament rooted in contract that gave it the authority to act in an emergency situation to fill a vacancy on the throne, just as, Atwood argues, the king-in-Parliament is the supreme power in the normal course of constitutional operation.[20] Atwood followed Pufendorf in arguing that popular sovereignty was incompatible with his most cherished ideas about sovereignty, the nature of contract, and the character of the English Constitution.

The third and perhaps most influential defense of the Glorious Revolution settlement was James Tyrrell's *Bibliotheca Politica*. This massive volume of thirteen dialogues, first published in separate segments but finally compiled in 1694, stands as a tour de force among the moderate Whig apologies for the revolution.[21] In the series of exchanges between Mr. Meanwell, a Tory, and Mr. Freeman, a Whig, Tyrrell advanced an argument for the essentially moderate and conservative character of the revolution. He reiterated his argument from *Patriacha, Non Monarcha* establishing that the English Constitution must be understood as a limited monarchy. While generally avoiding natural law arguments or the idea of original contract, Tyrrell maintains that the essence of the compact between king and people regulates monarchical authority through Parliament's role in legislation and taxation and

---

[19] William Atwood, *The Fundamentals of the English Government* (London, 1690): 100–1 and Samuel Pufendorf, *De Jure Naturae et Gentium Libri Octo* (Oxford: Clarendon Press, 1934): bk. 7, ch. 7, p. 9 (hereafter DJNG, bk., ch., pages). Cf. Julian Franklin, *John Locke and the Theory of Sovereignty* (Cambridge: Cambridge University Press, 1978): p. 106.

[20] Nenner, *The Right to Be King*, pp. 235–6.

[21] See Kenyon's high praise for *Bibliotheca Politica* (*Revolution Principles*, p. 69). Tyrrell published a fourteenth dialogue to defend the Glorious Revolution against latter-day critics in 1704.

by certain fundamental laws.[22] Tyrrell has Freeman rehearse a long passage from Pufendorf's *De Jure Naturae et Gentium* to the effect that resistance to royal power is justifiable only if the king's actions subvert the Constitution established in the express compact of subjection. Moreover, Tyrrell rejects the Lockean idea of dissolution, arguing instead that the legally established institutions of Parliament are authorized to restore the constitutional order by filling a vacancy on the throne.[23] He is also at pains to dissociate the actions of the Convention from the radical populism in the Lockean or Sidneyan idea of resistance, reminding the reader frequently that the people as such, or the "rabble" and "Vulgar or Mobile," possess no moral right to revolt and do not become the repositories of political power through a dissolution of government. Only the various estates represented in the institutions of government can provide the legal sanction to legitimize resistance.[24] Just as with Burnet and Atwood, Tyrrell's reasoning in *Bibliotheca Politica* is replete with Pufendorfian assumptions about the nature of contract and the limits of obedience. Tyrrell fused a Pufendorfian conception of legal sovereignty in Parliament with a conservative understanding of the fundamentally restorative purpose of resistance to produce a defense and rationale for the Glorious Revolution that not only echoed the arguments of Burnet and Atwood but, perhaps more importantly, struck a deep chord among most English Whigs and gave voice to their most fundamental political instincts and philosophical commitments.

Although moderate Whiggism provided the intellectual nerve running through the revolution and the settlement, radical Whigs and Tories did not go gently into that good constitutional night. They continued to rage, after a fashion, during the crucial days in the winter of 1689 and well afterward. The radicals, while marginalized in the formation of the final product of the Convention Parliament, were not without articulate spokesmen and leaders in the Convention such as Sir Robert Howard, John Wildman, and John Hampden in the Commons and Delamere, Macclesfield, and Wharton in the Lords. Generally speaking, the radicals argued that the Convention should act as a constituent assembly authorized by the people to enact a major constitutional revision. As we have seen, the tenor of the moderate Whigs in the Convention and in the writings of Burnet, Atwood, and Tyrrell was to conceptualize the proceedings of the Convention as an extraordinary, but by no means unprecedented, act of constitutional restoration by the Houses of Parliament to fill a vacancy on the throne and reestablish the Constitution. And while Locke appears to have supported the radicals' view of the populist foundation and ambitious possibilities for the Convention,

---

[22] James Tyrrell, *Bibliotheca Politica* (London, 1718): p. 704 (hereafter BP). Cf. Kenyon, *Revolution Principles*, pp. 35–7.
[23] Tyrrell, BP: 696, 781. Cf. Pufendorf, DJNG 7.7.7, 10.
[24] Tyrrell, BP: 182, 690, 773, 778, 781.

Lockean philosophical principles were typically ignored or rejected by most respectable Whigs at the time.[25] To the extent that radical Whig ideas suffered from the association with republicanism in an England still haunted by the memory of 1649 and deeply hostile to the idea of a republic, it is not surprising that moderate Whiggism would be more appealing to the broad center of the political spectrum in the revolution period. Yet while the radicals may have seen their political program calling for severe restrictions on executive power and harsh penalties on hard core Tories and sympathizers of the Stuarts systematically defeated, a persistent voice of radical Whig dissent to the Williamite Junto Ministry persisted throughout the 1690s. A submerged but nonetheless very real countertradition to moderate Whiggism can be seen in the Lockeanism of Bishop Hoadly, in the arguments by the anonymous author of *Political Aphorisms*, and in William Molyneux's employment of Lockean arguments in his case for self-government in Ireland.[26] In addition, a distinctively Sidneyan opposition Whig tradition based on the necessity of frequent and broadly elected Parliaments, and a hostility to executive power and standing armies, would flower toward the end of the century and, fusing with elements in the Tories, become a central ideological component of the emerging country party.

The central paradox in the radical Whig ideology in Britain in the postrevolution years lay in the fundamental tension between the two most common arguments employed by the radicals. On the one hand, there was the argument that something revolutionary had occurred in 1688–9, namely, the deposition of an aspiring tyrant by a broad-based national uprising. On the other hand, radical Whigs often appealed to the countervailing logic of the argument that the Convention had not been truly revolutionary, or had not seized the opportunity to institute the dramatic constitutional reforms required to establish the English Constitution on a more populist and natural rights foundation. The inability of the radical Whigs in Britain to harmonize fully the rationale underlying their view of the moral and political claims

---

[25] For arguments affirming the irrelevance of Lockean ideas in the revolution, see John Dunn, "The Politics of Locke in England and America," in *John Locke: Problems and Perspectives*, John Yolton, ed. (Cambridge: Cambridge University Press, 1969); M. M. Goldsmith and Richard Ashcraft, "Locke, Revolution Principles, and the Formation of Whig Ideology," *The Historical Journal*, vol. 26, no. 4 (1983): pp. 773–800; Kenyon, *Revolution Principles*, pp. 1–4; and Martyn P. Thompson, "The Reception of Locke's Two Treatises of Government, 1690–1705," *Political Studies*, vol. 24, no. 2 (1976): pp. 184–91. For the argument that Locke's irrelevance in this period is frequently exaggerated, see Schwoerer, "Lockean Ideas," and Zuckert, *Natural Rights*, esp. ch. 10.

[26] The best treatment of the radical or "Real Whig" opposition to the Junto is Goldie, "Roots of True Whiggism." For Hoadly's Lockeanism, see Reed Browning, *Political and Constitutional Ideas of the Court Whigs* (Baton Rouge: Louisiana State University Press, 1982): pp. 81–2 and for the Lockeanism of *Political Aphorisms*, see Zuckert, *Natural Rights*, pp. 289–91, 293. Interestingly, after the public furor produced by it, Locke publicly condemned the radical arguments of his friend William Molyneux's *The Case of Ireland's being Bound by Acts of Parliament in England* (1698).

implicit in the revolution and their dissatisfaction with its settlement made the Glorious Revolution a historical phenomenon they could neither simply repudiate nor wholly embrace.

If radical Whig opposition to the revolution settlement continued only on the margins of English political opinion, the same cannot be said for the Tories. Tory unease with the revolution and its results reflected deep and abiding strains in English public sentiment. The unpopularity of William and his ministries often translated into a more serious disaffection with the revolution itself. While only hard-core Jacobites and clerical nonjurors utterly rejected the revolution, most Tories only reluctantly accommodated to the new political reality after 1689.[27] However, the internal tensions in the logical premises of Tory ideology were as fundamental as those embedded in the position of the radical Whigs. Filmerism persisted as the philosophical bedrock of Tory opposition to the Whigs in church and country until well into the eighteenth century. But the two central premises of Filmerian divine right, the principle of indefeasible hereditary right and the doctrine of nonresistance, were difficult to reconcile with the events and aftermath of the revolution. Tory efforts to rationalize the new political reality, one that many Tories were complicit in creating, were often a painful exercise of soul searching and self-justification. Some Tories tentatively embraced the argument that William could be accepted as a legal conqueror in the Grotian sense, thereby allowing the rigidly scrupulous to transfer their allegiance with few moral qualms. But after an initial flurry of interest, both Tories and Whigs rejected the conquest idea as a rather distasteful way to construe the events of 1688–9.[28] Ultimately, most Tories in the decade after 1689 adopted a quasi-Filmerian stance toward the revolution. They accepted William and Mary as de facto rulers, and thus as the proper objects of obedience, but could not bring themselves to abandon entirely the principle of indefeasible hereditary succession by recognizing them as "rightful and lawful" sovereigns. No doubt the two major underlying motivations in the Tory de facto argument were simply fear of civil war and a deep distrust of a

[27] Dickinson, *Liberty and Property*, ch. 1 and Kenyon, *Revolution Principles*, pp. 3–4 and chs. 5 and 9. Goldsworthy perhaps identifies the Tory acceptance of the idea of parliamentary sovereignty prematurely at 1700–1 with the Act of Settlement debate (*Sovereignty of Parliament*, p. 164). As Holmes demonstrates, many Tories were still wedded to indefeasible hereditary right as late as 1714–15 (Geoffrey Holmes, "Harley, St. John and the Death of the Tory Party," in *Britain after the Glorious Revolution*, Geoffrey Holmes, ed. [New York: St. Martin's, 1969]: pp. 232, 234–5).

[28] See, for example, the negative reaction to Charles Blount's fabulously titled *King William and Queen Mary Conquerors* (1693) in Kenyon, *Revolution Principles*, pp. 31–2. For good treatments of the use of conquest theory as it was employed by leading Tory apologists for the revolution such as Charles Blount, Robert Sherlock, and Edmund Bohun (Blount's licensee), see Mark Goldie, "Edmund Bohun and *Jus Gentium* in the Revolution Debate, 1689–1693," *The Historical Journal*, vol. 20, no. 3 (September 1977): pp. 573–86 and Martyn P. Thompson, "The Idea of Conquest in Controversies Over the 1688 Revolution," *Journal of the History of Ideas*, vol. 38, no. 1 (January–March 1977): pp. 33–46.

return to England by the Catholic James II, of whom most Tories were happy to be unburdened. One particularly interesting strain of reasoning among Anglican royalists after 1689 rested on a version of the Filmerian idea of divine providence. These Tories argued that there was divine sanction for James' removal (but not a popular right of resistance); hence obedience to William and Mary was compatible with the divine ordination of political rule.[29] In this respect, the Tory dilemma after 1689 resembled Filmer's moral anguish in the Engagement controversy of the 1650s, with the added twist that many Tories, unlike Filmer under the Commonwealth, were themselves partly the reluctant accomplices in the creation of this new order. The provisional character of the Tory view of allegiance to the revolution settlement would contribute to the continuing political instability of the country for decades until 1714.

Two major developments in the period spanning the Glorious Revolution and the Hanoverian accession that exposed the important philosophical cleavages in England were the Standing Army controversy of 1697–9 and the trial of Henry Sacheverell in 1710. The context of the Standing Army controversy was the debate over the reduction in the size of William's army following the Peace of Ryswick with the French in 1697.[30] The Tories under the leadership of the former Whig Robert Harley had by this time assumed the role of champions of the landed gentry, who bore the major costs of William's continental wars through the land tax. The Tories and anti-Junto Whigs displayed an unprecedented degree of cooperation in their successful efforts to decrease dramatically the size of the army against strong opposition from William and the Junto ministry. Animating the anti-army forces was the fear that a standing army in peacetime could be used by an unscrupulous court to intimidate Parliament by a show of force and corrupt it through the distribution of patronage. Anti-army pamphleteers such as the old Whig John Trenchard and the Scot Andrew Fletcher made Sidney's argument concerning the inherent danger a standing army in peacetime posed for the delicate constitutional balance in a limited monarchy.[31] The counterargument of the pro-army establishment Whigs such John Somers and Daniel Defoe that Parliament's control over taxation was a

---

[29] Gerald Straka, *The Anglican Reaction to the Revolution of 1688* (Madison: State Historical Society of Wisconsin, 1962): esp. ch. 6.

[30] For a comprehensive treatment of the context of the controversy, see Lois Schwoerer, *No Standing Armies! Anti-army Ideology in Seventeenth Century England* (Baltimore: Johns Hopkins University Press, 1974).

[31] For a fuller treatment of Fletcher and the other anti-army spokesmen, see Hiram Caton, *The Politics of Progress: The Origins and Development of the Commercial Republic, 1600–1835* (Gainesville: University of Florida Press, 1988): pp. 301–4; J. G. A. Pocock, *Virtue, Commerce and History* (Cambridge: Cambridge University Press, 1986): pp. 235–9; Paul Rahe, *Republics Ancient and Modern: Classical Republicanism and the American Revolution* (Chapel Hill: University of North Carolina Press, 1992): pp. 341–4; and Schwoerer, *No Standing Armies*, pp. 180–1.

sufficient safeguard to the constitutional order did not carry the day, and by 1699 William's army was seriously reduced in size and his beloved Dutch Guards were sent packing.

The significance of the Standing Army controversy was threefold. First, it generated a degree of partisan mobilization not seen in England since the days of the Exclusion crisis. Former Whigs Paul Foley and Robert Harley (the future earl of Oxford) cobbled together a disparate coalition of groups in opposition to William that included new Whigs like themselves, as well as Tories and radical old Whigs disaffected by the Junto. On the other side, William's supporters, including Montague (later the earl of Halifax), Somers, and John Churchill (soon to be duke of Marlborough) pursued a vigorous campaign on their leader's behalf. Harley's anti-army parliamentary opposition showed remarkable political skills and organizational abilities that proved to be infectious, as diverse groups of kindred spirits began meeting regularly in political clubs in coffee houses all over the capital such as the famous Grecian Coffee House.[32] In many respects, Harley's success in resisting the crown and the ruling Whigs in the Standing Army controversy foreshadowed his even bolder and unsuccessful attempt to impeach Somers a few years later. The Standing Army controversy not only produced the nucleus for the party machinery that would emerge in postrevolution Britain, it also adumbrated the ideological cleavages already forming around the interpretation of the meaning of revolution. Harley's new Whigs and Tories feared the idea of a large standing army in time of peace principally because of the implications they saw in it for constitutional balance and the dangerous expansion of royal prerogative. The issue for Harley and the Tories, as it would be later for the country opposition, had much more to do with preserving their conception of the institutional design of the Constitution than with William's foreign policy.[33] For their part, radical Whigs during the Standing Army controversy such as John Trenchard and Walter Moyle not only feared that prerogative endangered the power of the Commons, they also worried that a standing army would effectively nullify the natural right of revolution so central to radical Whig philosophy.[34] As would be the case with the country party of Bolingbroke in years to come, the anti-army coalition held together, however loosely, partisans of often widely divergent political persuasions.

In addition to the practical partisan dimensions of the debate, another important element in the Standing Army controversy was its impetus to a rebirth of interest in republican and radical Whig thought among a certain

---

[32] Schwoerer, *No Standing Armies*, p. 161.
[33] Ibid., p. 162. As Linda Colley observes, England successfully prosecuted a very large and very expensive continental war during the period of Tory strength in the Commons in the early 1700s (Linda Colley, *In Defiance of Oligarchy; The Tory Party, 1714–1760* [Cambridge: Cambridge University Press, 1982]: p. 16).
[34] Schwoerer, *No Standing Armies*, pp. 180–1.

segment of Whigs. The radical John Toland republished works about and by the commonwealthmen Ludlow, Milton, and Marvell, as well as publishing the first full edition of Sidney's *Discourses* in 1698.[35] Thus, the legacy of the Standing Army controversy was complex. It not only had great symbolism for the emerging country ideology as an example of a parliamentary bloc successfully defying the court and ministry. It also sparked a new interest in radical literature that would leave its mark on the coming years. With respect to both of these legacies, the Standing Army controversy brought the adequacy of the postrevolution settlement into question.

The impeachment trial of Henry Sacheverell a decade after the Standing Army controversy forced to the forefront once again crucial constitutional issues and heated speculation about the nature and meaning of the Glorious Revolution. The immediate context of the trial was the angry reaction of the Whig government to a controversial sermon by the outspoken high Anglican clergyman Henry Sacheverell at St. Paul's Cathedral on November 5, 1709, in which he castigated the revolution on the Filmerian grounds of the immorality of the resistance to James II and thereby challenged the legitimacy of the entire revolution settlement. Whig leaders in the government determined that this brazen attack casting "black and odious colours" on the revolution in the capital and on the anniversary of William's landing at Torbay could not go unchallenged and unpunished.[36] The quandary for the Whig establishment, however, was that in defending the resistance to James, they ran the risk of legitimizing more radical principles than they deemed consistent with the revolution. What followed in the impeachment trial in early 1710 was a classic statement of the moderate Whig conservative interpretation of the revolution. The Whig trial managers took the opportunity to clarify definitively the Whig position on the events of 1688–9. They largely eschewed the language and logic of radical contract theory and scrupulously avoided the argument that James had been deposed for violating the original contract. The Whigs cautiously affirmed the right of resistance narrowly construed in Pufendorfian terms as an emergency measure taken out of dire necessity to restore, rather than radically revise, the constitutional order.[37] A young Robert Walpole, one of the trial managers and a rising star in the Whig establishment, expressed the deep ambiguity felt by many Whigs

---

[35] Ibid., p. 174–6. Cf. J. G. A. Pocock, *The Machiavellian Moment: Florentine Political Thought and the Atlantic Republican Tradition* (Princeton: Princeton University Press, 1975): pp. 427–46 and Blair Worden, *Roundhead Reputations: The English Civil Wars and the Passions of Posterity* (London: Penguin Press, 2001): pp. 131–3.

[36] The general consensus appears to be that Sacheverell was intentionally provocative in his sermon (e.g., Reed Browning, *Political and Constitutional Ideas of the Court Whigs* [Baton Rouge: Louisiana State University Press, 1982]: p. 15; Kenyon, *Revolution Principles*, p. 131; and J. H. Plumb, *Sir Robert Walpole: The Making of a Statesman* [Boston: Houghton Mifflin, 1956]: pp. 146–7).

[37] Dickinson, *Liberty and Property*, pp. 76–7 and Kenyon, *Revolution Principles*, pp. 134–6.

toward the principle of resistance, arguing that while "resistance is nowhere enacted to be legal but to be subjected by all laws now in being to the greatest penalties; [it] ought never to be thought of but when an utter subversion of the realm threaten the whole frame of the constitution and no redress can otherwise be hoped for."[38] Walpole's commonsense recognition of the legitimacy of resistance in extraordinary circumstances and his defense of principled moderation stand firmly in the moderate Whig tradition voiced by Burnet, Atwood, and Tyrrell.

Although Sacheverell was narrowly convicted by the Lords, the whole affair was a public relations disaster for the Whigs. Sacheverell's conciliatory posture in the trial and the popular outrage at the perceived vindictiveness in the Whig government's handling of the affair culminated in two nights of rioting in London. The fact that the Lords reduced Sacheverell's punishment to a merely symbolic gesture also contributed to a loss of face for the Whigs. In the elections of 1710 they suffered a crushing defeat at the hands of the Tories. Despite the tactical miscalculation in their dealings with Sacheverell, the moderate Whigs did achieve the more strategic aim of setting forth a rigorous and comprehensive interpretation of the revolution that would in time dominate the English political landscape.

The accession of George I and the installation of the Hanoverian line after Anne's death in 1714 marked a sea change in English political history. The solid Whig support for the Hanoverians and the Protestant succession ushered in a period of Whig hegemony that defined the political system for most of the eighteenth century. The Tory renaissance in the closing years of Anne's reign after 1710, already endangered by their palpable hesitation about the transfer of the crown to the Hanoverians, absolutely collapsed with the repercussions of the abortive Jacobite rising in 1715. The public's and the crown's association of Toryism with Jacobitism diminished the Tories as a political force throughout Bolingbroke's ascendancy as leader during the long Walpole administration. With the evisceration of Tory political power, the early period of the Whig establishment after 1714 witnessed a renewed battle within Whiggism between its ruling moderate bloc and its radical fringe. The long-simmering tension between these two elements of Whiggism was exacerbated by the passage of the Septennial Act in 1716, in which a solidly Whig Parliament annulled the Triennial Act increasing its own life from three to seven years. The growing tension between moderate Whig ideas about parliamentary sovereignty and the more radical ideas of contract and popular representation of the Whig opposition motivated much of this internal Whig conflict. The first radical Whig champion to lay a glove on

---

[38] Quoted in Plumb, *Walpole*, p. 149. In contrast to Caton, I argue that the philosophical principles underlying the Whig idea of contract and resistance presented at the trial is based on the more conservative conception associated with Pufendorf than that of Locke or Sidney. For a Lockean reading of the Sacheverell Whigs, see Caton, *Politics of Progress*, pp. 267–9.

Britain's ruling Whigs, the complacent children of the spirit of 1689, was *Cato's Letters.*

Cato's Letters

Cato's Letters were a series of 138 short essays published by John Trenchard and Thomas Gordon under the pseudonym Cato between November 1720 and July 1723. The partnership between Trenchard, the radical veteran of the Standing Army controversy, and Gordon, a somewhat mysterious young Scotsman, began as a scathing criticism of the public officials and company directors involved in the financial scandal known as the South Sea Bubble. The South Sea Company originally established by Harley's Tory government in 1711 proposed eight years later to assume most of the national debt in exchange for monopoly trading privileges and a handsome rate of interest. In the fever of speculation and the precipitous crash that followed, many fortunes were ruined and the Sunderland government was rocked.[39] In the investigations that followed Walpole's rise to power and his plan to restore the system of national credit, several members of the former government and influential courtiers were implicated in a vast bribery and corruption scandal. While the *Letters* began as an impassioned appeal to punish severely the government officials and company directors involved in the scandal, they grew into a sustained campaign calling for new elections and ultimately into a collection of general reflections on the character and importance of political, civil, and religious liberty and the meaning of the Glorious Revolution. Trenchard and Gordon used these letters to redefine the legacy of the revolution in a more radical direction than the moderate Whig trial managers in the Sacheverell affair. *Cato's Letters* represent an effort to rehabilitate radical Whig theory in England – in effect, to reclaim the Whig mantle for the radicals so as to firm up resistance to court corruption, reexamine the idea of constitutional balance, and restore the notion of the importance of freely and regularly elected Parliaments.

Cato's Letters hold an important place in the radical Whig tradition for a number of reasons. First, they signify a seminal instance in the development of opposition Whig thought, whereby the establishment moderate Whigs were attacked, as it were, from the left by a radical Whig opposition. In the *Letters* we see an early instance of the events and theoretical implications of the Glorious Revolution interpreted through a radical Whig lens. Trenchard and Gordon offered a provocative counterargument to the prevailing

[39] For good discussions of the events surrounding the South Sea scandal, see Browning, *Court Whigs*, pp. 19–20; Caton, *Politics of Progress*, pp. 275–80; Ronald Hamowy, "Cato's Letters, John Locke, and the Republican Paradigm," *History of Political Thought*, vol. xi, no. 2 (Summer 1990): pp. 279–81; Jerome Huyler, *Locke in America* (Lawrence: University Press of Kansas, 1995): pp. 213–15; and Plumb, *Walpole*, pp. 293–328.

Pufendorfianism of England's ruling Whigs and their sense of the spirit of 1689. Second, the *Letters* were enormously popular in the American colonies, being published, republished, and widely distributed in every major colonial center.[40] Indeed, Cato gained much greater currency as an authority in America than in England. Third, in recent times, *Cato's Letters* have been keenly examined with respect to their role and place in the heated liberal versus republican revisionist debate.[41] The *Letters* have been claimed by both schools as support for their general positions.

I suggest that the fundamental significance of *Cato's Letters* is their position as a unique example of the attempt to combine the distinct strains of radical Whig constitutional and rights theory. The undeniable presence of both liberal and republican themes in the *Letters* suggests that radical Whig thought resists the dichotomy advanced by scholars today. What makes the *Letters* so interesting is this attempt to synthesize the distinct elements of radical Whiggism.[42] It is not difficult to detect the liberal and republican elements in them. Frankly, *Cato's Letters* often plagiarized important discussions in Locke (a not uncommon practice in the period) and devoted two entire letters to a verbatim and candidly attributed use of extended passages from Sidney's *Discourses*. So the question for us is not whether *Cato's Letters* drew

[40] For statements of Cato's influence in America, see Bernard Bailyn, *The Ideological Origins of the American Revolution* (Cambridge, MA: Harvard University Press, 1967): pp. 35–7, 44, 53; Colin Bonwick, "The United States Constitution and Its Roots in British Political Thought and Tradition," in *Foundations of Democracy in the European Union: From the Genesis of Parliamentary Democracy to the European Parliament*, John Pinder, ed. (New York: St. Martin's, 1999): pp. 45–6; Ronald Hamowy, "Cato's Letters, John Locke, and the Republican Paradigm," *History of Political Thought*, vol. xi, no. 2 (Summer 1990): p. 278; Forrest McDonald, *Novus Ordo Seclorum* (Lawrence: University Press of Kansas, 1985): pp. 47, 70, 77, 89, 93; and Gordon Wood, *The Creation of the American Republic: 1776–1787* (Chapel Hill: University of North Carolina Press, 1969): pp. 14–16. For views to the contrary, which suggest that Cato's influence in America has been exaggerated, see Steven Dworetz, *The Unvarnished Doctrine: Locke, Liberalism, and the American Revolution* (Durham: Duke University Press, 1990): p. 44 and Donald S. Lutz, "The Relative Influence of European Writers on Late-Eighteenth Century American Political Thought," *American Political Science Review*, vol. 78 (March 1984): p. 193.

[41] For Cato as an important part of the republican synthesis, see Bailyn, *Ideological Origins*, pp. 34–5; Pocock, *Machiavellian Moment*, pp. 468, 507; Caroline Robbins, *The Eighteenth Century Commonwealthmen* (New York: Atheneum, 1968): pp. 115–25; and Robert Shalhope, "Towards a Republican Synthesis," *William and Mary Quarterly*, vol. 29 (January 1972): p. 58. For Cato as fundamentally a Lockean liberal, see Shelley Burtt, *Virtue Transformed: Political Argument in England, 1688–1740* (Cambridge: Cambridge University Press, 1992), p. 81; Dworetz, *Unvarnished Doctrine*, pp. 85, 89; Hamowy, "Republican Paradigm," pp. 281–4, and 293; Jerome Huyler, *Locke in America* (Lawrence: University Press of Kansas, 1995): pp. 225–6; Rahe, *Republics*, p. 532; and Zuckert, *Natural Rights*, pp. 300–2.

[42] Others who have identified this synthezing character in Cato include Lance Banning, *The Jeffersonian Persuasion* (Ithaca: Cornell University Press, 1978): p. 55; Huyler, *Locke in America*, p. 224; and Zuckert, *Natural Rights*, p. 299.

on these radical Whig sources – Trenchard and Gordon emphatically did –
but rather why and how the authors employed these theoretical resources in
their dispute with England's ruling moderate Whig establishment.

The Lockean features of Cato's argument related primarily to the philosophical foundation of natural rights. For Cato, the source and purpose of
government must be understood in Lockean terms. Government originates
in the consent of free and equal individuals, and its proper end is the security of individual liberty and rights. The *Letters* present a distinctly Lockean
conception of the centrality of property for understanding rights, as well as
an emphatic endorsement of the principle of dissolution. The Sidneyan elements in the *Letters* are equally prominent. Cato shares Sidney's republican
sympathies and presents a theory of sovereignty stressing the need to reflect
the interests of the people as much as possible through such institutional
devices as regular Parliaments, rotation of delegates, and more equal and
numerous representation. In addition to a strong statement of a Lockean
conception of individual liberty, Cato presents a more Sidneyan ideal of political liberty emphasizing the importance of the public share in government
and reinterpreting the classical notion of republican virtue as the spirited
defense of rights. The *Letters'* fusion of Locke and Sidney produced a radical
defense of liberty, which went beyond merely criticizing the informal technique of royal "influence" and corruption, extending to a serious criticism of
the British Constitution itself as it was understood by the majority of English
Whigs.

Cato's Liberalism

A little over a year into the serial publication of the *Letters*, the authors
temporarily suspended their treatment of the specific issues surrounding the
South Sea scandal and its implications for British constitutional practice in
order to devote a series of ten letters to the general topic "the advantages of
liberty." Cato begins this discussion with a treatment of the philosophical
foundations of natural rights. Cato's natural rights are emphatically Lockean
in form and substance. Echoing Locke, Cato asserts:

All men are born free; liberty is a gift which they receive from God himself; nor can
they alienate the same by consent, though possibly they may forfeit it by crimes.
No man has power over his own life, or to dispose of his own religion; and cannot
transfer the power of either to anybody else.[43]

Thus, Cato premises the discussion of the advantages of liberty with a strong
endorsement of natural rights. In typical radical Whig fashion, Cato emphatically denies the Grotian or Pufendorfian version of natural liberty, which

---

[43] John Trenchard and Thomas Gordon, *Cato's Letters*, Ronald Hamowy, ed. (Indianapolis:
Liberty Classics, 1995): Letter 59, pp. 406–7 (hereafter letter and page number).

allows the possibility of an individual's freely contracting away or alienating his or her liberty. Actually, Cato states boldly what is left largely implicit in Locke or Sidney when he asserts: "liberty is the unalienable right of all mankind."[44] To the Grotian idea of absolute contract, Cato replies that even if an individual were to make such a contract, "he is relievable by the eternal laws of God and reason." In addition to denying the moral validity of absolute contract, Cato makes the characteristically Lockean connection between natural rights and natural law, deriving the latter from the former: the "first law of nature, that of self-preservation."[45] Cato thus begins his treatment of liberty on solid Lockean ground.

Cato's understanding of the origin and end of government is also infused with the concepts of Lockean natural jurisprudence. He asserts that government is rooted in consent and that the powers of government derive from the natural executive power of individuals. In Letter 60 Cato states: "Government...can have no power, but such as men give, and such as they actually did give, or permit for their own sakes: Nor can any government be in fact framed but by consent." The principle of consent, Cato concludes, excludes the possibility of establishing legitimate rule on the basis of conquest, heredity, or prescription.[46] Moreover, Cato also proclaims his support for Locke's "strange doctrine" of the natural executive power: "The right of the magistrate arises only from the right of private men to defend themselves, to repel injuries, and to punish those who commit them." By affirming this natural punishing power, Cato exemplifies the radical Whig departure from the older Christian-Aristotelian assumptions of scholastic and Calvinist consent theory and commits to the core Lockean liberal premises of the conventionality of political society and the fiduciary character of political power. He states: "What is government but a trust committed by all, or the most, to one, or a few, who are to attend upon the interests of all, that everyone may, with the more security, attend upon his own."[47] From this premise, Cato draws the Lockean conclusion that the scope and range of political power are inherently limited by its source, namely, "the measure of power, which men in the state of nature have over themselves and one another."[48]

[44] Ibid., p. 405. Cf. Simmons, who points out that Locke generally eschews the language of inalienability of rights, which has become so familiar to us as a central premise of the Declaration of Independence (see John Simmons, "Inalienable Rights and Locke's *Treatises*," *Philosophy and Public Affairs*, vol. 12 [1983]: pp. 176, 185–6, 192). Simmons' observation leaves us with the interesting possibility that Jefferson may have drawn the language of inalienability from Cato.

[45] Letter 60, p. 415; 33, p. 239.

[46] Letter 60, pp. 413–14; 59, p. 406.

[47] Letter 59, p. 407 (cf. 11, p. 87); 38, p. 267.

[48] Letter 60, p. 414.

For Cato, the ends and limits of political power are known by reference to the state of nature. This recourse to the state of nature in an explicit way further demonstrates the underlying Lockeanism of Cato's position. Sidney, we recall, did not advance a clearly articulated state of nature theory largely because he did not locate the primary unit of political analysis in the natural power of the individual, but rather in the collected power of individuals characterizing the natural democracy. Cato follows Locke by arguing that individuals form government and leave the state of nature because of "the distrust that men have of men," which produces in a state of "boundless liberty" perpetual "interfering and quarreling." In this natural condition, Cato affirms, individual rights are not secure: "everyman would be plundering the acquisitions of another." To get out of this state, individuals create a "mutual compact" agreeing on certain terms of society; thus, Cato claims, men "quitted part of their natural liberty to acquire civil security." Given the purpose for individuals quitting the state of nature, namely, the insecurity of their property and preservation, Cato determines that the sole end of government is "the mutual protection and defense" of individual rights.[49]

Cato's discussion of the "inconveniences" of the state of nature parallels Locke's emphasis on and concern for the natural right of property. Four of the ten letters Cato assigns to discussing the advantages of liberty deal largely or exclusively with issues relating to property.[50] One of the primary purposes for which individuals enter civil society, according to Cato, is to secure their property. Indeed, Cato practically equates the natural right of life and liberty to the natural property right: "Nor has any man in the state of nature power over his own life, or to take away the life of another, unless to defend his own, or what is as much his own, namely, his property."[51] By interjecting the issue of property into his discussion of the natural self-defense right (a classic Lockean move), Cato strongly suggests the profound connection between property rights and a more comprehensive notion of human liberty. Moreover, Cato derives the property right not from a Tyrrellian or Pufendorfian moderate Whig notion of occupancy, but rather directly from the Lockean principle of labor: "Nor could any man in the state of nature, have a right to violate the property of another; that is, what another had acquired by his art or labour."[52] In contrast to the moderate Whig view, which gave compact

---

[49] Letter 33, p. 236; 11, p. 87 (cf. 62, p. 429).

[50] Letters 62, 64, 67, 68. For Cato's Lockean view of property, see Dworetz, *Unvarnished Doctrine*, pp. 85, 89; Hamowy, "Republican Paradigm," pp. 281–4; and Zuckert, *Natural Rights*, pp. 300–2. I do not agree with Dworetz's claim that Cato's Lockeanism does not extend to the issue of consent and representation (p. 89). While Cato may say little about these issues in Letter 97 (the letter that Dworetz focuses on to draw Cato's connection to Locke), he has a great deal to say about these issues in Letters 59–61, and much of what he says is distinctively Lockean.

[51] Letter 60, p. 414.

[52] Ibid., p. 415.

considerable normative status in the determination of property rights, Cato shares Locke's emphasis on the naturalness of this right and its centrality to the very source and end of government.

It is in this discussion of property that Cato really earns his libertarian credentials. One way Cato defines liberty is the individual's control over his or her own actions and goods. Cato's presentation of this individualist view of liberty is saturated with references to the importance of private property:

> By liberty, I understand the power which every man has over his own actions, and his right to enjoy the fruit of his labour, art, and industry, as far as by it he hurts not the society, or any members of it, by taking from any members, or by hindering him from enjoying what he himself enjoys. The fruit of a man's honest industry are the just rewards of it, ascertained to him by natural and eternal equity, as is his title to use them in the manner which he thinks fit: And thus, everyman is sole lord and arbiter of his own private actions and property.[53]

A clearer statement of Lockean liberal economic individualism would be hard to imagine. Limited government is by its very nature one that protects individuals in the free enjoyment of their property. According to Cato, government exists merely to protect the private sphere, not to direct or manage it: "Let people alone, and they will take care of themselves, and do it best . . . to think what he will, and act as he thinks . . . to spend his money himself, and lay out the produce of his labour his own way; and to labour for his own pleasure and profit."[54] With this undeniable emphasis on private property and the close connection between civil, political, and economic liberty, Cato shows his true Lockean colors.

Perhaps the most striking Lockean feature in the *Letters* is its treatment of the dissolution of government. This discussion is telling inasmuch as Cato provides an account of the people's natural constitutive power, which is taken practically verbatim from Locke's *Second Treatise*. Cato demonstrates a commitment to one of the central tenets of Lockean constitutionalism, and a principle that was vociferously opposed by Trenchard and Gordon's moderate Whig opponents. Cato's discussion of the logic of resistance underlying dissolution is, however, ambiguous inasmuch as he does not advocate revolutionary action in the Britain of the 1720s. While the alleged corruption of the Walpole government was certainly vexing to Cato and his radical Whig readers, the broader constitutional context of the period does not have the seriousness of the heated, indeed overcharged, atmosphere of the Exclusion era. Locke and Sidney were willing to, and in a sense did, topple a reigning monarch, but Cato offers no such prescriptions for England's constitutional problems. The *Letters* represent the transformation of radical Whig thought in England from a revolutionary to a reformist or opposition stance. Though

---

[53] Letter 62, p. 427.
[54] Ibid., pp. 428–9.

Trenchard and Gordon were on the fringes of respectable opinion in their time, they can still be identified, in contrast to the hard-core Jacobites, as the loyal opposition.

Cato begins his treatment of the right of resistance with the perennial question "Who shall judge whether the magistrate acts justly, and pursues his trust?" He claims that neither the magistrate nor the aggrieved party is the proper judge. The former would produce tyranny, and the latter would place an authority above the sovereign authority. With this argument, Cato signifies his departure from the parliamentary resistance theory of the civil war era exemplified by Hunton and Parker, which gave the houses of Parliament the right to judge the crown, ostensibly a coequal element in the Constitution. Facing the prospect that no constituted body can settle the matter, Cato takes the familiar Lockean turn:

If neither magistrates, nor they who complain of magistrates, and are aggrieved by them, have a right to determine decisively... then everyman interested in the success of the contest, must act according to the light and dictates of his own conscience, and inform it as well as he can.[55]

The right of resistance, Cato maintains, is a natural right lodged in the conscience of every individual composing society. In language practically plagiarized from Locke, Cato contends: "Where no judge is nor can be appointed, every man must be his own; that is, where there is no stated judge upon the earth, we must have recourse to heaven."[56] By referring to the right of resistance as an extra- or transconstitutional right, an appeal beyond the authority of institutions to the ultimate authority of arms, Cato posits the radical Whig theory of resistance, which so disgusted and alarmed the moderate Whigs who practically framed the Glorious Revolution settlement.

The logical corollary of Cato's theory of resistance is, of course, the Lockean principle of dissolution. Cato argues that individuals surrender only part of their natural liberty to form society; thus, when government becomes injurious to securing life and property, "the individuals must return to their former state again" inasmuch as "no constitution can provide against what will happen, when that constitution is dissolved."[57] The contention that no constitution is a guarantee against dissolution was precisely contrary to what Pufendorfian Whigs like Tyrrell and Atwood maintained did occur in the event of a constitutional crisis. Cato denies the Pufendorfian proposition that all social compacts provide for the continuous and legal transfer of power in all cases. For Cato, as for Locke, when the trust between ruler and ruled is broken, the "power must return of course to those who gave

[55] Letter 59, p. 407.
[56] Ibid., p. 407–8 (cf. Locke, II:168, II:240–3).
[57] Ibid., p. 411 (see also p. 408 for Cato's example of republican Rome as an illustration of a constitutional dissolution). Notice that Cato appears to make the same logical leap from dissolution directly to the state of nature, which moderate Whig critics usually made.

it." Cato is careful, as was Locke, to demonstrate that dissolution theory is not an anarchic principle introducing instability into every and any government whatsoever. In language again almost identical to Locke's "long train of abuses" argument, Cato claims:

Obedience to authority is so well secured, that it is wild to imagine, that any number of men, formidable enough to disturb a settled state, can unite together and hope to overturn it, till the publick grievances are so enormous, the oppression so great, and dissatisfaction so universal, that there can be no question remaining, whether their calamities be real or imagined, and whether the magistrate has protected or endeavored to destroy the people.[58]

While Cato's calming assurance that people never (or almost never) revolt for light and transient causes may have been designed to massage the sense of propriety and love of order in his English audience, the more radical implications of his argument are unmistakable for his treatment of England's recent constitutional past. Despite the official moderate Whig portrayal of the Glorious Revolution as the very model of continuity and peaceful political change, Cato strongly implies that it did signify the dissolution of government. He repeatedly refers to James II as a "tyrant," implicitly doing what the Declaration of Rights pointedly avoided doing, namely, identifying James' tyrannical or abusive actions as the cause of his deposition.[59] In one of the last letters in the series, Cato strongly suggests the incoherence of the legal fiction of James' "abdication" and challenges his fellow countrymen to deny that "you yourselves did not help to expel him."[60] While Cato asserts the obviousness of the revolutionary character of 1688–9, it is nonetheless apparent that Trenchard and Gordon understood these events in much more radical terms than did the moderate Whig majority in the country at large. We are, in effect, left to consider whether Cato believed that the radical principles underlying the Glorious Revolution should result in a more popular form of government than the resulting restored mixed and balanced constitutional settlement of 1689.

Cato's Republicanism

We have seen that *Cato's Letters*, a central text in the republican revision's non-Lockean Whig canon, is deeply penetrated by Lockean ideas. This is not to deny, however, the strong republican elements in the *Letters*. Whereas Locke provided the theoretical foundation for Cato's ideas on natural rights and consent, Sidney's influence came to the fore in his treatment of the structure of government and the political implications of popular sovereignty.

---

[58] Ibid., pp. 412–13 (cf. Locke II:223, II:225).
[59] Letters 80, 94, 128 (cf. Dickinson, *Liberty and Property*, p. 175).
[60] Letter 132, p. 918.

Cato, if not an open advocate of abolishing the monarchy (a position unpalatable to even most opposition radical Whigs), nonetheless shares strong
republican sympathies with Sidney. In his treatment of the separation of powers, Cato echoes Sidney's argument that the popular element must anchor any
legitimate form of government. Moreover, Cato follows Sidney's dictum that
the interests of the governors must be united to those of the governed through
several institutional devices such as regular elections, rotation of delegates,
and numerous representation meant to guarantee popular sovereignty in a
constitutional order. In fundamental respects, Cato drew more emphatically
populist implications from Lockean natural rights theory than Locke did
himself.

Cato's reflections on constitutionalism appear at least very much as a
tribute to the Settlement of 1689, "our late happy Revolution." Cato confirms his heartfelt support for the major principles of that revolution, which
centered on the ideas of mixed government and parliamentary sovereignty.
The virtue of England's mixed government, according to Cato, is its proven
capacity to place legal restraints and checks on public power. In a moving
passage Cato states:

Power is naturally active, vigilant, and distrustful: which qualities in it push it upon
all means and expedients to fortify itself, and upon destroying all opposition.... It
would do what it pleases, and have no check. Now, because liberty chas-
tises and shortens power, therefore power would extinguish liberty, and consequently liberty has too much cause to be exceeding jealous, and always upon her
defense.[61]

This natural antithesis of power and liberty ensures that any government that
can plausibly be said to protect liberty must be one in which public power is
checked and restrained by law. England's mixed and balanced Constitution,
according to Cato, may be said to fulfill the criteria of free government because the different parts of the Constitution can legitimately check the power
of the others. Herein lies Cato's deep concern for the corrupting effect of royal
"influence." This element of Trenchard and Gordon's argument against executive corruption is perfectly compatible with the country party ideology.
When the crown employs patronage and bribery to acquire illegal or un-
constitutional control over the members of Parliament, the monarch is thus,
in effect, subverting the mixed and limited character of the Constitution. In
Cato's view, the dangerous consequences of official corruption should not
be underestimated. Political corruption, for Cato, is not understood in terms
of a personal failing or dismissed as a regrettable, but inevitable, demonstration of human frailty among public officials. Rather, political corruption in
England is a problem that strikes at the heart of the Constitution.

[61] Letter 33, p. 239.

The major difference between free and unfree governments is, according to Cato, that in the former "there are checks and restraints appointed and expressed in the constitution itself." In free governments, the limits on power are established by law and institutional checks rather than the personal discretion of a ruler or ruling body. Cato's analysis goes beyond an assessment of the unreliability of a ruler's good intentions, however; he argues in language foreshadowing Madison in *Federalist* 51 that free peoples constitute government and delegate power cognizant of the fact that private interests may be turned to public good. In Letter 60 Cato claims:

The power and sovereignty of magistrates in free countries was so qualified, and so divided into different channels, and committed to the direction of so many different men, with different interests and views, that the majority of them could seldom or never find their account in betraying their trust in fundamental instances. Their emulation, envy, fear, or interest, always made them spies and checks upon one another.[62]

It is this salutary and finely calibrated institutional distrust and rivalry that Cato believes is threatened by royal "influence." His solution to the problem of political corruption is the typically republican remedy of strengthening the popular element in the mixed government.

Cato sees strengthening and revivifying the Commons as the way to preserve England's constitutional balance. He expresses this goal in terms strikingly similar to those of Sidney, emphasizing the need to counter political corruption by returning to the "first principles" of the "original constitution."[63] Implicit in Cato's reasoning is the modern republican claim advanced by Sidney and Spinoza for the naturalness of democracy. To argue that the first principles of a mixed constitution are emphatically popular is essentially to propose the conclusion that moderate Whigs generally sought to avoid or at least mute, namely, that all the elements of the British Constitution, including the hereditary Lords and the crown, derive from this popular foundation. Cato urges for new elections ostensibly to replace the corrupt ministry in power that officiated over the South Sea scandal. His more fundamental and subtle intention, however, is to reveal and revitalize the popular foundations of the British government. In his appeal to the electors of Britain, Cato calls them, and pointedly not their representatives, "the first spring that gives life" to the government. This is not to suggest that Cato does not believe that the representative element in the British mixed government is the key to liberty – he emphatically does – but rather to observe that the people understood as *electors* are in Cato's view "the Alpha and Omega" of any and all legitimate government.[64] The renewal of popular consent expressed through

---

[62] Letter 60, p. 417. Cf. James Madison, *Federalist Papers* (New York: Mentor, 1961): #51, p. 322.
[63] Letter 69, p. 497 (cf. Sidney D 3.25.462).
[64] Letter 69, pp. 499, 503.

elections in the near future would, Cato hopes, remind parliamentarians that their positions and future security depend not on the favors of the crown or the ministry, but on the will of the people.

Thus, from Cato's reflections on the British Constitution, it appears that the fundamental problem of mixed and balanced constitutionalism, the subversion of the power of the Commons, can be remedied by measures perfectly in keeping with resources made available by the Constitution itself. If Cato can persuade the crown to dissolve the existing Parliament and call for new elections (admittedly a big if), then the electors can return delegates who will hopefully act independently of the executive. It is important, however, to recall that Cato quite explicitly limits much of this discussion to issues pertinent to "free monarchical constitutions" such as the one in England.[65] It is in this vein that Cato calls on England's electors to select men with the same interests as themselves, individuals constitutionally impervious to bribery and patronage. In this appeal for new elections and vigilant electors, Cato offers a means to strengthen the popular element in the Constitution in a way consistent with the principles of the mixed and balanced constitution.

However, in the places where the *Letters* abstract from the particulars of the British Constitution and focus instead on the more general philosophical issues surrounding representation and sovereignty, Cato's populist proclivities come into visible conflict with the principles of mixed and balanced constitutionalism. When Cato expressly limits his discussion to the English political context, namely, mixed monarchy, his call is to strengthen and renew the popular element in the government. But when he abstracts from the English situation to a more theoretical account, the tension between his republican populism and his professed admiration for mixed constitutionalism becomes more pronounced.[66] In his general treatment on the issue of representation, Cato's position comes very close to Sidney's reflection theory of sovereignty: "The only secret . . . in forming a free government, is to make the interests of the governors and of the governed the same, as far as human policy can contrive. Liberty cannot be preserved any other way."[67] For Cato, as for Sidney, the sovereign authority must reflect as directly and distinctly as possible the interests of the people collectively. In the theoretical, as opposed to particularly British, account, the means to achieve this goal is not, as we would expect, the separation and balance of the institutions and powers of government. Rather, Cato affirms: "Human wisdom has yet found out but one certain expedient to effect this; and that is, to have the concerns of *all*

---

[65] Letter 61, p. 421.

[66] Here I would disagree with Banning, *Jeffersonian Persuasion*, pp. 55, 64; Burtt, *Virtue Transformed*, p. 72; and Huyler, *Locke in America*, pp. 212–13. I maintain that Cato's defense of the British constitution is largely pragmatic, and not based on a commitment to mixed regime theory.

[67] Letter 60, p. 417.

directed by *all*, as far as possibly can be."⁶⁸ In this view, Britain's mixed government, with two important hereditary elements, would flow neither as a direct consequence of natural rights nor as a particularly effective product of "human wisdom."

What, then, is Cato's actual stance toward mixed and balanced constitutionalism in general and the British system in particular? It is ambiguous. On the one hand, at times he suggests that the Constitution needs little more than a tune-up, a renewal of consent through elections and some new blood in the system. On the other hand, he indicates that good government must operate on the principle that "the concerns of all [must be] directed by all, as far as possibly can be." This standard suggests that the British balanced Constitution has some way to go before it can satisfy the Catonic criteria for good government. Indeed, for Cato, as for Sidney, the three measures necessary to ensure that the government reflects the interests of the people are regular elections, increased representation "to make the deputies so numerous" that they can adequately represent the nation as a whole, and changing the delegates "so often, that there is no sufficient time to corrupt them."⁶⁹ Cato rages against the repeal of the 1694 Triennial Act limiting Parliaments to three-year terms and the replacement of this salutary measure by the pernicious Septennial Act that extended Parliament's life to seven years. Insofar as Britain's mixed Constitution was unable to guarantee even so basic a principle as regular elections, Cato suggests that there is a fundamental structural problem in the government.

One obvious source of concern for Cato is, of course, the monarchy. Cato shares Sidney's modern republican distrust of executive power. He often indicates that the checks and restraints on power in free government are typically directed against the executive.⁷⁰ Cato's call for a more popularized order amounts to a demand for legislative supremacy. When he offers an illustration of a good constitutional model based on the structural implications of natural rights, he does not point to the British Constitution of his time, but rather to "the constitution of our several great companies." In these corporations, Cato explains, "the general court, composed of all its members, constitutes the legislature, and the consent of that court is the sanction of their laws; and where the administration of their affairs is put under the conduct of a certain number chosen by the whole."⁷¹ Cato's model constitution, then, is composed of a legislature of all the society's members (or in this instance shareholders), which holds supreme power and an executive administration drawn from and responsible to the legislature. In addition to rejecting the principle of executive independence, Cato relates that the companies

---

⁶⁸ Ibid., p. 417 (emphasis mine).
⁶⁹ Ibid., pp. 418, 419.
⁷⁰ See, for example, Letter 59, p. 405 and Letter 60, p. 416.
⁷¹ Letter 60, p. 418.

originally incorporated a provision whereby "a third part of directors are to go out every year," thus establishing the principles of regular elections and rotation. This constitutional model, Cato informs us, while clearly not what resulted from the Glorious Revolution, was "the ancient constitution of England."[72] Again in the spirit of Sidney, Cato establishes that the original and true animating principle of Britain's free government was and still is its popular, rather than its mixed and balanced, character.

The Catonic emphasis on the popular foundations of limited government is closely connected to his argument for the importance of virtue in a free people. Cato's frequent appeals to the characteristically republican principle of virtue certainly give credence to those scholars who identify Cato as a champion of the republican idea of liberty and government. This appeal to virtue does not, however, denote a reliance on a classical conception of virtue and does not in any way make Cato, any more than Sidney, a direct opponent of Lockean individual natural rights. As we have seen, Cato quite unabashedly offers a thoroughly Lockean definition of liberty as the individual's control over his or her own actions. Moreover, Cato offers an assessment of the human passions that gives pride of place to self-interest. The classical notion of virtue as self-sacrifice is virtually nonexistent in Cato.[73] Cato also, though, and despite his melancholy assessment of the primacy of self-interest, advances a more decidedly republican notion of liberty as a public share in government than we see in Locke. Cato, like Sidney, believes that more populist implications flow from natural rights than did Locke, and as such they offer different analyses of the states of character and the institutional ethos required to preserve popular governments.

The unifying thread linking Cato's argument for liberty and his understanding of virtue is his notion of the public or common good. For Cato, the common good cannot be understood as requiring a subsuming or denial of private interests. He claims: "The chief inducement which men have to act for the interest of one state before another is, because they are members of it, and that their own interest is involved in the general interest."[74] In this view, the public interest is the accumulation of all the private interests in society. The republican modification of Lockean individualism is seen in Cato's assertion that the only way to protect the private interests of all is to give them all some meaningful share in the government. Thus, when Cato appeals to the virtue of Britain's electors, he is calling on them to be vigilant

---

[72] Ibid., pp. 418–19.

[73] See Letter 108 for Cato's utter rejection of the classical ideal of virtue. For good discussions of Cato's very modern and very natural rights based understanding of virtue, see Burtt, *Virtue Transformed*, pp. 70–1, 73–89 and Zuckert, *Natural Rights*, pp. 304–5. For the contrary view, which maintains that Cato does signify a classical conception of virtue, see J. P. Diggins, *The Lost Soul of American Politics* (New York: Basic Books, 1984): p. 19 and Pocock, *Machiavellian Moment*, p. 471.

[74] Letter 90, p. 643.

and spirited defenders of liberty against a corrupt and abusive crown and ministry. Virtue becomes inseparable from the defense of rights, and corruption is identical to violation or nonprotection of rights. As we have seen, one vital right Cato was convinced needed protection was private property. Cato's notion of virtue contains no hostility to capitalism. Given Cato's impassioned defense of economic liberty, it is not surprising that he includes with the "privileges of thinking, saying and doing what we please" the further right "of growing as rich as we can."[75] Even the classical republican bugbear luxury escapes Cato's censure. He points out that luxury is as much a spur to "invention and industry" as necessity, and may be said to have at least as much to do with the progress of the "arts and sciences, which alone can support multitudes of people."[76] Clearly, Cato is no threadbare republican.

Cato's fusion of Sidney and Locke, of republican and liberal ideas, crystallizes and unifies in a cohesive way the distinct notions of liberty among the radical Whigs. Liberty, for Cato, is good and noble, both instrumental to self-preservation and good in itself. This duality in Cato's idea of liberty reflects the underlying complexity of his understanding of human nature. On the one hand, Cato offers a very melancholy view of human nature. He opines: "It cannot but be irksome to a good natured man, to find that there is nothing so terrible or mischievous, but human nature is capable of it." The root of the problem that underlies "the violent bent of human nature to evil" and the "restless appetites of men" is self-love, or "an ill-judging fondness for themselves."[77] Despite the negative effects of self-love, this self-regarding passion also grounds "the first law of nature, that of self-preservation." In this view, liberty is instrumental: I must be free to preserve myself because I cannot trust anyone else to put my preservation before their own. On the other hand, Cato also maintains that the love of liberty, itself an intrinsic human passion, is a healthy form and expression of self-love. Cato even suggests that the love of liberty may touch a deeper chord in the human soul than concern for self-preservation. He claims: "The love of liberty is an appetite so strongly implanted in the nature of all living creatures, that even the appetite of self-preservation, which is allowed to be the strongest, seems to be contained in it." It is this love of liberty that is the source of such virtues as law-abidingness and the spirited defense of rights. Slavery is worse than death for more reasons than its tendency to endanger preservation – a position more consistent with Locke. It is repugnant to the deeper love of liberty, which contains and in some sense animates our preservationist concerns. For Cato, as for Sidney, the psychological effects of liberty, which support such things as the progress of the arts, sciences, and commerce, are simply good.

[75] Letter 62, p. 432.
[76] Letter 67, pp. 473–4.
[77] Letter 31, p. 221.

How then did Cato's argument for liberty as a public share in government affect his attitude toward the British Constitution? For one thing, Cato
defends the settlement of 1688–9 on the basis of radical Whig principles,
which were far more revolutionary than those of the architects of the settlement. The ultimate standard for judging the merits of a constitutional order
is, according to Cato, its capacity to protect natural rights: "The nature of
government does not alter the natural right of men to liberty, which in all
political societies is alike their due. But some governments provide better
than others for the security and impartial distribution of that right."[78] By
this standard, Cato concludes that Britain's Constitution, "if duly administered, provides excellently well for general liberty." Thus, the British system
of government appears to be basically sound.

The deep ambiguity in Cato's attitude to the mixed monarchy mainly
comes to light later in the crucial Letter 85. Here Cato claims to offer a
favorable comparison between Britain and the Dutch Republic. A careful
reading of Cato's argument, however, reveals that his defense of Britain is
largely pragmatic, and his criticism of Holland is not a condemnation of republicanism at all, but rather a specific criticism of the flawed federal system
in the United Provinces. In answer to the hypothetical question of whether
republicanism is superior to monarchy or vice versa, Cato finesses the issue
by cautioning that a relative "equality of estate" is necessary for a republic;
as such, "the distribution of property in England" at present makes republicanism not only impractical but more or less impossible. The point Cato
makes is that the "nobility and gentry have great possessions" in England
and thus are naturally inclined to support the current system, in which they
"have great privileges and distinctions by the constitution." The success of
Britain's mixed monarchy relies on its capacity to link the economic interests
and social status of certain classes with considerable political privilege. Cato
claims: "these must ever be in the interest of monarchy whilst they are in
their own interest."[79] While here Cato does appear to follow Harrington's
dictum that "power follows property," it would be a mistake to associate
Cato too closely with Harrington.[80] Cato's realistic assessment of the British
situation does not indicate partisan support for mixed government or suggest any incongruity between his Lockean understanding of property and
the political and constitutional implications of the unequal distribution of
property. The essence of Cato's argument is that Britain's chances of becoming a successful republic at present are seriously injured because of the deep
constitutional connection between property and political power. It is this
connection that threatens the integrity and vitality of the popular element in

---

[78] Letter 60, p. 416, and Letter 85, p. 616.
[79] Letter 85, p. 614.
[80] James Harrington, *The Commonwealth of Oceana*, J. G. A. Pocock, ed. (Cambridge: Cambridge University Press, 1992): pp. 52, 54–6.

the government, the one part of the Constitution so vital for securing liberty. Apart from the nobility and gentry, Cato's list of the other mainstays of the current mixed monarchy amounts to a veritable rogues' gallery drawn from the pages of the *Letters*: the established clergy, those with interests in the monopoly companies, place men with royal salaries, and court favorites.[81] Suffice to say that these are not Cato's kind of people.

Cato defends the British Constitution largely on pragmatic grounds. It does a reasonably good job of securing liberty, and it is just as well, because the obstacles impeding radical constitutional alteration are insuperable, at least in the near term. For Cato, the limited aims, and indeed achievements, of the Glorious Revolution testify to these practical obstacles to serious constitutional reform. With respect to the hypothetical question of whether limited monarchy or republicanism is the best form of government, Cato concedes that it is a moot issue because, with so many powerful interests behind the status quo, "it is impossible to contend against all these interests, and the Crown too, which is almost a match for them all." But Cato does not entirely relegate the question of republicanism to the realm of intellectual marginalia. In his own treatment of Holland he finds a regime where the people have the "real and natural power." For Cato, as for Sidney, Spinoza's Holland is the example of modern republicanism par excellence. The Dutch Republic does, Cato admits, have serious structural problems, primarily relating to issues of federalism, but it is important to observe that he also calls the Dutch Republic "the most virtuous and flourishing state which ever yet appeared in the world," as well as a "state which, ever since its institution, has been the champion of publick liberty."[82] This is higher praise than he ever extends to the British Constitution. Cato's qualified and pragmatic defense of Britain's mixed government speaks volumes when set beside his praise of the Dutch Republic. While Cato is careful to spare the sensibilities of his English audience, which would be shocked at the republican alternative in their own country, he does show his republican sympathies, sympathies probably originating in Cato's admiration for Algernon Sidney, whom he claims "has written better upon government than any Englishman, as well as foreigner."[83]

Cato's Letters stand as a classic expression of radical Whig political and constitutional thought. In the *Letters* we see a more fully articulated notion of individual rights than in Sidney combined with more robust populism and republican principles than in Locke. Trenchard and Gordon's attempt to synthesize Lockean liberal individualism and Sidneyan modern republicanism produced a much more volatile cocktail than most moderate Whigs in Britain could digest. Cato's endorsement of Lockean natural rights and dissolution

---

[81] Letter 85, pp. 615–16.
[82] Ibid., pp. 617–18.
[83] Letter 26, p. 188.

theory, as well as his support for seriously strengthening the popular element in the British polity, ran counter to the way most Whigs conceived of their Constitution. Cato's argument did, however, take firm root in the American colonies, where the *Letters* became a central part in the canon of American Whig thought. In order to defend limited government against the apparent and incipient abuses of the crown and the ministry, Cato reconceptualized the foundations of the British Constitution in terms of radical Whig philosophy. In the process, he exposed radical Whiggism's uneasy relationship with the mixed monarchy, a disquietude that would become even more vocal throughout the course of the imperial debate between the British government and the American colonists in the 1760s and 1770s.

11

Eighteenth-Century British Constitutionalism

The British Constitution in the middle of the eighteenth century in many respects attained its historical prime. Looking back on two decades of political stability and economic growth under the pragmatic administration of Walpole and his successors and the final demise of the Jacobite threat on the heath of the windswept fields of Culloden in 1746, the subjects of the now firmly United Kingdom understandably enjoyed a general spirit of contentment and self-congratulation. On the political level, the bitter partisan and theological divisions in the nation during the reigns of William and Anne and the early Hanoverian period were for the most part relegated to an unlamented past.[1] On the intellectual level, the British Constitution reached its zenith in philosophical circles with the praise of observers of such import as David Hume, Montesquieu, and later Sir William Blackstone. The philosophical framework and ideological commitments of the dominant forces in the British political nation during the imperial crisis with America were firmly installed, practically without domestic rival, during this period.

The conservative tendencies present in moderate Whig thought since the Exclusion and Glorious Revolution periods solidified throughout the first half of the century, further marginalizing radical Whig ideas and attaining a degree of theoretical sophistication hitherto unseen. When British political elites and the public faced the challenges of empire posed by American resistance to parliamentary sovereignty in the 1760s and 1770s, they understood the dispute over the order of the empire and the nature of the British Constitution primarily in terms of the philosophical and constitutional principles of moderate Whiggism that achieved ascendancy in Britain throughout the course of the eighteenth century. In order to understand the nature of the moderate Whig ideological hegemony in eighteenth-century Britain, it is important to trace the pattern of British constitutional development in the

---

[1] Isaac Kramnick, *Bolingbroke and His Circle: The Politics of Nostalgia in the Age of Walpole* (Cambridge, MA: Harvard University Press, 1968): p. 11.

Hanoverian period and consider the influential observations on the Constitution offered by some of the leading philosophical and legal minds of the
century.

The Moderate Whig Ascendancy in Eighteenth-Century Britain

The period from the Hanoverian accession in 1714 until the eve of the outbreak of the conflict with the American colonies in the early 1760s is often
characterized as the era of "Whig supremacy" in Britain. By this is meant
the period of political stability in which Britain was ruled by a Whig regime
brought to power by the installation of George I and then consolidated and
maintained under the leadership of Walpole and his successors. For more
than four decades, the ruling Whigs managed to drape themselves in the
mantle of the Glorious Revolution and convince the first two Georges that
all Tories were really Jacobites and could not be trusted with any share
of political power. One-party dominance was not, however, the cause but
rather the effect of deeper underlying sources of political stability in Augustan
Britain.[2] The most significant feature of the ideological development in the
period was the intellectual hegemony of moderate Whig principles across
the political spectrum. Both the crypto-republicanism of the radical Whig
Cato's Letters and Filmerian divine right were expelled from respectable political opinion in eighteenth-century Britain. The British political nation experienced a gradual process of philosophical and ideological homogeniza-
tion at the level of first political principles as the overwhelming majority of
Whigs and Tories, seventeenth-century antipodes, underwent an eighteenth-
century convergence regarding their fundamental philosophical and political
commitments.

Moderate Whig philosophy provided the dominant intellectual paradigm
through which all the politically relevant classes in Britain came to understand the Constitution. This meant that there was overwhelming agreement
with the moderate Whig interpretation of the nature, if not necessarily the
actual practice, of the constitutional order produced by the Glorious Revolution settlement. Britons almost universally recognized the political order
as a limited monarchy constructed on the basis of a Constitution balancing
the various classes, interests, and estates of the realm in a system of shared
legislative power including king, Lords, and Commons. This period also witnessed the emergence of an as yet inchoate but identifiable public doctrine
of parliamentary sovereignty as Britons of all political stripes increasingly
recognized the joint action of the constituent elements of king-in-Parliament
as the supreme legal authority in the nation. On a more theoretical level,

---

[2] For the classic treatment of the sociopolitical forces informing the emergence of this period
of political stability, see J. H. Plumb, *The Growth of Political Stability in England, 1675–1725*
(London: Macmillan, 1967).

moderate Whig philosophical principles defined the way people understood the origin of government. Neither Filmerian divine right political theology nor radical Whig contract theory remained credible accounts of the origins and nature of political power. The more conservative moderate Whig idea of compact rooted in Pufendorf's theory of natural sociability and the multiple layers of agreement and social context informing civil society, avoiding as it did the radical ideas of individualism, dissolution, and the general right of revolution as well as divine right absolutism and passive obedience, provided a conceptual model of political first principles that was well adapted to the British intellectual taste and temper in the years after 1714.

This is not, of course, to suggest that Britain in the first half of the eighteenth century did not experience a considerable degree of partisanship. What is significant, however, is the narrow range of philosophical ideas underlying these partisan positions. In the years of Whig supremacy, the nature and character of political divisions in Britain altered and reduced dramatically from what they had been in the seventeenth century. The moderate Whig convergence of political ideology produced a much less serious division than the theologically and philosophically based divide between Exclusion Whigs and Tories or Cavaliers and Roundheads. The Court and Country parties that emerged in a political order characterized by fundamental agreement on the nature of the Constitution superimposed a new set of issues, attitudes, and interests on the increasingly anachronistic Tory and Whig labels inherited from the period prior to the consolidation of the revolution settlement. Although there is some truth to the view that the eighteenth-century parties of competing interests replaced the seventeenth-century parties divided over principles as fundamental as divine right and natural liberty, it is important not to exaggerate the pragmatic character of Augustan politics or to diminish the depth of hostility possible in a partisan divide based on interest, policy, and even petty rivalries and personal frustrations.[3] Even if partisans of the Court and Country operated on a common set of received categories and fundamental assumptions about the virtues of balanced constitutionalism and limited monarchy drawn from the wellspring of moderate Whig thought, they disagreed bitterly about the political mechanisms and constitutional norms required to maintain the delicate constitutional balance and limits. They also battled over the virtues and vices of the new economic order of commercial interests, public credit, and taxes that survived the South Sea collapse and became an increasingly central element in the British polity.[4] These differences were keenly felt by large segments of the political nation and produced enough of a partisan edge

---

[3] See Harvey Mansfield, *Statesmanship and Party Government: A Study of Burke and Bolingbroke* (Chicago: University of Chicago Press, 1965): esp. ch. 1, in which Mansfield lays out the various approaches to this question.

[4] Kramnick, *Bolingbroke and His Circle*, ch. 2.

to Augustan politics to refute any impression of political quietism in the period.

A brief outline of the dynamic of the Court–Country division will expose both the fundamental continuity and the inherent cleavages in the British political system after 1714.[5] To the extent that both the loosely organized Court and Country parties expressed a fundamental commitment to the principles of the Glorious Revolution and to the balanced Constitution, they were philosophically in the moderate Whig camp. However, they disagreed seriously about how best to achieve and maintain the constitutional balance or even what was the greatest danger to this cherished balance. The Court Party, composed almost entirely of Whigs, believed in the need to strengthen the executive against the growing power of the commons, primarily by maintaining the king's prerogative in choosing ministers, ensuring a source of public money independent of parliamentary provision, and defending the use of royal patronage to secure parliamentary majorities. In the transformation of the Whigs from Shaftesbury's party of resistance to executive power in the 1680s to the governing party representing social order, royal influence, and the national debt after 1720, the pragmatic and conservative tendencies we have identified in moderate Whiggism from its earliest appearance became more pronounced with the quotidian vagaries of day-to-day administration.[6] With the responsibility of power, most Whigs shed the remaining traces of their radical heritage.

The Country Party, composed mainly of Tory country squires and disaffected Whigs, developed as the loosely affiliated opposition to the ruling Whigs. They believed the great danger to the constitutional balance lay in the extension of executive power through patronage or royal "influence" and the emerging system of cabinet government, both of which undermined the Country ideal of the independent landed Member of Parliament. The Country position sought to preserve the independence of the commons through measures such as Place Bills prohibiting membership in the Commons to anyone holding an office of profit under the crown and by repeal of the

---

[5] For more in-depth accounts of the Court–Country system there are many excellent studies, including Reed Browning, *Political and Constitutional Ideas of the Court Whigs* (Baton Rouge: Louisiana State University Press, 1982): esp. ch. 1; Hiram Caton, *The Politics of Progress: The Origins and Development of the Commercial Republic, 1600–1835* (Gainesville: University of Florida Press, 1988): pp. 246–50; H. T. Dickinson, *Liberty and Property* (London: Weidenfeld and Nilcolson, 1977): chs. 4, 5; Kramnick, *Bolingbroke and His Circle*, chs. 5, 6; J. G. A. Pocock, *Virtue, Commerce, and History* (Cambridge: Cambridge University Press, 1986): esp. "Varieties of Whiggism" (pp. 239–53); and W. A. Speck, *Stability and Strife: England 1714–1760* (London: Edward Arnold, 1977): chs. 6, 10.

[6] Dickinson, *Liberty and Property*, p. 125. For the classic sociological study of the oligarchic tendencies in modern political parties, see Roberto Michels, *Political Parties: A Sociological Study of the Oligarchic Tendencies of Modern Democracy*, Eden Paul and Cedar Paul, trans. (New York: Free Press, 1958).

Septennial Act, which Country spokesmen argued contributed to the insulation of Parliament from public accountability.[7] Moreover, they saw in the system of national debt and commercial interests dangerous innovations with serious implications for the proper relation of property and political power, innovations that undermined politically the independent gentry representing the Commons, transferred too much independence to the crown and its financial supporters, and allowed the corruption of Parliament by the number of civil offices now available to the crown. With their program of "economical" and electoral reform, the Country Party aspired to reverse what they took to be the oligarchic trend and the demoralizing effect the Court policies and practices had on the British constitutional order.

The causes of the Court–Country system and of the partisan divide operating at a level of abstraction from first principles were twofold. First, in one sense the Court–Country cleavage originated in the very structure of a balanced Constitution. Some form of partisan divide, however vaguely understood and loosely organized, is built into the logic of balanced constitutionalism. The process of retrenchment of the moderate Whig ideological commitment to the principle of constitutional balance did not preclude but actually contributed to the Court–Country division. General agreement on the importance of constitutional balance did not automatically resolve questions over the location and source of this balance. Which element of the Constitution requires particular safeguards to preserve its integral position in the larger framework, and which element is most likely to grow in strength of its own accord in extralegal ways and threaten encroachment on the other branches? Even if some measure of agreement can be achieved regarding a particularly vulnerable or predatory part of the Constitution, what measures may be needed to secure or limit these powers? The debates about the Peerage Bill in 1719 and the various Place Bills and economical reforms were of this nature.

Moreover, a balanced Constitution is, as Sidney and Trenchard and Gordon suggested, always in need of adjustment to changing social, political, and economic conditions such as those happening in Britain in the first half of the eighteenth century. Despite serious differences of interpretation about constitutional matters, neither wing of the Augustan era party divide embraced the radical Whig idea of popular sovereignty. The balanced Constitution they envisaged was composed of the politically relevant interests, classes, and estates of the nation. Much like the moderate Whig defenders of the revolution settlement in the 1690s, neither Court nor Country supporters countenanced the radical principle of dissolution or believed that

---

[7] For the long-term oligarchic effects of the Septennial Act on the electoral system, see Pocock, *Virtue, Commerce, and History*, p. 239. Cf. M. J. C. Vile, *Constitutionalism and the Separation of Powers*, 2nd ed. (Indianapolis: Liberty Fund, 1998): pp. 78–9.

Parliament represented the whole "people" in a direct way.[8] For example, the Country appeals for frequent Parliaments did not include demands for radical extension of the franchise or reflect the visceral hostility to the idea of monarchy seen in the Whig republicanism of Sidney or *Cato's Letters*.

The second major cause of the Court–Country divide had to do with the transformation of the party ideologies inherited from the seventeenth century. Both Whigs and Tories experienced significant changes in the Augustan period. For the Whigs, the transformation from Shaftesbury's party of exclusion to Walpole's party of administration involved, as we have seen, both the marginalization of radical Whig arguments in the post-1689 years and the gradual process of legitimization that came with the regular exercise of power in developing institutional norms. The transformation of the Tories in the years after 1714 was even more dramatic than that of the Whigs. Somewhere on the road from the Stuart Court to the Hanoverian Country, the Tories transformed from the party of Filmer and divine right into the Patriot Party of Bolingbroke and commitment to the idea of liberty and the balanced Constitution. It was the transformation of Tory ideology in the eighteenth century that, more than any other factor, made possible the domestication of party division into Court and Country. A brief examination of Bolingbroke's political and constitutional thought should suffice to illuminate the profound change in Toryism.

The colorful Viscount Bolingbroke was the intellectual voice of the Tory Party throughout much of the first half of the eighteenth century. Despite his own early flirtation with Jacobitism, this English Alcibiades did more in his writings to express the gradual Tory acceptance of the revolution settlement than probably any of his contemporaries. It is perhaps a good indication of the philosophical distance between Bolingbroke's Tories in the 1720s and 1730s and the Tories of the Exclusion, Glorious Revolution, and even Sacheverell trial periods that Bolingbroke deplored the continuing, and he argued anachronistic, distinction between Whigs and Tories favoring rather the dichotomy between a corrupt Court ministry and a virtuous Country. Under Bolingbroke's influence, the Tories finally rejected the Filmerian doctrine of divine right and embraced the principles of limited monarchy and balanced constitutionalism. Bolingbroke even identified Filmer's patron, James I, as the "anointed pedant" first responsible for bringing to England the "system

---

[8] Dickinson, *Liberty and Property*, pp. 189–92 and Kramnick, *Bolingbroke and His Circle*, pp. 150, 171–4. However, Kramnick does, I think, go too far in characterizing Walpole's court Whigs as Lockeans (117–19; see also Caton, *Politics of Progress*, pp. 316–20) on the basis of a few radical statements in the government press. As a matter of political and constitutional philosophy, Walpole demonstrated his moderate Whig credentials in the Sacheverell trial (see Chapter 10), and I find no suggestion that he became radicalized in the course of his long career in power. There is perhaps a problem in identifying precipitately the nascent bourgeois capitalist system espoused by the court with Locke's radical Whig philosophy of government.

of absurdity" that became divine right royalism.[9] His own account of the origin of political authority rested on the twin notions of natural sociability and compact more akin to the conservative contractualism of Pufendorf than the Lutheran political theology of Filmer.[10] The major implication of Bolingbroke's reorientation of the Tories away from divine right was an acceptance, and indeed a celebration, of the constitutional settlement following the Glorious Revolution. He praised "our present settlement" as one "built on the foundation of liberty." In a stunning co-opting and incorporation of standard Whig historiography, Bolingbroke identified the genius of the British Constitution in its traditional commitment to the ideal of constitutional balance: "In a constitution like ours, the safety of the whole depends on the balance of the parts, and the balance of the parts on their mutual independency on one another."[11]

In his bitter Country polemic against the Walpole administration, Bolingbroke positioned the Tory opposition as the defenders of the Commons against the corrupt Court practices of royal patronage and the concentration of parliamentary power in the ministry. What is most striking about Bolingbroke's Tories, given their party's origins in Filmerian divine right monarchy, is the expressed concern to resist the extension of executive power. In response to the Court argument that the monarch needed the advantage of royal influence to counterbalance the strength of the Commons and to "oil the wheels" of government by producing a proper degree of dependence on the crown, Bolingbroke claimed:

It is [the] division of power, [the] distinct privileges attributed to the king, to the lords, and to the commons, which constitute a limited monarchy.... The power which the several parts of our government have of controlling and checking one another, may be called a dependency on one another, [however]... this mutual dependency cannot subsist without such an independency... that the resolutions of each part, which direct these proceedings, be taken independantly [sic] and without any influence, direct or indirect, on the others.[12]

For Bolingbroke and his Country supporters, the independence and protection of the Commons from extraparliamentary executive influence was a

[9] Henry St. John, Viscount Bolingbroke, *The Works of Lord Bolingbroke* (Philadelphia: Carey and Hart, 1841): Vol. II, pp. 26–7, 29–30, "Dissertation on Parties," and pp. 372, 379, "Patriot King."

[10] Bolingbroke, *Works*, Vol. II, p. 390, "Patriot King." Cf. Kramnick, *Bolingbroke and His Circle*, p. 106 and Mansfield, *Statesmanship*, p. 75.

[11] Bolingbroke, *Works*, Vol. I, pp. 335, 306, "Remarks on the History of England." Cf. Kramnick, *Bolingbroke and His Circle*, pp. 127–36, 177–81.

[12] Bolingbroke, *Works*, Vol. I, pp. 332–3, "Remarks" and Vol. II, pp. 93–6, "Dissertation of Parties." Cf. Paul Rahe, *Republics Ancient and Modern: Classical Republicanism and the American Revolution* (Chapel Hill: University of North Carolina Press, 1992): pp. 434–7, 440 and Vile, *Separation of Powers*, pp. 80–1.

crucial ingredient for maintaining the limited monarchy. However, one measure of the ideological distance between Bolingbroke's Country opposition and radical Whig philosophy was his openness to the essentially monarchic solution to the problem of constitutional dependence and corruption offered by the "standing miracle" of a Patriot King who refused to use the prerogatives of his office to benefit a particular faction in Parliament.[13] In the idea of a Patriot King, we see that Bolingbroke's primary concern was to maintain the constitutional balance rather than the populist institutional foundation favored by Sidney or Trenchard and Gordon.

According to Bolingbroke's constitutional theory, the only legitimate kinds of influence the various elements of the Constitution can have on each other are determined by the legal forms and political structures embodied in the Constitution since the very origin of the English government in the age of Saxon liberty before the Norman Conquest and lately restored by the revolution against King James Stuart.[14] With this formulation of the British Constitution, Bolingbroke does more than simply mobilize Whig history in the Country cause; he also signals the Tories' new commitment to the principle of limited monarchy. In Bolingbroke we see a particularly vivid demonstration of the Tory transfer of allegiance from the Filmerian absolute monarch to the eighteenth-century moderate Whig doctrine of parliamentary sovereignty. With language and logic practically identical to those of the moderate Whig patron Pufendorf, Bolingbroke described the principle of sovereignty and limited monarchy:

The distinction should always be preserved in our notions, between two things that we are apt to confound in speculation, as they have been confounded in practice, legislative and monarchical power. *There must an absolute, unlimited, and uncontrollable power lodged somewhere in every government*; but to constitute monarchy . . . it is not necessary that this power should be lodged in the monarch alone. It is no more necessary that he should exclusively and independently establish the rule of his government, than it is that he should govern without any rule at all.[15]

Even if it would take some decades before the idea of parliamentary sovereignty became the established orthodoxy it was as the time of the crisis with America, it is clear that Bolingbroke offers evidence of a Tory movement in that direction that parallels the first seminal arguments for legal sovereignty in Tyrrell and the Glorious Revolution era moderate Whigs.[16]

---

[13] See Bolingbroke, *Works*, Vol II, pp. 372–429. Cf. Kramnick, *Bolingbroke and His Circle*, pp. 163–9 and Mansfield, *Statesmanship*, ch. 4.

[14] See Bolingbroke, *Works*, Vol I, pp. 317–19, 335, 363–98, 398–443, "Remarks on the History of England."

[15] Compare Bolingbroke, *Works*, Vol II, p. 382, "Patriot King" (emphasis mine) and Samuel Pufendorf, *De Jure Naturae et Gentium Libri Octo* (Oxford: Clarendon Press, 1934): bk. 7, ch. 6, sec. 1, 7 (hereafter DJNG, bk., ch., and sec.). Cf. Jeffrey Goldsworthy, *The Sovereignty of Parliament: History and Philosophy* (Oxford: Clarendon Press, 1999): p. 176.

[16] As Dickinson observes (*Liberty and Property*, pp. 182, 187), the Country challenged Walpole's ministry because they saw it as a corruption of Parliament; but the Country ideal is that of

Bolingbroke, the scourge of Walpole and the Court Whigs in the partisan battles of the 1720s and 1730s, reflects on the level of philosophical principles about sovereignty and the Constitution the more fundamental convergence of political ideology toward moderate Whig hegemony in eighteenth-century Britain.

The change in British politics that occurred upon the accession of George III in 1760 on the eve of the outbreak of the imperial crisis with America heralded the end of the long period of Whig supremacy.[17] The old party distinctions between Whig and Tory, which had become increasingly anachronistic since the time of Bolingbroke, were largely swept aside by a new quasi-Patriot King who offered the levers of power in the government to Whig and Tory alike, to a Bute, a North, a Grenville, or even a Rockingham. The formal legitimization of the Tories by George III signaled the final consummation of a process of convergence of fundamental philosophical principles between the parties that had been developing in some sense since 1714. While differences between and within the loosely identified parties persisted well into the 1760s and 1770s over the best means to preserve the British constitutional balance, these debates occurred within the context of a general philosophical framework informed by the moderate Whig principles of limited monarchy, balanced constitutionalism, parliamentary sovereignty, and the rejection of radical contract theory. By the 1760s, the Tories bore little less relation to their divine right forbears than the Whigs did to the radical elements in their philosophical heritage. In the spirit of Thomas Jefferson's First Inaugural Address delivered at the opening of a similar period of ideological consolidation in American history, the British were in a fundamental sense all Whigs and all Tories now.

Reflections on British Constitutionalism: Hume, Montesquieu, and Blackstone

When David Hume published his essays on political and moral issues in the early 1740s, he offered them not as a partisan of the Whigs or the Tories but as an unabashed "friend to moderation."[18] While he certainly challenged

---

a reformed Parliament, not popular sovereignty. See also Colin Bonwick for the distinction between parliamentary and popular sovereignty ("The United States Constitution and Its Roots in British Political Thought and Tradition," in *Foundations of Democracy in the European Union: From the Genesis of Parliamentary Democracy to the European Parliament*, John Pinder, ed. [New York: St. Martin's, 1999]: pp. 43–4).

[17] For two classic studies of the state of British politics at the beginning of George III's reign, see Lewis Namier, *England in the Age of the American Revolution* (London: Macmillan, 1930), and Richard Pares, *King George III and the Politicians* (Oxford: Clarendon Press, 1953). For a good discussion of how the breakdown of the period of Whig supremacy affected the various elements of the old Whig governing party, see John Brewer, "Rockingham, Burke, and Whig Political Argument," *The Historical Journal*, vol. 18, no. 1 (March 1975): pp. 188–201.

[18] David Hume, "That Politics May Be Reduced to a Science," in *Essays Moral, Political and Literary*, Eugene Miller, ed. (Indianapolis: Liberty Fund, 1985): p. 15.

the orthodox Whig interpretation of the British Constitution and of English history in a number of important respects, Hume's reputation as a Tory is unjustified. Certainly Hume's *History of England*, denying as it did some of the central Whig arguments for the ancient constitution, for example identifying the Norman Conquest as a conquest, was castigated by many Whigs as a Tory or even Jacobite revisionist history. Moreover, his scathing criticism of the writings of radical Whig luminaries including Locke, Sidney, and Hoadly as "the most despicable, both for style and matter," did not endear him to even the more moderate Whig establishment.[19] However, the central ideas in Hume's treatment of the British Constitution were many of the essential tenets of moderate Whiggism. For example, he lauded the genius of the constitutional system of "checks and controls" in Britain that made it "the interest even of bad men to act for the public good."[20] Hume's pessimism regarding human nature demonstrates the emphatically modern as opposed to classical basis of his thought, and it was this same political realism that located him in the moderate Whig camp.[21] Given his skepticism about the political reliability of moral virtue, Hume followed the moderate Whig path rejecting both absolute monarchy and popular government. Neither the people as a collectivity nor a single ruler could be expected to govern wisely, but a system including the firmly planted interests of king, Lords, and Commons could provide the basis for an arrangement of mutual checks and limits. He praised the British Constitution as a complex, compound instrument of government delicately balanced between the two objectionable poles of absolute monarchy and democracy. Moreover, he steadfastly maintained the importance of the independent executive and a body of hereditary Lords to counteract the growing strength of the commercial classes in the Commons, even advocating a salutary measure of royal corruption or "influence" and defending cabinet government as a way to ensure a "proper degree of dependence" of the Commons on the crown and ministry.[22] Hume, then, was less an adherent of the Tory tradition of Bolingbroke and Harley, and even less a disciple of Filmer, than a Court Whig with Country sympathies on some issues, such as the national debt and the question of a standing army.

---

[19] For a good account of Hume's philosophical history, see Duncan Forbes, *Hume's Philosophical Politics* (Cambridge: Cambridge University Press, 1975): pp. 233–323 and David Miller, *Philosophy and Ideology in Hume's Political Thought* (Oxford: Clarendon Press, 1981): pp. 167–72.

[20] Hume, *Essays*, "Politics Reduced to a Science," pp. 15–16 and "Of the Independency of Parliament," p. 42.

[21] Rahe, *Republics*, pp. 439–40.

[22] Hume, *Essays*, "Independency of Parliament," pp. 44–6 (cf. "Of the First Principles of Government," pp. 35–6). Notice also Hume's praise for the ameliorating effects of representation on the populist tendencies of the Commons in terms reminiscent of Tyrrell, Burnet, and Atwood fifty years earlier ("Politics Reduced to a Science," p. 16 and "Whether the British Government Inclines More to Absolute Monarchy or to a Republic," pp. 52–3). For Hume's court Whig credentials, see Miller, *Philosophy and Ideology*, pp. 173, 178–9.

The philosophical kinship between Hume and the moderate Whig tradition is seen most clearly in his criticism of the potent mixture of speculative principles and partisan politics. Hume's rejection of both the theology of divine right monarchy and the speculative philosophy animating the doctrine of popular sovereignty reflected an important Pufendorfian dimension of moderate Whig thought that elevated the moral claims of practical utility above abstract theoretical standards of legitimacy and supplied a compelling normative status for established governments.[23] Even Hume's scathing attack on the Whig idea of original contract did not cast him outside the orbit of moderate Whiggism, because as we have seen, most Whigs since the time of the revolution were quite prepared to jettison radical contract theory for fear of its populist implications. In most respects, Hume, like the moderate Whigs of two generations earlier, sought to defend the balanced Constitution of king, Lords, and Commons.[24] Hume's argument against the direct political relevance of state of nature theory and popular consent, and his emphasis instead on the "effect of established governments" and the authority of custom and opinion, had deep philosophical roots in the pragmatic natural jurisprudence of Pufendorf and his English followers.[25] Pufendorf's idea of compact, stressing the importance of social context and natural sociability, was much more in line with Hume's thinking than the radical individualism expounded by Locke. However, the constitutional thrust of Hume's criticism of Locke as a philosopher "who embraced a party" is that the Lockean political principles championed by radical Whigs were inimical to the delicate balance between liberty and authority achieved in Britain since the revolution. Here again Hume is no proponent of Filmerian Toryism. Hume had absorbed far too much of Locke's theological skepticism to ever countenance old school divine right. He balanced his rejection of the radical doctrine of resistance with an equally emphatic denunciation of the divine right idea of

---

[23] For Hume's critique of Locke's philosophical partisanship, see Dickinson, *Liberty and Property*, p. 137 and Rahe, *Republics*, pp. 537–40.

[24] We should note that in the "Idea of a Perfect Commonwealth" Hume proposed a model constitution that preserved the "opposition of interests" that was "the chief support of the British government," but did so on the basis of a pyramid-shaped federal scheme built on elected local institutions rather than a hereditary nobility and monarchy. Yet as a matter of practical reform in Britain, Hume suggested strengthening the Lords by increasing the number of life peers as a check to the crown and Commons (Hume, *Essays*, pp. 525, 527). This measure, Hume argued, would maintain the system of checks and balances while reducing the problem of faction.

[25] Hume, *Essays*, "Original Contract," pp. 456–66, 468–9. See also the *Treatise*, in which he calls the state of nature "a mere philosophical fiction" and an "imaginary state" (David Hume, *A Treatise of Human Nature*, L. A. Selby-Bigge, ed. [Oxford: Clarendon Press, 1967]: bk 3, sec. 2, pp. 493–4, 501). For Hume's rejection of radical contract theory, see Forbes, *Philosophical Politics*, pp. 91–101 (and 27–31 and 72 for Hume's agreement with Pufendorf's social context based understanding of property and the origin of society) and Miller, *Philosophy and Ideology*, ch. 4.

passive obedience, favoring instead the narrowly construed resistance right based on extreme necessity that had been a feature of moderate Whig thought since the time of Walpole at the Sacheverell trial and the defenses of the revolution in the 1690s.[26] Likewise, Hume's rejection of the Lockean argument for dissolution rested on the Pufendorfian grounds of its incompatibility with the requirements of social life rather than a refutation of the idea of natural liberty.

Hume celebrated the Glorious Revolution and the Protestant Succession, which together he identified as the "firmest foundation for British liberty," in terms practically indistinguishable from those of the moderate Whig architects of the revolution settlement. While rejecting the radical interpretation of the events in 1688–9, Hume eulogized the "happy effects" of the now firmly established constitutional order such as the commercial prosperity, political stability, public liberty, and flourishing of the arts and sciences enjoyed in mid-century Britain. For Hume, the partisan of moderation, the greatest tribute to the genius of the British Constitution, and implicitly to the moderate Whigs who fashioned it, was the gradual dilution of the fierce partisan and theological controversies that had plagued the kingdom for decades, and now were replaced by widespread agreement on the nature, if not the practical operation, of the Constitution.[27] Even if some potentially fruitful tension over the operation of the government and its policies continued to be manifest in the Court–Country partisan divide, Hume acknowledged the demonstrable fact that the balanced and complex Constitution was reasonably secure against the zealots of both divine right monarchy and radical popular sovereignty.

Perhaps the most dramatic celebration of the British Constitution by any major thinker at mid-century was Montesquieu's reflections in the *Spirit of the Laws*, published in 1748. England stood as the centerpiece of Montesquieu's teaching on moderate constitutionalism. In Walpolean Britain, Montesquieu found "a nation where the republic hides under the form of a monarchy."[28] It

---

[26] Hume, *Essays*, "Original Contract," p. 480 and "Passive Obedience," pp. 489–92. Cf. "Original Contract," pp. 472–3, for Hume's rejection of the principle of dissolution. For a good discussion of the moderate philosophy informing Hume's theory of limited resistance, see Nicholas Phillipson, "Propriety, Property, and Prudence: David Hume and the Defence of the Revolution," in *Political Discourse in Early Modern Britain*, Nicholas Phillipson and Quentin Skinner, eds. (Cambridge: Cambridge University Press, 1991): pp. 311–16. For Hume's fundamental agreement with Locke's secularizing project, see Rahe, *Republics*, pp. 537–40.

[27] Hume, *Essays*, "Coalition of Parties," pp. 500–1 and "Protestant Succession," p. 508. Cf. Dickinson, *Liberty and Property*, pp. 124–5.

[28] Charles Secondat Montesquieu, *The Spirit of the Laws* (1748), Anne Cohler, Basia Carolyn Miller, and Harold Summel, trans. and eds. (Cambridge: Cambridge University Press, 1989; hereafter *Spirit*): bk. 5, ch. 19, p. 70. For good general treatments of Montesquieu's account of the British Constitution, see Ann Cohler, *Montesquieu's Comparative Politics and the Spirit of American Constitutionalism* (Lawrence: University Press of Kansas, 1988): esp. ch. 5; Pierre Manent, *An Intellectual History of Liberalism*, Rebecca Balinski, trans. (Princeton:

was a free government to the extent that the British Constitution had "political liberty for its direct purpose," but this purpose was sufficiently channeled or "hidden" through a series of institutional devices that protected the individual from arbitrary government, whether monarchical or democratic.[29] Montesquieu shared Hume's distrust of emphasizing the contractual origins of government and his criticism of the twin evils of unrestrained democracy and absolute monarchy. Montesquieu saw in the eighteenth-century British Constitution a concrete manifestation of the sort of enlightened practical wisdom that evaded what he took to be the logical fallacy of radical republicanism, in which "the power of the people has been confused with the liberty of the people."[30] For Montesquieu, the moderate government in Britain contrasted favorably with the public-spirited and warlike democracies of classical antiquity, as well as with the system of centralized autocracy he identified with the Ottoman East but perceived to be spreading into the postfeudal monarchies of continental Europe, including France.[31] In both the austere virtues of the classical republics and the routinized terror of oriental despotism, Montesquieu recognized ruling principles that did violence to the human material composing government and society. In contrast, for Montesquieu, Britain's balanced Constitution, with its internal dynamic resisting the concentration of power, conformed admirably to the natural human desire for the comfortable and benign hedonism denied to the classical *demos* and the sense of physical security impossible to achieve in despotic regimes.

The core of Montesquieu's account of the British Constitution was his admiration for its system of checks and balances, especially the division of power between the independent hereditary executive and the bicameral legislature composed of Lords and Commons. Through its separation of the executive, legislative, and judicial powers, Montesquieu claimed, the British government could reliably avoid the arbitrary power of royal or democratic absolutism: "The form of these three powers should be rest or inaction, but

---

Princeton University Press, 1994): ch. 5; Thomas Pangle, *Montesquieu's Philosophy of Liberalism* (Chicago: University of Chicago Press, 1973): ch. 5; Rahe, *Republics*, pp. 293–7, 440–4 and "Forms of Government: Structure, Principle, Object and Aim," in *Montesquieu's Science of Politics: Essays on the Spirit of the Laws*, David W. Carrithers, Michael A. Mosher, and Paul A. Rahe, eds. (Lanham, MD: Rowman & Littlefield, 2001): pp. 71–2, 80–90, 94–7; and James Stoner, *Common Law and Liberal Theory: Coke, Hobbes, and the Origin of American Constitutionalism* (Lawrence: University Press of Kansas, 1992): ch. 9.

[29] Montesquieu, *Spirit*, 11.5.156.

[30] Ibid., 11.2.155.

[31] For Montesquieu's treatment of despotism, see *Spirit*, 2.5, 3.8–10, 4.3, and 5.13–15; for the classical republic, see 2.2, 3.3, 4.4–8, and 5.2–7. For Montesquieu's complex mixture of genuine admiration and profound revulsion at the severity of the classical republic, see Rahe, "Forms of Government," p. 75 and Schaub's excellent discussion (Diana Schaub, *Erotic Liberalism: Women and Revolution in Montesquieu's Persian Letters* [Lanham, MD: Rowman & Littlefield], 1995: pp. 19, 37, 137–42).

as they are constrained to move by the necessary motion of things, they will be forced to move in concert."[32] It is important to recognize that in his account of the British balanced Constitution, Montesquieu did not identify Britain as a mixed regime. The British separation of powers system was, according to Montesquieu, grafted onto historical institutions such as the hereditary Lords and monarchy, but it was in the decisive sense a product of political prudence embodied in the compendium of legislation including the Bill of Rights of 1689 and the Act of Settlement of 1701 that formed the revolution settlement. Montesquieu was as concerned to disavow the legacy of constitutional irregularity and instability of English civil war era mixed regime theory as were the moderate Whig architects of the revolution settlement.[33] The point of Montesquieu's admittedly idealized, and in some respects more prescriptive than descriptive, account of the British Constitution was to expose the theoretical foundations of the British system of legal sovereignty that emerged from the revolution of 1688–9. Montesquieu demonstrates that postrevolution Britain at the very least suggested the possibility of creating, through legislation and policy, the matrix of institutional power relations necessary to provide constitutional balance without the benefit of the intermediary feudal institutions he claims helped moderate other European monarchies such as France. The distribution of powers embedded in the moderate Whig idea of legal sovereignty had successfully, according to Montesquieu, shifted the emphasis in thinking about constitutional moderation away from the claims of societal representativeness by the various composite elements of the older idea of mixed regime toward the more sound principle of relying on the inevitable relations of legally interconnected and interdependent structures and institutions.[34] It was by virtue of the necessary interaction of the institutional elements of the British sovereign that the British Constitution was, in Montesquieu's assessment, the closest thing to a government truly of laws that had yet appeared in human history.

It was in light of the profoundly legalistic character of British constitutionalism that Montesquieu offered his most original and perhaps most significant contribution to the study of the British Constitution: his analysis of the judicial power. For Montesquieu, Britain's treatment of the judicial power, a power "so terrible among men," whereby the entire power of the state comes crashing down on the individual, pointed to an essential feature of moderate government. Montesquieu recognized in the British jury system, in which the power of judging is "exercised by persons drawn from the body

---

[32] Montesquieu, *Spirit*, 11.6.157–9, 11.6.164.

[33] See *Spirit*, 3.1.22, for Montesquieu's disparaging assessment of the results of the English civil war. Cf. Rahe, "Forms of Government," p. 103, n. 41.

[34] Perhaps this is one reason why, in contrast to his procedure in his regime analysis in Books III–VIII, Montesquieu does not offer a single "principle" animating the English regime. By virtue of the structural design of the Constitution, a multiplicity of passions necessarily acquire political saliency in Britain. Cf. Rahe, "Forms of Government," pp. 71–2.

of the people," an awareness of the important psychological dimension in the experience of political liberty. Montesquieu argued that the many legal and institutional supports for civil liberties in Britain encouraged in the individual "that tranquility of spirit which comes from the opinion each one has of his security."[35]

While his praise for the system of checks and balances presented a decidedly moderate Whig view of the balanced Constitution, Montesquieu's celebration of British civil liberties signified an element of Whig thought embodied in the Habeas Corpus Act of 1679, the Toleration Act of 1689, and the establishment of an independent judiciary in the Act of Settlement of 1701 that generally transcended the moderate–radical cleavage in the Whig ranks.[36] In Humean terms, Montesquieu positively evaluated the diluted partisanship in Britain, where he saw loose and ephemeral coalitions of interests colliding as Court and Country, rather than theological and fiercely ideological parties battling to the death over the fundamentals of government. In the partisan struggles characterizing midcentury Britain, Montesquieu saw real "hatred" that would endure precisely "because it would always be powerless" to alter the Constitution significantly in a monarchical or democratic direction.[37] In the established tradition of moderate Whiggism, Montesquieu emphasized the direct political relevance of considerations of utility: Does this system of government effectively protect individuals from each other and from the awesome power of the state? Of Britain in the eighteenth century, Montesqieu said, *mais oui*! In many respects, Montesquieu's high praise for the British commercial society established after the Glorious Revolution, with its enlightened system of criminal justice and its balanced Constitution, could only reinforce moderate Whig triumphalism at midcentury.

The last of the troika of important intellectual voices that did so much to articulate and define the way the British political nation understood itself and its system of government in the years leading up to and during the imperial crisis with America was the legendary jurist Sir William Blackstone. Blackstone's *Commentaries on the Laws of England*, published between 1765

---

35 Montesquieu, *Spirit*, 11.6. 157–8. Cf. Rahe's discussion in *Republics*, pp. 441–3. Rahe makes the interesting claim that insofar as individuals detached from their feudal institutional moorings experience, in Montesquieu's view, great uneasiness (*inquietude*) in their relations with others, the government of England "has an undeniable kinship with despotism" ("Forms of Government," pp. 83–4; cf. C. P. Courtney, "Montesquieu and English Liberty," in *Montesquieu's Science of Politics*, p. 284 for the contrary view). The qualitative difference, then, between English uneasiness and despotic terrorism would rest not only in the softening of mores produced by commerce in England but also, somewhat paradoxically, by the heightened vigilance the individual feels about ensuring the institutional and legal safeguards against government oppression (cf. Rahe, "Forms of Government," 94–6).

36 Rahe, *Republics*, p. 211. Cf. Montesquieu, *Spirit*, 6.17.92 for Montesquieu's praise for Britain's prohibition on torture.

37 Montesqieu, *Spirit*, 19.27.325. Compare Courtney, "English Liberty," p. 283 and Rahe, "Forms of Government," p. 88.

and 1769, were in many respects an echo of the ideological self-confidence of moderate Whig hegemony at midcentury. Blackstone's reputation as a Tory is perhaps even less justified than that of Hume. Even at the height of the imperial crisis, Americans referred to Blackstone as a champion of individual property rights against the abuse of legislative power.[38] Moreover, Blackstone never supported the unrestrained exercise of monarchal power. In a manner almost identical to that of Hume and Montesquieu, Blackstone celebrated the system of checks and balances characterizing Britain's complex and compound Constitution:

> Herein indeed consists the true excellence of the English government, that all the parts of it form a mutual check upon each other. In the legislature, the people are a check upon the nobility, and the nobility a check upon the people, ... while the king is a check upon both, which preserves the executive power from encroachments. And this very executive power is again checked and kept within due bonds by the two houses. ... Thus every branch of our polity supports and is supported, regulates and is regulated, by the rest.[39]

Blackstone emphasizes the importance of an independent hereditary executive proven by the legislative tyranny of the 1640s that "overturned both church and state," even as he advocates "more complete representation of the people" in the Commons. In classic moderate Whig fashion, Blackstone locates the genius of the British Constitution in its capacity to achieve a harmonious equipoise between absolute monarchy and democracy by balancing the great sociopolitical estates of the nation in the legal sovereignty of king-in-Parliament.[40]

While never explicitly rejecting the idea of the ancient constitution, Blackstone did reject the central tenets of radical contract theory. For example, he referred to the authority of Pufendorf to demonstrate that the Lockean state of nature in which individuals are "unconnected with other individuals" was a historical and logical nullity given natural human sociability. Much like the Whig managers at the Sacheverell trial, he understood the right of resistance in terms of extreme necessity rather than popular sovereignty, and he viewed the Glorious Revolution as an event occasioned

---

[38] H. T. Dickinson, "The Eighteenth Century Debate on the Sovereignty of Parliament," *Transactions of the Royal Historical Society*, fifth ser., vol. 26 (1976): p. 206 and Rahe, *Republics*, pp. 530–3. For a good treatment of the Americans' use of Blackstone as a champion of property rights, see Gerald Stourz, "William Blackstone: Teacher of Revolution," *Jährbuch für Amerikastudien*, vol. 15 (1970): pp. 184–200 and Glendon's argument for Blackstone's formative role in the development of the American understanding of property rights (Mary Ann Glendon, *Rights Talk* [New York: Free Press, 1991]: pp. 22–4). For a dissenting view that asserts the essential irrelevance of Blackstone in America, see David Mayer, "The English Radical Whig Origins of American Constitutionalism," *Washington University Law Quarterly*, vol. 70 (1992): esp. pp. 196–204.

[39] William Blackstone, *Commentaries on the Laws of England* (London, 1791): Vol. 1, pp. 154–5.

[40] Ibid., pp. 154, 171–2. Cf. Rahe, *Republics*, p. 439.

by "a palpable vacancy of a throne" in which, echoing Tyrrell, Burnet, and Atwood, he claimed that "the body of the nation, consisting of lords and commons, would have a right to meet and settle the government." Blackstone also shared Hume's deep distrust of the highly speculative theory of the dissolution of government advanced by "Mr. Locke and other theoretical writers." Blackstone concluded that "however just this conclusion is in theory, we cannot practically adopt it."[41] By this he did not mean that dissolution theory, while logically sound, did not apply to the conditions of 1688–9. Rather, Blackstone, following Atwood, adopted the identifiably Pufendorfian dictum that the principle of dissolution is antithetical to the very nature of organized social life: "No human laws will therefore suppose a case, which at once must destroy all law, and compel men to build afresh upon a new foundation; nor will they make provision for so desperate an event, as must render all legal provisions ineffectual."[42] Blackstone's opposition to radical dissolution theory, and its essential corollary, popular sovereignty, was then based on principle, not simply pragmatism, although the principle at issue was itself profoundly pragmatic.

However, Blackstone's most momentous contribution to British constitutional theory in the eighteenth century was his argument for parliamentary sovereignty. It was on the matter of parliamentary sovereignty that Blackstone's argument ran directly contrary to American colonial aspirations and interpretations of the imperial order and the meaning of British liberty. On the issue of sovereignty, Blackstone collected, formalized and solidified theoretical premises implicit in Hume, Montesquieu, and moderate Whig thinkers tracing back through Tyrrell to Pufendorf.[43] The structural limits on the British government supplied by internal checks and balances meant that Parliament could combine a claim of absolute legal sovereignty with a relative assurance against arbitrary power. While Blackstone agreed with

---

[41] Blackstone, *Commentaries*, pp. 43–8, 152, 161–2.

[42] Ibid., p. 162; see also p. 213 (cf. Pufendorf, DJNG 7.8.9; 7.7.9). Stoner (*Common Law*, ch. 10) and Storing argue that Blackstone fundamentally agrees with Lockean premises but offers a constitutionalist formula for Lockean natural rights (Herbert Storing, "William Blackstone," *History of Political Philosophy*, 3rd ed., Leo Strauss and Joseph Cropsey, eds. [Chicago: University of Chicago Press, 1987]: pp. 622–33). While there is much in these interpretations with which I agree, I believe Blackstone's rejection of the individualist and radical implications of Locke's dissolution theory reflects a fundamental disagreement with Locke over the natural constituent power of the people to form new societies that is so central to radical Whig ideology and thus seriously qualifies Blackstone's prudential Lockeanism.

[43] Stoner identifies Blackstone as a Hobbesian on the issue of sovereignty, whereas Vile argues that he is by and large a replica of Montesquieu (Stoner, *Common Law*, pp. 166–75 and Vile, *Separation of Powers*, pp. 111–12). While Goldsworthy (*Sovereignty of Parliament*, pp. 7, 188) is correct to dissociate Blackstone from the legal positivism of Hobbes, it is mistaken to derive his argument from the parliamentary theories of the civil war era, which had failed signally to achieve constitutional balance. In contrast, I contend that Blackstone's absolutism has a Pufendorfian root in the moderate Whig tradition.

Locke about the natural law limits placed on the legislature's interference with property rights, he seriously diverged from the radicals in his argument for parliamentary sovereignty against the claims of popular sovereignty. His argument for parliamentary sovereignty reflects the two central Pufendorfian ideas at the foundation of the moderate Whig constitutional theory. The first is Blackstone's reliance on the Pufendorfian principle that the essence of law is to be a command of a superior directed to an inferior: "Unless some superior be constituted, whose commands and decisions all the members [of society] are bound to obey, they would still remain in a state of nature, without any judge on earth to define their several rights, and redress their several wrongs."[44] Thus, in Blackstone's view, the voluntaristic basis of law makes the mutual coherence of a sovereign government and a sovereign people a logical and moral impossibility.

The second major element of Blackstone's argument for parliamentary sovereignty drew from Pufendorf's notion of the inescapable need for one legally constituted sovereign authority in any constitutional order. Blackstone claims that in any form of government "there is and must be ... a supreme, irresistible, absolute, uncontrolled authority in which ... the rights of sovereignty reside."[45] In Britain this sovereign authority, he continues, rests in Parliament, which has authority "in the making, confirming, enlarging, restraining, abrogating, repealing, reviving, and expounding of laws" and can "change and create afresh even the constitution of the kingdom and of parliaments themselves."[46] With Blackstone we see the hardening of the orthodoxy of parliamentary sovereignty identifiable as far back as the Convention debates and the Septennial Act, and even further back to

---

[44] Blackstone, *Commentaries*, p. 48. Cf. Pufendorf, DJNG 1.6.1–4; 8.1.1. See also John V. Jezierski, "Parliament or People: James Wilson and William Blackstone on the Nature and Location of Sovereignty," *Journal of the History of Ideas*, vol. 32, issue 1 (January–March, 1971): p. 100 and James Wilson, "Of Municipal Law," *American Political Writing during the Founding Era, 1760–1805, Vol. II*, Charles S. Hyneman and Donald S. Lutz, eds. (Indianapolis: Liberty Classics, 1983): pp. 1266–7, 1278, 1287, 1289 for Pufendorf's influence on Blackstone.

[45] Blackstone, *Commentaries*, p. 49. Cf. Pufendorf, DJNG 7.6.1,7; 4.7.9–13.

[46] Blackstone, *Commentaries*, pp. 160–1. Reid and Dickinson make the correct observation that in Blackstone's ideas of the 1760s we see "a new constitution of arbitrary parliamentary sovereignty" emerging in Britain (see Dickinson, "The Eighteenth Century Debate Over Parliamentary Sovereignty," pp. 190, 194–6 and John Philip Reid, *Constitutional History of the American Revolution: The Authority to Legislate*, [Madison: University of Wisconsin Press, 1991]: 4; cf. Jezierski, "Parliament or People," p. 96). I would only add with Goldsworthy (*Sovereignty of Parliament*, p. 7) the important caveat that the *idea* of parliamentary sovereignty had deep roots at the very origin of moderate Whiggism in the Exclusion era and the Glorious Revolution, even if the idea did not achieve general acceptance or mature articulation until a good deal later. However, in contrast to Goldsworthy, I would not trace this idea as far back as medieval theorists such as Dante, Marsilius, and Ockham who operated in a very different theologically charged period (Goldsworthy, *Sovereignty of Parliament*, pp. 18–19).

Tyrrell and the moderate Whigs in the Exclusion period. This was a process of ideological solidification that saw even the Tories transfer allegiance from absolute monarch to absolute king-in-Parliament.

What were the implications of Blackstone's argument regarding parliamentary sovereignty for the coming dispute with American Whigs in the years leading up to the revolution in the colonies? Blackstone explicitly extended the principle of parliamentary sovereignty to America, arguing that American colonists enjoyed a limited right of self-government but were "also liable to . . . the general superintending power of the legislature in the mother country."[47] Blackstone, then, not only advanced parliamentary sovereignty as the governing principle of the British Constitution, he also confirmed it as the principle by which Britain ruled the empire. In so doing, Blackstone crystallized ideas with deep roots in moderate Whig philosophy, conservative ideas about sovereignty and rights that had, if anything, only strengthened their hold on the British Whig imagination in the little less than a century since the Glorious Revolution. These ideas would play a major role in guiding British policy and informing British political ideology throughout the imperial crisis with America.

---

[47] Blackstone, *Commentaries*, p. 108. Blackstone voted against the repeal of the Stamp Act as a member of Parliament in 1766. Despite this opposition to the colonial position, Samuelson shows that Blackstone's authority as an expert in the common law gave him great influence among lawyers in the colonies (see Richard Samuelson, "The Constitutional Sanity of James Otis: Resistance Leader and Loyal Subject," *Review of Politics*, vol. 61, no. 3 [Summer 1999]: pp. 503–4, 510). For Blackstone's legacy as the authority in America on the common law, see Bonwick, "United States Constitution," pp. 52–3 and Stoner, *Common Law*, chs. 12 and 13.

PART THREE

THE WHIG LEGACY IN AMERICA

As we have seen, the common front against divine right absolutism that united the various strands of English Whig thought in the Exclusion era soon splintered when the Stuart line, or at least from the Whig perspective the most unsavory (i.e., Catholic) elements of it, were packed off to forced exile and eventual oblivion. The very term "Whig" came to represent differing, often conflicting, and eventually quite separate ideas of liberty and government. Our analysis of the distinct strands of Whiggism present at the origin of this diverse body of thought provides a conceptual framework by which we can trace the development of the modern politics of liberty in eighteenth-century England and America. I have argued that the diversity within the Whig school reflects the enormous impact of modern natural jurisprudence on English constitutional and political thought. Such thinkers as Pufendorf and Spinoza made their impact on Anglo-American thought largely indirectly through the medium of the Whigs. Imagine the foundational works of Tyrrell, Sidney, and Locke to be intellectual and philosophical genetic markers placed in the bloodstream of the tradition. In the following discussion, we will identify and analyze the full panoply of Anglo-American Whig thought including moderate, liberal, and republican strains of Whiggism as they emerged, intersected, and even quarreled in the twelve-year period spanning the beginning of the Anglo-American imperial dispute in 1764 and the American Declaration of Independence in 1776.

Whigs came in a variety of flavors, and the various strains of Whiggism made their presence felt in different times and among different groups. Ironically, the moderate Whiggism of James Tyrrell, by far the least celebrated of the major Exclusion Whigs today, reflected the conception of rights and sovereignty that governed England politically and philosophically throughout the eighteenth century. The Glorious Revolution of 1688–89, or at least the official Whig version of events, heralded the eventual triumph of moderate Whiggism in England. In the century that followed the Glorious Revolution, most Englishmen would understand and defend their constitutional monarchy in terms first articulated by Tyrrell. Through the medium of moderate Whigs like Tyrrell, Gilbert Burnet, and William Atwood, and later a modified version of moderate Whiggism through David Hume and William Blackstone, Britons imbibed Pufendorfian principles of sovereignty and law. These principles, once duly modified for the British political and constitutional context, provided Britain's ruling Whigs with the theoretical resources to resist the historical claims and philosophical pretensions of both royal absolutism and radical popular sovereignty. For its part, the radical Whig legacy of liberal individualism and populist republicanism survived on the margins of British political thought but took root in the rich soil of America, and came to revolutionary fruition in the imperial dispute of the decade or so prior to American independence.

It is perhaps an irony that the Anglo–American dispute preceding independence amounted to ideological internecine warfare among the Whig descendants of the Exclusion era heroes. British and American Whigs quarreled over fundamental questions of sovereignty, the character of rights, the importance of representation, and the best form of government. They did so, moreover, within the broad but identifiable framework of Whig philosophy established many decades earlier. All Whigs, moderate and radical, agreed on the principle of natural liberty and the contractual origins of government in consent. However, they differed over the constitutional, political, and moral implications flowing from these basic premises. The radical Whig philosophy of liberal individualism and populist republicanism, though marginalized in the official Whig ideology in Britain, became the fundamental political creed in the colonies. The American spokesmen drew on the theoretical resources and guiding principles of radical Whiggism identified with Locke, Sidney, and the opposition Whigs Trenchard and Gordon to justify their claims for colonial self-government. The British government countered with characteristically moderate Whig arguments drawn from the pages of Pufendorf, Tyrrell, and the architects of the settlement of 1689. In the colonial camp, American Whigs like James Otis, John Dickinson, Thomas Jefferson, and Tom Paine drew freely from both the liberal and republican strains of radical Whiggism, creating the complex, philosophically pluralistic, and intellectually heterogeneous whole that was to typify the early republic. In what follows, we shall see that the Whig legacy in America was a song of liberty with many parts and several distinct voices.

12

British Constitutionalism and the Challenge of Empire

The glorification of the British Constitution during the middle of the eighteenth century seen in Hume, Montesquieu, and Blackstone was not exclusively a British or even a European phenomenon. Deep admiration for the constitutional order produced by the Glorious Revolution was manifest in clear evidence on both sides of the Atlantic. Americans typically celebrated what they took to be the great virtues of British constitutionalism, such as the separation of powers, representative government, and the defense of civil liberties or "rights of Englishmen" with as much enthusiasm as their British brethren in the "transatlantic community" formed by the bonds of common sentiments, regular commercial contact, and, perhaps most importantly, a shared intellectual and political tradition.[1] From Hume, Montesquieu, Blackstone, and the host of Whig writers including Trenchard and Gordon, Locke, and Sidney, Americans took enormous pride in what they perceived to be their constitutional heritage. The success of the revolution settlement touched the colonies in a particularly palpable way when the British government, primarily under Pitt's energetic leadership, fought and won a global war with its old foe, France, from 1756 to 1763 that ensured British supremacy over most of North America. With the defeat of Bourbon France in the New World and the colonies thriving with their own experience of self-government, political stability, and commercial prosperity under the benign neglect of the mother country, Americans in the middle of the eighteenth century by and large enjoyed as much contentment and political self-assurance as their complacent Whig brethren in the Old World.

---

[1] For good discussions of the "transatlantic community" between Britain and its American colonies at midcentury, see Colin Bonwick, *English Radicals and the American Revolution* (Chapel Hill: University of North Carolina Press, 1977): ch. 2 and "The United States Constitution and Its Roots in British Political Thought and Practice," *Foundations of Democracy in the European Union: From the Genesis of Parliamentary Democracy to the European Parliament*, John Pinder, ed. (New York: St. Martin's, 1999): pp. 42–3.

The Challenge of Empire

With the last shot in the Seven Years War, the global power struggle between Britain and France, barely spent, a new constitutional and philosophical dispute simmered to the surface in the Anglo-American world over British and colonial interpretations of the empire. While both British and American Whigs lauded the virtues of British constitutionalism, it became increasingly apparent throughout the course of the crisis that they understood the meaning of the Glorious Revolution, the idea of sovereignty, and the character of rights very differently. Radical and moderate Whig ideas came in contact, and indeed conflict, in the imperial dispute in a direct and visceral way that had not occurred in Britain since the early Hanoverian period. The same radical ideas and principles that had been thoroughly marginalized by the moderate Whig hegemony in Britain shared a place with British balanced constitutionalism at the core of the political creed of American Whigs. American Whigs in the early stages of the imperial crisis incorporated radical Whig philosophical principles and moderate Whig political commitments to British constitutionalism in a delicate balance that would prove increasingly untenable under the pressure of events in the 1760s and 1770s. These events forced American Whigs not only to reconsider their commitment to British constitutionalism, but also to reexamine the first principles of government simply.

The immediate impetus to the imperial crisis was the effort of the Grenville ministry after the war with France to reorganize the colonial administration and to raise revenue in the colonies. The Grenville program brought to the fore questions surrounding parliamentary sovereignty in the colonies that had remained largely dormant during the long period of British neglect of colonial affairs prior to the Seven Years War. In the Sugar Act of 1764, Parliament extended its traditional power to regulate imperial trade, a power the Americans had always conceded, by designing trade policy with the explicit intention of raising revenue in the colonies. Initial colonial opposition to this blurring of the distinction between what they took to be Parliament's legitimate power over external trade policy and the illegitimate practice of internal taxation was largely confined to the northern colonies most directly affected by the duty on molasses.[2] However, with the passage of the Stamp Act in 1765, the colonists recoiled at Parliament's most assertive claim ever of sovereignty over the colonies. This act, which imposed duties on goods and services in the colonies to raise money for military expenses in America, represented an unambiguous claim for Parliament's power to impose an internal tax on the colonies. The easy passage of the bill through Parliament,

---

[2] For good treatments of the Sugar Act and its effects in America, see Bernard Knollenberg, *Origin of the American Revolution: 1759–1766* (New York: Macmillan, 1960): pp. 27–33 and Edmund S. Morgan and Helen M. Morgan, *The Stamp Act Crisis: Prologue to Revolution* (Chapel Hill: University of North Carolina Press, 1953): pp. 139–49.

with the Pittite Barré as the lone significant voice in opposition, indicates the general presumption in Britain of Parliament's authority over the colonies.[3] In the colonies, however, the hostility to the Stamp Act was overwhelming. Colonial opposition to the act was based more on the matter of constitutional principle than on the expense (which was minimal), and it took several forms. In major ports like Boston and Charleston, organizations such as the Sons of Liberty and the Charles Town Fire Brigade mobilized mass street demonstrations and orchestrated systematic intimidation of the crown-appointed stamp distributors. Colonial assemblies, against the opposition of royal governors, issued resolutions condemning the act and denying Parliament's right to tax the colonies. The Virginia House of Burgesses led the way for the other colonies, declaring: "The taxation of the people, by themselves, or by persons chosen by themselves to represent them, ... is the only security against a burthensome taxation, and the distinguishing characteristic of British freedom."[4] Champions for the colonial cause emerged during the crisis, such as Patrick Henry in Virginia and James Otis in Massachusetts. Otis originated the idea of uniting the various assembly committees into a single Stamp Act Congress, to which nine of the thirteen colonies sent delegates. And, perhaps most ominously from the British perspective, the colonists adopted retaliatory trade practices including the nonimportation of British goods.

With the alarming spread of civil disobedience in the colonies, the protests of influential British merchant groups, and the fortuitous replacement of Grenville with a ministry led by the Marquis of Rockingham, who was much more sympathetic to the Americans, the movement for repeal of the act gained ground in Britain in the winter of 1766. The dilemma confronting Parliament at this time was how to repeal the repugnant act without appearing to countenance the American challenge to the principle of parliamentary sovereignty over the empire. Ultimately Parliament decided to repeal the Stamp Act on prudential grounds, but resolved to maintain the ideological commitment to the principle of parliamentary sovereignty by passing almost simultaneously with its repeal the Declaratory Act, which affirmed that the British Parliament "had, hath, and of right ought to have, full power and authority to make laws and statutes, of sufficient force to bind the colonies

---

[3] See Colonel Barré's impassioned speech in the first parliamentary debate over the Stamp Act proposal (T. C. Hansard, *The Parliamentary History of England, Volume XVI: 1765–1771* [London: Hansard, 1813]: pp. 38–40).

[4] Hansard, *Parliamentary History*, pp. 120–1. For good discussions of the Stamp Act crisis in America, see Knollenberg, *Origin*, chs. 20, 21; Pauline Maier, *From Resistance to Revolution: Colonial Radicals and the Development of American Opposition to Britain, 1765–1776* (New York: Alfred A. Knopf, 1972): chs. 3, 4; and Morgan and Morgan, *Stamp Act Crisis*, chs. 8–11. For the general effect in Britain, see P. D. G. Thomas, *British Politics and the Stamp Act Crisis: The First Phase of the American Revolution, 1763–1767* (Oxford: Clarendon Press, 1975), and for the response of the radicals in Britain to the Stamp Act crisis, see Bonwick, *English Radicals*, pp. 57–61, 75, and 79.

and people of America, subjects of the crown of Great Britain, in all cases whatsoever."[5] Perhaps no single measure during the imperial crisis more clearly demonstrated the depth of the British political nation's commitment to the moderate Whig principles of sovereignty articulated by Blackstone, Tyrrell, and Pufendorf than the Declaratory Act.

The principle of parliamentary sovereignty was affirmed even by the Americans' strongest supporters in Parliament, such as Rockingham and Edmund Burke, with even Pitt never entirely rejecting the doctrine of parliamentary sovereignty.[6] Burke expressed the fundamental ambiguity in the Rockinghamite Whig position in a speech during the debate over the Declaratory Act in which he stated that with respect to the colonies "we have the clearest right imaginable, not only to bind them generally with every Law, but with every mode of Legislative Taxation, that can be thought on." However, he qualified this idea by cautioning that "the practical exertion of many clear rights may by change of time and circumstances become impossible, may be inequitable, may clash with the genius of the very constitution that gives them or at least may clash entirely with liberty."[7] While the initial response to the repeal of the Stamp Act was relief on both sides of the Atlantic, the more serious questions about Parliament's authority over the colonies remained unresolved. When asked under examination by a parliamentary committee whether repeal of the Stamp Act would induce the assemblies in America to acknowledge the right, even if only in theory, of Parliament to tax them, the most important colonial agent in London, Benjamin Franklin, replied unequivocally: "No, never."[8] The tumultuous consequences of Parliament's later, albeit more subtle, attempt to raise revenue in the colonies through the Townshend duties were clearly foreshadowed in the fundamental dispute over the nature of imperial sovereignty in the Stamp Act crisis.

The legacy of the Stamp Act debacle in Britain was complex. On the one hand, the repeal movement demonstrated that America had influential friends in the British government and polity. On the other hand, the support for the Declaratory Act expressed by mainstream British leadership and public opinion signified the hardening of the orthodoxy of parliamentary

[5] Hansard, *Parliamentary History*, p. 165.

[6] Bonwick, *English Radicals*, pp. 60, 66; H. T. Dickinson, "The Eighteenth Century Debate on the Sovereignty of Parliament," *Transactions of the Royal Historical Society*, fifth ser., vol. 26 (1976): p. 190 and Jeffrey Goldsworthy, *The Sovereignty of Parliament: History and Philosophy* (Oxford: Clarendon Press, 1999): pp. 192–3, 196. However, note that in some respects Pitt and his follower, Lord Camden, criticized the idea of parliamentary sovereignty in favor of Locke's popular sovereignty argument – if not with respect to all forms of legislation, at least with regard to taxation of the colonies (see Camden's speech in the Lords in Hansard, *Parliamentary History*, pp. 177–81).

[7] Edmund Burke, "Speech on the Declaratory Resolution, February 3 1766," *The Writings and Speeches of Edmund Burke, Volume II: Party, Parliament, and the American Crisis 1766–1774*, Paul Langford, ed. (Oxford: Clarendon Press, 1981): pp. 48–9.

[8] Hansard, *Parliamentary History*, p. 160.

sovereignty and the central role of this doctrine in the British vision for the future government of the empire. The legacy of the Stamp Act in America was momentous. It signified the most successful, broad-based resistance movement to imperial authority in American history up to that time. The colonial opponents to the Stamp Act developed sophisticated techniques to mobilize opposition groups and public sentiment, and effectively organized and administered extralegal institutions such as the Stamp Act Congress and later the Committees of Correspondence. Moreover, the colonial opposition to the Stamp Act demonstrated a degree of practical cooperation among the colonies hitherto unknown. In many respects, the Stamp Act Congress represented the seedbed of colonial union with the identification of a common American interest, as opposed to thirteen separate colonial interests, distinct from Britain.[9] But the most profound legacy of the first parliamentary attempt to tax the colonies occurred on the level of ideas. This was, after all, primarily a dispute about principle, and the gifted colonial spokesmen who championed the colonial cause in the early stages of the imperial crisis began the process of articulation, modification, and consolidation of philosophical principles that would mark the ever-widening ideological cleavage between British and American Whigs.

We can now begin to trace the radical Whig core of American resistance theory by examining the works of the two most influential colonial spokesmen in the early stages of the quarrel with Britain, James Otis and John Dickinson. These early colonial champions developed arguments for limited colonial self-government that rested on distinctively Lockean ideas of natural rights, property, and political representation. Where they differed from later and more radical colonial spokesmen like Thomas Jefferson and Thomas Paine, however, was in their ultimate, albeit reluctant, acceptance of the moderate Whig conception of constitutional sovereignty as it applied to the empire. They admitted that some legally constituted body must be sovereign in the empire, that is, a body with no higher body to command it, and they duly identified this sovereignty in Parliament. This distinctive combination of radical and moderate Whig principles would mark the early colonial attempts to devise a moderate theory of the empire, which tried to combine supreme sovereignty in Westminster with considerable self-government in the colonies.

Otis' Rights Asserted

Massachusetts lawyer James Otis' *The Rights of the British Colonies Asserted and Proved* (1764) was the first important work in the pamphlet war initiated by the imperial dispute between the British government and the American

---

[9] In a sense, the degree of colonial cooperation in the Stamp Act crisis made manifest the underlying thrust of the logic of Franklin's Albany Plan of Union devised a decade earlier.

colonists. The issue that prompted Otis' effort was the debate over Parliament's presumptive right to tax the colonies. The historical context of the *Rights* is the colonial opposition to the Sugar Act of 1764 and the colonists' anticipation of the Stamp Act the following year. Otis had first come to the attention of many in the colonies three years earlier, when he represented a group of Boston merchants in a suit challenging the extension of general writs of assistance. These writs, which had been introduced near the beginning of the war with France to stop illegal trade with the French West Indies, authorized colonial courts to permit customs officers to enter warehouses, stores, and even private homes in order to search for smuggled goods. Otis acquired widespread celebrity not only for his eloquent attack on the writs but, more importantly, for his willingness to claim that Parliament's right to legislate for the colonies was subject to limitations set by British constitutional practice and the principles of natural justice. He argued, echoing Sir Edward Coke's opinion in *Dr Bonham's Case* (1610), that regardless of parliamentary sanction "An Act against the Constitution is void: an act against natural equity is void." One portentous witness to the proceedings, a young John Adams, later reflected on the significance of Otis' argument: "then and there the Child Independence was born."[10]

Otis' argument in the *Rights* is in many respects an amplification of his position in the writs case. He provides a theoretical account for the philosophical foundations of colonial self-government that draws heavily on the natural rights teaching of John Locke. Using the logic of the Lockean principle of consent, Otis argues that only the colonial legislatures may legitimately tax the colonists, because these are the only bodies by which they have consented to be taxed and in which they are represented. Otis also interprets British constitutional principles and Anglo-American imperial history through a decidedly radical Whig lens. In this sense, the *Rights* provides a wonderful demonstration of how thoroughly Lockean liberal principles could be used to defend mixed and balanced constitutional forms.

However, Otis also reveals the complex relation between the radical and moderate Whig principles underlying the early colonial position in the imperial crisis. Otis offers glowing, often effusive, praise for the British Constitution and what he takes to be the principles of the Glorious Revolution. Even though the theoretical foundation of Otis' argument for colonial self-government was radical Whig rights and contract theory, his guiding authorities on matters of constitutional design and political architecture were the eighteenth-century moderate Whig apologists for the British

---

[10] Knollenberg, *Origins*, pp. 67–9 and James Stoner, *Common Law and Liberal Theory: Coke, Hobbes, and the Origins of American Constitutionalism* (Lawrence: University Press of Kansas, 1992): pp. 190–1. For Otis' prominent role as a political organizer and intellectual leader of the colonies in the Stamp Act period, see Morgan and Morgan (*Stamp Act Crisis*, pp. 34, 38, 104–5, 209–10, 273).

Constitution. In defending the mixed and balanced constitutional model as it applied to the colonial context, with the British crown an integral element of colonial constitutionalism, Otis rejected the radical republican conclusions advanced by Sidney and implied by Trenchard and Gordon, favoring rather the tried and tested compound government praised by Bolingbroke, Hume, and Montesquieu. Despite John Adams' assessment of the radical impact of Otis' arguments, the spirit of abiding moderation in the *Rights* made Otis an advocate for neither revolution nor independence as the solution to the imperial crisis. More importantly, however, Otis' radical rights theory is seriously qualified by elements of an essentially moderate Whig conception of sovereignty. While he denies Parliament the power to tax the colonies, Otis simultaneously affirms that Parliament is the supreme legislature in the colonies and as such is empowered to manage imperial affairs by regulating trade and coordinating defense policy among and between the various colonies and the mother country. Otis accepted the moderate Whig principle of parliamentary sovereignty, and the Pufendorfian ideas underlying it, but wanted to retain considerable autonomy for the subordinate colonial legislatures. He wanted to demonstrate in the *Rights* that a high degree of colonial self-government is not incompatible with either British constitutional principles or parliamentary sovereignty in the empire. It is this uneasy balance of the radical and moderate Whig elements in America's English political inheritance that characterized the early colonial position in the imperial crisis.

From the opening pages of the *Rights*, it is apparent that Otis is not averse to applying radical Whig natural rights theory to the issues facing Americans in the mid-1760s. Otis refers to Locke often and presents him as the chief authority for the colonial position. Indeed, Otis' introduction to the *Rights*, entitled "Of the Origin of Government," is a veritable compendium of Lockean radical Whig principles. Otis asserts that the natural human condition is one of perfect freedom and equality. With direct quotations from Locke's *Two Treatises*, Otis draws the fundamental premises: "There is nothing more evident, says Mr. Locke, than 'that creatures of the same species and rank, promiscuously born to all the same advantages of nature and use of the same faculties, should also be equal one among another without subordination and subjection" and "the natural liberty of man is to free from any superior power on earth, and not to be under the will or legislative authority of man, but only to have the law of nature for his rule." The starting point for any explication of the origin of government, then, is what Otis calls "the natural and original rights of each individual." Natural liberty, according to Otis, anchors the "great law of self-preservation," the natural law principle animating the purpose of government.[11] Otis' natural

---

[11] James Otis, "The Rights of the British Colonies Asserted and Proved" (1764), in *Pamphlets of the American Revolution, 1750–1776*, ed. Bernard Bailyn, ed. (Cambridge, MA: Harvard University Press, 1965), pp. 440, 439, 426 (cf. John Locke, *Two Treatises of Government*

rights are emphatically Lockean. They signify the natural liberty and equality of individuals.

Predictably, Otis' account of the origins of government also draws heavily from Locke. He frames his account of the origins of political society as a response to a series of objections to the doctrine of natural liberty. These objections amount to a rehearsal of Filmer's criticisms of contract and include Sir Robert's remonstrations against the feasibility and desirability of the universal consent of all individuals to government. In fine Whig fashion, Otis rejects practically out of hand the arguments that government originates in divine grace, in conquest, or in a proprietary right.[12] Otis' concern in this introduction to the *Rights* is to establish the principle of the contractual origins of government as the only basis of any rational discussion of politics. In other words, Otis assumes that British Whigs and the Americans could agree on this fundamental question. To be a Whig was, of course, to disagree with Filmer. However, rather than demonstrate through detailed analysis the truth of contract theory to British Whigs, who presumably would not quarrel with the idea of contract, Otis simply refers the reader to "Mr. Locke's discourses on government,... and their own consciences."[13] While it is unfortunate that Otis did not present a fuller account of the origins of government, it is important to note his explicit criticism of the Grotian position on the legitimacy of absolute contracts. Here Otis shows mildly, but firmly, an important departure from a theoretical possibility left somewhat unresolved in moderate Whig thought. Otis queries: "Is it possible for a man to have a natural right to make a slave of himself or his

---

(1690), Peter Laslett, ed. [Cambridge: Cambridge University Press, 1988]: II:4, II:22). For Otis' appeal to natural rights, see Robert Webking, *The American Revolution and the Politics of Liberty* (Baton Rouge: Louisiana State University Press, 1988): p. 25 and to Locke in particular, see Steven Dworetz, *The Unvarnished Doctrine: Locke, Liberalism, and the American Revolution* (Durham: Duke University Press, 1990): p. 85 and Thomas Pangle, *The Spirit of Modern Republicanism* (Chicago: University of Chicago Press, 1988): p. 304, n. 9. Given Otis' clear and articulate appeal to Lockean natural rights as the foundation of his argument in the introduction to the rights, John Phillip Reid's argument (*Constitutional History of the American Revolution: The Authority to Legislate*. [Madison: University of Wisconsin Press, 1991]: p. 5) that the American leaders appealed exclusively to rights defined by the British Constitution appear singularly unpersuasive.

[12] Otis, *Rights*, pp. 419–20 (cf. Jerome Huyler, *Locke in America* [Lawrence: University Press of Kansas, 1995]: pp. 221–2).

[13] Otis, *Rights*, p. 421. This probably says more about Locke's great stature in the colonies than about Otis' understanding of the mindset of the architects of British imperial policy in the 1760s. Alan Houston draws on Otis' other writings to make the interesting observation that Otis believed that Sidney was widely held in the colonies in the 1760s to be more radical than Locke (*Algernon Sidney and the Republican Heritage in England and America* [Princeton: Princeton University Press, 1991: p. 238). This is not surprising considering that Lockean principles were consistent with mixed monarchy – the system familiar to Americans – whereas Sidney's ardent republicanism would not really find an audience in the colonies until the publication of Paine's *Common Sense* in 1776.

posterity?" He later responds that natural liberty, "this gift of God cannot be eliminated."[14]

Otis' position on natural rights, then, follows that of the radical Whigs, especially Locke and presumably Cato, in affirming the ultimate inalienability of natural liberty. No absolute contract may be valid. In this way, Otis shows the vast conceptual chasm between the radical Whiggism of the American defenders of colonial rights and the Pufendorfian (and on this issue Grotian) assumptions of most English Whigs. The more generally restrictive character of Grotian and Pufendorfian compact theory drew from their reflections on the logical possibilities flowing from natural liberty. Even very bad contracts, or contracts gone bad, entail a binding obligation on individuals. Otis follows Locke in favoring popular sovereignty over contractual originalism. He asserts that the "supreme absolute power" in any government is found both "originally" and "ultimately" in the people.[15] Otis' understanding of the nature of contract and the origins of political society reflects the radical Whig notion that political power is "given in trust and on condition the performance of which no mortal can dispense with, namely, that the person or persons on whom sovereignty is conferred by the people shall *incessantly* consult *their* good."[16] Accepting the fiduciary character of political power leads Otis to endorse the principle of dissolution. This meant Otis supported, at least in principle if not in the immediate American context, a more radical right of revolution than the moderate Whigs who shaped the Glorious Revolution. This is important to keep in mind when we consider that Otis is, as we shall see, a relative moderate among the colonial spokesmen. Perhaps the most signal feature of the philosophical dimension of the imperial dispute is the fact that even the moderates in America effortlessly and naturally articulated principles that would have put them on the radical fringes of political discourse in England. Otis reminds us of the extent to which the American and British wings of Whiggism were talking past each other in the imperial crisis.

The end of government, the purpose for which individuals contract to form political society, is, in Otis' view, the "good of all the people." While the "supreme legislative and executive ultimately" reside in the "people or whole community where God has placed it," Otis concedes that the impracticality of "simple democracy" led to the necessity of establishing a system of representation.[17] Otis follows Locke in asserting that the original supreme legislative and executive power of the people is delegated to governing institutions. The choice of the form of government and the distinct institutional arrangement of this natural power rest with the people as a whole. Otis gives

[14] Otis, *Rights*, pp. 420, 440 (cf. p. 424).
[15] Ibid., p. 424.
[16] Ibid., (emphasis in the original).
[17] Ibid., p. 427.

no indication that the popular origins of government in consent necessarily lead to a republican or highly democratic form of government. Like Locke, Otis finds various forms of mixed government, including limited monarchy, to be fully consistent with natural liberty. The end of government, according to Otis, is "to provide for the security, the quiet, and happy enjoyment of life, liberty, and property" for every individual in society.[18] Individuals form limited government because neither the state of nature nor absolute monarchy can secure their life, liberty, and property. In the state of nature, Otis claims, insecurity is guaranteed without a "common, indifferent, and impartial judge." The Hobbesian solution of absolute monarchy is equally or more insecure than the state of nature inasmuch as "it is evidently contrary to the first principles of reason that supreme *unlimited power* should be in the hands of one man."[19] For Otis, the end of government necessarily implies limited government, though not necessarily republicanism.

Otis' discussion of property rights signifies one point where Locke's theory was particularly germane to the central issue in the imperial debate regarding the Sugar and Stamp Acts. Why is Parliament not legitimately able to tax the colonies? Otis does not appeal primarily to historical custom or constitutional precedent, but rather to natural rights. Echoing Locke, Otis contends that control over property is intimately connected to an individual's right to life and liberty: "If a shilling in the pound may be taken from me against my will, why may not twenty shillings; and if so, why may not my liberty and my life?" It is precisely in order to secure property that individuals leave the state of nature and form society.[20] For Otis, property is so central to liberty that no tax may be levied on any individual except by a body to which that individual has consented and in which he is represented. The violation of this principle of property rights and representation is an attack on the very essence of liberty. Otis charges: "The very act of taxing exercised over those who are not represented appears to me to be depriving them of one of their most essential rights as freemen, and if continued seems to be in effect an entire disenfranchisement of every civil right."[21] For Parliament to tax the colonists is, according to Otis, to trample on their most fundamental freedoms.

The aim of Otis' argument in this discussion is twofold. First, he wants to demonstrate that the right of property is natural and not derived solely or even primarily from compact. With this he rejects the Pufendorfian idea that property rights originate in the multiple layers of compact that form society. Given the natural basis of the property right in the more comprehensive

---

[18] Ibid., p. 425.
[19] Ibid. (emphasis in the original). Cf. Locke II:90–4.
[20] Ibid., p. 461; see also pp. 422–3. Notice that Locke makes the same point in practically identical language at II:17–18.
[21] Ibid., p. 447.

notion of natural liberty, Otis concludes: "It will never follow...that government is rightfully founded on property alone."[22] Rightful property claims originate in nature and provide the logic for the end of government; they do not originate concurrently with government. By following Locke as opposed to Pufendorf on the issue of property, Otis establishes the philosophical nerve of the argument linking the colonists' property rights and their right to representation. For Otis, the Americans did not, and logically could not, ever have consented to a government over which they had no measure of legal control. Second, Otis attempts to prove that Parliament's plan to tax the colonies is a violation of their natural rights and a dangerous departure from the proper end of government. Insofar as the connection between representation and legitimate taxation power is a natural one, only legislatures directly responsible to the colonists can tax them. Otis' use of Locke's notion of the natural right to property supports his claim that the lack of colonial representation in Westminster means that Parliament has no right to tax them. Moreover, by basing his claim on natural, as opposed to merely constitutional and historical, rights, Otis tries to put this issue beyond the realm of competing constitutional interpretations of the empire. However, Otis does grant Parliament sovereign authority to regulate imperial trade. He admits this right of Parliament on the grounds that "[i]t may be for the good of the whole that a certain commodity should be prohibited, but this power should be exercised with great moderation and impartially over dominions which are not represented in the national Parliament."[23] Otis accepts in principle that as the supreme legislative power in the empire, Parliament may prohibit the importation of certain goods into the colonies and restrict American trade with the rest of the world, although he advises as a matter of prudence that Parliament exercise this right cautiously. Otis views this regulatory power in Britain as the price, if you will, of membership in the empire, and in no sense as a justification for taxing the colonies directly. At the core of the moderate theory of empire expressed by Otis is the notion that the legitimate taxing power lodged in the colonial assemblies flows from natural rights, whereas Parliament's regulatory power is a matter of principle of a different order.

The Glorious Dissolution

In order to understand Otis' conception of the colonies' relations to Britain, it is necessary to examine his use of another key Lockean principle: the dissolution of government. Otis employs this standard Lockean idea in an innovative way. In the imperial context, Otis applies the theory of dissolution to give an account of the status of the colonial governments in the imperial

---

[22] Ibid., p. 423 (cf. Samuel Pufendorf, *De Jure Naturale et Gentium Libri Octo* [Oxford: Clarendon Press, 1934]: bk. 4, ch. 4, pp. 5–8).

[23] Ibid., pp. 460, 468.

order. Surprisingly, Otis does not, as we might expect, assert the colonists' right to dissolve the imperial connection. Rather, he appeals to dissolution theory to explain that connection. Unlike moderate Whigs in Britain such as Hume and Blackstone, Otis viewed the Glorious Revolution as an example of dissolution. In this respect, Otis is even more open in his Lockeanism than Cato. He asserts that the British Constitution was "reestablished" in 1688–9 in response to Stuart usurpations. Otis has great praise for the British constitutional model that emerged from this period. He argues that it is a stellar example of a government designed on the principles needed to secure liberty, claiming that "No country has been more distinguished for these principles than Great Britain, since the Revolution." Moreover, he glowingly cites long passages from the Declaration of Rights pointing to and detailing the rights of Parliament and the civil rights guaranteed therein.[24] Otis goes so far as to claim that with respect to the "grand political problem in all ages" of how to combine and distribute the supreme powers of legislation and execution, "the British Constitution in theory and in the present administration of it in general comes closer to the idea of perfection of any that has been reduced to practice."[25] Thus, Otis celebrates the settlement of 1689 and shows that he has no quarrel with the principle of parliamentary supremacy either in England's mixed monarchy or, by extension, in the empire at large.

Of course, to argue that the dissolution of the British government in 1689 resulted in a very good constitutional system is still not to square the imperial circle. Good government in England does not immediately translate into a settlement of how the Parliament should relate to the colonies. Otis' more fundamental point in this discussion is to demonstrate that not only was the British Constitution reformed in 1688, but so was the entire empire. Otis maintains that the events of the Glorious Revolution demonstrated the Lockean principle that the form of government is left to be settled by the individuals in society, who may alter or abolish it as they see fit. Otis claims that the actions of the Convention Parliament in 1689 were consented to and ratified by the entire free population of the empire. In contrast to later and more radical colonial spokesmen like Jefferson and Paine, who more or less denied any fundamental societal link between England and America, Otis includes Americans in the collection of "the people" that consented to the Glorious Revolution.[26] Otis affirms that through a form of tacit consent

---

[24] Ibid., pp. 449, 446–8, 430–4.

[25] Ibid., p. 428.

[26] Greene's observation that in the wake of the Glorious Revolution the colonies experienced increased localization of power and the growth of their own parliamentary institutions provides an experiential basis for Otis' argument, which gives it some air of plausibility, at least practically, if not theoretically (see Jack P. Greene, "The Glorious Revolution and the British Empire, 1688–1783," in *The Revolution of 1688–1689: Changing Perspectives*, Lois G. Schwoerer, ed. [Cambridge: Cambridge University Press, 1992], p. 269).

whereby had the people "not liked the proceedings it was in their power to control them," every individual in the empire except hard-core Tory "bigots to the indefeasible power of tyrants" consented to the settlement. Notice that in Otis' version of events, those not consenting to the Glorious Revolution are determined on ideological as opposed to geographical or jurisdictional grounds. By this logic, the Americans consented to "the present happy and most righteous establishment," which was "founded on the law of God and nature [and] was begun by the Convention with a professed and real view in all parts of the British Empire."[27]

Otis uses his treatment of dissolution to demonstrate two things: the legitimacy of parliamentary rule in England and the extension of that principle throughout the free parts of the empire. According to Otis, the Glorious Revolution affirmed the Lockean principle that in the event of an abuse of political power

[i]t devolves to the people, who have a right to resume their original liberty and by the establishment of a new legislative (such as they shall think fit) provide for their own safety and security, which is the end for which they are in society.[28]

Since it is a natural right, Otis concludes that this right to form new societies that was operative in Britain in 1689 must extend as much to the Americans, who are "entitled to all the natural, essential, inherent, and inseparable rights of our fellow subjects in Great Britain."[29] How, then, does Otis believe the Glorious Revolution impacted on the colonies? He claims that it left a double legacy. First, it established the formal constitutional principle of legislative supremacy. In Britain, this meant the sovereignty of Parliament and, by extension, Parliament's absolute legislative supremacy in the empire. This part of the legacy seems to offer little in support of the colonial position in the dispute over taxation. However, Otis contends that the revolutionary legacy in America also secured a more substantive constitutional principle, namely, that the purpose of government is to secure liberty and rights, especially property.[30] The question is then: Can Parliament secure this notion of substantive, as opposed to simply formal, justice for the Americans? Otis clearly answers, no. While it is not my intention to examine the argument for virtual representation made by British leaders, it suffices to note that Otis unhesitatingly rejects this idea. He claims that only the colonial legislatures, in which the colonists are actually represented, can fulfill this substantive principle of securing liberty. Only the colonial legislatures, which are, according to Otis, a product of the act of empirewide consent issuing in 1688–9, can provide the legitimate institutional devices for raising taxes and governing

[27] Otis, *Rights*, pp. 429–30, 441, 430.
[28] Ibid., pp. 434–5.
[29] Ibid., p. 441.
[30] Ibid., p. 446.

domestic affairs in the colonies. Thus, by appealing to Lockean dissolution theory, Otis seeks to guarantee the legitimacy of parliamentary sovereignty in Britain and, in a brilliant theoretical double move, to affirm the broader principle of legislative supremacy as the chief bulwark protecting the people's rights in the colonies as elsewhere. Otis concludes that fidelity to the broader and deeper substantive principle of legislative supremacy requires abridging and trimming the formal principle of parliamentary rule in the empire.

Delegation and Subordination

The main theoretical problem emerging for the colonial position from Otis' discussion of dissolution and the Glorious Revolution relates to how one can reconcile the formal principle of right (legislative supremacy) with the substantive principle of right (the security of rights only by a representative legislature) in the imperial context. In order to resolve this thorny question Otis turns, once again, to two characteristically Lockean ideas: the theory of delegated powers and the constitutional principle of subordination. When the *Rights* moves from the foundational discussion of natural rights and the Glorious Revolution to the specific question of the colonists' rights in the empire, Otis notes that the subject of the natural rights of colonists has been largely neglected or misunderstood by continental natural law theorists. He claims that in particular "Grotius and Pufendorf find themselves much mistaken" on this matter.[31] Given Otis' radical Whig sympathies, it is not surprising that he finds the characteristically Grotian and Pufendorfian argument that colonial rights are entirely subject to the specific compact resolved with the mother country far too restrictive to be palatable. Rather, Otis claims that the true teaching on the natural rights of colonists is "chiefly drawn from the purer fountains of one or two of our English writers, particularly from Mr. Locke." To determine the legitimate rights of colonists in general, and of Americans in particular, Otis adapts Locke's delegation theory of sovereignty to the British imperial situation.

As we have seen, Otis started his analysis of the natural rights of colonists from the Lockean premise that the people are the original and ultimate supreme power in any constitutional order. As such, the people can locate the supreme legislative and executive power wherever they wish, including, of course, in a supreme legislature in which the executive has a share of the legislative power, like the British mixed monarchy. This system of delegated powers, according to Otis, is precisely what was created in 1688–9. In order to explain the status of the colonial legislatures in the empire, Otis modified another feature of Lockean constitutionalism, the subordination

[31] Ibid., pp. 436–7.

of powers, and adapted this principle to the imperial context.[32] In Chapter thirteen of the *Second Treatise*, Locke claimed that the supreme legislative power can delegate some measure of its authority to "several subordinate Powers."[33] Otis adapted this Lockean idea to the imperial context by arguing that the colonial legislatures have subordinate legislative status with respect to Parliament's overarching supremacy in the empire. The principal role of these subordinate legislatures, in Otis' view, is to exercise exclusive power over domestic taxation in the colonies. Otis combined the Lockean notions of delegation and the subordination of powers to argue for the idea of co-ordinate constitutional powers, the Parliament and the colonial legislatures, with their own spheres of legitimate power and jurisdiction. In this way, Otis hoped to draw from Locke the theoretical materials necessary to accommodate colonial demands for self-government within a broader framework of imperial unity. Thus, when Otis claimed that Americans consented to the settlement of 1689, he meant that they agreed to an imperial constitution that reconciled obligations to Britain with considerable colonial self-government over domestic affairs.

Otis' defense of the natural right of the colonists to tax themselves is based on his idea of a three-pronged system of delegated powers. He claims that the people can create and arrange subordinate constitutional powers with relatively complete competence in their own defined jurisdiction. By this logic, the people of the colonies exercised their natural rights in order to produce a complex system whereby (1) they assigned supreme legislative power to Parliament for managing imperial relations through trade and defense policy, (2) they also delegated certain powers to the British crown to participate in the legislative process in the colonies through the veto and dissolution powers, and (3) they delegated certain powers exclusively to the colonial legislatures to raise taxes and govern domestic affairs with royal assent. In this multifarious system of consent and imperial constitutionalism, the people of the colonies retained ultimate sovereignty because each element of their government, domestic and imperial, could be traced back to a delegation of their natural power. Simply put, Otis presents the argument that the colonial legislatures exist by virtue of a constitutional agreement more

---

[32] The importance Otis and others attached to Locke as a constitutional authority supports Dworetz's claim (*Unvarnished Doctrine*, p. 70) that it was Locke the constitutional theorist, rather than Locke the prophet of property rights and capitalism, who primarily fired the colonial imagination during the imperial dispute. However, it should be noted that colonial spokesmen like Otis and Dickinson often emphasized the Lockean connection between property rights and representative government.

[33] Locke, II:151. It is important to notice that Otis uses the idea of subordination of powers in ways quite different from Locke. The "several" subordinate powers Locke imagines refer mainly to inferior magistrates, municipal corporations, or executives without a share of the legislative power (II:133, II:151). It is not at all clear that Locke would see the principle of subordination applying to colonies.

fundamental than an act of Parliament: a primary act of consent rooted in the natural rights of the colonists.

While it is true that Otis' argument is based on Lockean principles, it is important to note his significant modification of Locke's teaching. In Locke's understanding of subordinate powers, they are completely subject to alteration or abolition by the supreme legislative power. The practical implication of this principle in the imperial context – namely, that Parliament can alter or dissolve the colonial legislatures – is clearly a theoretical possibility that Otis wants to avoid. Otis seeks to balance two competing, perhaps ultimately contradictory, claims. On the one hand, he admits that the colonial legislatures are subordinate to Parliament in the sense that there is no higher legislative authority in the empire than Parliament, but, on the other hand, he claims that Parliament cannot legitimately legislate the internal affairs of the colonies through taxation. While conceding that the colonial legislatures are not supreme or independent of the British government, Otis maintains that they possess a legal and constitutional integrity of their own as a product of the people of the colonies themselves.

In Otis' complex formulation of the imperial constitution, he foreshadows something like a federal arrangement in which Parliament has its proper sphere of rule and the colonial legislatures have theirs. The central question regarding which body has the supreme power in the event of a conflict between two legally constituted bodies – essentially the issue in question in 1764 – is one Otis assiduously tries to avoid. This ambiguity in Otis' position comes to the surface in his account of the limits of legislative power. Otis presents this account as though it were taken verbatim from Chapter Eleven of Locke's *Second Treatise*. However, there is one crucial modification of Locke's argument in Otis' account. In his version of the second limit on legislative power in an otherwise faithfully Lockean list of limits, Otis imports the notion of subordination into the discussion. Otis claims that one crucial limit on legislative power is that "[t]he supreme national legislative cannot be altered justly till the commonwealth is dissolved, *nor a subordinate legislative taken away without forfeiture or other good cause.*"[34] Locke, of course, makes no mention of the distinction between national legislatures and any other kind. He also places no qualification on the supreme legislature's power to alter or abolish subordinate powers. In fact, Locke never discusses subordinate powers in his account of the limits on the legislative power. Even Locke's far from absolute commitment to the principle of legislative supremacy ensured that he would see no inherent right of subordinate bodies that the supreme legislature would be obliged to observe.[35] Otis imports the principle of subordination into Locke's discussion of the limits on legislative power in order to create an additional limit on the extent of

[34] Otis, *Rights*, p. 444 (emphasis mine). Compare with Locke II:134.
[35] See Locke, II:135–41 (cf. II:133, II:151).

supreme legislative power, a limit tailored to the imperial context but one not explicitly countenanced by Locke. Otis modifies Locke to argue that not only the supreme legislative power but also "the subordinate powers of legislation" should be "free and sacred in the hands where the community have once rightfully placed them."[36] Thus, in order to adapt Lockean principles to serve the colonial position, Otis departs from a strict construction of Locke's constitutional theory for the purpose of appealing to the deeper Lockean natural rights teaching underlying this constitutional theory.

The Moderate Theory of Empire

Otis employs a Lockean argument to demonstrate that only the ultimate and natural supreme power of the people can alter or abolish a subordinate legislature; the supreme constitutional legislative power cannot. Is this a tenable argument? Otis wants the subordinate colonial legislatures to have sole and inviolable authority within their proper sphere. This sphere includes the power of taxation rooted in the natural right of the colonists to protect their property by means of their own representative assemblies. Yet Otis does not want to assert the general supremacy of the colonial legislatures. He passionately denies that the colonies want "to assume the right of an independent legislative or state."[37] Thus, by admitting the supremacy of Parliament, Otis, albeit reluctantly, is forced to concede that the supreme legislative power, in this case Parliament, can *unilaterally* alter or dissolve the subordinate colonial legislatures in the event of "forfeiture or other good cause."[38] By admitting parliamentary supremacy in the empire, Otis does not, however, concede that Parliament's legislative authority is absolute or arbitrary. For Otis, Locke's natural law limits on legislative power apply as much to Parliament as to any legislative body. In keeping with the logic of his argument in the writs of assistance case, Otis contends that no legislature may legitimately endanger the lives, liberties, and property of the people. Otis claims that these constitutional limits on legislative power are as natural and self-evident as the proof that "[t]he Parliament cannot make 2 and 2, 5."[39] Thus the British government's right to rule the empire cannot in any way be construed to countenance the violation of the colonists' natural rights. Otis maintains that the colonial legislatures are an integral part of the panoply of constitutional structures set in place by the consent of the people of the colonies in order to secure their rights.

---

[36] Otis, *Rights*, p. 444.
[37] Ibid., p. 457.
[38] Ibid., p. 444. Cf. Goldsworthy, *Sovereignty of Parliament*, p. 205.
[39] Otis, *Rights*, p. 454; Locke II:135–42. Cf. Bernard Bailyn, *The Ideological Origins of the American Revolution* (Cambridge, MA: Harvard University Press, 1967): pp. 205–6.

The moderate theory of empire tried to combine parliamentary supremacy in the empire with a considerable measure of colonial self-government. The major problem in Otis' formulation of the theoretical foundations of the moderate imperial theory is the difficulty in reconciling the Lockean liberal idea of consent with the system of delegated powers in the imperial context. In particular, Locke's constitutional principle of subordinate powers did not have the normative bite that Otis sought in order to defend the legislative assemblies at the heart of his idea of colonial self-government. However, the deeper problem in Otis' imperial argument was his underlying commitment to the moderate Whig theory of constitutional sovereignty rooted in Pufendorf and refashioned for the Anglo-American transatlantic community of the 1760s by Blackstone. Whereas Locke's radical Whig account of sovereignty emphasized the natural constituent power of the people and the resulting ambiguity and difficulty in identifying political sovereignty, the moderate Whig position on sovereignty maintained by Blackstone and many prominent leaders on both sides of the Atlantic stressed the necessity of recognizing one legally instituted, easily identifiable, and duly constituted supreme power in any constitutional order. Drawing from the authority of Pufendorf, Blackstone argued that "there is and must be in all [forms of government] a supreme, irresistible, absolute, and uncontrolled authority, in which the *jura summi imperii*, or rights of sovereignty reside."[40] As we have seen, soon after the publication of the *Rights*, the British moderate Whig position on sovereignty would find its most extreme legal expression in the Declaratory Act of 1766, which affirmed Parliament's authority "to make laws and statutes of sufficient force and validity to bind the colonies and people of America... in all cases whatsoever."[41]

In his effort to defend some measure of colonial self-government, Otis clearly rejected the logic and spirit of the Declaratory Act's claim for Parliament's sweeping power to legislate for the colonies "in all cases whatsoever." But while he tried to maintain the constitutional integrity of the separate spheres of authority, in effect to combine parliamentary supremacy in the empire and limited colonial autonomy over issues of taxation and domestic affairs, Otis was driven by his commitment to the moderate Whig view of sovereignty to concede that as Parliament was the highest legislative authority in the empire, there was simply no legal or constitutional way to impede or reverse its will. As Otis stipulated: "The power of Parliament is uncontrollable but by themselves, and we must obey. They can only repeal their own acts." Should push come to shove, Otis and later Dickinson advocated passive resistance in America (for example, a voluntary embargo on British

[40] William Blackstone, *Commentaries on the Laws of England* vol. I (London, 1791 [1765]): p. 49; cf. pp. 108–9 and 160–1 for his argument in support of parliamentary supremacy in the empire.
[41] Henry Steele Commager, *Documents of American History* (New York: Appleton, 1963): p. 61.

imports) and diplomatic efforts to persuade Parliament to change its conduct toward the colonies.[42] For Otis, in keeping with the moderate Whig Blackstonian–Pufendorfian understanding of sovereignty, there must be one supreme legislative power in the empire, and that power logically and legally must lie in Parliament. In this respect, the arguments of Otis, and later of Dickinson, were much closer to the logic of the Declaratory Act than were the later arguments expounded by Jefferson and Paine.

In order to maintain logical consistency, Otis reluctantly concedes that Parliament can alter or abolish the colonial legislatures. He thinks he has to do this if he wishes to maintain the colonies' links with the imperial government in England. One way out of the imperial dispute, which Otis raises, is the possibility of colonial representation in an imperial Parliament. While Otis rejects the notion of virtual representation, he does propose this alternative to the present situation, which would, at least theoretically, meet the requirement of representation necessary for taxation.[43] Otis argues: "A representation in Parliament from the several colonies . . . can't be thought an unreasonable thing, nor if asked could it be called an immodest request."[44] Despite the obvious practical difficulties in securing effective representation in an assembly 3,000 miles across the sea in the eighteenth century, Otis demonstrates that this idea was not unthinkable among the colonists, at least in the very early stages of the imperial dispute. It is important to recall, however, that for Otis, parliamentary representation is not intended to replace the colonial legislatures, but rather to supplement them: "No representation of the colonies in Parliament *alone* would, however, be equivalent to a subordinate legislative among themselves."[45] Only the colonial legislatures close to the colonial situation and directly responsible to the people of the colonies could effectively secure "the end of increasing their prosperity." Perhaps Otis' ideal solution to the imperial dispute would involve maintaining exclusive taxation power in the colonial legislatures, and gaining American admission at Westminster to secure an American voice in the formulation of imperial policy. Predictably, this was a solution unacceptable to the British government.

---

[42] Otis, *Rights*, pp. 448–9.
[43] For good discussions about the complex issues surrounding the idea of virtual representation, see Dworetz, *Unvarnished Doctrine*, pp. 82–3; Jack P. Greene, "Origins of the American Revolution: A Constitutional Interpretation," in *Framing and Ratifying the Constitution*, Leonard Levy and Dennis Mahoney, eds. (New York: Macmillan, 1987): p. 37; and Webking, *American Revolution*, p. 27. Samuelson observes that in the period following publication of the *Rights*, Otis would propose an idea of imperial federalism similar to those devised years later by Jefferson, Wilson, and John Adams (Richard Samuelson, "The Constitutional Sanity of James Otis: Resistance Leader and Loyal Subject," *Review of Politics*, vol. 61, no. 3 [Summer 1999]: pp. 517–20).
[44] Otis, *Rights*, p. 445.
[45] Ibid. (emphasis mine).

In the final analysis, Otis' argument is characterized by an abiding moderation. While asserting the rights of limited colonial self-government, he also emphatically denies the alternative of full independence. He does not employ Lockean dissolution theory to justify revolt. Rebellion, for Otis, is a kind of doomsday scenario: "The ministry in all future generations may rely on it that British America will not prove undutiful till driven to it as a fatal last resort against ministerial oppression, which will make the wisest mad, and the weakest strong."[46] Though Otis affirms that it is the colonists' "duty to submit and patiently bear" whatever burdens the supreme legislative power in Parliament may place on them, he claims that "our mouths are not stopped" and that the people of America may plead, appeal, and shame the British government until it repeals its obnoxious measures.[47] If the colonists were to maintain an imperial presence characterized by parliamentary sovereignty in Britain and only subordinate or limited sovereignty in the colonies, they could do little else.

Dickinson's *Farmer Letters*

James Otis' impact on the defenders of the colonial position was palpable. A century later, Lord Acton would echo Adams in calling Otis "the founder of the revolutionary doctrine."[48] In the years immediately following the Stamp Act crisis, colonial spokesmen continued to advance their arguments on the basis of premises and principles originally articulated by Otis. While many of Otis' immediate successors lacked his relish and aptitude for examining philosophical first principles, they inevitably drew on the enormous theoretical resources of radical Whiggism that Otis had unearthed. Probably the most important of Otis' immediate successors was the Delaware native John Dickinson.[49] Although Dickinson was less apt to make direct appeals to the authority of radical Whig philosophy, his influential *Letters from a Farmer in Pennsylvania* assumed Otis' basic theoretical position but applied these principles to a different situation in the changing dynamics of the ongoing imperial dispute in the late 1760s. In the nearly four-year span between the publication of the *Rights* and Dickinson's *Farmer Letters*, much had changed in the colonial situation. The repeal of the Stamp Act in 1766 seemed to signal the apparent success of Otis' moderate appeal for limited colonial self-government. America's Rockinghamite and Pittite champions

---

[46] Ibid., p. 458.

[47] Ibid., pp. 448–9.

[48] John Emerich Edward Dalberg-Acton, *Essays in the History of Liberty* (Indianapolis: Liberty Fund Press, 1985): p. 200 and James Ferguson, "Reason and Madness: The Political Thought of James Otis," *William and Mary Quarterly*, vol. 36, no. 2 (April 1979): p. 194.

[49] For Dickinson's status as the authority on the colonial position in Britain in the late 1760s, see Bonwick, *English Radicals*, pp. 38, 44 61–2.

in Parliament successfully argued for the repeal of this act with great encouragement from the colonies. The British government, however, presented the repeal as a matter of political expedience and not as an implicit acceptance of Otis' argument. In keeping with its aim to assert the purely prudential character of its decision, Parliament took the bold measure of passing the Declaratory Act, which asserted an unqualified and legitimate right inhering in Parliament to make laws for the colonies "in all cases whatsoever." Parliament's position was clearly hardening on the principle, if not the practice, of British rule over the colonies.

The *Farmer Letter* appeared in the American press from December 1767 to February 1768. Dickinson offered them as a response to Parliament's passage of the Townshend duties, to be paid at American ports on goods imported from Britain. The Americans were also prohibited from importing these products from anywhere else except Britain. While the Townshend duties, unlike the stamp tax, were not a direct tax on American consumers, Dickinson believed that the principle behind these duties was no different from that of the Stamp Act, namely, to raise revenue from the Americans without their consent. Dickinson echoes Otis' argument that only the colonial legislatures could legitimately tax the colonies. He also agrees with Otis that Parliament, as the supreme legislative authority in the empire, has the power to regulate imperial trade policy. Dickinson worries, however, that the Townshend Act demonstrates that the distinction between the idea of direct internal taxation and external regulatory duties provides cover for Parliament to use its traditionally accepted power to regulate imperial trade in order to impose what really amounted to a tax on the colonies.[50] In response to the parliamentary command that American merchants buy British goods with a duty attached to them, Dickinson queries: "What tax can be more internal than this?"[51]

The theoretical grounding for Dickinson's defense of the colonists' right to tax themselves is radical Whig natural rights. He derives the core of the argument for self-government from the Lockean natural right of property. Dickinson argues: "If they have any right to tax us – then . . . There is nothing which we can call our own; or to use the words of Mr. Locke – WHAT PROPERTY HAVE WE IN THAT, WHICH ANOTHER MAY, BY RIGHT, TAKE, WHEN HE PLEASES, TO HIMSELF."[52] Like Otis, Dickinson follows Locke in linking the individual's control over personal property to a more comprehensive notion of freedom including the natural rights to life

---

[50] Webking, *American Revolution*, p. 48.

[51] John Dickinson, "The Letters from a Farmer in Pennsylvania," in *Empire and Nation*, William E. Leuchtenberg and Bernard Wishy, eds. (Englewood Cliffs, NJ: Prentice Hall, 1962): Letter 6, p. 24.

[52] Dickinson, *Letter* 7, p. 44 (capitalization in the original). Cf. Locke II:138 and Dworetz, *Unvarnished Doctrine*, p. 75.

and liberty. Dickinson fears that the imposition of even a minuscule tax by Parliament sets a very dangerous precedent. It will stand like "a sword in the scabbard," waiting to plunge at the heart of American liberty. Dickinson's fundamental concern is that British taxing of the colonies will undermine the position of the colonial legislatures. Like Otis, he believes that a free people must have control over "the purse strings."[53] The colonists' natural right to control their own property, according to Dickinson, means that the colonial legislatures were the primary guarantors of American freedom. Unlike Otis, however, Dickinson makes no appeal in the *Farmer Letters* for American representation in Parliament. The message of the *Farmer Letters* is simply an emphatic warning to the British government to leave the colonies alone to tax themselves. British rule over the empire, Dickinson argued, does not make the power of the colonial legislatures nugatory. Even more clearly than Otis, Dickinson expands the right of taxation to include the broader range of issues relating to self-government. He claims that if Parliament takes upon itself the "administration of justice" in the colonies, "what will they [the colonial legislatures] have to do, when they are met? To what shadows will they be reduced?"[54] Always present in the background of the dispute over taxes and duties is Dickinson's concern to defend the legitimacy and constitutional integrity of the colonial legislatures.

The theory of empire propounded in the *Farmer Letters* is profoundly influenced by the moderate Whig conception of sovereignty. Dickinson, no less than Otis, remains committed to the moderate Whig idea of parliamentary sovereignty over the empire. He consciously frames his argument as an appeal to British constitutional principles and practices enshrined by the Glorious Revolution.[55] The first letter is auspiciously dated November 5, the anniversary of William's landing at Torbay. Moreover, Dickinson has high praise for the British Constitution, claiming that it is "incontestably our duty, and our interest, to support the strength of Great Britain."[56] Despite minor differences in the manner and extent to which they applied Lockean principles to

---

[53] Dickinson, *Letter 9*, p. 50.

[54] Ibid., p. 57.

[55] Dickinson's status as one of the most important nonsigners of the Declaration of Independence has no doubt contributed to the debate over his status as a "conservative" revolutionary. Bailyn (*Ideological Origins*, p. 145) and Forrest McDonald (introduction to *Empire and Nation*, William E. Leuchtenberg and Bernard Wishy, eds. [Englewood Cliffs, NJ: Prentice Hall, 1962]: p. xi) make the case that Dickinson was the most conservative of the colonial champions. Webking (*American Revolution*, pp. 41–2) counters by arguing that insofar as Dickinson did not emphasize "sources of order" in the community such as institutions and precedents, he was "more radical, than the other major revolutionaries." While I agree with Bailyn and McDonald that Dickinson was clearly a moderate in important respects, I am also sensitive to Webking's objection, although I would locate the radical character of Dickinson's argument in his use of Lockean principles of property rights and representation, not in any supposed tendency to avoid discussing institutions or precedents.

[56] Dickinson, *Letter 12*, p. 82.

the particular situation they were addressing, the logical and practical implications of Dickinson's argument differ little from those of Otis. By affirming
parliamentary supremacy in the empire, Dickinson is driven by concern for
theoretical consistency and British patriotism to admit the incapacity of the
colonists to counter parliamentary abuses in a legal or constitutional way.
For Dickinson, the colonial options are seriously limited. He rejects the radical alternative of independence even more emphatically than Otis, claiming:

> If once we are separated from our mother country, what new form of government
> shall we adopt, or where shall we find another Britain to supply our loss? Torn
> from the body, to which we are united by religion, liberty, laws, affections, relation,
> language and commerce, we must bleed at every vein.[57]

With no certain legal or constitutional means of relief, Dickinson calls for
his fellow colonists to join in a sustained and voluntary American policy
of nonimportation of British goods to hit the ministry in the pocketbook.
Dickinson assumes that only then will they see not only the imprudence but
also the injustice of their actions.

Otis and Dickinson represent the fullest and most articulate expression
of the moderate formulation of colonial rights in the empire. Their arguments sought to accommodate the colonial demands and position within the
framework of the empire and British constitutional and imperial practice.
While they remained adherents to the moderate Whig idea of parliamentary
sovereignty, these early colonial spokesmen drew their most fundamental
ideas about rights and government from the radical Whig philosophy. Even
in the early stages of the imperial crisis, Americans were not afraid to employ core Lockean principles like natural rights, dissolution of government,
delegation, and subordination of powers in innovative ways. Indeed, they
applied Locke's teaching to their own colonial situation in order to defend
the exclusive powers of the subordinate colonial legislatures to secure limited self-government for the colonies. Their use of Locke reminds us that his
brand of radical Whiggism was both compatible with the principle of mixed
government and adaptable to understanding composite imperial structures.

However, Lockean principles, at least as they were applied by Otis and
Dickinson, had serious limits for the colonial position. When push came to
shove over the issue of sovereignty in the empire, Otis and Dickinson fell
back on the inherited moderate Whig notions of constitutional supremacy
and sovereignty, which elevated Parliament above the colonial legislatures.
Thus, despite the radical foundation of the early colonial position in Lockean
natural rights theory, Otis and Dickinson displayed an abiding moderation
in their view of the empire, seeing parliamentary supremacy in the empire as
the cost of maintaining the colonial links with Britain. They did so even as
they sought to defend a considerable degree of colonial autonomy. However,

---

[57] Dickinson, *Letter* 3, p. 18.

justifying American membership in an imperial order headed by Parliament left the rights of colonial self-government on tenuous ground. As the supreme legislative power in the empire and, by extension, in the colonies, Parliament could, by this theory, legitimately abolish or alter the colonial legislatures. The question of exactly what conditions would legitimate this forfeiture of colonial rights was a source of bitter dispute as the imperial crisis heated up in the 1770s. Ultimately, the later American position in the crisis represented by Thomas Jefferson and Tom Paine would remove this theoretical ambiguity, or even obstacle to colonial self-government, by denying that the colonies had any constitutional or legal connection, let alone subordination, to Parliament whatsoever.

13

Thomas Jefferson and the Radical Theory of Empire

Thomas Jefferson's *Summary View of the Rights of British America* differed in both form and substance from the work of earlier colonial spokesmen like Otis and Dickinson. Written in the highly charged atmosphere of 1774, the *Summary View* was originally intended as a set of instructions for the Virginia delegation to the First Continental Congress, a distinguished group including Patrick Henry, Edmund Randolph, and George Washington. It was, however, soon recognized to be much more than that, as much a statement of general principles underlying the colonial resistance to British rule as a specific set of proposals to resolve the imperial crisis. As such it was later published anonymously and was a major contribution to the pamphlet war between the colonists and Britain. In contrast to earlier colonial statements of their rights, the *Summary View* put much less emphasis on the painful details and dangerous implications of parliamentary efforts to tax the colonies, and dealt primarily with the constitutional and philosophical issues raised by the Coercive Acts disabling the Massachusetts Assembly and by the Act Suspending the New York Legislature. In this sense, Jefferson responded to the rapidly deteriorating situation affecting imperial relations in the early 1770s. By 1774 Otis and Dickinson's nightmare scenario, the theoretical possibility that Parliament could annihilate colonial self-government, had become a practical reality in at least two colonies and an increasingly likely possibility in the others.

Jefferson drew on the theoretical resources of Lockean political philosophy to articulate and support the American position in this critical period. In this respect he did not differ greatly from Otis and Dickinson, who also appealed to the authority of Locke. However, Jefferson's use of Locke signaled a departure from the position of his earlier compatriots. While both the early and later colonial positions were grounded on radical Whig natural rights theory, Jefferson drew from this foundation a different understanding of the colonists' relation to the British government than did Otis and Dickinson. Whereas most colonial leaders in 1774 were still inclined, in

Jefferson's words, to stop "at the half-way house of John Dickinson," admitting parliamentary authority to regulate American commerce but not to raise revenue in the colonies, in Jefferson's radical formulation of the empire Parliament could not legitimately govern the colonies in any form because there was no constitutional and legal link between the colonial governments and Parliament whatsoever.[1] The only connection between the colonies and Britain was the crown, which acted as the supreme executive power in both Britain and the colonies. For this reason, the *Summary View*, unlike Otis' *Rights* and Dickinson's *Farmer Letters*, is addressed to the king, not Parliament. Jefferson calls on the king to restrain the actions of an abusive Parliament. In the broader view of Jefferson's proposed theory of imperial federalism, the empire is seen as a collection of sovereign and equal commonwealths united only by their common acceptance of the same king. Thus, both constitutionally and in terms of natural rights, Jefferson argues, the legislatures of Delaware and Rhode Island, as well as those of the rest of the colonies, were equal to Parliament. This meant, of course, that Jefferson denied that Parliament had any legal status in the colonies, certainly not the potentially sweeping powers that Otis and Dickinson granted it as the supreme legislative power in the empire.

A Statement of "Our Rights": Emigration and Self-Government

The Lockean influence on Jefferson's expression of the core principles of natural rights and government in the *Summary View* is unmistakable. Jefferson grounds the claims of the colonists on "their rights, as derived from the laws of nature." These "rights of human nature" include, first and foremost, the power to create governments dedicated to securing liberty.[2] For Jefferson, government is the product of human artifice generated by the consent of free and equal individuals. In classic Lockean form, Jefferson asserts that the people are the ultimate supreme power in any constitutional order. The people are free to delegate their natural power to officers and institutions "appointed by the laws, and circumscribed with definite powers, to assist in working the great machine of government, erected for their use, and consequently subject to their superintendance [sic]."[3] This statement of popular

---

[1] Thomas Jefferson, "Autobiography" (6 January 1821), *The Writings of Thomas Jefferson*, 10 vols., Paul Leicester Ford, ed. (New York: G. P. Putnam's Sons, 1892–9): vol. 1: p. 12.

[2] Thomas Jefferson, "Summary View of the Rights of British America," in *Thomas Jefferson Writings*, Merrill Peterson, ed. (New York: Norton, 1984), pp. 121, 105 (hereafter Jefferson, SV, and page number). For good but too brief treatments of natural rights in the *Summary View*, see Harry Jaffa, *A New Birth of Freedom: Abraham Lincoln and the Coming of the Civil War* (Lanham, MD: Rowman & Littlefield, 2000): pp. 22–5 and David Mayer, *The Constitutional Thought of Thomas Jefferson* (Charlottesville: University of Virginia Press, 1994): pp. 35–7.

[3] Jefferson, SV, p. 105 (cf. p. 121).

sovereignty confirms the radical conventionality of this "great machine of government" and asserts the inherent limits on the legitimate use of political power. Throughout the course of the *Summary View*, Jefferson lays before his reader both the most important of the colonists' natural rights, "Our Rights," and the frequent, and increasingly dangerous, "violations of them" by the British government.

The primary natural right Jefferson treats in his opening salvo in the *Summary View* is the natural right of emigration. It is in this discussion that he most fully considers the philosophical foundations of natural liberty theory. The origin of the colonies, Jefferson argues, lies in the right of emigration, a "right which nature has given to all men." The individual's right "of departing from the country in which chance, not choice, has placed [him]" acts as both a logical and a practical demonstration of the state of nature, serving to illustrate how naturally free and equal individuals may be understood to come together and form political societies.[4] This natural right of emigration contains within it the ground of the Lockean principle that all government rests on consent. Implicit in Jefferson's argument is the notion that one alternative to consenting to a government is the exercise of the natural right to leave the sphere of that government.[5] This, according to Jefferson, is precisely what the original settlers of America and all immigrants since have done. Thus, when several of the "free inhabitants of the British dominions in Europe" chose to leave and then left their homeland, they effectively returned to a state of nature with full possession of all the natural liberties attending that state. Jefferson's aim here is to demonstrate that the act of emigration constituted a severing of the constitutional links and legal obligations of the colonists to Britain.

The deeper right embodied in the bare act of emigration is the natural right of free people to form "new societies under such laws and regulations as to them shall seem most likely to promote public happiness."[6] In this respect,

---

4 Jefferson, SV, p. 105. Jaffa, *New Birth of Freedom*, pp. 9–12 asserts with little textual or logical evidence that Jefferson's understanding of "public happiness" (and, for that matter, Locke's) was indistinguishable from the classical republican conception Jaffa identifies with Plato and Aristotle. However, Jefferson and Locke ground their idea of public happiness on the principle of securing rights, the logic of natural rights being alien and ultimately contrary to the classical idea of natural sociability and civic education (cf. Paul Rahe, *Republics Ancient and Modern: Classical Republicanism and the American Revolution* [Chapel Hill: University of North Carolina Press, 1992]).

5 Locke claimed that there was a natural right "of Men withdrawing themselves, and their Obedience, from the Jurisdiction they were born under, and the Family or Community they were bred up in, and setting up new Governments in other places" (John Locke, *Two Treatises of Government*, ed. Peter Laslett (Cambridge: Cambridge University Press, 1988): bk. II: sec. 115 (hereafter Locke, book, and section, e.g., Locke II:115).

6 Jefferson, SV, pp. 105–6. John Zvesper argues persuasively that Jefferson demonstrates the emphatically political character of his natural rights teaching in the *Summary View* by drawing from the Lockean assertion of natural freedom the idea that this freedom, in Jefferson's view,

Jefferson draws a Lockean natural rights teaching out of the actual experiences of colonial history: emigration, settlement, and government building. It perhaps goes without saying that the Lockean emigration right to which Jefferson appeals constitutes a milder form of the natural right of revolution. The first Americans, in Jefferson's view, showed their dissatisfaction with the British government by voting with their feet.[7] These first settlers were as free to establish their own form of government as England's "Saxon ancestors had, under this universal law, in like manner left their native wilds and woods in the north of Europe, had possessed themselves of the island of Britain...and had established there that system of laws which has so long been the glory and protection of that country."[8] By logically connecting the historical origins of the British Constitution in Saxon England and the America colonies in their first settlement, and citing these events as examples of the construction of new societies by free individuals, Jefferson attempts to demonstrate that by nature, Britain and the American colonies are free and equal with respect to each other.

Jefferson employs this discussion of the natural right of emigration to explain the colonists' relations with Britain and its government. Emigration replaces the Glorious Revolution as the fulcrum for the colonial position. Whereas an earlier colonial spokesman such as Otis could advance the claim that the Americans consented to the settlement of 1688–9, and thus consented to both subordinate colonial legislatures and parliamentary supremacy in the empire, Jefferson derives the colonial connection to Britain solely

---

is "valuable only because it is the freedom to form a people by establishing a government" (John Zvesper, "Jefferson on Liberal Natural Rights," in *Reason and Republicanism*, Gary McDowell and Sharon Noble, eds. [Lanham, MD: Rowman & Littlefield, 1997]: pp. 15–17). I concur with Zvesper's conclusion that Jefferson's robust and complex idea of natural rights may provide a salutary correction to the "unreasonable fear of nature and the ethical and political implications of human nature" (what Zvesper calls "physiophobia") seen in nineteenth- and twentieth-century critics of natural rights theories. Cf. Ralph Lerner, *The Thinking Revolutionary* (Ithaca: Cornell University Press, 1987): p. 61 and Jean Yarborough, "Thomas Jefferson and Republicanism," in *Thomas Jefferson and the Politics of Nature*, Thomas Engeman, ed. (Notre Dame, IN: University of Notre Dame Press, 2000): pp. 66, 74–5.

[7] Hannah Arendt suggests that Jefferson's emigrants settled what amounted to "breeding grounds for revolutionaries from the beginning" (Hannah Arendt, *On Revolution* [New York: Viking Press, 1963], p. 123). For a similar analysis, see Bernard Bailyn, *Ideological Origins of the American Revolution* (Cambridge, MA: Harvard University Press, 1967), p. 83; William Hedges, "Telling off the King: Jefferson's *Summary View* as American Fantasy," *Early American Literature*, vol. 22, no. 3 (Fall 1987): p. 166; and James Stoner, *Common Law and Liberal Theory: Coke, Hobbes, and the Origins of American Constitutionalism* (Lawrence: University Press of Kansas, 1992): p. 194.

[8] Jefferson, SV, p. 106. Cf. Algernon Sidney, *The Discourses Concerning Government*, Thomas West, ed. (Indianapolis: Liberty Classics, 1996): ch. 3, sec. 28, pp. 481–2, for a similar appeal to the libertarian origins of the British Constitution in the original Saxon democracy.

from the first settlements in America. Moreover, Jefferson's understanding of this connection is much more restricted that it was for Otis. He claims:

> The settlements having been thus effected in the wilds of America, the emigrants thought proper to adopt that system of laws under which they had hitherto lived in the mother country, and to continue their union with her by submitting themselves to the same common sovereign, who was thereby made the central link connecting the several parts of the empire thus newly multiplied.[9]

The natural liberty of the immigrants to America included the total freedom to establish whichever form of government they pleased. They chose to adopt the British system of laws, namely, representative assemblies and the common law, and they retained the British monarch as their supreme executive power. Whereas for Otis, asserting the colonial component in the empirewide act of consent to the Glorious Revolution settlement left the colonial legislatures in a theoretically unstable subordinate status vis-à-vis Parliament, Jefferson declares that each colonial legislature was made supreme by the people of the several colonies. In conformity with Locke's delegation theory of sovereignty, Jefferson argues that the colonial assemblies were the bodies to which the colonists delegated supreme legislative power. That they chose to retain their links with the crown was entirely, in this view, a matter of prudence, habit, or affection, not a preceding obligation or legal tie.

What, then, is Parliament's constitutional relation to the colonies? According to Jefferson, there is none. The colonies were not established by Britain: "America was conquered, and her settlements made, and firmly established at the expence [sic] of individuals, and not of the British public." Once again, Jefferson's central contention is that the first settlers of the colonies were free individuals who were, he states, quoting Locke, "free from any Superior Power on Earth, and not . . . under the Will or Legislative Authority of Man."[10] Subsequent actions of the British government, such as

---

[9] Jefferson, SV, p. 107.

[10] Jefferson, SV, p. 106 and Locke, II:22. Jefferson's claim that Britain and the American colonies constituted distinct states held together only by a common connection to the British crown was echoed in the months following the writing of the *Summary View* by John Adams and James Wilson (John Adams, "Novanglus Letters," *The Political Writings of John Adams*, George Peek, ed. [New York: Liberal Arts Press, 1954]: pp. 42, 46–7 and James Wilson, "Considerations on the Nature and Extent of the Legislative Authority of the British Parliament," *Selected Political Essays of James Wilson*, Randolph G. Adams, ed. [New York: Knopf, 1930]: pp. 66, 75–82). However, Jefferson's argument was more radical than that of Adams and Wilson inasmuch as the latter two both maintained that the American colonists remained subject to the crown before, during, and after they settled the colonies. In this view, the colonists were in no way subject to Parliament but had never ceased to be subject to the crown (Adams, "Novanglus," pp. 60–1; Wilson, "Considerations," pp. 76–7; cf. Anthony Lewis, "Jefferson's *Summary View* as Chart of Political Union," *William and Mary Quarterly*, vol. 5, no. 1 [January 1948]: p. 45 and Mayer, *Constitutional Thought*, p. 39). Thus Jefferson's use of the Lockean natural right of emigration had the effect of producing

sending troops to defend the colonies during the wars with France, should not, according to Jefferson, be construed as explicit or even implicit recognition of British sovereignty over America. "Such assistance," he argues, "they had often given before to Portugal, and other allied states..., yet these states never supposed that by calling in her aid, they thereby submitted themselves to her sovereignty."[11] Notably, it is on the basis of natural jurisprudence rather than British constitutional custom that Jefferson makes the astonishing claim that the American colonies are no more legally or constitutionally bound to the British government than are foreign allied states such as Portugal.[12] Jefferson asserts that despite the undoubted value of British assistance to America in the past, if such support had compromised American sovereignty, the colonists "would have rejected them with disdain, and trusted for better to the moderation of their enemies, or to a vigorous exertion of their own force."[13] Far from granting Parliament supreme power to regulate imperial trade and defense policy, in this radical formulation of the empire the colonies stand in relation to Britain as at most allies, and increasingly as estranged ones.

In his statement of colonial rights, "Our Rights," Jefferson claims a natural right of complete self-government based on the natural liberty of the first settlers in America. The retention of the British monarch as the supreme executive office in the constitutional orders of the various colonies is, he argues, in no way inconsistent with this natural liberty. The British king is the American king, "the chief officer" of the American people "appointed" by their laws.[14] His constitutional status in America, according to Jefferson, is in no way derived from the settlement of the British Constitution in the Glorious Revolution. Despite this statement of the natural rights principles informing "our rights," Jefferson uses much of the *Summary View* to illustrate the frequent and increasingly serious "invasions of them" by the British government. His treatment of the British violations of American rights is

---

an even more emphatic statement of colonial autonomy than these others, inasmuch as, in Jefferson's view, the connection to the crown was the function of a deliberate act of consent on the part of the colonists.

[11] Jefferson, SV, p. 106.

[12] Jefferson's explicit and articulate formulation of Lockean natural rights as the basis of the colonial position undermines Stephen Conrad's claim that Jefferson had no single, coherent notion of rights in the *Summary View*. While I agree with Conrad that Jefferson's rights teaching is complex, I do not believe this complexity indicates "the manifest contingency of rights talk" in the *Summary View* (Stephen Conrad, "Putting Rights Talk in Its Place: The *Summary View* Revisited," in *Jeffersonian Legacies*, Peter Onuf, ed. (Charlottesville: University of Virginia Press, 1993), p. 216 (see also pp. 262–3, 265, 273).

[13] Jefferson, SV, p. 106.

[14] Ibid., SV, p. 105. This presentation of the British monarch as the "chief officer" of the people is clearly as subversive of British moderate Whig constitutional theory as it is of British imperial policy (cf. Jaffa, *New Birth of Freedom*, pp. 8, 13–14).

divided into two parts: a discussion of past historical abuses and the more recent (and more dangerous) invasions of the 1770s.

Historical Violations of "Our Rights": Property and Trade

Jefferson's historical account of Anglo-American relations is little short of a litany of abuses perpetrated by Britain on the colonies. He uses this account to demonstrate the natural rights of the colonies by illuminating the principles of right violated in each particular instance. By demonstrating that imperial relations have not historically been as sanguine as Otis or Dickinson suggest, Jefferson tries to justify the radical implications of his theory of empire. That British constitutional practice and past imperial policy have consistently injured the colonists' natural rights does not in any way legitimize these injuries.[15] Just as Jefferson's discussion of the natural right of emigration effaced the normative status of the Glorious Revolution for the colonies, so too does his treatment of past British abuses undermine the legitimacy of claims to parliamentary sovereignty based on past imperial policy.

Jefferson's discussion of these past historical abuses extends back to the Stuart era long before 1689. The first issue he addresses is the customary practice of royal land grants dating back to the very infancy of the colonies. As we recall, a key part of Jefferson's argument, for the colonists' natural right to form new societies was his claim that the colonies were established by the blood and treasure of the individual emigrants, not the "British public."[16] However, after the first settlements, Jefferson argues, the "treasonable" Stuart kings "parted out and distributed among the favorites and followers of their fortunes" titles to lands in America. Maryland, Pennsylvania, and the Carolinas were all granted to these royal dependents by letters of the crown to right "in propriety" to American lands. These actions were taken generally without the consent of the inhabitants.[17] Jefferson charged

---

[15] Jefferson uses history as a supplement to his more fundamental natural rights argument. It is not his primary source for understanding the basis of colonial claims in the sense Colbourn suggests, nor is history used, as Conrad argues, simply to demonstrate the inefficacy of rights claims without constitutional and legal support (see H. Trevor Colbourn, "Jefferson's Use of the Past," *William and Mary Quarterly*, 3rd ser., vol. 15 [January 1958]: pp. 56–70 and Conrad, "Rights Talk," pp. 262, 273). For a good discussion of the way Jefferson used both historical and logical demonstration in the *Summary View* to support the natural rights foundation of the colonists' position, see Mayer, *Constitutional Thought*, pp. 29–37 and Robert Webking, *The American Revolution and the Politics of Liberty* (Baton Rouge: Louisiana State University Press, 1988): pp. 94–5.

[16] Jefferson, SV, p. 106.

[17] Ibid., pp. 107–8. Jefferson notes, however, that the Whig lords who were granted title to the Carolinas were only given the power to make laws and to tax "with the consent of the inhabitants." We recall that John Locke himself was the framer of the prototype "Fundamental Constitutions of Carolina" (see John Locke, "Fundamental Constitutions of Carolina," in

that this alleged royal power "of dividing and dismembering a country" has never occurred or been asserted "in his majesty's realm of England."[18] The natural right of the colonists to resist or prevent the dismemberment of their lands is as valid, according to Jefferson, as the right of Englishmen precisely because this is a natural right. With this argument, he makes the startling assertion that the natural right of colonial self-government has been threatened by Britain since practically the first settlement of America.

This discussion of the dismemberment of American lands by royal grants points to Jefferson's reflections on the natural right to property. He begins these reflections by taking "notice of an error in the nature of our land holdings, which crept in at a very early period of our settlement." The error was the introduction of the English system of "feudal tenures" into the colonies. According to the feudal system, which was established in England after the Norman Conquest in order to pacify and suppress the native Saxons, the fundamental notion of property rights was the general principle that "all lands in Europe were held either mediately or immediately of the crown." Prior to the Conquest, Jefferson claims, "our Saxon ancestors" held their lands on the basis of fee simple, that is, with none of the military and labor obligations associated with feudalism, and their personal property in "absolute dominion, disencumbered with any superior."[19] This pre-Conquest principle of property rights, which Jefferson terms the "allodial system," generally conforms to the Lockean idea of property rights as natural, deriving from an individual's labor.[20] By this principle, people in a state of nature can appropriate lands or goods through their own labor without the sanction of any higher authority. As a general principle of property rights in civil society, the allodial systems would establish proprietary rights in any vacant land on which the individual should choose to occupy and labor. Jefferson draws this distinction between the feudal and allodial systems to demonstrate that land in America is held on the basis of allodial right, not by feudal right as the original and mediate property of the crown. He argues: "America was not conquered by William the Norman, nor its lands surrendered to him, or any of his successors. Possessions there are undoubtedly of the 'allodial nature'."

Political Essays, Mark Goldie, ed. [Cambridge: Cambridge University Press, 1997]: pp. 160–82).

[18] Jefferson, SV, p. 108. Cf. Locke II:117.
[19] Jefferson, SV, pp. 118–19.
[20] See Locke II: ch. 5, esp. 25–7. Richard Matthews contends that Jefferson did not assert any natural right to property, but rather expounded solely a natural right of expatriation that implied the power to settle new positive laws regarding property in the colonies (Richard Matthews, *The Radical Politics of Thomas Jefferson* [Lawrence: University Press of Kansas, 1984]: pp. 24–6). I believe Matthews' mistake is to misread a moderate Whig Pufendorfian argument for property (as he identifies Jefferson with Blackstone on the issue of property) into Jefferson's decidedly radical Whig emphasis on the connection between labor and a natural, as opposed to purely civil, property right.

Even if, as Jefferson admits, "our ancestors . . . were farmers, not lawyers," and were unfortunately "early persuaded to believe" in "the fictitious principle that all land belongs originally to the king," this nonetheless did not in any way diminish the colonists' natural right to appropriate vacant land through their own labor or to establish a system of property laws consistent with this core Lockean principle.[21]

Jefferson's point in this discussion is not to illustrate that the Americans have a different system of property rights than the British. His aim, rather, is to demonstrate that the colonists possessed the natural right of self-government available to all people. And a central feature of self-government is a society's control over its system of property holdings. In a clear parallel to Locke's account of the civil status of property in a self-governing community, Jefferson argues:

From the nature and purpose of civil institutions, all the lands within the limits which any particular society has circumscribed around itself are assumed by that society, and subject to their allotment only. This may be done by themselves, assembled collectively, or by their legislature, to whom they may have delegated sovereign authority; and if they are allotted in neither of these ways, each individual of the society may appropriate to himself such lands as he finds vacant.[22]

Given that the purpose of "civil institutions" is to secure the property of the individuals in society, it is illogical to assume that any agent extrinsic to that society could exercise a form of control over its property. This Lockean principle had, of course, been at the core of the imperial dispute over taxation at least since the time of the Stamp Act.

The second major historical abuse of the colonists' natural rights by Britain had to do with the issue of trade. Jefferson argues: "The exercise of a free trade with all parts of the world, possessed by the American colonists, as of natural right, and which no law of their own had taken away or abridged, was next the object of unjust encroachment" by the British government.[23] Jefferson's assertion of a natural right of free trade sheds some light on the complex character of his rights teaching. His point is not to deny that certain natural rights, like trade, are never subject to legitimate public control or regulation; actually, he emphasizes that these natural rights may be "taken away or abridged" by law. The point Jefferson makes in this discussion is that only laws made by the colonists can regulate or restrict this natural right. In one fell swoop, Jefferson more or less demolishes the earlier colonial position, the "half-way house" of Otis and Dickinson, which admitted that Parliament had the right, to regulate imperial trade. This "natural right" of free trade means that only the colonial governments can legitimately place

---

[21] Jefferson, SV, p. 119.
[22] Ibid., pp. 119–20. See also, Locke II: 125, 127, 138–40.
[23] Jefferson, SV, p. 108.

any commercial restrictions on their citizens. The free trade right, and the broader issue of commercial freedom more generally, flow from Jefferson's fundamental premise of the individual natural right to property. From this bedrock Lockean principle Jefferson concludes that the Americans not only may manufacture "for our own use the articles we raise on our own lands with our own labor," they may also trade these goods with whomever is allowable by their own laws. He claims that the historical restrictions placed by Parliament on this natural right are "instances of despotism to which no parallel can be produced in the most arbitrary ages in British history."[24] From this discussion, it is apparent that Jefferson's emphasis on the natural basis of property rights perceptibly and logically extends to a broader treatment of the natural right of self-government. Inasmuch as the individuals in the colonies hold their property under a system of laws devised by themselves, Parliament has no ground to claim an antecedent right to regulate their trade.

Jefferson's discussion of the natural right of free trade is notable for several reasons. First, it signals his radical departure from the earlier colonial position of the 1760s. For Jefferson, in contrast to Otis and Dickinson, Parliament may well have passed laws regulating American trade, but it never had a right to do so. The general thrust of Jefferson's reasoning is to undermine the normative status of British imperial practice and to expose the many invasions of colonial natural rights, which have been accepted by the Americans themselves simply out of an uncritical and trusting respect for tradition and precedent. Second, Jefferson's opposition to Parliament's regulation of imperial trade demonstrates his willingness to abandon the conceptual distinction between internal and external controls. The earlier colonial position maintained that the internal affairs of the colonies should be governed by the colonial legislatures, but that external affairs – issues that could plausibly fall into the category of imperial affairs – afforded the British government considerable scope for regulating key aspects of life in the colonies such as commerce and trade. In Jefferson's view, however, the British government had always interfered with colonial internal affairs, not only by imposing trade restrictions and banning domestic manufactures, but also by such measures as "establishing a post office in America," in which the British government has "intermeddled with the regulation of the internal affairs of the colonies."[25] Once again, Jefferson does not legitimize the undeniable example of parliamentary intrusion witnessed in the creation of the post office. He does not even attempt to connect this action with any prior evidence of colonial consent. His point is not to argue against the utility of a continental postal service, but rather to focus on what he takes to be the

[24] Ibid., p. 109.
[25] Ibid., p. 110.

disturbing question of where the British government ever acquired the right to introduce such a system into the colonies.

The third important feature of Jefferson's historical treatment of Anglo-American relations is his attempt to demonstrate to the king and to his fellow colonists that legislative assemblies provide no guarantee against oppression. He claims: "History has informed us that bodies of men, as well as individuals, are susceptible to the spirit of tyranny."[26] Jefferson asserts that one important constitutional lesson emerging from Anglo-American historical relations is the potential for legislative tyranny arising even from representative bodies. This problem is emphatically more acute in the American situation, in which the legislature assuming this authority over the colonists is one in which they are not represented. In Jefferson's view, insofar as Parliament is not directly responsible to the colonists, "they are beyond the reach of fear, the only restraining motive which may hold the hand of a tyrant."[27] Fear and distrust of the oligarchical tendencies in even the most representative assemblies would come to mark Jefferson's general approach to the question of the proper limits on legislative power.[28] This fear of legislative tyranny, of course, takes on greater poignancy when the government resides 3,000 miles away from the people it aspires to govern and, as Jefferson suggests, cannot even claim to represent the entire British people in any meaningful sense. By this measure, the extension of parliamentary rule throughout the empire on the basis of the Glorious Revolution or any other pretense is simply illegitimate. Despite the seemingly inherent instability of Anglo-American relations since the very origins of the colonies, Jefferson argues that these historic abuses of the colonists' natural rights were tolerable inasmuch as they "were less alarming, because repeated at more distant intervals than that rapid and bold succession of injuries which is likely to distinguish the present from all other periods of the American story."[29] To Jefferson's account of the present period of the "American story" we now turn.

Recent Invasions of "Our Rights": Coercion and Dissolution

The theoretical innovation in Jefferson's position from the one advanced by the colonial moderates prior to the *Summary View* is linked to a material change in the character of the imperial dispute. In his treatment of the more

[26] Ibid., SV, p. 108.
[27] Ibid., SV, p. 112.
[28] See, for example, Jefferson's criticism of the 1776 Virginia Constitution for concentrating the legislative, executive, and judicial powers of government in the legislative branch: "The concentrating these in the same hands is precisely the definition of despotic government. It will be no alleviation that these powers be exercised by a plurality of hands, and not by a single one. 173 despots would surely be as oppressive as one" (Jefferson, *Notes on the State of Virginia* [New York: Penguin, 1999]: Query XIII, p. 126).
[29] Jefferson, SV, p. 110.

recent British abuses of the colonies, Jefferson asserts that by 1774 "a series of oppressions, begun at a distinguished period, and pursued unalterably
through every change of ministers, too plainly prove a deliberate and system-
atical plan of reducing us to slavery." The dire situation facing the colonists
at this time was caused by the specific nature of the recent parliamentary
actions. Whereas the debate in the 1760s had to do primarily with the issue
of taxation, by the 1770s Jefferson mentions the Stamp Act and Townshend
duties only in passing, focusing rather on parliamentary measures such as the
act suspending the New York legislature and the Coercive Acts, which struck
against the very existence of the colonial institutions of self-government. As
Robert Webking explains: "The taxation acts violated the principle of self-
determination, but the suspension of the legislature rejected it."[30] By the time
Jefferson added his own pen to the authors of the "American story," the issue was no longer simply dangerous precedents; now it was the arbitrary
dissolution of colonial legislatures and the practical imposition of martial
law in the colonies.

The two foci of Jefferson's account of the recent British violations of
American natural rights are the act suspending the New York legislature
and the Coercive Acts, the most important of which closed Boston harbor as
punishment for the illegal destruction of goods in the celebrated Tea Party of
1773. In describing the illegitimacy of the parliamentary measure suspending the New York legislature for its refusal to sanction the quartering of
British troops in the colony, Jefferson appeals far beyond imperial custom
and British constitutional practice to support his position. The standard to
which he appeals is nature: "One free and independent legislature hereby
takes upon itself to suspend the powers of another, free and independent as
itself; thus exhibiting a phoenomenon [sic] unknown in nature, the creator
and creature of its own power."[31] Here Jefferson's argument rests on the
Lockean teaching that the power of a legislative body derives from the natural executive power of the people who created it. Insofar as the people of
the colonies never delegated to Parliament any power over their assemblies,
this act is an unwarranted and unjustifiable violation of their natural rights.
Could Parliament dissolve the Cortes of Spain or the Diets in Germany and
Poland? Of course not. Then, Jefferson's reasoning goes, on what grounds
can the British government act so arbitrarily with respect to New York?
Any assertion of parliamentary authority over the colonies is a prima facie
violation of their natural rights.

The standard to which Jefferson appeals to criticize the suspension of one
legislature by the act of another is emphatically natural, not British constitutional custom and practice. He contends that the colonists would have
to renounce "the common feelings of human nature" if they were to admit

---

[30] Webking, *American Revolution*, p. 96.
[31] Jefferson, SV, p. 111 (cf. Locke, II:87, II:123–31).

"that they hold their political existence at the will of a British parliament."[32] The political existence of the colonies derives solely from the consent of the individuals inhabiting them. Thus, by suspending the legislature of the people of New York, in effect destroying their political existence, the people of this colony are "reduced to a state of nature." Jefferson suggests that the radical consequences of this act are dissolution of the government and devolution of political power to the individuals in the colony. This is precisely the Lockean principle that British constitutional theorists like the influential William Blackstone could not accept as the legitimate juridical or even logical consequence of Parliament's action.[33] Implicit in Jefferson's argument is the notion of the people of New York's absolute liberty to alter or abolish the old form of government and to establish a new political society. In pure Lockean form, Jefferson argues:

> While those bodies are in existence to whom the people have delegated the powers of legislation, they alone possess and may exercise those powers; but when they are dissolved by the lopping off of one or more of their branches, the power reverts to the people, who may exercise it to unlimited extent, either assembling together in person, sending deputies, or in any other way they may think proper.[34]

Jefferson claims that the practical consequence of Parliament's action is the theoretical possibility that British moderate Whig constitutionalists most abhorred: the dissolution of government. According to Jefferson, this consequence is inevitable given that "every society must at all times possess within itself the sovereign powers of legislation," and as such, the people of the colonies, who are reduced to this state of nature, must, and are perfectly free to, reconstitute the legislative power of their society.

This discussion of the suspension of the New York legislature exemplifies Jefferson's use of radical Whig theory to counter the intensified scope of Parliament's pretensions to ruling the colonies. Denying that the colonists have delegated any authority to Parliament provides Jefferson with stronger theoretical resources than were available to Otis and Dickinson. In straight Lockean terms Jefferson can, and does, insist on the independence of the colonial governments vis-à-vis Parliament. There is no question of subordinate powers for Jefferson. Otis and Dickinson's argument for a colonial subordinate legislative status may be a more reasonable explanation for the actual practice of Anglo-American relations than Jefferson's view – that to the naked eye, Parliament always looked like the biggest fish in the imperial pond and Americans seemed to accept it with some limitations, at least prior to the 1770s. Jefferson's argument, while counterintuitive given his

---

[32] Jefferson, SV, p. 111.
[33] For Blackstone's explicit criticism of Locke's argument for the principle of dissolution, see William Blackstone, *Commentaries on the Laws of England* (London, 1791): vol. 1, p. 213.
[34] Jefferson, SV, p. 118.

own admission of Parliament's constant interference in the colonies, does at least provide the theoretical resources to indict any British effort to legislate in the colonies. In the *Summary View* the logic of colonial resistance is simpler, less restrictive, and more internally consistent than in any previous statement of the colonial position.

The other recent example of British encroachments against the colonies that Jefferson cites is the closing of Boston harbor. This component of the Coercive Acts produced his longest discussion of any single British misdeed. By this act, he argues, "a large and populous town, whose trade was their sole subsistence, was deprived of that trade, and involved in utter ruin."[35] Here Jefferson introduces another dimension in his argument against Parliament. It is not surprising that he finds that Parliament has no legal or constitutional right to close Boston harbor, because it has no legitimate authority over the colonies whatsoever. However, Jefferson also goes on to muse: "Let us for a while suppose the question of right suspended, in order to examine this act on principles of justice."[36] It should be noted that Jefferson's distinction between matters of "rights" and matters of "justice" at this point in his argument does not indicate, as some have claimed, the secondary importance of natural rights in Jefferson's complex and multifaceted rights teaching. As is clear from the context of this discussion, namely, the closing of Boston harbor, Jefferson intends to illustrate how natural rights claims constitute the core of his understanding of justice. He goes beyond the issue of the constitutional or legal competence of Parliament's action regarding Boston harbor to examine the character of the legislation itself.[37] With this example, Jefferson addresses the question of whether not only Parliament, but any government, could legitimately take a measure like closing a city's harbor as a punitive action. In other words, Jefferson widens the lens of his analysis of this act in order to ponder whether even the Massachusetts legislature would be justified in closing down the commercial activity in one area under its jurisdiction as punishment for disobedience of its laws. The answer he gives is a resounding no.

First, Jefferson argues that this sweeping government action is completely out of proportion to the alleged offense. It is inherently wrong and contrary

---

[35] Ibid., p. 112.

[36] Ibid., Stephen Conrad ("Rights Talk," p. 266) takes this to mean that here Jefferson "moves beyond arguments based on 'rights' to arguments based on the larger, ultimate standard of 'justice'." Conrad (p. 269) even goes so far as to suggest that Jefferson's various uses of "rights" in the *Summary View* "evinces ambivalence and ambiguity to the point of incoherence." While I agree with Conrad that Jefferson's use of the concept of rights is very complex in this document, I believe Conrad exaggerates the importance of Jefferson's distinction between justice and rights. Indeed, I maintain that justice is the core principle animating Jefferson's rights teaching in the *Summary View*.

[37] Michael Zuckert, *The Natural Rights Republic* (Notre Dame, IN: University of Notre Dame, IN: Press, 1996): p. 262, n. 35.

to the principles of natural equity to punish an entire city for the crimes of a few individuals – in this case, the small band who "threw the tea into the ocean, and dispersed without doing any other act of violence."[38] Thus, according to Jefferson, if any government, even presumably an American one, had acted in this arbitrary and disproportionate way, it would have been unjustified. Second, and more importantly, Jefferson affirms that no government whatsoever may produce legislation that intentionally endangers the property and self-preservation of its people. Here he draws on Locke's first limit on legislative power, which states that the supreme legislative power may not act arbitrarily "over the Lives and Fortunes of the People." Locke even claims that there are serious natural law limitations on the right of conquerors in a just war with respect to confiscating property and restricting the economic activity of the rightfully conquered.[39] Jefferson argues that by passing a measure intended to reduce Boston, "that antient [sic] and wealthy town," from "opulence to beggary" and to force its citizens "on the world for subsistence by its charities," Parliament is assuming a power that no government, not even a victor in a just war, may legitimately exercise.[40] The Lockean premise underlying Jefferson's argument is that the purpose of government is to protect the lives and property of *all* the individuals in society. Government may not arbitrarily deny individuals the natural right to the means of self-preservation. Thus, Jefferson's purpose in discussing the closing of Boston harbor is to abstract somewhat from the particular question of parliamentary encroachments on the colonies in order to reflect on the fundamental Lockean teaching on the natural limits on government power. By this means Jefferson assimilates the concepts and universalist reasoning of Lockean philosophy into an examination of specific issues of right.[41] This discussion is clearly not anomalous in the *Summary View* because it serves to highlight the Lockean natural rights principles underlying Jefferson's comprehensive position.

Jefferson's account of the colonists' rights and the British government's frequent violations of these rights is replete with recourse to distinctively Lockean principles of natural rights and government. In effect, Jefferson employs historical analysis in order to demonstrate the natural, as opposed

---

[38] Jefferson, SV, p. 112.
[39] Locke, II:135, II:182–4.
[40] Jefferson, SV, p. 113.
[41] While I agree with Stoner that Jefferson displays a keen capacity to apply abstract notions of right to the settlement of particular issues, I am not convinced that this illustrates the workings of a "common law mind" (Stoner, *Common Law*, p. 189). The general thrust of the argument in the *Summary View* for the most part avoids appeals to the common law tradition. In the Boston harbor example, as well as in his fundamental treatment of the natural emigration right, it appears that Jefferson is relying on a natural, as opposed to a constitutional or common law, authority to explain colonial relations with the mother country.

to the simply constitutional or contingent, character of the violation of those rights. Through his detailed treatment of Parliament's historic abuses of the rights of American self-government from the infancy of the colonies up to the very brink of the revolution, Jefferson tries to prove that Parliament has undermined both the formal legal basis of the colonies' limited relations with Britain and the substantive principles of Lockean natural rights philosophy informing these relations.

The Problem of the British Executive

Whereas Parliament, according to Jefferson, has no legal or constitutional role in the colonies, in his version of the empire the British crown most emphatically does. A central aim of the *Summary View* is both to articulate the proper role of the king in the empire and colonies and to illustrate the obvious failure of the present king, George III, to perform the constitutional function assigned to him by the colonists. Jefferson claims that any serious reflection on the king's conduct as the holder of "the executive powers of the laws of these states" will "mark out his deviations from the line of duty."[42] One aspect of the monarch's deviation from his constitutional responsibility is his failure to recognize the inherently limited character of any delegated authority. This authority must be used nonarbitrarily and only for the public good. A prime example of this breach of trust is the stationing of troops in the colonies. Jefferson argues that the king, "in order to enforce the arbitrary measures" of Parliament, has sent to the colonies "large bodies of armed forces, not made up of the people here, nor raised by the authority of our laws."[43] He claims that the king was never granted the power to bring foreign troops to America, and as such, these troops are legitimately subject to American law made for the suppression of riots, sedition, and unlawful assemblies. Behind Jefferson's reasoning is the Lockean teaching and the "Old Whig" tenet that any people who do not have legal control over the public use of force are incapable of securing their lives, property, and liberty. The king threatens to place civil authority in the colonies under the British military. With rhetoric and logic deeply rooted in the radical Whig anti–standing army literature of the late seventeenth and early eighteenth centuries, Jefferson charges, "did his majesty possess such a right as this, it might swallow up all our other rights whenever he should think proper."[44]

---

[42] Jefferson, SV, p. 115.

[43] Ibid., p. 120.

[44] Ibid., Cf. Locke, II:90–4. A prime example of the Old Whig anti–standing army literature with which Jefferson was familiar is by *Cato's Letters'* coauthor, John Trenchard, entitled *An Argument shewing that a Standing Army Is Inconsistent with a Free Government* (London, 1697). Cf. Bailyn, *Ideological Origins*, p. 62.

In addition to violating the natural rights of the colonists by thrusting upon them an armed force to which they did not consent, Jefferson charges that the king's conduct shows a clear double standard in his behavior towards the colonies and Britain. He points out that when during the Seven Years War the king wanted to bring over Hanoverian troops to defend Britain against the French, he applied to Parliament first, which passed an act for that purpose that limited the number of troops and how long they could stay in the country. Jefferson claims that this supplies more than precedent, but is in fact the only legitimate course of action the monarch could have taken, and thus "in like manner is his majesty restrained in every part of the empire."[45]

Another example of the king's failure to attend to the limited character of delegated power, and his double standard toward the colonies, relates to the issue of dissolution. This power must be distinguished from Locke's dissolution of government theory. The king's dissolution power is a legal one, established in the Constitution, but consists only of providing the monarch with the capacity to dissolve a legislature with the purpose of providing for new elections whenever the public good requires them. Jefferson does not deny that the executive may exercise this power, but he specifies that it is restricted to occasions "when the representative body have lost the confidence of their constituents." Indeed, given that the frequent dissolution of the Exclusion Parliaments by Charles II was one of the key whig indictments against Stuart tyranny, Jefferson is more or less correct to observe that since the early part of the eighteenth century, "neither his majesty, nor his ancestors, have exercised such a power in the island of Great Britain."[46] The importance of a free Parliament was one of the core principles of the 1689 settlement. This, however, has not been the case in America, Jefferson argues, where the representative assemblies of "the colonies have repeatedly" been dissolved by the crown and its agents, who "after dissolving one house of representatives ... have refused to call another, so that, for a great length of time, the legislature provided by the laws has been out of existence."[47] By charging that the king has carried the dissolution power beyond "every limit known, or provided for, by the laws," Jefferson essentially accuses him of having done repeatedly in the various colonies what Parliament is now being called to account for in New York.

---

[45] Jefferson, SV, p. 120.

[46] Ibid., p. 117. For evidence that the architects of the Glorious Revolution era settlement were deeply concerned with the need to guarantee free and regular Parliaments, see Articles 1, 2, 4, 8, and 9 of the Declaration of Rights and especially Article 13, which stipulates, "For the redress of all grievances and for the amending strengthening and preserving of the Lawes, Parliaments ought to be held frequently" ("Declaration of Rights," in Lois Schwoerer, *The Declaration of Rights, 1689* [Baltimore: Johns Hopkins University Press, 1981]: pp. 295–8).

[47] Jefferson, SV, p. 118.

Jefferson's point here is not simply, or even primarily, to expose British hypocrisy toward the colonies, but rather to articulate the natural rights principles underlying American Whig reasoning in the crisis. The problem is not that the king is merely inconsistent in applying a perfectly legitimate constitutional power to Britain and the colonies. The fundamental problem is that in the colonies the king uses his dissolution power to invade the colonists' natural right to self-government as reflected in their laws. Jefferson's ultimate authority, the idea to which he assigns the highest normative status, here as throughout the *Summary View*, is nature: "From the nature of things, every society must at all times possess within itself the sovereign powers of legislation."[48] As such, the king's failure to call new assemblies in a timely fashion has undermined the purpose for which he was delegated the dissolution power in the first place.

Not only has the king broken the bounds of legitimate authority and acted in ways inconsistent with the spirit of the British Constitution, at least as he has acted toward the colonies, he has also neglected to do things he ought to do. For example, the king ought to give his assent to measures of the colonial legislatures manifestly directed to the public good. Rather than doing this, however, Jefferson charges, "for the most trifling reasons, and sometimes no conceivable reason at all, his majesty has rejected laws of the most salutary tendency." Once again, the crown's proclivity for vetoing colonial legislation is not in keeping with contemporary British constitutional practice, inasmuch as "his majesty, and his ancestors ... for several ages past have modestly declined the exercise of this power in that part of the empire called Great Britain."[49] Jefferson cites two important examples of the malignant consequences of this breach of British constitutional custom in the colonies. The first relates to the issue of slavery. Jefferson, speaking for the Virginia delegation, asserts: "The abolition of domestic slavery is the great object of desire in those colonies, where it was unhappily introduced in their infant state." The first step in such a project of abolition is the prohibition of the African slave trade. But Jefferson charges that every effort by the colonial legislatures to effectively ban this trade by imposing prohibitive duties has "been hitherto defeated by his majesty's negative." By placing the interests of a "few African corsairs" above the interests of the American people, the king, according to Jefferson, has violated "the rights of human nature."[50] This charge goes beyond a simple criticism of a specific royal action; it constitutes a stinging indictment of a constitutional actor brutally indifferent to the natural rights to life and liberty. Jefferson strongly hints

---

[48] Ibid.

[49] Ibid., p. 115.

[50] Ibid., p. 116. Jefferson leveled an almost identical charge against George III in the list of grievances in his original draft of the Declaration of Independence, which was later omitted by the Committee at the Continental Congress.

that the king's failure to use the veto power in the colonies in a measured, prudent, and morally enlightened way may force dramatic constitutional change in the form of "some legal restrictions" on the crown.

Another example of the king's failure to assent to clearly salutary laws is his instruction to his governor in Virginia not to agree to any law for the establishment of new counties "unless the new county will consent to have no representation in assembly."[51] The practical effects of such a measure are to restrict the westward expansion of the colony and to confine the legislative body in Virginia to its present number. The people of the western counties, which, Jefferson argues, are "of indefinite extent," would be substantially injured in their civil rights, often having to travel hundreds of miles to seek relief for injuries in their county courts. Apart from the obvious practical difficulties created by the crown's decision, Jefferson finds an even more serious objection to the king's willingness to violate the principle of representation. By denying many citizens of Virginia "the glorious right of representation," the crown threatens to tear away at a principle woven into the very fabric of colonial liberty. At the heart of the colonial rallying cry, Locke's dictum of "No taxation, Without Representation," lay the natural rights principle that government exists for the protection of life, liberty, and property.[52] The effect of creating new counties without representation in the colonial assembly is to impose taxes and laws on these individuals without their consent. In this sense, the Virginia county issue was the broader colonial issue writ small: In both cases, the abusive action of the king or Parliament worked to subvert the proper end of government.

The Radical Theory of the Empire

In the closing section of the *Summary View* Jefferson turns from recounting the crown's and Parliament's abuse of the colonies to constructing a positive formulation of the proper relations between the British and American constitutional orders. It is here in his closing statement, as it were, and only after he has treated the issue of natural rights and their violations in the colonies at considerable length, that Jefferson outlines his radical theory of the empire.

Jefferson's radical theory of imperial relations is a direct manifestation of his Lockeanism. As we have seen, it is based on three central principles.

---

[51] Ibid. Jefferson's complaint about the abuse of the principle of representation in the colonies also pointed to what he took to be serious inadequacies in the representative system in Britain at the time. In this respect, Jefferson's argument parallels the concern of British radicals such as James Burgh and Granville Sharp, who saw faulty representation as one of the deepest constitutional problems in Britain (see Colin Bonwick, *English Radicals and the American Revolution* [Chapel Hill: University of North Carolina Press, 1977]: pp. 145–9 and Mayer, *Constitutional Thought*, pp. 36–7).

[52] See Locke, II:140.

First, Parliament has no jurisdiction over the colonies whatsoever. Since the people of the colonies never delegated any of their natural executive power to the British Parliament, there can be no legitimate grounds for the British government to interfere in the colonies, even in the limited and historically exercised role of regulating imperial trade and defense policy. In this respect, Jefferson went further in denying parliamentary involvement in the colonies than earlier luminaries like Otis and Dickinson.[53] In Jefferson's formulation of imperial relations, any parliamentary effort to govern the colonies is tantamount to a state of war, or as Locke put it, the use of "Force without Right."[54] Second, Jefferson argues that the colonies retained the British monarch as the supreme executive power in their constitutional orders. In Lockean terms, the supreme executive is a power "vested in a single Person, who has also a share in the Legislative."[55] Thus, Jefferson allows that the king has a legitimate role in the colonial legislative process through such measures as the veto and dissolution powers. These powers are, however, delegated to the crown only on the condition that they are exercised demonstrably for the public good. Third, Jefferson contends that not only is the king, or his representative, a part of the colonial legislatures, but also that the king is "thereby made the central link connecting the several parts of the empire thus newly established."[56] As supreme executive power of the various units constituting the empire, the king thus plays a mediating role between and among them all; a kind of hereditary glue holding the empire together in a federated commonwealth of self-governing peoples, in which the legislatures of Rhode Island and Delaware are the constitutional equals of Westminster.

Jefferson's proposal for a remedy to the imperial dispute is based on this radical theory of the empire and focuses on two major issues: the king's position as supreme executive agent in the colonial governments and the king's role as the only juridical or constitutional link between Britain and the colonies. If, according to Jefferson's radical theory of the empire, the king is the sole constitutional actor with authority in both the colonies and Britain, it is apparent that Jefferson believes George III has done a shabby job. Clearly, one focus in the *Summary View* is to encourage the king to perform his role in the colonial legislative process better, with more attention to the specific needs of the colonies and with greater respect for the inherent limits

---

[53] Apparently Jefferson's theory of the empire was too radical for the cautious Virginia House of Burgesses in 1774–5, which did not support Jefferson's instructions to their delegates in Philadelphia. For good discussions of the immediate practical effect of the *Summary View* in America and England, see Conrad, "Rights Talk," pp. 256–9 and Douglas Wilson, "Jefferson and the Republic of Letters," in *Jeffersonian Legacies*, Peter Onuf, ed. (Charlottesville: University of Virginia Press, 1993): p. 53.

[54] Locke, II:19 (see also II:18).

[55] Locke, II:151.

[56] Jefferson, SV, p. 107.

on delegated powers. The deeper thrust of the logic of Jefferson's radical imperial theory is, however, to force the king to change the way he relates to Parliament. Jefferson calls on the king, as the only mediatory power between the several states of the British Empire, "to recommend to his parliament total revocation" of all acts injurious to the colonies.[57] His appeal to the king to defend the colonies against parliamentary encroachments extends so far as to encourage the king to veto parliamentary legislation affecting the colonies. Jefferson claims: "It is now... the great office of his majesty, to resume the exercise of his negative power, and to prevent the passage of laws by any one legislature of the empire which bear injuriously on the rights and interests of another."[58] This pointed statement is clearly directed against Westminster. Jefferson is calling on the king to use his veto power liberally in Britain while restraining his use of the same power in the colonies! In terms of British constitutional practice since the Glorious Revolution and of imperial policy since the first settlements in America, this would truly signify the world turned upside down. By Jefferson's own admission, the veto power had fallen into desuetude in Britain because monarchs since the demise of the hapless James II have come to recognize "the impropriety of opposing their single opinion to the united wisdom of two houses of parliament."[59] The clear implication of Jefferson's radical theory of the empire is that one of the core elements of the British constitutional principle of legislative supremacy must be altered, or even abandoned, if the king is to play his proper role as the mediatory power between the several states of the British Empire.

The logical peak of Jefferson's radical imperial theory is the postulation that the king must protect the colonists against parliamentary encroachment through the use of his veto power. Such a departure from British constitutional practice and the doctrine of legislative supremacy enshrined in the Glorious Revolution is necessary because of a "change of circumstances" caused by "the addition of new states to the British empire," which "has produced an addition of new, sometimes opposite interest."[60] The logic of this imperial theory runs contrary to Robert Dawidoff's claim that the *Summary View* represents Jefferson's attempt to reclaim the heritage of "English Constitutionalism" for service in the colonial cause.[61] The implication of

---

[57] Ibid., p. 115.

[58] Ibid.

[59] Ibid.

[60] Ibid. Webking (*American Revolution*, p. 97) suggests that Jefferson's claim that the king has not used his veto power properly "is far and away the most important of the grievances against the king that Jefferson offers."

[61] Robert Dawidoff, "Rhetoric of Democracy," in *Thomas Jefferson and the Politics of Nature*, Thomas Engeman, ed. (Notre Dame, IN: University of Notre Dame Press, 2000), p. 106 (and see also Jaffa, *New Birth of Freedom*, pp. 14, 28–9). By presenting Jefferson's argument in the *Summary View* as torn between competing commitments to Lockean natural rights and moderate Whig constitutionalism, Jaffa and Dawidoff attribute to Jefferson a position more

Jefferson's argument is that the 1689 constitutional settlement in Britain is untenable because of the imperial pressures produced by the inclusion of numerous colonial governments directed to securing the natural rights of their people. Jefferson forcefully argues that the practice of English constitutionalism must change dramatically in the new imperial order. Could the British government have accepted this formulation of imperial relations and the implications it would hold for the British constitutional order? Theoretically, yes. British leaders, including the king and Parliament, could have taken Jefferson's proposal as simply another colonial warning to Parliament to abandon its pretensions to ruling the colonies. Thus, if they had taken Jefferson's argument to heart and desisted from legislating for the Americans, then the king, again at least in theory, would never have to use his veto to protect the colonists. However, this scenario was always extremely unlikely, especially given the express language of Parliament's official statement on imperial relations in the 1766 Declaratory Act, which affirmed that it had the authority "to make laws . . . to bind the Colonists and People of America . . . in all cases whatsoever."[62] To retreat from this position to the one proposed by Jefferson would be almost unthinkable to the British government.

From the British perspective, the theoretical objections to Jefferson's radical theory of the empire cut to the heart of the way they understood their own system of government. To accept that the British king had a share in the colonial government that he held independently of the authority of Parliament, a share of rule in the colonies rooted, à la Locke, exclusively in the consent of the American people, would be to accept a principle of royal independence that could potentially subvert the power of the two houses in Britain's balanced Constitution. In order to accommodate the colonial formulation of the empire expressed by Jefferson, the British people would have to countenance a potentially dangerous reversal of the principle of legislative supremacy established in 1689. An imperial king with colonial sympathies who actively employed the veto in Britain could raise money or even troops in America for use in Britain. In British constitutional history prior to 1689, there were several important examples suggesting the dangers such royal independence posed for Britain's balanced Constitution.[63] In the celebrated

akin to that of Otis and Dickinson. Jefferson's argument in the *Summary View* is actually deeply subversive of the British constitutional tradition.

[62] Declaratory Act, 6 George III, c. 12 in Henry Steele Commager, *Documents of American History* (New York: Appleton, 1963): p. 61.

[63] Jack Greene and Paul Rahe also observe the subversive potential that Jefferson's imperial theory held for the British Constitution as understood at least since the Glorious Revolution (Jack Greene, "Origins of the American Revolution: A Constitutional Interpretation," *Framing and Ratification of the Constitution*, Leonard Levy and Dennis Mahoney, eds. [New York: Macmillan, 1987]: p. 52 and Paul Rahe, "The American Revolution," in *The American Experiment: Essays on the Theory and Practice of Liberty*, Peter Augustine Lawler and Robert Martin Schaefer, eds. [Lanham, MD: Rowman & Littlefield, 1994]: p. 45). Bonwick (*English*

Ship Money case of the 1630s and in the crown's use of Irish troops in the civil war, supporters of parliamentary supremacy in Britain saw dangerous historical precedents in the executive's use and abuse of the crown's control over the nation's foreign affairs and national security. In more recent times, in the secret Treaty of Dover concluded in 1670 by the penultimate Stuart king, Charles II drew on French money and promises of French troops with a plan of asserting royal independence from an obstructionist Parliament. These examples of royal pretensions to subvert the balanced Constitution seared painful lessons into the British Whig constitutional consciousness in the seventeenth and eighteenth centuries.

The core British constitutional principle since the Glorious Revolution was the nullification of any legal, and indeed irregular, means by which the crown could circumvent parliamentary assent in the raising of revenue or troops. Jefferson's radical theory of the empire threatened to make such constitutional safeguards nugatory. While the prospects of a British monarch using American taxpayers' money to circumvent parliamentary supply and employing American troops to form a standing army in Britain may have been rather improbable, even farfetched, there was much in this theoretical and juridical possibility, however unlikely, that struck at the very core of British constitutional theory and practice. An imperial king, perhaps in the future, could slip his British constitutional leash. In this sense, Jefferson appears to have made the British government an offer of a wide-ranging and innovative new theory of imperial relations, that it could never have accepted in 1774 and would not even begin instituting until the formation of the Commonwealth in 1931.[64]

Jefferson's *Summary View* is a classic example of the Lockean basis of the colonial position in the imperial dispute with Britain. However, his audacious assertion of the colonists' natural rights to self-government went far beyond the claims of earlier colonial spokesmen, extending to a call for the crown to use its constitutional power as supreme executive in the several states of the empire to nullify proposed parliamentary legislation. Jefferson's radical Whig principle of popular sovereignty collided directly with the moderate Whig tenet of parliamentary sovereignty. By proclaiming the independence of the colonial legislatures from Parliament, Jefferson established an imperial theory that would have enshrined the equality of all the legislatures in the empire. In this way, his position escaped the theoretical difficulties in justifying colonial resistance that faced Otis and Dickinson's admission that Parliament was the supreme legislative power in the empire. In the process, Jefferson cleared away some of the theoretical obstacles

---

Radicals, p. 251) observes that, for their part, British radicals also found cause to fear that the British monarch might use authoritarian measures in the colonies as a way to circumvent parliamentary control over revenue.

[64] Mayer, *Constitutional Thought*, p. 35.

to legitimizing American independence. Now the only link to be cut from Britain was with the crown, not the entire British system of government. Despite this theoretical achievement, Jefferson's argument offered less practical possibility for accommodating colonial self-government within the imperial system than did those of his earlier compatriots. It is more conceivable that the British would have been persuaded to see the prudence and rectitude of respecting the exclusive rights of America's subordinate legislatures than they would ever have acknowledged the equality of all the states in the empire. Thus, both in theory and in practice, Jefferson's efforts in 1774 did much to break the path for independence in 1776.

14

Tom Paine and Popular Sovereignty

In the opening days of 1776, Tom Paine's influential tract *Common Sense* rolled off the presses and rushed straight into the swirling firestorm that increasingly consumed the imperial dispute. The newly arrived English immigrant appeared on the scene as though sent from central casting as one of Jefferson's emigré revolutionaries in the *Summary View*, and promptly set his distinctive stamp on the events and philosophical debate in the six months or so prior to the formal declaration of American independence. By the time Paine's pamphlet reached his American audience, much had changed in even a few years, and what little goodwill that remained in Anglo–American relations after years of strain had largely disappeared. American blood had been shed by British troops, and a hastily recruited Continental Army lay siege to the British garrison in Boston. Quite in keeping with the turbulent passions of the time, Paine's incendiary rhetoric advanced the colonial position in a way hitherto unseen in the more than decade-long dispute between the colonists and the British government. *Common Sense* marked a departure from previous statements of the colonial position in several ways. First, Paine expressly and unambiguously made the case for American independence from the British Empire. He showed no desire to quibble over legitimate spheres of imperial jurisdiction or to engage in extended discussions of the colonists' legal and constitutional links with the mother country. For Paine, Britain ruled the empire, and the Americans should and must leave it. He drew both on natural rights theory and on realpolitik to argue that the separation of America from Britain was inevitable, and given the deteriorating relations between the two peoples, now more than ever it was desirable.

Second, Paine's philosophical and theoretical justification for independence was based on a potent blend of distinct radical Whig republican ideas. While Paine shared the view of the earlier colonial champions that government should be directed to securing rights, Paine combined this essentially Lockean notion of liberty as individual autonomy with a deep commitment to the modern republican notion of political liberty as popular control of government. In this regard, the Englishman Paine's explicit and determined advocacy of republicanism in *Common Sense* located his thought on the extreme fringe of British radicalism, from which many of his ideas originated but that for the most part rejected outright republicanism. The primary concern of the British radicals during the period of the imperial crisis was the movement for electoral reform and more equitable representation catalyzed by the Wilkes Affair of the late 1760s and 1770s, in which the notorious radical John Wilkes was repeatedly expelled from the Commons despite his repeated reelection in Middlesex. Most British radicals sought the more limited goal of fairer popular representation rather than quantum democratic change in the fundamental structure of the British Constitution.[1] Paine expressed republican ideals that displayed substantive connections not so much to the contemporary British radical reform movement as further back in the radical Whig tradition to seminal thinkers like Sidney, Trenchard, and Gordon. Like Sidney, Paine incorporated the classical republican hostility to monarchy and the principle of heredity into his natural rights – based theory of government. Gordon Wood suggests that Paine expressed antimonarchical sentiments "that had not been said before" in the colonies.[2] Perhaps Paine more than any other thinker ensured that the result and goal of the revolution in America would be emphatically republican.

Paine's unambiguous republicanism also marked an important departure from previous statements of the colonial position in the imperial crisis. Whereas Otis and Dickinson's moderate imperial theory expressed high praise for the British constitutional model, and while even Jefferson's radical theory of the empire still retained the British crown as the fulcrum linking the several states of the empire, Paine expressed little short of contempt for the British Constitution. Paine's strident republicanism dealt a powerful blow to American confidence in the British Constitution at a decisive

---

[1] Colin Bonwick, *English Radicals and the American Revolution* (Chapel Hill: University of North Carolina Press, 1977): pp. 21–3, 148–9, 259 and Gregory Claeys, *Thomas Paine: Social and Political Thought* (Boston: Unwin & Hyman, 1989): pp. 14–15. Bonwick (pp. 265–6) observes that in many respects the overwhelming majority of British radicals in the American Revolution period were committed to a "sentimentalized" version of the fundamentally conservative principles of the moderate Whig revolution of 1688–9. Unlike Paine, he argues, British radical reformers at the time, such as Price, Priestley, Sharp, and Cartwright, denied any association with republicanism and expressed a genuine fear of social and political upheaval.

[2] Gordon Wood, "The Democratization of Mind in the American Revolution," in *The Moral Foundations of the American Republic*, 3rd ed., Robert Horwitz, ed. (Charlottesville: University Press of Virginia, 1987): p. 117–18. Bernard Bailyn ("Common Sense" in *Fundamental Testaments of the American Revolution* [Washington, DC: Library of Congress, 1973]: pp. 8–9) argues that in early January 1776 only "a fool or a fanatic" openly advocated American independence. Therefore, Paine not only had to make his own radical case in a persuasive and coherent form, he also had to reverse deeply ingrained habits of thought and presumptions about government. Bailyn contends that Paine played a significant but far from determinative role in changing and shaping the worldview of the colonists ("Common Sense," pp. 18–19, 22).

moment in Anglo-American relations following years of growing frustration and resentment on both sides of the imperial crisis.

Common Sense accelerated and radicalized the process of American disenchantment with Britain and its system of government already manifest in Jefferson's *Summary View.* In contrast with the Lockean liberal delegation theory of sovereignty that was amenable to the construction of mixed constitutions, Paine followed the more clearly Sidneyan form of Whig republicanism, which deeply distrusted the principle of constitutional mixture and balance. In language much more critical than even that of Trenchard and Gordon's *Cato*, Paine rejected outright the British system of mixed government with its complex balance of king, Lords, and Commons. Paine was the first major colonial spokesman to criticize explicitly not only British policy toward the colonies, but the very concept of the British Constitution itself, the product of 1688–9 that was so revered for so long on both sides of the Atlantic. In a particularly potent sense, Paine was the first to say that the emperor, so long dishabille in America, really had no clothes.

Government and Society

In many respects, Paine's discussion of the origins of government is simply a collection of axioms drawn from radical Whig philosophy. Government is a product of consent and is properly directed to the security of individual rights. What is striking, however, in Paine's account of the origins of government is his radical separation of the concept of government from that of society. Paine practically begins *Common Sense* with the statement "Some writers have so confounded society with government, as to leave little or no distinction between them; whereas they are not only different, but have different origins."[3] Paine's point with this assertion is one not unfamiliar in radical Whig thought. He, like Locke and Sidney, wanted to demonstrate that government is emphatically conventional, a product of human will. But Paine goes beyond even Locke and Sidney in arguing that society and government not only constitute differing forms of human association with different legal and ethical claims on the individual, they actually reflect something like two moral poles in human experience. Simply put, Paine believes society is good and government is bad, or at least stands as a testament to human frailty. He argues:

Society is produced by our wants, and government by our wickedness; the former promotes our happiness *positively* by uniting our affections, the latter *negatively* by restraining our vices. The one encourages intercourse, the other creates distinctions. The first is a patron, the last a punisher.[4]

---

[3] Thomas Paine, *Common Sense*, Ronald Herder, ed. (Mineola, NY: Dover Publications, 1997): pp. 2–3 (hereafter Paine, CS, and page number).
[4] Ibid., p. 3 (emphasis in the original).

Society, then, is an informal system of human relations rooted in the natural communal passions and social sentiments, whereas government is a system of laws, commands, and coercive power embedded in the logic of rights and interests. Insofar as society reflects the deep human need and desire for community, Paine claims that it is "in every state . . . a blessing." For its part, government, being a regulator of the antisocial passions and the injurious effects of extreme self-interest, is "even in its best state . . . but a necessary evil."[5]

How are we to understand Paine's premising his theoretical account of the origin of government on this discussion of a radical dichotomy between government and society? One effect of his method of argumentation is to focus our attention on the limited goals of government. Given that, due to our fallible nature, the individuals composing society cannot flourish peacefully in an unregulated state for long, each individual "finds it necessary to surrender up a part of his property to furnish the means for the protection of the rest." The surrender of natural liberty necessary to form government is, according to Paine, at best "a necessary evil," and thus reflects the self-limiting character of political power and the utilitarian considerations that should guide our analysis of differing forms of government. In fine radical Whig fashion, Paine states: "security being the true design and end of government, it unanswerably follows that whatever form thereof appears most likely to secure it to us with the least expence and greatest benefit, is preferable to all others."[6] Government in general not only has a limited end, but also in its particular forms is subject to change, variation, and alteration based on its capacity to secure the rights of its citizens. The rhetorical effect of Paine's opening discussion is clear. When we follow Paine's lead and accept his account of government's limited aims and humble (not to say vicious) origins, the reader feels little desire or logical ground to revere any particular government, especially the British government then practically at war with America.

Paine's discussion of the government–society dichotomy thus appears to make two points. First, he wants to establish the theoretical claims for a form of human association that exists independently of formal constitutional government. There is a natural harmony of interests, according to Paine, but they are still individual interests.[7] Society is a realm of individuals bound

---

[5] Ibid.

[6] Ibid., p. 5.

[7] Francis Canavan, "Thomas Paine," in *The History of Political Philosophy*, 3rd ed., Leo Strauss and Joseph Cropsey, eds. (Chicago: University of Chicago Press, 1987): p. 681. David Mayer (*The Constitutional Thought of Thomas Jefferson* [Charlottesville: University of Virginia Press, 1994]: pp. 70–2) makes an interesting argument that Paine's natural society represents a synthesis between Lockean natural rights theory and Scottish moral sense philosophy. Eric Foner (*Tom Paine and Revolutionary America* [New York: Oxford University Press, 1976]: pp. 92–4) attributes Paine's natural society argument to a "Newtonian frame of mind" stressing

by habits, sentiments, and necessity in which rights are inherently insecure because of the fallibility of human virtue. Virtue plays a more significant role in Paine's analysis than in that of any of the other radical Whigs save Sidney and Cato. The end of government is not to replace the organic connections of society or even to supplement them; rather, government is meant solely to protect individual rights through law and punishment. The state of liberty characterizing society must be in part surrendered in the contract that establishes government. In this respect, Paine makes the very Lockean argument that government exists to secure the private realm of activities in society.

Paine's second aim in this discussion is to lay the theoretical foundation of the more polemical argument for American independence. The practical effect of Paine's conceptual bifurcation of government and society, especially in the turbulent early days of 1776, is to reinforce the idea for his audience that there is an American society that exists independently of Britain and its government.[8] According to Paine, America in 1776 is for all intents and purposes a society (or collection of societies) in want of a government. With Britain practically at war with the colonies, Parliament and the king had essentially forfeited any legal or constitutional right to govern America that they may or may not have possessed in the past. The legal rights of Parliament or the king over the colonies was by 1776 a moot point for Paine. Moreover, independently of the actions of the British government, America had no societal link with British society 3,000 miles away. This is particularly true, Paine claims, since American blood has been shed by British hands. What bond of affection and sentiment between the colonies and Britain could survive this strain? Paine asks.[9] By affirming that the constitutive power to form a government lies with the individuals composing society, Paine reinforces the idea that Americans can rightfully and should expeditiously abandon whatever association they had with Britain previously and form a new system of government.

Paine's concept of society plays a double role in his larger argument for independence. On the one hand, society represents a form of human association independent of the formal obligations and laws coincident with government. It thus stands as a principle to which Paine can have recourse in explaining the devolution of political power within the empire. The concept

---

cosmic harmony and, perhaps paradoxically, Paine's own observations of American society in the process of throwing off British rule. Given the eclectic and amalgamating bent of Paine's largely autodidactic mind, both Mayer's and Foner's suggestions are plausible. However as I argue in Chapter 7, one of the central features of modern Whig republican thought since Spinoza and Sidney was the conscious blurring of the distinction between nature and society. This is, of course, a theoretical postulation that can with only minor modification support an argument for the comparative naturalness of society in contrast to the strictly limited ends and scope of government.

[8] Foner, *Tom Paine and Revolutionary America*, p. 92.

[9] Paine, CS, pp. 23–4.

of society operates as an intermediary condition between government and
natural liberty. By severing its ties with Britain, America does not revert to a
state of nature because there is a society or societies on these shores entirely
derived from the circumstances and common life of the American people.
In this sense, Paine's notion of society serves to assuage the fears of those
reluctant patriots in the colonies who view separation from Britain as an
invitation to anarchy and disorder, the spectral nightmare of a loose collection of individuals existing with no legal and moral obligations whatsoever.
Paine assures these cautious colonists, with their essentially moderate Whig
antipathy to the idea of dissolution of government, that society without government is not a brutal state of nature. On the other hand, society operates in
Paine's thought as a seedbed for government. Society is not only the Lockean
repository to which political power would devolve in the event of separation, it also supplies the preexisting materials out of which government can
be established or reconstructed. Paine's vision of the promise for Americans
is one in which their government fully reflects their own society with no
admixture from Britain.

The Origins of Government

In order to demonstrate the constituent power of the individuals composing
society, Paine provides an account of a proxy state of nature based on the
experience of emigration and colonization. In a move strikingly similar to
Jefferson's in the *Summary View*, Paine contends that "[i]n order to gain a
clear and just idea of the design and end of government, let us suppose a
small number of persons settled in some sequestered part of the earth, unconnected with the rest, they will then represent the first peopling of any
country, or of the world."[10] This thinly veiled allusion to the first European
settlement of the New World operates as a quasi-theoretical construction
meant to demonstrate the origin of government in a manner loosely based
on the actual American experience of emigration and colonization. Whereas
Jefferson used this motif somewhat narrowly to establish the colonists' natural right of self-government, Paine extrapolates from Jefferson's premise to
produce a broader account of the complex social mechanisms contributing
to the formation of government. In this respect, Paine employs the American
experience as indicative of the primordial human relation to society and government. Of these "newly arrived emigrants," Paine argues, "society will be
their first thought." The first movement out of the "state of natural liberty"
is the transition to society, whereby the stirrings of the heart and the practical necessity of securing survival in a harsh and uncultured environment
will drive these individuals "to seek assistance and relief of one another."[11]

[10] Ibid., p. 3.
[11] Ibid.

The movement to the next stage, from society to government, is occasioned by "the defect of moral virtue," its inability to be a reliable guarantor of just action. As Paine understands it, government is necessary only after people have attained a degree of relative security. He claims: "In proportion as they surmount the first difficulties of emigration, which bound them together in common cause, they will begin to relax in their duty and attachment to each other; and this remissness, will point out the necessity, of establishing some form of government."[12] This discussion of the origins of government bears a more than passing resemblance to Rousseau's description in his *Second Discourse* of the transition from the golden age of simplicity and social cohesion to the corruption and inequality characterizing advanced government.[13] However, Paine, more emphatically than Rousseau, attempts to demonstrate the Sidneyan–Spinozist postulation about the naturalness of democracy. Paine's concern is to show that the condition of natural liberty and equality that human beings originally enjoy and the social experience of their intercourse in society produce more or less immediately a democratic form of government. Rousseau's argument that the first imaginative sparks of human vice necessarily, almost spontaneously, produce inequality in society, and between governors and the governed, is a conclusion Paine roundly denounces. He claims:

Some convenient tree will afford them a State-House, under the branches of which, the whole colony may assemble to deliberate on public matters. It is more than probable that their first laws will have the title only of REGULATIONS, and be enforced by no other penalty than public disesteem. In this first parliament every man, by natural right, will have a seat.[14]

---

[12] Ibid., p. 4.

[13] See Jean-Jacques Rousseau, "Discourse on Inequality," in *Rousseau's Political Writings*, Alan Ritter and Julia Conaway Bondanella, eds. (New York: Norton, 1988): esp. Part II, pp. 34–57. Paine is a fascinating example of the modifications and adjustments in English radical Whig thought after it has been exposed to philosophical influences from France. With his emphasis on society and on the sentiments generally, Paine shows the strong influence of Rousseau. But for Rousseau, in contrast to Paine, the golden age of social relations soon, and apparently inevitably, degenerated into a brutal state of war, out of which political society finally emerged. While Paine appears to imply that the original social harmony of the pre-civil period comes to an end when individuals "begin to relax in their duty and attachment to each other," he avoids the implication of a general state of war. Perhaps because he rejects this Rousseauian conclusion, Paine can assert the radically egalitarian character of the origins of government; that is, people do not need to select a warlord/chief to provide security; instead, they can institute broad-based self-government.

[14] Paine, CS, p. 4. Wilson Carey McWilliams observes that one of the most important moral implications of Paine's egalitarianism is his claim that political distinctions, as opposed to sexual and economic distinctions, are simply unnatural (Wilson Carey McWilliams, "On Equality as the Moral Foundation for Community," in *The Moral Foundations of the American Republic*, Robert Horwitz, ed. [Charlottesville: University Press of Virginia, 1987]: pp. 304–5). This observation supports my argument that Paine's antimonarchism denotes more than a criticism of the structural or institutional problems attending monarchy as a form of

The strong egalitarian root in Paine's natural rights theory produces distinct moral and constitutional implications. Paine's colonists assembled under "some convenient" oak play a role in his argument similar to that of the citizen-soldiers in Sidney's account of the Saxon democracy at the origins of the English regime. In both cases, the intention is to demonstrate the natural foundations of democracy. This is where for Paine, as for Sidney and to a lesser extent Cato, the individualist notion of natural rights and the characteristically republican argument for political liberty coalesce. Paine reveals that the necessary implication of the need for government as a means to secure individual liberty is a guarantee of general, if not even universal, political liberty. A public share in government is the natural precondition for securing rights. This is not simply a matter of employing citizenship instrumentally to secure private interests. In the preceding passage, Paine calls this individual share in government a "natural right." The principle and practice of representation, in this view, emerge only as a matter of "convenience" when the colony becomes too large and populous to allow a realistic way of calling a universal assembly of all the citizenry. Even so, Paine qualifies the idea of representation by cautioning that it will be necessary "to augment the number of representatives" as the colony grows and to guarantee "having elections often" in order to ensure that the representatives "well establish a common interest with every part of the community."[15] This modern republican understanding of the radical egalitarianism underlying the origins of government means that Paine's constitutionalism will be based on the principle of government reflecting the interests of all the naturally free and equal individuals composing society. Paine appeals to nature as the mother of political and constitutional art.

Another important feature of Paine's discussion of the origins of government is his treatment of moral virtue. One serious implication of Paine's argument for the moral and logical primacy of society over and against government is the ambiguous status of virtue in his argument. As we have seen, Paine believed that government is necessary because of "the defect of moral virtue." With an appeal to Miltonic rhetoric, Paine asserts: "Government, like dress, is the badge of lost innocence; the palaces of kings are built on the ruins of the bowers of paradise."[16] If we could count on conscience to direct

---

government. For radical Whig republicans like Sidney and Paine, monarchy is fundamentally a moral problem. It is unnatural because it requires suppression or distortion of the moral and political implications of natural equality and hence denies the naturalness of democracy. For Paine's view of the naturalness of democracy, see Gordon Wood, *The Creation of the American Republic, 1776–1787* (Chapel Hill: University of North Carolina Press, 1969): pp. 100, 222–4.

[15] Paine, CS, pp. 4–5.

[16] Ibid., p. 4. For Paine's rhetorical parallels with Milton, see, for example, John Milton, "Areopagitica," in *Areopagitica and Other Political Writings of John Milton*, ed. John Alvis (Indianapolis: Liberty Fund Press, 1999): pp. 17, 23 and *Paradise Lost*, ed. Christopher Ricks (New York: Signet Classics, 1968): Book IX, lines 1052–131, pp. 263–6.

human actions in a reliable way, then government would not be necessary. Paine concludes, in contrast to classical republican thinkers, that human beings are able to develop the moral qualities of "duty and attachment" without intense civic education and almost spontaneously by dint of their proclivity for mutual assistance and social intercourse. According to Paine, modern society rather than the classical polis provides the psychic plane on which moral virtue flourishes.[17] But given the psychology of the human passions, government will always be necessary to some extent. Implicit in Paine's argument is an assessment of human nature similar to that of Cato and Sidney. Self-interest, while in part a manifestation of our natural liberty, is also a feature of human nature that can distort our duty to refrain from injuring the rights of others. Paine's republicanism, his concern for political liberty and equality, flows from his assessment of this melancholy but ineradicable dimension of human liberty. Individuals must be directly involved in public affairs, even if through the means of representation, because it is both foolish and base to rely on others to protect one's own rights without this relatively direct and unmediated form of popular control. In this sense, for Paine, as for Cato and Sidney, the logic of rights and interests is not antithetical to the concern for civic virtue. While individual virtue may be too slender and brittle a reed to cling to in the hope of securing liberty, the direct participation of an entire citizenry in political affairs will, in Paine's view, provide some reliable guarantee that government will remain committed to the limited aim it is assigned by nature.

The British Constitution

This account of the origins of government lays the foundation for Paine's critical analysis of the British Constitution. The opening discussion of natural rights in *Common Sense* is distinctly Lockean. In the following treatment of British mixed constitutionalism, Paine injects a decidedly radical Whig republican dimension into his argument.[18] Herein lies one of Paine's most important departures from the position of earlier colonial spokesmen in the imperial dispute. He offers little or no praise for British constitutional

---

[17] Compare Paine's argument with Aristotle, *The Politics*, Carnes Lord, trans. (Chicago: University of Chicago Press, 1984): 1253a25–9.

[18] In this sense, I agree with Kramnick regarding his interpretive division of *Common Sense* by the Lockean character of the first section and the more republican arguments that follow (Isaac Kramnick, *Republicanism and Bourgeois Radicalism* [Ithaca: Cornell University Press, 1990]: p. 146). Where I differ from Kramnick is in his assessment that Paine's republicanism bears the formative influence of late eighteenth-century English dissenting radicals. My point is not to dispute the influence of dissenting Protestant radicals on Paine, but rather to trace the core elements of his republicanism back in the Whig tradition to Sidney and ultimately to Spinoza.

theory or practice. Whereas Otis, Dickinson, and even Jefferson all sought to defend colonial rights in terms consistent with the British constitutional model of mixed sovereignty, Paine rejects this notion outright.[19] His primary objection to British constitutionalism is twofold: its origins in clear violation of popular sovereignty and its adherence to what Paine takes to be the absurd doctrine of mixed sovereignty.

First, Paine traces the origins of the modern British government not to a universal act of popular consent, whether in 1689 or at any other date, but rather to the "dark and slavish times in which it was erected." That it may have been noble and enlightened for the time it was first established Paine grants. But this nobility is radically contingent on the context of "the dark and slavish times" in which the British Constitution emerged. Paine employs a notion of historical and intellectual progress akin to that of Sidney. His argument rests on the assumption that the central lessons of the radical Whig theory of government were only imperfectly understood by the people of early English civilization. As such, the historical development of British constitutional ideas and practice represents a distortion of the true egalitarian natural rights teaching. Paine claims that the British Constitution as it currently exists includes the "remains of two ancient tyrannies, compounded with some new republican materials."[20] In a sense, Paine agrees with the framers of the 1689 Declaration of Rights, who saw the constituent parts of the constitutional order as the estates – king, Lords, and Commons – and not as the individuals composing society. For Paine, however, the signal features of the British government are the remains of "monarchical tyranny" and "aristocratical tyranny" embodied in the king and Lords. Paine's point here is that these two historical tyrannies are not the product of popular consent. Indeed, he claims that inasmuch as they are still hereditary offices, the constitutional authority invested in the king and Lords is "independent of the people."[21] Moreover, Paine makes this claim in the face of the contrary position maintained even by other American Whigs like Otis and Dickinson, who looked to the Glorious Revolution, or in Jefferson's case to emigration, as the point at which the entire British people and the people of the empire consented to a certain constitutional and imperial arrangement.

The only salutary feature of the British Constitution, in Paine's view, is the "new republican materials, in the persons of the commons." It is this element of political or public liberty "which Englishmen glory in."[22] It is only this single element of the British government that can plausibly be said

---

[19] For good accounts of the revolutionary impact of Paine's harsh criticism of the revered British Constitution in the colonies, see Bailyn, "Common Sense," pp. 10, 12, 15–16; Claeys, *Thomas Paine: Social and Political Thought*, pp. 43–5; and Foner, *Tom Paine and the American Revolution*, pp. 76–7.

[20] Paine, CS, p. 6.

[21] Ibid.

[22] Ibid., pp. 6, 17.

to provide the continuous flow of popular consent necessary to secure free government. What Paine sees in the British Constitution, then, is a radically truncated form of popular government severely handicapped by two powerful institutions rooted in the country's "dark and slavish" feudal past. He repudiates the moderate Whig idea of balanced constitutionalism, arguing of the king and the Lords that "in a *constitutional sense*, they contribute nothing toward the freedom of the state."[23] By this Paine suggests that the hereditary offices are empowered by the Constitution to check, restrain, and ultimately emasculate the popular will expressed, albeit imperfectly, through the House of Commons. Needless to say, Paine equates the expression of popular will with the freedom of the state.

In order to understand Paine's antipathy to Britain's mixed regime, it is important to recall his account of the origins of government. In that discussion, Paine claimed that the move from natural society to political society eventuates in a radical democracy, a parliament where "every man, by natural right, will have a seat." What is notable in this account is Paine's silence regarding the institution of magistracy or executive power. Presumably, the executive power is created by the people as a definitively subordinate power, clearly subject to the people and/or their representatives in the legislative body. Paine's silence on the exact mechanics involved in the construction and delegation of executive power may be explained as an effort to make Sidney and Spinoza's point that the strength of government derives not from institutions, but from the collected power of individuals in society.[24] Paine says as much by arguing that "the strength of government, and the happiness of the governed" depend on the legislature's capacity to form a common interest with every part of the community, and "not on the unmeaning name of king."[25] Thus, British constitutional development marks a clear violation of Paine's argument for the popular foundations of government. The principle of natural democracy articulated in his theoretical account of the origins of government has, Paine argues, been distorted and effaced by English historical development from feudal times. Although the introduction of "new republican materials" to the constitution by the improved status of the Commons, at least since the revolutions of the seventeenth century, is clearly a salutary development, Paine suggests that these popular victories are fragile and dangerously diluted by the considerable constitutional powers of the nondemocratic elements in the government.

Paine's second major objection to the "much boasted constitution of England" flows from his opposition to the doctrine of mixed sovereignty.

---

[23] Ibid., p. 6 (emphasis in the original).
[24] Cf. Sidney, D 3.11 and D 3.45; Benedict Spinoza, *A Theologico-Political Treatise* and *A Political Treatise*, R. H. M. Elwes, trans. (New York: Dover, 1951) and Spinoza, *Ethics*, Edwin Curley, trans. (Amhert: Prometheus, 1989).
[25] Paine, CS, p. 5.

Paine follows Sidney and Spinoza in basing his objection to the idea of constitutional mixture on the basis of a certain understanding of nature. He
argues: "I draw my idea of the form of government from a principle in nature, which no art can overturn, viz. that the more simple any thing is, the
less liable it is to be disordered, and the easier repaired when disordered."
Paine claims that "the constitution of England is so exceedingly complex,
that the nation may suffer for years together without being able to discover
in which part the fault lies."[26] For Paine, the interaction of various constitutional actors with independent powers in a single complex system of
relations is anathema to the very essence of limited government. It was this
aspect of Paine's thought that drew the fire of one of his harshest American
critics, John Adams. Adams' defense of the principle of mixed constitutionalism in his *Thoughts on Government* may be seen in large measure as a
critical response to Paine and an effort to counteract the latter's influence on
early American constitution making.[27] Paine's objection to mixed government rests on several postulations. First, as we have seen, he believes that
complex constitutional structures obscure the responsibility of public officials to the people. When it is not entirely clear who or what body effects
measures injurious to the public or impedes the passage of salutary acts,
the security of the people will suffer. This concern resembles Cato's effort
to identify and punish the public officials involved behind the scenes in the
South Sea scandal.[28] For both Paine and Cato, the people must be able to
see public corruption *as it begins* so as to be able to defend their rights.

Paine's other major objection to the principle of mixed sovereignty is his
rejection of the notion of constitutional checks and balances. The central
tenet of Paine's radical Whig republicanism is the idea that political freedom
and individual liberty are best preserved by the body that directly reflects
the popular will. As such, he scorns the system of checks and balances in the
British constitutional model: "To say the constitution of England is a union
of three powers reciprocally *checking* each other is farcical, either the words
have no meaning, or they are flat contradictions."[29] He tries to demonstrate
both that on a practical level the powers in England do not reciprocally check
each other and on a theoretical level that the very idea of mixed sovereignty
is absurd. With respect to the practical question of whether the branches of

[26] Ibid.
[27] John Adams, "Thoughts on Government," in *The Political Writings of John Adams*, George
Peck, ed. (New York: Liberal Arts Press, 1954). For a good discussion of Adams' criticism
of Paine's support for unicameralism as well as Paine's unfortunate, but unintentional, role
in precipitating one of the nastier episodes in the stormy Adams–Jefferson relationship, see
C. Bradley Thompson, *John Adams and the Spirit of Liberty* (Lawrence: University of Kansas
Press, 1998): pp. 175, 205, 212–13, 270–3.
[28] See John Trenchard and Thomas Gordon, *Cato's Letters*, Ronald Hamowy, ed. (Indianapolis:
Liberty Classics, 1995): Letters #2–8, 11, 12.
[29] Paine, CS, p. 6.

government in England are coequal in their capacity to check each other, Paine baldly states: "That the crown is the overbearing part in the English constitution needs not to be mentioned."[30] Paine even goes so far as to suggest that the crown in England constantly threatens to swallow up what little power the Commons do have. In terms echoing Cato's fears more than fifty years earlier, Paine opines:

The corrupt influence of the crown, by having all places in its disposal, hath so effectually swallowed up the power, and eaten out the virtue of the house of commons (the republican part in the constitution) that the government of England is nearly as monarchical as that of France or Spain.[31]

This unflattering comparison of Britain to notorious absolute monarchies like France and Spain could only stun and enrage moderate and mainstream English Whigs and like-minded Americans.[32] But behind Paine's objection to the actual practice of British government, with its constant tendency to lurch toward absolutism, rests his suspicion that any notion of mixed sovereignty will ultimately reduce to a veil for monarchical hegemony.

On a more theoretical level, Paine contends that the principle of mixed sovereignty is a logical absurdity. If we accept the logical and moral premise that all power originates in the people, he argues, then how can they be said to create a power to check their own power, namely, the king, and then also create a power, the House of Commons, to check the power of the king? Paine claims:

To say that the commons is a check upon the king presupposes two things. First-That the king is not to be trusted without being looked after, or in other words, that a thirst for absolute power is the natural disease of monarchy. Secondly- That the commons, by being appointed for that purpose, are either wiser or more worthy of confidence than the crown.[33]

Paine asks, where did the king obtain this power, which cannot be trusted without legal restraint? If from the people, why would they grant such a dangerous authority? Moreover, if the people's representatives are wise and competent enough to check the king (who cannot be trusted, we recall), then why do we need a king at all? Clearly, the implication drawn from the check on royal power is the idea that the Commons can perform the role of government on its own. But, given the Constitution's assurance of a royal veto power on legislation, the clear intent of the Constitution is to prevent

[30] Ibid., p. 7.
[31] Ibid., p. 16.
[32] See Bailyn, *Ideological Origins*, pp. 287–91 and Foner, *Tom Paine and Revolutionary America*, pp. 120–3 for an account of the many enraged Tory and even moderate Whig responses to Paine that followed the publication of *Common Sense*.
[33] Paine, CS, p. 6.

such direct popular rule. Paine blurts out that the entire premise of the British system is "a mere absurdity!"

The Problem of Monarchy

The fundamental constitutional errors embedded in the British system of government are, in Paine's view, monarchy and the principle of heredity. Paine's detailed and impassioned account of the defects of monarchy is drawn practically straight from the pages of Algernon Sidney. The first and deepest problem with monarchy is its violation of the moral principle of natural equality. Paine compares the distinction between rich and poor, on the one hand, and monarch and subject, on the other:

Mankind being originally equals in the order of creation, the equality could only be destroyed by some subsequent circumstances; the distinctions of rich and poor, may in great measure be accounted for.... But there is another and greater distinction for which no truly natural or religious reason can be assigned, and that is, the distinction of men into KINGS and SUBJECTS.[34]

The unnaturalness of monarchy is, for Paine, a prima facie case against its inherent reasonableness. By "unnatural," however, Paine means that monarchy is inconsistent with the principle of equality; he does not suggest that it is rare. Quite the contrary, Paine argues that the historical ubiquity of monarchy has two explanations.

First, a people may in ignorance and primitive simplicity offer their voluntary assent to a king. Paine cites the example of the establishment of the Hebrew monarchy in I Samuel 8 to show the Bible's disapproval of monarchy.[35] The second explanation for the prevalence of monarchy is more ominous. Here Paine draws on English history to demonstrate that another frequent cause of monarchy is conquest and force. He claims that of the current kings of Europe and their noble lineage, if "we take off the dark covering of antiquity, and trace them to their first rise, ... we should find the first of them nothing better than the principal ruffian of some restless gang."[36] With a further allusion to William I of England, the dubious implication for the British Constitution and its origins is obvious as Paine continues: "A French bastard landing with an armed banditti, and establishing himself King of England against the consent of the natives, is in plain terms a very paltry, rascally original."[37] Contrary to the moderate Whigs of the Glorious Revolution period such as Tyrrell, Burnet, and Atwood, who sought to deny or deflate the importance of the Norman Conquest, Paine is brutally candid

---

[34] Ibid., p. 8.
[35] Ibid., pp. 10–12.
[36] Ibid., p. 13.
[37] Ibid., p. 14.

about the origin of England's monarchy and hereditary nobility. In his view, there was no fundamental act of popular consent to the Norman establishment. That these "remains" of feudal tyranny are still venerated in the country and remain key parts of the Constitution says more to Paine about the human capacity for self-deception than it does about the possibility of consenting to such a "rascally original."

Paine's republicanism is born of his moral objections to the principle of monarchy. While criticizing England's mixed monarchy, Paine is not shy about praising Spinoza's Dutch Republic.[38] If Paine believes monarchy is unnatural and morally objectionable, then perhaps it would be fair to say that he found the idea of hereditary office absolutely mystifying. The problems he identifies with heredity are legion. To start with, even good rulers cannot guarantee worthy successors. Nature simply does not generate merit in this way.[39] Moreover, the only even mildly plausible argument for heredity – that it clearly delineates lines of succession and thus prevents disorder – has, according to Paine, proved to be a dangerous fallacy. The manifest problems of regency demonstrate that succession by a minor will always be problematic. Beyond this, however, Paine argues that "the whole of English history disowns the fact that hereditary succession preserves civil peace." Far from securing peace, the prize of hereditary monarchy dangling before the eyes of proud and ambitious nobles produced devastating periods in English history like the War of the Roses. Paine concludes: "In short, monarchy and [hereditary] succession have laid (not this or that kingdom only) but the world in ashes and blood."[40] For Paine, the British constitutional system of mixed monarchy, this "house divided against itself," is not the product of enlightened popular consent and the prudence of brilliant statesmen. It is rather a sad species of habitual and unthinking reverence for institutions rooted in conquest, ignorance, and tyranny.

Paine's reflections on monarchy and the British Constitution are a scathing criticism of this "much boasted" system. The principal goal of Paine's rhetorical strategy in this discussion is to uproot the British Constitution's privileged status in the intellectual purview of politically minded American Whigs by means of a passionate and logical assault in language accessible to the general public.[41] There is no elegizing of 1689 in Paine's treatment of British history. He claims that the core structures of the British Constitution predate the halting Glorious Revolution and originate in England's "dark and slavish" past. As such, the Glorious Revolution and the domestic and imperial

---

[38] Ibid., pp. 9, 29. Cf. *Cato's Letters*, #85, pp. 616–18 and Sidney D 2.11.143 and 3.10.371.

[39] Paine, CS, p. 12.

[40] Ibid., pp. 15–16.

[41] For a good discussion of Paine's seminal role as a founder of modern republican political rhetoric designed to enlighten and mobilize a mass audience, see Foner, *Tom Paine and Revolutionary America*, pp. 80–7.

order it settled have no normative status or binding character for Paine's Americans. By discrediting the underlying principles of the British Constitution with language and arguments hitherto unheard in the imperial debate, Paine seeks to buttress the case for independence with his claim for the theoretical and practical superiority of republicanism over mixed government. Notably, Paine has no ideological or temperamental animus to the House of Commons. Of course, he believes it has no right to govern the colonies – that is a given – but what little praise he offers the British system is reserved solely for the popular body. Unlike Jefferson, Paine does not draw from the imperial dispute a lesson in the dangers of legislative tyranny.[42] Actually, Paine argues that the only reason England has not slipped into despotism is the vigilance of the people and their representatives in Parliament. He claims: "It is wholly owing to the constitution of the people, and not to the constitution of the government that the crown is not as oppressive in England as in Turkey." It is not the restraint on popular power promoted by moderate Whig mixed regime theory that ensures free government; rather, it is the character of the English people and their flawed but still crucial representation in the Commons.

The Case for Independence

The conclusion the reader is meant to draw from Paine's account of the fundamental constitutional errors in the British system of government is unavoidable: the British government rules the empire, and the British government is bad both in theory and in practice. Therefore America must leave the empire and go it alone. Needless to say, for Paine, going it alone means that the American states must adopt the republican form of government. Paine's case for independence, then, rests in part on a stinging indictment of the British Constitution and the principle of monarchy. In the context of the imperial dispute, the malignancy of the British government takes on a particularly poignant form. Paine argues that all government should be directed toward securing individual rights through a robust institutional expression of popular sovereignty. The British government, according to Paine, has clearly ceased to be a government for the colonies. He adduces the example of Boston to demonstrate how far the British government has departed from fulfilling even a modicum of its proper role in the colonies. It not only fails to secure American rights, it actively injures them. In a stirring passage, Paine intones:

Let our imaginations transport us for a few moments to Boston, that seat of wretchedness will teach us wisdom, and instruct us forever to renounce a power in whom we can have no trust. The inhabitants of that unfortunate city, who but a few months ago

---

[42] Compare Paine, CS, pp. 4–5 and Jefferson, SV, p. 108.

were in ease and affluence, have now, no other alternative than to stay and starve, or turn "out to beg," endangered by the fire of their friends if they continue within the city, and plundered by the [British] soldiery if they leave it. In their present condition they are prisoners without the hope of redemption.[43]

The British government, Paine argues, is at war with America. This obvious rhetorical appeal to popular emotion does, however, resonate with Paine's natural rights teaching on the fundamental relation between the individual and government. To those in the colonies who still seek reconciliation with Britain, even at this late stage in the quarrel, Paine questions whether an individual ever can or should be reconciled with a government that attacks the people over whom it claims jurisdiction: "Bring the doctrine of reconciliation to the touchstone of nature, and then tell me, whether you can hereafter love, honour, and faithfully serve the power that hath carried fire and sword into your land?"[44] For Paine, the time for any reconciliation has long passed.

Common Sense is unique among the important colonial statements not only because Paine so explicitly and unambiguously calls for independence but also because of the reasoning behind his argument. As we have seen, even colonial moderates like Otis and Dickinson defended the colonists' right to dissolve the imperial connection. While legitimating the principle of dissolution as a theoretical possibility for the colonies, they also, however, genuinely recoiled from what they saw as the disastrous consequences of independence. In the words of John Dickinson: "If once we are separated from our mother country, what new form of government shall we adopt, or where shall we find another Britain to supply our loss?"[45] For Paine, both the justification for and the bright promise of American independence are understood in emphatically naturalistic terms. He views independence less in terms of formal dissolution theory – that is, as the severing of legal links with the empire – and more in terms of the natural structure of power relations. That the British government has broken its trust with the colonies is for Paine a point clearly proven, but a deeper reason he cites for independence is that "it is repugnant to reason, to the universal order of things to all examples from former ages, to suppose, that this continent can long remain subject to any external power."[46] This appeal extends beyond a dispute over the particular structure of government and imperial relations to which the Americans may or may not have consented at some point in the past. Rather, Paine bases his analysis of the imperial situation and the natural rights of the colonists on the Spinozist–Sidneyan conception of nature and power. Paine is

---

[43] Paine, CS, p. 23.

[44] Ibid.

[45] John Dickinson, "The Letters from a Farmer in Pennsylvania," in *Empire and Nation*, William Leuchtenberg and Bernard Wishy, eds. (Englewood Cliffs, NJ: Prentice-Hall, 1962): Letter 3, p. 18.

[46] Paine, CS, p. 24.

such an interesting example of radical Whig republicanism precisely because the philosophical principles of nature underlying this brand of Whiggism are brought so forcefully to the surface in his argument.

Quite simply, Paine argues that the British do not have the power – the natural right, in the Spinozist view – to govern the colonies, and thus they should not. That Paine draws this normative conclusion from a principle of power inhering in raw nature sets him clearly in the Spinozist republican camp. Paine tries to demonstrate that there is something deeply perverse and unnatural about British rule in America. He argues:

> Small islands not capable of protecting themselves; are the proper subject for kingdoms to take under their care; but there is something absurd, in supposing a continent to be perpetually governed by an island. In no instance hath nature made the satellite larger than its primary planet, and as England and America, with respect to each other, reverses the common order of nature, it is evident they belong to different systems.[47]

In sum, British rule in America is, according to Paine, qualitatively different from imperial sovereignty over St. Helena or the Falkland Islands. The Americans can govern themselves; they have the raw natural power of over a million individuals to animate and defend their own governments. Should the Americans harness this natural power in the cause of independence, the British government will be unable to coerce adherence to its laws and recognition of its sovereignty over the colonies. Notice Paine's language in the preceding passage. He makes the case for independence by drawing graphic allusions to raw natural characteristics of size, strength, and volume. He suggests a certain affinity between human political and moral affairs, on the one hand, and nonsentient nature such as the relation of planets and orbiting satellites, on the other.[48] In a fundamental sense, Paine is a disciple of Spinoza's project to articulate an understanding of human things that is in harmony with the operation of power in the nonhuman physical universe. Paine and Sidney's modern Anglo-American republicanism is rooted in this Spinozist insight. They claim that monarchy and aristocracy violate the natural order of power relations that underlies popular sovereignty. Paine takes Sidney a step further to argue that it is as natural for a people to govern themselves domestically in a republican form as it is for America to govern itself independently of the empire. It is not a huge theoretical leap to transpose radical Whig republican theory into foreign relations. For Paine, monarchical rule over a naturally free people is an illustrative analogue to

---

[47] Ibid., p. 25.

[48] While Kramnick is correct to point out the almost messianic promise Paine assigns to America, its "world-historical mission," this interpretation rests mainly on Paine's rhetorical aims – which are certainly important – but largely overlooks his core argument for independence, which is profoundly naturalistic and in keeping with a Spinozist perspective on the character of power and natural rights (Kramnick, *Bourgeois Radicalism*, pp. 149–50).

British rule over America; both situations are a product of custom, habit, and unthinking allegiance, and both situations reflect a serious distortion of natural right.

The case for independence in *Common Sense* also has a decidedly practical dimension. Paine argues that independence is both natural and beneficial for America. Far from losing the protection of Britain, the American states would not only be able to defend themselves, they would actually avoid entanglements in Britain's European wars.[49] To those who fear the economic consequences of independence and the loss of imperial trade protection, Paine rejoins: "America would have flourished as much, and probably much more, had no European power had anything to do with her. The commerce, by which she hath enriched herself are the necessaries of life, and will always have a market while eating is the custom of Europe."[50] Apart from the issue of America's economic and politico-military viability as an independent state, Paine also tries to address the perhaps even deeper concerns of those in America who feared loosening the intellectual and moral bands of consanguinity, sympathy, and affection that underlay the transatlantic community. Paine responds to these concerns in a number of ways.

First, as we have seen, he argues that any emotional tie with a power that attacks one's own people is simply illusory and self-destructive. Second, he denies that there is any genuine societal link between Britain and America. Nature has set the two peoples at such variance that it is inevitable that Americans would develop customs, habits, and ways of life distinct from those of Britain. Once again, raw physical nature – nature in the Spinozist sense – plays its part in Paine's analysis of human affairs: "Even the distance at which the Almighty hath placed England and America, is a strong and natural proof, that the authority of one, over the other, was never the design of heaven." For Paine, continentalism replaces imperialism as the primary societal link among Americans. He claims: "Now is the seedtime of continental union, faith and honour."[51] The basis of this new continental consciousness is admittedly, at least in part, simply a manifestation of anti-British animus.[52] Paine claims that Americans have a common interest in resisting Britain because all are in danger of similar oppression. He does, however, frame the promise of a common American identity drawn not only from crisis and

[49] Paine, CS, p. 21.
[50] Ibid., p. 19. Cf. A. Owen Aldridge, "The Collapse of the British Empire as Seen by Franklin, Paine, and Burke," in *Revisioning the British Empire in the Eighteenth Century*, William G. Shade, ed. (London: Associated University Press, 1998): pp. 88–9.
[51] Paine, CS, pp. 22, 18. Cf. Aldridge, "The Collapse of the British Empire," p. 91.
[52] See Lincoln's assessment of the crucial role the original anti-British animus produced in the revolutionary period played in at least temporarily cementing American unity in the founding era (Abraham Lincoln, "The Perpetuation of Our Political Institutions: Address Before the Young Men's Lyceum of Springfield, Illinois, January 27, 1838," in *Abraham Lincoln: His Speeches and Writings*, Roy Basler, ed. [New York: Da Capo, 1990]: pp. 83–4).

war, but also from shared interests, common democratic principles, and a love of liberty. Moreover, this new American identity derives not only from one ethnic root, an English original, but also from the rest of Europe and the world. Paine envisions a new form of continental citizenship in which "all Europeans meeting in America, or any other quarter of the globe, are countrymen."[53]

The promise of continental union and a rising new American identity in *Common Sense* is also the promise of republican government. The republican emphasis on political liberty, the public share in government, is the guiding principle of Paine's constitutionalism. In his proposal for the creation of a government of continental union, all the republican elements in radical Whig thought come to the fore. With regard to the assemblies of the various states, Paine offers the modern republican formula for radical legislative supremacy. Given the displacement of royal power in the colonies that independence would create, Paine sees the opportunity to make the assemblies more democratic: "Let the assemblies be annual, with a President only. The representation more equal."[54] In addition to reforming the colonial legislatures, Paine also boldly proposes the creation of a continental congress with much greater popular representation than the one created in defiance of Britain in the years immediately preceding the outbreak of hostilities. This new continental congress would have at least 390 members, with at least 30 sent from each colony, which would devise a convenient number of districts to elect members. As a replacement for the royal executive power, each congress would choose a president drawn from one state delegation selected by lot on a thirteen-year rotating system, so that a member of each state delegation would hold office in successive years. The measure of legitimacy for Paine, as for Sidney, is the extent to which government action reflects the popular will. Thus, to ensure that a law "is satisfactorily just," Paine proposes an unambiguous standard of popular assent by agreeing that "not less than three-fifths of the Congress . . . be called a majority."[55] With these measures, Paine incorporates the central tenets of radical Whig republicanism into his proposed continental union. The intention of his proposal with its call for annual elections, broad representation, supermajorities, and severely restricted executive power is to ensure popular sovereignty and to guarantee that the government reflects the interests of the people and their will.

Tom Paine's *Common Sense* not only proposed a federal republic, it also foreshadowed the process of constitution making in the United States. He called for a "Continental Conference" to act as an intermediate body between the governors and the governed. The numbers were to be drawn from the Congress, the various state assemblies, and the people at large, and it

[53] Paine, CS, p. 20.
[54] Ibid., p. 30.
[55] Ibid., pp. 30–1.

was to be elected by "as many qualified voters as shall think proper to attend from all parts of the province for that purpose."[56] Paine hoped that the radically democratic character of this conference would ensure its legitimacy and responsibility. This conference would be charged solely with the responsibility of devising a national "Charter." Paine suggests that the "Charter of the United Colonies" would establish the manner of elections, parliamentary rules, and federal–state relations and jurisdiction, and, most importantly, would secure the right of "freedom and property to all men."[57] With this proposal, Paine went beyond even Sidney's suggestion for a rationalized republican system of laws by firmly connecting the principle of popular government with the idea of a written constitution. According to Paine's version of modern republican regime analysis, the British Constitution was barely a rational or legitimate system of government at all precisely because British institutions were not anchored in a written charter signifying popular consent.[58] In Paine's new continental republic the rule of law, Sidney's "invisible king," would now be visible on parchment for all to see. He claims: "In America THE LAW IS KING." However, Paine reminds his readers that the crown of law may be broken "and scattered among the people whose right it is."[59] In Paine's America, the people would be king.

[56] Ibid., p. 30.
[57] Ibid., p. 31.
[58] Bonwick, *English Radicals*, p. 260 and Claeys, *Tom Paine: Social and Political Thought*, p. 50.
[59] Paine, CS, p. 32.

15

Revolutionary Constitutionalism

Laboratories of Radical Whiggism

Within six months after Americans first heard Paine's clarion call for separation from the British Empire, the entire political landscape of the colonies transformed dramatically. In the Declaration of Independence in July 1776, the representatives of the colonies assembled in the Continental Congress announced the formal severance of their connection with Britain. It was an event many American Whigs still considered unlikely when Jefferson made his appeal for radical imperial reform in 1774 and almost unthinkable when Otis and Dickinson protested parliamentary duties and taxes in the 1760s. However, the rhetoric and logic of the Declaration of Independence, saturated as it was with radical Whig principles of popular sovereignty, essentially represented an extension of arguments drawn from the radical Whig philosophy that had supplied the theoretical foundations of the American Whig position from the very beginning of the imperial crisis with Britain.

The Declaration of Independence was in many respects a classic expression of radical Whig philosophy.[1] In contrast to the conservative formulation

[1] For an interpretation of the intellectual influences in revolutionary America that is diametrically contrary to mine and rejects the significance of radical natural rights philosophy altogether, see John Philip Reid, *Constitutional History of the American Revolution: The Authority of Rights* (Madison: University of Wisconsin Press, 1986). Reid argues that the American use of the language and logic of natural jurisprudence was largely rhetorical and thus "irrelevant" compared to the substantive core of the American position, which he identifies with the idea of English constitutional rights (pp. 5, 18, 87–92; See also Reid, "The Irrelevance of the Declaration," in *Law in the American Revolution and the Revolution in Law: A Collection of Review Essays in American Legal History*, Hendrik Hartog, ed. [New York: New York University Press, 1981]: pp. 46–89). While Reid is correct to observe that rights understood in the English constitutional sense since the Glorious Revolution were not derived from radical Whig thought, I believe he fails to distinguish adequately between the moderate and radical Whig conceptions of rights, and thus tends to overread British moderate Whig reasoning into American radical Whig arguments. The passing resemblance between moderate and radical rights theories can, as I have shown, be traced back to their common source in the fight against divine right monarchy a century before. For a detailed response to Reid,

of the English Declaration of Rights of 1689, which accused James II of violating the "knowne lawes and statutes" and the "antient rights and liberties"
of the English nation, the American Declaration of 1776 reached conclusions and pronounced principles of rights and government that had proven
to be politically unpopular and theoretically unpersuasive to their English
Whig forbears. It clearly identified an unexhaustive list of "certain unalienable rights" and boldly asserted a universal right of popular revolution. For
American Whigs the philosophical justification for revolution and resistance
lay not in the Pufendorfian moderate Whig principle of original compact,
but in radical natural rights theory. American radical Whigs proclaimed that
"whenever any form of government becomes destructive" of the proper end
of securing rights, then "it is the right of the people to alter or abolish it,
and institute new government." The Americans utterly rejected the moderate Whig logic underlying the legal fiction of "abdication" employed in
England in 1689. Instead they clearly identified George III as a tyrant and
utilized the Lockean "long train of abuses" argument to establish the moral
and prudential criteria for legitimate popular resistance and the creation of
a new government.

In several crucial respects, the principles of the Declaration of Independence flowed from the natural continuum of radical Whig arguments employed by the colonists since the earliest phases of the imperial crisis. In keeping with the model of colonial opposition exemplified by Jefferson, Adams,
and Wilson in the years immediately preceding independence, the Declaration operated on the premise that the only historical legal link between Britain
and the colonies lay in the crown. Thus the Declaration of 1776 directed its
primary criticism toward the British monarch, as seen in its direction of twice
as many grievances against the king as against Parliament.[2] If the immediate thrust of the Declaration was clear, namely, American independence, the
political and constitutional implications of the principles justifying independence were comparatively inchoate. The overwhelming majority of American
Whigs agreed that the process of separation necessarily entailed a hectic process of constitution making in the newly sovereign states. However, the natural rights-based justification for independence in 1776 did not immediately
or unambiguously prescribe the proper design, composition, or form of government in the states. The principles of the Declaration of Independence are
in a pivotal sense nonpartisan, in theory at least legitimating a diversity of
pure and mixed regime types including monarchical as well as republican.[3]

see Michael P. Zuckert, *The Natural Rights Republic* (Notre Dame, IN: Notre Dame University
Press, 1996): pp. 108–17.
[2] However, both in the *Summary View* and in the Declaration of Independence, even the
grievances against Parliament were framed as complaints against the king for allowing
Parliament to interfere with the colonies.
[3] Martin Diamond, "The Revolution of Sober Expectations," *The American Revolution: Three
Views* (New York: American Brands, 1975): pp. 57–85, esp. pp. 67–8.

Moreover, even though the general sentiment among American Whigs in 1776 was profoundly antimonarchical, there was no universal agreement in American political culture about the meaning of republicanism. Indeed, to many American Whigs at the time, republicanism still carried pejorative connotations inherited from the British political tradition dating back over a century to the civil war era in England.[4] The task of replacing royal or parliamentary sovereignty with new regimes based on popular sovereignty made necessary by the palpable American desire for independence in fact left many new theoretical questions and practical issues unresolved for American Whigs.

On one ground at least there was practically universal agreement among American Whigs. The Congressional Resolution of May 1776 and Paine's call in *Common Sense* for the several colonies to draft written constitutions as part of the process leading to independence reflected a firm commitment and general presumption in America regarding the importance of written constitutions. On a practical level, this predisposition was reinforced by the usefulness of the colonial charters in the conflict with the crown during the imperial crisis of the 1760s and early 1770s. The colonists frequently pointed to the charters to illustrate British violations of prescribed American rights. However, as we have seen with Jefferson and Paine, the heart of the mature American case against the crown and Parliament was based on natural, as opposed to charter, rights. On a more philosophical level, the American commitment to the idea of written constitutions reflected a fundamental connection in the American Whig mind between the principles of radical contract theory and the imperatives of constitutional government.[5] Despite the universal recognition of the importance of written constitutions, the American Whig political spectrum in 1776 established no single, definitive constitutional design. A proposal for the Congress to draft a uniform constitution for the several states never gathered much support. However, with the disintegration of royal authority in the colonies in the months preceding formal independence, the political reality on the ground spurred the process of constitution making with great rapidity and urgency.[6] Even if American Whigs did not voice universal support for Patrick Henry's assertion that the colonial government was dissolved and the colonists had now reverted to a "state of nature," there was in the early summer of 1776 a

---

[4] For the ambiguity about the meaning of republicanism in revolutionary America, see Willi Paul Adams, *The First American Constitutions: Republican Ideology and the Making of the State Constitutions in the Revolutionary Era* (Chapel Hill: University of North Carolina Press, 1980): p. 100 and Donald S. Lutz, *Popular Control and Popular Consent: Whig Political Theory in the Early State Constitutions* (Baton Rouge: Louisiana Sate University Press, 1980): pp. 16–17.

[5] Fletcher M. Green, *Constitutional Development in the South Atlantic States, 1760–1860: A Study in the Evolution of Democracy* (Chapel Hill: University of North Carolina Press, 1930): pp. 51–2.

[6] For a good account of the reversion of royal power to provincial congresses in this period, see Adams, *First American Constitutions*, pp. 27–48.

pervasive recognition of the need for drafting fundamental legal instruments to reconstitute government in the former colonies. American Whigs soon came to the conclusion that the twin goals of achieving military victory and establishing new state constitutions were, as Gordon Wood argues "the very essence of the Revolution."[7]

The period of revolutionary constitutionalism was unique in Anglo–American history. It was a time, as John Adams celebrated, "when the greatest lawgivers of antiquity would have wished to live."[8] In contrast to the moderate Whig architects of the Glorious Revolution, American Whigs in 1776 were self-consciously aware that they had been given an unprecedented opportunity to devise new systems of government on a foundation of natural rights philosophy in relative freedom from the pressures and constraints of deeply rooted customs, habits, and conventions. However, the philosophical fabric of the period was inherently complex, combining elements of great novelty and experimentation, as well as witnessing some enduring continuity of colonial political forms.[9] This combination of novelty and continuity cohered to locate nascent American constitutionalism within the intellectual and ideological folds of the Anglo-American tradition understood in the broadest and most inclusive sense. Whig political philosophy in all its various strains and dimensions provided a rich source of theoretical materials for American constitutional development.

While the Pufendorfian moderate Whig idea of parliamentary sovereignty was badly discredited in America during the imperial crisis, the British model of balanced government and the principle of representation based on historical socioeconomic interests still retained considerable attraction among many American Whigs after 1776. In some respects, the conservative philosophy of British moderate Whigs, which appeared to have been superannuated by the radicalization of the colonial position in external relations during the imperial crisis, actually reemerged with renewed significance during the

---

[7] Gordon Wood, *The Creation of the American Republic, 1776–1787* (Chapel Hill: University of North Carolina Press, 1969): p. 128.

[8] John Adams, "Thoughts on Government," *The Political Writings of John Adams*, George Peek, ed. (New York: Liberal Arts Press, 1954: p. 92.

[9] For accounts of the period that stress its novelty, see Willi Paul Adams, "The State Constitutions as Analogy and Precedent," in *The United States Constitution: Roots, Rights, and Responsiblities* (Washington, DC: Smithsonian Institution Press, 1992): p. 8; Wood, *Creation*, p. 134 and Zuckert, *Natural Rights Republic*. For accounts that identify sources of underlying continuity with the Anglo-American tradition, see Colin Bonwick, "The United States Constitution and Its Roots in British Political Thought and Tradition," in *Foundations of Democracy in the European Union: From the Genesis of Parliamentary Democracy to the European Parliament*, John Pinder, ed. (New York: St. Martin's Press, 1999): p. 49; George Dargo, *Roots of the Republic: A New Perspective on Early American Constitutionalism* (New York: Praeger, 1974); Green, *Constitutional Development*, pp. 97–8; Lutz, *Popular Control*, pp. 44–5 as well as Donald Lutz, *The Origins of American Constitutionalism* (Baton Rouge: Louisiana State University Press, 1988): esp. ch. 8; and J. R. Pole, *Political Representation in England and the Origins of the American Republic* (New York: St. Martin's, 1966): p. 508.

debate about constitution making within the states during the revolutionary period. For their part, the liberal and republican elements in the Whig political tradition that had seemed so harmonious in the struggle against parliamentary sovereignty rapidly became more discrete in the context of revolutionary constitutionalism. In contrast to both the moderate Whig supporters of parliamentary sovereignty and the Whig republican champions of radical legislative supremacy, the Lockean liberal advocates registered a repugnance to any concentration of political power whatsoever. The Whig republican concern to ensure popular control of government and the deep distrust of the idea of the separation of powers did not typically evince the same degree of concern for the concentration of power. Whig republican philosophy stressed the dangers of tyranny from the executive and oligarchy from an upper chamber of the legislature, but maintained that a single representative assembly regulated by populist procedural controls such as annual elections, broad franchise, and regular rotation of delegates could responsibly and accountably express what Sidney identified as the primal constitutional truth: "The Legislative Power is always Arbitrary."[10] Armed with the philosophical premises of Spinozist sociological naturalism, Whig republicanism presented an argument for direct and egalitarian democracy that was in some respects as distinct from Lockean liberal principles as it was from the more conservative ideas of moderate Whiggism.

The revolution era state constitutions were in effect laboratories of radical Whig philosophy in which American Whigs set to the task of constitution making with divergent, overlapping, and often even conflicting philosophical commitments regarding sovereignty, rights, and the principle of representation. In their effort to convert the doctrine of popular sovereignty into the practical reality of effective limited government, American Whigs drew on the various liberal, republican, and even moderate Whig elements of their English philosophical inheritance. To some extent, all the distinct elements of the Whig politics of liberty played a part in revolutionary constitutionalism as American Whigs grappled with the political meaning of natural rights, the proper formulation of the separation of powers, and the legal or institutional significance of popular constituent power. The end product of this first independent experience of American constitution making was an important step toward the development of a uniquely American conception of constitutionalism and divided sovereignty.

The American Declaration of Rights

The idea of a bill or declaration of rights was firmly embedded in the Anglo-American political tradition long before the celebrated Declaration of Rights

---

[10] Algernon Sidney, *The Discourses Concerning Government*, Thomas West, ed. (Indianapolis: Liberty Fund Classics, 1996): ch. 3, sec. 45.

of 1689. From the time of Magna Carta, the 1628 Petition of Right, and the earliest colonial charters, written statements of fundamental rights and laws had acquired considerable normative and political value in the Anglo-American constitutional tradition. A declaration of rights was also a feature of many of the first state constitutions, whether these declarations stood as a discrete statement of rights typically preceding the main plan of government or were included in it. By the end of the period of revolutionary constitutionalism in 1780, nearly half of the states had included a formal declaration of rights in their constitution.

The 1776 Virginia Declaration of Rights, drafted by George Mason, set the pattern for states such as Pennsylvania, Massachusetts, Maryland, and North Carolina. The preamble to the Virginia declaration presents it as a statement of the rights that form "the basis and foundation of government." Most of the declarations included a statement of the radical Whig natural rights philosophy, typically at the very beginning in Article 1. The scope of these natural rights statements ranged from the comprehensive treatment in Virginia, "That all men are by nature equally free and independent, and have certain inherent rights, of which, when they enter into a state of society, they cannot by any compact, deprive or divest their posterity..." to the more pithy Maryland statement: "That all government of right originates from the people, is founded in compact only, and instituted solely for the good of the whole."[11] The universalistic thrust of the American declarations stands in stark contrast to the particularism of the English Declaration of 1689, which explicitly limited itself to vindicating and asserting "the antient rights and liberties" and "knowne lawes and statutes" of the historic British realm.[12] The confident radical Whiggism of the American declarations thus represented a clear departure from the British model that stressed the moral saliency of continuity, original compact, and fundamental laws. In this regard, the inspiration for the American state declarations was less the British legal inheritance than the radical Whig spirit of the Declaration of Independence. In language strikingly similar to that of the Declaration of Independence, practically all of the state declarations enshrined some version of the natural right to revolution. Ironically, relatively conservative Maryland went beyond any other state by not merely asserting the people's right to "reform, alter, or abolish" tyrannical government, but even explicitly

---

[11] Virginia Declaration of Rights, 1776, article 1 and Maryland Declaration of Rights, 1776, article 1 (hereafter in notes, all state constitutions and declarations will be cited by article and, if appropriate, by section number). For all the revolution era state constitutions, see *The Federal and State Constitutions, Colonial Charters and Other Organic Laws of the States and Territories Now or Heretofore Forming the United States of America*, Francis Newton Thorpe, ed. (Washington, DC: U.S. Government Printing Office, 1909) or online at http://www.yale.edu/lawweb/avalon/states.

[12] British Declaration of Rights, 1689, in Lois Schwoerer, *The Declaration of Rights, 1689* (Baltimore: Johns Hopkins University Press, p. 296.

denouncing the Tory "doctrine of non-resistance, against arbitrary power and oppression" as "absurd, [and] slavish."[13] Thus, even the more moderate statements of American revolutionary philosophy rejected the premises of the English Whigs of 1689 and Walpole at the Sacheverell trial by attempting to incorporate the natural right of revolution into the fundamental law of the state.

Although all the revolution era declarations share a radical Whig universalistic basis, the precise substance of these bills of particulars was typically diverse, often decidedly eclectic. The variety of rights identified in the state declarations generally fell into three categories. First, there were restatements and amplifications of the rights listed in the English Declaration of 1689. These were rights that Whigs of almost all philosophical varieties and ideological hues considered foundational for any proper understanding of limited government. For example, the American declarations typically included a prohibition on the suspension and dispensing of laws and amplified the English right to petition against grievances into a more general right of assembly. Americans often repeated the British prohibition on standing armies in peacetime and universalized the right to bear arms, extending this right from the preserve of "qualified" Protestants to "the people" generally.[14] As a general rule, the state declarations amplified the British Country party animus against standing armies to cover a wide range of civil–military relations including clear statements of civil supremacy and the need for regulated militias.[15] Also, many English rights of criminal procedure were restated in the state declarations and, given the American experience of martial law in several of the colonies, were fortified with clear and emphatic statements regarding the importance of reasonable bail, jury trials, and the prohibition on cruel and unusual punishments. With respect to the British Declaration's concern to ensure free elections and frequent Parliaments, the American states uniformly adapted this principle to their own legislatures, echoing Article 13 of the 1689 Declaration, which sought frequent Parliaments in order to ensure "the amending, strengthening, and preserving of laws."[16] The American Whig concern for the rights of the accused, legal control of the military, and regular legislative assemblies reflected general continuity with the important underlying areas of broad consensus in Whig thought that more or less spanned the radical and moderate philosophical divide.

---

[13] Maryland Declaration, 1776, art. 4. In other respects, relatively conservative Maryland, with its statement that its inhabitants "are entitled to the common law of England," was singular among the states in its emphasis on custom and British legal convention (1776: art. 3).

[14] See, for example, the Pennsylvania Declaration, 1776, art. 13.

[15] See, for example, Maryland 1776 arts. 25–9, North Carolina 1776 arts. 17–18, and Pennsylvania art. 13.

[16] Compare the English Declaration of 1689, art. 13, with Massachusetts 1780, art. 22 and Maryland 1776, art. 10.

In other respects, however, the state declarations established a unique American contribution to the tenets of Whig constitutionalism. One element of this specifically American brand of constitutionalism related to the much deeper populist commitments in America than in Britain. For example, the state declarations uniformly asserted the principle of a broad franchise typically extending the right of suffrage to any free adult male possessing some measure of "property in and attachment to" the community.[17] The crucial issue of the suffrage that was neglected or avoided in the Declaration of 1689, and would prove to be a source of great frustration for English radicals in the second half of the eighteenth century, was settled in a decidedly egalitarian direction in the American states. The state declarations established broad suffrage rights as a veritable precondition of representative government and thus, not surprisingly, reaffirmed the American practice stretching back to the colonial period of a much broader franchise than in eighteenth-century Britain.[18] Other distinctly American contributions to the Whig idea of rights were clearly drawn from the painful lessons of British policy toward the colonies during the imperial crisis. For example, many state declarations asserted a Jeffersonian right of emigration, formally confirmed the Lockean principle of no taxation without representation, prohibited the establishment of monopolies, and guaranteed freedom of the press. They even frequently asserted a right of sole control over "internal police," in effect pointedly cautioning Congress against attempting any repeat of Parliament's Coercive Acts.[19] Thus, on matters of suffrage and crucial elements of public policy, the drafters of the state declarations radically transformed the more traditional British understanding of rights and in many cases even established new, uniquely American varieties of rights.

The third category of rights often seen in the state declarations were not so much rights in the conventional sense as general exhortations about right principles of government. These statements typically included general pronouncements that government exists for the "common benefit" and for the administration of "impartial justice." Many statements referred to the importance of the principle of separation of powers: "That the legislative and executive powers of the State should be separate and distinct from the judiciary."[20] Another striking feature of many state declarations is the almost ubiquitous exhortation regarding the importance of "frequent recurrence to fundamental principles."[21] The explanatory clauses following this statement in most declarations indicate the American intention to replicate the

---

[17] See, for example, Pennsylvania 1776, art. 7 and Maryland 1776, art. 5.

[18] Pole, *Representation*, p. 272.

[19] See, for example, Massachusetts 1780, art. 4 and Maryland 1776, art. 2.

[20] See Virginia 1776, arts. 3 and 5; Massachusetts, 1780 art 30; and Maryland art. 6.

[21] See, for example, Massachusetts 1780, art. 18; Pennsylvania 1776, art. 14; North Carolina 1777, art. 21; Virginia 1776, art. 15; and Vermont 1777, art 16.

Sidneyan modification of Machiavelli's teaching on first principles. This effort reflected both the republican emphasis on equality in America and the pairing of the idea of frequent renewal of consent with a concern for ensuring the justice, honesty, and virtue of the electors. In keeping with the Sidneyan–Spinozist modern republican tradition, the logical thrust of the state constitutions' affirmation of the importance of frequently recurring to "fundamental principles" was to establish consent as the essential condition of free government and civic virtue as a kind of vital corollary.[22] In contrast to the Lockean idea of revolutionary (and presumably infrequent) dissolution of government, the state declarations in the revolutionary period favored the Sidneyan model of "frequent recurrence" to the popular base of the regime.[23] Rather than the Lockean "long train of abuses" argument in the Declaration of Independence, the first state declarations generally affirmed the more direct and continuous notion of consent substantiated by frequent and regular elections.

The question remains, however, how precisely did the drafters of the state declarations envision the legal or practical constitutional effects of their statements of rights? Did they intend these declarations of rights to be understood as part of the constitution, with specific legal content, or were they meant primarily to be normative statements of sociocultural values? Donald Lutz points to the preponderant use of the aspirational "ought" rather than the imperative "shall" in the state declarations to demonstrate their largely symbolic or normative character.[24] Further proof that the declarations were not generally meant to be incorporated into the fundamental law is suggested by the explicit inclusion of the declarations into the plan of government in a few states such as North Carolina and Delaware. While the evidence clearly suggests that the declarations were in large measure intended to be normative rather than strictly legal statements of rights, there is sufficient indication that they were not intended to be merely symbolic or elaborate pronouncements of sociocultural values. For example, some states, such as Maryland and Pennsylvania, deliberately identified the legal, or even supralegal, character of the rights expressed in their declarations either by stating that their rights statements were amendable only in the same manner as the rest of the constitution or by explicitly placing these statements beyond the normal amendment process.[25] It is perhaps best to understand the declarations as being meant to illuminate the natural rights principles at the core of the

[22] For a contrary view that identifies the early American idea of virtue with Calvinist theology, compare Lutz, *Popular Control*, p. 57 and Lutz, *American Constitutionalism*, pp. 24–7 with Chapter 2.

[23] Thus, I believe Locke and Sidney are considerably more different on the idea of consent than Pole (*Representation*, pp. 13–27) suggests.

[24] Lutz (*Popular Control*, pp. 61–70), see especially the informative table on p. 67.

[25] See Maryland 1776, art. 42 and section 46 in the main body of the Pennsylvania Constitution of 1776.

early American idea of limited government. This process of illumination was meant both to limn the parameters of legitimate state action and to manifest the principles of right in which legal enforcement would be supplied through variable constitutional structures.

Reflection on the character of the stipulated rights in many state declarations reveals the underlying complexity of the revolution era American understanding of rights. Clearly, many of the rights were understood to be alienable. For example, the right to property was consistently qualified by the principle of taxation by consent and by the notion of just compensation. Even the "sacred" right of individual conscience was qualified in some states, such as Massachusetts and Maryland, by affirmations of the legitimacy of public support for religion.[26] Thus, to a considerable extent and in some major areas of legal and moral concern, the American declarations presented a seriously qualified notion of individual rights, in effect asserting the moral primacy of the community over and against individual rights claims.[27] However, it is important to recall that the state declarations frequently asserted a complex combination of various kinds of rights. The rights relating to broad suffrage and frequent elections, for example, tend to be expressed as absolute preconditions for representative government. Likewise, the rights relating to criminal procedure, while perhaps not absolute, certainly contain an emphatically individualist tendency. A prime example of this individualist rights reasoning is the clause in the Pennsylvania Declaration that identified a natural right of emigration: "That all men have a natural inherent right to emigrate from one state to another... that thereby they may promote their own happiness."[28] This statement, bearing clear echoes of Jefferson's argument in the *Summary View*, posits "vacant countries" as a proxy for the Lockean state of nature to which any individual may go and help establish new governments. This individual natural right to dissolve personal and political bonds with a given community, while not stated explicitly in all the state declarations, could not logically have been rejected except by refuting practically the same reasoning that justified American separation from the British Empire in the Declaration of Independence.

How, then, should we interpret the composite rights teaching in the first state constitutions? The distinct kinds of rights in the state declarations, resting as they did in delicate, sometimes uneasy, balance, were the complex philosophical inheritance of the Whig politics of liberty in America. One aspect of the American rights philosophy at the time paralleled the moderate Whig tradition in Britain. The repetition of rights pronounced by English

---

[26] Massachusetts 1780, arts. 2 and 3, and Maryland 1776, art. 33.

[27] Lutz, *Popular Control*, pp. 50–2 and Ronald M. Peters, *The Massachusetts Constitution of 1780: A Social Compact* (Amherst: University of Massachusetts Press, 1978): pp. 76–87, 137.

[28] Pennsylvania 1776, art. 15.

Whigs in 1689 and the attempt by some states to link these rights with a notion of fundamental law illustrate clear echoes of British constitutionalism. However, the preponderant thrust of the rights philosophy in the state declarations was much more radical than traditional moderate Whiggism. For example, practically all the states asserted the Lockean liberal principle of delegated powers and typically placed greater emphasis on civil liberties relating to property, the press, and the right to bear arms than did the English Declaration. The first state declarations also contained important modern republican elements. The formal statement of rights relating to broad suffrage and frequent elections was meant to assert the principle of popular control over government. However, the primary thrust of the declarations from the republican perspective was to play an educative function and provide an informed citizenry with an accessible measure for legitimate government action. As we have seen, in Whig republican thought, the concentration of power is acceptable, even desirable, as long as this power is popular. Thus written statements of rights are fully compatible with the republican distrust of the separation of powers insofar as modern republicans in the Sidneyan–Spinozist tradition saw popular vigilance as a better security of rights than institutional complexity.

The liberal and republican elements of American Whig thought in the period of revolutionary constitutionalism were in essence groping to establish the same thing: a way to limit government by basing it on a written constitution derived from the consent of the people and directed to securing natural rights. The question of how well the first state constitutions succeeded in achieving this goal and how successfully American constitutionalists blended their complex Whig inheritance would prove to be inextricably linked to the gradual development of a uniquely American idea of the separation of powers.

The Separation of Powers

The formal commitment to the principle of the separation of powers was, as we have seen, a prominent feature of most of the state constitutions and declarations of rights. But what did this mean? There was no universal agreement on the political or legal implications of this general constitutional principle. The diversity of opinion regarding the meaning of the separation of powers reflects the complexity and underlying ambiguity in the American understanding of representative government in the revolutionary era. On the one hand, many of the drafters of the state constitutions intended the separation of powers to mean no more than a prohibition on multiple office-holding.[29] This limited conception of the "separation of persons" was fully consistent with the moderate Whig view of parliamentary sovereignty, more

---

[29] Lutz, *Popular Control*, pp. 96–7 and Peters, *Massachusetts Constitution*, pp. 63–4.

a reflection of the legacy of the British Country Whig opposition to political corruption than a statement of principle regarding fundamental constitutional design.

The more expansive understanding of the separation of powers in America circa 1776 related to the idea of the due process of law. Many American Whigs believed that in order to secure what John Adams called "an empire of laws, not of men," constitutions had to carefully structure the interaction of a variety of institutions involved in the creation of laws. Drawing from the classic Whig anti-absolutist doctrine of the seventeenth century, most American Whigs supported the idea of institutional checks and balances designed to ensure the responsible formulation and impartial application of laws. Of course, this traditional Whig principle of due process took several different forms. Moderate Whigs in Britain envisioned the separation of powers in terms of historic institutions representing socioeconomic interests and classes in a balanced compound legislature. The Lockean liberal idea of the separation of powers emphasized the functional as opposed to the interest-based principle of separation and representation. Only radical republicans in America shared Sidney's modern republican distrust of the very notion of a meaningful separation of powers.

The development of the American idea of the separation of powers was inextricably linked to the larger debate over the proper structure of government in the revolutionary period. In its most general form, this debate was a dispute between the partisans of simple and complex structures. At one extreme in this debate were the radical republicans, most notably those in Pennsylvania. It was in Pennsylvania that the most radical and democratic ideas came to light in the revolutionary period.[30] Not surprisingly, it was here also that Paine's influence, both philosophically and even directly in the drafting process, was most palpable. The constitution adopted in Pennsylvania and imitated in Georgia and Vermont was the epitome of simplicity, with a unicameral legislature and very weak executive and judiciary. The debate over the structure of government in Pennsylvania, which had a tradition of unicameralism dating back to the colonial period, was more skewed in the radical republican direction than in any other state in America.

However, the republican argument in Pennsylvania was far from simply an imitation of Paine's philosophy or merely an endorsement of colonial history. In contrast to the ahistorical republicanism of Paine and Sidney, Pennsylvania radical leader George Bryan, writing under the pseudonym Demophilus, unapologetically appealed to the ancient Saxon constitution. Demophilus drew heavily from English radical sources such as Obadiah Hulme to support the case that the model for simple, democratic government was Saxon England

---

[30] Wood, *Creation*, p. 226. In revolutionary Pennsylvania at least, if scarcely anywhere else in America, *Common Sense* thoroughly discredited the British model of mixed government.

prior to the Norman Conquest.[31] In Saxon England, Demophilus discovered the historical evidence that supported Sidney and Spinoza's case for the naturalness of democracy. Demophilus argued that the model for Pennsylvania should be the democratic Saxons with their tradition of unicameralism, direct and broad representation, weak executive power, and emphatic localism. In the unicameral legislature proposed by Demophilus, with its annual elections and broad representation, the concentration of political power would be a reflection of the natural truth that "the elective power of the people is the first principle of the constitution."[32] For Demophilus, in keeping with the Whig republican tradition stretching back to Sidney, popular control over a simple governmental structure was a surer guarantee of liberty than a substantive separation of powers and institutional complexity.

At the opposite end of the spectrum in colonial thought in the revolutionary era was the Virginian Carter Braxton. This spokesman for the Tidewater faction in the state hoped to steer the constitution-making process in Virginia in a decidedly conservative direction with the publication of his *Address to the Convention*. In contrast to the simple form of popular government advocated by Demophilus and Paine, Braxton's address was a paean to the glories of the British model of mixed and balanced constitutionalism. He hoped to replicate as much as possible the "happy edifice" of the British Constitution on Virginia soil.[33] While criticizing the corruption of the present British system in fine Country opposition fashion, Braxton nonetheless extolled the purity of the 1689 settlement, from which more recent times should be viewed as degenerate. Rather than Demophilus' simple, freedom-loving pre-Conquest Saxons, it is the sober Whig and Tory gentry of 1689 who occupy the place of honor in Braxton's historical account of Anglo-American constitutionalism. For Braxton, the demonstrated utility and organic character of the British Constitution, with its unparalleled capacity to represent the divergent interests of society, was the touchstone of moderate government.

In order to best adapt the British constitutional model to the American context, Braxton advocated life tenure for the governor and the two dozen members of an upper-chamber Council of State. These institutions of order and stability were balanced in Braxton's plan by a regularly elected representative assembly modeled on the House of Commons. While admitting that a de jure policy of hereditary right would not suit the temper of revolutionary Virginia, Braxton believed that life tenure was necessary, especially for

---

[31] For the importance of the ancient constitution idea for British radicals of the period, see Colin Bonwick, *English Radicals and the American Revolution* (Chapel Hill: University of North Carolina Press, 1977): pp. 256–7.

[32] Demophilus (George Bryan), "The Genuine Principles of the Ancient Saxon, or English Constitution "(1776), in *American Political Writings During the Founding Era, 1760–1805*, Charles S. Hyneman and Donald S. Lutz, eds. (Indianapolis: Liberty Fund, 1983): pp. 342–3.

[33] Carter Braxton, "An Address to the Convention of the Colony and Ancient Dominion of Virginia" (1776), in Hyneman and Lutz, eds., *American Political Writings*, pp. 331–2.

the governor, to secure the "dignity to command necessary respect and authority."[34] By institutionalizing the kinds of reforms long advocated by the British Country opposition, Braxton hoped that Virginia could "adapt and perfect the British system" through the establishment of a government with carefully distributed powers that would still retain a connection with each other in the legislative process. In language strikingly reminiscent of that of the moderate Whig doyen James Tyrrell nearly a century earlier, Braxton suggested that the virtues of his plan would be as much of a counterbalance to the dangers of executive tyranny as to the leveling horrors of unqualified democracy.[35] Whereas Demophilus and Paine did seriously affect the process of constitution making, at least in Pennsylvania, Braxton's overt advocacy of an American quasi-monarchy and aristocracy was met by almost universal hostility in his home state.[36] In the broad range of ideas in revolutionary constitutionalism, most American Whigs saw Demophilus' unicameral popular assembly as too democratic and Braxton's surrogate British Constitution as practically reactionary. The voice of mainstream American Whig constitutional thought would come from elsewhere.

John Adams' *Thoughts on Government*, published in 1776, provided an articulate middle ground between the radical republicans and the conservatives in the states that was much closer to the natural predisposition of the American Whig mind than Demophilus or Braxton. Although it was written ostensibly as a critical response to the French champion of simple government, Turgot, Adams' primary target was actually the Pennsylvania constitutional model then in vogue in radical circles in America. Adams feared that the simple populist plan in Pennsylvania would establish itself as the authoritative expression of constitutional government.[37] Adams' plan called for a bicameral legislature, with both the executive and the upper chamber possessing a veto on the popular assembly. He argued that only a complex constitutional structure with interdependent parts could provide the institutional mechanisms needed to delegate power from the popular many to the representative "few most wise and good."[38] Adams excoriated the Pennsylvania idea of unicameralism, listing its many defects, including the inadequacy and imprudence of a single deliberative body, the inability

[34] Ibid., p. 333.

[35] Ibid., pp. 334–5.

[36] For the hostility to Braxton's constitutional proposal, including Richard Henry Lee's shot that it was "a contemptible little tract," see Green, *Constitutional Development*, pp. 64–5 and Wood, *Creation*, p. 204.

[37] Adams, *First American Constitutions*, pp. 121–4; Bonwick, *English Radicals*, pp. 176–7; Gregory Claeys, *Thomas Paine: Social and Political Thought* (Boston: Unwin & Hyman, 1989): pp. 51–3; and Edward S. Corwin, "The Progress of Constitutional Theory between the Declaration of Independence and the Meeting of the Philadelphia Convention," *The American Historical Review*, vol. 30, no. 3 (April 1925): p. 520.

[38] Adams, "Thoughts on Government," p. 86.

of a representative assembly to assume the executive and judicial functions, and, perhaps most importantly, the tendency of a single-chamber legislature to place itself above the constitution by exempting itself from the law and even enacting its own perpetuity.

The significance of Adams' *Thoughts* was manifold. He was one of the first voices to awaken Americans to the unexpected danger that the specter of parliamentary sovereignty was more likely to return to the states through the radical republicanism of Paine or Demophilus rather than the nostalgic conservatism of Braxton. Adams' argument for complex government reflected the mixture of diverse elements embedded in the Anglo-American constitutional tradition. On the one hand, he asserted the republican principle of popular control through annual elections, repeating the populist maxim "where annual elections end, there slavery begins."[39] On the other hand, he endorsed the Braxtonian conservative principle of carefully distributed and balanced powers in order to represent the various interests in society. But the most striking and innovative feature of Adams' argument was his effort to blend the traditional British idea of institutional complexity with the goal of mirror representation advocated by radical republicans. He advised that the representative assembly "should be in miniature an exact portrait of the people at large. It should think, feel, reason, and act like them."[40] In Adams' contribution to the evolving American idea of representation, the institutional mirroring of society meant reflecting not only the popular will, but also the variety of regional and socioeconomic interests in the land. He implicitly endorsed the British ideal of compound government and sought to incorporate into it republican elements such as a broad franchise and annual elections. In certain crucial respects, the English balanced constitution was still the model for Adams and for most American Whigs in 1776, although it was a distinctly Americanized version of balanced government including important popular elements adapted from radical Whig political philosophy.[41] This blending of the principles of constitutional balance and popular will would become the central feature of the American conception of the separation of powers as it developed in the hard political reality of constitution making in the revolutionary era.

The first wave of revolutionary constitutionalism occurred in the period immediately preceding and following the publication of the Declaration of Independence in July 1776. In that year New Hampshire, South Carolina, Virginia, Maryland, Delaware, Pennsylvania, and North Carolina drafted and ratified new constitutions. Rhode Island and Connecticut preferred to retain slightly revised versions of their old colonial charters, and New York, Georgia, Massachusetts, and the territory of Vermont, for a variety of

---

[39] Ibid., p. 89.
[40] Ibid., p. 86.
[41] Wood, *Creation*, p. 200.

war-related reasons, would not produce new constitutions until the following years. The immediate result of the spirited and highly publicized theoretical debate over the virtues of simple and complex government was that few states followed the Pennsylvania unicameral model propounded by Paine and Demophilus. The large majority of states in the first wave adopted bicameral legislatures, but this was far from indicating the formulation of a clearly developed separation of powers theory. The centerpiece of the first-wave constitutions was invariably the representative assembly, the same body that John Adams identified as the crucial component for securing mirror representation of society at large. First-wave assemblies were characterized by frequent elections, with annual elections being the norm and only South Carolina adopting biennial elections. Predictably given the emphasis on suffrage rights in all of the state declarations of rights, the franchise for elections to the representative assembly was typically very broad.[42] Property or other requirements for members of the assembly were generally minimal, and several state constitutions included provisions securing the right of petition and instructing delegates. The central premise of the first-wave constitutions was ensuring popular control over the central lawmaking body in an effort to make the engine of government reflect the thoughts, opinions, and feelings of the public as closely as possible.

The inevitable consequence of producing such strong popular assemblies was to diminish the other branches of government. In particular, the executive power in the first-wave constitutions was typically very weak. As Gordon Wood describes it, "the Americans' emasculation of their governors lay at the heart of their constitutional reforms of 1776."[43] Seven of the eight first-wave constitutions stated that the governor would be appointed by the assembly or by a combination of both legislative houses. The effect of depriving the executive of an independent source of authority was to make him a veritable creature of the legislature. The entire thrust of first-wave thinking about executive power was to control and minimize it by denying it an effective veto and establishing very short terms of office often with a strict system of rotations and exclusions. First-wave governors were also given little or no direct control over appointments and were typically saddled with some form of executive council, again generally appointed by the legislature.[44]

[42] Pole, *Representation*, pp. 515–16.

[43] Wood, *Creation*, p. 149; cf. Lutz, *Popular Control*, pp. 60–1, 92–3. For the contrary view, which maintains that Americans were remarkably attached to the idea of strong executive power even in the earliest phases of revolutionary constitutionalism, see Adams, "State Constitutions," p. 8.

[44] The only first-wave executives to enjoy more than one-year terms were those in Delaware (three years) and South Carolina (two years). Cf. Lutz, *Popular Control*, pp. 92–3 and Wood, *Creation*, p. 148.

The source of the real animus against the idea of an independent executive in the firstwave constitutions is twofold. First, in the turbulent opening year of the war, many constitutional framers in the states felt a palpable, almost reflexive, hostility to executive power given the colonial experience of mistrust and accusation toward crown officials in the years of the imperial crisis. In addition to this anti-British feeling, another source of American distrust of independent executive power was deeply rooted in the tradition of Whig political thought on both sides of the Atlantic. Both the more conservative elements of American Whiggism and the most radical republicans traced the intellectual lineage of their suspicion of executive power to elements in their English philosophical inheritance. Whether American Whigs in 1776 drew their distrust of executive power from the example of the Glorious Revolution and the Country party opposition to executive "influence" or from the robust republicanism of Sidney, the result, constitutionally speaking, was the same. As such, there was no coherent philosophical or political consensus in America in 1776 supporting the idea of a vigorous and independent executive power.

The status of the judiciary and the upper chamber or senate in the first-wave constitutions was little better than that of the executive. The judiciary was typically the creature of the legislature, which often had, as in Virginia, sole control over the appointment of the judges. The states generally adopted the British practice of life tenure for good behavior, a tradition also deeply rooted in colonial legal history, although radical Pennsylvania set a seven-year term for judges with a possibility of reappointment.[45] The senate in first-wave constitutions was intended to be distinct from the popular assembly. There were generally higher property qualifications for electors and members of the senate than for the assembly. Moreover, while practically all of the first-wave constitutions established annual elections for the general assembly, more than half of them preferred multiple-year terms and some form of staggered elections for the senate.[46] The drafters of the first-wave constitutions generally intended to design the senate to perform the primary role of protecting property interests. The early American idea of property representation was perhaps most clearly articulated by the Massachusetts political commentator Theophilus Parsons in the *Essex Result*. Parsons determined that on matters concerning the general welfare, the representative assembly was adequate, but on matters pertaining more specifically to property, large holders should have a distinct institutional voice directed

[45] Judges in Virginia were appointed by both houses of the legislature, and in Pennsylvania either by the president and the executive council or by the general assembly alone (see Virginia 1776, sec. 20 and Pennsylvania 1776, sec. 23).

[46] The terms for senators ranged across the first-wave states: New Hampshire, New Jersey, North Carolina (one year), South Carolina (two years), Delaware (three years), Virginia (four years), and Maryland (five years). Maryland and Delaware also had staggered elections. Cf. Lutz, *Popular Control*, pp. 87–91 and Wood, *Creation*, pp. 209–15.

exclusively to representing property interests.[47] Parsons' distinction between the proper modality for representing "persons" and "property" reflected the intellectual basis for the first-wave theory of representation in the Senate. By replacing the traditional British idea of estates and classes with the more fluid conception of property, first-wave constitutionalists established an important American modification of the British principle of representing the diverse socioeconomic interests in society.

In addition to the countermajoritarian role of the senate as protector of property interests, some states explicitly associated the more exclusive membership of the senate with an effort to introduce an aristocratic element into American constitutionalism. In conservative Maryland, for example, the senate was elected by its own select electoral college, which was designed with the aim of electing men the caliber of Adams' "wise and good," men of "the most wisdom, experience and virtue."[48] Most of the first-wave senates embodied this aristocratic principle to an extent, with longer terms and higher property qualifications intended to insulate the institution somewhat from popular pressures. Predictably, the twin justifications of senatorial institutional exclusivity – aristocratic virtue and property protection – were deeply connected in the minds of both the supporters of senatorial prestige and its opponents. However, regardless of how the drafters of the constitutions envisaged the precise qualities of the senate, it was almost universally expected to provide some kind of institutional check on the popular representative assembly.

One of the fundamental problems in first-wave revolutionary constitutionalism was that the outline of a formal separation of powers in the states bore little resemblance to the emerging political reality. The Whig principle of legislative supremacy in the state constitutions rapidly devolved to the practice of the popular assembly assuming and absorbing all the other functions of government. The dangers of concentrated power so dramatically exposed by Locke and Montesquieu were in clear evidence, as the state legislatures frequently assumed executive and judicial functions.[49] The weak first-wave executives possessing no veto or independent source of authority offered no real check on the legislature. Looking back on the track record of the Virginia Constitution of 1776 with a few years of hindsight, Jefferson described it as an "elective despotism" wherein "173 despots would surely be as oppressive as one." While in the bicameral first-wave constitutions the concentration of power in the representative assembly was a perpetual danger, in unicameral Pennsylvania and Georgia the supremacy of the popular

---

[47] Theophilus Parsons, "The Essex Result" (1778), in Hyneman and Lutz, eds., *American Political Writings*, pp. 481–2, 491–2. Cf. Pole, *Representation*, pp. 182–9.

[48] For the unique design of the Maryland senate, see Green, *Constitutional Development*, p. 88; Lutz, *Popular Control*, p. 113; and Wood, *Creation*, pp. 251–4.

[49] Wood, *Creation*, pp. 162–3.

assembly was virtually guaranteed. The main obstacle to an effective senatorial check to the assembly was, as Jefferson again perceptively observed,
that the upper and lower houses were typically "too homogeneous."[50] The
property qualification for the election of senators was too low to represent effectively a distinct propertied interest separate from the general public
will. In the relatively egalitarian socioeconomic conditions of revolutionary
America, the senate and the assembly were invariably elected by practically
the same people. The conundrum facing the first-wave framers was that in
setting sufficiently high property qualifications, the new constitutional order would face serious resentment from the public and run contrary to the
egalitarian spirit of the suffrage clauses in the state declarations of rights.
However, by settling for minimal requirements, the senate was unable to
fulfill its role as the representative guardian of the propertied interests.

The extent of legislative supremacy in the first-wave constitutions typically
extended beyond even the assumption of other strictly political functions.
The several efforts to preserve constitutional limits on legislative action such
as the explicit provisions in New Jersey and Pennsylvania proved to be inadequate. First-wave legislatures altered and amended their constitutions with
abandon in the revolutionary period. The variety of amendment procedures
in the first-wave states, such as the Pennsylvania Council of Censors that
was to convene every seven years, or the Georgia model of petitions from
the counties, or the Maryland idea of a delayed amendment process ratified
by two-thirds of a newly elected legislature, were all intended to preserve
the fundamental distinction between constitutional law and normal statute
law.[51] The desire of first-wave constitutionalists to check ephemeral legislative will by more fundamental popular consent embodied in the written constitution was practically universal. Even the radical republican Demophilus
confided that his greatest fear was that legislatures would alter the constitution illegitimately, thus distorting the popular foundation of government.[52]
However, the inability of first-wave constitutions to preserve constitutional
authority against the claims of legislative supremacy was rooted in philosophical principles not merely adventitious.

For many American Whigs in 1776, the legacy of inherited assumptions
about parliamentary sovereignty proved much harder to dislodge than the
fears of any vestigial attachment to monarchy. Overcoming the residual connection to the moderate Whig idea of parliamentary sovereignty, with its organizing principle of balancing interdependent, rather than clearly separated,

---

[50] Thomas Jefferson, "Notes on the States of Virginia," in *Thomas Jefferson Writings*, Merrill
Peterson, ed. (New York: Northan, 1984): pp. 125–6. Cf. Lutz, *Popular Control*, p. 292.
[51] Adams, "State Constitutions," pp. 15–16 and Green, *Constitutional Development*, pp. 96–
7. Cf. Jefferson's consternation about omnipotent state legislatures in the period operating
without regard for constitutional limits ("Notes on the State of Virginia," pp. 127–31).
[52] Demophilus, "Genuine Principles," pp. 360–1.

parts would prove to be a vital precondition for the development of a uniquely American theory of separation of powers. In many respects, the first-wave American legislatures exceeded even the Blackstonian idea of parliamentary sovereignty insofar as many first-wave constitutions gave the legislature power even over proroguing, assembling, and matters of war and peace.[53] Radical republicans proved no less susceptible to a version of the parliamentary sovereignty doctrine than the more conservative elements among American Whigs. The democratized legislature envisioned by republicans such as Demophilus and Paine could claim nearly absolute sovereignty as the only truly representative body in the new constitutional order. As such, first-wave constitutions were typically more concerned to ensure that the popular assembly was made accountable and responsible through annual elections and broad franchise than they were to limit the legislature's power.

The second wave of revolutionary constitutionalism began in New York in 1777 and concluded with the ratification of the Massachusetts Constitution of 1780. The framers in the second wave in large measure reacted to the problems and criticisms of their first-wave predecessors. A general loss of confidence in the legislature set in quickly in many of the first-wave states. The multiplicity of laws, the usurpation of executive and judicial power, and the frequent alterations of the constitution produced a curious phenomenon as the old popular suspicion of the crown often gave way to a new ambivalence and even hostility to the state legislatures.[54] The central thrust of the second wave was to rehabilitate the idea of executive power in America. New York, for example, established an executive with direct popular elections for three-year terms and a qualified legislative veto shared with the majority of a Council of Revision. Massachusetts also established direct popular election (but only one-year terms) and a veto with a two-thirds override clause. The main theoretical innovation in second-wave thinking about executive power was to provide a source of constitutional and popular authority independent of the legislature. While in principle the enhanced executive veto may be defended or criticized on the basis of a separation of powers argument, the clear intention of the second-wave framers was to establish a formidable and ultimately accountable check on legislative power. The flaws revealed in first-wave thinking had in fact confirmed the fears of the more conservative American Whigs such as Carter Braxton and John Dickinson, who worried

---

[53] Colin Bonwick, "The United States Constitution, and Its Roots in British Political Thought and Tradition," in *Foundations of Democracy in the European Union: From the Genesis of Parliamentary Democracy to the European Parliament*, John Pinder, ed. (New York: St. Martins Press, 1999): p. 43; Corwin, "Progress of Constitutional Theory," pp. 515, 523, 525, 530; and Wood, *Creation*, pp. 154–5. In contrast to Blackstone, however, first-wave constitutionalists often ran the risk of slipping back into the logic of English civil war parliamentary radicalism exemplified by Henry Parker, in which the elected assembly assumed the role of supreme representative of the nation as a whole.

[54] For the popular resentment against the first-wave legislatures, see Wood, *Creation*, pp. 404–9.

that the authority of the crown could not be replaced and thus that constitutional imbalance would be irremediable.[55] The framers in New York and Massachusetts sought to restore the executive power as a means to provide a new and generally more populist version of the separation of powers than seemed possible or even desirable in the America of 1776.

With respect to the senate the second-wave constitutions also adopted plans for strengthening the upper chamber in relation to the assembly. The rehabilitation of senatorial power in the second wave was not as dramatic as that of the executive, principally because even in the first wave there was a general tendency to try to set the upper house apart with higher property qualifications and longer terms. Both Massachusetts and New York continued or even extended this trend, with New York establishing four-year staggered terms and Massachusetts explicitly charging its annually elected senate with the job of representing property rights and providing a deliberative check on the popular assembly.[56] Ironically, the clearest indication of the shift in attitude regarding the senate came from unicameral Pennsylvania, where opposition to the constitution was particularly vehement and well organized. Pennsylvania anticonstitutionalists saw the lack of an upper chamber as one of the most serious defects in the Constitution of 1776. The most effective argument among Pennsylvania bicameralists was not, however, that a senate was required to protect property interests against popular passions. Significantly, the strongest case for a senate was based on the perceived fear of the concentration of power in any single institution, even one as emphatically popular as the Pennsylvania General Assembly.[57] This was a charge to which even radical republicans were sensitive. With the rehabilitation of executive and senatorial power in the second wave, American Whigs were clearly trying to reconceptualize the meaning of popular control over government in a way consistent with the Lockean liberal functional separation of powers. Whether or not second-wave constitutionalists believed that the senate had a unique societal role as property protector, the underlying assumption of all but the most extreme republicans was that stable government and civil liberty required a dispersal of political power among a multiplicity of institutions.

American constitutional theory and practice in the revolutionary period thus attempted to harmonize several distinct strains of Whig thought. The second-wave reaction to the perceived populist excesses of the republican first wave was at root a blending of the moderate Whig principle of constitutional balance with the Lockean liberal ideas of a functional separation of powers and the fundamental limits on the legislature. In their efforts to functionalize both separation of powers theory and traditional notions of

[55] Ibid., p. 205.
[56] Ibid., pp. 218, 433–6.
[57] Ibid., pp. 246–7.

constitutional balance, American Whigs were groping to devise an institutional means to preserve the Lockean distinction between constitutional authority and legislative will.

The central theoretical problem facing the framers of the first American constitutions – the difficulty in distinguishing effectively constituent and legislative power – derived from the fundamental tension between the two competing ideas of popular sovereignty in radical Whig thought. The Lockean liberal idea of popular sovereignty stressed the need to base all political authority on a written or at least notionally "fundamental" constitution produced by popular consent. In this view, the separation of powers was compatible with a plan of government reflecting the natural constituent power of the people. On the other hand, the modern Whig republican notion of popular sovereignty sought to base all legitimate power on the direct will of the people expressed through a more or less continuous process of consent. This view of popular sovereignty slanted heavily toward the supremacy of the representative assembly in any constitutional system and thus effectively undermined the principle of separation of powers. The first-wave constitutions assumed a greater degree of congruity between these two understandings of popular sovereignty than proved warranted. The fundamental challenge then confronting American Whigs in the second wave of revolutionary constitutionalism was not simply how to implement the separation of powers, but rather how to formulate and institutionalize a theory of consent that embraced and harmonized the liberal and republican conceptions of popular sovereignty. What was needed was an innovative American blend of the diverse elements of their Whig philosophical inheritance that combined a considerable measure of direct popular consent to and control over government action with a principle of foundational constituent consent to a supralegal instrument regulating, separating, and limiting the organs of government power. American Whigs in the revolutionary period strove for nothing less than an unprecedented new understanding of the idea of a written constitution.

Constitutionalizing Constituent Power

The central feature in the period of revolutionary constitutionalism was the effort to diagnose and remedy the problems in the nascent American doctrine of the separation of powers. The nature of the problem these early constitution makers were grappling with was the ambiguous relation between the legislature, especially the popular branch, and the constitution. For most American Whigs, a written constitution was meant to preclude tyranny from either the garden variety monarchical absolutism typical in history or the uniquely British (and admittedly more popular) configuration of absolute parliamentary sovereignty. The idea of a written constitution was strongly connected in the American Whig mind with the notion of a social contract derived originally from the consent of rights-bearing individuals. American Whigs intuited this connection viscerally, but how exactly did it work? All American Whigs may have agreed that political sovereignty derived from popular sovereignty, but what did that mean institutionally? Did popular sovereignty require that constitutions be drafted by special conventions or were elected legislatures competent to devise and revise the constitution? Did written constitutions require popular ratification to be legitimate, or again, would legislative imprimatur suffice?

During the period of revolutionary constitutionalism, American Whigs struggled to find a steady and settled understanding of the complex relation between the Lockean idea of natural constituent power and the principle of fundamental constitutional law. The first six constitutions were written and ratified by state legislatures. However, most first-wave legislatures showed little regard for constitutional niceties. This is not really surprising given that, in a concrete sense, the constitutions were the creatures of these same legislatures. In the transition phase from the first- to second-wave constitutions, Delaware, Pennsylvania, and New York held special conventions to draft their constitutions, but they were enacted by the legislatures rather than through a special system of popular ratification.[58] The basic problem of legislative supremacy in these early state constitutions can be traced back in large part to the fact that these constitutions came into force lacking a *fundamental* expression of popular consent. Given that the institutional devices intended to check the legislatures did not originate in natural constituent power in a direct sense, the predictable tendency was for the popular assemblies that did reflect popular consent in a direct, albeit ephemeral, way to ensure that, as Jefferson deplored, "the ordinary legislature may alter the constitution itself."[59] The idea and practice of strong, practically omnipotent, legislatures had, as we have seen, deep roots in both the radical republican and more conservative moderate Whig elements of the Anglo-American tradition. What was lacking throughout most of the period of revolutionary constitutionalism was the practical formulation of an idea foreshadowed clearly by Locke and somewhat ambiguously by Paine of a constitution with teeth in it, a source of sovereign authority derived from society at large understood independently of any of the particular institutions it articulated and limited.

In order to appreciate the depth and subtlety of the issues confronting the first state constitution makers, it is important to reconsider the intellectual context informing the period of revolutionary constitutionalism. As we have seen, the core of the debate between the colonies and Britain during the imperial crisis focused on the issue of divided sovereignty. The common thread unifying the early colonial position of the moderates Otis and Dickinson

---

[58] Adams, *First American Constitutions*, pp. 74–6 and Lutz, *Popular Control*, pp. 44–5.
[59] Jefferson, "Notes on the State of Virginia," p. 127.

with the later, more radical formulation of imperial relations advanced by Jefferson, Adams, and Wilson was the argument that the people of America lived under a system of divided sovereignty that was under threat from the ministry in London. American Whigs argued that the people of the colonies possessed the natural constituent power to delegate authority both to their colonial assemblies and to the British crown. The idea of divided sovereignty, then, derived its intellectual premises from the Lockean liberal principle of delegated powers that may be distributed to a variety of organs and, at least in principle, measured out with discernible limits deducible from the express will of the people. The heart of the matter in the process of revolutionary constitutionalism was the difficulty of adjusting and modifying the idea of divided sovereignty, which had been so crucial for the American idea of government in the imperial context, to the practical reality of internal constitution making in the states following independence.

The problem of divided sovereignty took two forms after 1776. First, there was the tortuous process of establishing institutions of continental union that culminated in the ratification of the Articles of Confederation in 1781. The need for a continental union of the states was the underlying national issue during the revolutionary period. However, the continental or quasi-federal structure embodied in the Articles could hardly be considered an example of divided sovereignty given that supreme power so clearly rested in the individual states. State legislatures sent delegates to Congress and reserved practically plenary power in relation to it. Montesquieu's idea of democratic federalism, which maintained that democratic republics were necessarily small and must form security alliances with other small democratic states, was the dominant philosophical paradigm informing the drafting and passage of the Articles.[60] Clearly, the Montesquieuian idea of federalism afforded a much less cohesive idea of national government than would emerge in America after 1787.

The second area in which the principle of divided sovereignty only gradually began to develop in the revolutionary period was internally within the states. The general rule, especially in the first-wave constitutions, was for the most directly representative body in the constitutional system to assume supreme sovereignty, even over the constitution itself. The frequent failure of the revolutionary era constitutions to preserve the principle of the separation of powers and to prevent legislative encroachments on the constitution left the idea of divided sovereignty inherited from the imperial context in tatters. The combination of diverging tendencies, of centripetal forces internally in the states and centrifugal forces in the broader federation, only reinforced the concentration of political power in the revolutionary and confederation

---

[60] See Baron Charles Secondat Montesquieu, *Spirit of the Laws* (1748), Anne M. Cohler, Basia Carolyn Miller, and Harold Summel Stone, trans. and eds. (Cambridge: Cambridge University Press, 1989): bk 9, chs. 1–3, pp. 131–3.

periods. The state legislatures were the only real power in their states and thus collectively in the federation as a whole.

With respect to the problem of divided sovereignty within the states, the central dilemma appeared to be how to make the idea of divided sovereignty consistent with popular sovereignty, especially in the republican sense of popular control over government. The experience of divided sovereignty during the colonial period may have left the imperial connection in shards, but the idea of distributing and limiting delegated powers had deep roots in revolutionary America. The Declaration of Independence asserted the natural constituent power of the people to make and indeed break forms of government. There was no widespread opposition to this radical premise among American Whigs. Braxton's emphasis on continuity between colonial and postindependence American political life was quite singular and largely unpalatable in the revolutionary period. The Declaration of Independence was explicit and emphatic in advancing the principle of delegated powers underlying the idea of divided sovereignty; however, it was much more reticent about the workaday practical reality of implementing this principle. British constitutional practice was no real help in the matter either. The conventions of 1660 and 1689 were, as we have seen, never widely understood to be reflective of the natural constituent power of the people. They were generally recognized as at most irregular parliaments assembled in extraordinary times (typically on the basis of monarchical disability) and charged with specific restorative tasks.[61] The custom of assembling conventions as understood in British constitutional practice was, then, much more in keeping with the moderate Whig emphasis on temporary measures to restore the original compact than it was to any radical understanding of natural constituent power and the dissolution of government. Thus, the first-wave failure to apply the principle of popular sovereignty directly to the process of constitutional ratification was partially a function of the novelty of America's situation in 1776 and partially a reflection of the deep ambiguity in the Whig understanding of consent.

The ambiguity in the Whig understanding of consent related to more than just the cleavage between moderates and radicals. In the context of 1776–80, the most important tension within American Whiggism lay in the difference between the republican and liberal understanding of consent. Both the liberal and republican strains of radical Whig thought made consent central to their argument, but they offered differing approaches to the question of the application of the principle of consent to the formation and operation of political institutions. The republican strain placed the emphasis on direct consent and majority rule as the legitimizing principle of government action. The institutional mechanisms prescribed by Paine and Demophilus to ensure

[61] Adams, "State Constitutions," p. 10; Bonwick, "United States Constitution," p. 55; and Wood, *Creation*, pp. 310–12.

democratic accountability provided no real check on majority rule. The Pennsylvania Council of Censors and the New York Council of Revision, foreshadowed by Spinoza's Council of Syndics, were also intended to provide an institutional check, a constitution-protecting counterforce, against straight majority rule populism.[62] While these innovative institutions designed to ensure constitutional fidelity on the part of the legislature proved to be unreliable, they clearly indicated that even American Whigs who were committed to the ideal of popular government questioned whether legislative enactment was the sole basis of legitimacy.[63] Given the hard lessons of the imperial crisis, American Whigs had imbibed an inherent distrust of Pufendorfian and Blackstonian legal positivism, even if it was dressed up in the populist garb of broadly representative assemblies.

In the first-wave constitutions, the republican desire to maintain popular control over government trumped the liberal aspiration to preserve the integrity of the written constitution vis-à-vis the legislature. This was the constitutional price many American Whigs were prepared to pay for populist goods. The second wave, however, saw liberal arguments acquiring a new saliency in the states. The second-wave corrections to the pallid first-wave separation of powers were largely salutary but ultimately inadequate on their own because the effective separation of powers means more than just a certain institutional arrangement. The idea of the dispersal of powers that became more urgent following the first wave rested on a notion of functional instrumentality for political institutions. This Lockean argument, however, rested on the deeper liberal premises about the requirements of limited government.

The core principle informing the renewed prominence of liberal ideas in the second wave was the distinction between government and society rooted in Lockean Whig philosophy. Lockean liberals tended to internalize and presuppose a more articulated state of nature theory than did Whig republicans. The Lockean state of nature was intended not only to demonstrate the grounds of individual political obligation but also to highlight the profound artificiality of government. Government in the liberal view was the result neither of a Pufendorfian pact of submission nor a republican direct conduit of popular will. Rather, government in Lockean liberal philosophy is properly understood as the product of a more variegated form of consent and delegation of power. The people may delegate their natural authority to different institutions performing various functions, but they may also delegate

---

[62] See New York 1777, sec. 3, in which the governor and at least two judges could veto legislation, and Pennsylvania 1776, sec. 47, in which the elected council of censors meant to assemble every seven years, could call a new constitutional convention with a two-thirds vote. Cf. Spinoza's proposal for a council of syndics that represents a prototype for the New York and Pennsylvania councils (Benedict Spinoza, *A Theologico-Political Treatise and A Political Treatise*, R. H. M. Elwes, trans. [New York: Dover, 1951]: p. 380).

[63] Wood, *Creation*, p. 455.

different forms of power with carefully defined parameters of legitimate spheres of action. Thus, the Lockean liberal strain of Whig thought provided a coherent account of the properties of political power that was compatible with the palpable predisposition of Americans for written constitutions. Lockean liberalism advanced a conception of consent that was more adaptable to the construction of complex governments than was Whig republicanism. In the Lockean model, some institutions could reflect relatively direct consent and others a more indirect form. This flexibility in applying the principle of delegated powers was related to the core Lockean idea that a society of rights-bearing individuals may regulate their political life by the known and general laws establishing the form of government.[64] In addition, the Lockean liberal emphasis on the centrality of property rights was generally shared by nearly all American Whigs in this period. However, the first-wave constitutions were unable to operationalize this principle effectively because success in the goal of protecting property rights, even against elected majorities, rested on the more fundamental idea of a conceptual space and a moral hierarchy distinguishing constitutional provision and statute law. It was this latter idea that remained to be substantiated in the second wave of revolutionary constitutionalism.

In some respects, the Lockean liberal idea of flexible consent and delegated powers was in tension with the general current of revolutionary constitutional thought. In the first wave, the liberal concern to distinguish popular and political sovereignty paled beside the republican passion to ensure that the supreme institutions were emphatically popular. The liberal constitutionalism that began to emerge in the second wave can be understood as a conscious effort to reaffirm the moral primacy of society above political institutions. By devising a method of indirect consent to institutions deriving their authority from a more fundamentally popular written constitution, American framers in the states hoped thereby to develop a means to check the absolutizing tendency of the popular will. The Lockean liberal strain of Whig thought offered at least a theoretical outline for a method of parceling out sovereign power in limited and more or less clearly defined units to various institutions. The experience of constitution making in the states in the first-wave and much of the second wave demonstrated with urgency the need to devise procedural mechanisms of consent to solidify the connection between society and the written constitution establishing a government.

The theoretical peak of revolutionary constitutionalism occurred in Massachusetts. The Massachusetts Constitution of 1780 remains the oldest (albeit much amended) written constitution in active use today. More significantly for our purposes, the Massachusetts Constitution represented the first fully articulated formulation of the uniquely American form of constitutional government. As we have seen, under the driving intellectual

[64] Peters, *Massachusetts Constitution*, pp. 155, 169, 173–5.

leadership of John Adams the Massachusetts Constitution, along with that of New York, revivified the Lockean idea of a functional separation of powers theory in America.[65] However, the key innovation in Massachusetts lay not in its plan of government, but rather in the process of its creation. Massachusetts was the first state to draft the constitution in a special convention and then submit the proposal for popular ratification in the many townships in the state. Moreover, this process of popular ratification of the constitution was no mere symbolic gesture or simply pro forma event inasmuch as the framers of the 1780 Constitution were keenly aware of the stinging rebuke dealt by the people to the previous constitutional proposal in 1778. No state prior to Massachusetts had attempted to determine fundamental popular consent for the constitution drafted by their conventions or the legislature, and the prickly, politically sophisticated, and demanding citizens of Massachusetts ensured that the process of popular ratification would have substantive meaning.

The process of popular ratification in Massachusetts represented the most ambitious effort in the revolutionary period to institutionalize and operationalize the Lockean liberal understanding of the origin of government. The constitutional and legal implications of the Lockean turn in revolutionary constitutionalism were twofold. First, the Massachusetts process of constitution making and ratification illuminated a new way to understand the relation between written constitutions and the instruments of government. In the prior efforts at revolutionary constitutionalism, the states were unable to demonstrate the direct and palpable connection between the will of the majority of individuals in society, what Locke identified as the natural law of "greater force," and the basic structure of government. Due to their incapacity to demonstrate direct popular consent to the *fundamental* rules of government, as opposed to the actual operation of the legislative power, these first state constitutions were unable to solidify the majoritarian social, in contrast to simply political, premises of Lockean liberal constitutionalism. The Massachusetts Constitution of 1780 was the first American constitution to elevate constitutional provision securely above normal statute law through popular consent, in effect to provide the constitution with the normative bite in law and the political culture to resist legislative encroachment.[66] By fleshing out the process required to distinguish the fundamental popular consent implied in the idea of natural constituent power so central to Lockean Whig philosophy from the operational consent required in quotidian governance

---

[65] For Adams' role in the drafting of the Massachusetts Constitution of 1780, see C. Bradley Thompson, *John Adams and the Spirit of Liberty* (Lawrence: University Press of Kansas, 1998): pp. 202–22.

[66] As Peters observes, the Massachusetts ratification process underlined the difference between constituent power and operational political consent by establishing a broader suffrage for the ratification process than it did for the normal electoral process (*Constitution of Massachusetts*, pp. 135–6). Cf. Lutz, *Popular Control*, pp. 81–3 and Locke II:96.

and normal legislation, the Massachusetts constitutional framers advanced the American idea of consent materially toward a coherent theory of divided sovereignty.

The second major advance in American constitutional theory produced by the Massachusetts model had to do with the evolving conception of the separation of powers. The general shift toward independent executives and judiciaries that occurred in the movement from the first to the second wave of revolutionary constitutionalism reached a level of theoretical sophistication in Massachusetts hitherto unseen in America. The idea of governors and judges, or for that matter senators, with a source of legitimacy independent of both the popular assembly and the electorate broadly speaking, became more plausibly consistent with popular government inasmuch as the Massachusetts constitutional ratification process provided these institutions with a representative function ultimately rooted in the authority of the people. In principle at least an independent executive, judge, or senator with multiple-year terms or an indirect mode of election and appointment was no less representative of natural constituent power than the popular assembly. In its precise formulation in Massachusetts in 1780, the separation of powers was still profoundly influenced by populist republican principles such as annual elections for all the political branches. However, this idea of direct consent through institutions was fused with the more indirect notion of foundational consent amenable to the Lockean liberal principle of separation of powers and the delegation theory of sovereignty. Even if the Massachusetts Constitution of 1780 was still wedded to some extent to republican and moderate Whig ideas in terms of constitutional structure and electoral process, it introduced a very flexible Lockean understanding of the principle of consent into American constitutionalism. With the broad popular base supplied by direct fundamental consent, not only did the idea of indirect consent to particular institutions and offices become more palatable to an essentially democratic people, but also future American constitutional framers were shown the practical application of means to distinguish between making, executing, and interpreting law more clearly than at any prior point in Anglo-American history.

The Massachusetts Constitution of 1780 marked the end of the period of revolutionary constitutionalism in the states. It also signified the first true example of the uniquely American form of constitutionalism with a powerful independent executive and judiciary, a bicameral legislature, and a system of popular ratification and amendment. As the theoretical peak of revolutionary constitutionalism, the Massachusetts example of popular ratification became the model for subsequent American constitutions including the U.S. Constitution of 1787. At the philosophical level, the Massachusetts Constitution of 1780 represented a watershed in the historical development of Anglo-American constitutionalism. The Lockean liberal principle of conceptually dividing society and government produced an idea of consent that was inherently flexible and could operate in a variety of ways, impacting diverse institutions with particular functions in the constitutional system. Under the guidance of Lockean liberal philosophy, American constitutionalists would begin to articulate and develop a notion of indirect consent and representation that was largely devoid of the aristocratic and class-based elements of British moderate Whig constitutionalism. While modern republican elements such as frequent elections, broad franchise, and suspicions about the oligarchic tendencies in the separation of powers would remain important features of American constitutional development after 1780, the republican idea that direct popular consent to legislative activity is the sole basis of legitimacy would no longer be the central tenet of American constitutionalism.

The modern theory of divided sovereignty was slowly and rudimentarily worked out internally in the period of revolutionary constitutionalism in the states. By the time of the creation of the last revolutionary era constitution in Massachusetts, a combination of advanced theoretical rigor and dearly bought lessons of experience pointed American Whigs toward a means to combine fundamental consent to a written constitution with the idea of effective operational consent to government. The combination of these two distinct aspects of consent produced the conceptual model for distributing and dividing sovereign power that would become the hallmark of American constitutionalism. Both the shortcomings and achievements of revolutionary constitutionalism prepared the theoretical ground for 1787 by providing flexible concepts of consent and delegated powers that would come to undergird the American idea of federalism and separation of powers, each fully competent within its own sphere. In time American Whigs would go beyond even the parameters foreshadowed by Locke by applying the principle of delegated powers to an unprecedentedly complex federal system of interconnected but relatively autonomous governments and jurisdictions. In the Confederation period following the Revolution, many Americans gradually came to the conclusion that further comprehensive adaptation of Lockean liberal principles to the American context would be necessarily federal in character.

Conclusion

A decade or so after the fires of revolution were expended in America, and as the first sparks of conflagration were beginning to spread in France, the self-professed Old Whig Edmund Burke identified a surprising source of ideological solidarity with the emerging New Whig radicals occupying the opposite end of the British political spectrum. He assured all concerned that "the old fanatics of single arbitrary power ... maintained, what I believe no creature now maintains 'that the crown is held by divine hereditary and indefeasible right'."[1] Burke's utterance and the political context from which it emerged exposed in a particularly acute manner the dual character of the Whig politics of liberty that formed the foundation of Anglo-American thought in the early modern period. I have tried to show that Whig political philosophy was both a capacious repository for practically all limited constitutionalist thought and sentiment in the seventeenth- and eighteenth-century Anglo-American world and a complex, heterogeneous body of divergent, distinct, and even conflicting ideas and philosophical commitments.

Burke perceptively identified the common source of Whig political thought in the constitutional and theological battles of seventeenth-century England. As we have seen, in their quarrel with Filmerian divine right and its political theology of monarchical absolutism and scriptural literalism, the first English Whigs built upon, modified, and in important ways departed from the venerable natural liberty tradition of their philosophical predecessors. Each of the various strains of Whig thought we have identified in Exclusion era England shared both this anti–divine right philosophical heritage and the goal of purging the classical and Christian elements of the anti-absolutist principles of contract and consent seen in Catholic and Calvinist early modern thought. The Whigs did so, moreover, while simultaneously trying to reform and disable the absolutist tendencies of Hobbesian

---

[1] Edmund Burke, *Reflections on the Revolution in France* (Buffalo: Prometheus, 1987): p. 30.

and Grotian natural jurisprudence in order to produce a version of modern natural rights theory consistent with limited government. The diverse and multifarious body of thought that emerged from this revolution in the doctrine of natural liberty shaped and animated the development of Anglo-American thought from the Glorious Revolution in England in 1688–9 to the revolution in America nearly a century later. So profound and pervasive was the impact of Whig thought on the Anglo-American tradition in this period that even fierce political rivals and ideological opponents such as Paine and Burke or Blackstone and Jefferson were each, in a sense, heirs of the Whig politics of liberty.

In this study, I have tried to cast our vision backward from the ideological cleavages in Anglo-American thought at the time of the American Revolution to their source in the philosophical battles of the turbulent seventeenth century in the expectation that by clarifying and examining these philosophical sources, we are better situated to appreciate various aspects of the Anglo-American tradition that are now often neglected or misunderstood. By exaggerating the influence of liberal or modern republican ideas and by hypersystematizing the elements of this tradition in rigid paradigms, we not only fail to account for the heterogeneity of philosophical influences on the development of Anglo-American thought, we also obscure the underlying threads of intellectual unity connecting Anglo-American democratic traditions with the broader Western philosophical heritage of political rationalism. In an age called to renewed contemplation of the meaning and promise of liberal democracy by new global challenges and threats to democratic principles, we thus run the risk of depriving the student of the Anglo-American tradition today of important sources of wisdom and reflection embedded in our political history.

The Lockean liberal, modern republican, and moderate Whig strains of thought we have examined in this study each played a role in establishing the philosophical foundations of our political and constitutional traditions. The formation of two competing doctrines within the British Empire, with the emergence of parliamentary sovereignty in Britain and popular sovereignty in America, reflected the gradual solidification of tendencies rooted in the philosophical premises of early English Whiggism. I have tried to demonstrate not only that the origin of American political and constitutional ideas lay in English Whig thought, but also that English thought was deeply penetrated by seventeenth-century continental natural jurisprudence. The English Whig tradition that produced the theoretical foundations of American political and constitutional thought was itself a hybrid of indigenous and foreign intellectual influences as the concepts, categories, and reasoning of continental thought were injected into English political, constitutional, and theological controversies by the philosophically minded Whigs. I have aimed in essence to restore a sense of the original depth and multiplicity of philosophical sources composing Whig thought that included not only such English luminaries as Locke, Sidney, and Tyrrell, but also at one remove important continental thinkers in Europe's natural law heritage such as Spinoza, Pufendorf, and Grotius, who are typically not associated with the Anglo-American tradition. The development of Anglo-American political and constitutional thought in the seminal period between the Revolution in England in the 1680s and the American Revolution in 1776 must be understood in the larger context of the Enlightenment philosophical project, of which the Anglo-American experiment in liberty proved a fruitful and world-changing branch.

I certainly do not believe that my tripartite structure of Whig thought fully explains every aspect of Anglo-American or modern political development beyond the eighteenth century, but I offer some conjectures as perhaps a useful heuristic. In America the U.S. Constitution of 1787 represented both the culmination of early modern Whig thought and a new beginning for a uniquely American version of constitutionalism. By the end of the period of revolutionary constitutionalism in America, the long-running battle between British and American Whigs over the moral, legal, and political meaning of natural rights, the Glorious Revolution, and the British Constitution quite obviously had moved to a different plane as the young American Republic assumed its place among the independent nations of the world. However, the formal and institutional triumph of the principle of popular sovereignty and written constitutionalism in 1787 also reflected a deeper underlying continuity of thought rooted in the diverse strains of the radical Whig inheritance in America. The American application of the elusive principle of divided sovereignty in the formation of a complex federal system delimiting the distribution of powers between the national and state governments represented an immense theoretical achievement with deep roots in the Lockean liberal strain of English radical Whig thought. The Framers of 1787 not only imitated the Massachusetts model for institutionalizing popular sovereignty through popular ratification of the written legal instrument, they also modified traditional notions of constitutional balance and the Lockean idea of a functional separation of powers to produce the elaborate system of checks and balances that has come to embody the American system of government. With regard to both the principle of federalism and the separation of powers theory, the Framers in Philadelphia sought to make manifest the great mystery of liberal constitutionalism: the independence of dependent things.

The modern republican elements of American Whig thought that had been so influential in the period of revolutionary constitutionalism did not, however, disappear from the American political landscape with the apparent triumph of Lockean liberalism in 1787. The Antifederalist opponents of the Constitution in the ratification debates of 1787–8 drew many of their most influential arguments from the philosophical resources of the republican strain of the radical Whig tradition. Recalling the words of Sidney, Spinoza, Trenchard and Gordon, Tom Paine, and the framers of the first state constitutions from the historical past for the polemical battles of the constitutional present, Antifederalists from the fishing villages of Massachusetts to the plantations of Georgia expressed deep concern that the establishment of a distant national government with a complex system of separation of powers would undermine the cherished American principle of popular sovereignty. Free government, in the eyes of these American Whig republicans, was synonymous with government close to the people, accountable to the electorate, and subject to the direct control of a vigilant and public-spirited citizenry. While the Antifederalists lost the immediate debate over ratification in 1787–8, the impact of their republican philosophy of popular sovereignty on the future of American constitutionalism was far from nugatory. Even with regard to the Constitution of 1787, important features of republicanism were grafted into the separation of powers in the national government and were woven into the fabric of the complex federal system. The regular election of members of the House of Representatives and of the president (albeit through the medium of the Electoral College) reflected the characteristically republican concern for frequent recourse to first principles of consent and for a significant degree of popular control over the national government. Moreover, within the federal system for long after 1789 (arguably until well into the twentieth century), most of the important matters of actual governing in America took place at the level of the state governments, which were subject to the authority of their own typically more populist constitutions expressing an egalitarian franchise and created and amended according to the sovereignty of the people in the separate states.[2]

American political and constitutional development can be understood in a fundamental sense as a result of the perpetual interaction of the liberal and republican elements composing the philosophical foundations of the regime. The amended Constitution, which extended the franchise to women and African Americans, and established direct popular election to the Senate and term limits on the president, further demonstrated the incorporation of essentially republican principles into the framework of a liberal Constitution. Even the development of extra-constitutional institutions such as the mass political party, a phenomenon practically invented in the early American republic, originated in the profoundly democratic impulses of the modern republican tradition with its palpable tension concerning the separation of powers and its characteristic concern to mobilize popular will and structure a more or less continuous flow of consent to the operation of government.

---

[2] Colin Bonwick, "The United States Constitution and Its Roots in British Political Thought and Tradition," in *Foundations of Democracy in the European Union: From the Genesis of Parliamentary Democracy to the European Parliament*, John Pinder, ed. (New York: St. Martins Press, 1999): pp. 54–5 and Donald Lutz, *Popular Control and Popular Consent: Whig Political Theory in the Early State Constitutions* (Baton Rouge: Louisiana State University Press, 1980): pp. 221–2.

Far from indicating the crushing victory of Lockean liberalism over all com-
ers, the process of constitutional framing in 1787–9 inaugurated patterns of
thought and political behavior signifying the synergetic relation of construc-
tive antagonism between liberal and republican principles that has historically characterized the core dynamic of American constitutional and political
development.

Beyond the shores of America, the strands of thought we have identified
in Whig political philosophy would emerge from their common Enlightenment source and appear in late-eighteenth- and early-nineteenth-century
Britain and Europe in various mutations, evolutions, and parallels. Lockean
liberal constitutional philosophy would by and large find the *ancien régimes*
of continental Europe in the late eighteenth and nineteenth centuries much
less suitable soil for implantation than the Anglo–American world. While
Lockean liberalism in this period would generally find its intellectual voice
on the Continent subsumed or drowned out by the fervent appeals of na-
tionalism and working-class radicalism, modern republicanism proved to
make a more immediate and even explosive impact. Notably in revolutionary France, the Spinozist roots of modern republicanism would, if anything,
be more apparent than in America. The democratic philosophy of revolution
in France, with its deep antipathy to executive power and its reliance on the
mass mobilization of ideologically charged artisan radicalism, would lead in
short order to the complete absorption of all the power and privileges of the
historical estates of the realm into the ideal of popular sovereignty expressed
through a single omnicompetent national assembly. Following the collapse
of constitutional republican government in revolutionary France lay the hy-
perexecutive populism and military *la gloire* of Bonaparte and eventually the
restoration of an eviscerated *ancien régime* with nowhere left to go but down.

For its part, across the channel in Britain, the deeply entrenched practice of
parliamentary sovereignty would undergo important liberalizing and even
republicanizing modifications through the electoral and constitutional reforms of the nineteenth and twentieth centuries, but it would persist in form
and substance as the central organizing principle of the British system of government through to the present-day debates over European integration and
Scottish and Welsh devolution. Throughout the eighteenth and nineteenth
centuries, the moderate Whig conservative natural law theory of Pufendorf
that lay at the core of eighteenth-century British political and constitutional thought also experienced important modifications as new philosophical doctrines emerged. The early- and mid-eighteenth-century rearticula-
tions of the moderate Whig rejection of radical rights and contract theory by
Bolingbroke, Montesquieu, Hume, and Blackstone provided in many respects the theoretical foundations for later British philosophical movements
in the direction of Burkean prescription and Benthamite utilitarianism. My
reading of the conservative natural law theory underlying British constitutional and political thought in the eighteenth century suggests that, ironically,

these bitter philosophical foes championing the conservative principle of pre-scription, on the one hand, and the progressive ideal of utility, on the other, shared a deeply rooted and largely obscured common intellectual source in the seventeenth-century moderate Whig rejection of radical natural rights theory.

This study intends to illuminate the complex philosophical heritage under-lying the Anglo-American political and constitutional tradition. By uncov-ering the roots of this tradition in the political and theological controversies surrounding the early modern idea of natural liberty and reexamining its development in the seventeenth and eighteenth centuries, this study suggests that in many ways contemporary modes of thought and patterns of political behavior are rooted in much deeper and richer philosophical sources than we generally realize. I hope that by restoring a vision of the original hetero-geneity and scope of moral and intellectual resources in the Enlightenment philosophical foundations of Anglo-American thought, twenty-first-century enlightened friends of liberal democracy will be able to draw on these re-sources in order to respond to the dangerous alternatives to our way of life in the world today, both fanatical and banal.

Bibliography

Aarsleff, Hans. "The State of Nature and the Nature of Man in Locke." *John Locke: Problems and Perspectives*. John Yolton, ed. Cambridge: Cambridge University Press, 1969: 99–136.

Acton, Lord Emerich Edward Dalberg. *Essays in the History of Liberty*. Indianapolis: Liberty Fund Press, 1985.

Adams, John. "Thoughts on Government." *The Political Writings of John Adams*. George Peek, ed. New York: Liberal Arts Press, 1954: 84–92.

The Adams–Jefferson Letters. Lestor J. Capon, ed. Chapel Hill: University of North Carolina Press, 1959.

Adams, Willi Paul. *The First American Constitutions: Republican Ideology and the Making of the State Constitutions in the Revolutionary Era*. Chapel Hill: University of North Carolina Press, 1980.

"The State Constitutions as Analogy and Precedent." *The United States Constitution: Roots, Rights, and Responsibilities*. Washington, DC: Smithsonian Institution Press, 1992: 3–22.

Ahrensdorf, Peter and Thomas Pangle. *Justice Among Nations: On the Moral Basis of Power and Peace*. Lawrence: University Press of Kansas, 1999.

Aldridge, A. Owen. "The Collapse of the British Empire as Seen by Franklin, Paine, and Burke." *Revisioning the British Empire in the Eighteenth Century*. William G. Shade, ed. London: Associated University Press, 1998: 76–101.

Allen, W. J. A. *English Political Thought, 1603–1644*. London: Archon, 1967.

History of Political Thought in the Sixteenth Century. London: Methuen, 1977.

Appleby, Joyce. *Capitalism and a New Social Order*. New York: New York University Press, 1984.

Aquinas, St. Thomas. *Summa Theologica*. Literally translated by the Fathers of the English Dominican Province. 3 vols. New York: Benziger Brothers, 1947.

Arendt, Hannah. *On Revolution*. New York: Viking Press, 1963.

Aristotle. *The Nicomachean Ethics*. H. H. Rackham, trans. Cambridge, MA: Harvard University Press, 1934.

The Politics. Carnes Lord, trans. Chicago: University of Chicago Press, 1984.

433

Aschcraft, Richard and M. M. Goldsmith. "Locke, Revolution Principles, and the Formation of Whig Ideology." *The Historical Journal*, vol. 26, issue 4 (December 1983): 773–800.

    Revolutionary Politics and Locke's Two Treatises of Government. Princeton: Princeton University Press, 1986.

    Locke's Two Treatises of Government. London: Allen & Unwin, 1987.

Atwood, William. *The Fundamentals of the English Government*. London, 1690.

Augustine, St. *The City of God*. New York: Penguin, 1984.

Bailyn, Bernard. *The Ideological Origins of the American Revolution*. Cambridge, MA: Harvard University Press, 1967.

    "Common Sense." *Fundamental Testaments of the American Revolution*. Washington, DC: Library of Congress, 1973: 7–22.

Balibar, Etienne. *Spinoza and Politics*. Peter Snowdon, trans. New York: Verso, 1998.

Banning, Lance. *The Jeffersonian Persuasion*. Ithaca: Cornell University Press, 1978.

    "The Republican Interpretation: Retrospect and Prospect." *The Republican Synthesis Revisited: Essays in Honor of George Athan Bilias*. Milton M. Klein, Richard D. Brown, and John Hench, eds. Worcester: American Antiquarian Society, 1992: 91–118.

Beard, Charles. *An Economic Interpretation of the Constitution*. New York: Macmillan, 1935 [1913].

Becker, Carl. *The Declaration of Independence: A Study in the History of Political Ideas*. New York: Knopf, 1942 [1922].

Bellarmine, Roberto. *De Laicis*. Kathleen Murphy, trans. New York: Fordham University Press, 1928.

    Supreme Pontiff. George Moore, trans. Chevy Chase, MD.: Country Dollar Press, 1951.

Bennett, Joan. *Reviving Liberty: Radical Christian Humanism in Milton's Great Poems*. Cambridge, MA: Harvard University Press, 1989.

Blackstone, William. *Commentaries on the Laws of England*. Vol. I. London, 1791 [1765].

Bodin, Jean. *The Six Books of the Republic* (1606). Trans. by Richard Knolles from the original *Les six livres de la republique* (Paris, 1580). K. D. McRae, ed. Cambridge, MA: Harvard University Press, 1962.

Bolingbroke, Viscount Henry St. John. *The Works of Lord Bolingbroke*. Philadelphia: Carey and Hart, 1841.

Bonwick, Colin. *English Radicals and the American Revolution*. Chapel Hill: University of North Carolina Press, 1977.

    "The United States Constitution and Its Roots in British Political Thought and Tradition." *Foundations of Democracy in the European Union: From the Genesis of Parliamentary Democracy to the European Parliament*. John Pinder, ed. New York: St. Martin's Press, 1999: 41–58.

Brailsford, H. N. *The Levellers and the English Revolution*. Stanford: Stanford University Press, 1961.

Braxton, Carter. "An Address to the Convention of the Colony and Ancient Dominion of Virginia" (1776). *American Political Writings During the Founding Era: 1760–1805*. Charles S. Hyneman and Donald S. Lutz, eds. Indianapolis: Liberty Fund, 1983: 328–39.

Brett, Annabel. *Liberty, Right, and Nature*. Cambridge: Cambridge University Press, 1997.

"Individual and Community in the 'Second Scholastic': Subjective Rights in Domingo de Soto and Francisco Suarez." *Philosophy in the Sixteenth and Seventeenth Centuries: Conversations with Aristotle*. Constance Blackwell and Sachiko Kusukawa, eds. Aldershot: Ashgate, 1999: 146–68.

Brewer, John. "Rockingham, Burke, and Whig Political Argument." *The Historical Journal*, vol. 18, no. 1 (March 1975): 188–201.

Browning, Reed. *Political and Constitutional Ideas of the Court Whigs*. Baton Rouge: Louisiana State University Press, 1982.

Burke, Edmund. *The Writings and Speeches of Edmund Burke, Volume II: Party, Parliament, and the American Crisis, 1766–1774*, Paul Langford, ed. Oxford: Clarendon Press, 1981.

Reflections on the Revolution in France. Buffalo: Prometheus, 1987.

Burnet, Gilbert. "The Measures of Submission (1688)." *The Struggle for Sovereignty: Seventeenth Century English Political Tracts*. Joyce Lee Malcolm, ed. Indianapolis: Liberty Fund Press, 1999: 850–64.

Burns, J. H. "George Buchanan and the Anti-Monarchomachs." *Political Discourse in Early Modern Britain*. Nicholas Phillipson and Quentin Skinner, eds. Cambridge: Cambridge University Press, 1993: 3–22.

Burtt, Shelley. *Virtue Transformed: Political Argument in England, 1688–1740*. Cambridge: Cambridge University Press, 1992.

Butler, Melissa. "Early Liberal Roots of Feminism: John Locke and the Attack on Patriarchy." *American Political Science Review*, vol. 72, no. 1 (March 1978): 135–50.

Calvin, Jean. *Institutio of the Christianae religionis*. Trans. from the 1559 Latin edition by Ford Lewis Battles. *Library of Christian Classics*, 2 vols. John T. McNeill, ed. Philadelphia: Westminster Press, 1967.

Canavan, Francis. "Thomas Paine." *The History of Political Philosophy*, 3rd ed. Leo Strauss and Joseph Cropsey, eds. Chicago: University of Chicago Press, 1987: 680–86.

Carr, Craig L. and Michael J. Seidler. "Pufendorf, Sociality and the Modern State." *History of Political Thought*, vol. 13, no. 3 (Autumn 1996): 355–78.

Caton, Hiram. *The Politics of Progress: The Origins and Development of the Commercial Republic, 1600–1835*. Gainesville: University of Florida Press, 1988.

Chapman, Richard Allen. "*Leviathan* Writ Small: Thomas Hobbes on the Family." *American Political Science Review*, vol. 69, no. 1 (March 1975): 76–90.

Cherry, George L. "The Role of the Convention Parliament (1688–89) in Parliamentary Supremacy." *Journal of the History of Ideas*, vol. 17, no. 3 (June 1956): 390–406.

Churchill, Winston. *A History of the English Speaking Peoples: The New World, Volume II*. New York: Dodd, Mead, 1956.

Cicero, Marcus Tullius. *The Republic and the Laws*. Niall Rudd, trans. Oxford: Oxford University Press, 1988.

Claeys, Gregory. *Thomas Paine: Social and Political Thought*. Boston: Unwin & Hyman, 1989.

Clarke, Captain John. "Speech during the Putney Debates." *The English Levellers*. Andrew Sharp, ed. Cambridge: Cambridge University Press, 1998: 102–30.

Cohler, Ann. *Montesquieu's Comparative Politics and the Spirit of American Constitu-tionalism.* Lawrence: University Press of Kansas, 1988.

Colbourn, H. Trevor. "Jefferson's Use of the Past." *William and Mary Quarterly,* 3rd ser., vol. 15, no. 1 (January 1958): 56–70.

The Lamp of Experience: Whig History and the Intellectual Origins of the American Revolution. Chapel Hill: University of North Carolina Press, 1965.

Colley, Linda. *In Defiance of Oligarchy: The Tory Party, 1714–1760.* Cambridge: Cambridge University Press, 1982.

Commager, Henry Steele. *Documents of American History.* New York: Appleton, 1963.

Conniff, James. "Reason and History in Early Whig Thought: The Case of Algernon Sidney." *The Journal of the History of Ideas,* vol. 43 (July 1982): 397–416.

Conrad, Stephen. "Putting Rights Talk in Its Place: The *Summary View* Revisited." *Jeffersonian Legacies.* Peter Onuf, ed. Charlottesville: University of Virginia Press, 1993: 254–80.

Corwin, Edward S. "The Progress of Constitutional Theory between the Declaration of Independence and the Meeting of the Philadelphia Convention." *The American Historical Review,* vol. 30, issue 3 (April 1925): 511–36.

Courtney, C. P. "Montesquieu and English Liberty." *Montesquieu's Science of Politics: Essays on the Spirit of Laws.* David W. Carrithers, Michael A. Mosher, and Paul A. Rahe, eds. Lanham, MD: Rowman & Littlefield, 2001: 273–90.

Cox, Richard. *Locke on War and Peace.* Oxford: Clarendon Press, 1960.

"Hugo Grotius." *History of Political Philosophy,* 3rd ed. Leo Strauss and Joseph Cropsey, eds. Chicago: University of Chicago Press, 1987: 386–95.

Cranston, Maurice. *John Locke: A Biography.* London: Macmillan, 1957.

Daly, James. *Sir Robert Filmer and English Political Thought.* Toronto: University of Toronto Press, 1979.

Dargo, George. *Roots of the Republic: A New Perspective on Early American Constitu-tionalism.* New York: Praeger, 1974.

Dawidoff, Robert. "Rhetoric of Democracy." *Thomas Jefferson and the Politics of Nature.* Thomas Engeman, ed. Notre Dame, IN: University of Notre Dame Press, 2000: 99–122.

Demophilus (George Bryan). "The Genuine Principles of the Ancient Saxon, or English, Constitution." *American Political Writings During the Founding Era: 1760–1805.* Charles S. Hyneman and Donald S. Lutz, eds. Indianapolis: Liberty Fund, 1983: 340–67.

Diamond, Martin. "The Revolution of Sober Expectations." *The American Revo-lution: Three Views.* New York: American Brands, 1975: 57–85.

Dickinson, H. T. "The Eighteenth Century Debate on the Sovereignty of Parliament." *Transactions of the Royal Historical Society,* fifth ser., vol. 26 (1976): 189–210.

Liberty and Property. London: Weidenfeld and Nicolson, 1977.

Dickinson, John. "The Letters from a Farmer in Pennsylvania." *Empire and Nation.* William E. Leuchtenberg and Bernard Wishy, eds. Englewood Cliffs, NJ: Prentice-Hall, 1962: 3–85.

Dictionary of National Biography. 24 vols. Leslie Stephen and Sidney Lee, eds. London: Oxford University Press, 1921–2.

Diggins, John Paul. *The Lost Soul of American Politics.* New York: Basic Books, 1984.

Dowling, Paul. *Polite Wisdom: Heathen Rhetoric in Milton's Areopagitica.* Lanham, MD: Rowman & Littlefield, 1996.

Dufour, Alfred. "Pufendorf." *The Cambridge History of Political Thought, 1450–1700.* J. H. Burns and Mark Goldie, eds. Cambridge: University of Cambridge Press, 1991: 561–88.

Dunn, John. *The Political Thought of John Locke.* Cambridge: Cambridge University Press, 1969.

"The Politics of Locke in England and America." *John Locke: Problems and Perspectives.* John Yolton, ed. Cambridge: Cambridge University Press, 1969: 45–80.

Dworetz, Steven. *The Unvarnished Doctrine: Locke, Liberalism, and the American Revolution.* Durham: Duke University Press, 1990.

Edwards, Charles S. *Hugo Grotius, the Miracle of Holland: A Study in Political and Legal Thought.* Chicago: Nelson-Hall, 1981.

Elshtain, J. B. *Public Man, Private Woman.* Princeton: Princeton University Press, 1981.

Engeman, Thomas. "Liberalism, Republicanism and Ideology." *Review of Politics,* vol. 55 (Spring 1993): 331–43.

Faulkner, Robert. "The First Liberal Democrat: Locke's Popular Government." *Review of Politics,* vol. 63 (Fall 2001): 5–39.

Ferguson, James. "Reason and Madness: The Political Thought of James Otis." *William and Mary Quarterly,* vol. 36, no. 2 (April 1979): 194–214.

Ferne, Henry. "The Resolving of Conscience." Cambridge: 1642.

Feuer, Samuel. *Spinoza and the Rise of Liberalism.* Boston: Beacon Press, 1958.

Figgis, J. N. "On Some Political Theories of the Early Jesuits." *Transactions of the Royal Historical Society,* new ser., vol. XI (1897): 89–112.

The Divine Right of Kings. New York: Harper, 1965.

Filmer, Robert. *Patriarcha and Other Writings.* Johann Somerville, ed. Cambridge: Cambridge University Press, 1991.

Fink, Zera. *The Classical Republicans.* Chicago: Northwestern University Press, 1962.

Finnis, John. *Natural Law and Natural Rights.* Oxford: Oxford University Press, 1980.

Foner, Eric. *Tom Paine and Revolutionary America.* New York: Oxford University Press, 1976.

Forbes, Duncan. *Hume's Philosophical Politics.* Cambridge: Cambridge University Press, 1975.

Ford, Paul Leicester, ed. *The Writings of Thomas Jefferson.* 10 Vols. New York: G. P. Putnam's Sons: 1892–9.

Fortin, Ernest. "St. Augustine." *The History of Political Philosophy,* 3rd ed. Leo Strauss and Joseph Cropsey, eds. Chicago: University of Chicago Press, 1987: 176–205.

Foster, David. "Taming the Father: John Locke's Critique of Patriarchal Fatherhood." *Review of Politics,* vol. 56, no. 4 (Fall 1994): 641–70.

Frankle, Robert. "The Formulation of the Declaration of Rights." *The Historical Journal,* vol. 17, no. 2 (June 1974): 265–79.

Franklin, Julian, ed. *Constitutionalism and Resistance in the Sixteenth Century: Three Treatises by Hotman, Beza, and Mornay.* New York: Pegasus, 1969.

John Locke and the Theory of Sovereignty. Cambridge: Cambridge University Press, 1978.

Furley, O. W. "The Whig Exclusionists: Pamphlet Literature in the Exclusion Crisis, 1679–81." *Cambridge Historical Journal,* vol. 13, issue 1 (1957): 19–36.

438Bibliography

Glendon, Mary Ann. *Rights Talk*. New York: Free Press, 1991.

Glenn, Gary. "Inalienable Rights and Locke's Argument for Limited Government: Political Implications of a Right of Suicide." *Journal of Politics* (February 1984) vol. 46, no. 1: 80–105.

Goldie, Mark. "Edmund Bohun and *Jus Gentium* in the Revolution Debate, 1689–1693." *The Historical Journal*, vol. 20, no. 3 (September 1977): 569–86.

"The Roots of True Whiggism 1688–94." *History of Political Thought*, vol. 1, no. 2 (Summer 1980): 196–236.

"The Reception of Hobbes." *Cambridge History of Political Thought*. J. H. Burns and Mark Goldie, eds. Cambridge: Cambridge University Press, 1991: 589–615.

"John Locke's Circle and James II." *Historical Journal*, vol. 35, no. 3 (September 1992): 557–86.

Goldsmith, M. M. and Richard Ashcraft, "Locke, Revolution Principles, and the Formation of Whig Ideology." *The Historical Journal*, vol. 26, no. 4 (1983): 773–800.

Goldsworthy, Jeffrey. *The Sovereignty of Parliament: History and Philosophy*. Oxford: Clarendon Press, 1999.

Goldwin, Robert. "John Locke." *The History of Political Philosophy*, 3rd ed. Leo Strauss and Joseph Cropsey, eds. Chicago: University of Chicago Press, 1987: 476–512.

Goodwin, William. "A Sermon Preached Before the King's Most Excellent Majestie" (1614). *The Struggle for Sovereignty: Seventeenth Century English Political Tracts*. Joyce Lee Malcolm, ed. Indianapolis; Liberty Fund, 1999: 21–52.

Gough, John. *John Locke's Political Philosophy*. Cambridge: Cambridge University Press, 1973.

"James Tyrrell, Whig Historian and Friend of John Locke." *The Historical Journal*, vol. 19, no. 3 (1976): 581–610.

Grant, Ruth. *John Locke's Liberalism*. Chicago: University of Chicago Press, 1987.

Green, Fletcher M. *Constitutional Development in the South Atlantic States, 1776–1860: A Study in the Evolution of Democracy*. Chapel Hill: University of North Carolina Press, 1930.

Greene, Jack P. "Origins of the American Revolution: A Constitutional Interpretation." *Framing and Ratification of the Constitution*. Leonard Levy and Dennis Mahony, eds. New York: Macmillan, 1987: 36–53.

"The Glorious Revolution and the British Empire, 1688–1783." *The Revolution of 1688–89: Changing Perspectives*. Lois Schwoerer, ed. Cambridge: Cambridge University Press, 1992: 260–71.

Grotius, Hugo. *De Jure Belli ac Pacis Libri Tres*. Vol. I, photographic reproduction of the edition of 1646, Amsterdam, and Vol. II, translation of the text by Francis Kelsey. Oxford: Clarendon Press, 1925.

Haakonssen, Knud. "Hugo Grotius and the History of Political Thought." *Political Theory*, vol. 13, no. 2 (May 1985): 239–65.

Haller, William and Godfrey Davis, eds. *The Leveller Tracts, 1647–1653*. New York: Columbia University Press, 1944.

Hamilton, Alexander, James Madison, and John Jay. *The Federalist Papers*. New York: Mentor, 1961.

Hamowy, Ronald. "Cato's Letters, John Locke, and the Republican Paradigm." *History of Political Thought*, vol. xi, no. 2 (Summer 1990): 274–94.

Hancock, Ralph. *Calvin and the Foundations of Modern Politics*. Ithaca: Cornell University Press, 1989.

Hansard, T. C. *The Parliamentary History of England, Volume XVI: 1765–1771*. London: Hansard, 1813.

Harrington, James. *The Commonwealth of Oceana*. J. G. A. Pocock, ed. Cambridge: Cambridge University Press, 1992.

Hartz, Louis. *The Liberal Tradition in America*. New York: Harcourt, Brace, 1955.

Hedges, William. "Telling off the King: Jefferson's *Summary View* as American Fantasy." *Early American Literature*, vol. 22, no. 3 (Fall 1987): 166–74.

Heylyn, Peter, "A Briefe and Moderate Answer" (1637). *The Struggle for Sovereignty: Seventeenth Century Political Tracts*. Joyce Lee Malcolm, ed. Indianapolis: Liberty Fund, 1999: 73–89.

Hobbes, Thomas. *Man and Citizen*. Bernard Gert, ed. Indianapolis: Hackett, 1991.

Leviathan. Edwin Curley, ed. Indianapolis: Hackett, 1994.

Hofstadter, Richard. *The American Political Tradition*. New York: Vintage, 1957.

Holmes, Geoffrey. "Harley, St. John and the Death of the Tory Party." *Britain after the Glorious Revolution*. Geoffrey Holmes, ed. New York: St. Martin's, 1969: 216–37.

Hont, Istvan. "The Language of Sociability and Commerce: Samuel Pufendorf and the Theoretical Foundations of the 'Four-Stages Theory'." *The Languages of Political Theory in Early-Modern Europe*. Anthony Pagden, ed. Cambridge: Cambridge University Press, 1987: 253–76.

Hooker, Richard. *Of the Laws of Ecclesiastical Polity* (1593). George Edelen, W. Speed Hill, and P. G. Stanwood, eds. Cambridge, MA: Harvard University Press, 1977–81.

Höpfl, Harro. *The Christian Polity of John Calvin*. Cambridge: Cambridge University Press, 1982.

Höpfl, Harro and Martyn P. Thompson. "The History of Contract as a Motif in Political Thought." *American Historical Review*, vol. 84, no. 4 (October 1979): 919–44.

Houston, Alan Craig. *Algernon Sidney and the Republican Heritage in England and America*. Princeton: Princeton University Press, 1991.

"Republicanism, the Politics of Necessity and the Rule of Law." *A Nation Transformed: England after the Restoration*. Alan Houston and Steve Pincus, eds. Cambridge: Cambridge University Press, 2001: 241–71.

Hume, David. *A Treatise of Human Nature*. L. A. Selby-Bigge, ed. Oxford: Clarendon Press, 1967.

Essays Moral, Political, and Literary. Eugene Miller, ed. Indianapolis: Liberty Fund, 1985.

Hunton, Philip. "A Treatise of Monarchie" (1643). *Divine Right and Democracy*. David Wootton, ed. Hammondsworth, Middlesex: Penguin Classics, 1986: 175–211.

Huyler, Jerome. *Locke in America*. Lawrence: University Press of Kansas, 1995.

Israel, Jonathan I. *The Dutch Republic: Its Rise, Greatness and Fall, 1477–1806*. Oxford: Clarendon Press, 1998.

"William III, the Glorious Revolution and the Development of Parliamentary Democracy in Britain." *Foundations of Democracy in the European Union: From the Genesis of Parliamentary Democracy to the European Parliament.* John Pinder, ed. New York: St. Martin's, 1999: 33–40.

Radical Enlightenment: Philosophy and the Making of Modernity, 1650–1750. Oxford: Oxford University Press, 2001.

Jaffa, Harry V. *A New Birth of Freedom: Abraham Lincoln and the Coming of the Civil War.* Lanham, MD: Rowman & Littlefield. 2000.

James I, King of England (James VI of Scotland). "Trew Law of a Free Monarchie." *Divine Right and Democracy.* David Wootton, ed. Hammondsworth, Middlesex: Penguin Classics, 1986.

Jefferson, Thomas. "Autobiography" (6 January 1821). *The Writings of Thomas Jefferson,* 10 vols., Paul Leicester Ford, ed. New York: G. P. Putnam's Sons, 1892–99.

"Summary View of the Rights of British America." *Thomas Jefferson Writings.* Merrill Peterson, ed. New York: Viking Press, 1984.

"Notes on the State of Virginia." *Thomas Jefferson Writings.* Merrill Peterson, ed. New York: Viking Press, 1984.

"From the Minutes of the Board of Visitors, University of Virginia," March 4, 1825. *Thomas Jefferson Writings.* New York: Viking Press, 1984.

Notes on the State of Virginia. New York: Penguin, 1999.

Jezierski, John V. "Parliament or People: James Wilson and William Blackstone on the Nature and Location of Sovereignty." *Journal of the History of Ideas,* vol. 32, no. 1 (January–March 1971): 95–106.

Jones, J. R. *The First Whigs: The Politics of the Exclusion Crisis, 1678–1683.* London: Oxford University Press, 1961.

The Revolution of 1688 in England. New York: Norton, 1973.

Josephson, Peter. *The Great Art of Government: Locke's Use of Consent.* Lawrence: University Press of Kansas, 2002.

Karsten, Peter. *Patriot Heroes in England and America.* Madison: University of Wisconsin Press, 1978.

Kendall, R. T. *Calvin and English Calvinism to 1649.* Oxford: Oxford University Press, 1979.

Kendall, Willmore. *John Locke and the Doctrine of Majority Rule.* Urbana: University of Illinois Press, 1965.

Kenyon, J. P. *The Stuart Constitution, 1603–1688.* Cambridge: Cambridge University Press, 1966.

The Popish Plot. New York: St. Martin's, 1972.

Revolution Principles: The Politics of Party 1689–1720. Cambridge: Cambridge University Press, 1977.

Kingdon, Robert. *Geneva and the Consolidation of the French Protestant Movement, 1564–1572.* Geneva: Librairie Droz, 1967.

"Calvinism and Resistance Theory, 1550–1580." *The Cambridge History of Political Thought, 1450–1700.* J. H. Burns and Mark Goldie, eds. Cambridge: Cambridge University Press, 1991: 194–218.

Kishlansky, Mark. *A Monarchy Transformed.* London: Oxford University Press, 1996.

Knollenberg, Bernard. *Origin of the American Revolution, 1759–1766.* New York: Macmillan, 1960.

Kramnick, Isaac. *Bolingbroke and His Circle: The Politics of Nostalgia in the Age of Walpole.* Cambridge, MA: Harvard University Press, 1968.

Republicanism and Bourgeois Radicalism. Ithaca: Cornell University Press, 1990.

Krieger, Leonard. *The Politics of Discretion: Pufendorf and the Acceptance of Natural Law.* Chicago: University of Chicago Press, 1965.

Lamont, William. "Arminianism: The Controversy That Never Was." *Political Discourse in Early Modern Britain.* Phillip Nicholson and Quentin Skinner, eds. Cambridge: Cambridge University Press, 1993: 45–66.

Lerner, Ralph. *The Thinking Revolutionary.* Ithaca: Cornell University Press, 1987.

Lewis, Anthony. "Jefferson's *Summary View* as Chart of Political Union." *William and Mary Quarterly,* vol. 5, no. 1 (January 1948): 34–51.

Lincoln, Abraham. "The Perpetuation of Our Political Institutions: Address Before the Young Men's Lyceum of Springfield, Illinois, January 27, 1838," in *Abraham Lincoln: His Speeches and Writings.* Roy Basler, ed. New York: Da Capo, 1990: 76–85.

Locke, John. *The Correspondence of John Locke and Edward Clarke.* Benjamin Rand, ed. Cambridge: Cambridge University Press, 1927.

Two Treatises of Government (1690). Peter Laslett, ed. Cambridge: Cambridge University Press, 1988.

"Fundamental Constitutions of Carolina." *Political Essays.* Mark Goldie, ed. Cambridge: Cambridge University Press, 1997.

Luther, Martin. *The Works of Martin Luther.* 6 vols. H. E. Jacobs, ed. Philadelphia: Muhlenberg Press, 1915–32.

Selections from His Writings. John Dillenberger, ed. Garden City, NY: Doubleday, 1961.

Lutz, Donald S. *Popular Control and Popular Consent: Whig Political Theory in the Early State Constitutions.* Baton Rouge: Louisiana State University Press, 1980.

"The Relative Influence of European Writers on Late-Eighteenth Century American Thought." *American Political Science Review,* vol. 78, no. 2 (March 1984): 189–97.

The Origins of American Constitutionalism. Baton Rouge: Louisiana State University Press, 1988.

Macaulay, Thomas Babbington. *The History of England from the Accession of James the Second.* London: G. P. Putnam's Sons, 1898.

Machiavelli, Niccolo. *The Prince.* Harvey C. Mansfield, trans. Chicago: University of Chicago Press, 1985.

Discourses on Livy. Harvey C. Mansfield and Nathan Tarcov, trans. Chicago: University of Chicago Press, 1996.

MacPherson, C. B. *The Political Theory of Possessive Individualism.* Oxford: Oxford University Press, 1962.

Madison, James. *Federalist Papers.* New York: Mentor, 1961.

Maier, Pauline. *From Resistance to Revolution: Colonial Radicals and the Development of American Opposition to Britain, 1765–1776.* New York: Alfred A. Knopf, 1972.

Makus, Ingrid. *Women, Politics, and Reproduction.* Toronto: University of Toronto Press, 1996.

Malcolm, Joyce Lee. "The Right of the People to Keep and Bear Arms: The Common Law Tradition." *Gun Control and the Constitution.* Robert J. Cottrol, ed. New York: Garland, 1994: 227–56.

To Keep and Bear Arms: The Origins of an Anglo-American Right. Cambridge, MA: Harvard University Press, 1994.

Manent, Pierre. *An Intellectual History of Liberalism.* Rebecca Balinski, trans. Princeton: Princeton University Press, 1994.

Mansfield, Harvey C. *Statesmanship and Party Government: A Study of Burke and Bolingbroke.* Chicago: University of Chicago Press, 1965.

New Modes and Orders: A Study of the Discourses on Livy. Ithaca: Cornell University Press, 1979.

"On the Political Character of Property in Locke." *Powers, Possessions, and Freedoms: Essays in Honour of C. B. MacPherson.* Alkis Kontos, ed. Toronto: University of Toronto Press, 1979: 23–38.

Taming the Prince: The Ambivalence of Modern Executive Power. New York: Free Press, 1989.

Machiavelli's Virtue. Chicago: University of Chicago Press, 1996.

Marshall, John. *John Locke: Resistance, Religion, and Responsibility.* Cambridge: Cambridge University Press, 1994.

Matthews, Richard. *The Radical Politics of Thomas Jefferson: A Revisionist View.* Lawrence: University Press of Kansas, 1984.

Mayer, David. "The English Radical Whig Origins of American Constitutionalism." *Washington University Law Quarterly,* vol. 70 (1992): 131–208.

The Constitutional Thought of Thomas Jefferson. Charlottesville: University of Virginia Press, 1994.

Maynwaring, Roger. "Religion and Allegiance" (1627). *The Struggle for Sovereignty: Seventeenth Century English Political Tracts.* Joyce Lee Malcolm, ed. Indianapolis: Liberty Fund, 1999: 53–71.

McClure, Kirstie M. *Judging Rights: Lockean Politics and the Limits of Consent.* Ithaca, NY: Cornell University Press, 1996.

McDonald, Forrest. *Novus Ordo Seclorum.* Lawrence: University Press of Kansas, 1985.

Introduction to *Empire and Nation,* William E. Leuchtenberg and Bernard Wishy, eds. Englewood Cliffs, NJ: Prentice Hall, 1962: i–xvi.

McWilliams, Wilson Carey. "On Equality as the Moral Foundation for Community." *The Moral Foundations of the American Republic.* Robert Horwitz, ed. Charlottesville: University of Virginia Press, 1987: 282–312.

Mendle, Michael. *Dangerous Positions: Mixed Government, the Estates of the Realm, and the Making of the Answer to the XIX Propositions.* University, AL: University of Alabama Press, 1985.

"Parliamentary Sovereignty: A Very English Absolutism." *Political Discourse in Early Modern Britain.* Nicholas Phillipson and Quentin Skinner, eds. Cambridge: Cambridge University Press, 1993: 97–119.

Henry Parker and the English Civil War. Cambridge: Cambridge University Press, 1995.

Michels, Roberto. *Political Parties: A Sociological Study of the Oligarchical Tendencies of Modern Democracy.* Eden Paul and Cedar Paul, trans. New York: Free Press, 1958.

Mill, John Stuart. *On Liberty.* New York: Penguin, 1985 [1859].

Miller, David. *Philosophy and Ideology in Hume's Political Thought.* Oxford: Clarendon Press, 1981.

Miller, John. "The Glorious Revolution: 'Contract' and 'Abdication' Reconsidered." *The Historical Journal,* vol. 25, no. 3 (September 1982): 541–55.

Milton, John. *Paradise Lost*. Christoper Ricks, ed. New York: Signet Classics, 1968.
  Areopagitica and Other Political Writings of John Milton. John Alvis, ed. Indianapolis:
  Liberty Fund Press, 1999.
Montesquieu, Charles Secondat, Baron. *The Spirit of the Laws* (1748). Anne M.
  Cohler, Basia Carolyn Milller, and Harold Summel Stone, trans. and eds.
  Cambridge: Cambridge University Press, 1989.
Morgan, Edmund S. and Helen M. Morgan. *The Stamp Act Crisis: Prologue to Revo-
  lution*. Chapel Hill: University of North Carolina Press, 1953.
Myers, Peter. "Equality, Property, and the Problem of Partisanship: Lockean Consti-
  tution as Mixed Regime." *Interpretation*, vol. 22, no. 1 (Fall 1994): 39–64.
Namier, Lewis. *England in the Age of the American Revolution*. London: Macmillan,
  1930.
Nelson, Scott. *The Discourses of Algernon Sidney*. Cranbury, NJ: Associated University
  Presses, 1993.
Nenner, Howard. *The Right to Be King: The Succession to the Crown of England, 1603–
  1714*. Chapel Hill: University of North Carolina Press, 1995.
Nichols, Mary. *Citizens and Statesmen: A Commentary of Aristotle's Politics*. Savage,
  MD: Rowman & Littlefield, 1992.
Oakley, Francis. "Christian Obedience and Authority, 1520–1550." *The Cambridge
  History of Political Thought, 1450–1700*. J. H. Burns and Mark Goldie, eds.
  Cambridge: Cambridge University Press, 1991: 160–92.
  *The Politics of Eternity: Studies in the History of Medieval and Early-Modern Political
  Thought*. Leiden: Brill, 1999.
Orwin, Clifford. "On the Sovereign Authorization." *Political Theory*, vol. 3, no. 1
  (February 1975): 26–44.
Otis, James. "The Rights of the British Colonies Asserted and Proved" (1764).
  Pamphlets of the American Revolution, 1750–76. Bernard Bailyn, ed. Cambridge,
  MA: Harvard University Press, 1965: 419–70.
Overton, Richard. "An Arrow against All Tyrants." *The English Levellers*. Andrew
  Sharp, ed. Cambridge: Cambridge University Press, 1998: 54–72.
Paine, Tom. *Common Sense*. Mineola, NY: Dover Publications, 1997.
Pangle, Thomas. *Montesquieu's Philosophy of Liberalism*. Chicago: University of
  Chicago Press, 1973.
  The Spirit of Modern Republicanism. Chicago: University of Chicago Press, 1988.
Pangle, Thomas and Peter Ahrensdorf, *Justice Among Nations: On the Moral Basis of
  War and Peace*. Lawrence: University Press of Kansas, 1999.
Pares, Richard. *King George III and the Politicians*. Oxford: Clarendon Press, 1953.
Parker, Henry. "Observations upon some of his Majesties late Answers and Ex-
  presses" (London: 1642).
Parry, Geraint. "Locke on Representation in Politics." *History of European Ideas*,
  vol. 3, no. 4 (1982): 403–14.
Parson, Theophilus. "The Essex Result" (1778). *American Political Writings During
  the Founding Era: 1760–1805*. Charles S. Hyneman and Donald S. Lutz, eds.
  Indianapolis: Liberty Fund, 1983: 480–522.
Pateman, Carole. *The Sexual Contract: Aspects of Patriarchal Liberalism*. Stanford:
  Stanford University Press, 1988.
  "'God hath ordained Man a Helper': Hobbes, Patriarchy and Conjugal
  Right." *Feminist Interpretations in Political Theory*. Carole Pateman and Mary

Shanley, eds. University Park: University of Pennsylvania Press, 1991: 53–73.

Pease, Theodore Calvin. *The Leveller Movement.* Gloucester, MA: Peter Smith, 1965.

Peters, Ronald M. *The Massachusetts Constitution of 1780: A Social Compact.* Amherst: University of Massachusetts Press, 1978.

Phillipson, Nicholas. "Propriety, Property, and Prudence: David Hume and the Defence of the Revolution." *Political Discourse in Early Modern Britain.* Nicholas Phillipson and Quentin Skinner, eds. Cambridge: Cambridge University Press, 1991: 302–20.

Plato. *The Republic.* Allan Bloom, trans. New York: Basic Books, 1968.

Plumb, J. H. *Sir Robert Walpole: The Making of a Statesman.* Boston: Houghton Mifflin, 1956.

The Growth of Political Stability: England, 1675–1725. London: Macmillan, 1967.

Plutarch. *The Lives of the Noble Grecians and Romans.* John Dryden, trans. New York: Everyman, 1952.

Pocock, J. G. A. "Virtue and Commerce in the Eighteenth Century," *Journal of Interdisciplinary History,* vol. 3 (1972): 119–34.

The Machiavellian Moment: Florentine Political Thought and the Atlantic Republican Tradition. Princeton: Princeton University Press, 1975.

Virtue, Commerce, and History. Cambridge: Cambridge University Press, 1986.

The Ancient Constitution and the Feudal Law. Cambridge: Cambridge University Press, 1987.

"The Fourth English Civil War: Dissolution, Desertion, and Alternative Histories of the Glorious Revolution." *The Glorious Revolution: Changing Perspectives.* Lois Schwoerer, ed. Cambridge: Cambridge University Press, 1992: 52–64.

"England's Cato: The Virtues and Fortunes of Algernon Sidney." *Historical Journal,* vol. 37, no. 4 (December 1994): 915–35.

Pole, J. R. *Political Representation in England and the Origins of the American Republic.* New York: St. Martin's Press, 1966.

Polybius. *The Histories.* Evelyn Shuckburgh, trans. Lake Bluff, IL: Regnery Gateway, 1987.

Pufendorf, Samuel. *De Jure Naturae et Gentium Libri Octo.* Vol. I, photographic reproduction of the edition of 1688, Amsterdam, and Vol. II, translation of the text by C. H. and W. A. Oldfather. Oxford: Clarendon Press, 1934.

On the Duty of Man and Citizen. James Tully, ed. Cambridge: Cambridge University Press, 1991.

Rager, John Clement. *The Political Philosophy of the Blessed Cardinal Bellarmine.* Washington, DC: Catholic University of America Press, 1926.

Rahe, Paul. "John Locke's Philosophical Partisanship." *Political Science Reviewer,* vol. 20 (1991): 1–43.

Republics Ancient and Modern: Classical Republicanism and the American Revolution. Chapel Hill: University of North Carolina Press, 1992.

"The American Revolution." *The American Experiment: Essays on the Theory and Practice of Liberty.* Peter Augustine Lawler and Robert Martin Schaefer, eds. Lanham, MD: Rowman & Littlefield, 1994: 27–55.

"Situating Machiavelli." *Renaissance Civic Humanism.* James Hankins, ed. Cambridge: Cambridge University Press, 2000: 270–308.

"Forms of Government: Structure, Principle, Object, and Aim." *Montesquieu's Science of Politics: Essays on the Spirit of the Laws*. David W. Carrithers, Michael A. Mosher, and Paul A. Rahe, eds. Lanham, MD: Rowman & Littlefield, 2001: 69–108.

Reid, John Phillip. "The Irrelevance of the Declaration." *Law in the American Revolution and the Revolution in Law: A Collection of Review Essays in American Legal History*. Hendrik Hartog, ed. New York: New York University Press, 1981: 46–89.

Constitutional History of the American Revolution: The Authority of Rights. Madison: University of Wisconsin Press, 1986.

Constitutional History of the American Revolution: The Authority to Legislate. Madison: University of Wisconsin Press, 1991.

Robbins, Caroline. "Algernon Sidney's *Discourses Concerning Government*: Textbook of Revolution." *William and Mary Quarterly*, 3rd ser., vol. 4 (July 1947): 267–96.

The Eighteenth Century Commonwealthmen. New York: Atheneum, 1968.

Rosen, Stanley. "Benedict Spinoza." *The History of Political Philosophy*, 3rd ed. Leo Strauss and Joseph Cropsey, eds. Chicago: University of Chicago Press, 1987: 456–75.

Rossiter, Clinton. *Seedtime of the Republic*. New York: Harcourt, Brace, 1953.

Rousseau, Jean-Jacques. *Rousseau's Political Writings*. Alan Ritter and Julia Conaway Bondanella, eds. New York: Norton, 1988.

Rudolph, Julia. *Revolution by Degree: James Tyrrell and Whig Political Thought in the Late Seventeenth Century*. New York: Palgrave, 2002.

Samuelson, Richard. "The Constitutional Sanity of James Otis: Resistance Leader and Loyal Subject." *Review of Politics*, vol. 61, no. 3 (Summer 1999): 494–523.

Schaub, Diana. *Erotic Liberalism: Women and Revolution in Montesquieu's Persian Letters*. Lanham, MD: Rowman & Littlefield, 1995.

Schneewind, J. B. *The Invention of Autonomy: A History of Modern Moral Philosophy*. Cambridge: Cambridge University Press, 1998.

Schochet, Gordon. *Patriarchalism in Political Thought*. Oxford: Oxford University Press, 1975.

Schwoerer, Lois. *No Standing Armies! Anti-army Ideology in Seventeenth Century England*. Baltimore: Johns Hopkins University Press, 1974.

The Declaration of Rights, 1689. Baltimore: Johns Hopkins University Press, 1981.

"Locke, Lockean Ideas, and the Glorious Revolution." *Journal of the History of Ideas*, vol. 51, no. 4 (October–December 1990): 531–48.

Scott, Jonathan. *Algernon Sidney and the English Republic, 1623–1677*. Cambridge: Cambridge University Press, 1988.

Algernon Sidney and the Restoration Crisis, 1677–1683. Cambridge: Cambridge University Press, 1991.

England's Troubles: Seventeenth-Century English Political Instability in European Context. Cambridge: Cambridge University Press, 2000.

Seliger, Martin. *The Liberal Politics of John Locke*. New York: Praeger, 1969.

Shalhope, Robert. "Towards a Republican Synthesis." *William and Mary Quarterly*, vol. 29 (January 1972): 49–80.

Shanley, Mary. "Marriage Contract and Social Contract in Seventeenth Century England." *Western Political Quarterly*, vol. 32, no. 1 (March 1979): 79–91.

Shapiro, Ian. *The Evolution of Rights Theories*. Cambridge: Cambridge University Press, 1986.

Sidney, Algernon. *The Discourses Concerning Government*. Thomas West, ed. Indianapolis: Liberty Fund Classics, 1996.

    Court Maxims. Hans Blom, Eco Haitsma Molier, and Donald Janse, eds. Cambridge: Cambridge University Press, 1996.

Simmons, John. "Inalienable Rights and Locke's *Treatises*," *Philosophy and Public Affairs*, vol. 12 (1983): 175–204.

Simmons, John. *The Lockean Theory of Rights*. Princeton: Princeton University Press, 1992.

    On the Edge of Anarchy: Locke, Consent, and the Limits of Society. Princeton: Princeton University Press, 1993.

Skinner, Quentin. "The Ideological Context of Hobbes' Political Thought." *Historical Journal*, vol. 9 (1966): 286–317.

    The Foundations of Modern Political Thought, Volume II. Cambridge: Cambridge University Press, 1978.

    "Machiavelli's Discorsi and the Pre-Humanist Origin of Republican Ideas." *Machiavelli and Republicanism*. Gisela Bock, Quentin Skinner, and Maurizio Viroli, eds. Cambridge: Cambridge University Press, 1990: 121–41.

    "Machiavelli." *Great Political Thinkers*. Oxford: Oxford University Press, 1992.

    Liberty before Liberalism. Cambridge: Cambridge University Press, 1998.

Slaughter, T. P. "'Abdicate' and 'Contract' in the Glorious Revolution." *Historical Journal*, vol. 24 (1981): 323–37.

Smith, Steven. *Spinoza, Liberalism, and the Question of Jewish Identity*. New Haven: Yale University Press, 1997.

Somerville, J. P. "From Suarez to Filmer: A Reappraisal." *The Historical Journal*, vol. 25, no. 3 (1982): 525–40.

    "John Selden, the Law of Nature, and the Origins of Government." *Historical Journal*, vol. 27, no. 2 (June 1984): 437–47.

    Politics and Ideology in England, 1603–1640. London: Longman, 1986.

Speck, W. A. *Stability and Strife: England 1714–1760*. London: Edward Arnold, 1977.

    The Reluctant Revolutionaries: Englishmen and the Revolution of 1688. Oxford: Oxford University Press, 1988.

Spinoza, Benedict. *A Theologico-Political Treatise and A Political Treatise*, R. H. M. Elwes, trans. New York: Dover Books, 1951.

    Ethics. Edwin Curley, trans. Amherst: Prometheus, Books, 1989.

Stoner, James. *Common Law and Liberal Theory: Coke, Hobbes, and the Origins of American Constitutionalism*. Lawrence: University Press of Kansas, 1992.

    "Sound Whigs or Honeyed Tories? Jefferson and the Common Law Tradition." *Reason and Republicanism: Thomas Jefferson's Legacy of Liberty*. Gary L. McDowell and Sharon L. Noble, eds. Lanham, MD: Rowman & Littlefield, 1997: 103–17.

Storing, Herbert. "William Blackstone." *The History of Political Philosophy*, 3rd ed. Leo Strauss and Joseph Cropsey, eds. Chicago: University of Chicago Press, 1987: 622–34.

Stourz, Gerald. "William Blackstone: Teacher of Revolution." *Jährbuch für Amerikastüdien*, vol. 15 (1970): 184–200.

Straka, Gerald. *The Anglican Reaction to the Revolution of 1688.* Madison: State Historical Society of Wisconsin, 1962.

Strauss, Leo. *Natural Right and History.* Chicago: University of Chicago Press, 1953.

Thoughts on Machiavelli. Glencoe, IL: Free Press, 1958.

Spinoza's Critique of Religion. New York: Schocken Books, 1965.

"German Nihilism." *Interpretation,* vol. 26, no. 3 (Spring 1999): 353–78.

Suarez, Francisco. *Selections from Three Works of Francisco Suarez, S. J.* Volume I, photographic reproduction of original editions, and Volume II, English version of the text prepared by Gwladys L. Williams, Ammi Brown, and John Waldron. Oxford: Clarendon Press, 1944.

Extracts on Politics and Government. George Moore, trans. Chevy Chase, MD: Country Dollar Press, 1950.

Sullivan, Vickie B. *Machiavelli's Three Romes: Religion, Human Liberty, and Politics Reformed.* DeKalb: Northern Illinois University Press, 1996.

"Muted and Manifest English Machiavellianism: The Reconciliation of Machiavellian Republicanism with Liberalism in Sidney's *Discourses Concerning Government* and Trenchard and Gordon's *Cato's Letters.*" To appear in *Machiavelli's Republican Legacy.* Paul Rahe, ed. Lanham, MD: Rowman and Littlefield.

Tarcov, Nathan. "Locke's Second Treatise and the 'Best Fence Against Rebellion'." *Review of Politics,* vol. 43 (April 1981): 198–217.

Locke's Education for Liberty. Chicago: University of Chicago Press, 1984.

Tarlton, Charles D. "The Exclusion Controversy, Pamphleteering, and Locke's Two Treatises." *The Historical Journal,* vol. 24, no. 1 (March 1981): 49–68.

Thomas, P. D. G. *British Politics and the Stamp Act Crisis: The First Phase of the American Revolution, 1763–67.* Oxford: Clarendon Press, 1975.

Thompson, Bradley C. *John Adams and the Spirit of Liberty.* Lawrence: University Press of Kansas, 1998.

Thompson, Cargill W. D. J. *The Political Thought of Martin Luther.* Brighton, MA: Harvester, 1984.

Thompson, Martyn P. "The Reception of Locke's Two Treatises of Government, 1690–1705." *Political Studies,* vol. 24, no. 2 (1976): 184–91.

"The Idea of Conquest in Controversies over the 1688 Revolution." *Journal of the History of Ideas,* vol. 38, no. 1 (January–March 1977): 33–46.

Ideas of Contract in English Political Thought in the Age of John Locke. New York: Garland 1987.

Thorpe, Francis Newton, ed. *The Federal and State Constitutions, Colonial Charters and Other Organic Laws of the States and Territories Now or Heretofore Forming the United States of America.* Washington, DC: U.S. Government Publishing Office, 1909.

Tierney, Brian. *The Idea of Natural Rights: Studies on Natural Rights, Natural Law, and Church Law, 1150–1625.* Grand Rapids, MI: William B. Eerdmans, 1997.

Tocqueville, Alexis de. *Democracy in America.* George Lawrence, trans. New York: Harper, 1966 [1850].

Trenchard, John. *An Argument Shewing That a Standing Army Is Inconsistent with a Free Government.* London, 1697.

Trenchard, John and Robert Gordon. *Cato's Letters.* Ronald Hamowy, ed. Indianapolis: Liberty Classics, 1995.

Tuck, Richard. *Natural Rights Theories*. Cambridge: Cambridge University Press, 1979.

"Grotius, Carneades, and Hobbes." *Grotiana*, vol. 4 (1983): 43–62.

"Grotius and Selden." *Cambridge History of Political Thought, 1450–1700*. J. H. Burns and Mark Goldie, eds. Cambridge: Cambridge University Press, 1991: 499–529.

Philosophy and Government, 1572–1651. Cambridge: Cambridge University Press, 1993.

Tully, James. *A Discourse on Property: Locke and His Adversaries*. Cambridge: Cambridge University Press, 1980.

An Approach to Political Philosophy: Locke in Contexts. Cambridge: Cambridge University Press, 1993.

Tyrrell, James. *Patriarcha, Non Monarcha* (London: Richard Janeway, 1681).

Bibliotheca Politica (London: R. Baldwin, 1718).

Vile, M. J. C. *Constitutionalism and the Separation of Powers*, 2nd ed. Indianapolis: Liberty Fund, 1998.

Waldron, Jeremy. *The Right to Private Property*. Oxford: Oxford University Press, 1988.

Walsh, Mary. "Locke and Feminism on Private and Public Realms of Activities." *Review of Politics*, vol. 57, no. 2 (Spring 1995): 251–77.

Walzer, Michael. *The Revolution of the Saints: A Study in the Origin of Modern Radical Politics*. Cambridge, MA: Harvard University Press, 1965.

Ward, Lee. "The Natural Rights Family: Locke on Women, Nature, and the Problem of Patriarchy." *Nature, Woman, and the Art of Politics*. Eduardo Velasquez, ed. Lanham, MD: Rowman & Littlefield, 2000: 149–79.

"Rhetoric and Natural Rights in Algernon Sidney's *Discourses Concerning Government*." *Interpretation*, vol. 28, no. 2 (Winter 2000–1): 119–45.

Weber, Max. *The Protestant Ethic and the Spirit of Capitalism*. Talcott Parsons, trans. New York: Vintage, 1958.

Webking, Robert. *The American Revolution and the Politics of Liberty*. Baton Rouge: Louisiana State University Press, 1988.

Weil, Rachel. "The Family in the Exclusion Crisis: Locke versus Filmer Revisited." *A Nation Transformed: England after the Restoration*. Alan Houston and Steve Pincus, eds. Cambridge: Cambridge University Press, 2001: 100–24.

West, Thomas. "Introduction" to *The Discourses Concerning Government*. Indianapolis: Liberty Fund Press: xv–xxxvi.

Western, J. R. *Monarchy and Revolution: The English State in the 1680's*. Totowa, NJ: Rowman & Littlefield, 1972.

Weston, Corinne. "Theory of Mixed Monarchy Under Charles I and After." *English Historical Review*, vol. 75 (July 1960): 426–43.

"England: Ancient Constitution and Common Law." *Cambridge History of Political Thought, 1450–1700*. J. H. Burns and Mark Goldie, eds. Cambridge: Cambridge University Press, 1991: 375–411.

Wilenius, Reijo. *The Social and Political Theory of Francisco Suarez*. Helsinki: Suomalaisen Kirjallisuvden Kirjapaino, 1963.

Wilson, Douglas. "Jefferson and the Republic of Letters." *Jeffersonian Legacies*. Peter Onuf, ed. Charlottesville: University of Virginia Press, 1993: 50–76.

Wilson, James. "Considerations on the Nature and Extent of the Legislative Authority of the British Parliament" (1774). *Selected Political Essays of James Wilson.* Randolph G. Adams, ed. New York: Knopf, 1930: 42–108.

"Of Municipal Law." *American Political Writing during the Founding Era: 1760–1805, Volume II.* Charles S. Hyneman and Donald S. Lutz, eds. Indianapolis: Liberty Classics, 1983: 1264–98.

Wolin, Sheldon. *Politics and Vision: Continuity and Innovation in Western Political Thought.* London: Methuen, 1969.

Wood, Ellen Meiskins. "Locke against Democracy: Consent, Representation and Suffrage in the *Two Treatises.*" *History of Political Thought*, vol. 13, no. 4 (Winter 1992): 657–89.

Wood, Gordon. *The Creation of the American Republic, 1776–1787.* Chapel Hill: University of North Carolina Press, 1969.

"The Democratization of Mind in the American Revolution." *The Moral Foundations of the American Republic*, 3rd. Robert Horwitz, ed. Charlottesville: University of Virginia Press, 1987: 109–35.

Wood, Neal. "The Value of Asocial Sociability: Contributions of Machiavelli, Sidney and Montesquieu." *Machiavelli and the Nature of Political Thought.* Martin Fleisher, ed. New York: Atheneum, 1972: 282–307.

John Locke and Agrarian Capitalism. Berkeley: University of California Press, 1984.

Woolrych, Austin. *Britain in Revolution, 1625–1660.* Oxford: Oxford University Press, 2002.

Wootton, David. "Leveller Democracy and the Puritan Revolution." *The Cambridge History of Political Thought, 1450–1700.* J. H. Burns and Mark Goldie, eds. Cambridge: Cambridge University Press, 1991: 412–42.

Worden, Blair. "The Commonwealth Kidney of Algernon Sidney." *Journal of British Studies.* vol. 24, no. 1 (January 1985): 1–40.

"Marchmount Nedham and the Beginnings of English Republicanism, 1649–1656," *Republicanism, Liberty, and Commercial Society, 1649–1776.* David Wootton, ed. Stanford: Stanford University Press, 1994: 45–81.

"Republicanism and the Restoration, 1660–1683." *Republicanism, Liberty, and Commercial Society, 1649–1776.* David Wootton, ed. Stanford: Stanford University Press, 1994: 139–93.

Roundhead Reputations: The English Civil Wars and the Passions of Posterity. London: Penguin Press, 2001.

Yarborough, Jean. "Thomas Jefferson and Republicanism." *Thomas Jefferson and the Politics of Nature.* Thomas Engeman, ed. Notre Dame, IN: University of Notre Dame Press, 2000: 59–80.

Zagorin, Perez. *A History of Political Thought in the English Revolution.* London: Routledge & Kegan Paul, 1954.

"Hobbes without Grotius." *History of Political Thought*, vol. 21, no. 1 (Spring 2000): 16–40.

Zucker, Ross. "Unequal Property and Its Premise in Liberal Theory." *History of Philosophy Quarterly*, vol. 17, no. 1 (January 2000): 29–49.

Zuckert, Michael P. "Fools and Knaves: Reflections on Locke's Theory of Philosophical Discourse." *Review of Politics*, vol. 36 (1974): 544–64.

"Of Wary Physicians and Weary Readers: The Debate on Locke's Way of Writing." *Independent Journal of Philosophy*, vol. 2 (Fall 1977): 55–66.

"An Introduction to Locke's First Treatise." *Interpretation*, vol. 8 (1979): 58–74.

Natural Rights and the New Republicanism. Princeton: Princeton University Press, 1994.

The Natural Rights Republic. Notre Dame, IN: University of Notre Dame Press, 1996.

Zvesper, John. "Hobbes' Individualistic Analysis of the Family." *Politics*, vol. 5 (October 1985): 28–33.

"Jefferson on Liberal Natural Rights." *Reason and Republicanism.* Gary McDowell and Sharon Noble, eds. Lanham, MD: Rowman & Littlefield, 1997: 15–30.

Index

Abraham, 158
absolutism, 8, 12, 19, 28, 34, 49, 52, 61,
    70, 72, 95, 100, 103, 111, 143,
    166, 172, 186, 234, 248, 267,
    317, 387, 417
Acton, Lord Emerich Edward Dahlberg,
    346
Adam, 25, 27, 31, 32, 36, 44, 49, 64,
    81, 82, 86, 113, 127, 157, 215–18,
    222, 227, 241
Adams, John, 332, 333, 346, 355, 397,
    399, 407, 409–10, 411, 413, 419,
    423
    critic of Paine, 386, 410
Alexander I, Tsar, 232
Allegiance Oath Controversy, 23, 134
Allen, W.J., 49, 55
American Revolution, 13, 16, 323, 427,
    428
ancient constitutionalism, 48, 49, 59,
    60, 62, 70, 97, 255, 320, 408
Anglican Church, 195, 203, 204, 219,
    272, 273, 278, 284, 286
Anne, Queen of England, 287, 305
anti-Catholicism, 20–1, 101–2, 271,
    272, 276, 284, 325
anti-federalists, 428, 429
Appleby, Joyce, 5
Aquinas, St. Thomas, 50, 238
Arendt, Hannah, 3, 354
Aristotle, 9, 35, 38–40, 58, 68, 77, 92,
    95, 97, 124, 138, 161, 162, 163,
    164, 168, 169, 189, 206,
    255
Articles of Confederation, 419
Ashcraft, Richard, 8, 130, 259
Athens, 147
Atwood, William, 14, 266, 278,
    279–80, 281, 287, 294, 321, 326,
    388
Augustine, St., 26, 29
Augustus, 179

Bacon, Sir Francis, 73
Bailyn, Bernard, 3–4, 376
balanced constitutionalism, 307, 308,
    309–10, 311, 313, 315, 316, 317,
    333, 372, 385, 399, 407, 408, 410
Banning, Lance, 7, 9
Barbeyrac, Jean, 74
Barclay, William, 23, 267–8
Barré, Isaac, 329
Becker, Carl, 2
Bellarmine, Roberto, 22, 33, 34, 35–6,
    37, 54, 62, 63, 75, 123, 124, 159,
    160, 161, 163, 173, 214, 215,
    217, 220
    on consent, 24, 34, 36
Beza, Theodore, 55, 56
Bill of Rights (1689), 277, 318
Blackstone, Sir William, 16, 197, 305,
    319, 323, 326, 327, 330, 427, 430
    on checks and balances, 320
    critic of Locke, 321, 363

Blackstone, Sir William (*cont.*)
  on parliamentary sovereignty,
    321–3, 344, 415, 421
Bodin, Jean, 22, 34, 61, 83, 111, 186
Bolingbroke, Henry St. John,
    1st Viscount of, 16, 285, 287,
    310–13, 314, 333, 430
Bonaparte, Napoleon, 232
Bonwick, Colin, 327, 376
Boston Tea Party (1773), 362
Brady, Robert, 95, 113, 279
Braxton, Carter, 408–9, 410, 415,
    420
Brett, Annabel, 42
British Constitution, 305, 312, 314, 317,
    318, 320, 327, 332, 338, 348, 354,
    368, 376, 384, 406, 408, 428
British Empire, 339, 340, 341, 352, 427
British radicals, 376
Buchanan, George, 57
Burgh, James, 3, 5
Burke, Edmund, 17, 330, 426, 427, 430
Burnet, Gilbert, 14, 153, 278–9, 281,
    287, 321, 326, 388
Bute, Lord, 313

Cain, 229
Calvin, Jean, 52–4, 57
Calvinism, 21, 50, 51, 74, 76, 79, 85,
    95, 98, 160, 189, 291, 426
Camden, Lord, 330
Canada, 260
Carneades, 74
Catholicism, 95, 98, 102, 110, 117, 123,
    160, 228, 272, 291, 426
Caton, Hiram, 52
Cato's Letters, 3, 312, 327, 333, 338, 376,
    379
  criticism of influence, 296–7
  impact in America, 3, 5, 17, 289,
    304, 428
  and liberal natural rights, 290–2,
    335, 382
  on property, 292–3, 301
  republicanism of, 290, 296,
    298–300, 303, 306, 310, 377, 386
  right of resistance, 293–5
  and virtue, 300–1, 383

Charles I, King of England, 20, 48, 51,
    57, 59, 96, 102, 140, 148, 153
Charles II, King of England, 99, 100,
    102, 103, 133, 135, 153, 155, 267,
    272, 286, 367, 373
Charron, Pierre, 73
Churchill, John (Duke of
    Marlborough), 285
Churchill, Sir Winston, 180
Cicero, 38, 81, 127
civic humanism, 1, 3–4, 5
civic republicanism, *see* civic humanism
civic virtue, 3, 5, 317
Cleves, Duchy of, 210
Coercive Acts, 351, 362, 364–5, 403
Coke, Sir Edward, 332
Colbourn, H. Trevor, 141
committees of correspondence, 331
common law, 204
Common Sense, 375, 377, 391, 394, 398
    (*see also* Paine, Tom)
Conrad, Stephen, 356, 364
consent, 420–2, 424, 425, 429
Contarini, Gasparo, 34
continental army, 375
convention parliament, 271, 274–8,
    279, 280, 281, 322, 338, 420
corruption, *see* influence
country party, 282, 285, 296, 307,
    308–10, 312, 314, 402, 407, 408,
    409, 412
court party, 307, 308–10, 311, 313, 314
Cromwell, Oliver, 71, 106, 153, 207
Cyrus, 170, 174

Daly, James, 34, 49, 73
Danby, Earl of, 102, 155, 210
Dawidoff, Robert, 371
de la Court, Jean and Pieter, 193
Declaratory Act (1766), 329, 330, 344,
    345, 347, 372
Declaration of Independence, 396–8, 401,
    404, 405, 410, 420
Declaration of Rights (1689), 276, 277,
    295, 338, 367, 384, 397, 400, 401,
    402, 403, 406
Defoe, Daniel, 284
Delamere, Lord, 281

Delaware, Constitution of 1776, 404, 418
democracy, naturalness of, 184, 196, 381, 385, 408
Demophilus (George Bryan), 407–8, 409, 410, 411, 414, 415, 420
Denmark, 45, 69, 152, 153
DeWitt, Jan, 194, 201
Dickinson, H.T., 104, 312
Dickinson, John, 17, 326, 331, 344, 346–7, 351, 352, 357, 359, 363, 370, 373, 376, 384, 391, 396, 415, 418
  and natural rights, 347–8
  and parliamentary sovereignty, 348–50
Diggins, John Patrick, 5, 6
divided sovereignty, 400, 418–20, 424, 425, 428
Dunn, John, 4
Dworetz, Steven, 5

Edward VI, King of England, 136
Edwards, Charles, 76
Elizabeth I, Queen of England, 61
England, Church of, *see* Anglican Church
English Civil War, 48, 71, 133, 152, 373, 398, 415
Essex, Earl of, 107, 155
Essex Result, 412
Euclid, 161
Eve, 216, 217, 222, 238
Exclusion Crisis, 7–9, 100, 101–4, 113, 136, 155, 191, 211, 270, 271–2, 273, 293, 305, 323, 325, 367, 426

Falkland Islands, 392
federalism, 342, 352, 419, 425, 428, 429
Federalist Papers, 138, 297
Ferne, Henry, 61, 64, 80
feudalism, 185, 317, 318, 358, 385, 389
Figgis, J.N., 28
Filmer, Sir Robert, 19–22, 97, 102, 113, 123, 139, 156, 186, 206, 220, 227, 284, 314, 334
  and absolute sovereignty, 61, 65, 66–7, 69, 105, 312, 426
  attack on classical republics, 39–40
  critique of consent, 46–7, 93, 120
  on divine providence, 44–5, 78, 82, 88–9, 124, 215
  and divine right monarchy, 8, 11, 19, 78, 148, 193, 202, 306, 307, 310, 426
  doctrine of obedience in, 30–1, 44, 53, 64, 79, 94
  patriarchalism of, 26–8, 32, 38, 40, 86–7, 120, 217
  rejection of natural liberty, 11–12, 43, 45, 46, 47
  scripturalism of, 22, 28, 33, 38, 58, 81, 87, 91, 223, 426
Finch, Sir John, 59
Fletcher, Andrew, 284
Foley, Paul, 285
Foner, Eric, 378
France, 100, 136, 152, 154, 210, 273, 284, 317, 327, 332, 356, 367, 387
franchise, 310, 376, 403, 406, 410, 411, 425, 429
Franklin, Benjamin, 330, 331
Franklin, Julian, 262, 266
French Revolution, 426, 430
Furly, Benjamin, 194, 211

George I, King of England, 287, 306
George III, King of England, 313, 366, 370, 397
Georgia, Constitution of 1777, 407, 413, 414
Germany, 55, 362
Glorious Revolution, 13, 16, 17, 113, 214, 270, 271–4, 283, 286, 288, 295, 300, 303, 305, 306, 308, 320, 323, 325, 327, 328, 332, 335, 338, 348, 354, 356, 357, 361, 371, 373, 384, 389, 399, 412, 427, 428
Goldie, Mark, 85, 282
Goldsworthy, Jeffrey, 322
Goodwin, William, 32
Gordon, Thomas, 288, 326 (*see also Cato's Letters*)

gothic constitution, 171, 185
Greene, Jack, 338
Grenville, Lord, 313, 328, 329
Grotius, Hugo, 11, 12, 71, 91, 110, 124,
    126, 136, 166, 187, 214, 215,
    217, 220, 227, 237, 267, 283,
    340, 428
  contractualism of, 75, 77, 79, 80, 82,
    84, 95, 111, 227, 251, 334, 335
  law of nations in, 77
  on natural law, 71, 73, 74–5, 90,
    145, 266
  on natural rights, 75–7, 238, 290,
    427
  on property, 77, 80–1, 127, 174,
    216, 220–1, 246
  and resistance, 79, 80, 188
  secularism of, 73–4
  on sovereignty, 82–5, 111, 135, 267

Haakonsen, Knud, 77
Habeas Corpus Act (1679), 319
Hale, Sir Matthew, 61
Hampden, John, 107, 155, 300
Hannibal, 179
Hanover, House of, 287, 305, 306, 310,
    328, 367
Harley, Robert (Earl of Oxford), 284,
    285, 288, 314
Harrington, James, 3, 4, 302
Hartz, Louis, 2
Hayward, John, 23
Henry V, King of England, 206
Henry VIII, King of England, 136
Henry, Patrick, 329, 351, 398
Heylyn, Peter, 33, 195
Hoadly, Bishop, 282, 314
Hobbes, Thomas, 12, 22, 61, 71, 85,
    108, 118, 126, 139, 147, 163,
    172, 173, 174–6, 180, 182, 186,
    187, 190, 196, 215, 220, 229,
    230, 234, 237, 239, 267
  contractualism of, 90, 92, 93
  on the family, 86–7, 88, 91
  on law, 97–8
  natural law in, 71, 89–90, 110
  natural rights in, 85–6, 87, 93, 145,
    181, 193, 231, 426

on sovereignty, 91, 92, 93, 94–7,
    111, 181, 194, 196, 234, 239,
    248, 251, 268, 336
Hofstadter, Richard, 2
Holland, 154, 193, 195, 211, 272, 273,
    302, 303
Hooker, Richard, 50, 81, 161, 226,
    237–8
Horn, Friedrich, 125
Hotman, François, 55–6, 171
Houston, Alan, 186, 199, 206, 334
Howard, Lord John, 107, 155
Howard, Sir Robert, 275, 281
huguenots, 55, 56, 57, 68, 101, 171
Hulme, Obadiah, 407
Hume, David, 16, 305, 313–16, 317,
    319, 321, 326, 327, 333, 430
  critic of Locke, 315
  and Glorious Revolution, 316
  moderate Whiggism of, 314–16
Hunton, Philip, 48, 49, 56, 62–7, 68,
    71, 76, 112, 113, 117, 137, 139,
    140, 145, 215, 217, 220, 222–3,
    294
Huyler, Jerome, 11, 58, 116

imperial trade policy, 333, 347, 359,
    360, 393
influence, 387, 412
interregnum, 70
Ireland, 152, 273, 282, 373
Isaac, 115
Israel, 260

Jacobites, 283, 287, 294, 305, 306, 310,
    314
James I, King of England, 19, 23, 32,
    51, 58, 61, 97, 136, 310
James II, King of England, 100, 101,
    102, 103, 107, 271, 272–4, 275,
    276, 278, 284, 286, 295, 371,
    397
Jefferson, Thomas, 18, 313, 326, 331,
    338, 345, 350, 351, 352, 375, 376,
    384, 396, 397, 398, 414, 418,
    419, 427
  on legislative tyranny, 361, 390,
    413

and Lockean natural rights, 352–3,
354, 362, 363, 365
on property, 358–60, 365
right of emigration, 353–5, 357, 380,
384, 403, 405
role of British king in empire, 355,
356, 366–9, 370–3
on slavery, 368–369
Jeffreys, Chief Justice, 155
John of Antioch, St., 36, 37, 38
Junto Whigs, 282, 284, 285

*King's Answer to the Nineteen
Propositions*, 60–1, 96
kingship, the idea of, 388, 395
Kramnick, Isaac, 5, 383

Laslett, Peter, 8
Laud, Archbishop, 51, 52, 67
Lee, Richard Henry, 409
Letters from a Farmer in Pennsylvania, see
Dickinson, John
Levellers, 134
liberalism, 1–2, 5, 289, 326, 427, 428,
429
limited monarchy, *see* balanced
constitutionalism
Lincoln, Abraham, 393
Locke, John, 7, 9, 101, 102, 103, 104,
106, 109, 130, 209–12, 272, 273,
276, 278, 279, 289, 291, 314,
315, 321, 322, 325, 327, 333, 377,
379, 413, 428
and consent, 216, 245, 421, 424
critic of divine right, 214, 215–18
critique of patriarchy, 222–3,
250
and executive power, 253–4, 257,
260, 263
formation of political society in,
247–51, 423
on Glorious Revolution, 281
impact in America, 2, 4, 5–6, 9, 17,
18, 331, 332, 340, 351, 369, 400,
416, 418, 419, 421, 422, 424,
425, 428, 430
law of nature in, 226–8, 231, 233,
240, 241, 242–4

on legislative power, 252–3, 255,
256–7, 258, 341, 407
natural executive power in, 15,
228–30, 231, 232–5, 237–40,
247, 253, 291
natural rights in, 2, 15, 241, 244,
246, 268, 269, 290, 300, 335
on property, 2, 15, 220–2, 240,
241–6, 248, 292, 337, 347, 358,
422
on prerogative, 258–61
revolution and dissolution in, 262–9,
274, 279, 281, 294, 337, 367,
397, 404
on slavery, 235–7
on sovereignty, 15, 219, 247, 256,
258, 259, 344, 355, 377, 417, 422
Louis XIV, King of France, 101, 154,
267, 273
Ludlow, Edmund, 286
Luther, Martin, 28–31, 33, 52–3, 70,
311
Lutz, Donald, 404

Macaulay, Thomas Babbington, 274
Macclesfield, Lord, 281
Machiavelli, Niccolo, 3, 4, 34, 156, 163,
167, 168, 169–71, 172, 174–6,
177, 193, 195, 205, 206, 404
MacPherson, C.B., 2
Madison, James, 297
Magna Carta, 178, 184, 401
Marvell, Andrew, 286
marxism, 1
Mary Stuart, Queen of England, 211,
212, 271, 274, 276, 283
Mary Tudor, Queen of England, 100,
136
Maryland, Constitution of 1776, 401,
404, 405, 413, 414
Mason, George, 401
Massachusetts, Constitution of 1780,
18, 405, 415, 416, 422–5, 428
Mayer, David, 378
Maynard, John, 275
Maynwaring, Roger, 33
Mendle, Michael, 51, 58
Milton, John, 99, 153, 382

Mill, John Stuart, 53
mixed government, 397
    and Calvin, 53-4
    in classical republicanism, 3, 39,
        165-6
    and Locke, 15, 212, 255, 262, 336,
        340
    in moderate Whiggism, 14, 112, 140,
        147, 277, 318, 333, 338, 390
    and parliamentary theory, 48, 49,
        57, 60, 62, 65, 69, 70, 71
    republican critique of, 14, 297-8,
        302, 383, 385
moderate Whigs in America, 380, 387,
    420, 424
Molyneux, William, 282
Monck, General John, 99
Monmouth, Duke of, 107, 155, 211,
    273
Montague, John (Earl of Halifax), 285
Montaigne, Michel de, 73
Montesquieu, Baron de, 16, 305,
    316-19, 321, 327, 413, 419, 430
    balance of powers in, 317-19
    on moderate government in Britain,
        317
Moses, 158, 169, 205
Moyle, Walter, 285

Nebuchadnezzar, 170
Nelson, Scott, 183
Nero, 180, 204
New York, Constitution of 1777, 18,
    415, 416, 418, 421, 423
New York Legislature, Act suspending
    the, 351, 362-4
Nichols, Mary, 164
Noah, 27, 32, 82
Norman Conquest, 312, 314, 358, 389,
    408
North, Lord, 313
North Carolina, Constitution of 1776,
    404, 418
Nottingham, Earl of, 276

Oakley, Francis, 12, 23, 50, 58
Oates, Titus, 102

opposition or "old" Whigs, 285, 288,
    296, 326, 366
Orange, House of, 155, 201, 207, 212
Orwin, Clifford, 94
Otis, James, 17, 326, 329, 331, 346,
    349, 351, 357, 359, 363, 370, 373,
    376, 384, 391, 396, 418
    delegation and subordination of
        powers in, 344, 345, 346
    departure from Locke, 342-3
    on the Glorious Revolution, 338-40,
        354, 384
    Lockean natural rights in, 333-6
    parliamentary supremacy in, 343,
        344-6
    on property rights, 336-7
Ottoman Empire, 317, 390
Overall, Bishop, 32
Overton, Richard, 134
Oxford Decrees (1683), 272

Paine, Tom, 5, 331, 338, 345, 350,
    375-7, 396, 398, 407, 408, 409,
    410, 411, 418, 420, 427,
    428
    and American independence, 375,
        379, 391-4
    critique of British constitution, 383,
        384-8, 389-90
    republicanism of, 376, 382, 389, 394,
        415
    and rights, 379, 381, 391
    separation of government and
        society in, 377-80, 393
    and virtue, 379, 381, 382-3,
        387
Pangle, Thomas, 5, 225
Parker, Henry, 48, 49, 56, 67-70, 71,
    112, 143, 188-9, 294, 415
parliamentary sovereignty, 17, 69, 305,
    306, 312, 329-30, 331, 333, 339,
    346, 373, 398, 399, 400, 406,
    410, 414, 417, 420, 427
Parsons, Robert, 23
Parsons, Theophilus, 412
Paul, St., 26, 30
Peerage Bill (1719), 309

Pennsylvania, Constitution of 1776, 18,
    326, 404, 405, 407, 409, 411,
    412, 413, 414, 416, 418, 421
  council of censors in, 414, 421
Petition of Right (1628), 401
Petyt, William, 95, 141, 275
Pitt, William, 327, 330, 346
place bills, 308, 309
Plato, 163, 164, 169, 206, 207
Plutarch, 167
Pocock, J.G.A., 3, 4, 141
Poland, 45, 69, 362
Polybius, 38, 167
Pompey, 166
popish plot, 102
popular sovereignty, 17, 18, 36, 68, 309,
    326, 335, 373, 390, 392, 398, 400,
    417, 418, 427, 428, 429, 430
Portugal, 356
Presbyterianism, 51
Price, Richard, 3, 5
Priestley, Joseph, 3, 5
protestant succession, 316
Prynne, William, 67
Pufendorf, Samuel, 14, 16, 108,
    109–10, 187, 220, 230, 237, 238,
    246, 267, 278, 315, 320, 321,
    325, 340, 428
  contractualism of, 111, 113, 251,
    276, 290, 294, 307, 311, 335, 336,
    397, 421
  on natural law, 110–11, 266,
    430
  and resistance, 112–13, 266, 278,
    279, 281, 286
  on sovereignty, 14, 111–13, 137, 139,
    147–50, 191, 196, 257, 267, 280,
    312, 322, 326, 330, 333, 344, 399,
    421
Putney debates, 134

Rahe, Paul, 10, 92, 319
Randolph, Edmund, 351
realpolitik, 375
Reid, John Philip, 396
republicanism in America, 398, 427,
    429

*Rights of the Colonies Asserted and
    Proved, see* Otis, James
Robbins, Caroline, 3
Rockingham, Marquis of, 313, 329,
    330, 346
Rome, 39, 147, 166, 167, 168, 176,
    178, 207
Roses, War of the, 184, 185, 389
Rossiter, Clinton, 2
Rousseau, Jean-Jacques, 174, 249, 381
Rudolph, Julia, 108, 114
Russell, Lord John, 107, 155

Sachaverell, Henry (trial of), 284,
    286–7, 288, 310, 316, 320, 402
Samuel, Book of, 148–9, 388
Saxons, 183–4, 185, 186, 192, 201, 312,
    354, 358, 382, 407, 408
Sawyer, Sir Robert, 275
Schochet, Gordon, 28, 45, 86
scholasticism, *see* Catholicism
Schwoerer, Lois, 277
Scott, Jonathan, 13, 194
Selden, John, 81–2, 113, 216
separation of powers, 400, 403, 406–7,
    413, 415, 416, 417, 419, 421,
    424, 425, 428, 429
Septennial Act (1716), 287, 299, 309,
    322
Settlement, Act of (1701), 318, 319
Seven Years War, 328, 367
Shaftesbury, Earl of, 100, 102, 106,
    107, 155, 210, 259, 272, 308, 310
Shakespeare, William, 153
Shalhope, Robert, 2
Shanley, Mary, 114
Ship Money Case (1638), 59, 67, 373
Sidney, Algernon, 3, 7, 9, 14–15, 101,
    102, 103, 104, 107, 152–5, 209,
    213, 234, 239, 248, 257, 258,
    268, 269, 272, 284, 286, 289,
    291, 297, 300, 303, 314, 325,
    327, 333, 376, 377, 379, 381, 384,
    428
  and classical republicanism, 163–7,
    169, 193
  and commerce, 206–7

Sidney, Algernon (*cont.*)
  civic virtue in, 164–5, 166, 189–91,
    198–200, 300, 383
  critic of English mixed regime, 156,
    176–80, 182, 184–5, 193, 203,
    388
  critic of Filmer's patriarchalism,
    157–60
  and Enlightenment philosophy,
    203–6
  impact in America, 9, 17, 18, 157,
    400, 404, 406, 407, 412, 428
  on natural liberty, 160–3, 278
  natural rights in, 172–6, 199, 382
  on popular sovereignty, 14, 15, 156,
    181, 182, 186–9, 197–8, 200–2,
    256, 259, 296, 298, 310, 312,
    377
  and property, 173–4, 246
  on revolution, 181–2, 201, 266
Sidney, Sir Philip, 152
Simmons, John, 236
Skinner, Quentin, 28
Somers, Lord John, 284, 285
Somerville, J.P., 35, 51, 81
Sons of Liberty, 329
South Carolina, Constitution of 1776,
  411
South Sea bubble, 288, 290, 297, 307,
  386
Spain, 362, 387
Sparta, 167, 168, 177
Spinoza, Benedict, 15, 109, 156, 172,
  174, 180–1, 187, 188, 190, 234,
  239, 297, 303, 325, 381, 385, 391,
  421, 428, 430
  critique of orthodoxy in, 205
  and Dutch republicanism, 194, 195,
    389
  influence on Sidney, 193–4, 195–7,
    198, 199, 207, 392
  natural rights in, 186, 196, 392–3,
    400, 408
Stamp Act (1765), 328, 329, 330, 331,
  332, 336, 346, 347, 359, 362
Stamp Act Congress, 329, 330
standing army controversy, 284–6, 288,
  314, 366, 402

state constitutions (*see also specific states*)
  bicameralism in, 412–13, 416
  executive power in, 411–12, 413,
    415, 416, 424
  first wave of, 410, 411, 414–15, 416,
    418, 419, 420, 421, 422
  legislative power in, 417, 418, 419,
    421
  second wave of, 415–17, 421, 422
Strauss, Leo, 2
Suárez, Francisco, 22, 23, 36, 37, 62,
  63, 75, 76, 123, 124, 159, 160,
  162, 163, 173, 238
  on Adam's economic power, 36, 38
  consent in, 42, 43
  on resistance, 41
suffrage, *see* franchise
Sugar Act (1764), 328, 332, 336
Sweden, 45, 69

Tacitus, 200
Tarcov, Nathan, 91
Test Acts, 272
Tierney, Brian, 12, 42
Tocqueville, Alexis de, 53
Toland, John, 155, 156
Toleration Act (1689), 319
Tories, 95, 107, 155, 215, 273
  in Exclusion crisis, 8, 19, 100, 102,
    103, 271, 307, 310
  indebtedness to Filmer, 19, 25, 101,
    102, 272, 283, 284, 286, 315
  in Glorious Revolution, 275, 276,
    277, 310, 339, 408
  in Augustan period, 283–4, 287,
    306, 308, 310, 313, 323
Townshend Duties, 330, 347, 362
Trenchard, John, 284, 285, 288, 326,
  366; (*see also Cato's Letters*)
Triennial Acts (1664 and 1694), 99, 100,
  287, 299
trimmers, 274
Tuck, Richard, 73, 76, 77, 81, 130
Tully, James, 8, 72, 265
Turgot, Jacques, 409
Tyrrell, James, 7, 9, 14, 95, 101, 102,
  103, 104, 105–9, 186, 187,
  209, 210, 213, 230, 232, 237,

238, 255, 266, 271, 272, 275, 321, 325, 409, 428
consent in, 120–4
contractualism of, 117–19, 123, 141
and Glorious Revolution, 278, 280–1, 287, 321, 388
indebtedness to Pufendorf, 118, 119, 125, 129, 130, 131, 134, 137, 140–1, 142, 145, 146
natural law in, 115–16, 119–20, 121, 227
natural rights in, 114, 116–17, 119, 122, 131, 145
on property, 122, 126–31, 242, 246, 292
on resistance, 143–5, 146, 264, 265, 294
on sovereignty, 124–6, 137, 139–41, 212, 257, 312, 330

United Provinces, *see* Holland
United States Constitution (1787), 424, 428, 429
Ussher, Archbishop, 105, 106

Vane, Sir Walter, 210
Venice, 207
Vermont, Constitution of 1777, 407
veto power, 140, 371, 372, 387, 411, 413, 415
Vindicae contra Tyrranos, 56, 63
Virginia, Constitution of 1776, 361, 401, 408, 413

Walpole, Robert, 286, 287, 288, 293, 305, 306, 310, 311, 313, 316, 402
Washington, George, 351
Weber, Max, 53
Webking, Robert, 362
Weston, Corinne, 58
Wharton, Lord, 281
Whigs, 6–7, 9, 19, 37, 94, 95, 96, 98, 100, 209, 325, 426
in Exclusion crisis, 97, 100–4, 107, 271, 307
in Glorious Revolution, 274, 276, 277, 279, 309, 399, 402, 406, 408
period of Whig supremacy, 306–8, 313, 320, 326, 328
radical philosophy of, 377, 378, 384, 392, 394, 396, 400, 401, 410
Wildman, John, 134, 281
Wilenius, Reijo, 42
Wilkes affair, 376
William I, King of England, 358, 388
William III, King of England, 211, 214, 271, 273, 274, 276, 278, 283, 284, 286, 305, 348
Wilson, James, 355, 397, 419
Wolin, Sheldon, 31
Wood, Gordon, 4, 376, 399, 411
writs of assistance, 332
written constitutions, 395, 398–9, 406, 417, 422, 425, 428

Zagorin, Perez, 73, 90
Zuckert, Michael, 11, 58, 116
Zvesper, John, 353